THE INDIAN THEOGONY

THE INDIAN THEOGONY

A COMPARATIVE STUDY OF
INDIAN MYTHOLOGY
FROM THE *VEDAS*
TO THE *PURĀṆAS*

BY
SUKUMARI BHATTACHARJI

CAMBRIDGE
AT THE UNIVERSITY PRESS
1970

Published by the Syndics of the Cambridge University Press
Bentley House, 200 Euston Road, London N.W.1
American Branch: 32 East 57th Street, New York, N.Y.10022

Library of Congress Catalogue Card Number: 79-96080

Standard Book Number: 521 07190 9

Printed in Great Britain
at the University Printing House, Cambridge
(Brooke Crutchley, University Printer)

To the memory of my father

CONTENTS

CONTENTS

PART IV. THE EPIC-PURĀṆIC TRIAD

PREFACE

THE present book is the result of ten years' work on the subject of the historical development of Indian mythology and its connection with parallel mythologies elsewhere, on which no satisfactory work exists in English. It was submitted as a doctoral thesis in 1964 in an earlier and different form. In 1966 Clare Hall, Cambridge offered me a Visiting Fellowship for the academic year 1966–7, thus making it possible for me to bring the material up to date. For the most part the book was prepared in India, where books on non-Indian mythologies and related subjects are comparatively few and difficult to procure. This naturally was a hindrance which was partly removed by my stay in Cambridge and I am thankful to Clare Hall for the generous offer of this opportunity. The Syndics of the Cambridge University Press kindly took an interest in the work and offered to publish it. In preparing the book for the Press I had Dr F. R. Allchin's unstinted cooperation and assistance. I can never be sufficiently grateful for the patience and thoroughness with which he went through the entire work and for his many valuable suggestions. I had long and frequent discussions with him at Churchill College which were invariably pleasant and profitable for me.

At the end of September 1967 I returned to India to my teaching post at Jadavpur University, Calcutta. Technical problems of all sorts cropped up when editorial work on the book began in the Press. Since I was no longer at Cambridge to deal with them a prolonged correspondence ensued with those who looked after the publication of the book. I owe a deep debt of gratitude to them; but for their patience the book would never have been published.

In the early stages of the work my teacher Dr Suniti Kumar Chatterji (National Professor of Humanities) helped me greatly by lending me books from his vast collection—books which are otherwise difficult to obtain here. I also learned much from discussions on allied subjects which I had with him from time to time. Dr Radhagovinda Basak encouraged me frequently when I despaired of ever finishing the work; the example of this venerable scholar was itself an inspiration. I am thankful to Prof. Giuseppe Tucci, one of the examiners of my thesis, for his extremely valuable suggestions for preparing the book for publication.

PREFACE

A work of this kind must naturally be based on the researches of scholars of social anthropology and Indology and of my colleagues in the field, Indian and foreign. The merit of the book, if any, is largely theirs; for the errors which must be many, I am solely responsible.

SUKUMARI BHATTACHARJI

Calcutta

ABBREVIATIONS

PRIMARY SOURCES

AĀ	*Aitareya Āraṇyaka*
AB	*Aitareya Brāhmaṇa*
ĀDS	*Āśvalāyana Dharma Sūtra*
ĀGS	*Āśvalāyana Gṛhya Sūtra*
Āp.DS	*Āpastamba Dharma Sūtra*
Āp.GS	*Āpastamba Gṛhya Sūtra*
Āp.ŚS	*Āpastamba Śrauta Sūtra*
ĀŚS	*Āśvalāyana Śrauta Sūtra*
AU	*Aitareya Upaniṣad*
AV	*Atharva Veda*
BĀU	*Bṛhad Āraṇyaka Upaniṣad*
BGS	*Baudhāyana Gṛhya Sūtra*
Bh.G	*Bhagavad Gītā*
Bh.P	*Bhaviṣya Purāṇa*
CB	*Chāndogya Brāhmaṇa*
CU	*Chāndogya Upaniṣad*
GB	*Gopatha Brāhmaṇa*
GBU	*Gopatha Brāhmaṇa Uttarabhāga*
GGS	*Gobhila Gṛhya Sūtra*
HGS	*Hiraṇyakeśin Gṛhya Sūtra*
HV	*Harivaṃśa*
ĪU	*Īśa Upaniṣad*
JB / *JUB*	*Jaiminīya (Upaniṣad) Brāhmaṇa*
JU	*Jaiminīya Upaniṣad*
KB / *KUB*	*Kauṣītaki (Upaniṣad) Brāhmaṇa*
KU	*Kena Upaniṣad*
KP	*Kūrma Purāṇa*
KŚS	*Kātyāyana Śrauta Sūtra*
KYV	*Kṛṣṇa (Black) Yajurveda*
Mait. U	*Maitrāyaṇī Upaniṣad*
Matsya P	*Matsya Purāṇa*
Mbh.	*Mahābhārata*
MS	*Maitrāyaṇī Saṃhitā*
MU	*Muṇḍaka Upaniṣad*
NP	*Nīlamata Purāṇa*
PGS	*Pāraskara Gṛhya Sūtra*
Rām.	*Rāmāyaṇa*
ṚV	*Ṛgveda*
ŚB	*Śatapatha Brāhmaṇa*

ŚGS	*Śāṅkhāyana Gṛhya Sūtra*
ŚŚS	*Śāṅkhayana Śrauta Sūtra*
SV	*Sāmaveda*
Śvet. U	*Śvetaśvatara Upaniṣad*
ŚYV	*Śukla* (*white*) *Yajurveda*
TĀ	*Taittirīya Āraṇyaka*
TB	*Taittirīya Brāhmaṇa*
TMB	*Tāṇḍya Mahābrāhmaṇa*
TS	*Taittirīya Saṃhitā*
TU	*Taittirīya Upaniṣad*
VS	*Vājasaneyī Saṃhitā* (of the *ŚYV*)
Vāyu P	*Vāyu Purāṇa*
Viṣṇu P	*Viṣṇu Purāṇa*
YV	*Yajurveda*

GENERAL

ABORI	*Annals of the Bhandarkar Oriental Research Institute*
ERE	*Encyclopaedia of Religion and Ethics*
HOS	Harvard Oriental Series
IC	*Indian Culture*
IE	Indo-European
IHQ	*Indian Historical Quarterly*
JAOS	*Journal of the American Oriental Society*
JCOI	*Journal of the Cama Oriental Institute*
JGIS	*Journal of the Greater India Society*
JRAS	*Journal of the Royal Asiatic Society*
NIA	*New Indian Antiquary*
SBE	Sacred Books of the East

INTRODUCTION

ORTHODOX Indian religion contains much that must have been assimilated from primitive bases but Indian mythology as we have it has very little that is overtly or recognizably primitive. Hence theories of sociologists who worked in the field of primitive societies could not be applied to Indian religion and mythology without considerable modification and then only within a very limited scope. Because generations of mythographers have gone on adding, altering, selecting, rejecting, embellishing and 'modernizing' the myths, the traces of animism, totemism, manism or fetishism—so apparent in primitive myths—have been buried under the Indian material till there is hardly any obvious or incontrovertible evidence of these left. The ethnographer's approach to Indian religion will bear fruit only after much more investigation is done on the racial constituents of the Indian population and on the mythological correlative of their material experience. Even then, it is extremely doubtful whether it can yield any concrete or plausible results; first, because the necessary relationship between race and religion is now generally discredited, and secondly, because many of the ancient contributions of the various racial elements are now irretrievably lost in subsequent syncretism.

Two trends of research in the last two centuries had direct bearing on the exploration of Indian mythology—the social anthropological school of E. B. Tylor, Herbert Spencer, Lévy Bruhl, Andrew Lang and E. Durkheim and the Indologists' school of Max Müller, J. J. Meyer and A. Bergaigne.[1] The former carried on researches among primitive, tribal people and arrived at totemistic, animistic, manistic, fetishistic, solar, lunar or astral theories of the origin of myths. The latter, while subscribing to one or other of these theories, interpreted Indian myths relying chiefly on linguistic evidence. Coming to more recent time we again have two trends: the first represented by S. Freud, C. G. Jung, W. Schmidt, J. G. Frazer, Jane Harrison and S. H. Hooke, and the second by scholars like G. Dumézil, L. Renou, J. Gonda, H. Zimmer and A. Coomaraswamy. The first group drew their material from primitive and classical cultures and the second were primarily Indologists aware of the researches of social anthropologists.

[1] For these and subsequent references in the Introduction see the bibliographical note at the end of the chapter.

Jung, whose work was mainly based on Freud's, put forward his theory of archetypes; the human mind, he believed, thinks in terms of archetypes which are buried deep in the collective unconscious, and myths are a projection of these archetypes. This theory as an explanation of the origin of myths has an obvious difficulty: it ignores the fact that mythological thinking existed side by side with rational thinking, as modern scholars state emphatically. It also underestimates the value of ritual, the volitional correlative of myths. Frazer showed that primitive beliefs based on contiguity and similarity gave rise to magic and religion. All subsequent work was profoundly influenced by him. The ritual school of Jane Harrison, Gilbert Murray and S. H. Hooke made a reassessment of the interrelation of ritual and myth and interpreted myths with reference to their relation to corresponding rituals.

Although these researches opened up large vistas for the mythologist, not many scholars in social anthropology brought their theories to bear upon Indian myths. The reason is twofold. First, archaeology has not yet yielded the requisite amount of data for the material infra-structure which threw up the mythological superstructure of ancient India; and secondly, India was culturally too far away from primitive societies as well as from classical European cultures—the main areas of social anthropological study. Indian mythological material was used for illustration in works of Western mythology but there has not been any systematic or historical study of Indian mythology itself.

Max Müller's philological school of interpretation predominated in the study of Indian myths until modern Indologists like G. Dumézil, J. Gonda and L. Renou appeared in the field. H. Zimmer and A. Coomaraswamy were mainly philosophical and idealistic in their approach to myths and sought a symbolical correlative of myths on the metaphysical plane.

Mircea Eliade for the first time used the findings of all the allied and relevant disciplines in the field of mythology, avoiding the extremes of philological, historical, metaphysical and symbolic schools on the one hand and the unimaginative and comparatively barren approaches of many of the social anthropologists on the other. He traces common patterns in different mythological systems and probes into the cultural roots of these patterns. These, together with the inner structural organization (as emphasized by Lévi-Strauss), can explain the nature of the change, growth and development of the contours and dimensions of myths. His work assumes that myths are projections of vital experiences of a people; but he goes deeper than Malinowski and seeks to reveal the vital experiences which make myths the only valid medium for externalizing these experiences. This approach has greater potentialities for my material than those pursued so far, and in my book I have explored some of these lines to establish a pattern of the evolution of the Indian mythology from the Vedic to the epic-Purāṇic period. I have traced how the myriads of gods in the Vedic pantheon gradually converged into the epic-Purāṇic triad of Brahman, Viṣṇu and Śiva.

Regarding the parallels between Indian and non-Indian myths I adhere to Lévi-Strauss's view, viz. that diffusion within the limits of historical probability should be the natural explanation of similarities in myths of different areas, and when this fails the archetype in the collective unconscious should be accepted as the reason for such similarities. 'If history, when it is called upon unremittingly (and it must be called upon *first*) cannot yield an answer, then let us appeal to psychology, or the structural analysis of forms; let us ask ourselves if internal connections whether of a psychological or logical nature, will allow us to understand parallel recurrences whose frequency and cohesion cannot possibly be the result of chance' (Lévi-Strauss, *Structural anthropology*, p. 248).

In the first part the Vedic-Brāhmaṇical and epic-Purāṇic components of Śiva, Varuṇa, Yama, Nirṛti, Agni, Kāla, the mother-goddess, Kārttikeya, Gaṇapati, Kāma and Pūṣan, are treated. Their rise to prominence and their decline is shown and their contributions to some traits of the emergent epic-Purāṇic divinity, Śiva, are discussed. Some of these gods fade out, leaving one or two traits for Śiva, others are transmuted to form important and abiding factors of the Śiva-complex. Still others rise out of insignificance and become vital aspects of this hierophany. The resultant figure of Śiva is that of a sectarian god who stands for different things and is worshipped in a different manner. The Vedic, non-Vedic, Aryan, non-Aryan composition of the god, his emotional, philosophical and cultic associations are analysed and the processes of this growth, change and development traced with reference to similar gods in other mythologies.

Part II studies the rise of Viṣṇu. The component gods—the Vedic solar gods Savitṛ, Sūrya, Vivasvat, Mitra, Aryaman, Bhaga, Aṃśa, Dakṣa, Mārtaṇḍa, Indra, and Viṣṇu together with the epic-Purāṇic incarnations of Viṣṇu (with their Vedic precursors) are analysed. The process by which the minor Vedic god Viṣṇu eclipses other demiurges, the Ādityas, by absorbing their traits—fighting some, making alliances with others, pushing yet others into insignificance—is traced. The rise of sectarianism, with its special demands, accounts for some of these changes; different cults obtaining among different sections of the people account for others. Many distinct cults and sects mingled under the Viṣṇu-Kṛṣṇa complex and these are held together by some fundamental link which one might call the essence of the new god. The resultant figure is the object of the worship, devotion and contemplation of a vast section of the people.

With Brahman (part III) the picture is different. In the Vedic-Brāhmaṇical gods—Bṛhaspati, Brahmaṇaspati, Prajāpati, Viśvakarman, Hiraṇyagarbha, Puruṣa, Skambha, Parameṣṭhin, Pitāmaha, and Brahman—we do not get a very tangible figure, far less that of a sectarian god. These merge into the Brahman, Prajāpati or Pitāmaha of the epic-Purāṇic literature, but fail to answer to the definition of a sectarian god, so that no cult grows around the resultant image, and the central concept is transferred to philosophy which is thus enriched at the cost of theology. Brahman (m.) remains an attenuated figure, too unconvincing to have a real cult of his own.

In part IV the general characteristics of the Purāṇic pantheon are analysed. Here, on the one hand, there are innumerable regional, functional divinities, tutelary gods and goddesses, village- or disease-gods, and also gods for different occasions in life, while on the other hand there is the lofty Triad, which, thanks to the predominance of philosophy, is frequently stated to be three facets of the same supreme being. These latter belong to the official 'high religion' while the former remain the low gods. Thus the Hindu pantheon has struck a compromise and has made room for all. The 'high religion' explains the minor gods as manifestations of the central triad thus establishing it in unquestionable power and prominence.

II

And ponder it well in thy mind, that from the same origin sprang gods and mortal men (Hesiod, *Works and Days* I. 107).

Men and the gods above one race compose (Pindar, *Nemean Ode* 6. 1–7).

In Indian mythology, Kaśyapa is the progenitor of both gods and men. Thus we see that the Indo-European mind did not imagine the gods as very high, distant or different from men. Their god-making impulse stemmed from awe, wonder and admiration, an impulse unlike the other impulse of fear and misgivings which tends to create gods as very distant and formidable. All generalization is apt to be exaggerated and hence to some extent false, but if we try to probe into the fundamental attitude of the mythopoeic mind it will perhaps strike us that the Indo-European gods are friendly, living not very far from mortals, helpers in need, sharing faults and frailties with men. The Indo-European gods are not perfect; they are not above anger, malice, boastfulness, wile and jealousy.

The Indian pantheon as found in the *ṚV* is predominantly a legacy of the Indo-European pantheon. From the late tenth Maṇḍala, through the *YV* and *AV Saṃhitās* down to the *Brāhmaṇas* we find new factors operating as formative influences in this pantheon. The gods change their character mainly through the impact of the non-Vedic population. Exogamy introduced non-Aryan wives who brought their own gods together with the mode of their worship into their husbands' homes as Rachel brought Laban's gods into Jacob's household. As neighbours, too, the non-Vedic people influenced the newcomers. The result of this ethnic and cultural intermixture is first noticed in the tenth Maṇḍala and the process reaches a culmination in the *Brāhmaṇas*. When under the Guptas Brāhmaṇism again came into its own it was set up on a richer and more complex level. Thus we can trace three strata in the Indian pantheon: the Indo-European, the Vedic-Brāhmaṇical and the epic-Purāṇic.

The first stratum belongs to the history of the Indo-Europeans before their advent in India. For the second phase, that is, the Vedic-Brāhmaṇical, northern India—modern Punjab and Uttar Pradesh—was the centre of the Vedic Indians' myth-making activities. Between the seventh and sixth centuries B.C. heterodoxy flourished strongly in what is now south-eastern Uttar Pradesh and Bihar. The Brāhmaṇical religion was introduced rather later in that region and consequently the population there was little affected by the earlier Aryan social, or religious systems. Yakṣas, Nāgas and other local, chthonic deities were worshipped at sacred groves or chaityas (mounds), even after the Aryan religion had arrived there. The social structure was different, administration and forms of government were also different; an opulent merchant class lived in comparative economic security, while the free peasants and artisans, constituting the bulk of the population, enjoyed quite a high standard of living. The old tribal structure was disintegrating, older administrative institutions were crumbling and a number of petty principalities had arisen in which something of the tribal political structure was retained in the republic type of administration. Confederacies became powerful and although, through Aryan infiltration, new modes of social or religious life were absorbed slowly but surely, this did not happen without considerably altering the character of the Vedic religion itself and largely casting it into an indigenous mould. The development of organized state-machinery and the advance of material culture ran concurrently with the rapid spread of new religious and philosophical movements—the Upaniṣadic upheaval, Buddhism, Jainism, Yoga, Sāṃkhya and Vedānta. In the tremendous ferment of the succeeding ages the contribution of this 'new thought' was largely incorporated into the emergent religion and remained fundamental to all subsequent religious thought in India.

The chief characteristics of this 'new thought' were: a deep dissatisfaction with the existing state of affairs in the religious and philosophical world, an other-worldliness, a growing crystallization of the theory of rebirth and Karman (action), greater preoccupation with release from the chain of existence, increasing detachment and emphasis on non-violence and non-enjoyment. About two centuries after the Buddha there arose a cult which filled in the hiatus of the negative aspect of these doctrines—viz. the Bhāgavata cult. According to some, Kṛṣṇa, its first teacher, later became the central divinity of the cult and ended up by becoming an avatāra (incarnation) of Viṣṇu. In the next period (*c.* 200 B.C.–A.D. 300), when religious thought was at its most active and when the later mythological sections of the epics and early *Purāṇas* were being composed and redacted vigorously and briskly, we notice the rise of other sects—Śaiva, Vaiṣṇava (Nārāyaṇīya) and Saura. This period is characterized by a greater accent on the doctrine of reincarnation, the concept of the impersonal Brahman and the personal soterial god, Īśvara, the authority of the Smṛtis (religious conventions) alongside the Śrutis (Vedas), increasing stratification of caste and the four stages of life, the emergence of the triad (Brahman, Viṣṇu and Śiva), the reincarnation of the supreme being (avatāra), different levels of spiritual ability (adhikāra), rituals and image worship (pūjā), pilgrimages, shrines and temples and finally the slow but sure resurgence of the indigenous gods in different syncretistic shapes. It was a period of spiritual turmoil and achieved an astonishing transformation in Indian mythology.

III

Śaunaka says that gods are to be praised by their name, form, actions and (together with their) friends. (Stutistu nāmnā rūpeṇa karmaṇā bāndhavena ca, *Bṛhaddevata* 17.) The object of this worship is stated as heaven, long life, wealth and sons; this is called Āśīh (Svargāyurdhanaputtrādyāirarthairāśīstu kathyate, *ibid.*). In this passage we have a glimpse into the object of Vedic worship: gods were praised for material well-being. By the time of the *Purāṇas* much of this had changed. Some of the old gods had faded out altogether, some had grown more important while others were less so than before, and many new gods had appeared in the new pantheon. These new gods and the changed old gods were worshipped differently.

Several factors in this far-reaching change can be ascertained with some degree of certitude.

One characteristic of some of these gods is conspicuous from the Brāhmaṇical literature. From the *Brāhmaṇas* onwards certain gods are spoken of as guardians of certain quarters. A study of this relationship brings out an important fact:

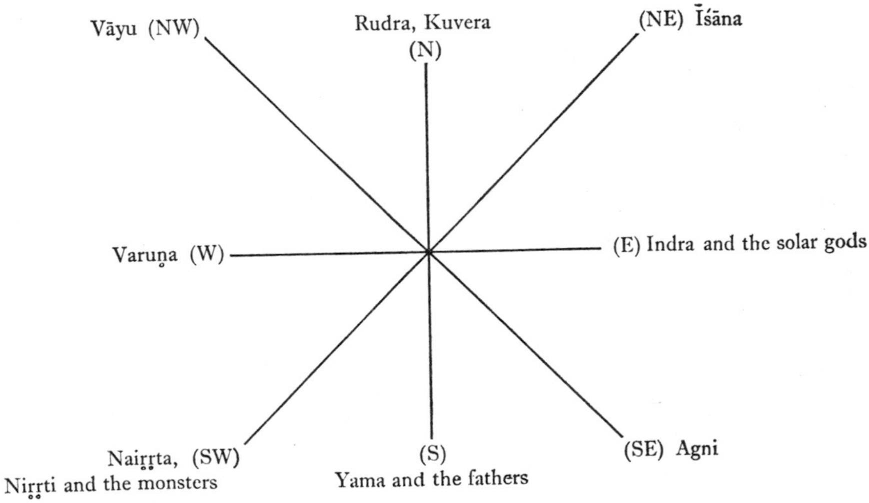

Indra and the solar gods rule only one quarter, the east (regarded mythologically as Aditi who gives birth to the Ādityas). In sharp opposition the west is ruled by Varuṇa. Varuṇa, when included among the Ādityas, symbolizes the setting sun and, as such, is more closely allied to the gods and powers of darkness than to those of light. Varuṇa is gradually absorbed in the Śiva-complex and the west is allotted as his quarter. Agni, in the *ṚV*, is both beneficent and sinister; as havyavāhana he is with the solar gods, as Kavyavāhana and Kravyād he is with the gods of darkness. Īśāna, too, has both divine and sinister bearings. He is a product of the *Brāhmaṇas* and is clearly an intermediary between the gods and the other powers. Rudra is a Vedic god, but with time he comes to take on dark and malevolent associations. Kuvera, his friend, is subdivine, with some links with the camp of the gods through his friendship with Rudra. He is the lord of the Yakṣas, who again are a species of Sondergötter. Between Rudra and

Varuṇa is Vāyu, a god who leans more to the dark gods than to the dwellers in the east. In the south is the region of Yama and the fathers. Yama, too, like Rudra and Varuṇa was a god like any other god in the *ṚV* but came to be associated with dark and destructive functions and character from the *Brāhmaṇas* until in the Purāṇic age he is almost a malevolent figure. When Yama rules in the south, his subjects are the fathers, that is, the dead ancestors. Between Yama and Varuṇa is the Nairṛta Koṇa, the south-west quarter, where Nirṛti rules and where monsters (Nairṛtas) dwell.

Analysing the residences of the gods we see that while Indra and the Ādityas command only one quarter, the seven other quarters are presided over by gods who somehow oppose the solar forces. What connects the other seven guardians of the quarters is their association with death, decay, destruction and the fathers. This is a vitally important characteristic of the Indian pantheon.

Most of the Vedic Ādityas died out by the time of the epics. We no longer hear of Savitṛ, Bhaga, Aryaman, Dakṣa, Aṃśa, Pūṣan or Mārtaṇḍa. Vivasvat becomes unconvincing, mythologically the Asyins are as good as forgotten, while Varuṇa changes his character to a great extent. Indra, too, dwindles in power and significance. The Ādityas gradually become less powerful. Only Viṣṇu grows, but even he grows as a culture-hero of the Indian people, not as an Āditya. The east remains the region of light, life and growth, but the pantheon is slowly moving away from the east.

The seven other quarters are connected with gods who are associated with death, destruction and decay. Their connection with the fathers binds them together, and the fathers in Vedic religion evoke a distinct set of associations. All through ritual gods and fathers are opposed to each other. In the first nine books of the *ṚV* the fathers do not play an important part; they come into prominence (together with their overlord Yama) only in the tenth book and increase in stature until they dominate a great part of ritual and mythology.

The *ŚB* says: 'the east is the quarter of the gods...the north of men... the south is the quarter of the deceased ancestors' (I: 2: 5: 17). We are also told that spring, summer and rainy seasons belong to and represent the gods, while autumn, winter and the dewy season belong to the fathers. The fortnight during which the moon waxes represents the gods and that in which it wanes represents the fathers. The day belongs to the gods, the night to the fathers, the morning to the gods, the afternoon to the fathers (*ŚB* II: I: 3: I). The contrast and opposition between the worship of the gods and that of the fathers is clearly discernible in such passages. Thus while the Vedic Aryans were preoccupied with the cult of the solar gods who stood for light and life, the non-Vedic people had been pre-eminently concerned with rituals to the ancestors who dwelt on the other side of life, whose time was the afternoon, the night, the fortnight during the waxing of the moon and the dull seasons. The division cannot be mathematical or precise or even mutually exclusive. Even among the Vedic Aryans an ancestor-cult must have existed since the impulse which prompts ancestor-ritual is universal and timeless. But the first nine books do not record much of this; they are primarily concerned with the gods on whose bounty depended their material existence and well-being. Perhaps these hymns record the chants of collective worship because ancestor-worship is, almost necessarily, a private affair of the family concerned. 'The two lines of religious development which were found in the Indo-European period, namely, the worship of ancestors and the worship of the "heavenly ones" continued throughout the Indo-Iranian period, for they appear in both the *ṚV* and the *Avesta*' (H. D. Griswold, *The religion of the Rigveda*, pp. 22–3). But the emphasis shifts, even in the period of Vedic literature, for while the *ṚV Saṃhitā* is predominantly occupied with the heavenly ones, in the other *Saṃhitās* and *Brāhmaṇas* the fathers figure more and more prominently. All through the ritual the gods and the fathers stand for opposite sets of values. In the major part of the *RV* the gods predominate, in the later Brāhmaṇical literatures the fathers also come into the limelight; in the later *Saṃhitās* and earlier *Brāhmaṇas* a balance is struck when gods and fathers receive almost equal attention.

IV

Another distinction exists between the religions of these two periods ('early Vedic' and 'later-Vedic to Brāhmaṇical'). While in the first the worship of the male gods predominates, in the latter the goddesses, too, become powerful. Vedic society, was basically patriarchal. If a nation's pantheon can be taken as a more or less faithful index of its human level of existence, then, the fact that gods dominate the early Vedic pantheon and are more numerous than the goddesses is significant. Uṣas is a minor goddess; Ilā, Bhāratī and Sarasvatī are hardly convincing as theophanies, Aditi is much better known because of her sons, and Pṛthivī because of her consort. In pre-Vedic Indian society, goddesses were equally, if not more, powerful and plentiful; this is shown by the artefacts found in the excavations of prehistoric sites. At the first clash of the two peoples, the pantheon of the indigenous population, like their worshippers, suffered a defeat and went underground. But with time the old gods steadily regained lost ground and retrieved their lost prestige. Thus in the *Brāhmaṇas* we have the first signs of the return of the mother-goddesses into power. Nirṛti, Śacī, Mīḍhuṣī, Yamī, Ambikā, Rudrāṇī, Śrī, Lakṣmī, Sarasvatī (or Vāc) re-emerge as mother-goddesses. One reason of the Aryans' partial religious surrender is the pre-Aryan worship of images; the visual appeal of the gods captured the imagination of the Aryans who worshipped ideas. Besides, Pūjā (worship of idols) is much more colourful than Yajña, although Yajña might well have been more awe-inspiring. Pūjā has a greater and more direct appeal to man's aesthetic sense.

V

The Aryans were a nomadic people and so had no temples or images. The primitive sacrifices must have been of a rough and ready sort although the Brāhmaṇical ritual was a much more elaborate affair. But they had to compete with visible images, which naturally increased their hold on the popular imagination. Besides, images and their worship had infiltrated into the Aryans' homes through their non-Aryan wives. The result was a compromise: the superior beauty of the hymns, their language and poetry retained its hold while the concrete images were adopted because of their immediate and inescapable aesthetic appeal and greater realism. Many of these images were female figures and they filled a gap in the Aryan pantheon. The goddesses gained in stature and significance. 'History became a conflict between these two forces: the old, stable unawakened matriarchal powers against the new, mobile, liberating tendencies of the equestrian peoples which were rising into consciousness' (Karl Jaspers, *The origin and goal of history*, p. 16).

This distinction between the patriarchal and matriarchal pantheons is linked to the other distinction of the Āgamic and Nigamic religions.[1] In the current Āgamas Śiva and Pārvatī hold a discussion, approved of by Vāsudeva. The Āgamic element embodied in the popular and perhaps the

[1] In this book I have sometimes used the terms Āgamic and Nigamic, terms which are quite familiar in India with accepted usage in religious terminology. In *Mbh.* XIII: 145: 61 we read: 'Āgamā lokadharmāṇām maryādā pūrvanirmitā' (the Āgamas are the previously ordained confines of the popular religions). In actual usage 'Āgama' generally signifies Śaiva texts and also all pre-Vedic (i.e. popular, indigenous and hence non-Vedic) religious treatises, chiefly oral and chthonic in character. Vedic Aryan religion was mostly sun-oriented and this was Nigama, i.e. Vedic. Later, the *Tantras*, i.e. scriptures of the mother-goddess (Śakti) were called Āgamas, and still later, certain Vaiṣṇava texts, too, called themselves Āgamas.

pre-Vedic oral religion (as the name indicates) gradually infiltrated the accepted official religion. With the close of the Brāhmaṇical period it had reached the culmination of its first phase when the Aryan gods ruled the pantheon, and the popular gods occupied a subordinate position.

Buddhism made its influence felt in the next period. The Buddha acknowledged the existence of Vedic deities. They were regarded as powerful agents somewhat above men who were subject to the laws of nature and had to be redeemed by the Buddha, for they were far from being perfect. Sometimes they symbolize the various powers of the Buddha. Asaṅga the famous Mahāyāna author introduced the Brāhmaṇical gods as agents to whom men could pray for worldly objects. It was a compromise with Hinduism. As a result the images of the Bodhisattvas came to be many-handed like the Indian gods. When Buddhism revived the Brāhmaṇical gods, the old Āgamic gods—the mother-goddess, tutelary deities, tree and animal-spirits, spirits of cremation grounds and funerary-mounds—all were revived. This had to be so, for Buddhism came at a time when the Brāhmaṇical society had a top-heavy religious hierarchy and there was apathy at the base; Buddhism fought this apathy by spreading its roots further down and these popular gods, once they were incorporated into Buddhism, brought with them numerous devotees, thus increasing the following of the new religion.

Later when Tantrism combined Śaivism, Śaktism and Buddhism it had a following from all these sections. 'It was not until towards the end of the twelfth century that the Buddhism then coming from Bengal had been so much altered by the upsurge of pre-Aryan ideas in Tantrism, while syncretism with Śaivism had made such strides, that what then passed for Mahāyāna Buddhism could be really adapted to the ancestor and chthonic aspects of the Devarāja cult' (H. G. Q. Wales, *Prehistory and religion in South East Asia*, p. 171). Thus we have among the 'low-goddesses' who came to be recognized after Buddhism, the Śākinīs and the Ḍākinīs.[1] The popular religion could afford to be catholic because the people had a greater need of syncretism in the pantheon—a product of the ethnic and cultural amalgamation.

Ancestor-worship, with all its chthonic associations, was acknowledged by Buddhism. The popular gods, with their rituals, brought the subdivine supernatural beings—products of animism and spiritism—the Yakṣas

[1] Of these 'the Śākinī refers to the Śakas and the Ḍākinī to the Dags of Dagistan in Central Asia' (P. C. Bagchi, *The Tantras*, p. 51). This suggests the extraneous influences which were operative in the formation of the low gods. The Ḍākinīs may, however, have come from the *AV* Ghoṣiṇīs, female attendants of Rudra.

(guardians of mineral treasures hidden in the earth), Yakṣīs (tree spirits), Apsarases (water-spirits), Nāgas (spirits of water-serpents), etc.

These changed their names and shapes after the decline of the first phase of Buddhism in India, and in the Purāṇic age they survived as regional and tutelary gods, with different names.

In the Rupnath edict of Asoka we read: 'Those gods who up to this time had been unassociated (with man) in Jambudvīpa have now been made associated with them' (E. Hultzsch, *Inscriptions of Asoka* (Clarendon Press, Oxford, 1925), p. 166 (for Rupnath), p. 169 (for Sahasram), and p. 174 (for Maski)). In the Sahasram edict: 'Men in Jambudvīpa who up to this time had been unassociated with the gods have (now) been made associated with gods'; and the Maski rock edict reads: '(These gods who) were (not) formerly (associated with men) in Jambu (dvīpa)...have now been made associated with them.' Thus the rival and growing popularity of the gods who had been neglected for centuries proves that more and more of the old Āgamic gods were being incorporated in the new pantheon.

As time went on the number of gods increased rapidly. Instead of reducing them to many manifestations of one, two or three abstract ideas it is safer in mythology to adopt the attitude of Yāska's yājñikapakṣa, which believed that there were as many gods as there were names. Thus Paśupati and Śiva were distinct hierophanies originally, so were Viṣṇu and Nārāyaṇa. Some fundamental link connected the names and combined the godheads. The classification of all the hierophanies into three major gods came later and was acknowledged only by a few; to the vast majority of the people gods remained many and to them this was desirable; they respected the functional and regional variations because they needed them.

VI

Indian mythology was not a static affair, neither was it a luxury; it was linked with the vital spiritual urges and needs of the people, who projected their most haunting dreams, hopes and cravings into their myths. The changes were not wrought overnight nor easily. From the earliest times the pantheon is the product of a continual clash and friction, not only with gods of other ethnic groups, but among those of various clans and families of the Aryans themselves. Each family seems to have had its weakness for its own god or gods. Those gods who could represent larger segments of life and experience, who could mobilize greater strength and significance, and, later, who could annex other gods by virtue of their greater potentialities, grew, while others faded out. This very fact of the gods changing—growing or diminishing in significance—is a proof of the continual influx of new ideas and a creative conflict with existing ideas. 'The background of the hymns is a troubled one, a scene of passionate rivalries and internal struggles, where great dangers had been faced and surmounted, the abandonment of the surā, the establishment of universal allegiance to Indra by gods and men alike, the eclipse of Varuṇa, the acceptance of the Aśvins, the advent of Rudra: none of these events could have been accomplished without great upheavals' (Louis Renou, *Religions of India*, p. 20). This turmoil continued through the ages until around the Gupta era a pantheon emerged which received universal recognition.

In this period sectarian religions were gradually replacing the older Brāhmaṇical religions. This new approach to the gods remodelled their characters. The gods which could adapt themselves best to the changing needs of the times survived. One way by which they did so was changing their Vedic character and shedding those characteristics which were found unsuitable. Another was sycretism with such regional and tutelary gods as were already being worshipped in this new mode (i.e. pūjā).

Only those gods could adapt themselves who had been 'minor' in the *ṚV*, who did not have too detailed characteristics, i.e. those whose personalities had the necessary vacuum which could be filled in with suitable traits. Gods like the Aśvins whose characters, functions and achievements had been too vividly described to afford the introduction of new traits were found unsuitable and were quietly dropped by the epic literature. On the other hand gods who were too transparently the personifications of natural phenomena could not be transformed into sectarian gods; thus Agni, Vāyu-Vātāh, Parjanya, Sūrya, Soma, Mātariśvan, Savitṛ or Uṣas had to be abandoned. Gods who were too dim as personalities and who had no potentialities to grow from, whose natural base was vague, and spiritual traits hazy were also unsuitable; hence Pūṣan, Bhaga, Aryaman, Dakṣa, Aṃśa, Mitra, Varuṇa, Dyaus, Vivasvat faded out. Only those whose characters were not explicitly known, and who, at the same time offered one or two significant traits which could be developed into rich and complex mythology, survived.

VII

Only Viṣṇu and Rudra fulfilled these conditions: they were suitably vague and indistinct with few or no definite achievements to their credit so as to allow new feats to be ascribed to them; at the same time they had certain features in their characters indicating the direction along which they would develop. Thus Viṣṇu had the nucleus of the 'tripādavikrama' (the three steps), his dwarfish figure, his solar nature, friendship with Indra, his 'most high' station, vague, insinuating references to his unparallelled might —all this could be developed into a concrete and coherent mythologem. He had no actual achievements, but potentially he could perform any feat. His unmistakable solar character aligned him with the solar gods whose traits enriched him. From Indra he imbibed the demon-killing character; from Sūrya and Savitṛ, brilliance and association with gold; from Mitra, kindly and benevolent attitudes to men, and from Bhaga the fortune-bestowing trait. From the solar gods in general he inherited his association with Devayāna, and consequently his role as a saviour. The *Brāhmaṇas* begin the process of introducing new traits through surreptitious syncretism, while the *Purāṇas*, through the 'avatāras' introduce open syncretism. The resulting figure of Viṣṇu-Kṛṣṇa is an eminently successful sectarian god. The component Vedic gods disappear one after another after bequeathing their mythologically potential characteristics on their successor. They last as long as there is any living mythological trait which remains spiritually valid for society, as long as any feature can be fruitfully developed to enrich the myth. When this mythological potentiality is exhausted they depart, leaving an heir to whom all their living features accrue.

In the case of Śiva, too, the same thing happened. The Vedic Rudra was a minor god—mighty, a giver of gifts, an archer, and a formidable god whose wrath was feared and whose darts were to be avoided. This Rudra had no feat to his credit. In his wrath and potential malevolence he came to resemble the later-Vedic Yama, the lord of the fathers; together they gave rise to the concept of Kāla. The *YV* associates him with Ambikā an early prototype of his consort Pārvatī and the mole (later, Gaṇeśa's mount). Varuṇa's function as a punitive god devolves on Rudra as Varuṇa takes his leave from the pantheon. The Maruts are transmuted into the fierce host of Śiva. Nirṛti—Yama's associate in some of her aspects—grows into Kālī, the awesome hierophany of Durgā, Śiva's consort. When the *Brāhmaṇas* select this figure (i.e. Rudra) to work upon, they develop his formidable and fearful traits into a sinister personality. Regional gods with similar evocative features are naturally absorbed by him. In the *Purāṇas* many local gods with dark and lunar associations merge into Rudra to give rise to a really impressive and formidable god.

Of the five important sects in India—Saura, Gāṇapatya, Śākta, Śaiva and Vaiṣṇava—the first two were only regional and shortlived. Of the last three the Śākta began as an offshoot of the Śaiva but very soon started developing as a separate sect. It became a focus for all the different mother-goddess epiphanies. Assimilation with Tantrism changed its orientation, and a complex cult emerged as Śaktism.

Brahman, as we shall notice, never had much hold on the popular imagination, never had any significant sect or following, did not inspire iconography or any devotional literature, and devotion is a prerequisite of the epic-Purāṇic cult. What could have been Brahman's own in religion was diverted into philosophy, into the abstract concept of the Vedāntic supreme being Brahman. It was, however, a two-way traffic. While the mythological Brahman's supreme monistic character was borrowed by metaphysics, the metaphysical Brahman's thin attenuated personality (cf. his epithets nirguṇa, nirañjana, and avyakta, i.e. beyond qualities, traits or manifestation) influenced the mythological Brahman, robbing him of a vivid or tangible personality which alone could grow into a sectarian god. His lofty station, neutrality, Olympian distance and grandfatherly detachment make him unconvincing as a god, and utterly unacceptable as a cult or sectarian god. The little following he must have had as a demiurge even in the period when Buddhism flourished (he was incorporated in the Mahāyāna pantheon) dwindled and in the Purāṇic age he was unceremoniously abandoned, or if not exactly abandoned he was retained only as the least effective and potent member of the triad.

Viṣṇu and Śiva, as supreme epiphanies were inherently opposed to each other. To begin with, Viṣṇu is pre-eminently a solar god while Śiva is a lunar god. The necessary corollary from this is that Viṣṇu stands for the day and light, Śiva and his associates for the night and darkness. Through their associations they are connected with different things—Viṣṇu with gold, Śiva with silver. Viṣṇu's mount is the heavenbound bird Garuḍa, Śiva's animal (according to the *YV*) the earth-bound mole. In later literature Viṣṇu in his Kalki incarnation is connected with the slim and swift horse and Śiva with the stout and slow bull; Śiva's associates—Yama and Nirṛti—have the buffalo and the ass, beasts with nefarious evocations. Viṣṇu is associated with the sea and water, Śiva with the mountains. Viṣṇu's mount Garuḍa is an eater of serpents which are entwined around Śiva's frame; Śiva belongs with death, Yama and the fathers, Viṣṇu with life and the gods. Śiva is connected with Pitṛyāna and reincarnation, Viṣṇu with Devayāna and liberation. The sacrifice (a rite to the gods) is identified with Viṣṇu; Piṇḍa and Pitṛkarman (rites to the fathers) are connected with Śiva. Viṣṇu was himself incarnated several times, Śiva had no incarnations

(Lakulīśa may not have been an incarnation of Śiva); Viṣṇu and gods of his group are generally polygamous, Śiva is monogamous. Woman appeared primarily in the role of lover in the Vaiṣṇava religion, but pre-eminently as a mother in Śaivism; Lakṣmī as mother is pale beside Durgā.

Both Viṣṇu and Śiva have fertility associations; Viṣṇu because he is a solar god, Śiva because he is a chthonic god. And fertility associations are essential for gods who were worshipped in agrarian communities; they enhanced the sectarian gods' cultic appeal and power. Thus while Viṣṇu symbolized the sunbeams which ripen the crops from above; Śiva and Yama, associated with the fathers who grant crops, symbolize the dark processes which go on underneath the soil to nourish the young shoot. As a god connected with the fathers (who are regarded as the guarantors of the harvest), and with the Earth and the mother-goddess who create life out of matter, Śiva stands for that phase of growth which continues unseen under the soil. Viṣṇu and the solar gods on the other hand stand for the sun, ripen the crops, beautify the plants and give colour to fruits and flowers.

Viṣṇu as the culmination of the solar hierophany symbolizes the concept of the Ādityas who belonged to the east, where the sun rises. They were 'the bright ones' (devāh), the prime connotation of Vedic Aryan gods. Later they found a rival set of powers worshipped by the Austrics and Dravidians (perhaps of the same stock as the Mediterranean peoples) who worshipped Pitarah, the Manes, the Earth and Mother goddesses. A clash followed, subtle, and long drawn out. The Indian pantheon, and its final culmination in the triad, is the result of this clash. What the Aryans found here was to a great extent antithetical to their own beliefs of gods and worship. The Āgamic religion came into conflict with the Nigamic; the religion of the patriarchal and solar gods connected primarily with the matriarchal and lunar pantheon. As a result of the clash, many new gods emerged and many of the old gods did not pass the test of fitness, i.e. the power to change, grow and assimilate. Discarded hierophanies were revived, and in the turmoil that followed only two gods emerged unscathed and triumphant. Gods who had inherited all the rich, potential and living traits of predecessors of their group and who had an almost infinite capacity for imbibing traits of similar regional gods survived. In the final synthesis Viṣṇu and Śiva remained as gods demanding not sacrifices but pūjās, i.e. as sectarian gods.

A note on the derivation of the names of gods

The prevalent tendency of scholars to derive god-names from one particular root with one particular meaning has an essential drawback, it limits the connotation to one particular time and meaning. Mythology, as long as it has any validity, has dynamism, and to confine a name to a fixed significance is to deaden it for all subsequent time. Thus when scholars derive Varuṇa from *vṛ*, *vār*, *ver* or *uer*, each attaches one particular meaning to the connotation of the name. When a name is first created its creator has an etymology in mind. The etymology is not circulated, only the name. When others in the community worship the god they are not aware of the etymology in which the name originated. Also in Vedic times in north India the society which accepted the god-name was composite, heterogeneous and amorphous, without a central religious organization like a church, but split up into communities which were united only through the major community (Śrauta) sacrifices. Hence there was complete freedom for each section (clan or phratry) to impute an etymology to a god-name. These different interpretations would multiply with time and with their dissemination to different countries. The absence of a universally accepted etymology is apparent in Yāska's Nirukta and Sāyaṇa's commentary on the *RV* god-names and in the *Brāhmaṇas* and the Purāṇic sections of the *Mahābhārata* and in the *Purāṇas* themselves, which are full of fantastic and sometimes apparently grotesque etymologies. But since the name was important, each section of the community may have derived any name differently, and from the worshipper's point of view—which alone can be the valid point of view in mythology—each derivation was as correct as another. Mythologically all possible and probable derivations—all, that is, that explain something of the nature or function of the god in question and do not conflict with the total image must be accepted. A search for the 'original' root of a god-name is a dangerous case of 'Kākadanta-gaveṣaṇa-nyāya' (i.e. seeking for a crow's teeth), since etymologies as much as morphological or phonemic entities are in all cases secondary abstractions: the name itself is the primary source of the connotation. I have adopted the theory of multiple derivations. A completely abstract derivation which is presented as the only acceptable one, though acceptable to an advanced and learned section of a society would be absolutely meaningless and hence unacceptable to the bulk of the worshippers. Mythologically speaking these were the people who made any cult a vital, living thing. If the common people understood only an abstract notion by any god-name, that god would be denuded of anthropomorphism and would become unfit for a cult. Thus, while such an abstraction may have been a valid concept to the highest sections of a society, to the people at the base it would not make much sense. The people would fill the name out with more concrete concepts to make the god cult-worthy.

A note on the principal Indian texts mentioned in this book

Chronologically the *Vedas* are divided into four sections—*Saṃhitā*, *Brāhmaṇa*, *Āraṇyaka* and *Upaniṣad*. Each of the four *Vedas* (*Ṛc*, *Sāman*, *Yajus* and *Atharvan*, again more or less in the chronological order) has these above sections. The *Ṛk Saṃhitā* (hymns), the earliest Vedic texts, are generally agreed to have been composed between 1200 and 900 B.C. The other three *Saṃhitās* belong to a period roughly between 1000 and 700 B.C. The *Brāhmaṇas* (prose directives for rituals and exegetical anecdotes) were composed between 800 and 500 B.C. By the beginning of the eighth century B.C. the Aryans had reached eastern Bihar and Bengal and a new phase of cultural amalgamation and religious fusion began; it was around this time that the *Āraṇyakas* and *Upaniṣads* (cosmogonic and philosophical treatises) were composed between 700 and 400 B.C. The earlier Brāhmaṇical *Upaniṣads* (Aitareya, parts of the Bṛ.Ā, Chāndogya, Kauṣītakī, Kena and Taittirīya—mainly prose) belong to the earlier part of this period, while the later *Upaniṣads* (Kaṭha, Muṇḍaka, Śvetāśvatara, Praśna, Māṇḍūkya and Maitrāyaṇī—mainly verse) belong to the latter half. The *Sūtras* which came after the period of the 'revealed literature' (i.e. *Saṃhitās* to *Upaniṣads*) were mainly of four types: (A) *Śruata* (codes for the major, communal sacrifices); (B) *Gṛhya* (for the minor family sacraments, like ceremonies at birth, marriage and death); (C) *Dharma* (codes of conduct governing the four āśramas, i.e. the four stages of life: (1) Brahmacarya, studenthood; (2) Gārhasthya, householder's life; (3) Vānaprastha, retirement to the forest, and (4) Yati, hermithood; as well as laws of conduct for the four castes, Brāhmaṇa, Kṣattriya, Vaiśya and Śūdra), and (D) *Śulva* (sacrificial architecture). These sūtras were in the main codified between 600 and 200 B.C.

The major Buddhist texts of the Pāli Canon were composed between 500 B.C. and A.D. 200. The two epics (*Rāmāyaṇa* and *Mahābhārata*) belong to the centuries immediately before and after Christ. The *Rāmāyaṇa*, as we have it, is thought to have been completed between 200 B.C. and A.D. 200. The *Mahābhārata*, whose inception belongs to *c.* 400 B.C. or even earlier, did not assume its present shape (i.e. including the later Purāṇic interpolations) until the fourth century A.D. or a little later. The epics were not overtly scriptures, yet posterity regarded them as such and in their final redactions they themselves laid down such a claim. The bulk of the heroic tales of both belong to the same period (200 B.C.–A.D. 200), but the antennae reach beyond the upper limit and the interpolations continued in the succeeding period of brisk activity of Purāṇic texts when the epics were reshaped so that the *Rām.* became a *Rāma Purāṇa* and the *Mbh.* a *Kṛṣṇa-Purāṇa.*

Māhāyāna Buddhist texts which deify the Buddha and introduce a new Buddhist pantheon are contemporaneous with the heroic sections of the epics. The earliest *Purāṇas* belong to the early Gupta age when the first and seventh books of the *Rām.* (where Rāma is deified) and the innumerable interpolations of the *Mbh.* appear to have been inserted. Roughly about this time we have the earliest codification of the Sāṃkhya, Yoga and Vedānta philosophies. The early *Purāṇas*, whose roots go back to the antiquity of oral traditions, were composed between the third and eighth centuries A.D. The *Harivaṃśa*, a supplementary work on the biography of Kṛṣṇa was composed during this period. The *Purāṇas* are sectarian scriptures, each of which magnified the cult and character of Śiva, Brahman or one or other of the incarnations of Viṣṇu. After this we have a new phase of Hinduism and Buddhism—represented by the *Tantras*, which sought to combine all earlier religious tendencies, formulated a new cosmogony and created new esoteric and mystery cults around the figures of Śiva and Pārvatī. By then the *Purāṇa* composers had achieved their end—i.e. the religious unification of India through a pantheon accepted all over the country. They had also succeeded in giving fixed shapes and characters to the theophanies, which have changed little since. With the defeat of the Hindus under Prithvīrāj at the hands of Muslim invaders in A.D. 1192, Buddhism disappeared as an organized force in India and neo-Brāhmaṇism established through the *Purāṇas* during the Gupta era (later termed Hinduism) became the religion of the Indian people. The gods which constitute the core of this religion were more or less fixed in their character and function by the early *Purāṇas*, hence the scope of this book extends up to the Gupta period.

Among ancillary Vedic texts I have used are Yāska's *Nirukta* (traditional etymology of Vedic names) and Śaunaka's *Bṛhaddevatā* (a traditional account of the Vedic gods, their characters and functions); the dates of both are uncertain. Yāska is considered to belong to the fourth century B.C. or earlier and Śaunaka somewhat later. I have used the Poona text of the *Ṛgveda*, the Vaidik Saṃśodhana Maṇḍala and Gorakhpur texts of the other Vedic and Purāṇic works, the Poona critical text of the *Mbh.* and the Gorresio and Bengal recensions of the *Rāmāyaṇa*. All the translations of Sanskrit texts are mine, except for the *Śatapatha Brāhmaṇa* for which I used Eggeling's translation.[1]

Bibliographical note on the Introduction

Bergaigne, A. *La Religion védique* (1878–97).
Coomaraswamy, A. *Myths of the Hindus and the Buddhists* (1913).
Dumézil, G. *Mitra-Varuna* (1940).
Les Dieux des Indo-Européens (1952).
Déesses Latines et mythes védiques (1954).
L'Indologie tripartite des Indo-Européens (1958).
Durkheim, E. *The elementary forms of religious life* (tr. 1915).
Eliade, M. *Patterns in comparative religion* (1958).
Myths, dreams and mysteries (1960).
Myth and reality (1964).
Frazer, J. G. *The golden bough* (1911–15).
Freud, S. *Totem and taboo* (1919).
Moses and monotheism (1939).
Gonda, J. *Aspects of early Visnuism* (1954).
Change and continuity in Indian religion (1965).
Harrison, Jane. *Themis* (1911).
Hooke, S. H. (ed.). *Myth and ritual* (1933).
Jung, C. G. *Introduction to a science of mythology* (1951).
The archetype and the collective unconscious (1959).
Lang, Andrew. *Custom and myth* (1884).
Myth, ritual and religion (1887).
Making of religion (1898).
Lévy-Bruhl. *Primitive mythology* (1923).
L'Expérience mythique et les symboles chez les primitifs (1938).
Lévi-Strauss, C. *Structural anthropology* (1964).
Malinowski, B. *The function of myth in primitive society* (1922–32).
Meyer, J. J. *Gesetzbuch und Purana* (1929).
Müller, Max. *Selected essays on language, mythology and religions* (1881).
Natural religion (1888).
Renou, L. *La Poésie religieuse de l'Inde antique* (1942).
Vedic India (1957).
Schmidt, W. *Origin and growth of religion* (1935).
Spencer, Herbert. *Principles of sociology* (1876).
Tylor, E. B. *Primitive culture* (1871).
Zimmer, H. *Myths and symbols in Indian art and civilization* (1963).

[1] All dates are more or less conjectural, deduced from internal evidence. I have primarily adopted the dates put forward by the linguistic evidence of Prof. T. Burrow, *The Sanskrit language*; K. W. Morgan, *The religion of the Hindus*, who co-ordinates various dates; Belvalkar and Ranade, *History of Indian philosophy*; M. Winternitz, *History of Indian literature*, vol. 1 and P. V. Kane, *History of Dharmaśāstra*.

PART I

GODS OF THE ŚIVA GROUP

CHAPTER I

VARUṆA

THE Indian pantheon as we have it in the *ṚV* is primarily a carry-over from the Indo-European period, but it is also specifically Indian; that is to say, the Indo-European content is modified through foreign and indigenous influences. Thus in Varuṇa we have an Indo-European base on which the structure of the Vedic, later-Vedic and epic-Purāṇic Varuṇa is built.

In almost all mythologies the primeval concept of a god begins with that of the sky-god. In all probability Dyaus was the first sky-god. But Dyaus had always been an abstract deity—the natural side of his character was permanently in the background and he is simply a consort of Pṛthivī. In the hymns Dyaus was almost inalienably paired with Pṛthivī and together they symbolized the heaven-and-earth couple, i.e. the visible world. In the *BĀU* (IV: 4: 20) there is a marriage-vow, 'Dyauraham pṛthivī tvam'—'I am Dyaus (the sky) and you are Pṛthivi (the earth)'. One is reminded of Ouranos and Gaia or the Egyptian Geb-and-Nut pair. This hierogamy of Dyāvāpṛthivī constituted the entire personality of Dyaus. But a sky-god, to be convincing, has to be a real divinity with creative attributes besides being merely married to another hierophany. Dyaus lacked any such convincing traits, so that as a sky-god he remains a minor figure with an arrested personality.

This attenuation of Dyaus coincides with the rise of Varuṇa, the new sky-god. It is like the attenuation of Tiwaz before Odin could become supreme. Varuṇa is called the protector of the firmament in *MS* IV: 3: 4. In the *Avesta*, Varuṇa is 'Varana the all-embracing sky', 'Asura Viśvavedas, the all-knowing Lord', 'Ahura Mazda, the Lord of high knowledge ...his concrete name Varana which became his usual name in India (Varuṇa) was lost in Iran and remained only as the name of the material heaven' (Introduction to the *Zend Avesta*, *S.B.E.*). Thus the Indo-Iranian identity of Varuṇa as the sky-god is established from Avestan evidence. Varuṇa, Uru-va-na-asil in the Boghaz-keui inscription, is the Indo-Iranian parallel of Greek Ouranos. But unlike Dyaus, Varuṇa was not merely a sky-god. He was much more. His Avestan parallel gradually became lost in Iran and remained only as the name of the heavens. Later the word indicated a mythical region, the Varana, the seat of the mythical fight between a storm-god and a storm-fiend. The term 'Asura', mainly an epithet of Varuṇa in the earlier part of the *ṚV*, was applied to the six Amesha Spentas—associates of Ahura Mazda. Ahura Mazda, though supreme in status, needed the assistance of these six asuras. But the Avestan 'Ahura Mazda' is not more different from the great Asura-Varuṇa. Thus the Mitra-Ahura of the *Avesta* corresponds to the Mitra-Varuṇa pair of the *ṚV*.

As a successor of Dyaus the sky-god Varuṇa flourished for a time in India, because, compared with Dyaus, his was a more tangible and vivid personality, with positive characteristics, definite relationships with gods and men and a specific cosmic function and concrete achievement.

As a sky-god Varuṇa is different from Ouranos, who preserved his cosmic character, i.e. he was the sky itself. But at the same time Ouranos was the procreative god. He is chiefly mentioned as such in Hesiod's *Theogony*. The other sky-gods resembling Varuṇa in overlordship and cosmic functions are all procreative. For example Thor began as a sky-god but he was also the champion of heroes; so were Odin and Zeus. But Varuṇa's evolution was not through physical power or prowess but through māyā—magic power. 'The celestial god sees everything and therefore knows everything and this knowledge, being of a supernatural order, is, in itself, a power' (M. Eliade, *Myths, dreams and mysteries*, p. 133). Yet, although in the *ṚV* Varuṇa remains supreme and the symbol of kingship, his status declines with time.

Even as an Indo-European god Varuṇa was supreme; he was the creation of primitive monotheism which demands 'a supreme deity, wholly beneficent, omnipotent and omniscient. It demands the complete exclusion of all other gods. The world in its minute details is regarded as his work, as having been created out of nothing in response to his wish' (Paul Radin, *Monotheism among primitive peoples*, pp. 15–16). In the Edda mythology Varuṇa's parallel was Odin as Tiwaz was Dyaus's. The fact that Odin is one-eyed also suggests that he is the sky-god. 'The All-father came there (i.e. to the spring-well Hvergelmir) and asked for a single drink from the spring, but he did not get it until he had given one of his eyes as a pledge.' As the sky-god his one eye is the Sun.

Varuṇa's Mesopotamian parallel is Anu, a very old sky-god. 'When the Sumerians arrived in 3000 B.C. they (the Mesopotamians) had already developed a highly organized pantheon under the leadership of Anu, whose name meant "heaven"...Anu lifted it (i.e. the universe) out of chaos and anarchy and made it an organized whole, for he was the supreme power in the sky, the father and king of the gods, the prototype of all earthly rulers and the ultimate source of their authority and of natural law' (E. O. James, *The ancient gods*, p. 303).

The sky-gods are all supreme because the sky encompasses the earth. Varuṇa, as the sky-god and the successor of the dim Dyaus, also became a sovereign god and he is frequently called Samrāj (= emperor) as opposed to rājan (= king), an appellative of Soma and many other gods. An *AV* passage praises Varuṇa kathenotheistically. It says that Varuṇa becomes Agni in the evening and rising in the morning he becomes Mitra. As Savitṛ he shines in the firmament and as Indra he shines in the centre of the sky (*AV* XIII: 3: 13). He is called Samrāj (*ṚV* I: 136: 1; VIII: 42: 1; together with Mitra, Samrājā, I: 2: 7). He is said to be a king (*ṚV* VII: 34: 11), a king of the gods (*MS* II: 21, *TB* II: 5: 7: 6; III: 1: 2: 7; 8: 18: B), dressed in shining golden attire (*ṚV* I: 25: 13). He is the king of the territories (rājā rāṣṭrāṇām, *ṚV* VII: 34: 11). The royal consecration is said to be the consecration of Varuṇa (*TS* V: 6: 2). In the *TMB* (XXIII: 9: 23) we hear that he attained sovereignty through chanting the Varuṇa Sāman. In the *ŚB* we are told that Varuṇa took away Śrī's universal sovereignty (XI: 6: 1: 13). The Rājasūya sacrifice belongs to Varuṇa (V: 4: 3: 1). The horse which everywhere is a symbol of sovereignty is to be slaughtered for Varuṇa (*ŚB* VI: 2: 1: 5, VII: 5: 2: 18); Varuṇa became the king of the gods by performing the Rājasūya sacrifice (II: 196). Another passage (*JB* III: 152) relates that Varuṇa, desiring supremacy, composed a hymn and became the divine overlord. The *Rāmāyaṇa* also regards Varuṇa as a king and mentions him as one of the five gods whose likeness kings bear (IV: 17: 26); he is invoked as a king (*Rām* II: 25: 22). The *Mbh.* describes Varuṇa's court with its royal splendour in II: 9. The *HV* mentions Varuṇa as having performed the Rājasūya sacrifice; after him it was performed by many other victorious sovereigns (III: 2), The *ŚŚS* says, 'He who desires sovereign lordship should offer as did Varuṇa in a similar situation' (XV: 21: 2). Varuṇa is the supreme Kṣattra (*ŚB* II: 5: 2: 34, *Mait. U* I: 6: 11). The worshippers feel like slaves in his presence (*ṚV* I: 25: 1). This awe and an attitude of profound humility is not found in connection with any other Vedic god.

As emperor Varuṇa is mighty and awe-inspiring. He is called Riśādas, the destroyer of enemies (*ṚV* I: 2: 7), 'tuvijāta' and 'urukṣaya' mighty (*ṚV* I: 17: 1). His might and speed are unequalled by birds or falling streams (*ṚV* I: 24: 8). He is strong as a white deer (*ṚV* VIII: 86: 6). The *KB* says, 'Varuṇa is the lordly power' (XII: 8). 'Varuṇa has a strong stomach which nothing can harm' (*ŚB* V: 1: 2, also *Rām.* V: 78: 12). He bound Prajāpati's creatures who ate up his barley but let them off when they performed a sacrifice (*ŚB* v: 1: 21). His power is connected with sanctity, for the garment of initiation belongs to Varuṇa (*ŚB* v: 3: 2: 8) and 'he is called Dharmapati, lord of righteousness' (*ŚB* v: 3: 3: 9).

Varuṇa is called Kavi, seer (*ṚV* I: 2: 9), chiefly because his vision and knowledge are stressed throughout the *ṚV*. The *AV* (v: 11: 4) says that there is no better Kavi than Varuṇa, none wiser than he. At XVIII: 33: 4 Varuṇa is said to be omniscient. This is because Varuṇa is seen as having many eyes, and consequently as all-seeing. He is Viśvadarśata, all-seeing (*ṚV* I: 25: 18), or Urucakṣasa, many-eyed (*ṚV* I: 25: 5). The sun is identified with the eye of Mitra and Varuṇa, to whom men should bow (*ṚV* x: 37: 1). Varuṇa shares a trait, in common with Odin, in the Edda. For Odin, 'the All-father', too is one-eyed, evidently the sun is his only eye. Varuṇa's eye is in the sky, svardṛśa' (*ṚV* v: 63: 2). He is thousand-eyed, sahasracakṣah (*ṚV* VII: 34: 10). He knows the cosmic secrets in the upper regions (*ṚV* I: 25: 7, 9) and all deeds, done or not done (*ṚV* I: 25: 11); he sees the truth and falsehood of men (*ṚV* VII: 49: 3). Together with Mitra he is nṛcakṣa, seer of men (*ṚV* VII: 60: 2). He notices all malice (*AV* I: 10: 2), and where two persons sit and hold a converse King Varuṇa the third knows it (*ṚV* IV: 16: 2). He can see everything because he has many eyes, which, if we remember his character as the sky-god—and especially the god of the night sky—are easily seen as the stars. But he is also assisted by the spaśas, spies. All through the Vedic literature Varuṇa is invariably associated with his spies. These he has placed all around him (*ṚV* I: 25: 3). Together with Mitra, Varuṇa employs spies in trees (presumably fireflies) and in men and these watch unwinkingly to see if men walk in the righteous path (*ṚV* VII: 6: 3).

The word *spaśa* which originally meant Varuṇa's spies, i.e. which indicated his all-seeing power and omniscience, before whom nothing in the universe—material or mental—could be kept secret, underwent a philological change in the later-Vedic literature where we no longer hear of the spies but of his noose (*pāśa*). The Indo-European root *spəc* gradually lost its meaning and Varuṇa came to be associated not with spies (who went over to Yama) but with a noose. Varuṇa holding the noose is not as formidable as the omniscient Varuṇa who employed the unwinking spies to catch miscreants. With time, as Varuṇa lost his early grandeur and awe-inspiring character, and spies were not essential for his reduced stature, it was enough if he had a noose instead. Thus philology only covered up the process of the attenuation and decentralization of his spiritual power.

By this time Varuṇa's entire personality had undergone a more thoroughgoing mythological transformation. From a benevolent sky-god Varuṇa had gradually become a sinister god with dark associations—not only the judge but the punisher of the transgressor. The Indo-European sky-god is now assuming a clearer form. Long prayers are addressed to him for forgiveness and the remission of sins (*ṚV* VII: 86) for he is feared as a severe punisher. From the time of the *AV* onwards we frequently hear of Varuṇa's pāśa (*AV* II: 10: 1). In the *TS* it says: 'I loosen this bond of Varuṇa' (I: I: 10). We also have a prayer, 'Unloose from us O Varuṇa, the highest, the lowest, the midmost knot'; 'Varuṇa seizes him who accepts the horse' (offerings of horses should be made for freeing him from Varuṇa's noose, *TS* II: 3: 12). In the *MS* his pāśa figures more frequently and we have quite a number of references to it. Even when the pāśa is removed it is still feared and regarded with awe (*MS* I: 2: 6). The Gāyatrī metre is one of his nooses (*MS* II: 3: 3), the day and night are others (*MS* III: 7: 8). Everything is subject to Varuṇa's control and authority and he takes everything; when the Soma offering is performed men are released from Varuṇa's noose (*MS* III: 9: 1; *TB* III: 3: 10: 1). Varuṇa, however, has two nooses—one terrible and the other beneficent (*MS* III: 9: 6). The *AB* says: 'so long as he is tied up, Varuṇa is his deity, so long as he proceeds to the closed places' (I: 3: 13). In the *KB* we are told that Prajāpati's offspring—who were created not born—ate Varuṇa's barley, Varuṇa seized them with his nooses. At their request Prajāpati devised the Varuṇapraghāsa sacrifice and they were released also from all ills (*KB* V: 3). The *TB* says: the human system composed of the five elements has to be released from Varuṇa's pāśa for health and also for independence of Varuṇa (*TB* I: 5: 9: 7, also *TB* I: 6: 5: 6). The *ŚB* mentions the noose together with the rope (*ŚB* II: 5: 2: 41, III: 6: 3: 20); 'that rope is Varuṇa's, therefore, he thus binds it with the rope of sacred order and thus the rope of Varuṇa does not injure' (III: 7: 4: 1). The sling also belongs to Varuṇa (*ŚB* VII: 5: 2: 18). By the time of the *Rāmāyaṇa* the noose had become inseparably associated with Varuṇa (*Rām.* II: 122: 22, also *Rām.* III: 54: 9, IV: 3: 58, VI: 51: 32); but he also carries a disc (*Rām.* I: 57: 9). In the *Mbh.* he has a specific Vāruṇāstra which he grants to Arjuna (III: 42). But the epics also mention his pāśa; at Brahman's request he had the demons tied with his pāśa and cast under the ocean in order to prevent an imminent battle (*Mbh.* V: 126). The river Parṇāśā, mother of Varuṇa's son Śrutāyudha asked Varuṇa for her son's immortality (this reminds us of Thetis seeking immortality for Achilles), but Varuṇa merely bestowed his club on his son.

This club was a divine weapon (*Mbh.* VII: 67). Varuṇa's pāśa binds the man who fails to keep his promise of a gift; this man is punished by Death himself (*Mbh.* XIII: 62: 75). The *HV*, a later epic-Purāṇic work, too, knows Varuṇa as holding his noose (III: 61), so does the *Matsya P* (CXXXV: 76). By this time Varuṇa had ceased to be the moral supervisor of the world, he had become merely the punisher, with the noose, the sling, and disc and the club.

The *ṚV* god of the firmament, the successor of Dyaus, was omniscient. As the embodiment of the sky itself the whole universe was spread beneath his vision. The natural corollary was that he watched and punished men's iniquity and was therefore an awesome god. But his formidable character had another source of power in the *ṚV*; he was the guardian of Ṛta the moral order in the universe.

Varuṇa himself is said to be the creator of Ṛta, as the boundary of creation which all nature observes (*ṚV* II: 28: 4). Through his Ṛta nature moves in an orderly manner, the luminaries are kept in their own fixed orbits (*ṚV* V: 62: 1), by Ṛta men cross iniquity as by a boat and are not caught unawares by Varuṇa's noose (*ṚV* VII: 66: 3). Varuṇa and Mitra are the keepers of Ṛta in the highest heaven (*ṚV* V: 63: 1).

Here (*ṚV* VIII: 35: 13; also *MS* III: 9: 1), besides Ṛta, Dharma is also mentioned as being in the keeping of Mitra and Varuṇa. Elsewhere, too, Dharma is said to be Varuṇa's law, prayer is made for absolution from the sin of flouting Dharma (*ṚV* VII: 88: 5). Varuṇa separates Ṛta from anṛta—the true path from the false (*ṚV* X: 124: 5). It is remarkable that in the later tenth book of the *ṚV* we meet the word anṛta, which in later literature came to mean falsehood and is already inclining towards that meaning. But the early Vedic Ṛta is distinctly the firm, fundamental and inherent law of nature. This is clear in *ṚV* IV: 24: 8: 9. The *AV* calls it Dharma (VI: 132) and uses it in a curse. The *TS* says, 'Thou art Varuṇa who guardeth law' (I: 2: 11). The *MS* says that to Varuṇa belongs the seat of Ṛta (I: 2: 6), and calls him the lord of Dharma (II: 6: 6). Together with Mitra he is the guardian of law (III: 8: 9). In the *Avabhṛtha Homa* Varuṇa is called dharmāṇām pati, lord of all righteousness (*JB* III: 11: 4: 1). The *ŚB* mentions Varuṇa's noose of sacred order (III: 7: 4: 1). In the *Avesta* there is no Varuṇa, but there is a god who performs the vital function of Varuṇa, that is, watching the sacred order, Ṛta. Paul Thieme says, 'Not Varuṇa but a great many ideas connected with the Vedic Varuṇa, e.g. the Avestic Ahura Mazda do correspond. Of the four chief Ādityas Varuṇa, Mitra, Aryaman and Bhaga, there are Miθra, Airiyaman and Baγa, but Varuṇa is conspicuously lacking. Ṛta, the ethical concept most intimately associated with Varuṇa in the *ṚV* is...in its Avestic form ṛta/aša, a central concept of Zoroastrian religion. The *Avesta* has not a trace of the god Varuṇa' (*JAOS* 80, no. 4 (1960), 45). But his ethical function is taken up by Ahura Mazda—and Ahura Mazda is supreme. This clearly shows that at least in the Indo-Iranian period gods needed ethical functions in order to become supreme.

In the Tell-el-Amarna inscription we have the word 'arta' from which is derived the Avestan Aša/Urta/Arta variants of Ṛta. This brings out his relationship with Ṛta even in the Indo-Iranian period. His rise and prominence even in the Indo-European and Indo-Iranian period may be due to his ethical responsibility. Together with Mitra, Varuṇa more than any other god is in charge of the established order of the universe—both moral and physical. It is said to Agni, 'Thou dost become Varuṇa when thou strivest for Ṛta' (*ṚV* x: 8: 5). This shows the almost exclusive connection of Varuṇa with Ṛta. The Avestan Ahura Mazda resembles Varuṇa in this, for 'Ahura Mazda and Varuṇa are both ethically developed and important' (M. M. Ghosh, 'Varuṇa, His Identification', *IHQ* xxv, no. 4, Dec. 1959). Heinrich Lüders too, in his *Varuṇa* (Göttingen, 1951, p. 35) says, 'Als Schützer des Ṛta mußte er mit seiner Macht alles überstrahlen, war schon das Ṛta gar nicht anders denn als ein Allherrscher angesehen werden. So erklärt sich, wie ich meine, auch das Königtum Varuṇas gerade als seinem Charakter als Eidgott.' Varuṇa inspired awe and reverence through Ṛta and became great because of his connection with it.

The word Ṛta can be derived from the root *ṛ* = to go. But as primitive man's basic word stock was economical and had only one word for one meaning, synonyms were ruled out because each word expressed a different shade of meaning. Hence the root *ṛ* is not the same as the root *gam* which meant simple going. The root *ṛ*, as is clear from later derivations, meant a particular kind of going, that is 'going straight or regularly, or along a fixed course', from which the auxiliary meaning is derived. This is also borne out by substantives derived from it,—'conforming to a norm'. *Ṛta*, a derivative from *ṛ*, means 'any settled point of time, fixed time, right or fit time' (Monier Williams: *Sanskrit–English dictionary*). The regular rotation of the seasons establishes a manifest principle of universal law. Again *Ṛju* meaning 'straight' appears to be another derivative from *ṛ* formed with the suffix *ju* (like *sarju*, *sṛ* plus *ju* equals lightning, that which moves fast). The word *Ārya* (one who conforms to an accepted, noble, straightforward code of conduct) is also derived from *ṛ*. In all this we notice the emphasis on straightness and regularity. He whose conduct was irregular or crooked (= evil) was an anārya. So we get Ṛta from *ṛ* (with *kta* in the passive voice like *gata* meaning 'going, gait'). The combination *ṛ* plus *ta* must have yielded two forms, *rta* and *arta*, the first retained in India and the second in Iran in Urta/Arta/Aša. Ṛta was personified quite early. Duchesne-Guillemin in his book *Symbols and values in Zoroastrianism* mentions words which have 'ṛta' as a component part: artammanya, artasumara, artadama, artamna, artasari and artaxshathra. It has a secondary sense or association of regular or straight going—like the ploughman's regular and fixed course along his field. One remembers the Lithuanian *arti*, a derivative from the same root meaning 'to plough'. *Ṛta*, in Monier-Williams is a fixed or settled order, law, rule, sacred or pious action or custom, divine law, faith, divine faith. One is tempted to see in Hooker's *Ecclesiastical polity* a statement of this old Indo-European concept of divine ordinance. Hooker's subject in book I is stated as 'Of the Law which God from before the beginning hath set for himself to do all things by'. This is the theistic definition of *Ṛta*, for 'God' according to Hooker and his contemporary tehologians 'is only a law unto himself'. His definition of this law is 'That which determines the kind of working, moderates the force and power of working, appoints form and measure of working of each thing is a law' (Hooker, *Of the laws of ecclesiastical polity*, ed. Keole, 3rd edn. 1845). Thus we see that down the centuries this faith is rooted in man's ethical consciousness; he obeys rules because nature herself does so, and this obedience is at the bottom of the essential cohesion in nature and human society, and morality becomes a matter of inner compulsion in response to the operation of Ṛta in external nature. And, because all this is so, there is peace and harmony in nature. Man, too, in order to have peace and prosperity should observe some fixed principles and behave according to some accepted code of conduct. He would be a true Ārya if he did so and the Ārya's gods would look after his well-being. But he did not always do so and when he transgressed the norm of Ārya's conduct, broke faith and failed gods and men, he offended against a vital fundamental principle—Ṛta. Varuṇa, who watched men's intentions and actions, condemned him. In primitive religion the supreme being did this, and as long as Varuṇa was supreme (i.e. during the first phase of composition of the *ṚV* hymns) he discharged this function.

Keith says 'the idea of Ṛta is one which, like the moral elevation of Varuṇa, has no future history in India, pointing irresistibly to the view that it was not an Indian creation but an inheritance which did not long survive its new milieu' (*Religion and philosophy of the Vedas and the Upanisads*, p. 35).

The inevitable corollary of judgement is punishment of the evil-doer. And from the *Brāhmaṇas* onwards we have a dark, wrathful Varuṇa. Even in the earlier portion of the *ṚV* we are acquainted with his wrath, but it is the wrath of a just god. In *ṚV* I: 24: 9 his anger is sought to be mollified. One entire hymn, *ṚV* VII: 86 is a prayer for forgiveness of sins of drink, dice, temper and falsehood. Another hymn is a prayer for absolution from the sin of flouting 'dharman', or Varuṇa's immutable ordinance (*ṚV* VII: 88: 5). His wrath and vengeance are referred to in *ṚV* IV: 24: 8, 9. Vengeance is the exclusive domain of Varuṇa; we can almost hear 'Vengeance is mine, I will repay'.

An *AV* prayer addressed to Varuṇa asks him to release the worshipper from the bonds of Varuṇa in all spheres, from sin and evil dreams (*ṚV* VII: 83: 1: 4). The *TS* says, 'Varuṇa is the exactor of recompense' (I: 5: 2). Again, 'Thine anger, O Varuṇa, would we avert with reverence, with sacrifices, with oblations. Ruling, O wise Asura, O king, Do thou unloose the sins we have committed, unloose us, O Varuṇa, the highest, the lowest, the midmost Knot, then may we, O Āditya, in thy rule, be guiltless before Aditi' (*TS* I: 5: 11). The horse which has ever been an emblem of kingship and solar associations was in the early stage Varuṇa's symbol, because he was the sun-eyed sky-god. Thus we read 'vāruṇo vā aśvah', the horse belongs to Varuṇa (*TB* II: 2: 5: 3; III: 8: 20: 3); the horse was to be slaughtered for Varuṇa (*ŚB* VI: 2: 1: 5), for it is Varuṇa (*ŚB* VII: 5: 2: 18). Varuṇa is jealous of this symbol, 'Prajāpati led the horse to Varuṇa, it went to its own deity...Varuṇa seizes him who accepts the horse. Varuṇa is a destroyer of foes (*TS* V: 6: 20).[1] He binds and bondage is another mark of his power. Hence, 'the Soma when bought and tied up is connected with Varuṇa' (*TS* VI: 1: 11; also *AB* I: 3: 13). The *KB* says: 'Varuṇa being pleased freed offspring from the nooses (of Varuṇa) and from all evil' (V: 3: 14). The Varuṇapraghāsa sacrifice (second of the periodical oblations) is offered at the full moon of Āṣāḍha for obtaining redemption from Varuṇameni, i.e. Varuṇa's wrath or vengeance. 'The evils (i.e. remissnesses) of a sacrifice are atoned through Varuṇa' (*JB* II: 230). Varuṇa catches a man in his lies (*TB* I: 7: 2: 6) and then, unless Varuṇa is duly propitiated, great harm befalls the offender, as he caused emaciation to the

[1] Varuna later had association with seas and significantly enough the Greek sea-god Poseidon was also associated with horses. Poseidon's son by Alope was called Hippothsoon, who in his infancy was twice rescued by a mare. His son Bellerophon owned Pegasus. Assuming horse-shape Poseidon begot Arcion and the Arcadian Despoina from the Tilphusian Erinys. Another interesting connection with Varuṇa is Poseidon's name Epoptes, 'the watcher', which he shares with Zeus. Again Poseidon, too, received human sacrifices and this grim trait connects him with Varuṇa in the latter's gruesome aspect.

sacrificers until they hid behind their respective sacrificial gifts (dakṣiṇā) and then Varuṇa could not harm them (*TB* II: 2: 5: 1). Once, we read in *TMB*, the Vrātyas performed a sacrifice with Sthapati (architect) Budha as their priest. As they were initiated without first supplicating Devayajana, Varuṇa cursed them: They were not to find sacrificial offerings nor to know the path of the gods, Devayāna (XXIV: 18: 2). 'When a woman who belongs to one (man) carries on intercourse with another, she undoubtedly commits (a sin) against Varuṇa' (*ŚB* II: 5: 2: 20). Varuṇa bound Prajāpati's creatures because they ate his barley, but later let them off when they offered a sacrifice (*ŚB* V: 1: 21), the two-fold expiatory Varuṇapraghāsa sacrifices (*JB* II: 231). In some passages we have clear hints of his character. After the avabhṛtha bath at the Agniṣṭoma sacrifice the performer turns away and does not look back so as to escape from Varuṇa's notice (*TS* VI: 6: 3: 5 and *MS* IV: 8: 5). The solemn sin-offering, Varuṇapraghāsa, is another proof of his dreadfulness. In the Paśuyāga the heart-spit is buried with a verse imploring Varuṇa to forgive sin.

The punishments meted out by Varuṇa usually took the shape of diseases which afflicted those who offend against him, and he cured them only when he was placated. This, however, is as is to be expected, for, an offence against the god of the norm is punished by a disease which is abnormal. Thus the man who refuses to offer Mitra and Varuṇa is punished with Yakṣman, tuberculosis (*ṚV* I: 122: 9). In *ṚV* II: 28 we have a prayer for the appeasement of Varuṇa's destructive anger. It mentions physical deformity and premature decay as punishments from Varuṇa (verses 5–8). He is prayed to for removal of fears also (verse 10). The word Varuṇagraha, seizure by Varuṇa, means paralysis. In an *AV* hymn Varuṇa is invoked together with Mitra and Aryaman for removing unlucky marks in a woman (I: 18). He, however, not only inflicts diseases as punishments but can cure them as well. Thus we hear...A hundred remedies are thine, O King, (Varuṇa) a thousand...verily he makes medicines for him (the sacrificer)—(*TS* VI: 6: 3). The *TB* says Varuṇa should be worshipped Bheṣajatvāya, nirvaruṇatvāya (I: 5: 9: 7), for health, for freedom from (the scourge of) Varuṇa. Another passage calls him physician (II: 6: 17: 7). Keith says that in Fiji, as in England, people believed that swelling was healed by the royal touch (A. B. Keith, 'Varuna and Ouranos', *IC* 1937–8). In *ṚV* VII: 50 we have a hymn for casting out poison; it is dedicated to Varuṇa and Mitra. In *AV* VII: 83 88 there is a prayer to Varuṇa for release from sin and from leprosy. Traces of similar faith in the efficacy of the royal touch are recorded in Shakespeare's *Macbeth* (Act IV, scene 3, ll. 143–5). Varuṇa's bhisajah (drugs) are said to expel Nirṛti (*ṚV* I: 24: 9); this introduces us to a very important aspect of his personality, namely, his association with Nirṛti and forces of evil. In all mythologies we have gods who, when angry or offended, cause certain diseases, but when appeased can also heal them. They can, in other words create and remove evils. Varuṇa is one such high god who can bless, cure and reward and at the same time curse and punish. The *MS* tells us that Varuṇa has two kinds of pāśas (nooses), one terrible and the other beneficent (III: 9: 6). In his malevolent aspect Varuṇa is unlike most other gods of Vedic literature, for he is terrible and sinister.

In the first place, throughout the Vedic literature Varuṇa is associated with the night. Even an early passage bears this out—he encompassed the nights and bore light with his magic power (*ṚV* VIII: 41: 3). But in the early Vedic texts his association with darkness is not stressed; he is then the star-eyed night sky. In later Vedic literature his dark and malevolent associations emerge clearly. A *YV* passage brings out Varuṇa's association with the night and fierceness.

Varuṇa became the night and swallowed beasts (*MS* I: 5: 12). The *TMB* clearly states that Varuṇa is the night; the fortnight in which the moon wanes is devoted to Varuṇa (XXV: 10: 10, also I: 7: 10: 1). Here his connection not only with the night but particularly with darkness is apparent. It is this association with darkness that grows with time and gradually transforms him into a sinister god. For example all that is malformed, decrepit and ugly is associated with him.

This happens because, though initially Varuṇa symbolized the sky in all its aspects, he later came to be the symbol of the night sky with its thousand stars as his eyes. The day sky became solely associated with Mitra who became the god of sunlight, still later Varuṇa was connected with the dark and sinister aspects of the night. Thus while Mitra signified truth, brightness and benevolence, Varuṇa came to be associated with the dark, malevolent and gruesome aspects of life and nature. The oblations to Varuṇa are connected with deformity and ugliness. 'To Varuṇa (the sacrificer) offers on ten potsherds in the house of the ministrel; the sacrificial fee is a great castrated ox' (*TS* V: 6: 11). 'The humped, the bull, the dwarf (animal), these are for Indra and Varuṇa' (*TS* V: 6: 14). 'There are three black-spotted (beasts) for Varuṇa; to Varuṇa the king are (to be offered) three red-spotted; to Varuṇa the destroyer of foes, three ruddy-spotted' (*TS* V: 6: 20). Foulness is also his: 'The stagnant (waters) are seized by Varuṇa' (*TS* IV: 4: 2). In later literature Varuṇa becomes the lord of waters, so his association with water in this passage is not surprising. What is remarkable is his association with 'stagnation'. Heat and force are connected with oblations to Varuṇa. Thus 'what is hot is to be used (in oblations) for Varuṇa' (*MS* IV: 5: 8). The *TB* says Varuṇa is Jumbaka—this is his mysterious name, and to this Jumbaka Varuṇa, at the time of the purification, offerings should be made on the head of a white-spotted bald-headed man with protruding teeth and reddish brown eyes; for that is Varuṇa's form. By that form the sacrificer thus redeems himself from Varuṇa (*TB* III: 9: 15: 3, also *ŚB* XII: 3: 6: 5). His association with subnormality is borne out by his being mentioned as the father of two apes—Hemakūṭa and Ṛṣabha (*Rām.* VI: 6: 26; VI: 16: 28).

Whenever Varuṇa is described in his royal splendour he is shown to be surrounded by nāgas, probably water-snakes. Thus the *Mbh.* describes his court built and decorated by Viśvakarman, where he sits with his wife Vāruṇī together with the nāgas (*Mbh.* II: 9). In the *HV* he is said to have fought the demon Vipracitti, assisted by the nāgas (III: 61). The *PGS* says: 'In the Śrāvaṇa sacrifice one should thus address the serpents, "Drive away, O white one with thy foot...these seven children of Varuṇa and all the daughters of the king's tribe".' In this passage 'king' means Varuṇa, and his daughters are snakes. Snakes being symbols *inter alia* of death and danger, their association with Varuṇa is significant.

Bhṛgu is said to be Varuṇa's son, whom Varuṇa taught herb and cattle lore and also about belief, unbelief and wrath (*ŚB* XI: 6: 1: 13; *VS* XXV: 9; *TB* III: 9: 15: 3). If we remember that the *Brāhmaṇas* tell us of Bhṛgu's descent into hell, his vision of the gruesome tortures there and a glimpse of the dark and sinister king of hell (*ŚB* XI: 6: 1; *JB* I: 42–4, XV: 234–8), we become immediately aware of an indirect connection of Varuṇa with death and the dead. Odin, a dim parallel of Varuṇa in the Edda mythology is also associated with death and danger. Among his various names we read Grim (Flame-eyed one), Bölverk (worker of evil), Ygg (terrible one). Varuṇa, like the one-eyed sky-god of the Edda, clearly belongs to the group of primitive gods who sat above in royal splendour and detachment and were feared and revered because of their might, majesty and omniscience.[1] In ancient Sumerian mythology we find another god of this group in Anu the sky-god (E. O. James, *The ancient gods*, p. 303). In the Enneadie pattern of the Mesopotamian pantheon Anu

[1] 'When the Sumerians arrived in 3000 B.C. they already had a highly organized pantheon under the leadership of Anu, whose name meant heaven...he was the supreme power in the sky...the prototype of all earthly rulers and the ultimate source of their authority and of natural law. It was his sovereignty to which Marduk, in due course, succeeded when all power was bestowed upon him by the gods' (E. O. James, *The ancient gods*, p. 303). Later Enlil assisted Anu in upholding the moral order.

the maker of the cosmic law (known as Ṛta in India) is assisted by another god, Enlil, in its operation. In India however, Varuṇa combines both functions, in early Vedic times, and it is only in the later Vedic period that these functions are separated and are discharged by different gods.

The secret of Varuṇa's supernatural power is called māyā in early Vedic literature. Indra, Agni and sometimes some other gods are said to have māyā, but in the first phase of *ṚV* literature it is almost inseparably and exclusively connected with Varuṇa, who is called Māyin and Asura. *Asu* means 'life of the spiritual world or of departed souls' (Monier Williams, *Dictionary*). In *ṚV* x: 15: 1 it is used in connection with the 'pitarah', the dead ancestors. If we remember the later dark associations of Varuṇa, his connection with death, Nirṛti and the other world, this power of life of the spiritual world or of departed souls becomes quite understandable. The epithet Asura means 'spiritual, incorporeal, divine or supreme spirit', and in this sense it is used of Varuṇa in the *ṚV* and *YV*. Later, when Varuṇa ceased to occupy a position of supremacy, 'asura' came to mean 'chief of the evil spirits' (*ibid.*)—as in *ṚV* II: 30: 4 or VII: 99: 5. It is as a lord of supernatural spiritual power that Varuṇa is called Asura, and this power is called māyā. Thus he sends rain in the sky through asura's māyā (*ṚV* v: 63: 3). With Mitra Varuṇa protects the earth through Dharman and Asura's māyā, he envelops the night and creates the dawn with asura's māyā (*ṚV* VIII: 41: 3). The asuras, i.e. demons of later Vedic literature, are said to have lost their māyā through Varuṇa's power. The *TS* mentions 'the woolly wiles of Varuṇa' (IV: 210). Varuṇa's Eddic parallel Odin is also pre-eminently connected with magic power.

Māyā means 'wisdom, extraordinary or supernatural power' (only in earlier language) but later it comes to mean 'illusion, unreality, deception, fraud, trick, sorcery, witchcraft and magic' (Monier Williams, *Dictionary*). Varuṇa wields supernatural power in the early Vedic literature. Later, with the rise of Prajāpati to prominence, he loses this asura's māyā, which is then shared by gods and demons in two different forms: Prajāpati (and still later Viṣṇu), being identified with the sacrifice, becomes the sole proprietor of āsurī māyā, in other words, white magic beneficial to gods and men. The demons, on the other hand, wield black magic in their efforts to harass the gods.[1] A *JB* passage leaves a hint to this transition. 'The asuras', it says, 'consecrate Varuṇa, Soma's brother, because they see in him the form (rūpa) of their father Prajāpati' (III: 152). Here Varuṇa's

[1] Lá proposition fondamentale de la Bonne Religion est, selon les écrits pehlevie, que le créateur est autre que le destructeur. Cela implique que les daeva ne peuvent être

mastery of āsurī māyā is still remembered, but the demons also share it, through being descendants of Prajāpati, who in the Brāhmaṇic period is the overlord of magic power of all kinds. Varuṇa's losing this supernatural power, māyā, to Prajāpati and also to the demons is symptomatic of his decline and attenuation as a god. It is interesting to note that in the epic the demon Maya has this magical power, with which he builds spendid mansions. He may have been a personification of the abstract concept of māyā, or the reverse may be true.

Varuṇa's might is great and unequalled by birds or falling streams (*ṚV* I: 24: 6) and he is as strong as a white deer (*ṚV* VII: 86: 6); he prepared a wide path for the sun (*ṚV* I: 24: 8), and is the helper of Indra in Indra's exploits. Rainfall is due to him and Mitra (*ṚV* V: 63: 1). Together with Indra he saved protégés like Sudas (*ṚV* VII: 85). He revealed the secret of the word (i.e. speech) to his worshippers (*ṚV* VII: 86: 4) and prepared a golden hammock (i.e. the sun) in the firmament (*ṚV* VII: 86: 5). He is fond of his devotee Vaśiṣṭha the sage. He helps the thirsty Vaśiṣṭha (with water) in the midst of an ocean (*ṚV* VII: 89: 4) and it may not be an accident that the seventh Maṇḍala, where we hear most of Varuṇa's achievements, is composed almost exclusively by Vaśiṣṭha. Varuṇa's friendship with Vaśiṣṭha may refer to the fact that the Vaśiṣṭha family is a very old clan of Varuṇa worshippers. Vaśiṣṭha's Iranian name Vañhiṣṭha is another proof of the clan being at least as old as the Indo-Iranian period. Aša Vahiṣṭha (one of the six Amesa Spentas of the *Avesta*) would, in the *ṚV* language, be Ṛta Vaśiṣṭha, and here we have a connection of Vaśiṣṭha with Ṛta, perhaps a dim recollection—at least verbal—of the close association of the Vaśiṣṭha clan with Ṛta and hence with Varuṇa as well. Mitra and Varuṇa are said to see paths better than (human) eyes (*ṚV* VIII: 25: 9). Varuṇa's throne is invulnerable (*ṚV* VIII: 35: 9). Varuṇa is the keeper of nectar (*ṚV* VIII: 42: 2). He separates Ṛta from anṛta, night from day (*ṚV* X: 124: 5; VII: 87: 1). He settled the earth and the constellations (*ṚV* VII: 86: 2). This idea is repeated in the *TS* 'The bull hath stabilized the sky, the atmosphere; hath meted out the breadth of the earth; hath set him in all the worlds as king. All these are Varuṇa's ordinances. He hath stretched out the sky over the woods; hath placed strength in horses, milk in kine. Varuṇa hath set skill in the heart, Agni in dwellings, the sun in the sky, the Soma on the hill' (I: 2: 8 also VI: 6: 3; *MS* IV: 3: 4).

des créateurs, que le Créateur est autre que le destructeur. Implicitement, le dualisme iranien—et indo-européenne—entre le ṛta et la māyā étudie et mise en relief par M. Dumézil ('Ordre, fantasie, changement dans les pensées archaïques de l'Inde et de Rome', *Rel.* 32 (1954), 139–62), quoted by M. Molé in *Culte, mythe et cosmologie.*

When, with time, overlordship power and glory depart from Varuṇa, he becomes somewhat different in his exploits. The cosmic functions are no longer his; from a supreme sky-god inscrutable in his ways, omnipotent and omniscient, he becomes one of the many Brāhmaṇic and later epic-Purāṇic gods. He is still powerful, but this is the power of one member of a powerful team subservient to the Almighty Prajāpati, and later to Viṣṇu. Now he is a partisan in the fight between gods and demons. His court is described as splendid and gorgeous, prepared by Viśvakarman (*Mbh.* II: 9). His weapon is still the pāśa (*Rām.* II: 122: 22; IV: 11: 12). To Daśaratha he gave two bows (*Rām.* II: 31: 24). The Vāruṇāstra is still coveted (*Mbh.* III: 42). Varuṇa saved sage Ṛcīka from a predicament when the latter sought to marry Gadhi's daughter Satyavatī and was told to fetch one thousand horses each with one dark ear (ekatah śyāmakarṇa), Varuṇa supplied him with such horses (*Mbh.* XIII: 4). When Aurva waxed mighty, Varuṇa together with Indra and Soma offered to kill him so that the demons might be finally crushed (*HV* I: XLV: 76–7), also accompanied by Soma he fought the demons (*HV* I: XLVI: 14–19). In the *HV* he stoops to the position of the keeper of Bāṇāsura's cattle; when Kṛṣṇa wanted to plunder them Varuṇa fought Kṛṣṇa and his followers. As Kṛṣṇa was about to destroy Varuṇa the latter sang a hymn to Kṛṣṇa (*HV* II: CXXVII), thus finally yielding the last semblance of might and glory to his Purāṇic successor. The *HV* records his ultimate degradation. He is almost a non-entity—his past glory is remembered as belonging to an extremely remote past and is considered to be quite insignificant. That he was once the supreme overlord is referred to; for instance in passages where he is said to have instituted the Rājasūya sacrifice, after Soma, but before a number of earthly kings, all of whom became victorious emperors through the merit of the sacrifice. Varuṇa thus becomes the prototype of imperial glory—but he is no longer mentioned as the sole emperor.

In post-Vedic literature Varuṇa's nature and functions undergo a major change; he becomes the lord of waters. In the *ṚV* he was connected with water, but these were the celestial waters. Thus he conjured up rain water in the sky with his magic power (*ṚV* V: 63: 3). Varuṇa the terrible, the thousand-eyed declared (i.e. determined) the current of rivers (*ṚV* VII: 34: 10). He is the king of countries, the peśa i.e. architect (of the courses) of rivers (*ṚV* VII: 34: 11), the lord of waters and he regulates their courses (*ṚV* VII: 87: 1; *AV* V: 24: 4). He cut out a path for the river Sindhu (*ṚV* X: 75: 2); rain water is sent by him (*ṚV* X: 125: 7; *AV* IV: 7: 12). The portion of a dead man that goes to the waters belongs to Varuṇa (*AV* III: 3: 3).

He is not only the overlord of waters but has a secret golden chamber in the waters (*AV* v: 24 and vii: 83: 1). The stagnant (waters) are seized by Varuṇa (*TS* vi: 4: 2). Waters are Varuṇa's, so is the wind (*MS* iv: 8: 5). Varuṇa's son is called Puṣkara which means water (*Mbh.* v: 97), and the waters Varuṇa's wives (*TB* i: 1: 3: 8), Agni pursued them, his seed was spilled and became gold. Varuṇa (lives) in the water (*TB* i: 7: 26; *TS* i: 8: 12, ii: 3: 12, iii: 4: 5). In this connection one is reminded of Okeanos, the god of water, one of the primeval Greek gods, son of Gaia and Ouranos, and thus in the language of mythology an aspect of the hierophany of Ouranos himself. In Greek mythology, too, Okeanos like Varuṇa is associated with the dead (cf Everyman's *Smaller classical dictionary* on Okeanos).

Later Varuṇa's suzerainty in the pantheon is lost and he is only one of the ten dikpālas reigning in and over water. Although the *HV* makes Varuṇa reside in Dvarakā (ii: 102: 33) in common usage the term Varuṇālaya is a palace in the bottom of the ocean surrounded on all sides by aquatic animals (*Rām.* iii: 60: 18), as sometimes he is said to dwell in a lake (*Rām.* iv: 43: 59), sometimes he is the lord of the sea (*Rām.* vi: 6: 26), the salilarāja (*Rām.* vi: 51: 32). It is also significant that he assumed the shape of a waterfowl—the goose—when Rāvaṇa had encroached upon King Marutta's sacrifice and blessed the goose with a fair complexion and it was told to refresh itself in water, Varuṇa's element (*Rām.* vii: 18: 28–30). Again he is made the keeper of the lower waters in *Rām.* vii: 73: 4. It is interesting to note that the last two passages are from the spurious and later parts of the *Rāmāyaṇa*. In the *Mbh.* Varuṇa's court is 'antahsalila'—beneath or within water, where he resides with Vāruṇī, his wife, surrounded by nāgas or water-snakes, by all the seas, rivers and ponds which appear anthropomorphized (*Mbh.* ii: 9). In the Mahākalpadāna, a vow of charity, the image of Varuṇa is to be seated on a fish (*Matsya P.* ch. 286). This proves the god's inseparable connection with water. In another passage Varuṇa holds the noose and is accompanied by crocodiles and fishes (*HV* iii: 61). We hear that once all the gods came and made Varuṇa the lord of the waters (*Mbh.* ix: 46) or that Śiva made him so (*Mbh.* xii: 122). Passages like these indicate that Varuṇa was not the lord of the waters from the beginning, he was 'made' so, by the gods or by Śiva. In other words, his ancient status and function were still a disturbing memory because they had been usurped by other gods so that he had to be 'made' something in order to occupy a semi-respectable position in the later pantheon. Such passages signify his subservience to the rising epic-gods, who invest him with power merely over the waters. The episode of Kṛṣṇa drowning Varuṇa in the Lohita lake (*HV* II: 102: 33) is another proof of the epic Varuṇa's humiliation at the hands of the rising epic-god Viṣṇu-Kṛṣṇa. Garuḍa says to Kṛṣṇa that he (Kṛṣṇa) is also called Varuṇa because he, too, was born in the water (*HV* II: 172: 33); Varuṇa's power and glory are clearly passing away from him.

Once Varuṇa is relegated as the lord of the waters he is inevitably associated with snakes. This is also a consequence of the dark and sinister associations which he gradually acquires between the *Brāhmaṇas* and the epic-Purāṇic age. The *Mbh.* describes him and his palace as surrounded by nāgas. His daughter Vāruṇī (who came out of the churned ocean, *Rām.* I: 46: 26) he sent to Balarāma, an incarnation of the Śeṣanāga or Anantanāga, and told her to please him (*HV* II: 41: 21). She gave him a blue dress (the colour of the ocean), an ear-ring (kuṇḍala) and a necklace. This episode is repeated in the *Viṣṇu P.* In the *Bh.P*, Sura (i.e. Vāruṇī, Varuṇa's wife) arose from the churning of the ocean. Varuṇa fought demon Vipracitti together with his nāga-retinue (*HV* III: 61).

In the *NP* we hear of Varuṇapañcamī in place of Nāgapañcamī, a festival of the nāgas, establishing an identity or association with snakes. In Buddhist works like the *Mahāvyutpatti* and the *Jātakas* Varuṇa is called Nāgarāja. His association with snakes is unquestionably accepted in many other heterodox works. A Nepalese legend makes him a great Nāga. Even as early as *ṚV* III: 69: 11 there is a passage—'Yet in the small pool he lies'—and this may have a reference to his connection with water-snakes. In Bāṇabhaṭṭa's *Kādambarī* the childless queen Vilāsavatī, desiring a son, bathes in a pool infested with snakes. She obtained a son, presumably through the boon of Varuṇa, the lord of snakes.

The earlier Vedic literature does not describe Varuṇa as a concrete figure. But later, when image worship came into vogue, there are directions for sculptured images of Varuṇa. The *Bṛhatsaṃhitā* says that Varuṇa should be made slightly pot-bellied, seated on a chariot drawn by seven swans, a four-armed figure holding the lotus, the noose, the conch-shell and a jewelbox with his consort Gaurī on his lap. Gaṅgā and Yamunā should accompany the group. In the Rajārāṇī temple in Bhubaneswar (Orissa) there is an actual image of Varuṇa, where he is two-armed, and seated on a makara (a mythical sea-animal or a crocodile). From the *Bṛhatsaṃhitā* description certain important features of the concept of Varuṇa emerge. His pot-belly indicates his association with the Śiva-group in which many popular non-Aryan gods were assimilated. Kuvera the god of wealth is pot-bellied; so is the popular Śiva of certain regions, so also is Gaṇeśa and the

Yakṣas. Like Kuvera he has a jewelbox in his hand. The chariot drawn by seven swans, the lotus, the conch-shell, Gaṅgā and Yamunā, the makara in the Rajāraṇī temple in Orissa, all indicate his close connection with water.

When Varuṇa becomes definitely a water-god, and practically nothing more, he also comes to be known as a Dikpāla, the guardian of the west. It is in the *AV* that we hear for the first time that Varuṇa is connected with the west. Thus it says 'the west direction, of which Varuṇa is the overlord' (*AV* III: 27: 3, IV: 40: 5, XII: 4: 57). The *Rāmāyaṇa* knows him as a Dikpāla (III: 44: 41), the keeper of the west and it is as such that all later epic-Purāṇic and Buddhist literature knows him. We shall come to the significance of the west later on. But being in the west connects him with Yama, Rudra, Vāyu, and Agni, Kuvera and Nirṛti, that is with all the dread gods.

Of these Yama belongs to the south, of which quarter he is the guardian. Varuṇa's emissary, an active (i.e. fluttering) bird with golden wings, is said to rest in Yama's nest (*AV* XVIII: 3: 66). The *AV* hymn I: 14 has for its god Varuṇo Yamo vā (Varuṇa or Yama) thus identifying, or at least connecting, Varuṇa with Yama. The *TMB* calls Varuṇa Preti, death (I: 8: 2); the *MS* says that buffaloes (and the buffalo is Yama's mount in later Vedic literature) should be offered to Varuṇa (III: 14: 10). These connect Varuṇa with Yama, who in later literature is invariably associated with death, and the buffalo which he uses as a mount. Yama and Varuṇa both belong to the larger pattern of the Śiva complex. In *TS* I: 2: 4 the group of gods mentioned—Vāyu, Varuṇa, Nirṛti and Rudra—establishes their common characteristics. Varuṇa is connected with Soma in many *TS* passages. Hillebrandt and Oldenberg identify Varuṇa with the moon (Soma).

But Varuṇa is also a god with solar associations. He is one of the Ādityas, the solar gods (*ŚB* V: 2: 11). He is a great friend of Mitra and Aryaman, with whom he is frequently grouped in the *ṚV*; they are invoked together to destroy sin and ignorance in *ṚV* VII: 66: 4. This moral function is continued in verses 5 and 6 in the same hymn. Varuṇa is also identified with Sūrya and Mitra and the worshipper worships the sun, the eye of Mitra and Varuṇa (*ṚV* X: 37: 1). Varuṇa is also identified with Savitṛ and Indra in *AV* XIII: 3: 13. With Mitra a man settles the well-offered oblation of a sacrifice, with Varuṇa the badly-offered oblation (*TB* I: 2: 5: 3; *JB* II: 230). Varuṇa is invoked as Savitṛ and truth (*TB* I: 7: 10: 3).

In many *TB* and *ŚB* passages Varuṇa is associated with the horse, which in all ancient mythology is an emblem of the sun. According to *KŚS* the Kṣattriya is to kindle his sacred fire after Varuṇa's rules and the Rājanya after Indra's rules; the frequent mention of Varuṇa in connection with the Rājasūya sacrifice is also indicative of his royal and solar bearings.

Like the one-eyed Odin Varuṇa must originally have been the sun-eyed sky-god. It was only later that he came to be identified with the night sky and gathered dark associations. In the first phase, however, all passive sky-gods later became sun-gods as well, and, still later, on account of their essential passivity, they made way for active and warlike sun-gods. Thus Varuṇa, too, before he yielded to the superior claims of Indra and Viṣṇu-Kṛṣṇa, was himself an Āditya.[1]

Of all the Vedic solar gods Varuṇa is the most closely related to Mitra and Aryaman with whom he is invoked in the *ṚV* hymns I: 122, I: 141, with Mitra in I: 136, V: 62. Together with Mitra, Varuṇa is the keeper of Ṛta and Dharman (*ṚV* VIII: 25, also *MS* III: 8: 9 and *ŚB* V: 3: 5: 34). Mitra creates the firmament and Varuṇa is the king of all creation (*ṚV* X: 132). With Mitra Varuṇa is implored to allow a person to die only when he is old (*AV* II: 28: 2). Varuṇa becomes Agni in the evening, and rising in the morning becomes Mitra (*AV* XIII: 3: 13). Even down to the *Rāmāyaṇa* Mitra is remembered as assisting Varuṇa (VII: 56: 12: 23–6). In later literature the alliance between Mitra and Varuṇa had become so proverbial that it was used in similes as in the *Mbh.*: Dhṛṣṭa-dyumna became the leader of the Pāṇḍavas, covered by Bhīṣma as Varuṇa was by Mitra (*Mbh.* XIV: 59: 15). In the *HV* Devakī with her sons Kṛṣṇa and Balarāma is compared to Aditi with her sons Mitra and Varuṇa (*HV* II: 101: 10).

The *ṚV* connects Mitra mainly with law and order—Ṛta and Dharman as in *ṚV* III: 59: 1, V: 81: 4, VIII: 52: 3, X: 8: 4. In this he is identical with Varuṇa who is also the upholder of law and order. But in the *TS* we hear that Mitra created the day, Varuṇa the night (IV: 4: 8: 3). Here we

[1] The *Avesta*, however, omits Varuṇa although it includes the other three Vedic solar gods. 'Of the four chief Vedic Ādityas, Varuṇa, Mitra, Aryaman and Bhaga, there are Miθra, Airiyaman and Baga but Varuṇa is conspiciously lacking...The Avesta has not even a trace of the god Varuṇa', says Paul Thieme in 'The Aryan gods of the Mitanni treaties', *JAOS* 80, no. 4 (1960). And from this he concludes, 'We can, then, by no means be sure whether there existed a Proto-Aryan Varuṇa, much less of a Proto-Aryan dvandva Mitrāvaruṇau'. But in the Avesta *ərəta/aša* is a central concept which is attributed to Ahura Mazda. Bearing in mind that the Vedic Varuṇa is an Asura, then the fourth important Vedic Āditya, Varuṇa, was possibly assimilated in the supreme Avestan godhead Ahura Mazda and is therefore not known by his older name. Besides the Boghazkeui inscription knows an Uruvaṇuna or Proto-Varuṇa. Greek mythology knows Ouranos, Varuṇa's Greek counterpart, so that instead of considering that Varuṇa vanished into the thin air in the Iranian mythology, it would be a more plausible surmise that Varuṇa assumed supreme grandeur in Avestan mythology along with his new name Ahura Mazda. As Paul Thieme points out, Miθra-Ahura is an older compound than Ahura-Miθra, therefore Ahura was gaining importance. And Ahura's solar characteristics are only too apparent.

have two different sets of associations for the two gods. Varuṇa, as we have seen, was originally the hierophany of the entire sky in all its phases. But later his manifestation became limited and he symbolized only the night sky with its thousand stars, which became his thousand eyes or spies watching the secret activities of men at night. At this period the day sky came to be symbolized by Mitra. Thus while Varuṇa began to assume dark, malevolent traits Mitra symbolized light. The *TS* advises a person who is ill for a long time to offer a white (beast) to Mitra and a black one to Varuṇa (II: 1: 9: 3). It also said that Mitra pacifies the cruel Varuṇa ('Mitro hi krūraṃ varuṇam śāntaṃ Karoti'; *TS* II: 1: 9: 5). Thus the opposition between the personalities of Mitra and Varuṇa is brought out. Vedic Mitra closely answers to his Avestan parallel Miθra. In the *Avesta* Mithra is the light of Varuṇa, i.e. Ahura Mazda, because the latter as the supreme spirit could have no rival. Hence Mithra became his creature. 'He is a judge in hell in company with Rashnu, "the true one", "the god of truth", a mere offshoot of Mithra in his moral character' (Introduction to the *Zend Avesta*, *SBE* IV, lxi, n. 1). It is interesting to note that since Varuṇa is not a god in the *Avesta*, but is merely the material heaven, his ethical function is discharged by his Vedic associate Mithra.

There is an inherent ethical duality in the Avestan religio-philosophical thinking which is expressed in the duality and opposition of the conceptual antinomies—Ahura Mazda and Angra Mainyu. The Indian counterpart to this duality is to be found in Mitrāvaruṇau, where the light-and-darkness polarity is concretized.

Varuṇa is also intimately related to Agni, the god of fire, another night-god. He is identified with Agni or called Agni's brother in *ṚV* IV: 1. Three shining tongues are said to reside inside Varuṇa's mouth, among them the middle one is the vaśā cow, which it is wrong to capture (*AV* X: 10: 28). Although in this passage the author intends to warn against forcible seizure of a vaśā cow, the imagery—that of three shining tongues inside Varuṇa's mouth—has an evocative power. It recalls the fire whose flames are later deified and given names, so that the passage connects Varuṇa with Agni through imagery. The *AB* says 'Varuṇa is Agni, this also is declared by a seer' (VI: 26); the declaration obviously refers to *ṚV* V: 3: 1. When the *ŚB* declares that nothing hurts Varuṇa's stomach (V: 1: 2) he is made one with Agni who in later literature is caller sarvabhuj, all-eater.

As Varuṇa's antecedents can be traced far back in the dim Indo-European period it is difficult to say what the original derivative meaning of the word was. Nevertheless, if the Boghazkeui tablet by the word Uruvan-nas-sil means Varuṇa and his followers, then his existence can safely be assumed as pre-Iranian and it can surely be connected with its Greek counterpart Ouranos.[1]

We have seen that the name Varuṇa is derived by some from the root *vṛ*, to cover, and that this would tend to make him the sky, the meaning which lingers on in the Avestan Varena, the sky. This must have been the earliest, i.e. the IE derivation because this was the earliest phase of Varuṇa's hierophany. Keith's proposed derivation of Varuṇa from the same root as Sanskrit *vāri* and Avestan *vār* (= water) must at least be of Indo-Iranian antiquity, thus establishing Varuṇa's association with water, for as early as the *Brāhmaṇas* Varuṇa is a god of water. The sea-god (corresponding to Okeanos, Poseidon, Nereus or Neptune) could very easily have derived his name from a root meaning water. Przyluski's derivation of Varuṇa from palaeo-Asiatic *Baru* with the Austro-Asiatic sense of the sea-god must have been added to the Varuṇa-concept on the Indian soil, thus connecting him with the sea-spirit, to which, as Przyluski suggests, a section of the Indian people always remained faithful. Lastly, even in the Indo-European period the derivation of Varuṇa from a root meaning 'to fasten' (Dumézil) and the root *uer* (= to find; Peterson) must have been prevalent. The all-encompassing, all-seeing sky-god had this moral function of judging. The gradual syncretism of similar gods with ethical characteristics was accreted to him. He punished the transgressor by fastening or binding him (with the pāśa in later Vedic literature). This explains the anxious prayers against the activity of his omniscient spies, and later 'against his pāśa (derived

[1] One remembers the Armenian word *Garuna* meaning the 'sky', a counterpart to 'Ouranos'. Keith says 'We may refer the term (Varuṇa) to the base seen in Sanskrit *vāri*, water, Avestan *vār*, rain' ('The god Varuṇa', *IHQ* IX (1933)). Roth, Darmesteter, Hopkins, Schröder, and Bloomfield, on the other hand, agree to take Varuṇa to be originally the sky-god who was transformed into the god of water only later, on the Indian soil. As a sky-god his name can be derived from the root *vṛ*, to cover—that which encompasses this world, i.e the sky. G. Dumézil, again, says that Varuṇa is derived from a root which means 'to fasten' and compares Varuṇa with Hesiod's Ouranos in this point. Przyluski believes that Varuṇa is god of the sea and sky, *JRAS* (1931). He is of the opinion that 'the name of the god Varuṇa is derived from a Palaeo-Asiatic root *Baru* which denoted originally that which is outside human society'. He connects this with 'the pre-eminence of the sea-spirits in the Austro-Asiatic mythologies... In the Vedic religion a sovereign deity could not reside at the bottom of the ocean: he had to be enthroned on high... Nothing forbids us to affirm that a section of the Aryans always remained faithful to the Austro-Asiatic Varuṇa, god of the sea'. H. Peterson is inclined to derive Varuṇa from the Indo-European root *uer* = to bind. One is reminded of Sanskrit *varaka* = cloth, *varaṇḍa* = string of a fish-hook, *varatra* = strap, thong, *varutra* = upper and outer garment. Lithuanian *weru* means 'to thread', = to embroider, Russian *verenica* means 'broken thread'. Varuṇa's Greek parallel Ouranos binds his enemies. Paul Thieme proposes to derive Varuṇa from the root word *ver* = to speak; the word *Varuṇa*, he says, means 'true speech' (*Mitra and Aryaman*, p. 70).

from *spaś*, the same root as that of 'spy'). Thus the sky-god was imperceptibly assimilated into the water-god and later into the judge-and-punisher-god. Stage by stage the different derivations were accreted to the nucleus of the IE Varuna-Ouranos. All the derivations appear to be partially correct, since each contributed conceptually to the formation of a growing, changing divinity, for Varuṇa's figure was not static and the *ṚV* Varuṇa is hardly recognizable in his epic-Purāṇic counterpart. So it would seem idle to derive the name of such a mobile concept once and for all. Hence with each successive change and addition, a suitable derivation from a different root must have been apprehended in order that this complex godhead might emerge. As each of these roots yielded a resultant form 'Varuṇa', there is no difficulty in associating a new concept through it, a concept which gave the god new functions and characteristics. For Varuṇa from *vṛ̥*, = to cover, could not give us the punisher-god except through far-fetched and devious means. Far more plausible seems the assumption that Varuṇa from *uer*, to fasten, should contribute this new moral function. Again, as neither the all-encompassing Varuṇa nor the fastener Varuṇa could possibly, through these derivative meanings, be conceived as the water-god, the derivation from the root of *vāri* or *vār*, also the Austro-Asiatic *Baru* would seem likelier to yield the new attributes, so that the totality of the conceptual complex seems best derived from multiple roots all converging into a concrete, changing god.

By 3000 B.C. men 'had associated the "divine" category with power and the act of creation. The empirical necessity of a single head for any complex organization had led them to infer a single power behind the complex manifestations of the universe. This power appears in various forms and with various limitations, but in each case a high god is the head of the cosmos to his worshippers' (W. F. Albright, *From Stone Age to Christianity*, p. 177). The Egyptian Rā, Indian Dyaus-Pitṛ, Greek Ouranos are all cosmic high gods of this order.

In the dim and remote past Dyaus was the supreme sky-god, but already in the *ṚV* mythology his figure is essentially attenuated, and apart from the compound Dyāvāpṛthivī there is very little of a tangible god in Dyaus. The reason is not far to seek. Hierogamy, omniscience and creativity, are absent. "Varuṇa is omniscient and that is his advantage over Dyaus. His spies or eyes are ever watchful—he sees and knows all secrets, judges and punishes men through this knowledge. This makes him the true overlord through a superior type of knowledge and power in a way foreign to the concept of Dyaus. But here ends his theophany. He also is weighed and, found wanting, for he is not hierogamous and thus not reproductive. It is, therefore, his fate to submit to a successor who fulfils these requirements. Varuṇa's failure seems to be due to 'the serene, sacred', almost passive quality of his 'power'. That is to say, power is his by right because of his very nature. This power enables him to act through 'magic', through 'the power of the mind', 'through knowledge' (M. Eliade, *Patterns of comparative religion*, pp. 71–2). But this is hardly enough; 'As Dumézil has shown, the primitive IA double picture of the "magic sovereign" and the "hero sovereign" the possessor of spiritual power and of physical power is preserved here' (*ibid.* p. 81).

This can be regarded as a reflection of the history of the Indo-European people whose supreme god was a passive sky-god while they were a stationary pastoral people in their original habitat. This passive omniscient god, with spiritual and magic power, dispensed justice and inspired their awe and reverence. But there came a time when this people started moving away from their homeland, facing hostility and opposition at every step of their way and in every place of their settlement. They fought their way and frequently the battles were bitter and hard, challenging to the utmost the heroism of which they were capable. Victory was theirs only if they fought tough battles arduously. They could survive only by subjugating the indigenous population. At this period a passive Father-god, although omnipresent and omniscient, was hardly sufficient to inspire the heroic qualities in them, especially when this god had no exploits to his credit in the ancient mythology. Small wonder, therefore, that everywhere these passive Ouranos-Varuṇa gods made way for the warrior gods of the second generation. Thus Thor supplanted Odin, and Indra Varuṇa. There is a very close parallel between the Indian and Eddic mythology in this respect. In the Edda we have Tiwaz, who occupies the same position as Dyaus (the very names appear to be cognates); then Odin, whose parallel is found in Varuṇa. Both Odin and Varuṇa were pushed out of supremacy by Thor and Indra, the former with his magic hammer Mjöllnir, the latter with his magic thunderbolt vajra. These new gods won by their 'maleness', they were hierogamous with a divine spouse whose emblem was almost everywhere the cow corresponding to their partners' bull-emblem. They were also rain-and-storm gods, the 'tornado divinities' as M. Eliade calls them (*Patterns of comparative religion*, p. 85), symbolizing the fecundity aspect of the sky-god and also the most boisterous phenomenon in the sky, thus symbolizing the warrior traits in them. Quite frequently they are the vanquishers of demons of drought or obstruction—a direct reflection of the hero-leader's role. 'These sky-gods, these divine figures tend to disappear from the cult. Nowhere do they play a leading part, but have become remote and been replaced by other religious forces. It is noteworthy that such substitution always means a more concrete, more dynamic, more fertile divinity or religious force' (Eliade, *op. cit.* p. 109). In the case of Varuṇa he had supplanted Dyaus by his richer personality, since he took upon himself more important tasks—those of dispensing justice and imposing punishment. As Varuṇa succeeded where Dyaus had failed, so other gods came in where Varuṇa stopped short. 'The supreme beings progressively lose their religious importance and...are replaced by other divine figures nearer to man, more "concrete" and more "dynamic"—solar gods, Great Goddesses, mythic ancestors etc. These divine figures may end by usurping nearly the whole of the religious life of the tribe' (M. Eliade, *Myths, dreams and mysteries*, p. 136). As we have seen, although Varuṇa had IE antecedents and has supplanted Dyaus, almost immediately after the dispersal of the IE peoples, yet his growth and development took place chiefly in the Indo-Iranian period. After the settlement of the IE people on the Indo-Iranian soil, the god who took over from Varuṇa was Indra, also of Indo-Iranian origin. One remembers how Zeus came to imbibe the attributes of Ouranos. 'For upon the bounteous earth Zeus has thrice ten thousand spies, watchers of mortal men and these keep watch on judgements and deeds of wrong as they roam clothed in mist all over the earth' (Hesiod, *Theogony*, Loeb edn. p. 21). This was a trait of Varuṇa in India, later taken over by other solar gods including Indra after Varuṇa had faded out. Indra is Varuṇa's warrior-successor emerging in power and glory after Varuṇa's dynamic growth had been arrested. Indra's personality as a warrior-god must have been evolving while the Aryans were fighting their way into India. In the first phase he is a mighty tornado-divinity symbolizing storm and rain in the early Vedic literature. He fulfils all three conditions of the real sky-god—hierogamy, omniscience and creativity—and his personality answers more fully the demands of a fighting people desiring their apotheosis of the experiences. His wife Indrāṇī, too, is a more fully developed personality compared with Varuṇa's wife who is rarely mentioned and is hardly anything more than a mere name. Indra is omniscient and also the creator-god. In many hymns the creation of the universe is ascribed to him. As a rain-and-storm god he is a god of reproduction too. And so for a time he reigns supreme, as the vast majority (over 250) of *ṚV* hymns addressed to him prove. But even a warrior-god has a limited span of life allotted to him. When the warlike people's adventures are over and the period of settled agricultural and pastoral life follows, the boisterous storm-god gives way to vegetation-gods, of quieter rituals, and to abstract ideas symbolical of spiritual power. Thus on the one hand Viṣṇu, the solar-vegetation god succeeds Indra on the cultic plane, and on the other hand the semi-abstract Prajāpati, symbolic of spiritual power, takes over from Varuṇa on the philosophical plane. In the next phase, i.e. in the Brāhmaṇical period, Varuṇa's jurisdiction is divided into two distinct spheres, and Viṣṇu and Prajāpati together inherit Varuṇa's glory and majesty. It is significant that in the *Brāhmaṇas* both Viṣṇu and Prajāpati are identified with Yajña, sacrifice, since in that period sacrifice was of supreme interest and importance, just as warfare had been in the immediately preceding period. Indra the warrior-god became dim in this period of settled agrarian-pastoral life. In Prajāpati we have a repetition of the Dyaus-Ouranos phase but on a new, richer and more complex plane. Varuṇa's various functions are distributed among other gods of the Rudra group in the epic-Purāṇic age. In and through the evolution of Varuṇa we see the spiritual symbols of the three stages of the Indo-European people—the Ouranos-Varuṇa stage of a settled pastoral people, the Zeus-Indra stage of a warring people and finally the Apollo-Viṣṇu stage of a settled agricultural people. The Greek Kronos-Rhea stage seems to be simply an extension of the Ouranos-Gaia phase and cannot be traced clearly in the Indian mythology. In the Eddic mythology, too, the Odin stage is followed by the Thor period, which again is succeeded by the Heimdall-Baldr group. In Mesopotamia Anu the sky-god was the supreme divinity and is invoked in the code of Hammurabi as 'il Shame' (sky-god), 'ab Shame' (sky-father) and 'shar Shame' (sky-king). 'But as time went on, the feast of the New Year was consecrated to Marduk, a younger god (his rise dates from the time of Hammurabi, about 2150 B.C.), more dynamic (he battled with the sea-monster Tiamat and killed her) and more important still, a creator-god (Marduk created the world out of Tiamat's body). This change over of Anu's principal feast to Marduk corresponds to the promotion of the storm-god Enlil Bel to the rank of the Supreme God of the Babylonians' (M. Eliade, *Patterns in comparative religion*, p. 66). The institution of the New Year Festival in favour of the more dynamic Marduk, after his more static predecessor Anu's regime was over, indicates a projection of the national experience into mythology. Thus Varuṇa, too, belonged to a chain of evolution, and if he continued after his inner content, i.e. mythological potentiality, was exhausted he could only be pensioned off as a dikpāla (a guardian of the west quarter) and a god of the waters, occupying a minor rank in both capacities.

CHAPTER 2

YAMA

Of Varuna's many functions in the Brāhmaṇical period Yama absorbed some in order to grow in stature, for Yama was quite a minor god in the early Vedic period with only a few hymns addressed to him.

He is invoked by the worshipper to come with the fathers and Aṅgiras borne thither by laudatory hymns sung in his honour, to sit on a seat of Kuśa grass and taste the oblation (*ṚV* x: 14: 4, x: 14: 5), to appear with Agni for his messenger (*ṚV* x: 14: 13). In an *AV* passage we have 'Worship the son of Vivasvat, the gatherer of men, with oblations, he who was the first of the mortals to die, he who first entered this world' (*AV* xviii: 3: 13). This is a very significant passage establishing that the son of Vivasvat was a mortal at first, but was the first to die and enter the other world (and become an immortal presumably) and that he then became a gatherer of the people, i.e. of departed souls; afterwards he was accorded divine honour, i.e. oblations in sacrifices. This career of the apotheosis of Yama is variously recorded in Vedic literature. 'The gods and Yama were in strife over this world, Yama appropriated the power and strength of the gods; hence his name, Yama. The gods reflected, 'Yama here has become what we are' (*TS* ii: 5: 11). Here too it is evident that Yama had not always been an immortal like the other gods, but after some struggle with the established gods he wrested power and authority and was raised to the rank of a god. The above is a Yajurvedic passage and thus chronologically later than the *ṚV*, in which no record of any such strife exists. This shows the process through which a comparatively minor god rises in importance, as also the inevitable opposition from devotees of other orthodox gods in the struggle for power. Yama's immortality was not a *fait accompli* in the earliest period. It was established later and through a struggle. It is significant that Yama figures most prominently only in the tenth book of the *ṚV* and this book was compiled last. There had already started the process of racial and cultural amalgamation before this book was compiled, and Yama's rise to power may be the outcome of this process. It is a most unusual history for a god and it makes Yama somewhat unique. In sacrifices, in the *ṚV* and *AV*, Yama is invoked together with the fathers and the Aṅgirasas, just as Indra is invoked with the Maruts and Vasus, or Rudra with the Rudrāsah.

The *AV* says clearly that Yama is the overlord of the fathers (Yamah pitṛṛṇāmadhipatih, *AV* v: 5: 13: 14). From the south, his quarter, he is asked to come to the sacrifice, accompanied by the fathers, in order to bestow benefits to the worshipper (*AV* xii: 3: 3). The fathers are also invoked as preparing a region, a path for the worshipper (*AV* xviii: 34: 25). Obeisance unto that Yama, Death, who is the master of the two-footed and the four-footed (*AV* vi: 28: 3). In the ritual for the departed, the living kinsman sweeps the ground with a Palāśa branch saying: 'May Yama grant him an abode; for Yama has the power over the abode in this earth and it is him, Yama, that he solicits for an abode therein for this (dead man)' (*ŚB* xiii: 8: 2: 4).

An *AV* prayer says, 'Those of our fathers' fathers and our grandfathers who are most excellent and have ran after (Yama), let Yama, desiring oblation, taste together with them who also desire it and be satisfied' (*AV* xviii: 34: 52). Many such prayers invoke Yama to come to the sacrifice together with the fathers and enjoy oblation. In return Yama is besought for happiness and long life and even for immortality (*ṚV* x: 14: 14). *AV* iv: 9 is a hymn with the title 'Atimṛtyu' (beyond death) addressed to Yama.

The five sections of society are said to have scattered (prepared) dwellings for Yama so the worshipper prepares an abode where they can flourish (*AV* xviii: 4: 54). Yama's father Vivasvat, too, is implored to let the devotee pass through death into immortality (*AV* xviii: 3: 62). Together with Yama, Soma, Varuṇa, the Aśvinas and Pūṣan, too, are prayed to for immortality (*AV* xix: 35: 3: 4), or abundant life (*AV* xviii: 3: 63, xviii: 5: 54). All such prayers presuppose a kindly, benevolent god who has passed over to the other side of death and is occupied with providing the living with longevity and the dead with proper food and shelter. The dead are his companions whom the living place in his hands trusting him for their well-being in the other world.

The *TB* has a prayer for deliverance from deaths, addressed to King Yama (*TB* i: 8: 6). Another is for safe conduct (apparently from this life to the next) and for deliverance from sins through due oblations (*AV* iii: 2: 11). Death is sought to be warded off through Yama's help, and the worshipper desires reassurance (*AV* iii: 14: 4). The man who worships Death with due reverence, uttering svāhā, is loosened from the clutches of death, and it can only be avoided through respectful obeisance to Death while one is yet alive (*AV* iii: 15: 1, 2). The idea is to give Death its due in the form of worship and oblations so that he will by-pass the worshipper.

Thus we read, 'the sacrificer becomes under a debt to Yama in that he strews the altar with plants; if he were to go away without burning (them) they would drag him about bound by the neck in the yonder world' (*TS* III: 3: 8). The sacrificer then is equally under debt to the gods as to the fathers and he remits that to the fathers by observing certain rules and by performing certain sacrifices. Death is not only a phenomenon peculiar to this life, but wherever a man happens to be born, in whatever region, Death awaits him and is sure to claim him at the end of his span. So the only way Death can be deceived or warded off is by acknowledging Yama's inalienable claim and by worshipping him duly in this life so that his grace spares the worshipper in the next. This idea is behind the worship of Yama in many hymns. By worshipping Yama in the proper manner through due sacrifices one is loosened from the thousand snares of Yama, with which he entangles the mortal in Death (*AV* III: 8: 2). If a man worships Yama, with hymns which belong to him, he wins the region of the fathers (*AV* V: 4: 11, IX: 8: 4; *JB* I: 345). Through one such hymn Yamī herself had sent (the dead) Yama to heaven (*AV* IX: 10: 21). Therefore these hymns, peculiar to Yama, must be chanted in the faith that since they were efficacious in the case of Yama himself, they should be efficacious for the worshipper too. Yama himself attained sovereignty through a hymn which is still powerful for the worshipper (*AV* XI: 10: 21).

Ever since the early *Brāhmaṇas* Yama is quite frequently called Death (mṛtyu) or the Ender (Antaka). His domain is over those souls whose earthly span is complete. But with the prevalence of the ideas of reincarnation the jurisdiction of Death was extended; whenever a man was reborn, in whatever time and place, in whatever form or shape, Death would claim him. This theory was coincident with the rise of the sacrifice in importance, for man could only quit his existence, be free from the regime of successive rebirths and deaths through the sacrificial ritual. Thus we have in the period of the flowering of the doctrine of reincarnation (i.e in the Brāhmaṇical period) continual harping on sacrifice as the sole channel of release. Man could make his final exit by performing the proper sacrifice, thus obtaining his release from recurinrg lives and consequently from recurring deaths. The emphasis on the sacrifice presupposes a threat—viz. that of reincarnation, which involved repetition of the miseries of existence culminating in the final misery of death, in each life. If man desired to snap the chain of existence, elude the clutches of recurrent deaths, his only way was to perform the proper sacrifices. Hence, while on the ideological, Upaniṣadic plane we have the elaboration of the reincarnation-and-karman theory with all its complex disquisition, on the ritual level sacrifices were being multiplied *ad infinitum* to provide a solution for all conceivable earthly predicaments. It was, therefore, at the time of the composition and compilation of the more elaborate *Brāhmaṇas* that Yama actually comes into his own, i.e. becomes a really formidable god, not only for the dead but also for the living, demanding oblations in return for freeing man from his biggest fear, viz. the fear of reincarnation. Existence in time is constant and inescapable involvement with death, hence time is to be feared.

The year, doubtless, is the same as Death, for he it is who by means of day and night destroys the life of mortal beings and then they die: therefore the year is the same as Death, his life that (year) does not destroy, by day and night, before old age, and he attains his full (extent of) life...And he, (i.e Yama) indeed, is the Ender, for it is he who...is...life. The gods were afraid of this Prajāpati, the Year, Death, the Ender, lest he, by day and night should reach the end of their life.

By Agnihotra, Darśapurṇamāsa, Cāturmāsya and Somayāga the gods did not attain immortality. Prajāpati's body was divided into 360 parts. Death was afraid lest all should become immortal and said,

He who is to become immortal either through knowledge or through holy work shall become immortal after separating from the body...But they who do not know this, or do not do this holy work, come to life again when they die and become the food of him (Death) time after time. But when he builds the fire-altar, he thereby gains Agni, Prajāpati, the Year, Death, the Ender whom the gods gained' (*ŚB* x: 4: 3: 1–11).

'Whatsoever is on this side of the sun, all that is held by Death' (*ŚB* x: 5: 1: 4); but 'within Death is immortality' (*ŚB* x: 5: 2: 4). 'Verily, there was nothing here in the beginning: by Death this (universe) was covered, by hunger, for Death is hunger' (*ŚB* x: 6: 5: 1). 'These two are the Arka and Aśvamedha, but these indeed become again one deity...Death. And, verily, whosoever knows this, conquers recurrent Death...Death is his own self, he attains all life and becomes one of those deities' (*ŚB* x: 6: 4: 1). Mere knowledge, however, can hardly be enough from the ritualistic point of view of the *Brāhmaṇas*. Holy work (i.e. sacrifices) is necessary in order to elude the grasp of rucurrent death. 'That "vaṣat" call being yonder shining (sun) and he being the same as Death—he thereby consecrates (the sacrificer) after death and causes him to be born from out of it and he is delivered from that death. And the sacrifice indeed, becomes his body; thus having become the sacrifice he is delivered from that death' (*ŚB* xi: 2: 2: 5). Again to drive the fear of recurrent deaths home, we have in another passage: 'Verily, there are deaths connected with all the worlds and were he not to offer oblations to them, Death would get hold of him in every world: when he offers oblations to the Deaths, he wards off Death in every world, even Hunger: it is him he wards off in yonder world' (*ŚB* XIII: 5: 1, 2). 'The gods who were in heaven were afraid of death and rushed to Prajāpati who instituted the Daśarātra sacrifice for them...also the Viśvajit (sacrifice), and then they defeated death and became immortal' (*JB* II: 329–31).

In the *Rām.* the concept of Yama is developed and his functions are distributed between Yama, Antaka, Kāla and Mṛtyu, each symbolizing a specific aspect of the older composite personality of Yama. We have the story of Yama attaining immortality through a physical fight and victory. Yama fights Mṛtyu for seven long days and the fight is fierce. This was when Rāvaṇa had attacked Yama's kingdom in the nether world. Mṛtyu finally asks Vaivasvata's (i.e. Yama's) leave to kill Rāvaṇa as he (Vaivasvata) alone killed and destroyed, and is called Dharmarāja (i.e. Yama) and lifts the Kāladaṇḍa (i.e. the rod of death). Then, as is usual in such stories, Brāhman intervened, requesting Yama not to render futile his boon to Rāvaṇa, and Yama had to desist from the attempt (*Rām.* VII: 22).

In the *Mbh.* tale of Ruru and Pramadvarā, Yama, called Dharmarāja complies with the angel's proposal that Pramadvarā, dead from snake-bite, should be revived with half of Ruru's life (*Mbh.* I: 9). Almost a parallel of this is found in Euripedes' *Alcestis*, where

> the fatal goddess allowed
> Admetus to escape the moment of his death
> by giving the lower power someone else to die
> instead of him... (11 ff.)

Yama's benevolent life-giving aspect is not lost sight of. Once the sage Gautama practised stiff penance for a very long period, Yama approached him unbidden and taught him how to be free from the debt to one's own parents and thus ascend to higher grounds (*Mbh.* XII: 127). Yama granted Satyavat's life to Sāvitrī after a long argument (*Mbh.* III: 281). Also in the Naciketas episode he obliged the sincere seeker by directing him to higher spiritual spheres in a nightlong trance and through visions (*Mbh.* XIII: 71). Again, when the Brahmin Śarmin was fetched by mistake by Yama's messengers, Yama courteously rose from his throne, greeted Śarmin and at his (Śarmin's) wish taught him the merits of charity (*Mbh.* XIII: 69). In this episode Yama is not thought of as a god above error, at least his emissaries are not. But, as we all know, these late passages are incorporated in order to dilate upon prescribed righteousness, so the context is not very important or significant. In this episode Yama is used as a mere peg to hang the discourse upon. In all the above passages Yama is a benevolent god granting immortality, or longevity, or higher knowledge. But the one Ṛgvedic god is many now: Yama, Kāla, Antaka, Mṛtyu and Dharma. Together they form the Yama-complex.

In the tale of Gautamī's son, who to all appearance died prematurely (*Mbh.* XIII: 1), we have all the different aspects of Yama's theophany dwelt upon. This is not because of any ritual complexity but because by now Yama means much more to the popular mind than he did in the Ṛgvedic time. He is Dharma, the king of the righteous (*Mbh.* XII: 92: 38). He was made the king of the departed ancestors, we are told by Śiva himself when the latter created Daṇḍa (punishment) at Brahman's request (*Mbh.* XII: 122). This is significant, since in earlier literature nobody ever 'made' him the king of the Pitṛs—he either 'was' their king or fought for and attained this rank. But now, in a sense he is being subjugated, not by another god as it strikes us at first, but by an idea-complex.

Let us probe into this at some length. Yama, if he 'is' the lord of the fathers becomes supreme in his jurisdiction by his own right as it were. But if he is made so by Śiva, whose mount the bull is also called 'Dharma' (*Mbh.* XII: 91: 13), an appellate of Yama in this context, then Yama as the lord of the fathers becomes an integral part of the Śiva-complex. And here is the crux of the matter. Yama on his own is a minor god with limited jurisdiction confined to the after-life and consequently he cannot directly control the land of the living. Whereas by being associated with the Śiva-complex he becomes an organic part of a much bigger whole, for, although Yama is frequently called Kāla, it is only as he imbibes the attributes of the Śiva-complex more and more that he becomes the true representative of Time, for Śiva is Mahākāla. And behind this we have the tremendously powerful philosophical concepts of Karman, rebirth and metempsychosis. As Yama fits into the larger pattern of a theophany which controls these philosophical ideas, his stature grows and his functions become multiple. Consequently he himself becomes a myriad-faced god. This is most clearly brought out in the legend of Gautamī's son who died of snake-bite because his actions (Karman) had exhausted his span of life. The snake pleaded not-guilty because it was merely an agent of Death, a tool in the hands of Mṛtyu. Death shifted the onus to Kāla (time) who wields supreme power; even the gods, he said, are subservient to Kāla. Time (Kāla) pointed out that the real agent was Karman which actually determines human destiny (*Mbh.* XIII: 1). Thus Death could not directly touch the victim, but only through the latter's own actions. These actions measure out a specific span and through these man signs his own death-warrant, as it were. Then Kāla comes in to pronounce the verdict and to usher in Mṛtyu or Antaka the executioner. Behind the whole action stands Dharma, the judge, who surveys life, checks up and weighs all man's actions, determines their fruits and sees that the effect is proportionate to the cause. Thus Yama becomes a nullity in his ultimate essence; he can operate only within the framework of fatalism, and fate works within certain categories, for each of which we have a distinctly designated hierophany—Dharma, Kāla, Antaka and Mṛtyu. Yama's functions, then, and jurisdiction are correlated to the operations of the ineluctible mechanism of fate. And it is in this direction that he grows in the epic-Purāṇic age. Vedānta with its Karman-doctrine and transmigration-dogma had come to stay and was gradually becoming the dominant pattern of man's religious belief—and within this framework Yama grows in stature. This explains why the one Yama of the *Vedas* had to become the multiple personality—because thus alone could he survive and retain his power. The mere god of the dead had no further mythological potentiality.

The *ṚV* has prayers addressed to Yama for release from his bondage, his fetters (*ṚV* x: 97: 16). In *ṚV* x: 135 Naciketas, the seer of the hymn tells his story. His father had sent him to Yama, who was rejoicing together with other gods under a leafy tree. Grieved at first that his father had sent him to the dead he had a vision of Yama and then desired to be with him. Then Yama told him that his father had behaved in an unnatural manner in sending him to the land of the dead, even though he had really meant the boy to return. When the father's temper cooled down, Yama showed him a path of return—a ritual path. This story seems to be the nucleus of the Yama-Naciketas episode which repeats itself in the *Upaniṣad* and in the *Mbh.* As yet it contains little of eschatology. Yama is very much like any other god here, only his region is beyond death. It is noteworthy that most of the *ṚV* Yama hymns are found in bk x, the latest book. But even so they depict a kindly god, who is more to be adored than feared. He is specifically a god of the dead, and not a god of death. This new facet merges for the first time in the *AV*. There we read, 'Svāhā to Yama, to Antaka, to Death' (*AV* xviii: 7: 8). In another place Death is said to be Yama's clever emissary who sends lives (that is souls) to the Pitṛs (*TS* xviii: 27). Yama is identified with Mṛtyu, Nirṛtha and Śarva in the *AV* (vi: 92: 2, vi: 66: 2, vi: 84: 3). In the 'mekhalābandhana' (tying on of the girdle) ceremony the preceptor symbolically releases the Brahmacārin from the clutches of Death by tying the girdle. Yama is called the Ender and Death (Antak'osi mṛytyu-ṛasi, *AV* VI: 46: 2, XVI: 5: 3), or simply Death (*AV* VI: 63: 2), or Fire (*TS* III: 3: 8) and through his identity with fire he is connected with Śiva.

A *TB* passage reads, 'Let Yama the king purify me through destructions' (*TB* I: 4: 8: 6). Yama had desired and conquered the world of the fathers and thus become its overlord (Pitṛṛṇām rājyamabhijayeyamiti, *TB* III: 1: 5: 14). Again, the gods had ordained him king (of the next world, the world of the fathers) (*TB* III: 1: 2: 11). As Dharma he is the overlord (*TB* III: 9: 16: 2). As Death he is (out) to kill mortals; through sacrifices men seek to free themselves from Yama's fetters (*TB* III: 10: 8: 2). In a passage in the *CB* we have Yama's name explained in the early commentary of Guṇaviṣṇu as Yame dharmarāje (in Yama the lord of righteousness, *CB* II: 2: 1), Sāyaṇa explains Yama as the restrainer (niyamayitṛ). Guṇaviṣṇu seems to accept this interpretation in other passages too (cf. II: 3: 20). In the *JB* Yama is identified with Agni. In the *Rām.* he is described as sitting with Agni before him (VII: 21: 2). He is also Time as expressing itself in the year, Saṃvatsara, of which the seasons are the mouths. He who does not realize this dies (*JB* I: 12, I: 246; *Mbh.* XIII: 43: 10, XIII: 148: 40, I: 1: 187–90). This idea is clarified in the *ŚB*: 'The Year (Saṃvatsara) doubtless is the same as Death, for he it is who, by means of day and night, destroys the life of mortal beings and then they die: therefore the Year is the same as Death, his life that (Year) does not destroy, by day and night before old age and his full (extent of) life...And he, indeed, is the Ender, for it is he who ends life' (*ŚB* X: 3: 1–9). The *Mait. U* dilates on the idea of Kāla as 'the cook of creatures', i.e. as ripening them with time, presumably to be fit to be swallowed by Death. It is significant that the word *Kāla* means both time and death. In the *Mbh.* Yama as Kāla assumes greater dimensions. 'He ever knows day and night and the seasons, also the good and evil works of a man.' As Kāla, he is painted black, with red eyes and holding a staff in his hand.

In the episode of Uttaṅka's vision of the Nāgaloka, Dhaumya explained the parable to him when he emerged from the nether regions:

> 'The two women are providence and the ordainer. Those dark and white warp and woof are the night and the day. The twelve-spoke wheel turned by the six boys are the six seasons (turning the twelve-month) year. The man is rain-cloud. The horse is fire. The ox you saw on your way is Airāvata, the lord of the elephants. The one mounted on it is Indra. The ox-dung you ate is nectar' (*Mbh* I: 1: 187–90).

The equation of Yama, Agni and Mrtyu is carried to its logical conclusion in 'Agni is Mṛtyu' (Agnirvai mṛtyuh, *JB* I: 332).

Mṛtyu, another aspect of Yama, is also called the overlord and his complexion is said to be red (*JB* III: 348; *GBU* IV: 4; *Mait. U* VI: 14, V: 15). Again 'King Yama is the same as the Gārhapatya (fire), because day by day they take that fire to the south, therefore, indeed they say that day by day Naḍa Naiṣadha carries King Yama (further) south.' Eggeling in his footnote on the passage says, 'Here Yama is apparently taken as the god of death and destruction, caused, ...by the warlike expeditions of Naḍa, king of Niṣadha in the south'. As the Aryans, under the leadership of Naḍa Naiṣadha, moved southwards, perhaps setting fire to the jungle tracts on the way (with the fire kindled from their own Gārhapatya fire), and as incendiary and havoc followed, it is said that the Gārhapatya fire is none but Yama, the god of death and destruction. While the Gārhapatya fire is kindled Yama is invoked and the place is swept with a Palāśa branch, an emblem of Yama (cf. *ŚB* VII: 1: 1: 1). In the Agnihotra sacrifice for the fathers, cinders from the Gārhapatya are thrown towards the south (*ŚB* XII: 5: 1: 7). Thus 'those who perform at the southern fire go down to the world of the Fathers...He thereby commits the fathers to Yama' (*ŚB* XII: 8: 1: 19, 20). In the Puruṣamedha sacrifice described in the *ŚB*, symbolical victims are offered to the many sinister aspects of Yama. Thus we hear 'to hell a manslayer, to Fate a rope-maker, to death a huntsman, to the End, Antaka, a dog-keeper, to the ogress of the waste lands a Niṣāda, to Yama a barren woman, to Yama (Yamī in the *TB*) one who bears twins, to the End Antaka a cow-slayer, to the night a black one with yellow eyes (*ŚB* XIII: 6: 1:1–13).

The *Rām.* combines the various aspects of Yama to create a fearful image of Time-End-Death. Thus in the epic imagery a formidable hero slaying his enemies is frequently referred to as Kālāntakayamopama: 'like Time, the Ender and Yama' (*Rām.* III: 32: 5). The idea of Antaka as the Destroyer is reflected in imagery where he is depicted with a gaping mouth (vyāttānanamivāntakam, *Rām.* III: 36: 8). Rāvaṇa is described as Mṛtyu or Kāla the inescapable (*Rām.* III: 68: 49). Again, in another image like Yama, like Death, like Time and like Fate (*Rām.* III: 69: 20). In the epic Mṛtyu, Kāla, Antaka and Yama are quite frequently used as abstractions and at the same time they are also introduced as much more tangible and vivid personalities than in the Vedic literature. Vidhi or Fate is another aspect of the same god in this epic. Thus it says, 'Verily for our destruction Fate has stretched his hands' (*Rām.* VI: 1: 3). Kāla is also used in the sense of preordained Fate, as in the passage where Lakṣmaṇa consoles Rāma for his misfortunes and miseries (*Rām.* VII: 106: 2).

The most majestic aspect of Yama, however, is his appearance as

Dharma, or Dharmarāja. In this form he is the 'great legislator and judge'. Yama himself is shown as the dispenser of justice, as the witness of human actions in the hearts of men (*Mbh.* I: 66: 30).

In order to elevate Dharma in his austere aspect, he is made to pierce the right breast of Brahman and come out in a human form—bestowing happiness on all (*Mbh.* I: 60: 60). In the Aṇīmāṇḍavya episode Dharma himself is at fault, dispensing justice according to the letter and not according to the spirit of true righteousness. The result is that the pious sage curses Dharma at the moment of death and even Dharma had to pay the penalty for his error. This episode is partially narrated to introduce Yudhiṣṭhira as Dharma's son, and to show Vidura as Dharma himself, but it also proves that the laws of righteousness are immutable and cannot be violated with impunity even by the supreme judge. Dharma was invoked by Kuntī, who requested him to beget a son in her (*Mbh.* I: 114); this son was Yudhiṣṭhira. Yama is the moral supervisor of the universe and as such he declined to admit Mandapāla into heaven on the ground that the latter had not raised children (*Mbh.* I: 220). This illustrates Yama's function of maintaining order in the universe—an order which ensures the propagation and continuation of the human race.

Human existence on the earth is beset on all quarters with sufferings and extremes of experience, from which spring sorrow and unrest. Man strives to step beyond these experiences to attain a lasting equanimity, but he never attains it here. But when we are introduced to Yama's court in the other world, this dream becomes a reality. This court, fashioned by Viśvakarman, is free from the polarities of heat and cold, from sorrow, hunger or thirst. Yama as Dharma is a fair and impartial judge. King Somaka found his priest (who had offered Prince Jantu so that the king, his father, could have a hundred sons) in hell and offered to go there in his stead. Yama replied that this was not possible, but allowed Somaka to share hell with his priest so that afterwards both could go to heaven (*Mbh.* III: 128). Here we have the Karman theory superimposed with free-will, for the effects of one's actions can be voluntarily shared by another. A similar episode is found in *Mbh.* XII: 19: 31. Yama, Kāla and Mṛtyu appeared as three distinct entities before Kauśika as he sat meditating (on Sāvitrī's instructions) when at Dharma's direction he refused to go to heaven without the body although Dharma had wanted him to do so. Kauśika greeted the three respectfully. Then came Ikṣvāku and asked for a portion of Kauśika's meditations, and Kauśika obliged him. A long argument took place over this gift: the Brahmin said that he had nothing to ask of the king, and the king in his turn maintained that as a King he was a bestower and not a recipient. As a proof of their innate righteousness they were approved of by Yama and his followers and were both admitted in heaven. Here as in the Sāvitrī–Satyavat episode Yama appears as a prover of the human heart, as Dharma, before punishment or reward is meted out. Therefore past actions are not always accepted on their face value. Yama, Dharma, the judge and dispenser of justice, weighs the human heart before pronouncing the verdict. In the Kapotalubdhakakathā, Dharma appears as a dove—a symbol of innocence, and teaches the hunter the true path (*Mbh.* XII: 141–5).

Entrance into heaven is strictly on the basis of righteousness—either through action or through true realization. A certain Brahmin came to Brahmaloka; Kṛṣṇa questioned him regarding mokṣadharma (liberation) and he instructed all by repeating a dialogue between Kaśyapa and himself (*Mbh.* XIV: 16). Thus the Brahmin earned his right to Brahmaloka by true knowledge and realization, and paid his dues to Dharma. Dharma appeared to Yudhiṣṭhira as a crane, said that he was a Yakṣa and set him ethical problems which Yudhiṣṭhira solved successfully, thus proving his claims to piety (*Mbh.* III: 297). Vidura was Dharma incarnate and at his death his essence entered Yudhiṣṭhira, because the latter was Dharma's son. Vidura, as we notice, throughout his career was meek as a dove and yet strong and wholly incorruptible. Born of a slave-woman he was shorn of worldly pedigree or glory, yet was a favourite of Kṛṣṇa's, who accepted his hospitality rather than that of the haughty Prince Duryodhana'. In Vidura we have an eternal verity as opposed to the time-serving values of the Kṣattriyas as a class. The same thing is found in Yudhiṣṭhira, who ever postulates eternal human values against the class-values of the warriors. And yet the human element in Yudhiṣṭhira had to be fully tested before he could be admitted to heaven in his mortal body. Dharma appeared as a dog, followed him and tested his loyalty and hospitality before he was finally passed by the high judge of the next world (*Mbh.* XVIII: 3). At the sight of the torments of his brothers in hell, Yudhiṣṭhira cursed Dharma (*Mbh.* XVIII: 3); the gods themselves descended and explained eschatology to him so that the scales fell from his eyes and he was filled with the true knowledge regarding the operations of Dharma. Although Indra confessed that Yudhiṣṭhira's vision had been illusory, yet from the point of view of his ethical perfection it had been a necessity. When the Pāṇḍavas are taken to their respective fathers, Yudiṣṭhira and Vidura enter Dharma (*Mbh.* XVIII: 4).

In the late passages of the epic we have rather strange notions regarding

Dharma, presented through apparently puzzling or paradoxical episodes. Oghavatī, the wife of Sudarśana (son of Agni), is commanded by her husband to entertain guests in every manner. A Brahmin appears in her husband's absence and demands her. She yields because of her husband's instructions. The guest fails to provoke the husband's jealousy, and later turns out to be no other than Dharma (*Mbh.* XIII: 2). In the *Kaṭhopaniṣad* we have a version of the Yama–Naciketas story built on the *ṚV* legend but with a different purpose. In the entire first vallī (section) of the first chapter of this *Upaniṣad* Naciketas is tested by Yama, tempted with temporal gifts, covetable but fleeting. Naciketas resists the temptation and is firm in his stand. Life had deceived him, his own father had said 'I give you over to Death', so to Death he had come, fasting for three days, in his insatiable desire to know the ultimate truth. Nothing short of a revelation would satisfy him. Yama tried to dissuade him from his quest, but in vain. He was weighed and was not found wanting. So Yama in his Dharma-aspect obliged this earnest seeker by revealing to him what is kept a dark mystery from the living—the intransitory essence of the soul, the true meaning of existence, the search and the realization that makes life worth living. In the *Mbh.* story of Yama and Naciketā, the young boy was cursed by his father Uddālaki: 'see Yama' (yamam paśya) because he could not 'see' the gift-objects his father had bidden him to fetch. Naciketā fainted at the curse, his father wept over him all night. When he revived in the morning Uddālaki asked him about his night-long trance. He related his experience at Yama's house. Yama had greeted him in his court (the Vaivasvatī sabhā) where Naciketā, at his own wish had been shown the pious, i.e. those who had given proper gifts to Brahmins (*Mbh.* XIII: 71–4). It is clear that the old *ṚV* nucleus had been used in the *Kaṭhopaniṣad* in order to establish spiritual truths and eschatological doctrines; whereas in the *Mbh.* it is given a new orientation, viz. to impress upon the people the merits of giving gifts to the Brahmins. But the character of Yama as Dharma is present in both legends. Through an error of his father the young boy crosses the boundary of life and death, approaches Yama face to face and ultimately learns deep secrets. These mysteries are different but in both instances Yama is the all-knowing preceptor revealing mystic truths to the eager enquirer.

As Kala, too, Yama is sometimes identified with Dharma in his functions. Thus in the Uttaṅka episode he tried and tempted Uttaṅka by offering him nectar (i.e. immortality) in an obnoxious form (ox-dung). There Kāla is shown as composed of day and night, months and seasons, rotating along a wheel turned by seasons which in their turn are caused by rainfall. Indra, seated on his elephant Airāvata (as the god of rain), controls showers by which seasons are divided. This is the most concrete shape of time. The same idea is repeated: 'Kāla ripens creatures forcibly by turning months and seasons, changes their names, with the fire of the sun and the fuel of day and night, with the fruits of one's own actions as witness' (*Mbh.* XII: 309: 90). Kāla is also said to ripen creatures and gather them. The word Kālyamāna means 'being killed'. Here, we have Kāla identified with Death, the gatherer of men. He is shown as the personified agent of Fate in *Mbh.* I: 1. In Jaratkāru's vision of his forefathers hanging on branches of trees with feet up and heads down, Time is symbolically shown as a mouse 'gnawing at the roots of existence' (*Mbh.* I: 41). Here too, Kāla is the ender of life as well as Dharma, because Jaratkāru, the successor, failed to do his duty by his ancestors by raising a family and had thus been a defaulter, and hence they were suffering. We must remember that ancestors suffering for an heir's fault is not an uncommon idea. Kāla judged and dispensed justice as Dharma. 'And Kāla, it is said, is not artificial, i.e. unreal, Kāla is the supreme god' (*Mbh.* V: 111: 20). The inevitability of fate as represented by Kāla is brought out in Valin's speech on Kāla: 'There stands the dark, cruel and inescapable One, with me bound as a beast with ropes' (*Mbh.* XII: 220: 82).

Mṛtyu's origin is extremely significant. We are told that Mṛtyu (feminine) was created by Brahman out of his consuming wrath. She vigorously protested against the duty allotted to her, and went and practised penance in spite of Brahman's command to kill creatures. When Brahman rebuked her, she wept, cupped her palms and held her tears there. The tears were transformed into fatal diseases by Brahman (*Mbh.* XII: 250). This story is retold in different versions. But from an analysis of the legend certain things emerge. First, here and here alone is Death made a woman and a compassionate woman, revolted at the task she is commissioned to perform. Thus the supreme moral judge is not a cruel heartless figure. But Brahman is not to be swayed from his purpose by a woman who shrinks from her duty; he sees that there has to be death, in order that life continues unhindered. Yet Death is loth to discharge her cruel assignment, so she is spared from the task of directly destroying men. Her compassion symbolized by her tears provides a subterfuge: she would not have to kill creatures, diseases would carry them off. The concept of fate and death is here presented in an acceptable garb. In the *HV* this task is allotted not to a female Mṛtyu but to Death's daughter Sunītha (*HV* V: 2; *Mārkeṇḍeya P* II: 13: 11).

Yama is called by his various names in the *Purāṇas*—Dharmarāja, Mṛtyu,

Antaka, Vaivasvata, Kāla and the Great Destroyer (*Matsya P* 102: 22). But in most places he is referred to as Dharmarāja and Kāla (*Matsya P* 107: 27, 135: 76, 136: 5). When Hariścandra sees Yama in the disguise of a Caṇḍāla, the latter is called Dharma (Dharmas-caṇḍālarūpadhṛk, *Mārkaṇḍeya P* VIII: 80).

In his multiple aspects Yama becomes more interesting and significant. For it is not merely the case of one personality assuming different functions, but there is a parallel thought-pattern behind the concept. As has already been observed, the theory of Karman and transmigration wrought important changes in theology, for, instead of a god imposing justice from above, man now becomes the architect of his own fate. Thus Karman is of supreme importance. When a man's action nears final fruition, his span of life is measured accordingly—if his actions demand that his opportunities of life-on-earth are over, then Kāla, Time, comes in. Death as the Ender (Antaka) announces the end and Death as Mṛtyu carries him off to the other world. But who is to guarantee fair play in all this? This is the special province of Yama as Dharmarāja whose code of justice is immutable and infallible. Thus Karmavāda (theory of Karman) is shown to be the only irrefutable truth regarding life, death and after-life.

The concept of Time as Kāla is found in *AV* XIII: 2: 39 ff. Rohita is there a solar deity identified with Kāla and Prajāpati. One is reminded of Yama also having solar bearings for he is the son of Vivasvat, the sun. 'The two hymns about Kāla, who is said to enclose Brahman, must, therefore, belong to a period when the idea of Brahman had been developed and they denote an opposition to the teaching of the Brahman being the highest essence' (O. G. von Wesendonk, 'The Kālāvada and Zervanite System', *JRAS*, 1931). Kāla, as the supreme deity naturally sought to oust Brahman Bhāgavata from a position of supremacy, for philosophy and cosmogony tend to occupy the position that Brahman had. The *Bh.P*, for example, makes Viṣṇu act through Kāla, thus assigning the god a subordinate position to that of an idea. In the *Mait. U* time is a substance identical with the Brahman (I: 4, VI: 14–16). In the *BĀU* time only proceeds through the sky (Ākāśa), thus becoming co-eternal with an eternal and almost insubstantial element (*BĀU* III: 8: 6–10). The *Śvet. U* I: 2 also mentions Kāla with Ākāśa, the sky. The Zervan concept of time in Mithraism, is also 'the apotheosis of Time as the First Cause' (Franz Cumont, *The Mysteries of Mithra*, p. 148). 'This was the capital doctrine that Babylon introduced into Mazdaism: belief in Fatality, the conception of an inevitable destiny controlling the events of this world and inseparably conjoined with the revolution of the starry heavens' (*ibid.* p. 124). We have figures of Zervan when Rome adopted Mithraism and spread the mystic cult over Europe. On the plane of ideas Zervan somehow brought back the Greek Aion (Time), only in Greek mythology this figure is not very vivid or tangible. In Mithraism Time assumed supreme significance and was sculpturally reproduced. This concept of personified Time is important, because 'mystery worships spread enormously through the Mediterranean during the first three centuries A.D., and in the west as much as in the east from where they came' (*ibid.* pp. 182–3). It is significant that the epic-Purāṇic age is the time of the growth and development of the Kāla-Yama-Dharma, both theologically and philosophically, and is coincident with the rise and spread of Zervan-Saturn worship under the auspices of Mithraism. What spread as a mystic cult in Europe attained the support of full-fledged theology and philosophy in India, thus becoming an organic part of an intelligible whole.

The rise of Yama in importance is marked by his being referred to as king in a physical sense in the epic-Purāṇic age. In the Vedic age Yama was 'king of the fathers' ruling in the next world, but there was very little concrete description of him as king. We are, however, told that he is the king of the next world, although in the beginning it was not so, for 'Agni was in yonder world, Yama in this. The gods said "Come, let us interchange them. With food the gods invited Agni, with kingdom the Pitṛs (invited) Yama"' (*TS* II: 6: 6). Thus the Pitṛs or fathers, because they needed a king to rule over them 'in yonder world', offered Yama their kingdom and Yama became their sovereign. This tallies quite well with the *AV* passage 'Yama was the first mortal to die' (yo mamāra prathamo martyānām), and thus he is fittingly made the sovereign of those who die after him. But as he becomes a multifunctional god working within the framework of fatalism he is described as an actual king. Thus in the *Rām.* we have a lengthy description of the material splendour of Yama's vast kingdom. Beyond his capital is great darkness. Inside is his capital shimmering and resplendent—with golden pillars and seats of diamond and cat's-eye, surrounded by bowers. 'There on the judgement seat sits Lord Vaivasvata the king...This is the fearful end of the world—there is nowhere to go beyond it' (*Rām.* IV: 42: 66–70). The kingdom of Yama is still remembered as the land of the dead (*Rām.* III: 54: 28 and III: 55: 52; so also is vaivasvatakṣaya, Yama's abode, *Rām.* III: 73: 32). The *Mbh.* also gives a physical description of Yama's court fashioned by Viśvakarman. But this time there is a tinge of idealism mingled with it, for it is the symbol of the unattainable dream—free from pain, hunger, thirst or age—free also from the polarities of experience. Yama was surrounded by his retinue just like a mortal king. Yama's kingdom as Gautama describes it is also idealistic for there truth alone is spoken and the weak torment the strong (*Mbh.* XIII: 102: 16). Such heavens are common to all the mythologies of the world and are the product of man's dream of the unattained and unattainable, a reverse of actual experience. This dream is very old; its first expression is perhaps found in the old account on a tablet from Nippur. 'It describes how, when the world was young and the work of creation had only just begun, Dilmun was a place where "the croak of raven was not heard, the bird of death did not utter the cry of death, the lion did not devour, the wolf did not rend the lamb, the dove did not mourn, there was no widow, no sickness, no old age, no lamentation"' (Introduction to *The Gilgamesh Epic*, Penguin edn. p. 39). The mention of the raven, the bird of death, and the dove are significant, since these symbols are all associated with death. This Dilmun is reflected in the Garden of Eden of the Bible, in Yima's Var in the *Avesta*, and in Asgard in the Edda. The *HV* makes Yama the king of the fathers, mothers, of vows, mantras, cows, yakṣas, monsters and men (*HV* IV: 6–7). In the *Vāyu P* Yama's court (vaivasvatī sabhā) is called Śubhāvatī, and his city is called the City of the Restrainer (Saṃyamana pura).

Sitting in his magnificent court Yama performs his administrative function as Dharmarāja, the supreme judge and punisher. It is interesting to note that this aspect of Yama's personality emerges clearly for the first time in the later Brāhmaṇic period. Thus in the *ŚB* we have: 'indeed they place him (the dead man) on the balance in the yonder world and whichever of the two will rise that he will follow, whether it be the good or the evil. And, verily, whosoever knows this, mounts the balance even in this world and escapes being placed on the balance in yonder world, for his good deed rises and not his evil deed' (XI: 2: 7: 33). In the *Chāndogya* and *Gopatha Brāhmaṇas* we come across a new idea regarding Yama: it says that a man pays the interest (Kuṣīda, presumably on his debt) to Yama by offering oblations to Agni, by strewing the altar for Yama (*GBU* IV: 4). Thus the ethical life of man is controlled by certain obligations, or debts to Yama, and by discharging them faithfully he will escape torments in 'the yonder world', he will be spared the extortions and torments. Underneath this debt theory is the concept of Yama as Dharmarāja—the moral overlord who extorts his dues from mortals. The *Rām.* describes Yama as sitting in his Judgement Hall, sifting the good and evil of man (*Rām.* IV: 42: 69).

The *Mbh.* pushes the idea of a supreme judge inwards and creates a judge who judges from within (I: 68: 30). Yama is there described as punishing the evil deeds of men (*Mbh.* I: 68: 31). Indra explained eschatology to Yudhiṣṭhira, who felt bewildered at finding his miscreant Kaurava cousins in heaven and his pious brothers in hell: 'Hell is to be visited by all kings. He who enjoys (the fruits of) his good works comes to hell afterwards; he who suffers hell first comes to heaven afterwards (*Mbh.* XVIII: 3: 11–13.) Again, the kingdom of Yama is described as a plane of retribution. When Indra, disguised as Dhṛtarāṣṭra, stole Gautama's elephant, the latter told Indra that he (Indra) would have to make good this theft in Yama's kingdom. Indra said that was a region of punishment and torments for hedonists, the faithless sinners given to enjoyment of sensual pleasures (*Mbh.* XIII: 102: 14, 15). Suffering death at the hands of Yama's men, also sorrow and recurring births—these are the punishments of the evil-doer (*Mbh.* XIII: 111: 36). There is nothing unusual in this concept, for the dread god of the underworld is painted thus in all mythologies. The moral judge weighs men and if they are found wanting, he pronounces the verdict against them and his officers execute the torments. The Babylonian god Nergal may have become connected with the underworld. He, like Mṛtyu is a god of plague and fever, close to Era the plague-god proper and is often identified with him (*Hastings encyclopaedia of religion and ethics*: Babylonian Religion).

Yama's kingdom is fierce and full of torments (*Mbh.* XIII: 111), and Yama exhorts men, telling them of the merits of charity which will bear fruit in the next world (*Mbh.* XIII: 130). Pindar's eschatology, as expressed in the Second Olympian and the Threnoi, tells us that at death the souls are judged, the good dwell with Pluto and Persephone, the evil must suffer and be purified, sent back again to earth and at death judged once again. Those who, in three successive lives, live righteously are allowed into the tower of Kronos. In the *Avesta* Yima's four dogs, acting as his agents, separate the good from the bad. These dogs, watching at the head of the Cinvat bridge, scare fiends with furious barking.[1] In the *TA* we read that the good and bad are separated before Yama (VI: 5: 113). The *ŚB* says the separation is to be made by fire (II: 7: 33), after which the evil are punished with torments in hell (I: 9: 3: 2).[2]

[1] Incidentally, the root *ci* of the *cinoti* class means 'to arrange in order', and *ci* of the *ciketi* type means 'to observe', 'perceive', 'investigate', 'search through'. In either group it yields a meaning of judgement, separation and arranging or piling in order. Thus the word *Cinvat* itself has the sense of separating the souls according to their merits.

[2] In Matthew XXV. 31–41 we have a similar description of the sifting of the good and the evil before the former are rewarded and the latter punished. P'an Kuan in Chinese and Osiris in Egyptian mythology are judges of the dead. In Plato (the *Gorgias* myth) we hear of similar division of the dead into the blessed and the damned. Minos the Cretan king also became a judge of the dead.

CHAPTER 3

YAMA AND ESCHATOLOGY

MAN reaches Yama's domain through and after death. Judgement there is followed by reward and punishment. Of reward we do not have many records; only that the blessed live on with Yama in bliss. The cremation ground itself is sanctified by Yama with days, nights and water and he gives it to the dead for whom an incantation is chanted (*ṚV* x: 14: 9). The dead are also seen as inhabiting the earth, the air and the sky (*AV* xviii: 4: 55–6). Or they are in the south enjoying themselves in Yama's company (*AV* xii: 3: 8). King Yama followed the fathers (in their sojourn from this life to the next) providing them with food through the svadhā call (*AV* xv: 14: 13). The Vaśā cow provides happiness to the soul in Yama's kingdom (*AV* xii: 3: 3). The souls delight in the abode and under the command of Yama (*AV* xviii: 1: 34). The soul is asked to enjoy its fill in Yama's kingdom, where Savitṛ gives it a dwelling; there it can live on unharmed (*AV* xviii: 4: 31, 32).

The man who cooks vistārin brahmaudana (a large meal for the Brahmin) goes to Yama, to the gods and enjoys himself with Gandharvas connected with Soma (*AV* iv: 34: 3).

This is the picture of life in the next world for the blessed. The damned on the other hand are punished. In the first phase of Vedic literature, i.e. in the Saṃhitā and early Brāhmaṇa period, the reward and punishment appear to be final—thus judgement, too, is executed once and for all, presumably because this period precedes the rise of the theory of Karman and reincarnation. Yama, in this period, rewarded the good by conducting the souls safely from this world to the next and by leading them to happiness or misery there according to their manner of life on earth. But whereas the pleasure was provided by Yama himself the punishment was executed by his agents. The Aṅgirases who practised the cult of their ancestors regarded the departed as semi-divine. One is reminded of the Greek 'Angelos'—messenger—for Yama is always invoked accompanied by the fathers and the Aṅgirases (*MS* iv: 9: 8), who are his followers. Evil spirits dwell with the spirits of the (wicked) dead (*AV* xviii: 2: 28), and evil spirits are enemies of men (*AV* viii: 6: 5). After death comes a separation through judgement. Bliss or torment follows and those who are assigned to hell suffer torments from Yama's men.

Hell is a concept not found explicitly in the early Vedic literature, except in references of dubious meaning. Of the few truly Vedic references one is found in the account of Bhṛgu's descent into hell and his vision of the horrors there. The lord of hell appeared as a black man with yellow eyes, holding a staff, with two women at his side, one fair and the other called atikalyāṇī (surpassingly fair or beyond beauty, i.e. not-fair—*JB*: 42–4, also XV: 234–8, and in *ŚB* XI: 6: 1). This was perhaps one of the first of the series of hell visions to which Dante's *Inferno* and Milton's description of hell in *Paradise Lost* belong. It is clearly depicted only in the epic-Purāṇic age. Thus in the *Ram.* we have an account of Daśaratha in hell (II: 71: 10–19). It describes the torments of Daśaratha, dressed in black, seated on a black, iron seat, being beaten by black women and seated in a chariot drawn by asses dressed in red robes and garlands. Again, hell is described in the *Rām.* when Nārada announces Rāvaṇa's arrival to Yama. Rāvaṇa enters and sees creatures suffering or enjoying according to their works; Yama's fierce soldiery at work, cruelly torturing the evil-doer; the miserable wail of the sufferers who are being gnawed by worms and devoured by dogs; the heart-rending cries of people seeking to cross the Vaitaraṇī and being scorched on its hot sand-banks, or sawn in half; thirsty people begging for a drink of water and the hungry for food in the different hells; pale, emaciated spectres running to and fro. The blessed, on the other hand, are enjoying music and sumptuous dishes, in fair mansions, surrounded by well-dressed women. These were those who shone brilliantly because of their works (*Rām.* VII: 21: 10–20). This is a very elaborate account of the fruits of the good and evil works of this life in the next.

In the *Mbh.* Yama is described as being accompanied by death and looking fearsome, surrounded by a hundred diseases (*Mbh.* III: 221: 9). Sāvitrī saw him as a dark figure, with red eyes, holding the noose and looking fierce (*Mbh.* III: 281: 16). Yama forcibly wrenched out Satyavat's life, in the shape of a thumb-sized man. When the Kurukṣetra battlefield is described as a river of blood and death the image seems to be one of hell, and Yama is indirectly described as a voracious monster swallowing men whose span of life is over (*Mbh.* VII: 85: 18).

In *KB* XI: 3 we hear that a man is devoured by the same animal in the next world that he has devoured here. Again when a particularly bloody battle is fought, the field is compared to Yama's capital in its grim appearance (*Mbh.* VIII: 36). Then follows a description of death and horror on the battlefield—and the image of Yama's region of torment is behind the whole scene. A very striking episode is narrated in the *Mbh.* XV: 40, 41.

When Vyāsa offers water to the departed heroes they appear before the Pāṇḍavas, Dhṛtarāṣṭra, Kuntī and Gāndhārī; they were all purged of the dross of malice and ill-feeling. They lived one night with the survivors. In the morning Vyāsa said that if the wives so desired they could live with their husbands; to do so they should bathe in the water. They did so and were magically carried to their husbands. This vision recalls another—Odysseus' vision in the region of Erebus.

Another late account of hell is found in *Mbh.* XVII: 2: 25. Here hell is dark, full of hair, foul-smelling, full of raw flesh and blood, corpses, worms, deformed animals with night-and-darkness associations and ghosts of hideous shape. Various horrors are peculiar to different hells. The Kumbhīpāka had iron pans with oil boiling in them (to cook miscreants alive). The Śālmalī hell had tortures of a different order. Yudhiṣṭhira, to whom this vision was shown, was turning away in disgust when the sufferers called out to him imploring him to stay on because his stay ameliorated their pain. Later, Indra confessed that all these visions were illusory and Yudhiṣṭhira was taken to heaven. He goes down into the Svargaṅgā and leaves his body there. This story reminds us of the Biblical story of Lazarus and Manes. The *Purāṇas* make Yama owe his overlordship of the next world to Śiva, and also his position of moral judge (*Matsya P* XI: 20: 21). Janamejaya is said to have fought Yama, who was accompanied by the diseases of hell (*Matsya P* XI: 50). Hell is murky—full of dry-bones that in thirst run hither and thither, desiring others' food, tormented in different hells—Śālmalī, Vaitaraṇī, Kumbhīpāka, Iddhavālukā, and Asipatravaṇa (*Matsya P* CXLI: 67–72). Yama's messengers are of horrid appearance and deed (*Mārkaṇḍeya P* VIII: 136).

Hell is mentioned in certain *ṚV* passages of dubious meaning: *ṚV* VII: 104: 3, 7, 11; II: 29: 6; IX: 73: 8, 9; IV: 5: 5. The *AV* mentions Naraka loka (hell) in XI: 4: 36. But we do not have any clear reference to hell until later in the Upaniṣadic period. But the Upaniṣadic seers were not Ṛgvedic and the distinction is very significant, for in the first phase of Vedic composition eschatology is vague and nebulous, it is only much later in the epic-Purāṇic period that people paid attention to life-after-death. A hell of darkness, torments and wailing is then created. It is interesting to note that the later, interpolated book VII of the *Rām.* and the later books of the *Mbh.* full of non-heroic matter have a very vivid hell. This was the period of the composition of the early *Purāṇas*. This period is post-Buddhistic, a period of consolidation of Brāhmaṇism; and one of the forces which helped to mould this new pantheon and the neo-Brāhmaṇical creed was the growth of Yama into sinister dimensions and the creation of a hell as a place of torment and suffering. But this hell appears as not altogether a creation of the Indian mind in the epic-Purāṇic age. The *Mahāvastu* is a work whose compilation probably began in the second century B.C. but was not completed until the third or fourth century A.D., according to J. J. Jones in his edition of the *Mahāvastu* (1949). In the first section of the *Mahāvastu*, the venerable elder Kolita paid a visit to hell and found various circles of hell—Kālasūtra, Saṃghāta, Raurava, Mahāraurava, Pratāpa, Kukkula, Kunap, Kumbha and Sañjīva—each with a different kind of torment. Tracing these different hells to factors from outside India, we come upon the Chinese Buddhistic literature—which is a mixture of Buddhism with indigenous Chinese eschatology and ancestor worship. China could not very well give up such an old belief, rather she transformed the ancestors into the Yen-kings who punished miscreants. And in the traffic of Buddhism between China and India these numerous punishing gods exercising their authority in different hells came to be incorporated into Indian mythology. Thus Kern, in his discussion of the Buddhist cosmic system mentions that, according to this system, the universe consists of innumerable spheres—between these spheres are situated certain hells...the lowest of which is the abode of six classes of gods. The third class of gods is called the Yamas. The very lowest of the thirty-one abodes of the living beings are the hells of punishment. Above these is placed the animal kingdom. Higher than that is the abode of ghosts and spectres, which are placed in the Lokāntarita hell (Kern: *Manual of Indian Buddhism*).

The *JB* tells us of three hells and three heavens, so it is clear that the number of hells grew with time until there was one separate hell for each specific sin.

The spiritual world in the Buddhist scheme of the universe is clearly demarcated into zones or tiers. 'The first of them or the third of heavens is inhabited by beings called Yamas...They are called "strifeless" because they have not to take part in the war constantly being waged by the gods of the two lower heavens against the demons (asuras) who are unable to advance into the regions above Meru' (Monier Williams, *Buddhism*, p. 207). Thus eschatological concepts emerge clearly during the period when Buddhism flourished. Even when it declined and Brāhmaṇism was revived as Hinduism under royal patronage, these concepts seeped into Hinduism and influenced the epic-Purāṇic eschatology. Yama came to stay as an awe-inspiring and sinister character who frightened men into piety. Thus in the *Mudrārākṣasa* and *Harṣacarita* we hear of Yamapaṭikās—scrolls depicting hell-torments, which were shown around in order to inspire fear until sinners repented of their evil ways and adopted the accepted code of behaviour. The medieval paintings of the devil and his tortures in hell served the same purpose. Hell in the period of the revival of Hinduism, i.e. under the Guptas, when the later parts of the epics and the earlier parts of the *Purāṇas* were being composed, came to play a very significant part in the popular imagination. It confirmed the eschatology of neo-Brāhmaṇism by means of its horrors and threats on the popular plane—while the fear of reincarnation achieved the same end on the philosophical plane.

Deities of daily oblation include Yama's men in the Gṛhyasūtras. But their fearful aspect is not dwelt upon at any length until much later. In the *Avesta*, Zarathustra says to Ahura-Mazda: 'Where are the rewards given?' Ahura Mazda replies: 'When the man is dead, when his time is over, then the wicked, evil-doing Daevas cut off his eye-sight'...'The soul enters the way made by Time and open both to the wicked and to the righteous. At the head of the Kinvat bridge made by Mazda, they ask for their spirits and souls the rewards for the worldly goods which they gave away here below' (*Fargard* v, 218–20).

In the *Zamyad Yast* we are told that there are three hells—Evil Thought, Evil Word and Evil Deed which are enveloped in endless darkness.[1]

The *AV* hymn I: 14 is addressed to Yama or Varuṇa. It consists of an imprecation against spinsterhood (Kulapā Kanyā) and Yama is mentioned frequently. One is reminded of Antigone's words: 'I shall be the bride of Acheron' (*Antigone* 810–14). Perhaps a girl remaining unmarried was called 'the bride of Yama', i.e. as good as dead, and her stay in her father's house was likened to that in the other world.

A picture of Osiris in E. A. W. Budge's *Osiris and the Egyptian resurrection*, p. 20, has the god holding 'in his left hand the flail or whip, in his right the crook'. This picture of Osiris almost combines the weapons of Varuṇa and Yama, of the judge and the punisher in the nether world.

In Virgil's *Aeneid* VI: 724 ff. we have an account of the Roman eschato-

[1] In Egyptian mythology Nabu (announcer) was 'a writer of destiny'—an assistant of the god of death. We have in the later Indian figure of Citragupta, Yama's clerk, a parallel to this figure. Torture and horror as concomitants of hell are also found in Eddic eschatology. We hear that Odin 'threw Hel into Niflheim and gave her authority over nine worlds on condition that she shared all her provisions with those who were sent to her, namely men who die from disease or old age. She has a great homestead there...Her hall is called Eljudnir (= damp with sleet), her plate Hunger, her knife Famine...the stone at the entrance Drop-to-Destruction, her bed Sick-bed, its hangings Glimmering Misfortune. Hel is half black, half flesh-colour, and is easily recognized from this; she looks rather grim and gloomy' (*Prose Edda*, p. 56). The Valkyries are Odin's men whom he sends 'to every battle and they choose death for the men destined to die' (*ibid.* p. 61).

logical concepts, 'Therefore are they schooled with penalties and for olden sins pay punishment, some are hung stretched out to the empty winds, from some the stain of guilt is washed away under swirling floods or burned out in fire (Loeb edn.).

Yama is helped in his task in the underworld by his messengers commonly called Yamadūta. The word *aṅgiras*, bearing close resemblance to the Greek word *angelos* meaning angel or messenger, may refer to Yama's oldest assistants. We hear that Mātali grew with Kavya and Yama with the Aṅgirases ('Mātali Kavyairyama aṅgirobhih...vāvṛdhānah', *AV* XVIII: 33: 47).

In Theocritus we have an account of Angelos: 'Hera bore to Zeus a girl named Angelos and Zeus gave her to the nymphs to nurse. When she grew up she stole the myrrh that Hera used to rouge her face with. When Hera found out she was going to punish her but the girl ran away to the house of a woman who had just given birth and from there to some men who were carrying out a corpse. Then Hera gave up the pursuit and Zeus told the Kabeiroi to take charge of the girl and cleanse her; so the Kabeiroi took her away and cleansed her in the lake of Acheron' (II. 12).

Two things make the tale significant from our point of view. First, the impurity of childbirth and death attached to Angelos thus connecting her with death. Second, the Kabeiroi cleansed her, and these are the metalworkers, sons of Hephaestos or Vulcan, and this connects her with the parallel of Agni, with which the Indian Aṅgirases were early connected. Thus the Greek myth definitely connects Angelos, and through her the Aṅgirases, with gods of the Śiva-Yama-Agni group. The lake Acheron also connects her with the nether world. The Aṅgirases grew dim with time and we hear of Yama's agents, messengers and associates (*AV* VIII: 8: 10–11). Agni is also referred to as Yama's messenger (*AV* II: 12: 7, XII: 2: 8). His messengers are sought to be driven away from the living (*AV* V: 30: 6).

The *AV* mentions a bay horse of Yama (V: 5: 8). In the *ṚV* we meet Yama's dogs called Śyāma and Śabala who guard Yama's path (*AV* VIII: 1: 9). These are called Mithūdṛśā, i.e. seeing or appearing alternately—both could not see at once. This reminds us of the Graeae who had only one eye between the three of them. In a passage in the *ṚV* and another in the *AV* we have a prayer to the dogs of Yama, beseeching them not to devour the departed, who are advised to bypass these two dogs. In the *PGS* we have a dog-spell, requesting the dogs (evidently of Yama) to leave the child alone. 'Verily, your mother is the celebrated Saramā, your father is Sīsara: and Śyāma and Śabala are your brothers' (I: 16: 24). In *HGS* we have mention of a dog-demon called Sīsaramā (clearly a compound of Sīsara and Saramā). The fact that he is a demon whose sons, according to the *PGS* passage are Yama's messengers connects these dogs with sinister associations. They are described as long-nosed, relishing in blood, powerful or copper-coloured—the two messengers of Yama (*ṚV* x: 14: 10–12; *AV* xviii: 11: 13). The description is significant because of its fierceness and also because, as early as the *ṚV*, Yama is not actually associated with acts of cruelty. The mystery becomes somewhat clearer when we remember that these dogs have a Greek parallel—Kerberos: 'Kerberos who eats raw flesh, the brazen-voiced hounds of Hades, fifty-headed, relentless and strong' (Hesiod, *Theogony*, 311–13). And the name is striking because Kerberos is three-headed, and Śyāma and Śabala are two, but in other passages two four-eyed dogs are mentioned. Kerberos is allied to the word Karbara—spotted and variegated; this again yields a later form Śabala, which means the same thing. Kerberos is described as having serpents entwined round his body, which would naturally make him look variegated.

Thus Yama's dogs appear to be of Indo-European origin. This is borne out by the Avestan Yima's four dogs—dividers of the souls of the good and bad. Again in the Edda we hear, 'Managarm (Moon's dog) became the most powerful member of that family; he gorges on the flesh of all who die' (*Prose Edda*, p. 39). Thus the proto-Yama of the Indo-European peoples had gods, who were fierce in appearance and function, and Śyāma and Śabala are a mere carry-over from olden times. In Egyptian mythology Anubis is this dog—the conductor of the dead—and Anubis is called jackal-faced, which adds to his horrid look. In one single passage we hear that Yama has a brown horse (*AV* v: 5: 8). The word used is Śyāva which is connected with Śyāma, one of his dogs' names. In the *TB* we hear that Yama's messengers bring victims forcibly and torment them (i: 5: 15). The four-eyed dog of Yama is mentioned again in the *TB* (*AV* iii: 8: 4: 1). The *Rām.* simply mentions Yama's messengers without specifying them as human or bestial (ii: 66: 58). Elsewhere we hear of Yama's servants (*Rām.* vi: 53: 55). In the *Mbh.* we hear of agents of Yama (i: 220). The word *Yamadūta* or *Yamadūtaka* however means a crow.

[1] Yama's association with the dog, although of pre-Indian origin, had become more sinister in the age of the *Brāhmaṇas* and in the early epic period, possibly because of an oblique mythological projection of the Caṇḍāla caste in his personality. The Caṇḍāla, an outcaste in Indian society, is traditionally cruel, a hunter by profession and is invariably associated with dogs. Yama in his Dharma aspect becomes an image of this Caṇḍāla (cf. Dharmaścaṇḍālarūpadhṛk, *Mārk. P*: viii: 80). Yudhiṣthira, Dharma's son, in his last sojourn is followed by a dog, the picture evokes the image of the prototype, viz. Yama with his dog.

Besides dogs and messengers other creatures associated with Yama are mentioned. For example the treacherous green parrot is to be offered to Yama by one who desires long life (*GBU* I: 24). The owl and the vulture are called Yama's messengers in *TĀ* IV: 28, *HGS* I: 16: 19 and in the *Kauśikasūtra* 129.

Kapota and Śakuna, the dove and the vulture—birds of ill-omen—are associated with Nirṛti, Yama's female counterpart in many ways (*AV* VI: 27). They are called Dūto Nirṛtyāh—Nirṛti's messengers (*AV* VI: 28). The owl together with the dove is mentioned in connection with Yama as his and Nirṛti's messengers (*AV* VI: 29). Death as Yama and Nirṛti are most frequently connected with birds and the reason is perhaps not far to seek... 'The idea that birds were manifest forms of the spirits of the dead continued to be persistent in later Greek religion. We can assume that birds derived their religious sanctity from totemic associations' (R. F. Willets, *Cretan cults and festivals*, p. 73).[1]

Even in Indian folklore the crow, a dark bird, is held to represent deceased ancestors and is given food in memory of the dead. Birds have been associated with ancestral spirits all through the ages.

The owl together with the dove is mentioned again in connection with Yama, as his and Nirṛti's messenger (*AV* VI: 29; *ṚV* X: 165: 4). To Yama is appointed the task of collecting the souls of those whose time on the earth is over. In this capacity he is called sandaṃśa, tongs—that which forcibly draws souls from this life to the next (*JB* II: 169).

If Yama is the king of the next world, his subjects are the fathers over whom he rules. As man has his debt to pay to King Yama, so has he a debt to his dead forefathers. This belief in one's duty to one's dead predecessors is as old as human consciousness and is spread all over the world. The fathers are called the region-finders and pathfinders (*AV* XVIII: 34: 25), because they, passing through death, led the way to the next world; and living there

[1] Even in Byzantine sculpture executed during the reign of the emperor Theophilus the bird-motif seems to have symbolized ancestral spirits:

> set upon a golden bough to sing
> To Lords and ladies of Byzantium
> Of what is past, or passing or is to come.

Again,

> Miracle, bird or golden handiwork,
> More miracle than bird or handiwork,
> Planted on the starlit golden bough,
> Can, like the cocks of Hades crow.

In Yeats's association with the cocks of Hades (cf. Byzantium) these birds are immediately connected with ancestral spirits, as the whole tone of the 'Byzantium' and 'Sailing to Byzantium' proves.

in Yama's company found shelter for those who will follow. They also protect the living as a *TS* prayer indicates: 'May the Pitṛs whose lord is Yama, together with the Pitṛs, protect them in the south' (v: 6: 5).

The essentially this-worldly tone of the early Vedic literature, which repeatedly bursts forth into joyous praise of this life, led inevitably to regarding the dead as objects of pity. They are deprived of the good things of life, they are confined to darkness, let us look after them. When one remembers the numerous *ṚV* prayers for long life and a vision of the sun, one is not surprised by this tone of gentle commiseration for the dead—who are lighted not by the sun, but by the moon because they live on the other side of the sun (*MS* i: 10, 77). The day is symbolic of the gods, victory over dark and evil death (*TB* i: 5: 9: 6). But even the fathers are gods of one sort who deliver the living from sin (*TB* iii: 7: 5: 4; ii: 6: 16: 2). The fathers reside in a very lofty region usually referred to as 'the third region' (*TMB* ix: 8: 5). In the *Avesta* Yima was commissioned to prepare a place, not explicitly for the fathers but a place free from sorrow and suffering.

Yama is the leader of the fathers in the next world whom they sought out there (*JB* iii: 383). The fathers are the subjects of Yama, the king. Thus we read that while the Gārhapatya fire is kindled, Yama is invoked; the place is swept with a Palāśa branch (*ŚB* vii: 1: 1: 1) and an invocation is addressed to Yama: 'Yama hath given the settlement on earth (to this sacrificer) for Yama indeed rules over the settlements on this earth and it is he who grants to this (sacrificer) a settlement on this earth. The fathers have prepared this place for him for Yama is the Kṣatra (nobility or ruling power) and the fathers are his clansmen' (*ŚB* vii: 1: 1: 3–4). In the *TS* we read: 'Go away, O Soma-loving Pitṛs, on your majestic ancient paths, then reach ye the kindly Pitṛs who carouse in company with Yama' (i: 8: 4). Thus Yama entertains his people in his own kingdom. The Agnihotra is a sacrifice for the fathers: the cinders from the Gārhapatya are put towards the south, the direction of the fathers (*ŚB* xii: 5: 1: 7). '...those who perform at the southern fire go down to the world of the Fathers...He thereby commits the Fathers to Yama' (*ŚB* xii: 8: 1: 19, 20).

Everywhere in the Brāhmaṇical literature the south is said to belong to Yama and the fathers. In later literature, when Yama's personality undergoes a thorough transmutation during the period of the rise of the theories of Karman and transmigration, Yama becomes the overlord of the south. Strangely enough the Avestan Yima too rules in the south and whenever he is hard pressed for space he presses the magic ring given to him by

Ahura Mazda on the ground and the land of the Vara extends toward the south. Even in the *AV* Yama is assigned the south quarter and the fathers too are said to dwell there. Thus we read in the *AV* that Yama entertains his guests in his region in the south (*AV* XIII: 26: 3: 8), for 'the south is the (direction) of the deceased ancestors' (*ŚB* I: 2: 5: 17). The *ṚV* does not mention Yama in connection with the south, though the notion may have existed even in *ṚV* times. Also, Soma together with the Rudras are supplicated in order that the sacrificer may be delivered from the south, and Soma and the Rudras are allied gods (*AV* XIX: 35: 3, 4). The same idea is repeated in *AV* XII: 4: 56. Another prayer mentions the fathers together with their overlord Yama in the south (*MS* IV: 9: 5). In the *TS* we read: '...in the southern quarters may the months, the fathers, make (me) bright' (I: 6: 5), and 'the gods who sit in the south led by Yama' are mentioned in *TS* I: 8: 7. Because the south is Yama's direction it is called sinister (*GB* II: 19); also because in the south the demons destroyed the sacrifice of the gods. In the Trirātra sacrifice, 'if the released cow goes southwards, let him know the sacrificer will quickly depart from this world' (*ŚB* IV: 5: 8: 11). Here there is an indirect connection between death (hence Yama) and the south.

In the *Rām.* Yama is mentioned as a Dikpāla, guardian of the south (III: 44: 41). The southern quarter is said to be protected by Yama (*Rām.* IV: 51: 32). In the *Mbh.* episode of Sāvitrī, Yama forcibly wrested Satyavat's life and went towards the south (III: 281: 17). By the time of the *HV*, the south is not even mentioned by name, but only as Yama's direction (*HV* XLVI: 50, also *GBU* II: 1). Again, Yama is said to be made the lord of the south by Mahendra himself (*HV* III: 37: 22). Together with Yama the fathers themselves are assigned to the south (*Vāyu P* LXXVI: 34).

Yama as a god of lunar associations connected with the Śiva group controls the path of the fathers through the moon to repeated births (Pitṛyāṇa), as opposed to the solar Viṣṇu, who leads the righteous through the sun to find liberation. The Anatolian god Men 'is a lunar god and also a god of the underworld, because the moon was frequently brought into connection with the sombre kingdom of the dead' (Cumont, *Oriental religions in Roman paganism*, p. 61). These concepts were extremely elusive in the early Vedic literature, and only in the Upaniṣadic literature do we meet some clarification and elaboration into proper dogma. Those who perform pious deeds become Yama's courtiers (*AV* III: 29: 1). It is said of the departed soul that it has fled via the path of Ṛta through the moon to the south (*MS* I: 3: 37). The moon is the eye of the fathers, lighting up the path of the Pitṛayāṇa (*MS* IV: 2: 1). He who knows this knows the path of Pitṛyāṇa (*MS* IV: 2: 1). The sacrificer seems to be free from his debt to ancestors both from those who are 'rotating in the Pitṛyāṇa path into recurrent birth and from those who have moved on to final liberation (*TB* III: 7: 15: 4). Another prayer says that unless a man offers proper oblations, death will seize him in his successive existences in different regions. Here we are confronted with a fundamental concept of later Brāhmaṇism, for the bulk of the *ṚV* knows nothing of successive lives, as reincarnation as a doctrine was not yet formulated. It is in the late tenth maṇḍala that we first have a prayer mentioning devayāna, obliquely hinting at Pitṛyāṇa too as 'different from Devayāna, a path of Yama's own' (*ṚV* X: 18: 1). This new doctrine appears to be a compromise with the old belief of crossing through death to the happiness of Yama's kingdom. Liberation and reincarnation are posited as antinomies, like the sun and the moon, and two mutally opposed sets of gods govern them. The contrast is apparent in the opposition of the sun and the moon, light and darkness, knowledge and works, rebirth and release. This presupposes the flowering forth of the Sāṃkhya and the Vedānta systems and the emphasis on knowledge as the truly liberating agent but as unattainable to the mass of the people who progress slowly through Karman and reincarnation.

Death was afraid lest all should become immortal and said, 'he who is to become immortal either through knowledge or through holy work shall become so after being separated from the body. But they who do not know this or do not do this holy work come to life again when they die, and they become the food of death time after time' (*ŚB* X: 4: 3: 1–10). Metempsychosis 'was a tenet of faith by the time of the Buddha, and making all allowances for differences of schools and place, it can hardly be denied that its development must fall in the sixth century B.C., when portions of the *Upaniṣads* reflect its existence' (Keith, *Introduction to the Taittirīya Saṃhitā*, H.O.S. p. clxxi). The Upaniṣadic doctrines which form the core of Vedānta philosophy presuppose the rise and growth of doctrines of metempsychosis. In *ṚV* IX: 7: 113 and IX: 7: 8 we read a prayer: 'Soma, bring me to the region where there is resplendence, where the sun is placed, where there is no death or decay, where Vivasvat's son is king, where men enter the sun, where wide rivers flow; make me immortal there.' This clearly anticipates a prayer for attaining the solar path (of Devayāna) to liberation.

This distinction is connected with the two halves of the year and we remember Bhīṣma waiting patiently for the Uttarāyaṇa as the proper time to die so that he might enter the sun. He says: 'the moon wanes day by day and again waxes to fulness, but the sun ever shines brilliantly and never gets weaker, so I would enter the shining sun' (*Mbh.* XII: 318: 54–6). And this was because 'the sun is the final goal of the deceased' (*ŚB* I: 9: 3: 15).

The late Roman belief in the soul's progress through the moon, i.e. through rebirths for purification until its merger in the sun amounting to final liberation, may have been an echo of Pitṛyāṇa and Devayāna.

By the time of the epics the distinction between these two yānas had become clearer as they symbolically represented two approaches to truth (via knowledge, jñāna, and via holy deeds, karman), two modes of future existence (liberation and reincarnation), and also two sects Vaiṣṇavism and Śaivism represented by the two most important epic gods (the solar Viṣṇu and the lunar Śiva). With the bifurcation of the two sects (Vaiṣṇava and Śaiva) with sectarian dogmas and cultic practices on the one hand, and the innate opposition of two philosophies (Vedānta and Sāṃkhya) developing with ever-widening differences on the other, the distance and distinction between Devayāna and Pitṛyāṇa became greater, because these were but reflections of the above differences on the eschatological plane. Thus we read: 'Devayāna is Viṣṇu's path, the path of Pitṛyāṇa is dark; these are the two paths after death—the one leading upwards the other below' (*Mbh.* XII: 315: 30). The inferiority of Pitṛyāṇa to Devayāna was widely recognized. In Roman religion, too, reincarnation was held to be a punishment; 'the only penalty which can overtake the sinning soul is, according to these Neo-Pythagorians, Metempsychosis which forces it to reincarnate itself in a fleshly prison' (Franz Cumont, *After life in Roman paganism*, p. 78).

Those who wish to attain to Pitṛyāṇa perform sacrifices and those who desire Devayāna seek salvation (*Mbh.* XII: 17: 14).[1]

Just as man has an obligation to the gods, so has he a debt to his fathers. In Iranian (Avestan) mythology the ancestors called the Fravashi actually asked for libations. We read, '(The Fravashis) go along there asking thus: Who will praise us? Who will offer us a sacrifice? Who will receive us with meat and clothes in his hands and with a prayer worthy of bliss? Of which of you will the soul be worshipped by you with a sacrifice? To whom will the gift of ours be given that he may have an unfailing supply of food for ever and ever?' (*The Farvardin Yast*). It also recalls the *Mbh.* episode

[1] In Egyptian mythology, too, 'the waxing and waning moon was also equated with Osiris, typifying death and resurrection' (E. O. James, *The ancient gods*, p. 208). And Osiris, we remember, bears resemblance to Yama and Śiva—gods of the lunar group.

of Jaratkāru, whose ancestors insisted on his raising a family so that their supply of oblations would never cease (*Mbh.* I: 41). But there is an opposition between oblation to the gods and libation to the fathers. Thus the sacred thread is worn over the right shoulder for the Pitṛs and over the left for the gods (*TS* II: 5: 11 and *ŚB* I: 8: 1: 40). The obsequies of the Piṇḍapitṛyajña are to be offered on the Amāvasyā night when there is no moon, at the southern fire, the sacrificer's thread should be over the right shoulder and all movement should be from right to left (as opposed to devakriyā, worship of the gods, when movement should be from left to right). The gods invoked are Soma' Kavyavāhana (Agni), and the Pitarah. In the Mahāpitṛyajña the gods invoked are Soma, Pitarah, Agni, Yama and the Aṅgirasah.

In Roman ritual, too, we have similar offerings made. 'It was also at the approach of the spring that the Romans and the Athenians used to offer annual sacrifices to the dead. The souls of the dead were supposed to partake of the new life then beginning to circulate through nature. That had also been dead through the long months of winter (footnote on the *Fravardin Yast* by J. Darmesteter, SBE edn. of the *Avesta*).

The fathers are to be given not dhānāh (parched grain) but 'mantha' (mixed beverage, *MS* I: 10; 17). Sometimes the worship of the fathers is emphasized and made superior to the worship of the gods in order to inculcate in the worshipper the sense of its obligatoriness. The distinction between the two is again brought out in the 'svadhā' call being proper to the fathers and the 'namah' call to the gods (*MS* I: 10: 17). The fathers are also equated with the gods (*TB* III: 7: 5: 4). The rites to the fathers are to be performed in the afternoon, in the dark fortnight (*GBU* I: 24). The half-moon which increases represents the gods and that which decreases represents the fathers. The day belongs to the gods, the night to the fathers; the forenoon to the gods, the afternoon to the fathers (*ŚB* II: I: 3: I). Thus there is a clear contrast between gods and fathers, and it is basically a contrast between solar and chthonic (i.e. lunar) gods, for ancestor worship is fundamentally chthonian. In Greece, too, there were similar differences between the Olympian and chthonian worship. In Olympian sacrifice the animal was slain with its throat upwards (so that the blood would spurt upwards while the animal in the chthonian worship was killed with its throat downwards so that its blood could soak the earth). The altar for the Olympian was the high Bomos, and for the chthonian the low Eschara. The victim of an Olympian sacrifice was a white ox, of the chthonian a black pig or ram—animals with expiation associations. The Olympians' shrine was of the famous classical design that for the chthonians was a subterranean cave or adyton (which may originally have been a tomb). Offerings to the Olympians were by day, those to the chthonians were by evening or midnight. The officiant's gestures, too, differed: the hand raised palm upwards for the Olympians, lowered with the palm downward for the chthonians. The high religion and ritual involving sacrifices to the gods were thus opposed by probably a more antique chthonous ritual to the fathers, which may or may not have been of Indo-European origin. Of the Ṛgvedic seer class we hear only of the Aṅgirases as practising the cult of ancestors where the ancestors were regarded as semi-divine. It is also significant that the Aṅgirases were invoked together with the gods and the fathers at the Mahāpitṛyajña, and they were the only human clan thus invoked, besides those to whom the ritual properly belongs. When we remember that the Atharvaveda was originally called the Atharvāṅgirasa, and that there was a fierce hostility against the inclusion of this Veda among the revealed texts, we are probably confronted with the *ṚV* seers' ingrained hostility to chthonic cults.

According to Dr S. K. Chatterjee, *Indianism and the Indian synthesis*, the Indian synthesis was rapid between 1270 and 500 B.C., the period which, he says, saw the emergence of the Indian man. It is significant that even outside India, in contiguous regions, this was a period of very brisk activity in the formation of mythology, the rise of many new religions and the turmoil in the world of philosophy. We shall see in the course of this study how the gods of the lunar group associated with ancestor worship gradually grew in stature after the amalgamation of the Vedic people with the indigenous population which practised this cult of the fathers. Hence it appears to be a plausible surmise that the *AV*, originally the scripture of the non-Vedic Aryans and the non-Aryan indigenous population, was considered as alien because of its cult of the fathers. It should also be noticed that it is only in the tenth book of the *ṚV*—the latest book—that Yama and the fathers receive a full and clear treatment. This again points to the late development of eschatological doctrines, possibly through a process of racial and cultural amalgamation.

The actual worship of the fathers varied according to the nature of the deceased. The term 'Pretāh' indicates the immediate ancestors and 'Pitarah' the remote ones. Technically a Preta is one for whom the obsequial rites have not been performed. Thus, the rites from cremation to śrāddha are those proper to the Preta. Then the twelve monthly śrāddha ceremonies followed by annual śrāddhas are offered. In this as well as in the Piṇḍapitṛyāna and the Mahāpitṛyajña the remote ancestors are offered libations. In other mythologies the ancestors were not satisfied with the draught of water. 'If the dead ask for fresh water with which to quench their insatiable thirst, they are above all eager for the warm blood of victims' (Franz Cumont, *After life in Roman paganism*, p. 57). In Syria, as late as the seventh century of our era, Christians insisted, in spite of episcopal obligations, that the faithful remained persuaded that the dead found no happiness in the other life unless the blood of victims had been made to flow for them on days fixed by tradition (*ibid.* p. 52). The goddess Nirṛti symbolizing the chthonic associations connected with the cult of the dead is the goddess who is invariably invoked in all these ceremonies.

CHAPTER 4

YAMA AND HIS FEMALE COUNTERPARTS: NIṚṚTI AND YAMĪ

ABOUT the Anustaraṇī cow that is slaughtered and laid out on the corpse, limb on limb, for cremation, it is said:

They (gods) put her (the strong cow Yama had chosen) in the waters saying, 'Come out for Yama'. She came out in the shape of an aged, stupid and utterly bad animal. Therefore, one should offer as the funeral cow one that is aged, stupid and utterly bad (*TS* VIII: 1: 6).

When Indra was about to kill Vṛtra, Vṛtra offered his strength to Indra which Viṣṇu received on Indra's behalf thrice. This was a thousand cows which they divided into three parts: Indra took two and Viṣṇu one part...Yama heard of Indra and Viṣṇu's gain and asked for one cow, one filled with the milk of the thousand cows. They agreed on condition that this cow yielded a third of its milk to Soma the king. She became a dappled brown-eyed cow—the Somakrayaṇī (the price of Soma). With another third she offered to Indra as a three-year old Śabalā-dappled cow. With the remaining third she turned into an old, leprous, hornless, smoke-coloured cow, short from the hips—the Anustaraṇī cow for Yama (*TMB* XX: 15: 6, 7; XXI: 1).

One notices the dark associations. The Dharmaśātras lay down injunctions that such a cow is to be killed, chopped up and portions of its flesh and omentum are to be heaped on the corresponding limbs of the deceased before the corpse is cremated. This apparently is an offering the departed one carries to appease the dogs of Yama. The custom appears to be very old and quite widespread. Even Yama in this context is connected with dark, old and misshapen things. Thus a dark animal is to be slaughtered for Yama, or for Mṛtyu and also for the night (*MS* III: 14: 19). For Death is Yama, Death is the name of serpents (*MS* III: 4: 6, III: 2: 6).

NIṚṚTI

Niṛṛti's form is dark, her dress is dark, her sacrificial fees are dark husk (*TB* I: 6: 1: 4). In the Naramedha (human) sacrifice, 'life' should be offered to Yama (*TB* III: 4: 1: 10). Herodotus in *The Histories* (bk VII) mentions a similar instance. Xerxes' wife Amestris in her old age buried alive fourteen Persian boys of distinguished family, by way of a present to the supposed god of the underworld who, she thought, would accept these instead of herself.

On the identity of Niṛṛti the scriptures are not very clear. One passage says that Niṛṛti dwells in the south in a self-produced hollow; 'for Niṛṛti is this (Earth); whomsoever she seizes upon with evil, him she seizes upon with destruction (Niṛṛti)...Niṛṛti does not seize upon him while (he is) being consecrated' (*ŚB* v: 2: 3: 3). *ṚV* hymn x: 59 is a hymn to Niṛṛti imploring her to leave the sacrifice alone and to depart from the place of sacrifice so that no harm may come. The refrain of the hymn is a prayer to Niṛṛti to leave the sacrifice and go. A wife that is without a son is possessed with Niṛṛti...The fee for this (oblation) consists of a black decrepit, diseased cow, for such a one is also possessed with Niṛṛti (*ŚB* v: 3: 1: 13). Niṛṛti is called evil in *ŚB* vii: 2: 1: 3. We have an account of a rite for Niṛṛti:

They are black, for black was that darkness, and black in truth is Niṛṛti's corruption ...he thus places corruption in a (point) of the earth set aside for Niṛṛti...him who neither presses Soma nor makes offerings Niṛṛti indeed visits;—of the thief do thou follow the way, of the robber!...he thus turns Niṛṛti aside by rendering homage to her, 'Homage be unto thee full well, O sharp-edged'...it is with an iron bond that Niṛṛti binds...'thee, O awful (goddess) into whose mouth I offer'—Niṛṛti is indeed awful and into her mouth he now offers...'for the unloosing of these bonds'...'thee whom people rejoice in calling Earth'—'but I know thee to be Niṛṛti everywhere,...Now Niṛṛti is this earth, and this earth makes him decay who becomes corrupted' (*ŚB* vii: 2: 1: 7–11, 15).

Pain is associated with Niṛṛti, for we read: 'south-western is Niṛṛti's region, he thus consigns pain to Niṛṛti's region' (*ŚB* ix: 1: 2: 9). The dark and malevolent bearings of Niṛṛti are also symbolized by Asunīti, another form of Niṛṛti; the name means 'she who bears life away'. Evidently she is conceived here as a spirit charged with the task of carrying the dead man's life across to the other world. In *ṚV* x: 59: 6, the prayers are addressed to Soma and Asunīti; she is implored to leave the mind in the sacrificer. The superstitious fear with regard to Niṛṛti is already present in passages like this: 'the pan is connected with Niṛṛti, if he (the sacrificer) were to step on it he would hand himself over to Niṛṛti' (*TS* v: 6: 5). Since Niṛṛti means ruin and death, she is regarded with superstitious fear and apprehension.

Niṛṛti also figures as Mṛtyu in the *Mbh.*, where we read of her as a goddess of the south, a dark goddess dressed in red, the whites of her eyes reddened, a fierce creature commissioned by Brahman to destroy creation (*Mbh.* xii: 274).

All this brings us to a vital question: who is Nirṛti? As an answer let us examine her identity as stated by the scriptures—Nirṛti is the earth. And in one place it says, 'Yama doubtless is Agni and Yamī is this Earth' (*ŚB* VII: 2: 1: 9). Thus the later Vedic people knew her to be of chthonic origin. The name Nirṛti immediately reminds us of Ṛta; it is the opposite of Ṛta, but primitive concepts are not so linear and simple—she is not lawlessness; she is the evil spirit that grapples men when they violate Ṛta and it is significant that she is nowhere associated with Varuṇa even as the negation of Ṛta. As a dark goddess she may be of more primitive origin than the high god Varuṇa.

Tracing this goddess we reach a very old tradition which reaches back to beyond the first millennium B.C. and beyond the territories of India.

In the Maurya period, finds from different sites include a small female figure which once was interpreted as the Vedic earth-goddess. The nakedness of this goddess contrasts sharply with the Harappa figurines and connects it, on the other hand, with some of the later west Asian materials as we know the naked goddess was a favourite in Mesopotamia as also in the countries on the Mediterranean shore in the first millennium B.C. Thus a new tradition entered Indian soil with this type, which though not proved as Vedic may have been derived from Western Asia (Heinz Mode, *The Harappa culture and the west*, Calcutta Sanskrit College Research Series no. XVI, Studies no. 6).

The mother-goddess with snakes and dove is a motif found in Harappa, Mohenjo Daro, Lothal, Crete (Mycenae) and Tepe Hissar. 'Thus they form part of an older tradition which is the common background for Indian and Syro-Aegean culture' (*ibid.*).

Thus Nirṛti becomes an integral part of a larger pattern of theophany; the earth-goddess. But we must not lose sight of her essential characteristic of being the earth. Also, 'Cybele was the immeasurably ancient Earth Mother of Asia Minor' (Michael Grant, *The world of Rome*, p. 192). As earth-goddess she is one of the most primitive theophanies. 'Three great goddesses play the part of Mother of the world—Tethys, Nyx and Gaia' (C. Kerényi, *The gods of the Greeks*, p. 33). As we have noticed before, Nirṛti also came to be regarded as the female counterpart of Yama or Death. In Greek mythology Death is known by three names—Moros, Ker and Thanatos, and Moros is masculine of Moira (fate)—a brother of Hypnos and Nemesis and Geras (Jarā in Sanskrit). Now Svapna (Hypnos) is made a son of Yama, and Yama's relationship with Nirṛti becomes clearer when we remember that *ṚV* X: 164 is called Duhsvapnanāśana (warding off evil dreams) but the hymn actually aims at warding off Nirṛti and the god invoked for this purpose is Yama (*AV* VI: 46: 1, 2; and XVI: 5 the whole hymn). In another passage 'duhsvapna' is called the son not only of Niṛṛti but also of Abhūti and Nirbhūti (*AV* XVI: 5: 4), thus establishing a relation between Niṛṛti and Abhūti—adversity and ruin. Together they belong to the complex concept of perdition. Now Niṛṛti's oblations, as we have mentioned, include the ill-formed and decrepit creatures because such is her form, rūpa. Thus this association of decay and decrepitude as an aspect of death has always been connected with Niṛṛti. In one of her aspects she represents not only death but also decay, a natural precondition of death. If we bear in mind that interment was a very old mode of disposal of the corpse, the connection between the earth-goddess Niṛṛti, and decay and death becomes very clear. This is borne out by the *ŚB* (VII: 2: 11). Purūravas says to Ūrvaśī that if she does not come back 'he will lie in Niṛṛti's lap or the fierce wolves will devour him' (*ŚB* XI: 5: 1: 8). Now the first of these passages identifies death and corruption with Niṛṛti, the earth, and we can clearly visualize the burial behind the image, while the second passage describes two types of destruction—'lying in Niṛṛti's lap' and 'being devoured by wolves', again indicating that lying in the lap of Niṛṛti, the earth, is the same as being buried.

One remembers the Omphalos at Delphi with Gaia's figure and the tumuli at Lauriya Nandangarh, as also a gold statuette of the mother goddess, Pṛthivī, with its fecundity aspect emphasized. This recalls the *ṚV* burial hymn which, addressing the deceased, says: 'Go to thy mother'—obviously meaning the earth. As the condemning goddess, the punisher of the offender against Ṛta, she is a counterpart of Nemesis. 'The name (Nemesis) means righteous anger, which is directed against those who have violated order, especially the order of nature, and have disregarded nature's law and norm. Should Themis (Law of Nature, Norm) be disregarded, then Nemesis is there' (C. Kerényi, *The gods of the Greeks*, p. 105). In Indian language, should Ṛta be disregarded, Niṛṛti is there. She is nature's revenge on the offender against Ṛta.

The Indian picture of Niṛṛti is one of a dread goddess; she binds the offender with a strong rope around his neck; freedom from this knot means long life, strength and vigour (*AV* VI: 63: 1, 2). 'That is thy road' (*TS* IV: 2: 5). In another passage Niṛṛti is identified unequivocally with the earth. In the *Matsya P.* Bhagavatī is called Duhsvapnanāśinī (LX: 179). In the *ṚV* hymn X: 164 Yama is the god invoked for dispelling evil dreams. Again Niṛṛti-putra Kapota (the Dove, the son of Niṛṛti) is the seer of

ṚV x: 165; and the dove is associated with Yama as his messenger (as in *ṚV* x: 165: 4). The *ṚV* hymn x: 189 is addressed to Sarparājñī, Queen of the serpents, and the *TB* indirectly connects Nirṛti with the Queen of serpents (*TB* II: 2: 6: 2). The chaff that is thrown into the fire is the portion of the lord of the house and also of Nirṛti (*AV* XI: 1: 29). For Nirṛti are earmarked the dove with lop-ears and the hyena (Tarakṣu). She also receives the fallen portion on a piece of salt ground in the south at the Rājasūya sacrifice. While the fire altar is set up bricks for Nirṛti are put in place without actual contact, for the worshipper avoids touching them. The dread associations of Nirṛti are clearly brought out by this instance of avoidance of tactual contact. The other instances show that she had ever been considered as of ill-omen.

Nirṛti also stands for death. An ass was to be offered to Nirṛti by the breaker of the vow of chastity who desires thus to regain what he has wasted. At the Rājasūya sacrifice three mantras (incantations) are part of the offering to Nirṛti: with the first an offering is made in the Gārhapatya fire to appease Rudra; then the sacrificer goes south with an ember from the fire to where there is a natural cleft and deposits his ember there and offers oblations with the second mantra; he then retires by the same path and offers in the Gārhapatya fire with the third mantra. Keith in his footnote on this passage in his edition of the *TS* suggests that this might have a significance of life, death and rebirth. As death stands at the middle point of this process it is quite natural that this part of the sacrifice is addressed to Nirṛti as the female partner of Yama the god of death. Again 'To Nirṛti (he offers) an oblation in the house of the neglected wife (an oblation) made up of rice broken by the nails; the sacrificial fee is a black hornless (cow)' (*TS* I: 8: 9). This passage recalls the Kulapā Kanyā of the *AV* who is associated with Yama on account of her old spinsterhood. This indicates Nirṛti's association with the barren, the decrepit and the thing of ill-omen or ill-repute: 'Also that which is burnt belongs to Nirṛti' (*TS* II: 6: 4).

It is significant that Nirṛti's figure as such vanishes in the epic age. But in the *Rām.* we have the description of death as a woman in Trijaṭā's dream of Yama. She saw Rāvaṇa seated on an ass-drawn chariot, being forcibly carried away...by a woman in red, who held him by the scruff of his neck—a dark woman with large eyes pulling him to the south (*Rām.* V: 37). One notices the ass-drawn chariot and remembers the ass that was to be offered to Nirṛti by the breaker of the vow of chastity and then the undercurrent of associations become clear. In present-day Bengal the goddess of smallpox, called Śītalā, seated on an ass, is worshipped during the season of the smallpox epidemic, and paradoxically is said to deal smallpox to her devotees. The ass and the disease with its virulence and the toll it takes every year connect her with Nirṛti. Heti, the monster seeking a bride, married Bhayā the fearful, a sister to Kāla (*Rām.* 7: 14: 16). When the Pāṇḍavas went to the forest, priest Dhaumya sang the Yāmya and Raudra hymns after setting the Nairṛta grass (*Mbh.* II: 71: 7), indicating that these hymns (to Yama and Rudra) connected with Nirṛti (cf. the Nairṛta grass) would be sung when the Kauravas died in battle after fourteen years. Nairṛta, a derivative of Nirṛti, assumed the meaning of monsters in later literature, in the *Mbh.* passage just quoted it represents death. Thus the death-association of Nirṛti is still there, only her figure has apparently vanished. We shall see that by the time of the epics and *Purāṇas* her name had become legion.

In the *Matsya P* we hear of Viṣṭi—the child of Sūrya and Chāyā—who was fierce and became (a personification of) Kāla ('Ghorātmikā tadvat kālatvena vyavasthitā', XI: 22). Again, Yama's sister is called Mārtaṇḍa's daughter ('Yamasya bhaginī puṇyā martaṇḍaduhitā tathā', *Vāyu P* LXXVII: 70). These are Purāṇic replicas of the Vedic Nirṛti. In the *Vāyu P* Nirṛti is the name of a Rudra and is thus definitely associated with the Śiva-complex of theophanies. In the *HV* she is the wife of Adharma (unrighteousness) and mother of Bhaya, Mahābhaya and Mṛtyu (Fear, Great Fear and Death). Elsewhere she is the daughter of Adharma and Hiṃsā (unrighteousness and cruelty) and the mother of Naraka and Bhaya (Hell and Fear) (*Mārkaṇḍeya P*). She is again Death or the genius of Death in the *Bhaviṣya Purāṇa*. These connect her with dark and deadly associations and she definitely belongs to Death.

Although Nirṛti virtually disappears in the epic-Purāṇic age, her functions are discharged by other deities and her evocative associations are distributed among goddesses like Kālī, Karalī, Cāmuṇḍā, Chinnamastā, Manasā and such other minor, sectarian and regional goddesses. The reason is not far to seek. As the Brāhmaṇical religion was being transformed into Hinduism after the decline of Buddhism on Indian soil and the revival of the orthodox religion under the Imperial Guptas, the religion of the indigenous population had to be incorporated into the new composite religion in order to render it acceptable to all sections of the masses.

Other similar regional cultic practices raised their heads and demanded admission into the neo-Brāhmaṇism later called Hinduism. This led to syncretism and the gradual emergence of a new pantheon—the pantheon of the *Purāṇas* which has come to stay through all these centuries. In this new pantheon some of the high Vedic gods receded making room for the new popular deities. In this process Nirṛti faded into the background, leaving her form, functions and associations to other dread goddesses. But the essence of Nirṛti corresponded to some archetypal pattern rooted too deep in the human consciousness to be discarded as an image, and thus other minor regional goddesses took over the vital evocations to which there was a fundamental response in the human mind. What Nirṛti represented as a single hierophany these other Purāṇic 'Hindu' goddesses symbolized as multiple hierophany, but dread and dark associations never ceased to find concrete anthropomorphism.

In the Greek mythology Ker is the goddess of death and is thus an analogue of the Indian Nirṛti. So also is Moros (the masculine of Moira the fate-aspect of Nirṛti). These determined and controlled human destiny and were consequently regarded with fear and awe. The Greek earth-goddess Demeter, the mother of Persephone (the wife of Pluto), is another manifestation. The dread Cybele, imported into Rome from Anatolia, had similar gruesome rituals connected with her and as an earth-goddess is allied to Nirṛti. In Celtic mythology we have Morrigan 'the Danaan goddess of death and destruction' (T. W. Rolleston, *Myths and legends of the Celtic race*, p. 172). In Greek mythology we meet the Katachthonioi Theoi—the subterranean deities called the the Erinyes connected with the tomb. As such they represent the earth-Nirṛti in so far as she symbolizes the burial ground, where death is followed by decay. The Erinyes are guardians of the tomb. In one of her dread aspects Demeter the mother-goddess of the Minoans was called Demeter Erinyes.

The subterranean spirits or tomb spirits appear in a slightly different context in the Greek dramas. Thus the nether world is referred to in Sophocles' *Electra* (120) as the 'House of Death god, house of Persephone'. In Euripides' *Iphigeneia in Tauris* (1259–79) we hear that the earth created dreams against Apollo's oracles. Again in Aeschylus' *Eumenides* (783–4) we read of the Eumenides' claim:

> the vindictive poison
> dripping deadly out of my heart upon the ground.
> (Phoenix edn.)

and also (at 831–2) their 'spells that will ruin everything which might bear fruit'. The offering of the barren cow to Nirṛti, her association with the house of the neglected woman, the old spinster, the barren woman, her connection with snakes (when she is represented as Sarparājñī) are all brought back—and the Eumenides become indubitably associated with Niṛṛti. In Euripides' *Alcestis* (11 ff.) we read:

> the fatal goddesses allowed
> Admetus to escape the moment of his death by giving
> the lower power someone else to die instead of him.
> (Phoenix edn.)

This reminds us of the *Mbh.* story of Ruru who shared a half of his life-span with his wife Pramadvarā (1: 9), and Queen Amestris sending substitutes (to the god of death) for her own life.

In Sophocles' *Oedipus at Colonus* (273) these dark spirits are described as

> Inviolable, untrod; goddesses
> Dread brood of Earth and Darkness, here abide.
> (Loeb edn.)

The Furies in the *Eumenides* are 'black and utterly repulsive' (50) and 'Goddesses beneath the ground' (115). One sees in these passages the repeated emphasis on the dread aspect of the Eumenides. In the *Libation Bearers* they are described as 'goddesses beneath the ground', thus bearing strong resemblance to the earth-goddess Niṛṛti, who is frequently invoked as a subterranean deity and is called the Queen of serpents, serpents who dwell in holes under the earth. Besides, snakes too are symbols of dead ancestors buried underground who emerge as snakes (see George Thomson, *Studies in ancient Greek society*, pp. 118–19). Demeter too was a Minoan snake-goddess.

These fatal goddesses are no doubt allied to Niṛṛti. Alcestis when she is restored to life has 'obligation to the gods who live below' (1144) till the third morning—a parallel to the Indian 'aśauca' (state of impurity for the survivors) for a minimum period of three days.

As Niṛṛti definitely belongs to the lunar group of gods she bears resemblance to Hekate, the goddess of the moon as well as of witchcraft.

> At the end of the month when there was no moon in the sky, the Greek housewife used to sweep her floors and take the rubbish to a crossroads, where she threw it down with averted eyes and returned without looking back. Such deposits were known as 'Hekate's suppers'...On the sixteenth of the month, when the moon had just passed the full, the women used to go to the crossroad and offer Hekate round cakes stuck with candles which they called 'shiners' (amphiphontes). (George Thomson, *Studies in ancient Greek society*, p. 229.)

Small statues of Hekate were placed at the crossroads, where these offerings were laid. In the *Lalitavistara*, a Buddhist work, we read: some perform austerity in cremation grounds and at cross-roads (XVIII).

In ancient Roman religion we have a parallel of this custom, '...compitum, or crossroads. Here it was customary to set up a little chapel of the Lares of the crossroads, Lares Compitales, open in all four directions so that the Lar of each Farm might have free egress to the common shrine' (H. J. Rose, *Ancient Roman religion*, p. 38). One notices the stress on the cross-roads, perhaps symbolizing the meeting point of life and death. In the nature of the offerings to Hekate, viz. the sweepings, one notices the similarity with those offered to Nirṛti, the scum, the ill-omened, the refuse —these are her portion. In the ritual to Hekate, as in that to the Lares and Nirṛti and also to the fathers, the sacrificer comes away without looking back—a sign of fear and foreboding of evil.

In Indian mythology the fathers are most frequently called Somavat, 'having Soma', and Soma is also the moon. The sun is not related to that world of resurrection, the moon being the symbol *par excellence* of regeneration. So is the serpent, because it sheds its slough and is regenerated.

The image of the snake shedding its slough as a symbol of reincarnation and hence indirectly of eternal youth and immortality may have come from the ancient world of the third millennium B.C.—the world of the *Gilgamesh epic*. Gilgamesh, on his way back from Utanapishtim where he received the rejuvenating plant, 'saw a well of cool water and he went down and bathed; but deep in the pool there was lying a serpent and the serpent sensed the sweetness of the flower. It rose out of the water and snatched it away and immediately it sloughed its skin and returned to the well' (*The Epic Gilgamesh*, Penguin edn. p. 114). A very close parallel is the famous passage in the *Bhagavadgītā* where a man's death and rebirth are compared to his shedding of the old garment and donning a new. The serpent's behaviour may have suggested the image and the idea. The moon's growth, decay, death and rebirth must have suggested similar phases in man's destiny in early Egypt, where the moon is connected with so many rituals. Lunar calculation of the calendar in the ancient world proves close acquaintance with the moon's phases and course.

The three-faced Hekate (inscribed on a gem reproduced by W. H. Roscher in *Ausführliches Lexicon der griechischen und römischen Mythologie*, Leipzig, 1884–1934) is six-handed, holding weapons and torches, and carried on a pole drawn by two serpents. This connects her definitely with snakes and brings her into the family of the Erinyes and the Sarparājñī-epiphany of Nirṛti. 'The snake is the dead man's double...these serpentine Erinyes were spirits of the dead' (G. Thomson, *op. cit.* p. 117). The *KB* says, 'the serpent is this earth, for she is the queen of what creeps'

(XXVII: 4). The earth is Niṛṛti. So the obvious deduction is that Niṛṛti is the Sarparājñī, the serpent queen.

The gruesome and sombre associations of Niṛṛti also became apparent in the rules laid down in the *TS* for the Agnicayana. At the foundation of the altar, it is stated, should be deposited a lotus-leaf, a gold disc (both with solar associations), a golden man (probably reminiscent of the human sacrifice), two wooden ladles, a perforated brick, a brick of durvā grass, a living tortoise (lunar and aquatic association, the tortoise being the form of Dharma in the popular Dharma cult), the heads of dead creatures including those of a horse, a bull and a man, a pan in the middle of which the head of a man is placed, together with the head of a snake (*TS* V: 2: 6–9). The base of the altar is to be constructed in this manner and Niṛṛti seems to be indirectly connected with all this—as the heads of the dead animals, the man and the snake suggest. Her mount, like Kuvera's (another god of this group), is a man.

In the *Matsya P.* one of the forms of the Devī is called Śivadūtī and we have her description: 'Of distressed appearance, withered, especially in the body, many-armed, surrounded by serpents, with a small chain around her neck, fearsome because she is holding bones, fox-faced—thus must the auspicious goddess be sculptured.' It is one of the many forms in which Niṛṛti survived after her disappearance from the Brāhmaṇical pantheon. The *Matsya P* describes Ekānaṃśā as a dark variant of Umā (LX: 17). Śiva is said to have created 'the mothers' (mātṛkāh) to drink the blood of Andhakāsura. He commissioned them to protect creation but they devoured creatures (*Matsya P* LX: 155 ff.). This episode presents the fearsome aspect of the primitive mother-goddess. One thinks of the bloody rituals of Cybele. The dark complexion of Ekānaṃśā is significant, as it suggests a Dravidian origin.

Dr J. N. Banerji, in his book *The development of Hindu iconography*, mentions Bhīmādevīs (referred to in the seventh century A.D.) on soapstone discs found in Patna. Five of them contain the figures of the nude mother or fertility-goddess associated with various animals and birds (p. 175). The Nalanda seals no. 9RIA depict Niṛṛti, Cāmuṇḍā and Mahākālī. Niṛṛti here is a skeleton-goddess holding in her four hands a skull, a sword, a scythe, and a trident; she is seated on a dead body (Pretāsanā) facing right. Thus iconographically Niṛṛti continues to evoke gruesome associations.

In the *BGS* Jyeṣṭhā Alakṣmī is referred to as a goddess who is variously described as Jyeṣṭhā (elder), Kapilapatnī (Kapila's wife), Kumbhī (pitcher), Jyāyā (elder), Hastimukhā (elephant-faced), Vighnapārṣadā, and Niṛṛti.

Now, the emphasis on being elder is significant. She is older than Lakṣmī, an Aryan goddess of corn and prosperity. In the Lakṣmī Pūjā, even in present-day Bengal, a rough and ready image of Alakṣmī is fashioned out of cow-dung or clay and is chased away by a small winnowing fan before the proper rites for Lakṣmī begin. Jyeṣthā is the southern counterpart of the northern Śītalā (goddess of the smallpox). Jyeṣṭhā Alakṣmī, otherwise known as Alakṣmī or Nirṛti, is described by the manual of iconography *Suprabhedāgama* as having a crow ensign, seated on an ass, the wife of Kali and is to be two-armed, long-nosed, with sagging lips, long and pendulous breasts and belly and with a lotus in her hand. This description gives us back many of the old associations of Nirṛti: the crow (as it is a symbol of dead ancestors in many parts of India still); the ass, which was already connected with Nirṛti; her aged and decrepit appearance indicating that she symbolized decay. Her sagging lips and generally withered looks also indicate decrepitude. She is called Jyeṣṭhā or Jyāyā (older or elder) and these are relative terms: older than whom? The obvious answer is older than the Aryan Lakṣmī who is beneficent and of a pleasing appearance. The non-Aryan, probably Dravidian, mother-goddess associated with death, burial and decomposition was generally pushed out of existence and after the racial and cultural amalgamation remained only as a spectre of fearful and obnoxious appearance, to be disposed of summarily before the more aesthetically satisfying worship of an Aryan mother-goddess commences. The image of Cāmuṇḍā too is to be fashioned as four-armed, with an emaciated body and shrunken belly, with a skull-chain round her neck, seated on a dead body, with bare teeth, sunken eyes with round protruding eyeballs, bald head with flames issuing from it, holding a chopper, a śūla and a skull. The emphasis is on hideousness, emaciation, shrunkenness and death evocation—and these create a very vivid picture of Nirṛti as the *Brāhmaṇas* painted her. But she has grown more gruesome with time, as she has gone on imbibing trait after trait of indigenous mother-goddesses. She is still connected with death and is moreover called a mātṛkā, a mother. Thus the chain of associations embodied in earth-and-death recurs. The new iconographical traits may have been added after the rise of Tantrism.

One may mention in this connection the late hymn in *ṚV* addressed to Aśrīnāśa (destruction of the goddess of the inauspicious). The first two stanzas describe her as stingy, blind, ugly, making harsh sounds; and end with the prayer: 'let her depart from our quarters'. She is also connected with a pregnant woman whose female organ is impure (stanza 4). The Viniyoga (ritual application) for the hymn says that it is directed to the destruction of the deity of the inauspicious (Alakṣmīnāśana). The hymn is late, being in the tenth maṇḍala, and has an obvious reference to an old pre-Aryan goddess whose banishment is sought. Such an image is found at Ellora. In the *Viṣṇudharmottara P.* we read that Virūpākṣa's wife called Niṛṛti should also be sculptured.

Georges Dumézil (in his review of *Déesses latines et mythes védiques* in *JAOS* 80, no. 1, Jan./Mar. 1960) writes of the Roman goddess Lua Mater associated with Saturnus (who would be a parallel to Śani and Kāla) as she is described in Livy VIII. 1. 6 as the goddess of destruction. Consul Plautius gave the enemies' arms to her after the victory of Aemelius Paulus over Perseus. These arms were burned after prayers to Mars, Minerva and Lua Mater. Lua Mater is a parallel of Niṛṛti.

The dark and sinister traits of Niṛṛti are confirmed in her Greek parallel Persephone; for her 'sacrifices consisted of black sheep and the person offering it had to turn away his face...One is immediately aware of the similarity with the Indian ritual to the ancestors where, too, the sacrificer is bidden to turn away his face and sometimes to avoid direct contact by touch.'

The great image of Isis when she speaks to the transformed ass in Apuleius says, 'I am Nature, the universal mother', and 'the queen of the dead'; in both traits she resembles Niṛṛti. Thus she still remains the mother-goddess who is associated with the dead. It is also striking that she reveals her identity to a transformed 'ass'—so that the old connection with the ass, whether as a victim for immolation to her, or her mount or her devotee still persists.

Heinz Mode's theory of the origin of the Great Mother-Goddess in the Indo-Mediterranean region is borne out by Prof. E. O. James in *The ancient gods*, p. 54. Dr Mackay may also be correct in thinking that the images were household deities kept in a niche in the wall in almost every house in the Indus Valley cities, just like their present day parallels in the houses and villages. In the older uncritical edition of the *Mbh.* we have a reference to such a goddess—Jarā—decrepitude: she it was who put together the two separate halves of Jarāsandha. She introduces herself as a monstress who dwells in every mortal dwelling; Brahman created her of old as one of the divine Penates for the destruction of the demons. He who inscribes her youthful image faithfully on the wall, together with her son, will flourish; otherwise he will come to ruin (*Mbh.* vulgate edn. II: 18). There are several contradictions in this image. First she is called Jarā and she describes herself as youthful; then, she calls herself a rākṣasī and says that she is divayarūpiṇī (of divine appearance) and that prosperity comes through her. This anomaly is resolved if we bear in mind that she is trying to rationalize her pre-Aryan existence within the pattern of an essentially Vedic Aryan pantheon. This she succeeds in doing by mentioning that Brahman created her 'of old'—thus attaching antiquity to herself—and antiquity is a sort of sanction or passport in the epic pantheon. But she is really very old, older than the Vedic gods, for most probably she is of Austric origin, and because she corresponds to the Brāhmaṇical Nirṛti she finds a place in the new scheme of the epic-Purāṇic pantheon.

Nirṛti's parallels are found all over the world. 'At the Hagia Triada... the emblems suggest the cult of the goddess in a funerary setting with her priestesses the officiants in a sacrificial oblation on behalf of the deceased... perhaps with the blood flowing down to the earth through bottomless vessels as an offering to Mother Earth as the ultimate source of rebirth' (E. O. James, *Prehistoric religion*, pp. 164–5). This ritual is very much like the Roman Taurobolos instituted in honour of the imported west Asian Cybele. In many countries where the indigenous cults and rites had been pushed underground by the religion and ritual of the invading Aryans these ancient gods and goddesses rose and took their full revenge at a later period. The Indo-European religion was essentially a religion of 'gods' (as opposed to goddesses) as their society too was patriarchal. But in a period even later than the amalgamation of Indo-European and non-Indo-European religions, came the mystery cults, when the older cultic practices with their millennium-old chthonic and mother-goddess emphasis re-emerged and swept over the country. This happened in a very marked degree in Rome and in India. The occult rituals of Mithraism, Orphism, Dionysiac and Eleusinian mysteries together with other minor cults of similar order swept Rome, whereas Tantrism and veneration of the mother-goddess in many forms swept India and left an indelible mark on her religion for centuries to come. Gilbert Slater in his book *The Dravidian element in Indian culture* says of the south Indian *Magna Mater* Gaṅgāmmā or Mariāmman or Mariyāttal (who bears some resemblance to north Indian Durgā or Caṇḍī and also to the old earth-mother-goddess Nirṛti) that 'she rejoices in blood and demands wholesale sacrifice of male animals... but most of all in male buffalo' (p. 92). This is a faint echo of Taurobolos, only the buffalo is substituted for the ox.

The Black Demeter of Phigalia and the Demeter Erinyes of Thelpusa had similar dark associations, for Demeter had very strong connections with the dead.

YAMĪ

Niṛṛti is frequently identified with Yamī in the *Brāhmaṇas*, chiefly because they both are represented as Yama's partners. Yamī appears in a famous hymn (x: 10). It is a dialogue hymn in which Yamī desires Yama to oblige her by uniting with her as with a wife. Yama disagrees on the ground that they are brother and sister, and he has no desire for her. The gods will be offended at such an unnatural deed, they cannot escape their ever-watchful spies (*ṚV* x: 10: 8).

Yamī seeks to persuade him, says that none need know of it (*ṚV* x: 10: 6) and speaks contemptuously when he rejects her suit altogether. The *AV* gives a slightly different version. There Yama says that brother and sister sleeping together is something at which his mind revolts (*AV* xviii: 33: 14). Also, all the gods will know of this heinous crime, even the sun will open its eyes and know this and proclaim the unbrotherly act (*ṚV* x: 10: 9). In both *ṚV* and *AV* Yamī argues that since they have lain together once—in their mother's womb—doing so a second time cannot possibly be wicked.

Socially, the hymn may indicate the stage when incest was discouraged or looked down upon for fear of inbreeding. In the *Avesta* Yima marries his sister Yimak and produces mankind but is eventually killed by Azi Dahâka for this sin. This version combines the origin story together with the later taboo on incest. But what is striking is that in both versions the hymn ends abruptly and inconclusively. This is significant because it is not an isolated version, but is related to cosmogony myths all over the world, and in other mythologies the incest is committed for the sake of creation.

Thus we have androgynous creatures in all mythologies to whom the creation of the human race is ascribed. In Plato the idea behind this myth is stated clearly as one half of a soul yearning and searching for the other half.

In Ovid's *Metamorphoses* we read of the pair Byblis and Caunus—a parallel to Yama and Yamī. The *Avesta* has Yima and Yimeh or Yimak. In Egypt we have Osiris and Isis—brother and sister again, and Osiris corresponds very closely to Yama as the lord of the other world. The Greek pair Deukalion and Pyrrha recreated the human race after the annihilation by deluge.[1]

[1] In the Japanese *Kojiki* (compiled in A.D. 712) and *Nihongi* (compiled in A.D. 720) we have an account of cosmogony. After the Kami gods and other gods had passed away there came Izanagi (male who invites) and Izanami (female who invites) and created an island

Sometimes we hear of a spirit (Prajāpati in Indian mythology) who immolates himself or divides himself into two for the sake of creation. The *Brāhmaṇas* are full of such myths. R. N. Dandekar writing on 'Yama in the Veda' (in the *B. C. Law Commemoration Volume*) speaks of 'The primitive motif of the immolation of an androgenous primeval being for the sake of the creation of the universe'. In the Biblical myth of Adam and Eve there may have been an altered version of such a pair. Mircea Eliade in *Myths, dreams and mysteries* writes of 'the absence of hierogamy in archaic religions ...their supreme beings were androgyne, at once male and female, both Heavenly and Earthly' (p. 174). Adam for example was regarded as an androgyne. The Bereshit Rabba (1, 4, fol. 6, col. 2) affirmed that he was 'man on the right side and woman on the left side, but God has cloven him into two halves' (p. 175).

It is now clear why the Yama–Yamī episode had to end abruptly: in order to avoid the inevitable mythological truth, namely, their incest. For where social inhibition was absent the story reached its logical end and the incest motif is preserved and justified on grounds of creative expediency. In India Prajāpati became the creator, and so the Yama–Yamī pair were not united in a myth.

Ovid in his *Metamorphoses* (bk IX), giving the story of Byblis and Caunus, has to change the original incest motif, for Byblis, madly in love with her brother Caunus, pursued him through various lands, till at last, worn out with sorrow, she was changed into a fountain. This version preserves the male partner's aversion to incest and eventually manages to evade the conclusion through her metamorphosis. Vedic mythology, which knows no metamorphosis and yet has social revulsion at the idea of such an incest, leaves the dialogue unfinished. The story was so old and so widespread that the seers had to incorporate it in their scripture, perhaps because collective memory demanded it as an indispensable archetypal pattern.

The idea of creative activity with ritual promiscuity appears to have been

to which they descended and created other islands and afterwards other gods and goddesses. The Mexican mythology makes many of its god-pairs creator gods and hence their names are cognates like Yama–Yamī's. Thus Mictlantecutli, lord of 'a grim and shadowy realm', is represented by the bat. He had a spouse Mictecaciuatl. 'Souls passed ordeals before reaching Mictlantecutli' (L. Spence, *The myths of Mexico and Peru*). Another pair, Ometecutli and Omecuatl (also known as Tonacatecutli and Tonacaciuatl), are given the first place in the Nahua calendar and resemble Kronos and Gaia, but are actually 'two beings of a bisexual nature dominating the genesis of things' (*ibid.*). In the Hebrew *Zohar* (quoted by C. G. Ginsburg in *The Kavvah, its doctrine, development and literature*, p. 116) we read, 'Each soul and spirit, prior to its entering into this world, consists of a male and female united into one being. When it descends on this earth the two parts separate and animate two different bodies'. One remembers the Norse god Twisto whose name is derived from a word with 'twin' associations.

very old. In societies of primitive peoples this can still be observed. People believe that crops will be blessed if they practise ritual promiscuity sometimes in the cornfields. Promiscuity must have been the normal sexual relation in very old times, and an ancestral practice so to speak. With time the social taboo was enforced, consanguinity was considered injurious to the racial stock and sexual union was prohibited between certain prescribed relationships. But the old customs were ritually practised at certain junctures for specific purposes. In Fiji, 'after the initiation a public festival takes place in which all rules of exogamy and rights of property are suspended...Brothers and sisters, who in ordinary life are forbidden even to touch one another, behave as man and wife' (George Thomson, *Studies in ancient Greek society*, p. 67). Seen in this light the Yama–Yamī episode appears to belong to the period when the social taboo was gradually descending on the practice, yet the ritual lingered in public memory.

In later Indian mythology, whenever a pair is raised above the average in mythical significance, function or status, they usually bear cognate names, or are conceived as bisexual or alternately bisexual, or androgynous, Thus the name of the Jaratkāru couple is both masculine and feminine. Śikhaṇḍa–Śikhaṇḍī, Ila–Ilā are such cognate names. The Jaratkāru pair were the parents of the sage Āstīka and as such played an important role in the ancient serpent-lore. They also continued the line at a critical period of its history. Śikhaṇḍī is important because Bhīsma the chief hero of the major part of the epic battle could only be killed through him. Ila–Ilā were alternately male and female. Ilā became the wife of Budha and the mother of Purūravas. In the Ila–Ilā pair there may have lurked an idea of the primeval cognate couple Yama–Yamī as certain derivatives from the word indicate. Thus Ilāvarṣa was the name of 'the highest and most central part of the old continent' (Monier Williams, *Lexicon*), and a study of mythologies tells us that this part is the centre of creation (cf. the Garden of Eden or the island where Izanagi and Izanami descended). Thus indirectly Ilā's name indicates the creator couple as in the unfinished Yama–Yamī hymn Yamī insists on having a child by Yama and perhaps suggesting that they should multiply and replenish the earth. 'Ilikā' means the earth, and the name is a parallel to Yamī's who has been identified with the earth. In the *Vāyu P* 'Ilinā' is the name of a daughter of Yama. 'Ilya' is the name of a mythical tree in the other world. All these derivatives point to the Ila–Ilā pair being a mythological replica of Yama–Yamī. Again Śiva in his Ardhanārīśvara aspect is called Jagatpitṛ and Jaganmātṛ (compare the opening stanza of the *Raghuvaṃśa*). (See Rudra-Śiva (2).)

Yamī is the author of *ṚV* x: 154. The hymn is addressed to dying sacrificers; different drinks are offered to them in the next world—Soma to some (the Saman-singers, according to *TA* II: 20), Ghṛta, clarified butter, to others (the Yajus sacrificers, *ibid.*), and Madhu, honey, to yet others (the Atharvans, *ibid.*). The hymn is addressed to Yama.

That Yamī is the same as Nirṛti, at least that they were originally the same, is clear from passages like: 'Yama is Agni, Yamī is this earth' (*TS* III: 3: 8), for Nirṛti has frequently been identified with the earth too—'As "earth" men know thee, as Nirṛti I know thee on every side' (*TS* IV: 2: 5).

There is a charming episode of Yama and Yamī in the *MS*. Yama had died, the gods sought to console Yamī. She said, 'he died but today'. They then said, 'she will not endure it thus, let us create night'. At that time there was only day and no night. They created night, it became yesterday, then she could endure (her bereavement) (*MS* I: 5: 12).

Yamī's mourning for Yama has the Eddic parallel in Nanna mourning for Baldr when he died, and Baldr has faint resemblances with Yama, for of his abode Briedablik we hear that 'nothing impure can be there'; and 'it is a characteristic of his that once he has pronounced a judgement it can never be altered' (*Prose Edda*, p. 51). This irrevocability of judgement establishes his identity as closely similar to that of Yama. He dies and is mourned over by Nanna—a picture which calls to the mind Yamī mourning over Yama's death.

Freya also mourns for Od her husband. 'Od went away on long journeys and Freya weeps for him' (*ibid.* p. 59). It is significant, firstly, that she thus becomes the dead Odin's partner in this sinister business of sharing the dead; secondly, the man she marries bears the name Od which suggests Odin (a god of the Varuṇa-Yama group); and thirdly she mourns bitterly for this Od. Thus Freya resembles Yamī both in personality as well as in function.

This inevitably reminds one of Isis mourning for her brother-husband Osiris. In native Egyptian accounts corroborated by that of Plutarch Isis mourned for the dead Osiris, and this became a typical lamentation for the Egyptian women at the time of the ritual of Osiris. 'Come to thy sister, come to thy wife...'

When Osiris died through his brother's machination Isis fanned the corpse with her wings uttering the charms Thoth taught her: he revived and from then on reigned in the other world as the king of departed souls. A similar tale is told in the *TMB*: 'With this hymn Yamī helped Yama ascend to heaven' (XI: 10: 21–2); so that here too we have the twin sister sending the dead brother to heaven through certain spells.[1]

In Indian mythology Yama is connected with the last lunar mansion called Apabharaṇī. This is characterized by certain stars known as Yama-nakṣatrāṇi (*TB* I: 5: 1: 5, I: 5: 2: 7). Under these stars Yama is king—they are said to bear away sins (*TB* III: 1: 2: 11).

The connection of Osiris and Isis with the season of the flood in the Nile valley and consequently with the coming harvest has a deeper substratum of significance; the god of the underworld is the guardian of the ancestors and it is the ancestors who guarantee crops. This idea is current in many ancient mythologies. From the point of view of the season of ancestor-rites it is significant that the lamp that is offered on the food-offering to Hekate ('cakes stuck with candles') has a parallel in Indian rituals.

In the dark fortnight preceding the Durgāpūjā (worship of the chief mother-goddess), libations are offered daily to the ancestors and in the next month (Kārttika) lamps are set up on poles to light the ancestors. It is striking that the very next month is the month of harvest and is called Agrahāyaṇa, the first month of the year according to old calendar calculations, when the harvest marked the beginning of a year. The Durgāpūjā itself was originally a harvest festival as is evident from the greetings on the last day of the Pūjā and also from the goddess's name Śāradā (autumnal). From all this it emerges that the ancestor-worship preceding the harvest is no accident, for all over the world there is a belief that the ancestral spirits help the growth of the crops.

The month Kārttika is named after the six mythical sister-stars, the Kṛttikās. They are called Dulā, Nitatnī, Cupuṇikā, Abhrayantī, Meghayantī and Varṣayantī (*TS* IV: 4: 5: 1). The last three names are unambiguously connected with rainfall. Nitatnī and Cupuṇikā are of uncertain origin, but Dulā seems to be derived from the Semitic Hebrew root *dili*

[1] What is the significance of the personality of Osiris-Yama? 'The divinity whose worship was started at Alexandria by Ptolemy was the god that ruled the dead and shared his immortality with them...a god governing both vegetation and the underworld' (Franz Cumont, *The Oriental religions in Roman paganism*, pp. 74, 77). Certain things become clearer if we pursue the cult of Osiris as it was practised in Egypt. 'A useful clue to the original nature of a god or goddess is often furnished by the season at which his or her festival is celebrated...For in the early days of Egyptian history...the splendid star of Sirius, the brightest of all the fixed stars, appeared at dawn in the east just before sunrise about the time of the summer solstice, when the Nile begins to rise. The Egyptians called it Sothis, and regarded it as the star of Isis, just as the Babylonians deemed the planet Venus the star of Astarte. To both peoples apparently the brilliant luminary in the morning sky seemed the goddess of life and love come to mourn her departed lover or spouse and to wake him from the dead' (J. G. Frazer, *The golden bough*, pp. 368–70).

(a pot for pouring water), whence the Arab *ḍālā*, to pour. Thus four of these six stars are definitely rain-bearing. The month Kārttika was thus the month of the late showers which ripen the corn; it is also the month of the annual ancestor-ritual.

'The period of the Roman ancestor-ritual Lemuria was considered unsuitable for marriage, also the All Souls' Day when honour was paid...to the tombs, people were enjoined thus: Appease the souls of your fathers and bring small gifts to the extinguished fires...Not that I forbid larger offerings.' Lemuria was also 'the day on which due worship was paid to buried ancestors'. (Ovid, *Fasti* 540 ff.)

The month of Kārttika is also unsuitable for auspicious ceremonies, presumably because this month was set apart for reverentially approaching the spirits of the dead who would guarantee good crops. The association of the Kārttika group of constellation with rain-crops harvest is a parallel of the rising of the Nile—for on it depended the agriculture and prosperity of Egypt as they did on the showers in India.[1]

It is no accident, therefore, that Isis was called Sochit or Sochet, i.e. cornfield, and that twin Yama–Yamī, too, recalled the annual death of the corn-spirit—the field of stubbles (the earth–Nirṛti–Yamī) which remained barren for long months until in autumn the ancestral spirits (of whom Yama was the overlord) came up as young shoots, guaranteeing the reappearance of the corn-spirit and the continuation of the human species. The autumnal harvest festival is thus the festival of the fulfilment of promise, the triumph of reincarnation, the resurgence of life after death.

Yamī, however, is chiefly thought of as a twin-sister to Yama; and the early *Saṃhitās* emphasize this fact. In the *Brāhmaṇas* the concept behind Yamī becomes increasingly complex—she becomes malignant as Nirṛti and yet retains her original personality as Yama's twin sister. Thus in the Puruṣamedha sacrifice while a barren woman is to be offered to Yama, to Yamī should be offered one who bears twins (yamyai yamasūm) (*ŚB* III: 8: 1: 4). In the *TB* too this is the case: twins for Yamī is the rule (III: 4: 1: 11); while life is to be offered to Yama (*Yamāyasum* III: 4: 1: 10).

[1] Significantly enough the word *vapus*, body, seems to be derived from *vap*, to sow, for in burial the body is sown and the crops rise out of it. The image is found in Christian mythology. 'It is sown in corruption; it is raised in incorruption. It is sown in dishonour; it is raised in glory. It is sown a natural body; it is raised a spiritual body' (1 Cor. xv. 42–4). One notices the image of 'sowing' and 'raising' (i.e. gathering in the harvest) running through the whole passage. It illustrates the fundamental associations of body-ancestors-crops image. Sayings like 'the mortal matures like the corn and like the corn is born again' (*Bh. G*) evince the belief in recurrent birth and death of mortals, a belief generated and fostered by the observation of similar phenomena in nature.

Thus we notice that in the early times Yama was conceived chiefly as a twin, with Yamī as his female counterpart. As he grew complex in stature, taking on malevolent traits, she also as his partner became a malign goddess, Nirṛti, taking over the dark non-Aryan earth-goddess's functions and chthonic characteristics.

In the *Purāṇas* Yamī becomes the river Yamunā—the river of dark water—or Kālindī the sister of Yama in his Kāla aspect. She thus retains the dark traits, her other traits being forgotten. It is significant that when her chthonic and mystic cults had been taken over by the other major goddess during the new upheaval of Hinduism under the Guptas, she was still remembered only as a dark goddess. The echo from the *TB* still rings true—dark (are her) garments, dark chaff her sacrificial fee—this is the appearance of Nirṛti (*TB* 1: 6: 1: 4). The dark traits of this primeval goddess persist even when all her functions are quite forgotten or redistributed.

CHAPTER 5

YAMA'S IDENTITY

YAMA and most of his parallels in other mythologies died once and were revived afterwards—in the other world. Yama was the first of the mortals to die; he then became the king of the dead (through Yamī's spell). Osiris died and rose up king of the departed. Pluto (or Dis), the son of Kronos and Rhea, was swallowed and later disgorged by Kronos (Apollodoros: *Bibliotheke*, vol. I, p. 7). Transmigration or metempsychosis demanded that the god who was the guardian of the dead should himself pass through death.

In almost all mythology Yama or his parallel figures are sons of the sun. Yama is the son of Vivasvat, Yima of Vivanghant. Incidentally we have an account of Aditi ascending to heaven with seven of her eight solar sons, leaving only Mārtaṇḍa or Mārtāṇḍa behind (*ṚV* X: 72: 8). Now the name Mārtaṇḍa has in other places been explained as 'springing from a dead egg and coming to life afterwards'. Thus one of the Ādityas—solar gods—actually sprang from a dead egg. Decoding the mythological language we have a solar god who passed through death. The image of an egg is significant for it indicates two existences—one, as an egg; the other, when the shell is broken, as a bird: and all solar gods are likened to birds. Thus through his connection with a dead egg Mārtaṇḍa becomes associated with a chain of existences (egg entity–death–living bird) and this connects him with the birth–death–resurrection chain. The death of the egg brings him in very close relation with Yama, the god who passed through death and later became an immortal, the lord of the deceased ancestors, Yama, son of Vivasvat, the sun. In the *Mbh.* Mārtaṇḍa is the son of Yama (I: 70: 10). In the *ŚB* we read: 'That man in yonder (sun's) orb is no other than Death and that glowing light is that immortal element, therefore Death does not die, for he is within the immortal' (X: 5: 2: 3). 'Yama...is he who shines yonder, for it is he who controls everything' (*ŚB* XIV: 1: 3: 4). It is clear that Yama is connected with the sun through time: the sun by his daily rotations creates time and in time men decay and approach death, hence Yama (death) is a product (the son) of death. This is the Kāla aspect of Yama. In the *AV* Yama is identified with the sun and as such is called the supreme god.

In the *Rām.* Yama is called Sūryātmajo nṛpah, king (Yama), the son of Sūrya (VII: 20: 23).

The *JB* equates Yama with the Year (Saṃvatsara), Yama is time and the seasons his faces (mouths?) (*JB* I: 246). Here Yama becomes the same as Prajāpati who is very frequently called the Year in the *Brāhmaṇas*. In another passage we are told that Mṛtyu was created by Prajāpati and was crushed by the metres (*JB* I: 283). Thus Yama is connected with the supreme god of the *Brāhmaṇas*, for it was at this period that his stature began to grow and change.

In the age of the epics and *Purāṇas*, Yama became a Dikpāla, a guardian of the south, a more or less static ruler, and this diminishes his stature to some extent for he now fights and loses battles to others. Thus in the *Rām.* he is once defeated by Rāvaṇa (III: 44: 28); at another time he is called Rāvaṇa's brother (III: 47: 8), presumably because of the destructive roles of both. Yama's defeat at the hands of Rāvaṇa is dwelt upon at some length: the battle was long, Yama's army was vast, the fight was fierce, yet Yama could not withstand Rāvaṇa's might (*Rām.* V: 78: 12–13, VI: 35: 21). Still another passage makes Kāla a son of Rāma in a previous birth. In the *HV* Kṛṣṇa goes to Yama's city and returns with the four dead sons of his preceptor restoring them to the father. Yama had to yield his own to Kṛṣṇa, something he had never done before. This clearly indicates a curbing of his former glory, just as it indicates the rise and growth of the Kṛṣṇa cult. But Kṛṣṇa could not have made Yama relinquish his claim over what was his own by rights (i.e. the dead) unless Yama had fallen from power.

As a god Yama has some relation with Varuṇa. The latter part of the hymn *AV* XVIII: 34 is addressed to the man who is recently dead. He is told to hasten to the other world where he will see Yama and Varuṇa (*ṚV* X: 14: 7, *AV* XVIII: 34: 6). But the real connection between the two is through Nirṛti; Varuṇa is the lord of Ṛta and Yamī, Yama's consort in one of her aspects is Nirṛti—the opposite of Ṛta. In the *AV* Nirṛti is called Varuṇānī, where Svapna or Duhsvapna (dream or bad dream) is called Yama's son by Varuṇānī (*AV* VI: 46: 1, 2). In another place Yamī-Nirṛti is called Grāhi (seizure), and Bad Dream is called Yama's son by her (*AV* XVI: 5: 1–3). Grāhi is almost a synonym for Nirṛti. Duhsvapna is in the next passage called the son of Nirṛti, Abhūti and Nirbhūti. Now Yama's son by Varuṇānī is rather intriguing—why not by Yamī? The simple answer is: that would be incest, and the Vedic seers fought shy of incest as is clear from the unfinished Yama–Yamī hymn (*ṚV* X: 10).

So Yama could not possibly have a son by Yamī. We have a Yaminī, too, formed with the feminine suffix which yields the meaning of 'wife of'. The *AV* prayer in hymn III: 6: 28 is addressed to Yaminī, where she is clearly identified with the malevolent, destructive goddess injuring animals out of spite and ill-will (*AV* III: 6: 28). If there is a Yaminī, Yama's consort, then it is rather striking that Yama should have a son not by her but by Varuṇānī. It appears the seer preferred adultery rather than risk incest. 'Karaṇa putra' has come to mean a child by parents of two different castes—and Yama's 'Karaṇa' son may have reference to some such alliance.

The word 'Araru', the name of Yama's Karaṇa son, is not explained by commentators and lexicographers. Perhaps we have to look beyond the territory of India to find an explanation of the term. In Sumerian mythology we have a goddess who bears close resemblance to Nirṛti called by different names, Māh, Ninmāh, Inanna, Ishtar, Nintu and Aruru (E. O. James, *The ancient gods*, p. 60). It is a well-known fact in mythology that gods and goddesses often change their sex in different times and places. Thus the merciful Buddha has become the goddess Kannon or Kwannon in the Japanese pantheon. Similar instances are plentiful in other mythologies. Hence it is quite probable that Araru travelled from Sumeria to India; what this deity retains is of more vital importance—viz. the connection with the underworld and the dark and earth-goddess traits. As Duhsvapna, Araru (as he was known in India) became the precursor of death, for evil dreams were interpreted as forebodings of imminent death or destruction—and this made him Yama's son. One may note in passing that this is the only instance where Varuṇānī is mentioned in Vedic literature.

Among other relatives Sāyaṇa commenting on *ṚV* x: 15 mentions Śaṅkha, the sage, as one of Yama's five sons. The *ṚV* hymn x: 18 is ascribed to Yama's son Saṃkusuka. Amṛta (nectar) is said to be Yama's son too (*AV* xx: 25: 5)—this perhaps really means that immortality comes through death.[1] Yama and Śaṅkha are both said to be authors of scriptures.

Saraṇyū is called Yama's mother (*ṚV* x: 17: 1; *AV* XVIII: 1: 53). The gods hid Saraṇyū and created another like her for Vivasvat. Saraṇyū bore Yama and Yamī; and the Aśvins she bore to Vivasvat in the shape of a mare (*ṚV* x: 18: 2). This story of Saraṇyū bearing Yama and Yamī goes down through Vedic to epic-Purāṇic literature in different versions. Vivasvat's wife Saraṇyū bore Yama, Yamī and Manu, and then, because she

[1] In *ṚV* x: 99: 10 and *TB* III: 2: 92 Araru is the name of a demon (four-footed in *ṚV*) whom Indra killed. It is significant that Yama is called the father of this apparently subhuman and malign demon whom Indra the solar hero slaughtered.

could not bear his brilliance, she fled to her father's house leaving her double, Chāyā, behind, instructing her never to divulge the secret to the husband. She consented on the condition that he would not man-handle her. She bore him Sāvarṇi Manu and Śani. Yama suspected that she was a stepmother from her preferential treatment of her own children. After an altercation he struck her with his foot. She revealed her identity, Vivasvat struck her, she fled cursing Yama that the foot would fall on the earth. Vivasvat modified the curse, said the foot would be afflicted with a putrid running sore, but that worms would take bits of flesh from it and fall on earth, thus fulfilling the curse symbolically (*HV* IX: 32; *Matsya P* XI: 12). Yama deeply grieved, turned righteous through penance and became Dharmarāja, king of righteousness. The whole story is significant, because—apart from the mention of Tvaṣṭṛ's daughter Saraṇyū bearing Yama and Yamī to Vivasvat, leaving Chāyā with her husband to whom she bore the Aśvins in the shape of a mare—the whole of Vedic literature is silent about the rest of the legend. Some scholars have connected Saraṇyū with the Greek Erinyes, thus establishing the dark associations of the chthonic goddesses with those of Yama's mother. The episode of Yama being cursed by her stepmother because of his fit of temper has a remote parallel in the *Avesta*: 'soon he (Yima) changed this (his immortality) to death by the fault of his tongue (when he took delight in the words of falsehood and error)' (*Zend Fragment*, p. 262). Thus to the Iranians, too, Yama had been at fault, although he never became evil or personification of evil like Angra Mainyu, yet he fell from his early glory and his first millennial reign came to a close. The association of sores, putrefaction and worms is a creation of Indian mythology in the Purāṇic age—perhaps signifying that he bore corruption, putrefaction and torments in his own person which he inflicted on the inmates of hell.

In the Purāṇic age Manu is Yama's brother—both children of Saraṇyū and Vivasvat. Of the two brothers Manu is the lord of the living, and Yama of the dead.[1]

Manu like the Old Testament Noah was saved from a deluge. He was the first to formulate a code of social, religious and political laws and thus became not only the progenitor but also the guardian of the human race.

[1] *Manu* is derived from the same root from which is derived the Gothic form *Mannu* or the Germanic *Mannus* mentioned by Tacitus, also the German *Mann*, *Man* or English *man*. It indicates 'man', especially in his role as a thinking animal (cf. root *man*, to think), as opposed to *vīr*, the reproductive man (cf. Sanskrit *Vīra*, *Vīrya*; Avestan *vir*; Engl. *hero*, *virility*; Lithuanian *Vyras*), or *aner* the tilling man (cf. Sanskrit *nara*, Greek *Aner*, Avestan *ner*, Old Latin *Nero*). Manu is thus the progenitor of *homo sapiens* in Indian mythology.

In this function he is complementary to Yama, who is the guardian of the departed souls. Together these sons of Vivasvat are in charge of humanity, living and dead.

But Yama's solar connections gradually became dim, and he came to be increasingly related to the lunar group, and it is as a lunar god that his stature grows. As Śiva is the principal god of this group, Yama's connections with him are important.

Yama is characterized by epithets which are normally used of Śiva: Babhru (reddish brown), Nīlaśikhaṇḍa (blue-tufted) and Śarva (one who shoots śaru, darts) (*AV* VI: 10: 1). The *Mbh.* calls Yama Somātman (whose essence is Soma) and Vṛṣa, the bull, both epithets of Śiva (*Mbh.* XII: 47: 24, XII: 91: 13). In the *Matsya P* Yama received his overlordship of the fathers, his guardianship of the (southern) quarter, the rank of a judge of the world and also of the departed from Śiva as a boon (XI: 20, 21). Thus he is definitely connected with Śiva, as whose regent he reigns over the dead.

A relief image of Hades is one of the finds at Hatra. 'In the lower right corner', writes Dr Shinji Fukai, 'three dogs with snakes for their tails and having a common body' are seen. In high relief, low relief and line-carving these dogs are executed with a black body, the first head black, the second red and the third unpainted. The man holding them is the master of hell. He has a hideous look with abundant dishevelled hair. In his raised right hand he holds a double-edged hatchet the point of which is a snake cocking its head. A pair of snakes issues from both sides of the forehead, another one at his foot, and a further couple of snakes crawl to his right with a fourth pair on his left side. At his right waist is a dagger. Between the fore and hind legs of the three-headed dog is a vermilion lion, and a lady sits on a leonine pedestal above the three-headed dog. She has a dove with spread wings on her diadem. In the centre of the pedestal is a pair of fish (*East and West*, vol. 11, nos. 2–3, 1960).

As these finds are dated between the first two centuries of our era, it is striking that, in this group, Yama-Hades is unambiguously connected with the lunar group of gods, and is particularly closely connected with Durgā, Śiva's consort.

The formidable appearance, the snake-infested atmosphere, the three-headed dog (cf. Kerberos, or Śyāma and Śabala), the hatchet and dagger, the lion pedestal of the goddess, the dove and fish motifs—all these are clearly associations which evoke the Yama–Śiva–Durgā group of the lunar gods. The Hatra finds clearly establish the parallels and formative influences operative on the myth-making processes in India.

Yama's relationship with Śiva is established via two other gods: Agni and Soma. They belong to the lunar group and are specific manifestations of the Śiva theophany. In later mythology Agni becomes a minor god, but in the early Vedic literature he is a major god invoked by many names—one of which is Kravyād, the consumer of corpses. In this aspect he is associated with the dead bodies and hence with Yama. A *ṚV* hymn calls Yama the leader of the gods who reside in the south. These 'gods' are apparently deified ancestors, the Lares, and are also connected with Agni (*VS* IX: 35: 36). Bright Agni is known by Yama to be variously residing in waters and herbs (*ṚV* X: 51: 3). In an *AV* hymn addressed to Agni Pāpamocana (the remitter of sins) Agni is supplicated for unbinding the cords of death from which the Brahmacārin (novitiate) seeks to be freed. The *TS* tells us unambiguously that Yama is Agni (III: 3: 8). With the Agniṣṭoma sacrifice (lit. praise of Agni) one wins Yama's kingdom (*MS* I: 8: 6). The *JB* says clearly that Agni is death, and that Mṛtyu's form is red (*JB* I: 332, III: 348). The *ŚB* (III: 1: 1: 37) says: 'King Yama is the same as the Gārhapatya (fire)'. Thus while the Gārhapatya fire is kindled Yama is invoked and the place is swept with a Palāśa branch (*ŚB* VII: 1: 1: 1), and the palāśa is an emblem of Yama. In this Brāhmaṇa, too, Yama is unequivocally identified with Agni: Yama doubtless is Agni (VII: 2: 1: 7).

The Egyptian hymn in *The Book of the Dead* entitled 'Bringing charms unto Osiris Ani' refers to the pool of fire in the underworld. The Christian hell as described in the New Testament, Dante and Milton is also a place of fire. The epic hell in the *Mbh.* or *Purāṇas* and the Buddhist hells are all full of flames of fire, and, through this fire also, Agni is connected with Yama the ruler of the underworld.

Along with Varuṇa, the Aśvins, Yama and Pūṣan, King Soma is also prayed to for deliverance from death, and to save the worshipper from the south—the quarter of Yama (*AV* XIX: 20: 1). In the other world he who cooks the vistārin Brahmaudana (rice for the Brahmin priest at a sacrifice) lives with Yama delighting himself in the company of the Apsarases (nymphs) who are connected with Soma (*AV* IV: 34: 3). The *MS* calls Soma the god of the fathers, thus indirectly identifying him with Yama; Candramas (i.e. Soma, the moon) is called the eye of the fathers (*MS* I: 10: 17, IV: 2: 1). The fathers are said to belong to Soma, and thus Yama is connected with Soma too (*TB* II: 6: 16: 2). The *JB* says very clearly that Yama resides in the heart of the moon, thus establishing his lunar bearings (*JB* I: 246). The *ŚB* frequently calls the fathers Somavantah or states the reverse, i.e. calls Soma Pitṛmat (*ŚB* II: 6: 1: 4; *Mbh.* XII: 318: 54). This confirms Yama's relationship with Soma, for Yama is the god of the Fathers, *par excellence.* In a *Mbh.* passage (XII: 293) Soma is used as an image of the chain of births; and it seems possible that passages affirming faith in rebirth on the analogy of the moon, which waxes and wanes periodically (*Mbh.* XII: 318: 54), give the underlying link through which the moon became an image of transmigration of the soul, a path of the fathers (pitṛyāṇa) and an associate of Yama who supervises the soul's course after death. The *JB* equates the mythical 'hare in the moon' with Yama (I: 2: 8). At the offering of Piṇḍapitṛyajña to the fathers Soma is invoked as Kavyavāhana, bearer of the libation, usually an epithet of Agni. Soma is always invoked in connection with the rituals for the ancestors.

When we called Yama a lunar god, his connection with Soma becomes fundamental, and wherever we have transmigration or metempsychosis in any form the moon is behind the concept and thus becomes inseparably connected with the god of the next world and with the progress of the soul after death: 'The waxing and waning moon was also equated with Osiris, typifying death and resurrection' (E. O. James, *The ancient gods*, p. 208). In a Śrāddha ceremony one should say, 'to Soma with the fathers' (*Mbh.* XIII: 92). The lunar eclipse is supposed to produce uncleanness, and a person must cleanse himself properly; it is significant that prayers are addressed to Yama for this purification (*Matsya P* LXVII: 11). The ancient Phrygian god of the underworld, Men, is a lunar god; so is the Egyptian Osiris. Thus we notice that the Yama type of gods have lunar bearings in other mythologies too.

Yama has connections with another minor god, Kāma, whose Buddhist parallel is Māra. In Indian mythology this relationship is not stated clearly but is merely implied. Monier-Williams in his *Buddhism* writes of the Buddhist conception of the cosmos and its different spheres which he calls 'tiers'. The sixth tier is inhabited by Paranirmitavaśavartidevāh, 'who are also called Māras. One of them is Kāma, superior even to Indra. Antaka, god of death is sometimes identified with Māra or with Yama "ruler in hell"' (p. 27). Thus in Buddhist mythology Yama is identified with Māra, the enemy of the soul *par excellence.* Hindu mythology knows no Māra, but Kāma (passion) is there, who leads men to destruction. The *Prabodhacandrodaya* a late drama (eleventh century) has an antagonist, Mahāmoha (great delusion), opposed to the protagonist Viveka (conscience), and the chief minister to Mahāmoha is Kāma (passion, lust). Indian mythology knows no absolute evil like Satan or Angra Mainyu. The nearest approach is the Buddhist Māra who endeavours to damn the human soul. Kāma as a synonym of Māra in the Buddhist mythology, a god who is identical with Yama becomes the closest approximation to evil in Indian mythology. But the fundamental difference should be remembered: Yama never bears the onus for damnation, for, with the doctrine of Karman, man becomes the architect of his own fate. Yama as Dharma, supervises retribution and punishment and to some extent inflicts it through his attendants and agents. Kāma, although introduced in the *ṚV* as the creative principle (*ṚV* x: 129: 4), is a late and minor god in Indian mythology, rising to full stature only in the *Purāṇas*. He is represented as the son of Dharma and husband of Rati in the *Mbh.*, *HV* and *Vāyu P.* Kāma is a name of Agni in *VS*, *TS*, *KŚS*, *ŚŚS*, and Yama is also equated with Agni. Thus Kāma definitely belongs in this theophany. The destructive, evil side of Māra is absent in the concept of Kāma, because abstract evil is conceptually alien to Indian mythology; but Kāma and Māra are both enemies of man, both are vanquished by Śiva. Kāma in Purāṇic mythology is consumed by fire issuing from Śiva's third eye, and Death also (Mṛtyu) was vanquished by him—hence Śiva's name Mṛtyuñjaya. Māra and Mṛtyu (from stem *mṛ*) are kindred concepts, although Mṛtyu, as symbolized by Yama, is not evil or an enemy of man as Satan or Angra Mainyu is. Through the impact of Buddhism Yama, in his Māra-Mṛtyu aspect, came to assume the function of an adversary and in later literature there is an inescapable element of evil connected with the concept of Kāma. Only in post-Vedic literature is Kāma associated with evil; in some earlier Vedic hymns Kāma, love or desire, is personified and praised as the prime mover of the universe, the impulse behind creation, i.e. existence (*ṚV* x: 129: 4; *AV* III: 2: 5: 1, IX, XII, XIX). One is reminded of a parallel in Orphic mythology: Nyx laid an egg out of which came Eros, also called Protogonos, the first-born.

Tracing the evolution of Yama from the *ṚV* down to the epic-Purāṇic age we notice that in the early period Yama was not thought of as a god of death. The first concrete attribute had very little to do with death itself. He was one of a pair of twins and it is as a twin brother of Yamī that he figures chiefly. This seems to be an Indo-European concept. Yamī mourning for her dead brother has a very close parallel in Nanna mourning for Baldr in the Edda. Egyptian and Sumerian concepts too offer similar myths in Isis–Osiris or Nergal–Ereshkegal. As we have endeavoured to show earlier, this twin image symbolizes the two phases of crops: the barren field from which cultivation has disappeared is the picture of the death of a chthonic twin, the corn-spirit, and the earth-goddess mourns long and inconsolably. Then they are united again after an arid period and the ancestral spirits guarantee the growth of vegetation from under the earth. This episode of union is absent in Indian mythology, but present in others.

In the early phase Yama is thus inseparably connected with the twin sister Yamī. His name is therefore akin to later Sanskrit Yamau, Yamaja or Jamajātakau, which probably meant twins of both sexes. Later the name lost its earlier significance; burial was discontinued, the corn symbolism was divorced from the theophany and the word came to be derived from root *yam*, to control, to torment (cf. 'Yama' or 'niyama', in *Yoga* = control; or *yantraṇa* = pain, distress, suffering). He thus became the god who controls the dead as well as the living (through fear and by the ethical code), as also the god who torments souls in hell. The twin-aspect, the vegetation symbol was entirely lost sight of and Yama gradually moved towards the Kāla-Dharma pattern of divinity and was relegated to the sphere where Śiva was the central deity—to whom Yama became an associate.

It is significant that his stature assumes clear dimensions in the tenth Maṇḍala of the *ṚV*, the first product of the cultural commingling of the Aryans and non-Aryans and by the time of the later *Brāhmaṇas* his benevolent *Saṃhitā*-personality is overshadowed by the malign Yama (derived from *yam*), till in the epic-Purāṇic age he is definitely a dread and formidable divinity, the chief assistant of Śiva, the god of destruction.

CHAPTER 6

RUDRA-ŚIVA (1)

THE central god of the lunar group is Rudra, later known as Śiva—a minor god in the *ṚV* with only two and a half hymns to him—yet one of the triad in the later pantheon. He is described as Kapardin (with matted or braided hair, *ṚV* I: 114: 1, 5); Suśipra (with a well-formed jaw) and Babhru (reddish brown in complexion, *ṚV* II: 33: 5, 8). He has a Niṣka (a gold necklace) round his neck (*ṚV* II: 33: 10) and is multiform, strong-limbed, terrible and tawny (*ṚV* II: 33: 9). Kapila (tawny) is the colour of Īśāna devata (*GB* I: 25). Śiva is three-eyed or born of three mothers (Tryambaka, *VS* III: 57), and is described as a giver of nourishment, of good perfume and clothed in animal skin (*VS* III: 61, III: 58). He is Nīlagrīva (blue-necked), sahasrākṣa (thousand-eyed) and Hiraṇyabāhu (golden-armed) (*VS* XVI: 7, 13, 17). His reddish complexion is emphasized, for he is called Rohita (red, *VS* XVI: 19) as also Tāmra and Aruṇa (tawny and reddish, *VS* XVI: 39).

Sometimes he is called Uṣṇīṣin (having a crown or head-gear). The *VS* calls him Śitikaṇṭha (white; or blue-throated), Vyomakeśa (with a shaven head). Hrasva or Vāmana (short of stature and a dwarf), and Varṣīyas or Vṛddha (old). Nīlalohita (blue-red) is a frequent epithet of Śiva, as also Nīlaśikhanda (blue-tufted) in the *YV* (*AV* II: 27: 6, VI: 93: 1, XI: 2: 7). One of his unexplained names is Krivi (*VS* X: 20). He is described as seated in a chariot (gartasad).

The epics know his shining (Dīptāni) as well as terrible (ghorāṇi) appearance. But he has changed along the lines of the *YV* Śatarudrīya hymn and has grown progressively sinister till, in the epic-Purāṇic period, very little of his original appearance remains. Thus he is now smoke-coloured instead of tawny, and one-eyed (*Mbh.* VII: 201: 120, 129); he is Tryambaka because he worships three goddesses—the sky, water and the earth (*Mbh.* VII: 201: 131). He is Vyomakeśa because the brilliance of the sun and the moon has become his hair (*Mbh.* VII: 201: 134). He is now three-eyed, for he created a third eye when his other two were closed (*Mbh.* VII: 201: 138). Below his thighs is Agni's region, above is Soma's. He is called Rudra (fierce) because whatever is burning, sharp, harsh and mighty in flesh, blood and marrow is his (*Mbh.* VII: 201: 144). He now carries a trident, is fair, with matted locks, clad in bark and in animal skins, thousand-eyed and wondrous-limbed (*Mbh.* VII: 78: 39). He also carries the Pināka-bow, the thunder, a flaming trident, a club, an iron dagger and a pestle—yet he carries the moon in his head and a fair armlet, and a garland of akṣa ṣeeds around his neck; in splendour he is like the sun (*Mbh.* VII: 200: 63–71). Contradictory descriptions grow rife, for he is described as brilliant like the sun as well as very dark (mahākṛṣṇa, *Mbh.* VII: 201: 7, 11). Gradually epithets are heaped on contradictory epithets until the picture becomes utterly blurred, undistinguished and unconvincing. He now rides a bull, carries a bull-ensign, is golden-bodied, is the sun, Gaṇeśa, eleven-bodied, delighting in the bow, with three matted locks, three-headed, greedy for dramatic performance, a patron of songs and instrumental music, his body entwined with serpents; he himself is the cluster of clouds, the peals of thunder and the lightning itself (*Mbh.* XII: 284: 56). He now has a garland of Karṇikāra flowers, instead of the Vedic gold necklace (*Mbh.* XIII: 17: 32). His quiet, well-dressed, fair form is forgotten and he is made to appear as a lunatic, and yet a formidably shaped almighty creator. He became four-headed trying to obtain a better view of the nonpareil of beauty, Tilottamā (*Mbh.* I: 211: 28). Later he became even five-faced.

In the later books of the *Mbh.* he looks like a lion, a tiger and even a banyan-tree (XIII: 17: 58), and also like a bird, obviously imbibing traits of tree and animal worship from fading hierophanies. His abnormal proportions and shapes are described in XIII: 17: 86–9. In short the aim of these passages seems to be to make him appear as 'Everything'. Thus he is fair, light complexioned and dark (XIII: 14: 162). In his bull-shape he has strong, sharp golden horns, as if gnawing the earth with their pointed tips, his (i.e. the bull's) body entwined all over with a gold chain, his face, hooves, nose, ears and middle are fair to look upon, his shoulders are massive, so is his hump; in brilliance he is like a thousand suns (*Mbh.* XIII: 14: 240–3). Brahman had given him the bull ensign to placate him when he became furious because the spurting milk of the cows (just created by Brahman) had touched him (*Mbh.* XIII: 141: 12). Elsewhere he is described as Śrīkaṇṭha, Indra had hurled the thunderbolt at him, and Śiva's throat retained the mark (*Mbh.* XIII: 141: 8), a mark, no doubt, of conflict and coalition of two cults. Another version says that the mark of Nārāyaṇa's hand remained on Śiva's throat and so he became Śrīkaṇṭha (*Mbh.* XII: 337: 62). This may indicate a conflict and compromise between the Śaiva and the Nārāyaṇīya sects. The *Rām.* knows him as matted-haired, and red-blue. In the *Mbh.*, when Arjuna was fighting the Kālakaya demons, as he took up the Raudra weapon, he saw a three-headed, six-armed man, with hair as bright and shining as the sun, and with hissing snakes for his headgear (III: 170: 39). This figure is familiar, and the clue to his identity is supplied by the coincidence with the hurling of the Raudra (Rudra's) weapon. His armour is mentioned in *Mbh.* VII: 69; when the gods were molested by demon Vṛtra, Brahman sent them to Śiva who gave Indra his own armour together with its charms. This armour had grown in his body (gātraja).

When Śiva had destroyed Dakṣa's sacrifice the angry Dakṣa, through the power of concentrated meditation created a third eye in Rudra's forehead; Uśanas plucked Śiva's hair when he had been initiated for the annihilation of Tripura, his locks turned into snakes; these snakes choked him and his neck turned blue. An alternate version has it that his neck turned blue when he was throttled by Nārāyaṇa's hand (*Mbh.* XII: 329: 14–15). He is described as draped in dripping animal hide (ārdracarmāvṛta), serpent-form, ill-clad, lunatic, short of stature, ithyphallic, four-faced and carrying skulls (*Mbh.* XIII: 17). Out of his four faces, with the eastern face he is Indra, with the northern he indulges in dalliance with Umā, with the benign western face he provides happiness to all creatures (Saumya, sarvaprāṇisukhāvaha) and with the fierce southern face he 'gathers up' all creatures (Bhīmasaṃkāśam raudram saṃharati prajāh, *Mbh.* XIII: 141). In XIII: 161 we hear of his Śivā and ghorā tanūs—benign and malign forms, symbolized by Soma and Agni respectively.

In the *Matsya P* we are told of his eight manifestations: in the sun, earth, water, fire, air, sky, the yajamāna (sacrificer) and the moon (XXVII: 189). Of these his solar form is called Raudrī tanū. The same purāṇa knows him as ten-armed (XXX: 196). The *KP* describes him as having created the Rudras in his own image: with matted locks, fearless, three-eyed, blue-red, with eyes in the forehead; (faces) covered with thick clusters of matted hair, holding tridents (VII: 29). He is fierce-toothed, dancing in the sky, fire emitting from his mouth, with thousands of feet, eyes and heads (XVI: 193). We shall discuss the significance of these images later.

In iconography Śiva is variously depicted. 'A terracotta seal', says Dr J. N. Banerji, 'in the collection of Dhir Singh Nahar, having on it a Śivaliṅga (*the phallus form of Śiva*) with subdued realism, described as Pādapeśvara (*lord of trees*) in Gupta characters' (*Development of Hindu iconography*, p. 114). Also on the coins of Wema Kadphises, Śiva is shown as two-armed, holding a trident in his right hand, with the left hand hanging downwards, carrying a water vessel. 'The four-armed god on some copper coins of Kaniska holds a noose in lower right hand.' Of the Huviska coins in the Punjab museum one has two figures—one male, the other female—the inscription describing them as Oeso (Bhavesa ?) and Nana (the Syrian or Elamite Nanaia, or the Babylonian Inanna). Another Huviska coin calls them Oeso and Ommo (Uma ?). Ommo holds a cornucopia instead of a lotus. Of the Ujjaini coins one represents Śiva in a human form, another in phallic form, and a third in the bull-shape; of these the human shape seems the earlier. Seal no. 764 depicts him in Ardhanārīśvara (androgynous) form. An Ekapādamūrti (i.e. one-footed, either Śarabha or Śarabheśamūrti. Śarabha is a mythical eight-footed beast like Odin's Sleipnir) depicts a man-bird-beast syncretism attacking the Nṛsiṃha (man-lion) with his claws, possibly because Hiraṇyakaśipu (whom the man-lion manifestation of Viṣṇu was attacking) was a devotee of Śiva. Here too we have the clash of cults projected in iconography.

It is clear that beneath the changing and mobile images there cannot be traced the evolution of a personality in any specific direction. What really happens is the syncretism of many Aryan, non-Aryan (and perhaps even non-Indian) gods, each bringing his own cultic image, traits, totems and functions, until in the resultant figure hardly a distinctive feature remains—and Śiva becomes at once a sectarian god (of the Śaivas and Pāśupatas) as also the kathenotheistic concept of the supreme being. The process was long, tortuous and complex and many of the factors can only be traced conjecturally now.

The *ṚV* Rudra is frequently invoked as a protector of animals—both bipeds and quadrupeds (dvipade catuṣpade, *ṚV* I: 114: 1). The *VS* addresses him as the lord of animals (*VS* IX: 39, XVI: 17, XXIV: 3). The *AV* has a whole hymn addressed to Paśupati (II: 34); the epithet is very common as found in *AV* XI: 2: 2, XI: 2: 28, XV: 5: 7. He is said to have found cattle as Rudra (*AV* XV: 14: 11).

Again, throughout the Vedic literature we have prayers supplicating Rudra not to harm the worshipper's cattle (*VS* XVI: 16). He looks after sheep and ewe, men and women and cattle (*ṚV* I: 43: 6). As the father of the Maruts he is called the overlord of cattle (*AV* V: 24: 2). Most of the *ṚV* prayers know him as the patron of cattle. One almost inevitably remembers the Mohenjodaro seals depicting a male god, horned and three-faced. On one seal he is surrounded by four beasts, the elephant, the tiger, the rhinoceros and the buffalo, with two deer by the throne at his feet.

Sir John Marshall interpreted it as the prototype of the great god Śiva, the lord of the beasts.

The special relation obtaining between Rudra and cattle is borne out by many Vedic passages. We are told 'He who practises witchcraft should offer a red (cow) to Rudra...it has Rudra as its deity' (*TS* II: I: 7). Rudra is described as red, reddish brown or tawny, hence the 'red' cow for him. Again, Rudra has the bull for his ensign, hence the cow is his symbolic female counterpart. Another episode tells us that Manu deprived Nābhānediṣṭha of a share and told him to help the Aṅgirases in a Satra sacrifice. They gave him cattle. Rudra approached him as he went about with his cattle in the place of sacrifice, saying: 'these are my cattle'. Rudra asked for a share in the sacrifice and received it. 'Then indeed had Rudra no designs against his cattle' (*TS* III: I: 9). The *AB* has a variant version for this episode. Nābhānediṣṭha Mānava deprived of his father's property (during studenthood) came to his father, who advised him to perform the Aṅgirases' sacrifice, especially the confusing rite of the sixth day. The Aṅgirases gave him a thousand cows when they went to heaven. 'As he was gathering it together, a man in black garments coming from the north, said to him, "Mine is this; mine is what is left on the place (of sacrifice)"... Nābhānediṣṭha questioned his father who said "His it is, my boy, but he will give it to thee". Nābhānediṣṭha spoke the truth to the man and got it' (V: 14). In this variant we find the Rudra cult appearing more clearly—Rudra comes from the north, is dressed in black, and claims the left-over in the sacrifice, especially cattle, which seem to be his exclusive portion. Thus the cult of Paśupati Rudra seems to be well established.

A third variant is found a little later in the same Brāhmaṇa. Here the man in black from the north claimed Nābhānediṣṭha's cows. Nābhānedistha's father said that the wealth in the Vāstu (i.e. the site of the sacrifice) belonged to him but that he would give it to Nābhānediṣṭha, which he did (V: 9: 22). Another passage says that Rudra chose a boon: the overlordship of animals (*TS* VI: 2: 3). The *MS* also knows Rudra as the lord of animals (*MS* II: 6: 6). Rudra's proper dakṣinā is the cow (*TB* II: 2: 5: 2). Of the Āhavanīya fire it is said, 'when in the cow, it is Rudra's' (*AB* V: 26). Again in another aspect Rudra is called Agni sviṣṭakṛt from whom cattle are made to disappear (or hide themselves) (*TB* III: 9: 12: 3). The *ÇB* knows Rudra as the overlord of cattle who draws calves along a long cord (i.e. grants numerous calves which are held together with a cord); prayer is addressed to him so that he does not injure the sacrificer's cattle (*ÇB* II: 4: 3).

The *TB* identifies Rudra with the horse and lays down that cattle are to be offered to Rudra (*TB* I: 115: 8–9). Rudra had also desired to possess cattle (*TB* III: I: 4: 4). He goes on being called lord of the cattle (*TB* III: II: 4: 2). The cow belongs to Rudra (Rudrāya gām, *TMB* I: 8: 3). 'Her (the cow) he gave to Rudra the hotṛ (priest)' (*ŚB* IV: 3: 4: 25). Again, Rudra is longing for (the cow) which is killed here in this hall (*ŚB* V: 3: I: 10). Rudra is to be worshipped for cattle (*ŚB* V: 3: 3: 11), a man brings cure to his cattle with the words: 'Blessing to our cattle, purify us in the season when Mahādeva kills the cattle' (*TMB* VI: 9: 7). Even plants are said to become smeared with poison in the season when Mahādeva slaughters cattle (*TMB* VI: 9: 9). The gods while distributing cattle hid Rudra, and they (the cattle) are disregarded in the stotra (hymn) of Vāmadeva (*TMB* VII: 9: 16). Also 'Paśupati...Rudra, the lord of beasts' (*ŚB* V: 3: 3: 7). The *MS* also pays homage to Rudra as Paśupati (Rudrāya paśupataye, II: 6: 6). The *AB* says that the gods gathered together their virtue and brilliance (potency) and created Bhūtavat (the possessor of creatures), who asked for and received the overlordship of the animals and became Paśumat (III: 9: 10).

In these passages we are introduced to a new aspect of the relation between Rudra and the cattle: he destroys the offender's cattle. A great number of prayers are addressed to assuage his wrath against cattle. His arrows and missiles are sought to be averted from the cattle. From such prayers one suspects that he, Rudra, is just as much an enemy of the cattle as he is Paśupati, the lord of cattle; the offender's cattle are his prey and he destroys them. Agni is said to make the cattle disappear (*TMB* XII: 4: 25); and Agni is identical with Rudra (*TMB* XII: 4: 24). To Mahādeva one should offer with animals; he (Mahādeva) will slaughter half of these animals, verily these are his oblations (ilā) (*JB* I: 301).

This apparent enmity or cruelty to animals is not noticed so clearly in the *ṚV* where he is mostly depicted as the benign patron of animals. But these traits multiply with time till Mahādeva is credited with the general massacre of animals. In later literature Rudra is remembered as annihilating animals in a freak of vengeance and wrath. Perhaps one ought to see in it the reminiscence of certain myths which are found in seals from western Asia. Both these aspects, the tamer or dominator (overlord) of animals as also the fighter of animals, are found inscribed on seals in India, western Asia, Crete and Egypt. From Mohenjo Daro we have a seal depicting the Proto-Śiva in his Paśupati aspect, and from Chanhu Daro we have another seal showing a bull over a prostrate body apparently the scene of a fight between man and beast.

The god as dominator or protector of animals, in a similar frontal attitude is found on a cult relief from Assur feeding two goats, and on a relief in Minet el Beida, on the Syrian shore...A sculptured slab from Karkemish shows a kneeling man surrounded by animals, evidently a slightly changed repetition of our Indian prototype. The last example comes from a metal vase from Gundestrap and is supposed to represent Celtic art. Here again the Mohenjo Daro group is repeated' (H. Mode: *The Harappa culture and the West*, p. 12).

Behind these two attitudes of man to animals is perhaps the long history of man as a hunter and a tamer of animals—two definite stages in his evolution between savagery and barbarism. In Dr Shinji Fukai's article on 'The artifacts of Hatra and the Bactrian Art' (*East and West* II, 1960) we read of a relief image of 'a god on the point of killing a goat by stabbing it with a dagger'. According to Dr Fukai its meaning is 'the struggle between man and animal—one of the oldest subjects in the Orient...In those days the theme usually represented the idea of Zoroastrian dualism with the king standing for Ahura Mazda and the beast for Angra Mainyu.' This image is thus a link in the chain of myths and images of man-versus-animal theme. In one of the world's earliest epics, the Gilgamesh epic, we have the image of Enkidu who 'ate grass in the hills with the gazelle and jostled with wild beasts at the water holes; he had joy of the water with the herds of wild game' (*The Epic of Gilgamesh*, Penguin edn. p. 61). But soon after 'Enkidu had become a man...he took arms to hunt the lion, so that the shepherds could rest at night. He caught wolves and lions and the herdsmen lay down in peace' (*ibid.* p. 66). The attitude changed. Later Enkidu fought Humbaba and the Bull of Heaven created by Ishtar and the lions in the passes of the mountain. He became a hunter. Thus the two pictures—the wild Enkidu, friend and tamer of animals, and the urban Enkidu, enemy and hunter of animals—depicted on ancient seals may have parallels in the Rudra-Śiva myth in the two apparently contradictory attitudes of Śiva towards animals. In his hunter aspect Śiva resembles Dionysus Zagreus.

Rudra retaliates with cruelty against those who intend to injure his devotee's cattle (*JB* III: 11).

Of the Sviṣṭakṛt rite (in the Aśvamedha sacrifice) is said: 'The Sviṣṭakṛt is Rudra: he (the sacrificer) thus shields the cattle from Rudra, whence Rudra does not prowl after the cattle where this oblation is offered at the Aśvamedha' (*ŚB* XIII: 3: 5: 3). According to the *HGS* the Śūlagava sacrifice is meant to propitiate Rudra and avert plague among cattle, and according to the *PGS* it is so called because Rudra is the spitbearer and through cattle-sacrifice the worshipper obtains cattle—a common theme of magic by affinity. During the fast of a vow, if the initiate 'were to eat, Rudra would plot evil against his cattle' (*TS* I: 6: 7). One notices that Rudra's blessings and curses come to the worshipper in the form of welfare or injury to the cattle. And he expects to be offered cattle by the performer of a sacrifice. 'To Rudra (he, the sacrificer offers) an oblation of Gavedhuka in the house of the thrower of the dice; the sacrificial fee is a speckled (ox) with raised tail' (*TS* I: 8: 9). Rudra is pleased if cattle are offered to him with the prayer that he should not slaughter the sacrificer's cattle (*TB* I: I: 8: 4). One should perform due rites to the Vāstavya fire, otherwise Rudra will slaughter one's cattle. 'If Rudra is so minded he will slaughter cattle by sending a blighting disease among them (Yadi rudrobhimanyeta, rogotpādanena praṇaśayet) hence it is safer to offer the eight potsherds to Agni Rudravat and slay some animals (for them)' (*TMB* XXI: 14: 13).

Rudra's connection with animals persists through the epic-Purāṇic age. The *Mbh.* calls him the lord of cows (VII: 201: 34). Reason is given for his name Paśupati: he delights in cattle (*Mbh.* VII: 20: 123, VII: 78: 53). He is called Govṛṣeśvara, the lord of cows and bulls (*Govṛṣeśvara* XIII: 17: 140; XIII: 14: 321–2), a lion among wild animals. Thus his close ties with the animal world are never forgotten, but are harped on through the literature of many centuries. On the other hand his antagonism to animals is also remembered. His specific exploits in this field are never mentioned, but by the time of the epics, his slaughter of animals appears to be such an established fact that it is used in similes: Bhīma's club resembled Rudra's Pināka when the latter slew animals (*Mbh.* VI: 58: 58). Arjuna boasts: 'I shall to-day lay these low as Rudra slew beasts' (*Mbh.* VII: 18: 3). Once this general massacre is mentioned as taking place on Doomsday (*Mbh.* VII: 18: 35).

The epic battle is compared to Rudra's havoc, when all creatures fell at his hand (*Mbh.* VII: 100: 39), also when beasts perished as Śiva danced (*Mbh.* VIII: 21: 42). Aśvatthāman brags: 'I shall course through the Pāñcālas slaying them like the holder of the Pināka-bow among beasts' (*Mbh.* X: 3: 29).

The *HV* remembers him as the lord of wild and tame animals (II: 74: 23). His slaughter of animals in a fit of rage is referred to in the *Purāṇas*. The *Vāyu P* uses it in a simile (LXXXVIII: 135). Even Patañjali in his *Mahābhāṣys* says that Rudra should be worshipped with an oblation of animals.

Professor E. O. James describes Teshub the ancient god of Hatti, the male partner of the mother-goddess, 'On a lentoid bead seal found near Canea (the site of the ancient Kydonia) represented as the Master of the

Animals standing between two sacral horns with a daemon to the left... To his right is a winged goat with the tail and hind quarters of a lion' (*The ancient gods*, p. 104). Although the accompanying animals are mythical, the basic figure is clearly recognizable as that of a god similar to the proto-Śiva-Paśupati. In almost all mythologies we have some god who is the overlord of animals, but nowhere else is this god as great and important as Rudra-Śiva in India.

Early in the *ṚV*, Rudra, like the rest of the gods of the Aryan pantheon is a benign god to whom people fled in distress, seeking grace and protection, wealth and welfare. Such prayers are very common (*ṚV* I: 114: 7, 8, II: 33: 4). He is called bhūrerdātṛ (the giver of plenty, II: 33: 12) and the protector (I: 43: 3, VI: 28: 7, VII: 40: 5, VII: 46: 3, 4, X: 66: 3). Good things of life flow from him. Thus he is invoked for long life, food, progeny, prosperity, good sons and heroism—in *VS* III: 63. He has a benign form, and people in distress take resort to him (*VS* XVI: 48–9). His army, says the devotee, should destroy elsewhere, 'not us'. One is almost reminded of Jehovah of the Psalms, 'Fight against them that fight against thee...Let destruction come upon him unawares' (Ps. xxv. 1, 8). 'Let Rudra's weapons pass us over' (*VS* XVI: 50; *AV* XI: 219, XVIII: 1: 40).

'The fire', says the *TS* 'is Rudra, his are three missiles; one that comes straight on, one that strikes transversely and one that follows up...Agni is Rudra: just as a tiger stands in anger so he stands' (V: 5: 7). The dark, malevolent and ominous presence of Agni-Rudra is amply brought home through the image of the tiger, against which man was powerless, to whom he succumbed as to an all-powerful enemy. Rudra in the early period forgave sins. Prayers to this effect are found in *ṚV* II: 33: 3, 7, V: 51: 13; *AV* VII: 42: 1, 2. Bhava and Śarva (two names of Rudra) are invoked to be gracious, to grant happiness, remove sins and lengthen life (*AV* VIII: 2: 7); peace, well-being and prosperity form the subject of a prayer to Śiva in *AV* VI: 93. From all this it is clear that at one period at least Rudra had very few malignant traits and he was chiefly invoked as a gracious god.

Rudra is praised kathenotheistically as early as the *YV*; he is invoked as 'Rudra, king of the sacrifice, true offerer, priest of both worlds' (*TS* I: 3: 14). Together with Soma he is invoked for release from evil. 'O Soma and Rudra, do ye drive away the evil spirit that hath entered our abode... do ye give to us. In our bodies release all these remedies and remove the evil that we have done and that is bound within our bodies (*TS* I: 8: 22). In the *Śatarudrīya* we read a hymn in praise of Rudra in his various aspects: 'Homage to thine arrow...thy most kindly arrow. To that body...which is kindly...Bluenecked and ruddy...the greenhaired, wearer of the cord. Bhava...the lord of the moving world, Rudra the lord of fields. Homage to...the turbaned wanderer on mountains...Homage to you...Śarva and Paśupati...to Śipiviṣṭa...to him at peace...Homage to Soma and to Rudra. The Bhavas in this great ocean, the atmosphere. The Śarvas of black necks and white throats who wander below the earth.' The plural number in these passages is interesting; it indicates an animistic belief which makes Rudra the apotheosis of a species of malevolent spirits that roam unseen seeking to injure men. 'To Rudra in the fire, in the waters, in the plants, the Rudra that hath entered all beings, to that Rudra be homage.' (*TS* v: 5: 1–7.)

The *MAU* reiterates several names for Rudra—Īśāna, Śambhu, Bhava and Rudra (vi: 7: 8). In the *KB* it is said in connection with the recitation of the Evayāmāruta and Āgnimāruta hymns that 'Rudra is the oldest and best of the gods' (xxv: 13). Regarding the Tryambaka offering offered by the Asuras it is recorded that 'thereby he delivers from Rudra's power both the descendants that are born and those that are unborn and his offspring is brought forth without disease and blemish' (*ŚB* ii: 6: 2: 2).

To his devotees Rudra-Śiva gives weapons, and assurance of victory. To Indrajit who had offered a sacrifice to him Śiva had granted a boon promising prowess (*Rām.* v: 78: 18). When Rāvaṇa's Puṣpaka chariot got stuck and would not budge Nandin warned him that it was so because he had disturbed Śiva while he was with Pārvatī. Angrily Rāvaṇa lifted mount Kailāsa, Śiva stayed it with his toes, Rāvaṇa was wounded and was advised by the gods to propitiate Śiva. Śiva would not relent until Rāvaṇa had yelled for a thousand years (and received the name Rāvaṇa, the yeller). Śiva was finally pleased and made Rāvaṇa invulnerable to all but men and also gave him the Candrahāsa sword (*Rām.* vii: 16). Śiva blessed Hanūmat with invulnerability from him and his weapons (*Rām.* vii: 36: 18). The demon Madhu's penance pleased Śiva, who gave him a spike made out of his own Śūla (*Rām.* vii: 61: 5–14).

Jayadratha asked for a boon from Śiva; to kill the Pāṇḍavas. Śiva refused but said that he (Jayadratha) would fight them all except Arjuna (*Mbh.* iii: 256). At the gate of the Pāñcāla camp Aśvatthāman saw a fierce figure (Śiva in his Kāla aspect). From his brilliance emanated Viṣṇus by the thousand. Aśvatthāman sought to wound him with weapons but failed, and was driven to praising Śiva for deliverance. There appeared a golden altar with a blazing fire on it and from the fire appeared fierce creatures, deformed and beast-shaped. These were Śiva's retinue devouring flesh and sucking blood, rejoicing and singing hymns to Śiva. Aśvatthaman was overwhelmed and offered himself to Śiva by flinging himself into the fire. Then spoke Śiva: 'Kṛṣṇa worshipped me in due form and I am well pleased with him; for his sake and in order to test you I concealed the Pāñcālas. But their end has come.' He gave Aśvatthaman a brilliant sword and disappeared (*Mbh.* x: 7). Demon Hiraṇyakaśipu was Śiva's protégé; his son Mandara fought Indra for long years and through Śiva's boon even Viṣṇu's Sudarśana disc would not hurt him. Demon Vidyutprabha became lord of the three worlds through Śiva's boon...Śiva was pleased with Demon Śatamakha's penance and granted unparalleled supernatural powers to him. Demon Bāṇa propitiated Śiva who granted him his desire, i.e. Bāṇa became Śiva's son and ruled in Śoṇitapura. He antagonized all through his inordinate pride. Śiva said he would fight when Bāṇa's flagstaff broke of itself. Ill omens appeared and the flagstaff broke; Śiva fought Kṛṣṇa on his protégé Bāṇa's behalf with his Vāruṇa, Paiśāca, Rākṣasa and Raudra weapons, sent his chariot to help Bāṇa and bestowed two boons on him (*HV* II: 116–26). Haṃsa and Dimbhaka, sons of King Brahmadatta, received invincibility and supernatural weapons from Śiva (*HV* III: 102).

On the eve of killing Jayadratha, Arjuna, at Karṇa's advice, praised Śiva (*Mbh.* VII: 78: 20, VII: 79: 24). To Arjuna Śiva gave the Brahmaśiras weapon (which came to be known as the Pāśupata weapon from the giver's name) and taught Arjuna its use and mystery (*Mbh.* III: 40). Śiva himself had obtained it through penance; it rose out of ambrosia (*Mbh.* III: 91: 11). The story of the Pāśupatāstra is repeated in III: 168: 18–56. Of the Śakti weapon which Yudiṣṭhira hurled at Śalya it is said that Tvaṣṭṛ himself had fashioned for Śiva the weapon which consumes the body and life of enemies (*Mbh.* 9: 17: 44). Paraśurāma became virtually invincible through the fatal axe and other weapons which he received by placating Śiva through long and dire penance (*Mbh.* XII: 49: 33). Śiva, when pleased, grants even immortality, and such prowess as would lay even Indra low (*Mbh.* x: 17: 1).

In the hoary past, when there was chaos in the midst of creation Brahman had approached Śiva and requested him to create Daṇḍa, punishment, so that harmony and order would return. Śiva meditated and created it (*Mbh.* XII: 122: 24). The Khaḍga, scimitar, was created out of a sacrifice and was then handed over to Śiva by Brahman for the destruction of unrighteousness (*Mbh.* XII: 166: 45–6). After this Śiva was transfigured and became terrible; his host danced and sang in joy and put up a macabre show. Then Śiva gave the sword smeared with the demons' blood to Viṣṇu (*Mbh.* XII: 166: 65).

Siva's trident (Śūla) is mentioned in connection with Daśaratha's and Kuvera's sacrifice (*Rām.* I: 30: 7). He blessed Viśvāmitra with the knowledge of the secret of weapons (*Rām.* I: 56: 13–18). His Raudra and Pāśupata weapons are mentioned in *Rām.* I: 57: 6. The bow of Janaka had belonged to Śiva with which he had killed gods at Dakṣa's sacrifice (*Rām.* I: 68: 9–12), he gave it to Janaka (*Rām.* III: 4: 25) and Śiva alone could wield it (*Rām.* I: 69: 9). Paraśurāma, armed with the bow and arrows, looked like Śiva (*Rām.* I: 76: 20). Of the two bows fashioned by Viśvakarman one was given to Śiva at the time of Tripuradahana (burning of the three demon cities) (*Rām.* I: 77: 15). His angry appearance at the time of the slaughter of animals is mentioned in the *Rām.* (IV: 5: 30).

Śiva's prowess as a mighty killer had so passed on to later literature that similes are based on it. When Kumbha died with his chest split with a blow, he looked like one seized by Śiva (*Rām.* VI: 55: 88). Rāma boasting of his strength as a warrior said Śiva alone was his equal (*Rām.* VI: 73: 40), 'Śiva alone can bear the brunt of the shower of my arrows', says Arjuna (*Mbh.* III: 40: 31, VII: 32: 11), and his might as a warrior is mentioned in *Mbh.* VII: 32. Śiva had killed demons in a battle with the Pāśupata weapon, says Karṇa to Arjuna (*Mbh.* VII: 57: 16), and when they approach Śiva for a divine weapon, he says that his bow and arrows are in a pond nearby; there the heroes are met by two serpents who turn into bow and arrows and Śiva grants them to Arjuna.

Of Śiva's exploits the best known are the Tripuradahana (destruction of the three demon cities) and the destruction of Dakṣa's sacrifice. The embryo of the Tripuradahana episode is found in the *TS*. The gods besieged Tripura (the three cities). 'They made ready an arrow, Agni as the point, Soma as the socket, Viṣṇu as the shaft. They said "who shall shoot it?" "Rudra", they said, "Rudra is cruel, let him shoot it".' Rudra afterwards chose a boon and became the overlord of the animals. The core of the story probably reaches back before the beginning of the process of amalgamation of the Aryans with the indigenous population begins. The Tripuradahana episode is narrated in *Mbh.* VIII: 24, and XIII: 160. When the gods plagued by the demon brothers Tarakākṣa, Kamalākṣa and Vidyunmālin, who ruled invincible in cities of gold, silver and iron, came and sought protection, Brahman directed them to Śiva who alone, he said, could fulfil the necessary conditions and destroy them. The gods were unable to bear even half of Śiva's strength. He borrowed half of their combined strength instead. (Hence he was called Mahādeva.) Together the gods fashioned a unique chariot and weapons for him. Brahman acted as charioteer, the other gods assisted in subservient capacities. Śiva waited for a thousand years till the cities revolving in mid-air fell in one line, and then, unaided, he pierced them with a single arrow. Terrific tumult and havoc followed. The vulgate edition says: when the cities burned, Pārvatī came to see it with a child in her arms. Indra grew jealous of Śiva's achievement and immediately his arms were paralysed. The gods supplicated Brahman, who revealed that the infant was Śiva. The gods paid homage to him and Indra was healed. The point of the spurious passage is clear: strength and paramountcy are passing from the Vedic-Brāhmaṇic Indra to the epic-Purāṇic Śiva; there is a brief and futile protest, but it is immediately quelled.

The Anuśāsanaparvan (*Mbh.* XIII) variant also has a vulgate emendation. Here, when the chariot starts to move, Śiva's bull roars and the chariot is about to sink from the commotion. Then Viṣṇu assumes the shape of a bull and rescues it. Here, too, the point is to make the two major sectarian gods share the glory of this extraordinary feat. If Śiva accomplished the destruction of the three cities alone, the Śaivas would score a point over the Nārāyaṇīyas. The brief interpolation restores balance and amity between the two sects. This episode emphasizing Śiva's deftness as an archer is rather striking, especially because specific episodes indicative of Śiva's markmanship or fighting skill are entirely absent in pre-epic literature. The *ṚV* mentions his bow and arrows in a conventional way and we are not given one instance of his career as a warrior. Śiva is not a demon-killer in the Vedic literature, and in this he belongs to the minority, which is also evident from the fact that only two and a half hymns are addressed to him in the *ṚV*. Moreover these demons, as well as their cities are rather unusual. Further excavations may throw some light on an indigenous hero-god credited with destroying rival neighbouring cultures, with skill in the smelting of gold, silver and bronze or iron. As yet we can only affirm safely that this episode is a class by itself and has no mythological parallel, except perhaps the faint echo of Viṣṇu's dominating the three regions with three steps. This feat of Śiva is necessary for playing up the figure of a comparatively unimportant god and to inflate his stature into that of a major god. This feat of dexterity earned Śiva such fame that in subsequent literature he came to have a permanent designation—Tripuraghna or Tripurāri. Whatever be the factual base of this story it helped to increase the stature of an otherwise passive god.

The other important feat is Śiva's destruction of Dakṣa's sacrifice. The account is given in *Mbh.* X: 18, XII: 274 and is mentioned in XII: 329 and XIII: 1: 32. The story of Dakṣayajña is the product of the epic imagination but its core is found in the *Brāhmaṇas*. The first mention, however, is found in the *TS*: 'the gods excluded Rudra from the sacrifice; he pierced the sacrifice, the gods gathered round it, (offered a well-offered sacrifice). That is why Agni is called the well-offerer Sviṣṭakṛt (II: 6: 8). Here the clue to the whole series of narratives is found: Rudra was denied his share in the sacrifice by the gods. In the *ŚB* we read: 'Once upon a time the sacrifice escaped the gods, and assuming the shape of a black antelope it roamed about. The gods having thereupon found it and stripped it of its own skin they brought it (the skin) away with them' (*ŚB* I: I: 4: I). Another episode gives us the clue for another constituent part of the Dakṣayajña tale:

Now by means of the sacrifice the gods ascended to heaven. But the god who ruled over the cattle was left behind here. Hence they call him Vāstavya for he was then left behind on the (sacrificial) site (vāstu)...He saw what occurred and said, 'I have been left behind; they are excluding me from the sacrifice'. He went up after them and with his raised weapon rose up on the north...The gods said, 'Do not hurl!' He said, 'Do ye not exclude me from the sacrifice! Set apart an oblation for me'; they replied, 'So be it'. He withdrew his weapon and did not hurl it, nor did he injure any one. (*ŚB* I: 7: 3 ff.)

In the *GB* we read: Prajāpati deprived Rudra of the sacrifice. He pierced it (the sacrifice) and it became Prāśitra. Bhaga became blind as he looked upon it. Savitṛ lost his arms as he held the pot (golden arms were provided for him and he became Hiraṇyapāṇi), Pūṣan lost his teeth as he tried to eat it; he became Piṣṭabhājana (eater of mashed food, *GBU* I: 2). These three tales together supply the core of the Dakṣayajña narrative. The first does not mention Rudra at all, but tells us of the sacrifice escaping the gods in the shape of an antelope. In the second the sacrifice does not escape, but Rudra is denied his rightful share and can get it only by threatening and intimidating the gods. In the third narrative the story is more developed, for Bhaga, Savitṛ and Pūṣan lose their limbs. Inherent in the third tale is the conflict of Rudra and the solar gods, whose domination in the Aryan pantheon may have been responsible for the exclusion of the lunar Rudra. The epic poet's imagination pieced together these bits deftly and the tale is spun round Rudra as the central figure. The *TS* seems to be the first religious composition 'after' the racial, cultic and cultural amalgamation of the Aryans and non-Aryans had begun, and it is significant that Rudra is here denied a share in the oblation.

Once the gods performed a sacrifice and allotted no share to Śiva, who grew angry. He took up his bow and arrows and marched to the venue of the sacrifice. The earth and all its creatures suffered from his heavy footsteps. He came and shot the sacrifice; it escaped (together with the sacrificial fire) in the shape of a deer and fled to the sky. Rudra followed it even there, he cut off Savitṛ's arms, Bhaga's eyes and Pūṣan's teeth. The gods protested and the power of their words broke Śiva's bowstring. He cast his wrath in a pool where it burns as fire. In the Śāntiparvan (bk. XII) account Śiva complains that the gods refused to grant him his due share in a sacrifice (*Mbh.* XII: 274: 26). Here as Śiva pursued the sacrifice fleeing in the shape of a deer, a drop of sweat fell from his brow, out of which rose a demon, fierce, dark and deformed, and consumed the sacrifice. The earth shook, the gods begged Brahman to withdraw this demon, Fever (jvara), whom the earth was unable to endure in his entire form. Brahman divided it into many objects, and the earth could then endure it. In this version Umā is not related to Dakṣa, and does not visit this sacrifice, does not die (of grief at the insult of her husband), the sacrifice is not restored, and Śiva is not promised a share in the oblations. The third place which mentions this episode says that Dakṣa, mortified and filled with wrath at the havoc in his sacrifice, concentrated in meditation and created a third eye in Rudra's forehead (*Mbh.* XII: 329: 14), presumably to disfigure him. Only the bk XIII account says that Śiva received his proper share by destroying (Dakṣa's) sacrifice (*Mbh.* XIII: 1: 32). The *Rām.* does not narrate the episode but refers to it quite frequently.

One or two points in the episode demand attention. The Sauptikaparvan (bk. X) episode says that the sacrifice in which Śiva was deprived of his share was offered, not by Dakṣa but by the gods; while the Śāntiparvan for the first time makes it Dakṣa's sacrifice, and the Anuśāsanaparvan confirms this. The earliest version of the story does not connect it in any way with Umā or Dakṣa.

The vulgate edition of the *Mbh.* has a different story; Pārvatī saw a procession of gods moving towards Dakṣa's sacrifice; these had been invited, she and her husband had been ignored. Śiva in supreme indifference and unconcern informs her that it had been ordained that he should have no share in the sacrifice. He, however, noticed her mortification and decided on action—revenge. Rushing to the venue in burning wrath and terrific destructive strength he smashed up the sacrifice. The vulgate recension in a later chapter of the Anuśāsanaparvan repeats the episode. Here Dakṣa purposefully leaves Śiva out of the list of guests. Dadhīca warns him, reminding him of Śiva's position and power and admonishes him for the proposed insult of such a god. Dakṣa laughs the caution away saying, with

Śiva as a guest the sacrifice would be neither righteous nor worth its name. Besides Dakṣa says that they have eleven Rudras, all with matted locks and all holding Śūlas, but he knows no Mahēśvara (*Mbh.* vulgate XII: 283: 38). In this version it is not Śiva himself, but Vīrabhadra and Bhadrakālī, monsters born of their master's wrath, who act at their master's bidding and destroy the sacrifice completely. Dakṣa is presented as a devotee of Viṣṇu. In the *HV* account, when Śiva destroyed Dakṣa's sacrifice terrible havoc followed and Viṣṇu fought him—and later Śiva became Nīlakaṇṭha when Viṣṇu embraced him. At last Viṣṇu allowed him a portion of the sacrificial oblation (*HV* III: 32 ff.).

In these accounts we notice not only the rivalry between the two sects but also a reluctance on the part of official Brāhmaṇical religion to admit an unfamiliar god into the recognized pantheon. The anomaly is rather striking, for a Vedic god being deprived of his share in the sacrifice is simply inconceivable. Oblations to every member of the Vedic pantheon were obligatory, and Rudra is a Vedic god. Now after enjoying his rightful share of oblation for centuries Śiva is suddenly denied it, and, at least in one version, is quite reconciled to it, saying that it is ordained so. This is a somewhat strange phenomenon. In every version, whether in the gods' sacrifice or in Dakṣa's, he has to fight his way into the sacrifice; and whether at Pārvatī's mortification or at his own initiative has to wreak fearful vengeance on the perpetrator of the sacrifice. Even then it is not clearly mentioned that he does receive his share of the oblation, except in one instance. This fierce hostility cannot be against an old and recognized deity, it can only be turned against an interloper, an upstart. And the epic-Purāṇic Śiva was largely that.

Among Śiva's minor feats may be included his slaughter of demon Andhaka. Brief, almost passing mention is made of this feat (*Mbh.* vulgate II: 284: 1, 11; VII: 200: 71; critical edn. VII: 57 as also in other hymns). In the *Purāṇas* the story is spun out and Andhaka becomes a son of Śiva's, born blind because Pārvatī had playfully shaded Śiva's eyes when she conceived him. Later Andhaka grew up into a nuisance, pestering and tormenting gods and men so that eventually Śiva himself had to kill him. What is unique is that in other myths of this type it is never the patron of the demon who kills the miscreant, some other god is commissioned for the task. The exception in Śiva's case may be due to his ruthlessness. The *Rām.* also mentions Śiva's killing of Andhaka on the Śvetaparvata (cf. *Rām.* III: 35: 93).

The *ṚV* knows Śiva as a dread god (cf. X: 126: 5); the *VS* calls him

Ātatāyin (with a drawn bow, XVI: 18); he is frequently called Bhīma (mighty). The Vedic Rudra carries bow and arrows, the bow is golden and kills by the thousand (*AV* XI: 2: 12). His cruelty is referred to in the *TS* nucleus of the Tripuradahana episode. A *JB* narrative says: the gods decided to leave behind whatever was cruel in them; they put the dross on potsherds; in it was born this god. Because he was born on Śarāvas (potsherds) he is thus called (Śarva) (*JB* III: 26: 2). This again mentions Śiva's cruelty.

Of Śiva's other feats the most significant and important is his holding the Gaṅgā on his head. The Vedic literature contains no reference to it, perhaps because the Gaṅgā did not attain its sanctity in that period and the holiness of the pilgrimages strewn on the banks of this river had not been so established and recognized a fact as in the epic-Purāṇic age. Thus its first mention is found in the epics.

The *Rām.* giving the story says that Śiva agreed to hold the descending Gaṅgā on his head (I: 37: 20–1). The descent is described in vivid language. Gaṅgā, it is significant to note, is the elder sister to Umā (I: 37: 16–19). Brahman instructed Bhagīratha about Gaṅgā's descent and also tells him that Śiva alone could hold the tumult of the descending torrent. Arriving on the earth, she becomes Bhagīratha's daughter and is called Bhāgīrathī (I: 45: 56) and Bhagīratha praises her. In the *Mbh.* the river asks Bhagīratha to beg Śiva to hold her (III: 107: 8, 9). He does so, Śiva agrees, and is called Jāhnavīdhṛk (XIII: 13: 137). The 60,000 sons of Sagara who lay burnt to ashes are saved through the contact of the river. The episode clearly has one purpose: to emphasize the power and sanctity of Śiva. Incidentally it appears as essentially bound up with the epic-Purāṇic religion, which has idol-worship, temples, vows and pilgrimages with all of which the rising Śaiva cult is connected. Śiva-culture flourished along the banks of the Gaṅgā. Vārāṇasī is on its bank and Śiva is called Kāśīnātha, which is probably a reminiscence of a local Śaiva cult with its central shrine in Vārāṇasī. The addition of the story of the purging of the ashes in the place now called Sāgara (i.e. the Bay of Bengal, south of Bengal) indicates the south-eastern course of the Aryan peoples' progress; it also includes all the region along the banks of the river. From Kailāsa, the epic home of Śiva, via Vārāṇasī, Prayāga (Allahabad) down to the Bay of Bengal the entire course of the river is included in the tract over which Śaivism spread and flourished.

A god seeking the command of an entire community—its worship, devotion and ritual ceremonies—has to have certain exploits to his credit, exploits which make manifest his power in a way that will raise him indisputably over other gods. And Śiva, with his meagre Vedic antecedents, lacked such exploits. He was fierce and turbulent, but he had to be shown as uniquely powerful. It was here that the Tripuradahana episode and this anecdote of his holding the Gaṅgā came in useful. When Brahman himself instructs Bhagīratha to approach Śiva as the only god able to bear the onrush of the powerful torrent, Śiva's might appears unquestionable. Thus this story is a very useful lever by which the Śiva cult is lifted to a higher plane in mythology.

Besides the gift of weapons, Śiva throughout the Vedic and epic literature is represented as a benign giver of diverse gifts. Later literature knows him as Āśutoṣa (easily pleased) and his protégés bank on this. Śiva blessed Viśvāmitra with the secret knowledge of weapons, especially of the Raudra and Pāśupata weapons (*Rām.* I: 57: 6). Propitiated by the awe-struck and humiliated gods at Dakṣa's sacrifice he restored the lost limbs to all (*Rām.* I: 68: 9–12). He granted progeny to Prabhaṅkara, king of Manalūra (Manipura), and Citrāṅgada was born (*Mbh.* I: 207). Propitiated by Sagara Śiva bestowed on him 60,000 sons by the one wife, but by the other wife only one son through whom the line would continue (*Mbh.* III: 104). Vāsudeva propitiated Śiva with long penance and received a son, Sāmba (*Mbh*, XIII: 14). When Kṛṣṇa sought an interview with Śiva Upamanyu would not let him in, but finally did so when Kṛṣṇa chanted a hymn to Śiva. Yājñavalkya became famous through Śiva's grace, so did Vedavyāsa. The Vālakhilyas, offended at Indra's scornful conduct, propitiated Śiva through penance and created Suparna Somahartṛ (the Soma-stealing eagle), a rival of Indra. The waters had become polluted through Śiva's wrath and could only be purified when Śiva was gracious again. Atri's wife conceived and delivered a son through Śiva's favour even after she had left her husband in anger. Through Śiva's grace and bounty Vikarṇa became famous, Śākalya and Sāvarni became authors, and Nārada a musician. Upamanyu, the son of sage Dhaumya, received favour in Śiva's sight by propitiating him through long penance (*Mbh.* XIII: 14).

Once during a drought the Saptarṣi (seven sages) went to collect fruits leaving Arundhatī (Vaśiṣṭha's wife) behind. Śiva approached her for food, she offered him some plums; he asked her to cook them tender while he told her stories. In the meantime the drought passed, the sages returned, the god revealed his identity and blessed her before he took his leave (*Mbh.* IX: 47). This episode, known as Vadarapacana (cooking of the plums), reveals a kind and tender god who tests the loyalty of his devotee, but usually does not set too hard a test, and blesses abundantly when he is satisfied. A girl once practised stiff penance for obtaining a husband. She begged Śiva five times for a husband; he took her literally and bestowed five husbands on her. In the next life she became Draupadī, wife of the five Pāṇḍava brothers (*Mbh.* I: 189).

This aspect of Śiva remains prominent through all Purāṇic and post-Purāṇic literature: whenever anybody is in distress or hard pressed for something he supplicates Śiva and the god sees him through his trouble. Thus Viśvamitra became a Brāhmaṇa through Śiva's boon. When through Indra's curse Dharma was lost, Asita Devala revived and received it from Śiva. Gṛtsamada told Ajamīḍha that in Śakra's sacrifice he (Gṛtsamada) had mispronounced a verse of a hymn and was cursed by Variṣṭha, into becoming a deer to roam about in deserts; he fled to Śiva, who alleviated his misery. Jaigīṣavya was blessed with supernatural powers by Śiva at Vārāṇasī, Garga with knowledge and longevity. Parāśara craved for a famous and righteous son, Śiva bestowed Vedavyāsa on him. Aṇīmāṇḍavya, wrongly punished to die on a spike, was relieved of pain and reached heaven through Śiva's grace. Gālava was a neglected son of his father, but Śiva blessed him and his father grew fond of his son (*Mbh.* XIII: 17, 18). Once Umā had playfully shaded Śiva's eyes with her hands, a terrible fire escaped from the third eye which consumed the Himalaya instantly. She was frightened, he then restored life and shape to the mountain by looking favourably at it (*Mbh.* XIII: 140).

The *ṚV* knows Śiva as a healer—he holds medicines in his hand (I: 114: 5). His drugs are called Jalāṣabheṣaja (*ṚV* II: 35: 7; *AV* II: 27: 6, VI: 44: 6), a phrase not explained satisfactorily yet. He is called the first exponent of divine remedies (*VS* XVI: 5). His drugs are soothing and kindly, they are efficacious for removing arrows and healing wounds (*ṚV* II: 33: 2, 12, 13; *AV* VI: 90: 1, VI: 57: 1, VI: 59: 3). His drugs are solicited by Manu (*ṚV* II: 33: 16). He is invoked for the remedy of various diseases including consumption (*ṚV* VI: 93: 1, VI: 141: 1; I: 43: 2, V: 42: 11, VII: 46: 2). The *ŚB* praises Rudra for his remedies which are potent for beasts: 'Thou (O Rudra) art a remedy for the cow, the horse, the ram and the ewe' (II: 6: 2: 11). Another passage hints at his remedy in a rather cryptic fashion: 'Thereby they cut out (i.e. extricate) his (Rudra's) darts from their bodies. If they fail to catch them, they touch those that have fallen to the ground, thereby they make them medicine and hence if they fail to catch them they touch them' (*ŚB* II: 6: 2: 10, 11).

The iconographic representation of Śiva on the coins of Wema Kadpheses, where he, almost invariably, holds a water-vessel with his left hand is perhaps a reminiscence of his Vedic description 'jalāṣabheṣaja': divine water efficacious for diseases. The practice of sprinkling sanctified water on the sick appears to be world-wide. 'Manasā', the snake-goddess (so-called because she was Rudra's daughter born of his mind, or thought, manas) is still worshipped in various forms in India. In Bengal she is invariably associated with a pitcher, is sometimes symbolically worshipped in the water-vessel, and, after the ritual is over, the water contained in the pitcher is believed to be charged with medicinal properties. Some old ideas may have percolated into this rite and belief—ideas connected with jalāṣabheṣaja.

Benign Rudra as the healing god appears to be the obverse of the malevolent Rudra sending blighting diseases to men and beasts. And this is quite the usual thing in mythology: a particular god has power and potency over a particular domain of life; pleased, he grants man happiness of that specific kind; angry, he punishes by depriving man of that happiness.

Besides being connected with the animal world, Rudra has indirect association with the plant world, too. When he slaughters animals, we are told in the *TMB*, the plants also get smeared with poison (VI: 9: 9). The *Mbh.* calls him lord of the trees, Vṛkṣapati (VII: 201: 34), Vanaspatīnām pati (VII: 201: 47). He is called by the names of various trees (*Mbh.* XIII: 17: 110, 140). Rudra is often identified with Agni, and as Agni he entered the Aśvattha and Śamī trees (*Mbh.* XIII: 85). A terracotta seal 'in the collection of Dhir Singh Nahar has a Śivaliṅga with subdued realism described as Pādapeśvara (Lord of Trees) in Gupta characters' (J. N. Banerji, *The development of Hindu iconography*, p. 114). Professor E. O. James, in his *Prehistoric religion*, writes of 'the ithyphallic statue of Min... carried in procession on poles by priests beneath a canopy preceded by a white bull, the sacred animal of Min and, followed by bundles of lettuce, his plant' (p. 186). Min corresponds to Śiva very closely—he is ithyphallic, has the bull for his animal, is lunar by nature, and is associated with plants. An *AV* hymn reads: 'Homage to Rudra, Agni, who has entered in the fire, the waters, the plants and creepers, who has fashioned all this world' (*AV* VII: 87). 'The worship of plants', says Rafael Karsten in *The origins of religion*, 'is intimately connected with the belief in souls animating trees and plants. In essence, this plant-soul seems to be the same as the soul or spirit animating man' (p. 93). Thus the root of the belief which connects plants with Rudra seems to be the concept of a single subterranean vital spirit which animates plants and men. And this spirit is fed by the corpses which enter the subsoil. This chthonic spirit (which Rudra and his group symbolize) fosters vegetation; hence Rudra is conceived of as an indwelling spirit of the plant and vegetation world.

Rudra as we have observed belongs to the lunar group of gods and this group is everywhere connected with the vegetation world. Gods like Yama and Soma are the links through which Rudra and his parallels in other mythologies are connected with vegetation. Death is at the root of this belief; for from observation man early arrived at the belief that matter does not perish altogether, but is conserved and converted into a different form. Hence death does not utterly destroy life but the buried body is regenerated in the shape of whatever comes out of the soil—plants or snakes. These are corpses regenerated in a different form and shape. Vitality is energy, and energy also does not die but merely changes its form. Thus what is lost to life above the earth is gained by life under the soil and is reborn as vegetation. This explains the very close connection of ancestor-worship and harvest. J. G. Frazer in his *The golden bough* has brought forward innumerable instances of harvest-rites being connected intimately with ancestor-rites. We have already observed the time-sequence of these two: ancestor-worship precedes the harvest. This lunar group of death-ancestor gods are associated with the dark and mysterious processes which go on underneath the soil—processes which are essential for the regeneration and recurrence of crops and vegetation.

The earth as Nirṛti, the chthonic mother-goddess, receives the corpse, the seed. Then follows a long and invisible process of decomposition and dissolution of the corpse and its conversion into sap, manure and vitality which resuscitate the soil, and the mother-goddess conceives from the seeds and brings forth the plants. Primitive people may have observed that corpses provided manure, and the good crops that resulted from it. The fact that cornfields, contiguous to burial grounds, yield better crops may have been a pointer to this theory. Somehow, slowly but surely the belief emerged, and was strengthened through experience, which became deep-rooted and progressively illustrated and elaborated in ritual and mythology until all over the world it was accepted as a self-evident truth. Śiva and Yama, with Durgā and Yamī-Nirṛti as their consorts, controlled the world of the departed souls as well as the buried bodies and later came to control the vegetation world, too. The association was strengthened by their lunar links, because the moon, as we have seen, confirmed man's faith in the indestructibility of matter, in its convertibility—in the conservation of energy and the transformation of life and form. Thus as lunar gods Śiva and Yama (together with their consorts) belong to the group of gods who symbolized the chain of existence, the cycle of life, and the regeneration of vitality on different planes and in different forms.

CHAPTER 7

RUDRA-ŚIVA (2)

ŚIVA's name 'Śarva' (a derivative from *Śara* or *Śaru*, arrow) means the 'god who kills people with arrows'; it is his dread and killer aspect. The *Avesta* has a demon called Sauru (or Saru) which literally means death, and the arrow. The Avestan demon Ishus Hvathakhto (lit. the self-moving arrow), and Asto Vidotus, i.e. the bone-divider who holds a noose around the neck of all living creatures, are figures parallel to the Indian Yama, Śiva's chief associate. In Avestan mythology Śarva is Angra Mainyu's associate and symbolizes tyranny, thus opposing Ahura Mazda's associate, Ksathra Vairya (good government), one of his six associates, the Amesha Spentas. Thus already in the Indo-Iranian mythology Śarva is an evil god; a daeva or demon in the *Avesta* and a malevolent god in India. The word occurs for the first time in *TS*, where a new Śiva is first introduced. Monier-Williams in his *Buddhism* says that Śiva was associated with the Buddha in the northern Śākta, Tantric and magic cults and becomes Mahākāla, Bhairava and Bhīma. It was in this aspect of Kāla that Śiva assumes new dimensions and also partially the functions of Yama the god of death. As an emerging member of the trinity of the neo-Brāhmaṇical triad he had to eclipse his minor predecessors and discharge their functions. Death, one of the major starting points of both magic and religion, had to be symbolized by a major god—and here Śiva stepped in. From the *TS* onwards his sinister and dread characteristics grew until he symbolized Death and Time in his person, for Kāla means both Time and Death. Later he came to be known as Mahākāla, with Mahākālī for his consort.

His Vedic followers are called Rudrāh, Rudrāsah and Marutah. 'Three and thirty in troops the Rudras frequent the sky and earth, the destructive ones, eleven, seated on the waters; may all of them accept the Soma pressed for the pressing' (*TS* I: 4: 11). He is invoked together with the Rudras in the *ṚV* I: 58: 6, I: 100: 5, I: 101: 7, III: 32: 3, VII: 5: 9, VII: 10: 4, VII: 35: 6, VII: 106: 14, X: 32: 5, X: 66: 3, X: 99: 5, X: 125: 1 as also in numerous other places. The *VS* invokes his followers as 'those whose arrows are the wind'. Rudra is called the father of the Maruts (I: 114: 6, 9), these he begot in the white womb of Pṛśni (*ṚV* II: 34: 2, V: 60: 5). They are called Rudra's men (*ṚV* I: 64: 2, V: 5: 7), Rudra's son or sons (*ṚV* I: 64: 12, v: 42: 15, i: 85: 1, vi: 50: 4, vi: 66: 3, 11, vii: 56: 1, also Rudrāh, dual no. *ṚV* i: 158: 1, v: 73: 8, v: 75: 3, viii: 22: 14, also i: 158: 1). Sometimes Gau instead of Pṛśni is mentioned as the mother of the Maruts (*ṚV* viii: 101: 15). Rudrāh, the plural of Rudra, is used in the sense of the latter's followers, retinue or associates. Taken in this light the Maruts come to be associated with death, spirits who hover in cremation grounds and are the natural companions of Rudra who begot them in Pṛśni. Anthropomorphically the Rudras may have been storm-spirits (anthropomorphized) who accompany Rudra, the storm-god.

The Maruts should be distinguished from Vāyu or Vātāh which are merely the wind and blast personified. Vāyu is described in the *ṚV* as riding a chariot drawn by the Niyuts, a team of horses, or as riding red (horses) in *ṚV* i: 134: 1. He is the mightiest among the gods, a white animal is to be slaughtered for him (*MS* ii: 5: 1), Vāyu is invoked together with Indra or Parjanya, a weak personification of the rain cloud.

Vātāh is the same as Zoroastrian Vata or Oado on the coins of Kaniska and Huviska, symbolizing strength, and fit emblems for invaders and conquerers. In the *Viṣṇudharmottara P.* Vāyu or Vāta is described anthropomorphically as two-armed, a figure holding the two ends of the scarf he wears thus symbolizing by his breeze-blown garments, a strong gusty wind; his hair is dishevelled (lviii: 1–6). Nothing in this description makes him anything more than the mere element personified.

In the *Rām.* Vāyu is a somewhat clearer figure. He falls in love with the daughters of Kuśanābha and curses them with humps when they reject him (i: 1, 17, 35). Hanūmat and Sampātin are Vāyu's sons by Añjanā (iv: 1: 32, v: 2: 17–22, v: 3: 27–34). In the spurious portions of the *Rām.* Vāyu is described as handsome and well-decked out in ornaments. His valour is much dwelt upon, but he never assumes a real presence or personality. In the *Mbh.* he is Bhīma's father—the notion of his might and speed persist behind the myth—but that is about all. In the *HV* he is the king of smell, winds, disembodied shapes, of sound and space and of the mighty ones. But here Vāyu is merely an element without any distinct personality.

With the Maruts the case is utterly different. Even as early as the *ṚV* the Maruts clearly belong to the Śiva group through their links with gods who belong to that group. Apart from the fact that as natural phenomena they are conceived of as mighty winds—and as such are associated with Indra, who in his natural aspect needs the aid of strong assistants and hence is called a friend of the Maruts—the Maruts are not confused with Vāyu-

Vātāh, i.e. they are never mere wind-gods. They are strong and powerful (*MS* I: 6: 5; *ṚV* I: 39: 7–11, I: 166: 5), have golden jaws and headgears and dappled cows or mares for mounts (*ṚV* II: 34: 3) and are credited with certain feats of strength which they performed alone or with other gods. They carry chisels, knives, bows, arrows in quivers and swords and ride on fine steeds and chariots (*ṚV* V: 58: 3). Sometimes they usher the thunderstorm, sometimes the rain cloud. But this is about all. The rest of the description of the Maruts definitely associates them with Rudra who begot them in Pṛśni—explained as a water-skin or the celestial cow which pours rain (*ṚV* V: 52: 6). They are Pṛśnimātarah (Pṛśni's sons, *ṚV* I: 38: 4, I: 168: 9), Rudriyāsah (Rudra's sons, I: 38: 7) a horde of the Maruts (Marutām gaṇa, *ṚV* I: 38: 15, I: 64: 12).

What definitely connects them with the Rudra-group is the reference to Śaryāṇavat in the Ṛjīka country (*ṚV* VIII: 7: 29), for we are told that Soma grows by the banks of Śaryāṇavat (*ṚV* I: 84: 4, VIII: 6: 93, VIII: 7: 29). Sāyaṇa, the commentator, says that Śaryāṇavat is a lake in the country of Kurukṣetra. Wherever Śaryāṇavat may be, it connects the Maruts with Soma, and with the Rudra-group; to Rudra they are openly and frequently related as sons. The *AB* says that the Maruts occupy the atmosphere and are the subjects (viśah) of the gods (II: 10). In the *Rām.* we are told that the Maruts were born of a cut-up foetus (I: 46, 48). The story is elaborated in the *Matsya P* where we are told that Indra, scared at Diti's penance (for a son who would kill Indra because Indra had killed her sons, the Daityas), sought and found a loophole in her austerity, entered her womb and cut up the foetus into forty-nine parts. Coming out he confessed, and they began to weep. He consoled them, said they would be given portions at sacrifices; hence they are called the Maruts (*Matsya P* VII: 62).

The derivation of the word Marut reminds us of that of Mārtaṇḍa or Mārtāṇḍa, who, we are told was left behind when Aditi took her seven other children, the Ādityas, to heaven. The word seems to be connected with *mṛ*, to die, and Mārtaṇḍa was the semi-mortal son, so Aditi left him behind. The Maruts are also sons of Diti, the mother of demons; they are howling tornado-divinities, and if they are derived from *mṛ* (= to die, probably a cognate of the Greek verb *maraino*) they may symbolize the spirits of the dead who hover in the atmosphere in Rudra's company, for mid-air is their sphere according to the *AB*. The *HV* account, retold in the *Purāṇas*, of how the Maruts were being practically killed (when Indra chopped the foetus) also connects them with death. We remember that as associates of Śiva who is garbhamāṃsaśṛgāla (greedy like a jackal for foetus-flesh) they were themselves nearly dead even as foetus, and perhaps they help Śiva to destroy foetuses. These dark associations are quite common with Śiva in his destructive element.

Of the Rudras we further hear: 'the Rudras which in thousands lie around this (earth) in the quarters, their wrath do we deprecate' (*TS* IV: 5). Indra is said to have consulted with the Rudras (*AB* I: 7: 4). The Rudras are identified with Agni (*TB* II: I: 10: I). To the Rudras belong the Triṣṭubh metre and the midday pressing (*JB* I: 281). The *Mbh.* knows eleven Rudras, sons of Rudra (*Mbh.* XII: 122: 30, 34). This number is inherited from the Vedas, but the names are supplied by the epic: Mṛgavyādha, Śarva, Nirṛti, Ajaikapād, Ahirbudhnya, Pinākin, Dahana, Īśvara, Kapālin, Sthāṇu and Bhava (*Mbh.* I: 103: 9). When Aśvatthāman had the vision of the blazing golden altar, out of whose fire emanated deformed beast-faced creatures, these are stated to be Rudra's retinue (*Mbh.* X: 7: 13–47). They devoured human flesh and drank blood, praised Śiva and made merry. The Śāntiparvan (*Mbh.* bk XII) tells us that Rudra was himself an irate god, and that he created ten others; these eleven are the different manifestations of Rudra (*Mbh.* XII: 327: 31). The *TS* lays down: 'Three red gallinules, these are for the Rudras' (V: 5: 9). Through the colour red the Rudras are linked with their leader Rudra, for to him also a red cow is to be offered.

Saṃvarta, describing Śiva's followers, says that they are dwarfish and deformed and roam the earth, but their permanent headquarters are in Vārāṇasī where they live with Śiva and Gaurī (*Mbh.* XIV: 7). They are animal-shaped, deformed, resemble various abhorrent and ferocious creatures and behave in obnoxious, funny and repulsive manners. In general they look hideous, disfigured with grotesquely distorted or maimed limbs—they are abnormal and hellish in looks and outlandish in dress and conduct. The vulgate edition has a fuller description of this macabre host. One has the impression that they do not belong to the world of the living or to the plane of normality. Hence one is driven to the conclusion that this sombre and dread god is surrounded by spectres, spirits who have 'passed on'—a belief which lingers even now, for Śiva is Bhūtanātha, and the word *bhūta* which originally meant 'being' or 'creature' has come to mean ghost, as Śiva is also Pramatheśa—lord of the Pramathas, and these are undoubtedly spirits. These terms connect Śiva with the spectre world, where the ghosts roam at his bidding, ghosts with whom he lives in the cremation-ground.

The *HV* clearly states that Śiva is the lord of all creatures and evil spirits (Piśācas) (*HV* IV: 8). The *HV* account of the havoc at Dakṣa's sacrifice says it was this dread and spirit retinue of Śiva which perpetrated the destruction (*HV* III: 32). In the *HV* the genealogy of the Rudras is given: Surabhi brought forth the eleven Rudras from Kaśyapa, through Mahādeva's favour, as well as Ajaikapād, Ahirbudhnya, Tvaṣṭṛ and Viśvarūpa. The eleven Rudras were Hara, Vahurūpa, Tryambaka, Aparājita, Vṛṣākapi, Śambhu, Kapardin, Raivata, Mṛgavyādha, Sarpa and Kapālin (*HV* III: 49–52). It is interesting to note the additions and omissions: Hara, Vahurūpa, Aparājita, Vṛṣākapi, Sarpa and Raivata are new names, while of the old group Nirṛti, Pinākin, Dahana, Īśvara, Sthāṇu and Bhava are omitted. One notices that the cult is changing and growing perhaps with regional variations. We are further told that there are hundreds of infinitely powerful Rudras with whom the whole earth is filled (*HV* III: 53). Thus by the time of the *HV* they have almost independent stature of their own and have grown 'infinitely powerful'. The *Matsya P* enumerates a different list of the eleven Rudras: Ajaikapād, Ahirbudhhya, Virūpākṣa, Raivata, Hara, Vahurūpa, Tryambaka, Sāvitra, Jayanta, Pinākin and Aparājits (VI: 29–30). The new additions are Virūpaksa, Sāvitra and Jayanta. They are called gaṇeśvaras, lord of the gaṇas. The *Vayu P* knows Śiva as the lord of the Rudras (LXVI: 70). The *KP* states that Śiva with his mind created Rudras like himself, fearless blue-red creatures with three eyes and matted hair (VII: 29). Thus with time the Rudras grew in importance and became replicas of Śiva himself, resembling him in appearance and functions, multiplying in number and dimensions until they appear to be sovereign of a particular domain, with Śiva as the central Rudra. They now have distinctive features and hold important positions, and remind one very closely of Pramathas and Piśācas, ghosts and spectres.

Their appearance and functions confirm the notion that there is a substratum of departed souls in the concept. These associates of Śiva, sometimes described as death-like and ghostly in appearance, sometimes as pleasant, seem to represent the spirits of the blessed and the damned. At the back of these spirits metempsychosis may have been at work, for 'we find this worship of the dead among the Hellenes, among the Latins, among the Etruscans, we also find it among the Aryans of India' (Fustel de Coulanges, *The ancient city*, p. 102). Thus these ancestor-spirits became the constant companions of Pramatheśa, lord of the Pramathas; and Pramatha literally means 'churner' or 'tomentor', but is used to denote a class of demons attending on Śiva. From the same Indo-European root the Greek name of Prometheos (the bringer of fire) is derived; Śiva, too, is intimately connected with fire.

Rudra had early been connected with dark characteristics. From the Ṛgvedic period he is a dreaded god whose darts and missiles are sought to be warded off, but the impression of the *ṚV* Rudra hymns is more of a powerful and formidable god than a malevolent or dark deity. The *YV* first presents before us a god with dark and mysterious associations. 'To Bhava is to be offered Yakan (the liver), to Śarva the matasna (the internal organs of the body), to Īśāna, Manyu (wrath), to Mahādeva the antahpārśavya (flesh between the sides), to the Ugra Deva (fierce God) the Vaniṣṭhu (entrails), to Vaśiṣṭthahanu the Kośas in the Śingin (the testicles out of the entrails). To Ugra should be offered red (blood?), to Mitra piety, to Rudra impiety and to the Ugra Deva the entrails; to Indra sport, the Maruts might, the Sādhyas delight. The neck-part belongs to Bhava, the flesh between the sides to Rudra, the liver to Mahādeva, the entrails to Śarva and the intestines to Paśupati (*VS* XXXIX: 8: 9). 'The god Rudras are praised with the summer season' (*VS* XXI: 24). This passage associates the obnoxious articles, and the oppression of heat with the different manifestations of Śiva. In *AV* II: 34: I Rudra is bought off and sent to his portion—this illustrates the fear connected with him and his rites. Bhava and Śarva are to hurl their lightning weapon on those who sin and practise sorcery (*AV* X: I: 23). It is significant that gods other than those of the lunar group are offered pleasant things—sport, might and delight—while those belonging to the Rudra group are offered gruesome oblations. 'He who practises witchcraft should offer a red (cow) to Rudra...it has Rudra as its deity' (*TS* II: I: 7). It is striking that he who practises witchcraft should endeavour to propitiate Rudra, thus establishing this god's connections with witchcraft; this is also evident from numerous *AV* hymns which are addressed to Rudra or his various other manifestations. 'To Agni and the Rudras he should offer a cake on eight potsherds when he practises witchcraft; Rudra is his dread form' (*TS* II: 2: 2). 'Vāstospati is Rudra. If he were to go on offering to Vāstospati the fire becoming Rudra would leap after him and slay him' (*TS* III: 4: 10). This presents a formidable and terrible god.

But the *YV* introduces an altogether new type of Rudra, hitherto unknown and unforeseen. For, in the famous *Śatarudrīya* hymn an unexpected side of his character is brought to light: 'Homage to the cheater, the swindler, to the lord of the burglars...the glider,...the wanderer around; ...the lord of the forests; the bearer of the sword, the night rover, the lord of the cut-purses...the turbaned wanderer on the mountains, the lord of the pluckers...to him who dwelleth with Yama and to him at peace...

The Śarvas of black necks and white throats, who wander below on the earth' (*TS* IV: 5; *VS* XVI). He is also associated with various professions and is called the god of architects, councillors and merchants. Here we have for the first time a god who rudely shakes our notion of divinity, for the whole hymn contradicts, and is utterly foreign to man's concept of godhead. This Rudra is evil, positively malevolent and abhorrent, he is physically outlandish, unfamiliar; his conduct is repulsive and his associations are obnoxious. Yet we have a frequently recurring refrain of 'namah' (homage to...) throughout the whole hymn. This appears more a product of fear—fear of the unfamiliar—rather than of reverence. Eggeling in his introduction to the translation of the *ŚB* says of the Śatarudrīya that it contains altogether '425 oblations to Rudra', the representative of the fearful aspects of life and nature—and calls it a 'dismal litany...reflecting ...the popular belief in demoniac agencies to which man is completely exposed'. It is true that the first perusal of this litany brings a shock, so utterly unlike it is to anything in the previous Vedic literature. No Ṛgvedic god ever inspired an emotion akin to this, for no Ṛgvedic god was so utterly gruesome. At the same time this god is praised kathenotheistically—he is the god of the universe, the god who enjoys supreme position and paramount importance; he is everything, good and evil, more evil perhaps than good—but he symbolizes all creation, animate, and inanimate, human and subhuman, moral and immoral. The various nefarious professions associated with him are balanced by his identification with all phenomena, and all levels of existence. In this hymn we actually have the effort for (or perhaps the success of) blending various non-Vedic and non-Aryan gods with the Vedic Rudra. In the *TS* we are introduced to his several names, here we have his several functions. Rudra is cruel (*TS* VI: 2: 3), the cruellest among the gods, his form is cruel (*MS* I: 10: 20, III: 8: 1). In the Nābhānediṣṭha episode we have the description of his inauspicious form: a man in black garments (*AB* V: 14).

Of his several names we have a history in the *KB*: 'then arose he of a thousand eyes, of a thousand feet, with a thousand fitted (arrows)'. He grasped his father Prajāpati for a name and wrenched out from Prajāpati one name after another: Bhava (of the waters), Śarva (fire), Paśupati (air), Ugra (plants and trees), Mahān Deva (the sun), Rudra (the moon), Īśāna (flood), and Aśani (thunder) (*KB* VI: 1–9). Here his thousand eyes, feet and arrows raise him to the rank of a supreme god, as also his identification with the elements and luminaries. His description as ghora (fierce), manyu (wrath), paśughātuka (animal-slayer), hara (brilliance or heat) in the *TB* associate him with what is fierce and fearful. 'The dried (or parched) oblations are to be offered to Rudra' (*TB* I: 7: 8: 5), thus his connection with heat is confirmed.

Rudra's various names are found in another passage in the *ŚB*. 'That (offering) then is certainly made to "Agni", for, indeed, Agni is that god—his are these names: Śarva as the eastern people call him; Bhava as the Bāhīkas (call him); Paśūnām pati, Rudra and Agni. The name Agni, doubtless, is the most auspicious (śānta) and the other names of his are inauspicious' (I: 7: 3: 8). In this passage we have an inkling as to the regional origins of some of Rudra's names—as also the nature of the syncretism. Thus a god of the eastern people, Śarva, or more probably a god whom the easterners (with their propensity for palatals) called Śarva (but who probably was kindred to the Avestan Sarva (or Saurva), the archer (with a dental 's') came to be blended with Rudra, perhaps because of his dread and cruel character. Another god Bhava of the Bāhikas (mispronounced perhaps into Bhāvikas, 'a despised people of the Punjab' as Monier-Williams's lexicon calls them), probably the god 'Oeso' (Bhaveśa) of the Kuṣāna coins was also assimilated. Pali texts corroborate this statement of differences between the east and west. This clue helps us to guess the process and tendencies at work behind the formation of the composite god. Some of the important organic components of the epic concepts of Śiva must have been lent him by the various tribal gods who were slowly being absorbed in the Aryan pantheon. A *ŚB* passage states Śiva's fearsome traits: 'And if anyone (Kṣattriya) desires to consume food (belonging to others)—even as Rudra seeks after these creatures, now with distrust, now with violence, now in striking them down—let him offer them: and assuredly he, who, knowing this offers them...obtains that food' (II: 3: 2: 9). The Tryambaka oblation is mentioned as being offered by the Asuras (*ŚB* II: 6: 2: 2). In these we have Rudra portrayed as a violent and revengeful god. Manyu (wrath) is identified with Rudra:

> when Prajāpati had become disjointed the deities departed from him. Only one god did not leave him...Manyu. Prajāpati cried and the tears settled on Manyu, who became the hundred-headed, thousand-eyed, hundred-quivered Rudra. And the other drops that fell spread over these worlds in countless numbers by the thousand (and) were called Rudras...Rudra with his bow strung and his arrow fitted to the string inspired fear, being in quest of food. The gods were afraid of him.

Prajāpati told the gods to give him food. This food is the Śatarudriya offering (*ŚB* IX: I: I: 7). Two *ŚB* passages describe Rudra as 'black' and as the same as 'Manyu' (wrath) with a 'devī' (goddess) on either side (IX: 1: 1: 6, XI: 6: 1: 12–13). All this brings out the cruel and sombre aspect of Rudra-Śiva. The *Rām.* describes Śiva as frequenting the cremation ground surrounded by Gaṇas and bhūtas (III: 31: 10, VI: 35: 3, 20) who are doubtless his ghost companions.

Śiva's dark and gruesome nature is evident in a rather unique episode: Jarāsandha offered human sacrifices (of Kṣattriya kings) to Śiva in order to propitiate him (*Mbh.* II: 20). This rather isolates Śiva as a god in the epic period, for human sacrifice had by then become obsolete, or if practised by the vulgar was discouraged by the official religion. No other epic god has any relish in human flesh. Śiva is fond of it and this trait, instead of being suppressed, is openly mentioned in hymns to him. This nauseating episode has a fitting conclusion: Kṛṣṇa chides Jarāsandha for it (*Mbh.* II: 22: 11). We can see the two attitudes of the two rising cults, Śaivism which was partially responsible for the origin of the Śākta cult, particularly in its Tantric aspect with its appetite for flesh-offerings, and Vaiṣṇavism with its abhorrence for meat and pronounced predilection for vegetarianism. Yudhiṣṭhira at the advice of Brahmins worshipped Śiva with caru (rice-and-butter oblation), sumanas (jasmines), modaka (sweetmeat), pāyasa (rice pudding), and māṃsa (meat) (*Mbh.* XIV: 64: 3, 4). The meat-offering was gradually becoming obsolete—so these instances are rather conspicuous. Śiva and his associate gods are almost invariably offered meat.

The demons and monsters prepare a kṛtyā (a sorcery ritual) through a sacrifice, and bid the demon Kṛtyā to fetch Duryodhana who had been downcast because of his discomfiture at the hands of the Gandharvas in Dvaita forest. When he appears the demons tell him that through their penance Śiva had created the upper part of Duryodhana's body out of the thunderbolt, but the lower half had been created by Devī out of flowers. As a result Duryodhana was tough and invulnerable in the upper half, but pretty and assailable in the lower. They make a false prophecy of ultimate victory to Duryodhana (*Mbh.* III: 240) much in the vein of the weird sisters' prophecy to Macbeth. In this episode Śiva is inalienably allied with witchcraft: he had fashioned the arch-villain of the epic almost as an accomplice of demons and monsters. This is a direct continuation of *AV* hymns on Kṛstyā which all have Rudra as their god.

Of the nocturnal massacre described in the Sauptikaparvan (bk X) of the *Mbh.* it is said that it should not be thought that Aśvatthāman was the author of this havoc, the real author was Śiva (*Mbh.* X: 18: 26). Again Śiva is associated with the night, treachery and cruelty and is conceived as the real power behind a gruesome scene. One remembers that it was Śiva who created Daṇḍa (punishment) and Asi (the scimitar) at Brahman's bidding, thus fulfilling his task as Kāla and Mahākāla, for, according to the apocalyptic passages in the *Purāṇas*, Śiva is the god in charge of the ultimate annihilation of all creation (Pralaya, or saṃhāra).

Śiva's appearance, too, is different from that of the traditional image of the gods, almost all of whom are dressed in impressive attire and decked out with precious gems. Śiva has no gems, and we have an anecdote to explain this lack. Both Bhṛgu and Śiva desired Umā, Himavat chose Śiva, Bhṛgu cursed him saying that he would never acquire precious gems (*Mbh.* XII: 329). This perhaps indicates the popular component god who wore no jewels. The epics call him Nīlakaṇṭha and the *Purāṇas* give us the story of the churning of the ocean and state that Śiva drank the venom that arose, and hence is blue-necked. His neck, or the neck of a component god of the Śiva-complex, must have had some peculiar mark for another anecdote makes him Śrīkaṇṭha, saying that he bears the mark of Viṣṇu's clutch on his throat (*Mbh.* XII: 330: 65), another mark of the conflict of cults. The blue neck may also indicate an amalgamation with cult of Kārttikeya whose mount was the blue-neck peacock.

Aṅgiras's son Saṃvarta was a follower of Śiva. He dressed and behaved like a lunatic. Describing Śiva's habitat and followers he reiterates their abominable traits. These belong to an apparently revolting set, with peculiar habits and practices. Aṅgiras, as we have noticed before, has dark associations, and is intimately connected with the Śiva-group through many links—chiefly through his connection with the ancestor-spirits. Saṃvarta's peculiar ways remind us of the Keśin-hymn in the *Ṛgveda*. Keśin holds fire and poison, heaven and earth... The Munis, wind-girt (i.e. naked), reddish brown (in complexion), clad in dirty (loin-cloth), follow the wind in speed. 'We are intoxicated with the vow of a Muni...we rush towards the winds...O ye men, look at our bodies...moving in the path (or gait) of the Apsarases, the Gandharvas, and the deer; Keśin knows desire and is a charming and fully-intoxicated friend. The inflexible wind churns and pounds the poison which Keśin, together with Rudra drank out of the chalice' (*ṚV* X: 136: 1–4, 6, 7). The exact import of this hymn may be obscure, but it can probably be safely assumed that it deals with a cult with Rudra as its deity and with certain dark and dangerous practices. This is perhaps the sole instance where the *ṚV* mentions Rudra's drinking poison—and it may have been imitated in a ritual symbol by the cult. We shall have occasion to return to this hymn later; for the present it illustrates

Śiva's association with poison-potion, and the Keśin of this hymn is perhaps the precursor of the lunatic-like followers of Śiva, as Saṃvarta describes them with dishevelled maenad-like hair. Significantly enough *AV* XI: 2, a hymn addressed to Bhava and Śarva, mentions Keśins and Keśinīs as companions of Śiva (verses 18 and 31).

Upamanyu's description of his vision of Śiva includes epithets which present a figure totally unvedic and almost unfamiliar. He calls Śiva Unmattaveṣapracchanna (clad in a lunatic's dress), ārdracarmāvṛta (girt with a wet hide), pretacārin (moving with or among ghosts), vāmana (dwarf), vyāghra (tiger), bhikṣu (beggar), durvāsas (ill-dressed). One remembers the irate epic sage Durvāsas who bore Śiva's epithet as well as some of his characteristics. This emphasis on 'a lunatic's dress' which is very noticeable in the later and spurious parts of the *Mbh.* and in the *Purāṇas* may not be accidental—it seems to be in the direct tradition of the Keśin hymn.

The *HV* gives us a naked, fasting Rudra, tawny in complexion, stooping and pleasing only to the fierce ones. It is significant that in the later epic and Purāṇic literature Rudra is a special friend and ally of demons and monsters—and helps many of them out of distress and difficulties. Gārgya, preceptor of the Vṛṣṇis and Andhakas, propitiated Śiva by eating iron-dust for long years. Later Śiva granted him the boon of a mighty son. The Yavana king heard of it, had Gārgya brought over and settled among cowherdesses where Gopalī, a nymph in disguise, conceived and delivered his son. All this happened at Śiva's command. This son was Kālayavana (*HV* II: 56). Again one notices the practices of austerity (eating of iron-dust) and self-mortification associated with the Śaiva cult.

The *Vāyu P* describes a Śiva who is old, pakvāmamāṃsalubdha (fond of cooked and raw flesh), huhuṃkārapriya (fond of howling noise), garbhamāṃ-saśṛgāla (greedy for foetus-flesh like a jackal) (XXX: 196–212). Tracing the history of the abominable side of Śiva's character one is struck with the fact that he progressively imbibes loathsome traits until there is something really revolting and obnoxious in his image.

Red is the colour of Rudra, and red is the colour of fire and blood. His reddish brown complexion is mentioned in *GGS* I: 8: 28; *Āp.DS.* II: 24: 23; *ŚŚS* IV: 19: 8; *HGS* I: 16: 8; and *PGS* III: 15: 7.

The *ṚV* describes Rudra as Paśupati in a more or less general way, although he is more closely connected with cattle. But the *AV* mentions cows, horses, goats and sheep, ravens and dogs (XI: 2: 9), also deer, ducks, birds and vultures (XI: 2: 24), dolphins, pythons and fish (XI: 2: 25). The

VS connects Rudra with snakes and monsters (XVI: 5) and also with the mole (ākhu). 'The mole is thine animal' (*ŚB* II: 6: 2: 2) and 'thine animal victim' (*ŚB* II: 6: 2: 10; *VS* III: 63). It is striking that the mole is offered to the earth (i.e. Nirṛti) in *VS* XXIV: 26, but the *Āp.ŚS* (VIII: 17: 1) again mentions it as Rudra's beast. This only proves that Nirṛti is one of Rudra's associate gods, discharging similar or supplementary functions. Later the mole is specifically allotted to Gaṇeśa, Śiva's Purāṇic and post-Purāṇic son, and Gaṇeśa still retains him. Śiva's two inseparable associates are Nandin and Bhṛṅgin; of these Nandin is described as monkey-shaped in the *Rām.* (VII: 16: 14). One passage states that Nandin is another form of Rudra (Śaṃkarasyāparā tanuh, *Rām.* VII: 16: 15). In this form Nandin is presumably thought of as a bull, his usual form, for the bull is Śiva's symbol and insignia throughout the epics. Gods, as we know, can be worshipped in their abstract, iconic, theriomorphic, kathenotheistic or incarnate forms. The bull is Rudra's theriomorphic form. Nandin is also a fierce, tawny, short-armed but very strong dwarf and the leader of Śiva's hosts. In Purāṇic literature and the Purāṇic interpolations of the *Mbh.*, Śiva is attended upon by ferocious and night-roving beasts. One remembers the Mohenjo Daro seal where he is surrounded by the tiger, the rhinoceros, the ox and the elephant. He is later credited with the killing of an elephant-demon and is depicted as dancing madly, girt with the fresh hide still dripping blood.

The *Śatarudrīya* references to 'the Rudras which in thousands lie around this (earth) in the quarters' and to 'the night rovers' may have obliquely meant ancestor-spirits who roamed about the earth in spectral bodies in Rudra's company. The *TB* has a passage mainly addressed to Rudra where it says, 'the seasons are the fathers, Homage to the fathers for sap, heat, for the svadhā call, for Manyu (wrath) and fierceness' (*TB* I: 3: 10: 5, 8). The *Mbh.* describes Rudra as living in a Karṇikāra garden on top of Mount Meru surrounded by ghosts (XII: 310).[1]

In Roman ancestor-cults, too, people believed that the spirits of the dead

[1] This figure of Siva with a night-roving horde brings to the mind the fierce Mexican figure of Huitzilopochtli, who also roamed about at night bringing harm and mischief. It is true that Huitzilopochtli resembles Agni more closely, but then Śiva and Agni have often been identified in Indian mythology. Like Śiva this Mexican god too is associated with the nether world, his shield of reeds anticipates Kārttikeya, born among the reeds. We shall notice many similarities between Mexican and Indian gods, due perhaps to a remote common stock which disseminated to the two lands carrying a common mythology. 'If any resemblances occur between the art forms or polity of its equal descendants in Asia and America, they are due to the influence of a remote common ancestry, and not to any later influx of Asiatic civilization to American shores' (Lewis Spence, *The myths of Mexico and Peru,* p. 3).

came out of the graves at night and roamed the streets of the city. The belief seems to be world-wide. In Indian mythologies Śiva's associates, the Rudras, hover in the mid-air; they are the lords of that sphere (*TB* III: 8: 18: 2).

In the *ŚB* we read: 'Now when he (the priest) cuts off the fore-portion he cuts out what is injured in the sacrifice, what belongs to Rudra' (I: 7: 4: 9). This strain of associating refuse or offals with Rudra is an undercurrent in the Rudra ritual from the Brāhmaṇical literature onwards. Thus we are told of Rudra: 'that god is (the recipient of) refuse (remains of an offering) and gavedhuka seeds are refuse' (*ŚB* V: 3: 3: 7). The gods from fear of Rudra allotted out of all the shares 'that good (share) which was incomplete or spoilt to him for ever' (*Mbh.* III: 114: 11). The *ĀGS* lays down that in the Śūlagava ceremony the cut-off portions are to be offered to Agni, Rudra, Śarva, Paśupati, Ugra, Aśani, Bhava, Mahādeva and Īśāna; in other words to the different forms of Śiva. The Śūlagava is so-called, says the *PGS*, because Rudra is the spit-bearer for the cattle. According to the *HGS* this ceremony is meant to propitiate Rudra so that plague among cattle may be averted. Hiraṇyakeśin says that the spit-ox or an image of Īśāna is led out to the southerly hut with the words: 'Come quickly to my offering, Śarva: Om!' Then the consort of the spit-ox (or an image of Miḍhūṣī) is led to the northerly part; and to the middle (space) between the two huts, is led a calf of those parents (or an image of Jayanta).

A sacrifice to Rudra if left unfinished can bring infinite harm (*Rām.* VII: 18: 16). It can extirpate a whole line of descendants as Marutta's priest tells him. Indrajit faced defeat and ruin because his sacrifice to Śiva was interrupted. Śiva's cult was associated with demons and monsters as we have noticed in the demons' Kṛtyā by which they had created Duryodhana, and later reassured him when he felt depressed.[1] Also the Tryambaka sacrifice is said to have been offered by the Asuras (*ŚB* II: 6: 2: 7). 'He offers with the central leaflet of a Palāśa leaf...' (*ŚB* II: 6: 2: 8). Palāśa literally means 'flesh-eating'—and we have noticed that Rudra is one of the few gods who delight in flesh-offering. Thus the leaf with indirect association with carnivorousness (perhaps through the blood-red Palāśa flowers) came to symbolize proper oblation for Rudra. Yama also was connected with the Palāśa tree. Rudra's preference for cattle and meat becomes obvious in passages like: 'Rudra is hankering after that (cow) which is killed here in this hall' (*ŚB* V: 3: 1: 10).

The Vedic Rudra imbibed characteristics from many kindred gods, and

[1] 'Savul' in Iranian mythology is one of the seven Daevas created by Angra Mainyu (*Sadar Bundahis* I: 5); each one of them is an enemy of one of the Amesha Spentas. Savul resembles Śarva in India.

absorbed many regional deities in his person. Some of these were non-Aryan and had a long tradition of cultic worship, and they brought the traits of those rituals. This explains to some extent the weird descriptions of Śiva, his followers and devotees. Śiva is night-roving, snake-shaped, Banyan-tree-shaped, holds a skull, is ithyphallic, lord or keeper of seeds, tiger and lord of cows and bullocks. Behind these terms we can see many gods—some of whom are totemic, others handed over from primitive tribal societies, some death-and-destruction gods, some chthonic and vegetation deities, reminiscences of tree and animal worship, ophiolatry, divinity-symbols of phallic rituals; animism, spiritism and many other forms of worship—all combined to produce this composite theophany. Each had a different code of rituals—but in the Śiva-syncretism each was given a place. At the same time it remains true that this complex Śiva is a mythological entity, nowhere a mere sum total of all his myriad aspects. Yet each of the component gods was locally worshipped, and only in theological works like the Śaiva *Purāṇas* or the interpolated portions of the *Mbh.* was Śiva presented in his multifarious functions or manifestations appearing in the totality of his characteristics. The result is that his figure becomes somewhat blurred, the distinctive features are submerged, a philosophy has to be spun about him and he has to become a supreme theistic god to combine all the different characteristics.

In the *Mbh.* a vision of innumerable Śivas is given to Upamanyu when he enumerates the 108 names of the god (XIII: 17). At the end of the hymn Upamanyu gives an extremely valuable piece of information; this revelation of the true identity of Śiva first dawned on Brahman's heart; he spoke of it to Śakra (Indra) who narrated it to Mṛtyu (Death) who again bestowed the knowledge to the Rudras and finally they deposited it with Taṇḍi. Brahman as the epic-Purāṇic supreme deity must be shown to be the originator of each cult in order to give it a halo of sanctity, antiquity and authority. Śakra is still remembered as the central deity of the *ṚV* and is an important deity in Buddhist literature, so to him must Brahman transmit it, for in that way the cult is pushed back to hoary antiquity. Then Death, an abstraction, becomes the next recipient—thus irrevocably connecting it with eschatological divinities and doctrines. The followers of Rudra (the Rudras) have to receive it from Death itself, and they are the divine followers, before the cult comes down to the earth. The first human being to receive the cult from the Rudras is Taṇḍi. This name is significant. From this word is derived the word Tāṇḍava (Śivas's dance) thus connecting the cult with dance.

All through the epic and Purāṇic literature Śiva is associated with dance and music. Both Upamanyu and Kṛṣṇa find his host singing and dancing in his abode at Kailāsa (*Mbh.* XIII: 14–15). The *Matsya P* lays down specifically that music and dancing should be performed before Śiva—thus indicating that it is part of a particular mode of Śiva worship. Śiva is greedy (or fond) of offerings of drama, is engaged in songs and music, is also fond of bells and garlands and has hundreds and thousands of bells about him (*Vāyu P* XXX: 196–212). His dance is described in the *Purāṇas*. He dances in mid-air, says the *KP* (divi nṛtyamāna, XVI: 193). This emphasis on dance, song, music, drama together with the popular practices of certain Śaiva cults (cf. the Gājan songs sung in Bengal in Śiva's name) and the ecstatic expressions which accompany them have a very remote parallel in the Greek Dionysiac cults.

This resemblance is so great and old that Megasthenes misinterpreted certain Śaiva practices and called them Dionysiac. According to Megasthenes there were Dionysiac festivals in honour of Śiva, in the Aśvaka district, north of the Kabul river, a region rich in vineyards. Arrian, too, calls Śiva Dionysus. In Ovid's *Metamorphoses* (ch. III) one reads of the vine God Liber or Bacchus who, like Śiva, had to fight his way into the accepted pantheon. Euripides records the conflict between Dionysus and Pentheus and gives an account of how Dionysus first ruined and then converted Cadmus (II. 42–54) which almost recalls the epic story of Dakṣayajña. One seems to understand the stiff opposition this wine god would face in a respectable pantheon, the feats he would be required to perform—the cruel havoc—before he converts worshippers of the 'high gods', and gains admittance. For, after all, a cult that allows intoxicating drinks to its followers, and indulgence in orgies as part of the necessary cultic ritual would be revolting to many who would sneer at its 'low' and popular base.

The Dionysiac festival had drinking as a necessary ritual. Pentheus scorned it for that reason. Śiva has all through been associated with intoxication and even in present-day India many Śaiva cults are connected with intoxication. The Osiris cult, or as the cult imported in Rome stood, had similar practices. Apuleius in his *Golden Ass* remarks on the mysteries of 'the invincible Osiris' (ch. XIX) and 'the nocturnal orgies of the Great God' (ch. XIX). In Rome in Apuleius' time this god had assumed a very impressive status: 'The God Osiris, the most powerful of all gods, the highest among the greatest, the greatest among the highest, the ruler of the greatest' (*ibid.* p. 293). Franz Cumont in his *After-life in Roman paganism* writes of 'the Bacchic communions in which wine was a drink of immortality' (p. 55). Thus both in the Graeco-Roman world and in India we have a wine-god whose cult included drunken orgies. When viewed in this context, Dakṣa's indignation at the mention of Rudra and his hosts is better understood. The *Matsya P*, describing the apocalyptic vision of the period of Kalki's incarnation, says that towns would then be full of spikes in market places, Śiva's spikes in crossroads, and even women's hair will be like spikes (*Matsya P* XLVII: 258). One remembers the Bacchic Maenads with their spiky hair described by Euripides and Ovid. Both the Bacchants and the followers of Śiva danced and sang and behaved like lunatics in a fashion that was revolting to the common man's sense of decency. We remember Śiva's epithet Unmattaveṣapracchanna: clad in the wild dress of a lunatic. Śiva's Purāṇic son Gaṇapati—a mythological projection of Śiva himself—is called Unmattavināyaka (leader of the lunatics) and Nṛtyagaṇapati (leader of the dancing host) in the *Agni Purāṇa*.

Keith in his introduction to the translation of the *AB* says of the admixture of the cult of the Aryan Rudra with that of the non-Aryan: 'We know that the *Aitareya Brāhmaṇa* treats Rudra as the great deity *par excellence*. It is true that the stories of Rudra in the *Aitareya* and *Kauṣītaki* are drawn bodily and are not necessary parts of the whole texts, but that is merely to say that the new religion was pervading the old traditional worship' (p. 37). Thus as early as the Ṛgvedic *Brāhmaṇas* (*Aitareya* and *Kauṣītaki*) the amalgamation of the Aryan and non-Aryan Rudras had started, but the non-Aryan Rudra cult was alien so that the process of assimilation was slow. The Śiva whom Dakṣa insulted was not the Vedic Rudra, but the supreme deity of the monotheistic Pāśupatas. Saṃvarta describing the Pāśupatas says that they were naked and wild. He says that Śiva's headquarters were in Vārāṇasī, and Jaigīṣavya was blessed by Śiva at Vārāṇasī (*Mbh.* XIII: 18).

Another trait of this cult was the preference for the cremation ground which at once connects it with death cults and the life of the disenchanted and detached mendicant.

Rudra's malevolent personality may have drawn some of its dreadness from the notion that 'Agni-Rudra bars the passage to the sun or beyond, to the soul, on the score of the evil a man has done, until he can satisfy the god of his merit which deserves heaven' (*JUB* I: 5). This Agni-Rudra resembles the Egyptian Osiris and like him is considered a dread god. The rituals to Rudra reflect this attitude to him. According to *GGS* at the end of a sacrifice a handful of straw is offered to propitiate him. The *ĀpDS* says that at the end of a meal the left-over is offered in the north to Śiva.

The *ŚŚS* lays down that Śiva should be offered the bloody entrails of the victim for he attacks men and beasts with disease and death. The *HGS* (I: 16: 8) and the *PGS* (III: 15: 7) state that in a place infested with snakes one should offer to Rudra who lives among snakes; at a mound of manure, to Rudra Paśupati; in a river, to Rudra who lives in the waters; at cross-roads and sacred trees, to Rudra of the roads. The Piśācas are presumably the darker damned dead as opposed to the 'Pitarah' who were the blessed dead. 'They are specifically of the ethnic type of theriomorphic ghouls of the dead' (Keith, *Religion and philosophy of the Vedas and Upanisads*, p. 238). The crossway is the scene of various magic rites, and the spirits of the dead were supposed to dwell there. Rudra is to be invoked when a man is on a path, at cross-roads, crossing a river, at a mountain, a forest, a burial ground and a stable (*HGS* I: 16: 8; *ĀpGS* IX: 3; *PGS* III: 15: 7; *ĀGS* IV: 8: 40). The offerings to Rudra were somewhat unholy. So were the offerings to the dead and the chthonian deities in Greece; for these rice-cakes to the fathers were not eaten but merely smelt. Oblations to Rudra were made in a part from which the village cannot be seen, as if even visual contact with such an offering could harm the villagers. The idea behind these cautions seems to be that when Rudra accepts an offering his host, i.e. the souls of the departed, also came to partake of it with him, and their contact was best avoided by the living for the *AV* says that evil spirits dwell with the spirits of the dead (XVIII: 2: 28).

One is reminded of the setting up of the fire altar for Nirṛti's bricks are also laid without actual contact. All rituals to the dead are performed in a manner reverse to that to the rites to the fathers. Thus at the Piṇḍapitṛyajña the sacred thread is worn over the right shoulder, and unlike the sacrifices to the gods which are performed in the bright fortnight and usually in the forenoon, these ceremonies are held on the Amāvasyā (the night of the new moon) and in the afternoon.

In the Mahāpitṛyajña (the great ancestor sacrifice), the cakes in a basket of Palāśa leaves are tied to a bamboo, placed on a tree and Rudra is asked to go away beyond the Mūjavat; the offering is made to Rudra the wearer of the quiver. Fever is also banished to the distant peoples of Gāndhāra and Mūjavats. And the Mūjavats were said to be Rudra's habitat.

The cross-roads are the scene of magic rites and are connected with a chain of superstitions all over the world. The departed souls were believed to live there. Rudra is to be invoked, among other places, at the cross-roads. The *ŚB* also lays down: 'He offers on a road—for on roads the great god roves; he offers on a cross-road, for the cross-road, indeed, is known to be his (Rudra's) favourite haunt' (II: 6: 2: 7). The *MS* tells us that the fire-brand is to be given to the Rudras, whose abode is in the cross-road (I: 10: 20). Comparing this with a Roman parallel we arrive at the conclusion that the cross-road–death-god association is very old; for Rose in his *Ancient Roman religion* writes of 'a compitum, or cross-roads' where a chapel to the Lares compitales was set up (p. 38). The *Gṛhyasūtras* mention 'a Rudra of the cross-way'. Symbolically the cross-road might have meant death—where the roads of life and death cross, and it was quite fitting that the living should perform their rite to the dead there.

The animal which symbolized Rudra most frequently was the bull, and this again is not an isolated phenomenon peculiar to India, but has parallels all over the world. In the Gṛhya ritual of the spit-ox (śūlagavahoma) water and food are offered to a bull, presumably a symbol of Rudra (since the cow and the calf stand for Mīḍhuṣī, his consort and Jayanta, his son). On the Ujjain coins Śiva is represented theriomorphically as a bull. The Ṛgvedic hymns mention Rudra generally as Paśupati without assigning any specific animal to him, but the ritual associates the bull or the ox or the cow with him. It is, however, in the epics that he is inalienably connected with the bull. The *Rām.* knows him as the god with the bull emblem (Vṛṣabhāṅka, II: 25: 36). Nandin, his attendant, mostly conceived in bull shape is called another form of Śiva (śaṃkarasyāparā tanuh, *Rām.* VII: 16: 15; *Matsya P* XLV: 3). In the Tripuradahana episode we see Śiva seated on a bull (*Mbh.* VIII: 24), and this is in sharp contrast to his Ṛgvedic prototype for there he was seated on a throne (gartasad, *ṚV* II: 33: 11). The bull is invariably mentioned in Rudra's context from the *Śatarudrīya* (*TS* and *VS*) onwards. Of Śiva himself we hear that he was Dharma in the shape of a bull (*Matsya P* XCIII: 66).

The closest parallels of Śiva are Dionysus in Greece and Osiris in Egypt and both are intimately associated with the bull. Of Zeus and Dionysus, C. Kerényi says in *The gods of the Greeks* that 'the more characteristic animals of these two gods were the serpent and the bull both of which appeared on the Mediterranean earlier than the horse' (p. 251). 'In Minoan times the bull, dove and snake had already achieved a special prominence in religious associations' (R. F. Willets, *Cretan cults and festivals*, p. 71). We shall see later that all of these creatures are intimately bound up with the Śiva group as emblems. In the *Viṣṇudharmottara Purāṇa* Śiva's mount is said to be the four-footed bull (III: 47: 1–18). As early as the Mohenjo Daro seal depicting the proto-Paśupati, Śiva is connected with, among other animals, the bull. Of Teshub the weather-god of Hatti, Professor E. O. James writes that he is shown as 'wearing a horned mitre, clad in a kilt and carrying a mace or club in his right hand, leading the male gods in procession'. This is Teshub as found in the rock sanctuary of Yazilikaya. Incidentally, Teshub's mace may have been the 'laguḍa' with which perhaps was connected the particular Pāśupata cult which called its deity 'Lagulīśa' or 'Lakulīśa'. This Lakuli sect thrived in north-west India and Bihar and is actually a subsect of the Pāśupata Śaivas. It flourished in the early years of the second century A.D. under a teacher Lakuli in Lāṭa (modern Kaṭhiawar), which was under the Saka Ksatrapas of Ujjain, therefore under Scythian patronage. Through the Sakas, it may have imbibed the reminiscence of the mace-bearing god from abroad. In another work Professor James describes Min: 'The ithyphallic statue of Min was carried in procession on poles by priests beneath a canopy preceded by a white bull, the sacred animal of Min' (*Prehistoric religion*, p. 186).

The Greek Dionysus is described by Euripides in *The Bacchae* as 'the bull-horned god' (920–3). After Pentheus imprisoned Dionysus and went inside the stable he found a bull instead of a god (1: 618, 1016 ff.). R. F. Willets in his *Cretan cults and festivals* says that the most important offering to Dionysus was a bull. In the Indus civilization the bull played a major role. 'Seals also show instances of bull and buffalo sacrifice...It is probable, therefore, that the Harappan religion embodied the worship of a horned god...attended by a ritual that included the...sacrifice of bulls' (D. H. Gordon, *The prehistoric background of Indian culture*, p. 68).[1]

The bull is a very old symbol of strength, vegetation and reproduction and has always been connected with the pantheon of the primitive agrarian communities. In Egypt Apis was 'the sacred bull worshipped in Memphis. When the sacred animal died a successor was chosen' (article on 'Apis', *Oxford classical dictionary*). In Herodotus we get a fuller account of the Apis bull, there were certain signs by which 'he' was chosen. 'They hold that Bulls belong to Epaphus and therefore test them thus...If there be as much as one black hair on them...the bull is deemed not clean...If it be pure in all these respects the priest marks it' (Herodotus, *The Histories*, bk. II, 38). Herodotus describes the bull sacrifice in which the head of the Epaphus bull is loaded with curses and taken away. Now over this

[1] Egypt offers a parallel god Osiris, represented theriomorphically as a bull. But representing gods by animals was of great antiquity in Egypt. There was practically no totemism in early Egypt although the raw materials existed out of which some form of totemism might have evolved. 'Nearly all the local gods, each of which was revived in a town or district, were represented in animal form. Many of these divinities were believed to be incarnated in some special individual beast, such as the Apis bull which became so well-known in later centuries' (W. F. Albright, *From the Stone Age to Christianity*, p. 179).

vast stretch of existences the god who reigned supreme was Osiris—symbolized by the bull, hence the supreme importance attached to the sacrifice of the bull to Osiris for the sake of the deceased. In present-day India there is a custom of dedicating a spotless bull to Śiva and also a bull released in honour of the deceased ancestor, a custom whose date of origin is unknown. The bull is depicted as a symbol on the reverse side of a coin of an Indo-Scythic king bearing the name in Greek and Kharosthi script—Tauros and Usabha (i.e. ṛṣabha) standing for Śiva. Osiris stood for the redemption of the departed soul on the other side of death, and on earth the Apis bull was his symbol. Śiva discharging similar functions in Indian mythology was theriomorphically conceived as a bull—also called Dharma. Analysing these mythological symbols we are left in no doubt that a god's mount and associate invariably symbolize some of his salient characteristics. The bull device also appears on the coins of the White Hun ruler Mihiragula with the legend 'Jayatu Vṛṣah' in the script of the period (J. N. Banerji, 'Śiva and his emblems on early Indian coins', *IHQ*, 1940), and this is clear identification of the god and his mount.

The other creature closely connected with Śiva is the snake. Early instances of this relationship occur in *HGS* I: 168; *GGS* I: 8: 28; *ŚŚS* IV: 19: 8; *ĀDS* II: 24: 23; *PGS* III: 15: 7. In all these scriptures we are told that offerings to Rudra are to be deposited in places infested with snakes. The Sūtra literature was taking its present shape in a period when the epics were already in the making. In the *Mbh.* we have the account of Kṛṣṇa and Arjuna approaching Śiva for a weapon that would be potent against the Kauravas in the battle. Śiva directs them to the pond where his weapons lie hidden. Kṛṣṇa and Arjuna chant the *Śatarudrīya* and are confronted with nāgas who were later transformed into the desired weapons (*Mbh.* VII: 57). The story is suggestive: nāgas or serpents are Śiva's weapons in disguise, and Śiva is connected with them. Early in the *Śatarudrīya* he has been connected with many dark and dread objects, including serpents, but in the epic-Purāṇic periods this connection becomes more essential and significant. We are told that when Śiva had come to be initiated for the destruction of the three cities, Uśanas plucked his matted locks, which were transformed into serpents; choked by these his neck became blue (*Mbh.* XII: 329: 14, 15). When Upamanyu enumerates the 108 names of Śiva he calls him serpent-form (*Mbh.* XIII: 17). Śiva is also frequently described as 'with his neck entwined with a serpent as with a sacred thread' (nāgopovītin).

The earth spirit is commonly thought of as assuming snake-form, perhaps because snakes come out of holes of the earth where corpses are deposited. That the souls of the ancestors live on in the snake is a world-wide idea. The *ĀGS* lays down a rule: blood should be offered to snakes (IV: 8: 27); significantly enough Dionysus is addressed as 'a snake with darting heads' (Euripides, *The Bacchae*, 1018 ff.).

The snake as an inseparable element in the Śiva cult has a long history and many parallels. Ahirbudhnya seems to form a link in the chain. Originally he belonged to the aerial region and was dangerous in character. In some aspects he resembled Agni. Ahirbudhnya and Aja Ekapād had their allotted shares in Gṛhya rituals. In the later epic-Purāṇic literature Ahirbudhnya was counted among the eleven Rudras.

Literally the word seems to mean the serpent (or the dragon of the deep). Cognates of Ophis and Puthon may have been the two component parts of the word. Or *Budhnya* meaning base, root, may yield the meaning of 'serpent of the root or deep'. It is curious that such a concept is widespread throughout the world. Popular mythology in India has it that the nāga Vāsuki holds the earth on its many-hooded head, and when he is tired and shifts the burden from one hood to another, we have an earthquake. Vāsuki dwells in Pātāla, the nether region, and is thus a serpent of the deep. Joseph Campbell writing of the immovable spot of the universe says: 'Beneath this spot is the earth-supporting head of the cosmic serpent, the dragon symbolical of the waters of the abyss which are the divine life-creative energy and substance of the demi-urge, the world-generative aspect of immortal being' (*The hero with a thousand faces*, p. 41).

In the *ṚV* we have the Ahi sometimes identified with Vṛtra. The *Avesta* has its parallel in Azi Dahaka. 'It seems, however, reasonably certain that the Ahi of the *ṚV* and the Azi of the *Zend Avesta* represent chiefs of widely spread sun-worshipping people, whose emblem was the many-headed serpent' (C. F. Oldham, *The sun and the serpent*, p. 41). It does not seem likely that Indra fought any sun-worshipping people, rather he and his solar assistants seem to have sought to extirpate a rival cult of worshippers of a chthonic deity of which the serpent is now proved to be a world-wide emblem.

The *Mbh.* in its opening chapters gives us an account of Janamejaya's snake sacrifice by which the king sought to exterminate the menace of not only snakes, but the snake cult. The failure recorded in the escape of individual serpents who became friendly with the Aryan gods may be a mythical expression of the historical compromise with the snake cult. Snake-worship was the religion of many primitive peoples and still persists in the aboriginal areas. Cults like that of Manasā in Bengal show the emergence of very old popular deities and the compromise seems to be evident when Manasā is described as Śiva's daughter. Vṛtra, however, may well have been the leader of a snake-worshipping tribe with his totemic emblem of an Ahi-Ophis.

Dr J. N. Banerji in his *The development of Hindu iconography* describes a figure on the reverse of Agnimitra's coins. A deity is shown standing between two pillars, with five flames for his hair, his right hand raised and the left on his hip; an object which looks like a sword or a club seems to project from his hip. Mme Bazin Foucher identified him with the Ādināga, the presiding deity of Ahicchatra of Pāñcāla. In Rajgir there are the remains of a snake temple called Maniar Math, where in the dilapidated bottom chamber was enshrined 'Maṇi Nāga'. This also seems to bear testimony to the snake cult, which must have been prevalent in that region.

'The serpent of the deep' has its parallel in many mythologies. In the Edda Loki is said to have begotten in the Giantess Angrboda Fenrir, Jormungand (= Midgard the serpent) and Hel. 'Later the All-Father flung the serpent into the deep sea which surrounds the whole world and it grew so large that it now lies in the middle of the ocean round the earth, biting its own tail' (*Prose Edda*, p. 56).

The apocalyptic vision of the Bible too corresponds to the fate of Midgard the serpent: 'And I saw an angel come down from heaven having the key of the bottomless pit and a great chain in his hand. And he laid hold on the dragon, that old serpent, which is the Devil and Satan, and bound him a thousand years...' (Revelation xx. 1, 2).

The *Avesta* has the same end for its serpent-fiend Azi Dahaka, who, because he could not be killed, was bound to Damavand by Thraetaona, there to lie in bonds till the end of the world, when he shall be let loose and later killed by Keresaspa. This Azi besides meaning Ahi (= serpent) had two snake-heads upon his shoulders, and was the most beautiful fiend created by Angra Mainyu.

Returning to the snake associations of Rudra we can turn to a remark by E. J. Chalmers Werner: 'The evil dragons are those introduced by the Buddhists who applied the current dragon legends to the nāgas inhabiting the mountains. These mountain nāgas...are harmful, those inhabiting lakes and rivers friendly and helpful' (*Myths and legends of China*, p. 208). It is significant that, whether in Muñjavat or Himavat, Śiva's abode is on a mountain and the snakes associated with him are venomous snakes, for Śiva is Nīlakaṇṭha, blue-necked, from the venom which rose from the churning of the ocean and which stuck to his throat. The snakes on his body are symbols of poison like much else about him that stands for the evil and poisonous.

It is significant that unlike other Aryan gods Śiva should be connected with poison; at the time of the churning of the ocean the good things that arose were distributed among other gods, and at their request Śiva drank the poison. This is in direct tradition of the Keśin hymn and his being deprived of oblation in Dakṣa's or the gods' sacrifice. The poisonous snakes around his body, his frequenting the cremation ground, are also illustrations to the point.

In Bali and Java we saw that the tendency was to consider the mountain as being the real home of the dead kings, though these could manifest locally through their images...the dead king was a god merely in his temple mountain. More probably he was considered to be manifest there in so far as he was united with that part or specification of the ancestor god which was concentrated in the centre of the microcosm that the capital was thought to be. (H. G. Q. Wales, *The mountain of God*, pp. 166–7.)

It is indeed significant that of all the Hindu pantheon, it is Śiva, the earth-god, who bears the epithet Giriśa, mountain lord (*ibid.* p. 88).

The snake cult in the primitive world is a much explored subject.

In very ancient times the serpent was the cult-sign or religious emblem of a tribe inhabiting a site in the (Egyptian) Delta. (Leonard Cottrell, *The anvil of civilization*, p. 41.)

In ancient India snakes were the Dravidian emblem of death and fertility, and in some archaeological specimens of the liṅga five-headed snakes formed a canopy of the liṅga. In iconography and literature Śiva is inseparably associated with snake and poison. Manasā the snake-goddess of modern Bengal is Śiva's daughter, perhaps because she took over the snake cult attached to her father. In the ritual of Manasā water-jars symbolize the goddess. We remember Demeter, the chthonic goddess of the ancient Greeks, who carried a jar round which was entwined a snake (statue in Pergamam Museum, Berlin). It is also striking that in medieval Bengali ballad poetry (like the Manasāmaṅgala) she also has to fight her way into a pantheon which is reluctant to grant her admission.

The *ṚV* first mentions Mūjavat hill as the abode of Rudra and Soma. The *YV*, too, mentions Mūjavat hill (*VS* III: 70). as his particular habitat. He is also called Giricara (mountain-rover), Giriśaya (lying in a mountain, *VS* XVI: 29, 44), also Giritra (protector of the mountain, XVI: 1).

In the Mahāpitṛyajña (great sacrifice to the ancestors) Rudra is asked to go away beyond the Mūjavats; Fever (born of Rudra's anger in the *Mbh.*) is also banished to Mūjavat and Gāndhāra. The *Rām.* however says Himavat is the father-in-law of Śaṃkara (*Rām.* IV: 9: 41). The *Mbh.* mentions Muñjapṛṣṭha (on the Muñja hill) as Śiva's habitat (*Mbh.* XII: 122: 4). In another place it says that he lived on the peak of Mt Meru (*Mbh.* XII: 310), and yet other passages mention Kailāsa as his abode. In later literature Kailāsa came to be his permanent address.

Mūjavat or Muñja as Rudra-Śiva's habitat is rather significant, for it is also the abode of Soma. It is clear that in early Vedic literature Soma was merely the plant out of which an exhilarating beverage was prepared—the drink of immortality, which has its parallel in many literatures. It is as such that Soma is praised in the *ṚV*, especially in bk. IX which is addressed exclusively to Soma. But there are certain ambiguous passages in which Soma may mean both the plant and the moon. The process through which Soma later became the moon is not clearly recognizable in our present state of knowledge. *ṚV* IX: 97: 9 addresses Soma and says that it is green by day and shines (clearly by night). Again *ṚV* IX: 97: 39 says that with the help of Soma the forefathers knew the cave where the Paṇis had hidden the stolen cows. Now in both these passages Soma as the exhilarating drink and the moon yields a meaning. Soma the plant has fibres, aṃśu, and the word also means 'ray'; thus Soma, itself, becomes ambiguous. Quite ordinary prayers for wealth and prosperity are addressed to Soma. Dadhyañc drank Soma, which enabled him to discover the secret place where the Paṇis had hidden the cows (*ṚV* IX: 108: 4); here the meaning is unequivocal. But when it says: Soma knows the way to the stolen cows (*ṚV* IX: 89: 3) it seems to mean the 'moonbeams' which revealed the path. Soma like other Vedic gods worked miracles: gave sight to blind Dīrghatamas, feet to the lame Parāvṛj, made Kakṣīvat tremble when he went to procure the Soma creeper, made Agni shiver when he hid in water (*ṚV* X: 26: 11, X: 61: 16). Soma himself is protected by the Vārhatas (*ṚV* X: 85: 4), they are therefore called Somapālas. Together with Indra Soma is the author of cosmic actions (*ṚV* VI: 72: 1, 2). Soma desired a wife, Savitṛ contemplated marrying his daughter Sūryā to Soma, but the Aśvins passed the test and married her (*ṚV* X: 85). Intoxicated with Soma Indra killed Śambara, Turvaśa and Yadu (*ṚV* IX: 61: 2). Soma himself is credited with demon-slaughter.

Soma's first home is in the sky—an eagle fetched it from heaven; his second home is on mountains (*ṚV* IX: 82: 3, IX: 48: 3: 4). Like many other gods Soma, too, is ubiquitous; his region is lofty and deep; his abode is in the upper region, on the earth and also on hills and in plants (*ṚV* I: 91: 3–4).

Soma however is connected with the lunar and chthonic gods by certain traits very early in Vedic literature. Thus the invocation to Soma of the fathers connects him with the Śiva-Yama complex (*ṚV* VIII: 72: 4). Again Soma is supplicated to prevent Nirṛti from injuring the worshipper (*ṚV* VI: 75: 2). Soma should deliver the devotee's enemy to the serpent or to the lap of Nirṛti (*ṚV* VII: 104: 9). Quite frequently Soma is addressed as Rakṣohan, demon-killer, an epithet of Yama and Agni, and through these links is connected with the Śiva complex. An eloquent prayer is addressed to Soma: 'Put me in the resplendent region where the sun is placed and where there is no death or decay, where Vivasvat's son is king, where men enter the sun, where wide rivers flow, make me immortal there. Where there is delight and satisfaction, in that place of the root (bradhna), where svadhā is, where there are joys and delights, where desires are satisfied (make me immortal there)' (*ṚV* IX: 113: 7–11). It is an early hymn (i.e before bk. X) and eschatological concepts are not clearly defined here. Consequently we have Devayāna and Pitṛyāṇa concepts both present in a confused order. Later, Soma is associated with Pitṛyanā alone. Vivasvat's son (Yama) and 'Svadhā' connect him with the Śiva-complex and the whole prayer reads like a transference of the intoxicated condition of ultimate bliss to the next world; it is significant that Soma is supplicated for bliss in the next world.

One Ṛgvedic passage says that Soma grows by the banks of the river, or the lake Saryāṇavat behind Kurukṣetra (*ṚV* IX: 65: 22); his father is Parjanya (*ṚV* IX: 82: 3) in other words rain water helps it grow. Soma is a plant as is evident in passages like, 'the plants whose king is Soma' (*TS* IV: 2: 6), or 'the gods slew Soma, it became putrified, Vāyu sweetened it for the gods' (*TS* VI: 4: 7). Soma is king (presumably of the plants, but later of the Brahmins. 'Soma the king is connected with plants, with plants they heal whom they heal, therefore, through the purchase of Soma the king whatsoever medicines there are, all these are resolved in the Agniṣṭoma' (*AB* III: 40). (The *GB* also says that Soma is the King of plants, *GBU* I: 17.) 'The gods said to Varuṇa, "with thee as helper we will slay Soma, the king"' (*TS* VI: 4: 8).

Like Rudra the offering to (or price of) Soma is a cow. 'Soma found a thousand (cows), Indra discovered it after him. Yama approached them and said to them, "May I, too, have a share in it"...Yama saw in one of the (cows) strength. He said, "This one has the strength of the thousand, this be mine, the rest yours".

They said..."Let us each have a portion"...They put her in the waters saying, "Come out for Soma". She came out in the shape of a red-brown cow of one year old, together with thirty-three others. Therefore let one buy the Soma with a red-brown cow of one year old' (*TS* VII: 1: 6).

In the sacrificial ritual a red-brown calf is the price of Soma; but the significant point is the colour red-brown which at once connects the Soma-ritual with the Rudra-ritual, for Rudra is red-brown, his oblation is red-brown too. 'The Soma-seller is not known, for the Soma seller is evil' (*AB* III: 12). Thus inauspiciousness, a common trait of this group, is shared by Soma too. Like Rudra's Jalāṣabheṣaja, and Varuṇa's power to heal or inflict diseases, Soma also is connected with ailments and drugs. In later literature he is both the moon and the plant and is associated with the plant world in both these aspects.

Śiva is invariably connected with the north, and so is Soma. 'That (north) indeed is the quarter of that god (Rudra)' (*ŚB* II: 6: 2: 5; *AB* I: II: 1: 8). Again of the north it says, 'for in that region lies the house of that god (Rudra)' (*ŚB* IX: 1: 1: 10). Soma, too, belongs to the north, of which quarter he, like Rudra, is the guardian (*AV* III: 27: 4). Like Varuṇa he is the guardian of the western quarter too (*AV* XII: 3: 9). Thus he is connected with two gods of this group.

The *KB* invokes Soma as five-faced thus anticipating the five faces of Śiva (*KB. Up.* II: 9); Prajāpati-Brahman, king, eagle, fire and an undefined fifth, with these five mouths he devours kings, subjects, birds, men and creatures respectively.

When we come to the epics, Soma has a distinct personality. He is good-looking and is undoubtedly the moon (*Rām.* I: 1: 6, I: 20, I: 17: 14). He has a wife Rohiṇī, and a son Budha (*Rām.* III: 3: 11, V: 31: 5, VI: 86: 4, VII: 88: 9). Sometimes his wife is called Dīkṣā (*Rām.* V: 31: 5). No trace of the plant is found either in the *Rām.* or in the *Mbh.* He is remembered only as the moon, or the spirit of the moon conceived anthropomorphically. In the *HV* we have an anecdote of the son of Atri. As a foetus he was borne by the ten quarters who, unable to bear, let him fall. Then Brahman put him in his chariot and went round the earth twenty-seven times. Of the nectar-rays which fell from him to the earth came the herbs and creepers. He practised penance; and Brahman made him king of the creepers. Afterwards he married the twenty-seven daughters of Dakṣa—the stars Aśvinī, Bharaṇī, etc. In the course of time he became arrogant, and eloped with Bṛhaspati's wife Tārā and would not return her to Bṛhaspati even when gods and sages begged him to do so. He fought the gods, and was defeated. Tārā returned to her husband pregnant with Soma's son Budha. For the sin of favouring Rohiṇī over the other wives Soma was cursed by Dakṣa with consumption and faced progressive emaciation. Eventually Atri cured him of it, and he shone brightly ever after. In this anecdote Soma is solely the moon in the sky. The twenty-seven days and twenty-seven wives all refer to the lunar month. And herbs and creepers are connected with the moon all over the world. His consumption and cure are mythological expression for the waxing and waning, and it is only as the moon that he is depicted in later literature. Commanded by Bṛhaspati Soma helps Varuṇa in the gods' battle against the demons (*HV* XLVI: 2–10), and is thus allied to the group of Rudra and his associate-gods. In order to bring into line the entire Soma mythologem from the *ṚV* onwards, the *HV* says that Soma was crowned the king of Brahmins, creepers, luminaries, of sacrifice and penance (*HV* IV: 2).

Mūjavat or Muñja is the mythical home of both Rudra and Soma. On this hill grew a plant which had inebriating properties. Soma, the same as Avestan Haoma, is described in its reaction on gods and men. Indra who is particularly addicted to the Soma drink is frequently described in his intoxicated condition. This Soma plant has been identified with *Ephadra Pachylada* by Sir Aurel Stein, who describes it as 'a tall shrub growing in the regions of western Himalayas and western Tibet', and says that this is the same plant mentioned as Haoma in the *Avesta*, and Huma in modern Persian (On the Ephadra, Huma and Soma plant, *Bulletin of the School of Oriental Studies*, vol. VI, 1931, pp. 501–14).

Intoxication is closely associated with Rudra-Śiva throughout his cultic career. His 'gaṇas' are described as behaving like lunatics, i.e. they are constantly in the state of intoxication. Even in present-day India the Śaiva cults (and the Tantrics as a later offshoot of Buddhist-Śaiva-Śākta cults) indulge in intoxicating drinks, dopes and opiates as part of their cultic ritual. Śiva's specific drug has changed with time (it is canabis indica at present), but he and his followers—on the popular plane of the cult—are not sober. One remembers Dionysus and the Bacchants and the cult which grew around wine. The Maenads also behaved like lunatics. Once Soma is said to have intended to oppress the Brahmins, and sin accrued to him (*ŚB* IV: 1: 2: 4). Such passages indicate the rise of the Brahmin caste, and Soma is called their king.

The eschatological importance of Soma lies in the path of reincarnation (Pitṛyāṇa), which is said to be through the moon.

The moon is common to both (Devayāna and Pitṛyāṇa) since the moon was often regarded as the home of the dead and in the *Upaniṣads* its waxing and waning are brought into connection with the movements of the souls: hence the path is the smoke, the night, the dark half of the month, the dark half of the year, the world of the Fathers in lieu of the year, the ether not the sun, the moon which is now not a stage of transit to the world of Brahman, but the highest place attained by the souls. The arrival of the souls fills up the moon. (Keith, *Rel. and Phil. of the Vedas and the Upaniṣ ads*, p. 576).

Various savage tribes...associate the heavenly bodies, especially the moon with the resurrection of the dead...Among the Greeks of the most ancient period Hecate was at one and the same time the goddess of the moon, the summoner of ghosts and the queen of the infernal realm...The belief was widely spread that the spirits of the dead went to inhabit the moon...We find it in India as well as in Manichaism which arose in Mesopotamia in the third century, but which admitted many ancient traditions into its doctrine...The association established in Syro-Punic religions between the moon and the idea of immortality is marked by the abundance in Africa of funeral monuments bearing the symbol of the crescent. (Franz Cumont, *After life in Roman paganism*, pp. 91–3.)

'A relief at Copenhagen shows the bust of a little girl within a large crescent surrounded by seven stars, thus indicating that she has risen towards the moon, the abode of the blessed souls' (*ibid.* p. 139). The crescent symbol of the lunar god appears on the head of many gods who control death and after-life, both in Egypt and Babylonia. Thus the Egyptian Hathor Isis and Ishtar, Iranian Anahita, Mesopotamian Sin, Indian Rudra (or Paśupati in the Mohenjo Daro seal), Greek Dionysus are all represented as horned. Śiva's Purāṇic and post-Purāṇic iconographic figures all show him with the crescent; he later came to be known as Candraśekhara (with the moon on his head). In American Indian mythology the moon is the first of the dead, resembling Yama of Indian mythology. The moon in all mythologies is associated with death, the next life, vegetation and the plant world—and in all these capacities the moon's function is essentially bound up with that of Yama and Śiva. Therefore Soma, when he was later relegated to a place in the Śiva-scheme, became an associate and later an ornament of Śiva, and the kindred gods share this trait in common. Soma, the plant, grew on the mountain (Mūjavat or Muñja), Śiva is specifically a mountain-dwelling god, and the later-Purāṇic Śiva is always represented with Soma the moon on his forehead. The facts are too pressing and too frequently mentioned to be accidental.

CHAPTER 8

RUDRA-ŚIVA'S CONSORT: THE MOTHER-GODDESS

In Kailāsa the epic Śiva lives in the mountains with his consort Durgā. The first mention we have of one of her many names (i.e Umā) is in the *Kenopaniṣad* (III: 12) where we are told that the ultimate mystery was revealed to her when other gods failed to reach the final revelation. Vedic literature does not offer a concrete prototype of this goddess. The *VS* tells us of Ambikā, Rudra's wife; Ambikā in the *TS* is given a share in the Triyambaka Homa with the words: 'This is your share, O Rudra, together with your sister Ambikā' (I: 8: 6 ff.), *TB* I: 6: 19: 4 has a commentary: 'Śarat or Ambikā is his sister; by her he harms whom he harms (śaradvā asyāmbikā svasā tayā vā eṣa hinasti yaṃ hinasti)'. Passages like these are significant for they reveal two things about Ambikā: first, that she was originally Rudra's sister, and, second, that she had cruel and malevolent associations. *TĀ* X: 18 tells us of an unnamed wife of Rudra; *TĀ* X: 1 of Durgā devī Vairocanī (Virocana's daughter); *TĀ* X: 1: 7 of Durgī, Kātyāyanī and Kanyākumārī; *KU* III: 12 of Umā Haimavatī. *TĀ* X: 18 has a parallel Dravidian text which makes Rudra Umāpati (Umā's husband). *MU* I: 2: 4 mentions Kālī and Karālī among the seven tongues of fire. The *ŚGS* II: 15: 14 and also *Manu* III: 89 mention Bhadrakālī. These texts, as is shown from their vagueness, are inconclusive even if taken in their totality; the epic-Purāṇic Durgā did not develop from any one of them, but from all of them and also from many other elements. The *Rām.* describes Umā as the daughter of Himavat and Menā (I: 37: 16) and also as Rudra's wife (I: 37: 20, 21). The Umā-Śiva myth is repeated in a contracted form in *Rām.* I: 38: 3. Throughout the epic the designation of Pārvatī as Śiva's wife follows. When Ilā begged Śiva for the recovery of his male form, Śiva had first refused, then Ilā begged Umā and she relented, but said she could only grant half a boon: Ilā would be man and woman alternately (*Rām.* VII: 87: 22–9). Kuvera saw her when she was with Śiva, she cursed him and he lost his left eye. *Rām.* VII: 12: 22–4. In the *Mbh.* she is said to have covered Śiva's eyes playfully and a third eye appeared on his forehead. This eye was fierce and burned the Himālaya;

Umā was sorry for her father so Śiva restored it to shape. He said the eye had appeared because creation would be enveloped in darkness if he did not look upon it (*Mbh.* XIII: 140). In a strikingly exceptional passage Gaurī is said to be Varuṇa's wife (*Mbh.* XII: 146). Umā is made to sermonize on the duties of the virtuous woman in a spurious passage (*Mbh.* XIII: 146). Once Uśanas offended Śiva's friend Kuvera and Śiva swallowed him up. Uśanas begged Śiva to show him a way out. At Śiva's command Uśanas came out through Śiva's organ: Śiva was about to kill him, but Pārvatī took pity and called him a son (*Mbh.* XII: 278). A later chapter describes her in Śiva's company on the peak of Mt Meru, in a Karṇikāra grove being surrounded by Śiva's host (*Mbh.* XII: 310). Pārvatī had been wooed by both Bhṛgu and Śiva; but Himavat, her father, chose Śiva (*Mbh.* XII: 330: 65). The *Mbh.* XIII tells us that at Śiva's marriage the gods asked Śiva not to deposit his seed in her. He agreed; but she in wrath cursed the gods with sonlessness (*Mbh.* XIII: 83).

In *HV* III: 88 we have the sory of Pārvatī's penance for obtaining Śiva as a husband—the story of the *Kumārasambhava*. Her position as Śiva's wife is accepted in the Sūtra literature, where oblations are offered to her as his wife. In the Śūlagava ritual she is symbolized by a cow, oblations are offered to her under the name Mīḍhuṣī. But it is at the very end of the Vedic period that Umā is recognized as Śiva's wife. On the Huviska coin Ommo undoubtedly refers to Pārvatī, Ommo could stand for both Umā and Ambā, and Pārvatī is invoked by both names. Ommo is shown as holding a lotus and cornucopia, symbols of beauty and prosperity and is thus the prototype of the later Purāṇic Lakṣmī, another manifestation of the mother-goddess.

The earliest texts which mention Umā do not state that she was the wife of Śiva. The relationship probably grew out of a number of factors which were operative in the syncretism of Śiva himself. First, he was a mountain-god, dwelling either in the Mūjavat or on the Himavat and she is first mentioned as Umā Haimavatī, a daughter of Himavat; but later she also becomes Vindhyavāsinī, dwelling on the Vindhya hills. Secondly, all over the world there was the cult of a holy family—composed of 'mother and son' at first, but later (when the man's contribution in the procreative process was recognized) of father, mother and son. In India this family consisted of Śiva, Pārvatī and Kārttikeya. Later the family grew to include Gaṇeśa, Lakṣmī and Sarasvatī, who constitute the group now worshipped in India in the autumn. In Egypt Osiris, Isis and Harpocrates composed this group. The Christian trinity of Father, Son and Holy Ghost may be the same group; for the Holy Ghost is symbolized by the dove and the dove is an invariable symbol of the mother-goddess all over the world. 'In Christian uncanonical phantasies...the Holy Ghost has feminine significance' (C. G. Jung, *Psychology of the unconscious*, p. 217). The earthly replica of the Holy Family was Joseph, Mary and Jesus. In the hey-day of the Indra cult there were Indra-Śacī and Jayanta, and in that of the Viṣṇu cult there were Viṣṇu-Lakṣmī and Madana. In the Nāga cult, too, we have a holy family—the Jaratkaru couple with their son Āstīka. Thus Pārvatī, a mountain-goddess, was essential to the cult of the Holy Family, which is a very old cult.

The earliest antecedents of Pārvatī connect her with Aditi and Nirṛti—the heaven mother and the earth mother respectively, as also the benign and malign aspects of the primitive mother-goddess, and throughout her entire career she retained this duality, the emphasis on the benign or malign traits varying regionally.

Aditi is an abstraction needed for the solar gods, the Ādityas, who were the chief deities in the Aryan pantheon. To the primitive mind the mother was the real channel through which the infant is born, the father playing only a subsidiary role and was not considered indispensable. The conquering hordes of the Aryans with their superior military equipment, their superior looks, language and pantheon, moving in their victorious course projected their existence and career to a group of solar divinities, gods of light and might—unhindered in their course. Hence they must also have a mother of a similar character. Physically Aditi can only be conceived as the point in the eastern sky where the light and the sun are born. Aditi is a vague and amorphous personality, but she has certain definite attributes which she shares with her sons, the Ādityas. She is the bestower of happiness (*ṚV* v: 51: 11, vii: 35: 9), well-being (*ṚV* ii: 29: 3, v: 51: 14, vi: 51: 11), gifts (*ṚV* v: 49: 3) and longevity (*ṚV* i: 94: 16). She protects her protégés (*ṚV* iv: 54: 6, iv: 55: 1, vi: 75: 12), answers their prayers (*ṚV* iii: 54: 20, v: 46: 6), pardons sinners (*ṚV* ii: 27: 14) and delivers supplicants from distress (*ṚV* viii: 25: 10, x: 36: 3, x: 39: 11). She is the guardian of an inviolable 'right order' (*ṚV* vii: 66: 6), and is an opposite number of Nirṛti. Aditi as the mother of the solar gods disappears after the *ṚV*, although she persists as a mother-goddess in the epics and *Purāṇas* where her husband is Kaśyapa. In the *ṚV* Aditi was closely associated with Dyaus (*ṚV* v: 59: 8, x: 63: 3), but the male partner was not considered essential for procreation, so a husband was not thought necessary. In the epics and *Purāṇas* her character and function are much more attenuated, and her personality becomes unconvincing.

The malign traits in her character are derived from her chthonic prototype Nirṛti, who as we have seen has her counterpart all over the world. In this aspect she takes over from Dyaus's earliest consort Pṛthivī, and as her characteristics unfold with time they bring about remarkable changes.

The chthonic part has another concomitant: the concept of Umā as the corn-goddess. In the first phase of the mother-goddess there was but one goddess who received the seed (i.e the corpse), conceived and delivered life out of herself (the crops), without any apparent help of a male agency. When the *ṚV* burial hymn says to the dead 'go to thy mother', it means the mother earth, the visible source of all life. To this goddess we perhaps owe the tumuli at Lauriya Nandangarh, where a gold statuette of a mother-goddess was found. This is no other than the earth herself.

The emphasis on the generative and procreative aspect became clearly formulated in a corn-goddess. In this aspect Umā or Durgā is the mother of the world. Later the connotation expanded to include the vegetation world which became an important aspect of the mother-goddess and in the *Mārkaṇḍeya Purāṇa* she says, 'I shall support the world with life-sustaining vegetables, which shall grow out of my own body during heavy rains' (*Devī Section*, *Matsya P* XCII: 42–3). Thus she is known as Śākambharī (bearing vegatables, the vulgate *Mbh.* VI: 23), and in her ritual (in present-day Bengal) is used the Navapatrikā—leaves of nine edible vegetables. Lakṣmī is invoked in the *Khila* (supplementary) *Sūktas* (section II, hymn no. 6); it is a hymn in twenty-nine stanzas. She is also mentioned in the *ŚB* XI: 4: 3: 1, and also in the *ŚGS* II: 14: 10 ff. Lakṣmī becomes the tutelary goddess of a primarily rice-growing agricultural population. She is addressed as Karīṣiṇī (the cow-dung goddess, and cow-dung is manure), her sons are Kardama (mud) and Ciklīta (moisture)—things essentially linked up with agriculture. Zimmer says of the Khilasūkta:

> a late and apocryphal hymn attached to the Aryan corpus of the *ṚV*; this mother of the world was actually supreme in India long before the arrival of the conquerors from the north. The conclusion of the Indus civilization together with its goddess queen must have resulted from the arrival of the strictly patriarchal warrior herdsmen and the installation of their patriarchal gods...Nevertheless, in the hearts of the native population, her supremacy was maintained. (H. Zimmer, *Myths, symbols, etc.*, p. 99.)

Iconographically Śrī is represented in Bharhut and Sanchi, where inscriptions in Brāhmī characters introduce her as Śirima Devatā. Dr S. K. Chatterji finds her parallels in Indonesia and Indo-China and says of the name, 'Here we have Śrī indicated by her two common names: Śrī, modified in Prakrit as Siri+Mā' (S. K. Chatterji, 'A Brahmanical deity in Indo-China and Indonesia', *J. N. Banerji*, p. 3). These figures belong to the Maurya period. There are also Gupta representations of this goddess on coins, holding, beside the cornucopia, lotuses (symbols of beauty) in her hand; thus the Indian Lakṣmī combines beauty with plenty and becomes the counterpart both of the Demeter-Persephone and Aphrodite. Demeter is black in Phigalia which signifies her dark associations and has a parallel in Kālī. The green Demeter, symbolizing the lush green corn, has a parallel in Śyāmā, while the yellow Demeter symbolic of the ripe corn recalls the Buddhist goddess Hārītī. Durgā is sometimes called Jagadgaurī, for 'gaura' besides meaning yellow is the name of several plants—like Priyaṅgu, Mañjiṣṭhā, Śvetadūrvā, Mallikā, Tulasī, Suvarṇakadalī and Ākāśamāṃsī. These connect the Gaurī aspect of Durgā (as represented in her projection in Lakṣmī) with the vegetation-goddess.

Lakṣmī has a synonym, Śrī, derived from the same root from which the Latin Ceres, the corn-goddess, is derived. Lakṣmī is especially connected with the rice-growing areas. Dr S. K. Chatterji has written on the Indo-Chinese and Indonesian parallels of Śrī, called Dewi Siri, and Vasudhārā, and Vasudhārā is one of the two wives of Kuvera the god of plenty according to the Mahāyāna pantheon. Dr Chatterji writing on these goddesses in the Far East has connected them with their Indian counterpart Śri or Lakṣmī (*ibid.*). These are goddesses of plenty and beauty. The *Amarakoṣa* lexicon giving synonyms of Lakṣmī mentions Mā. Now Mā is another name of the mother-goddess at Comana and she corresponds to Lakṣmī and Durgā. Almost everywhere the figures corresponding to Lakṣmī hold a sheaf of corn, or the Greek cornucopia in her hand, as Dr Chatterji found in the case of the Indo-Chinese figure.

It is significant that in present-day India in many auspicious rituals a mark (symbolic representations of a human figure) is made on the wall—and this mark is called Vasudhārā; perhaps this is how Lakṣmī with her Buddhist name has returned to bless an auspicious ceremony. The driving out of Alakṣmī (non-prosperity), one form of Nirṛti, before the Lakṣmī ritual proper begins may actually be reminiscent of the casting out of the non-Aryans' prosperity before the Aryan goddess's ritual started.

BGS gives various names of this goddess: Jyeṣṭhā (elder), Kapilapatnī (Kapila's wife), Kumbhī (pitcher-goddess), Jyāyā (elder), Hastimukhā (elephant-faced), Vighnapārṣadā (associated with obstacles) and Nirṛti (Shama Sastri's edn. pp. 294–6). Lions are attached to her chariot and tigers follow her. Manuals of iconography like *Aṃsumadbhedāgama*, *Supra-*

bhedāgama, *Viṣṇudharmottara-Purāṇa* and *Purṇakaraṇāgama* say that Jyesthā is two-armed, long-nosed (cf. Hastimukhā = elephant-faced, i.e. long-nosed), with sagging lips, long and pendulous breasts and belly and holding a lotus in her hand. The *Suprabhedāgama* says that she is is seated on a donkey and is Kali's wife. It is significant that she is called Jyeṣṭhā and Jyāyā, both names signifying her being the older and oldest. Older than whom? Obviously the goddess who supplanted her, the Lakṣmī of the Aryans; for following the iconographic descriptions we find that she is presented both as old and emaciated, as well as ugly and repulsive. But that she is the opposite number to the Aryan Lakṣmī is evident from her holding a lotus in her hand, in everything else she corresponds closely to Nirṛti which is actually one of her names. This non-Aryan goddess who symbolized non-Aryan prosperity had to be disgraced and chased out before her Aryan substitute could be safely enthroned. This drama of the Aryans' cultural conquest is enacted during the first part of the Lakṣmī-pūjā even today. Demeter and Ceres were the Greek and Latin counterparts of Lakṣmī—they symbolize fertility and crops in their persons as also in their daughter Persephone or Proserpine, who is seized forcibly and brought to the nether world by Hades or Pluto (cf. Pluto means plenty).

Thus Lakṣmī is one aspect of the Universal Mother, i.e. Durgā. In later mythology Durgā becomes Lakṣmī's mother, assuming the role of Demeter or Ceres herself, and Lakṣmī is relegated to that of Persephone or Proserpine. This later Lakṣmī becomes the wife of Viṣṇu. Lakṣmī and Nārāyaṇa have a son—Madana or Kāma. In this Lakṣmī answers to the concept of Aphrodite, whom she also resembles in having risen from the sea. Madana is an Indian counterpart of Eros or Cupid, that is love born of beauty. Aphrodite or Śri or Lakṣmī is the goddess of beauty who holds the lotus in her hand, for the lotus has ever symbolized beauty to the Indian mind.

A faint similarity to Uṣas the pretty maid of the *ṚV* may be traced in Lakṣmī. This may not be a conscious development, for Uṣas had long been abandoned mythologically before Lakṣmī was conceived. But there may be unconscious absorption of the Uṣas who was Svasar's (= the sun's) wife in the *ṚV*, for Lakṣmī too is a solar god's (Viṣṇu's) wife, and like Uṣas she too is beautiful, clothed in red, ever fresh and a benefactor of humanity.

The later Purāṇic Durgā has another daughter Sarasvatī. The *Vedas* know her as a river, invoked together with Ilā and Bhāratī, and also as Vāc (*Logos*) as she is called in the *Brāhmaṇas*. The river Sarasvatī may have been the river along whose banks Vedic and Brāhmaṇical culture had disseminated and this associated her inseparably with learning, until she actually became the goddess of learning in the Purāṇic age. Bhāratī also means Sarasvatī as does Vāc. The identity of the river Sarasvatī (as also of the goddess) has been much disputed. Many scholars identify her with the river Haraquaiti in Afghanistan, and it is quite probable that the Vedic Aryans named the small river in Madhyadeśa after the Afghanistani Haraquaiti. Sarasvatī is the mānasa-kanyā (born of the thought) of Brahman. In this she is like Athene or Minerva born of Zeus' or Jupiter's head.

In early Indian mythology we are told quite frequently that Brahman committed incest with his daughter; otherwise she is mostly conceived of as a virgin, like Athene or Minerva. She is thus an external projection of one aspect of the *prima dea*, for we know that a son or daughter, a brother or sister, even a husband or wife of a god or goddess is often the externalization of a latent characteristic through the mythological image-making faculty and that they also indicate the rise of separate cults which retain a degree of independence inside the total complex of a hierophany. Thus in mythological language Sarasvatī, the daughter of Durgā, is the Kumārī (virgin) aspect of Durgā herself. And this virgin goddess has many parallels. Athena was worshipped at the temple 'Parthenon', and the word emphasizes her virginity. The virgin became the mother in many mythologies (the Blessed Virgin Mary being the best example), while in other mythologies she remained a virgin. Durgā is called Kumārī, the pilgrimage at Cape Comorin is called Kanyā Kumārikā and Kanyākumārī (a virgin damsel) is a name of Durgā. She is still worshipped as a virgin (cf. Kumārīpūjā). The epic Durgā is frequently invoked in terms which do not connect her with a husband. Thus she is Vāsudeva's sister, Kṛṣṇā, Kumārī, Brahmacāriṇī (observing the nun's vow) (vulgate *Mbh.* IV: 6); again Gopendrasyānujā (younger sister to the cowherd-king), Kumārī (*Mbh.* VI: 23: 3–16). Her lunar prototype is found in Artemis or Diana. Nānā also is a virgin mother. Durgā as a mother-goddess has certain characteristics which she shares with her prototypes all over the world.

Durgā, as we have noticed, came to be Śiva's spouse. One of the factors contributing to this was that, as with Śiva, her residence is in the mountain. In the *Mountain of God*, H. G. Q. Wales says that sacred mountains are the centre of the earth and the source of its life-giving energies. Dr Heinz Mode in his article 'The Harappan Culture and the West' writes: 'in Crete and the Aegean the Minoan goddess assumed the guise of the mountain mother, the mistress of wild beasts with outstretched or uplifted arms, often holding or encircled by snakes, clad in a skirt with flounces, wearing a high crown. Near her are such symbols as the double axe, sacral horns, a pillar and her lions.' Another parallel is found in the Phrygian primordial goddess Kybele: 'In Greece the mother goddess was identified by Homer and Hesiod with Rhea, the wife of Kronos. From the fifth century B.C., she was associated with the Phrygian *magna mater* Kybele, while in Crete her affinities had been with the Minoan goddess in her threefold aspects as an earth–mountain–mother and a chthonic divinity guarding the dead' (E. O. James, *The ancient gods*, p. 298). 'From Middle Minoan times she was worshipped as the Mistress of Trees and Mountains and Lady of the Wild beasts' (E. O. James, *Prehistoric religion*, pp. 63, 164–5).

Durgā the cardinal mother-goddess of India is a mountain dweller; from this centre of the earth she draws her chthonic energy which she symbolizes in her person. She took a long time developing into her present dimensions. In her primitive stratum we have the fusion of a mountain-goddess of the Himālaya and the Vindhya region which explains her names Haimavatī and Vindhyavāsinī, together with a goddess worshipped by the nomadic Ābhīras as R. P. Chanda in his book (*The Indo-Aryan races*) suggests.

The Ābhīra goddess in Durgā is characterized by fierce and terrible traits, for Durgā is a dread killer of demons. All her prototypes in earlier mythologies share this trait with her. Artemis or Diana is a hunter. Earlier still we have prototypes in the Middle East who are huntresses. Among the Hatra finds recorded by Dr Shinji Fukai (in his article on 'The artifacts of Hatra and Bactrian art') we have report of a goddess who stands in the centre like an Athenian goddess in the attire of a soldier. She has a helmet on and holds a spear in her right hand. On the side of the shield there is a moon pattern. On the short coat on her breast there is Medusa's mask with a sinister look. On the front part of the pedestal is a lion. 'Originally Allat was a moon-goddess worshipped among the Arabs ever since the establishment of the Islamic empire.' With the eastern thrust of Hellenism Allat became Athena. But in the Hatra image we clearly have a prototype of Mahiṣamardinī Durgā, the warrior and the huntress. Many of the attendant features are common to both this Allat and Durgā: the warlike attire, the lunar association (cf. the moon pattern), the snake-motif (cf. the Medusa mask), and the lion. 'The great goddess, i.e the Minoan goddess, is represented in a rich variety of associations. She is a huntress and a goddess of sports; she is armed and she presides over ritual dances; she has female and male attendants. She has dominion over mountain, earth, sky and sea; over life and death; she is household goddess, vegetation goddess, Mother and Maid' (R. F. Willets, *Cretan cults and festivals*, p. 75).

Artemis shoots the arrow, the Middle Eastern goddess wields the battle-axe, Durgā kills with her scimitar. This dread aspect is symbolized in Nirṛti's figure, which is personified later in Cāmuṇḍā and Mahākālī. In the Nalanda seal no. 9RIA she is represented as a skeleton-goddess, holding in her four hands a skull, a sword, a scythe and a trident. She is shown seated on a corpse. Her weapons and her seat connect her with fierceness and killing. Of Isis we read that she was 'a goddess...of chase, and hunt and war' (*Hastings ency. of rel. and ethics*, vol. II). Durgā's counterparts in the Middle East include Ardvī. J. Przyluski in his article 'The "Great Goddess" in India and Iran', *IHQ* (vol. X, no. 3, 1934, pp. 423) writes: 'It seems that the cult of the Great Goddess was common to the Hellenic, Iranian and Semitic populations under the names of Ardvī, Anāhitā, Nanai and Artemis. In Vedic India the whip, like the rods in Italy and Greece, was the attribute of the Goddess mother and...perhaps there was scourging in her honour.' In the earliest Indian prototype of Durgā we perhaps have a hint of ritual flagellation in honour of the goddess: *AV* IX: 9 calls Aditi Madhukaśā.

Durgā is Caṇḍī in the *Mārkaṇḍeya Purāṇa* (*Devīmāhātmya* section) and Candī means irate, dread. She is the killer of the buffalo-demon. At Mamallapuram there is a seventh-century sculpture of Durgā smiting the buffalo-demon and there is an eighth-century sculpture on the same theme in Java. This indicates that the demon-killing feat was an established myth by the sixth century. We remember Bāṇabhaṭṭa's *Caṇḍīśataka* (seventh century) on this theme. As the life-giving mother it is quite in keeping that she should kill the buffalo, the symbol of Yama and death (just as her consort Śiva is Mṛtyuñjaya—victorious over death and Nīlakaṇṭha, symbolically holding death, i.e. poison in his throat). At the same time behind this image we can almost see a savage goddess, riding a lion, out on a hunting expedition, who kills a mighty snorting buffalo. Besides, these female deities when they rose to power, ascending the loftier seats in the Olympus, had to rise the same way as the traditional gods whose places they usurped: they had to have demon-killing feats to their credit, just as Indra or Agni had; Śiva too had to destroy Tripura or slay Andhaka or kill the elephant-demon before he could become great. The path of blood was thus the only path for a mother-goddess who had the ambition to usurp the place of honour and come into the limelight. Bāṇabhaṭṭa's *Caṇḍīśataka* is a litany to this demon-slaying mother-goddess, composed at a time when the non-Aryan mother-goddess was gaining predominance over the Vedic male pantheon.

Durgā also demanded flesh as part of her ritual. She is invoked as Sīdhumāṃsapaśupriyā (fond of wine, meat and animals, presumably slaughtered). She is Śiva's consort and he is 'greedy of cooked and raw flesh' and 'greedy like a jackal for foetus-flesh'. The *HV* describes Umā as a goddess of the outcasts who bring her oblations of cocks, goats, sheep, lions and tigers, because she is 'fond of wine and meat as oblations' (II: 3: 12). She is addressed as Śakunī (a hen-vulture), Pūtanā (the putrid monstress). Her ritual is observed by brigands who worship her with vessels filled with wine and meat (*HV* II: 22: 53–4). In Sophocles' (Loeb edn. vol. II) Artemis Ortygian is described as 'slayer of deer, with fiery brand, in either hand' (p. 275).

Artemis, the Greek counterpart of Durgā, the huntress, was worshipped with human blood (cf. Euripides, *Iphigenia in Tauris*, Phoenix edn. pp. 383–5).

Artemis was well-known for her cruelty. She was armed with a bow, quiver and arrows and sent plagues and sudden death among men, women and animals. Orion and Niobe's children were among her victims. The Brauronian Artemis was worshipped at Athens and Sparta, and Spartan boys were scourged at her blood-covered altar. In this ritual flagellation she resembles the cruel *primae deae* like Kybele, whose devotees, the Gallis, beat themselves with whips and whose male consort Attis was Papas to the Phrygians; and Aditi who perhaps enjoyed such horrible scenes as seems indicated by the reference to the Madhukaśā in the *AV*.

Gilbert Slater in *The Dravidian element in Indian culture* writes of Gangamma or Mariamman or Mariyattal (the Durgā of the Dravidians) that 'she rejoices in blood and demands whole-sale sacrifice of male animals...but most of all the male buffalo' (p. 92). In demanding the blood of males she resembles Artemis for whom 'boys' had to bleed, and in demanding buffalo-blood she resembles Durgā who killed the buffalo-demon and in whose honour buffaloes are killed ritually.

Durgā is herself described as a keen fighter both in the *Mbh.* and the *HV*; she is also to be worshipped by those who enjoy fighting. Besides killing the buffalo-demon she also killed two other demons—Śumbha and Niśumbha. Like Śiva she is Triśūlinī, bearing a trident (*HV*: II: 107: 11). She makes gifts of weapons: to Śambara she gave a club which he used against Pradyumna. Though auspicious, she is said to have appeared as inauspicious for the sake of demon-killing (*HV* II: 3: 12). This Vindhya-vāsinī and Kāntarvāsinī goddess (dweller in the Vindhya range or in the wilderness) is obviously a primitive goddess worshipped, as the *HV* says, by brigands and also by outcastes, living beyond the pale of Aryan Brāhmaṇical society. The *Mbh.* describes her as being worshipped by the Śabaras, Pulindas and barbarians. Their ritual was bloody and consequently Durgā's ritual came to be associated with blood-offerings.[1]

The closest parallel is the Taurobolium ritual in decadent Rome, where an animal's blood poured on to a devotee standing in a pit was supposed to cleanse him—the whole ritual was in honour of the Phrygian *magna mater* Kybele. In the present-day India a buffalo is beheaded in honour of Durgā (on the fourth day of the five-day ceremony), also to celebrate ritually her own feat of killing the buffalo. Spiritual explanations have ennobled the ritual by claiming that the buffalo symbolizes evil and darkness hence the worshipper is purged of his dross vicariously by partaking in the sin-and-expiation rite. But in actual practice the katharsis is really reached, the purgation-emotion rises to a frenzied pitch *only* when the worshippers smear themselves with the warm blood and dance in an orgy. This resembles the Kybele ritual very closely; in both we have a mother-goddess worshipped with blood, and the worshipper's body smeared with the blood of the bull or the buffalo as the case may be. When he is filled with emotional ecstasy he feels cleansed of his sin. Durgā as a huntress and a cruel goddess demanding bloody offerings resembles Bellona, the Roman goddess of war, the wife of Mars. Like the devotees of Kālī (an offshoot of the *prima dea*, thus another manifestation of Durgā) in the Tantric rituals, her priests, the Bellonarii wounded their own arms and legs when they offered sacrifices to her.

Durgā's mount is the lion; she is called Siṃhavāhinī. The lion, as we shall see later, is a symbol of solar bearings. Durgā, when her cult rose to high honour, came to imbibe certain solar characteristics so that she could be the supreme being to her votaries combining both solar and lunar traits. In the *Mbh.* she is connected with Kṛṣṇa and Nārāyaṇa, both solar gods. The lion is a symbol of kingship, authority and supremacy. Besides, many other goddesses corresponding to Durgā are seated on lions, and in a period of very far-reaching syncretism Durgā naturally imbibed many of their characteristics. Ishtar, in the later stage of her development, was associated with the lion, because she absorbed traits of goddesses who rode

[1] This becomes all the more striking when we remember that the Vedic sacrificial animal was choked to death, blood was not shed. 'At Hagia Triada...the emblems suggest the cult of the Goddess in a funerary setting with her priestesses the officiants in a sacrificial oblation on behalf of the deceased...perhaps with the blood flowing down to the earth through the bottomless vessels as an offering to Mother Earth as the ultimate source of rebirth' (E. O. James, *Prehistoric religion*, pp. 164–5).

on lions. Mother-goddess characteristics attached only after other mother-goddesses like Nintil and Damkina were absorbed by her. The lion, and the dove also, belong to her. The reason perhaps lies in the fact that in regions where the cultic fusion took place, the lion stood for supremacy, and the composite mother-goddess who subdued her regional rivals, leaving them dim as she herself came into the limelight, had to have this symbol of supremacy. Britomartis or Diktynnan was accompanied by lions. Kybele, the dread Phrygian goddess who had chthonic associations like Durgā, and like her was the mountain-mother, mistress of the trees, lady of the wild beasts and guardian of the dead, also rides in a lion-drawn chariot. Rhea, too, is seated on a lion throne. We remember Ariadne riding in a lion-chariot accompanied by her husband when he returned to Europe after victorious conquests in Ethiopia and India. The Cretan mother-goddess had lions by her. On the Middle Minoan seals she has a lioness by her; on the clay sealings in the central court of the Palace of Knossos she is represented between two lions. In Persia the lion-motif was the royal insignia. It was borrowed by the Mauryas; Asoka's lion-capital and the columns at Sarnath were borrowed from the Achamaenid decoration-motifs, the work of Achamaenid craftsmen whose predecessors created the Persepolitan columns (as Sir Mortimer Wheeler suggests in his *Early India and Pakistan*). In Persia the lion stood for sovereignty as it did in Egypt and the Middle Eastern countries, and when Durgā mounts the lion in the Purāṇic age she does so to establish her sovereignty over minor theophanies of the mother-goddess.

The bull is Śiva's emblem and consequently the cow is Umā's. But this also is not a matter of a simple corollary, for the mother-goddess is represented by the cow all over the world. In the Brāhmaṇa literature the cow is the symbol of Śiva's consort who is called Mīḍhuṣī in the Śūlagava sacrifice. Bhagavatī means both Umā and the cow.

R. F. Willets writes: 'At Knossos we have definite grounds for the view that there had once existed a ritual marriage of sungod and moon-goddess in bovine form' (*Cretan cults and festivals*, p. 253). Zeus chased Hera, they assumed the forms of bull and cow. She bore Epaphos the bull. The cow is also a lunar symbol—the pair of horns resembled the crescent. 'As the cow became a symbol of the moon, so the bull became a symbol of fertility' (R. F. Willets, *op. cit.* p. 100). In ancient Egypt the slaughter of the cow was forbidden. We read in Herodotus: 'They may not sacrifice cows, these are sacred to Isis, for the images of Isis are in woman's form horned like an ox as the Greeks picture Io' (*The Histories*, II: 41).

Of Io we read in Aeschylus' *Prometheus Bound* (Phoenix edn.) in the stage direction after l. 560: 'Enter Io, a girl wearing horns like an ox.' Hathor was the star-bespangled celestial cow. Neith, 'although she was represented with bows and arrows, she also appeared as a Cow-goddess with the head of a lioness' (E. O. James, *The ancient gods*, pp. 82, 84). In Neith the lion and the cow motifs combined, just as they did in the Indian Durgā. In Crete the earth mother was worshipped on horned altars. 'The classical moon-goddess Selene, the daughter of the Sun with whom Pasiphae is connected by her name, was figured as a cow-goddess with horns and in the legend the bull was the universal god of the sky and fertility' (R. F. Willets, *op. cit.* p. 295).

Thus Durgā's symbol, the cow, is not accidental nor is it peculiar to India. It is a necessary concomitant of Śiva's association with the bull, but it is also a lunar and vegetation symbol, which is shared by parallel gods all over the world.

'In Crete there were three outstanding forms of the mother-goddess—the snake-goddess, the dove-goddess and the lady of the wild creatures' (Donald A. Mackenzie, *Myths of Crete and Prehellenic Europe*, p. 59). 'Doves symbolized fertility and immortality while ravens were associated with destruction and death' (*ibid.* p. 291). In Greece a dove is said to have inaugurated the oracle of Dodona, a mother-goddess. The later *Purāṇas* describe how Śiva meditated at Kuśasthalī and became as emaciated as a dove and was called Kapoteśvara. Another account has it that Śiva and Pārvatī assumed dove shapes for the sake of dalliance and hence were called Kapoteśvara and Kapoteśvarī. Pārvatī is called Kokamukhā in Arjuna's litany to her in *Mbh.* bk. 6 and *koka* means a pigeon. We remember Dharma assumed the shape of a dove in the Śivi-Auśīnara legend, and Dharma is one aspect of Śiva-and-Yama. A son of Yama's is called Kapota. Thus we have the Yama–Śiva–Pārvatī group inalienably connected with the dove, as their symbol. Kapota is Nirṛti's symbol too.

Mother-goddess figurines found in Harappa, Mohenjo Daro, Lothal, Crete (Mycenae) and Tepe Hissar are all accompanied by the dove as well as by snakes. The Minoan mother-goddess has the dove, the bull, the lion and mythical creatures by her. Diodorus described Aphrodite as 'the Lady of the Dove'.[1]

[1] The Bible has the dove as a symbol of the Holy Spirit, the surrogate for the mother-goddess; for the Hebrew-dominated patriarchal mythology would not directly admit a mother-goddess. In Genesis i. 2 we read: 'And the earth was without form and void; and darkness was upon the face of the deep. And the spirit of God moved upon the face of the waters.' After that God said, 'Let there be light' and there was light. After the

In India the seven tongues of fire (Kālī, Karālī, Monojavā, Sulohitā, Sudhūmravarṇā, Sphuliṅginī and Viśvaruci) are mentioned in *MU* 1: 2: 4. These are all mother-goddess images, and the first two became so prominent that in Tantric times they became separate goddesses—dread aspects of Durgā, because Kālī also is Śiva's spouse. The dove is both a fertility symbol—and as such an invariable associate of the mother-goddess—and a symbol of love and the sexual impulse, the basic urge for procreation. Hence the dove was sacred to Aphrodite. The dove is a quiet bird, building its nest away from crowded spots, and in this it resembles lovers. In the Songs of Solomon the lover is frequently addressed as and compared with the dove.

It is clear from certain of the monuments, from the nomenclature of later deities, and from mythology, that the goddess (i.e the Great Minoan Goddess) was a moon-goddess as well as (or rather by virtue of being) a fertility goddess. The worship of the moon in its various phases is closely associated with time-keeping which is indispensable to any moderately advanced agricultural community... sacrificial animals offered by women to the moon universally belong to small species...chiefly the hare, goat, pig, the dove especially in Semitic women's cults. (R. F. Willets, *op. cit.* p. 78.)

This probably accounts for the frequency of the dove imagery in the Songs of Solomon in connection with love. The song itself is regarded as a primitive ritual song, with the prime progenitors invoking each other as lovers.

The *Vedas* have seen in Kāma, Eros, the primeval impulse for creation which existed before existence, i.e. which preceded creation as cause precedes effect. In this it resembles 'the spirit of God' in Genesis. 'It is the semen of the mind which existed before.' It is not actually called a god, but is raised to the level of one because of its prime creative character. In the epics there is no trace of this abstraction. In the *Purāṇas*, however, Kāma is introduced afresh and there it belongs to the Śiva group in an inverted relationship, for Śiva consumed Kāma. But in the same litany Śiva is called Madana, i.e. Kāma. He is called Kāma in the litany of book XII. Rati is Kāma's wife, a counterpart of Greek Psyche. Kāma was consumed by Śiva because of his presumption, and Rati mourned for him—thus re-enacting the role of Yamī mourning for Yama.

spirit of God had moved there was the act of creation. The whole image recalls gestation and parturition with the spirit as the mother. The Holy Ghost has been compared to the dove in which shape it came down on the head of Christ after his baptism (Matt. iii. 16; Mark i. 10; Luke iii. 22; John i. 32). The inherent concept of the Holy Spirit acting as the mother-goddess agent is also corroborated by the fact that it is also likened to tongues of fire—another exact image of the mother-goddess.

Goddesses corresponding to Rati have the pigeon (a variant of dove in mythology) consecrated to them. 'The pigeon belonged properly speaking to the goddess of love whose symbol it has remained above all to the people worshipping the goddess' (Franz Cumont, *The Oriental religions in Roman paganism*, p. 125). Śiva himself is Kāma and Kāmanāśaka, because any god assuming Śiva's magnitude has to have acknowledged antinomies cohering in him. In mythological language his destruction of Kāma led to his assimilation of the god on a higher level. With his triumph over Kāma and Rati, he and Pārvatī absorb the dove, the symbol of love. Love as the motive force behind creation is naturally associated with fertility, and the dove is a symbol of both in all mythologies.

Durgā or Umā, as we have noticed, was an insignificant goddess in the beginning, but she steadily grew in stature until finally she absorbed all her rivals in her personality and became the supreme mother-goddess. This was a slow but sure process and it has its parallels in the history of other goddesses in other parts of the world.

In Umā we have a mountain-goddess worshipped by tribal people who was either associated with the slaughter of a buffalo or whose cult overcame a rival cult of buffalo-worship. The Lakṣmī-Śrī aspect of her personality was a direct continuation or survival of the cult of an agrarian goddess. Śākambharī is a more generalized vegetation-goddess. Her demon-slaying as described in the *Devīmāhātmya* section of the *Mārkaṇḍeya Purāṇa* (chs. 81–93), where she becomes the creator of Brahman-Viṣṇu-Maheśvara and is called the Mother and Queen of the three worlds, echoes the Vedic Vāgambhṛṇīya, a hymn where the supreme goddess says 'I move with the Rudras, the Vasus...'

By slaying the demon, Devī Caṇḍī restored the gods' dominions to them, together with their sacrificial shares. In other words, most of the Vedic nature gods were reinstated after a fashion under her dominion; thus she connected Vedic polytheism with Śākta monotheism—as R. P. Chanda suggests (in his *Indo Aryan races*). Sarasvatī was the Kumārī, the virgin aspect of the *prima dea*, and Umā herself is Kumārī in one of her many manifestations. As Jagaddhātrī and Jagajjananī she is the Mother, as Durgā the supreme deliverer (cf. Durgāttārayase—you deliver us from difficulties, *Mbh.* IV: 6: 25). As Durgā-Lakṣmī she still retains her chthonic character, as is evident from a *HV* passage, which states that the lotus-seated goddess (Lakṣmī) is called the earth (*HV* III: 12: 4). As wilderness-dweller or dweller in the Malaya, Vindhya hills or Himālaya she is a wilderness or mountain goddess. As a goddess fond of wine and meat, to whom the brigands bring such oblations, she has nefarious connections, and is at best a goddess of marauders. As Ekānaṃsā she is said to be worshipped by the Vṛṣṇis (*HV* II: 4: 37–41). Her connection with the Vṛṣṇis becomes evident when she is called the daughter of Nanda the cowherd (Valadeva's sister, *HV* II: 2: 12). In the *Mbh.* she is a favourite of Nārāyaṇa, is born in the line of Nanda the cowherd, despoiler of Kaṃsa, sister to Vāsudeva, Nārāyaṇa's wife, and has a face like Valarāma's (*Mbh.* IV: 6, VI: 23). As Kauśikī she is worshipped in the Vindhya region (*HV* II: 2: 46–8). After killing Śumbha and Niśumbha she was promised oblations and animal sacrifices on the ninth day of the lunar month (*HV* II: 2: 52).

Her outlandish and apparently vulgar associations connect her with regional and primitive goddesses who had roots in the soil and were not elevated to a supreme deity. Thus she is described as Kṛṣṇā or Kṛṣṇa-cchavisamakṛṣṇā (dark as dark can be), an epithet that connects her with the non-Aryan tribes, she wears peacock-feather bangles, carries an insignia of peacock feather (*Mbh.* IV: 6: 1–25), and a raised trident, and has a loud laugh. She is said to dwell in 'jambhas', camps and funeral mounds (*Mbh.* VI: 23: 3–16). She is called death. One remembers that the Athenians called their dead Demetrioi (Demeter's men). Her hair is all dishevelled (*HV* II: 3: 12). Thus in her primitive, aboriginal and tribal roots she is a fierce mountain-goddess credited with hunting and warlike achievements, worshipped by the nomadic Ābhīras and shepherds and tribes of primitive hunters and tillers.

On the other hand she embodies the highest philosophical principles in her personality.[1] She is omnipotent, a creator of heaven and earth and of the gods as well, the primal energy (ādyāśakti), the supreme deliverer. In her deliverer aspect she is the Durgā of the Hindu pantheon, but she also embodies the Buddhist conception of the supreme female principle. When the Mahāyāna Buddhists sought a compromise with Hinduism they absorbed certain fundamental deities of the Hindu pantheon and sometimes converted them into Buddhist gods by calling them by different names. Thus the Buddhist adaptation of the Śākta Tārā, whom they call Tārā maulākṣobhyabhūṣitā (the saviour-goddess Tārā adorned with the chief of the Akṣobhyas, Akṣobhya, being the second of the five Dhyānī, i.e. meditating,

[1] With Tantrism the mother-goddess assumed greater significance. The Sāṃkhya and Vedanta philosophies supplied the mystic and metaphysical counterpart of the cosmic essence of the mother-goddess who now embodied the supreme principle in its final manifestation. Buddhist Tantrism ousted various theophanies to correspond to the metaphysical entity of the supreme being. These manifestations raised the mother-goddess to a height she had never attained before.

Buddhas). This particular goddess is a nāga in a Śākta Tārā (cf. Nāgarūpadhṛk) and a Buddha in the Mahāyāna Tārā. According to an anecdote given in the Mahacīnācāra Tantra Devī Buddheśvarī's rite was still current in China even after it had become obsolete in India. Goddess Tārā seems to have been incorporated into the Mahāyāna from the Śākta pantheon.

As early as the *Mbh.* Durgā is called Kālī and Mahākālī (IV: 6: 25). In this aspect she is the personification of the all-destroying Time (as Śiva the destroyer is Kāla and Mahākāla), and is a female counterpart of Aeon and Zervan. As Kālī she is fierce because she embodies the principle of destruction; her image is the dread image of a dark goddess standing upon the body of Śiva, holding death-dealing weapons in her many arms. In Buddhist mythology this image is variously called as Tāriṇī, Ugratārā, Ekajaṭā, Nīlā Sarasvatī (deliverer, fierce deliverer, having one braid of matted hair, and the Dark or blue Sarasvatī). This is a product of at least two factors—on the popular plane she is the dread (ghorā) aspect of Durgā, the familiar deadly goddess of the primitive people, who sends gruesome plagues, diseases dread and painful, senility and decrepitude, pain, torture, misery, fear and death and this side of her personality is a direct legacy from Nirṛti. On the conceptual plane she is the elevated idea of change as concomitant with time, mutability and ineluctible fate.

The process of Durgā's growth in stature was long and steady. One by one she absorbed the main traits of regional mother-goddesses, household deities who were worshipped for different things by different tribes. Some were fierce and awe-inspiring, others were mild, benign and motherly, yet others were embodiments of lofty ideas—all these were fused into one composite supreme goddess—Durgā. Each of the component deities brought with her a special ritual, specific cultic practices and a different mythological and religious significance to the devotee. A supreme goddess who commanded the whole-hearted allegiance of various types of people, had to combine in her personality all the different traits that would satisfy these manifold demands. The Vedic gods' functions had to be preserved, for the *Purāṇas* took great care to emphasize a continuous mythological tradition. The local goddesses' appeal to their worshippers also could not be ignored, for their tradition was equally old, if not older. In the age of the neo-Brāhmaṇism of the *Purāṇas*, when the six philosophical systems had sufficiently developed, abstract cosmic ideas came to play an indispensable role in moulding theological concepts. Thus Sāṃkhya demanded that a primordial creative couple corresponding to Prakṛti and Puruṣa should be reflected on the theological plane. Śiva and Durgā are an answer to this;

their androgynous image is a confirmation of this. The Yogīśvara Śiva who sits aloof satisfies the followers of the Yoga system; together with his active (huntress) wife, a direct illustration of the inactive Puruṣa and the active Prakṛti principles. Thus Śiva and Pārvatī satisfied the religious cravings at all levels of consciousness.[1]

Isis in Egypt had a similar history:

[She] belonged to the oldest creations of Egyptian theology and occurs frequently in the Pyramid texts of the Old Kingdom. Mythologically seen, she was always considered the devoted sister-wife of Osiris and the ardent loving mother of her son Horus... Little by little she absorbed and assimilated most of the religious and cultic functions of the other goddesses, and from the last centuries before our era her position as the great mother-goddess of Egypt was unchallenged. She was universally revered throughout the country and the ascent of the Ptolemaic dynasty meant the final acknowledgement of her official position in the new state cult. (Eric Iversen, *The myth of Egypt and its hieroglyphs*, p. 51.)

The best example of this syncretism of the regional mother-goddesses until there emerges one *prima dea* is found in Apuleius' *The golden ass.* The ass prays to Isis.

Blessed *Queen of Heaven* you are pleased to be known... *Ceres*, the original harvest mother who, in joy at the finding of your lost daughter Proserpine abolished the rude acorn diet of forefathers and gave them bread raised from the fertile soil at Eleusis; or as *Venus*...who at the time of the first Creation coupled the sexes in mutual love...whether *Artemis*, the physician sister of Phoebus Apollo... whether dread *Proserpine* to whom the owl cries at night, whose triple face is potent against the malice of ghosts, keeping them imprisoned below...you whose misty radiance nurses the happy seeds under the soil, you who control the wandering course of the sun and the very power of his rays. (Pen. edn. ch XVII.)

The goddess appears to Lucius and says:

I am *Nature the universal mother*, mistress of all the elements, *primordial child of Time*, sovereign of all things spiritual, *queen of the dead, queen also of the immortals, the single manifestation of all gods and goddesses that are.* My nod governs the shining Lights of Heaven...the lamentable silence of the world below.

T. R. Glover in *The conflict of religions in the Early Roman Empire* writes: 'It was during the second Punic War that Cybele was brought from Asia

[1] Durgā's rise to power is not a unique phenomenon. In other mythologies we have similar instances. Of Ishtar the *Hastings' encylopaedia of religion and ethics* writes: 'Starting with local cults in which she occupied the chief place, Ishtar came in the end practically to absorb all other goddesses of the Assyro-Babylonian pantheon so that her name became, even at an early date a Babylonian appellative for goddess.' Ishtar's cult was connected with astrolatry, and Venus (Ishtar) may have originally stood for the star. The mother-goddess characteristics were attached to her only after other mother-goddesses like Ningil and Damkina were assimilated by her.

Minor and definitely established as one of the divinities of the City... The Great Mother of Gods, she represented the principle of life and its reproduction' (p. 20).

In the Middle East the Great Mother cult seems to have been oldest. There she assumed several names varying with regions of different mother-goddess cults. Thus she was called Ninhursaga, (Sumerian) Mah, Nin-mah, Inanna-Ishtar, Nintu and Aruru. 'Inanna...having become queen of heaven as the wife of Anu by one of her many matrimonial alliances, seems to have gone to the underworld for his release' (E. O. James, *The ancient gods*, p. 78). Ishtar, Hathor, Allatu and Neith were regional variants of the same mother-goddess.

Durgā absorbed trait after trait of local, tutelary and household mother-goddesses, her cult embraced newer regions and different tribes till it became one of the major formative forces in Indian religion—for the Śākta and Tantric cults are direct offshoots of the universal popularity of the Durgā cults as also the sublimation of the Śivā and Ghorā (benign and malign) aspects of her personality on the philosophical plane.

Of all the mother-goddess's animal associates the snake appears to be the oldest and the most important. It is directly inherited from the Nirṛti-aspect of the *prima dea*. The snake is at once a chthonic goddess's symbol, the symbol of the deceased ancestors as well as a lunar and fertility symbol—and these, as we have seen, are closely interconnected.

> By far the most prominent Minoan domestic cult, however, is that of the snake, especially in association with the so-called snake-goddess. Such snake-cults are of world provenance, dependent on the belief that snakes are incarnations of the dead. But the snake also signifies immortality. Because it casts its slough and renews itself it becomes the symbol of the ability to be born again. Hence it is not only an object of reverence and dread, but also a beneficent spirit, a guardian of the house. (R. F. Willets, *op. cit.* p. 74.)

In their capacity as household spirits snakes became tutelary mother-goddesses worshipped everywhere in the world. The first book of the *Mbh.* gives us an inkling as to how widespread the snake cult was before the Aryans were fully amalgamated with the pre-Aryans. In the outer sectors of the Manu's Brahmāvarta, the cult still persists especially in the tracts of the Himalayan and Vindhyan foothills. Among the aboriginal tribes of Assam and Madhyapradesh the snake is a household deity. These household deities, i.e. mother-goddesses, are Durgā in her various names and aspects, Kālī and Lakṣmī, again in their many forms. But this holds good for the people within the Brāhmaṇical fold—in the outer region, it is quite frequently a snake symbolizing the ancestor, fertility, rejuvenation metempsychosis and immortality.

In the *Mbh.* Jaratkāru (feminine) is the wife of Jaratkāru (masculine). This female Jaratkāru became Manasā in the medieval dialect Purānas (i.e. Maṅgalakāvyas). Earlier representations call her Śrī Naini (i.e. Śri Nāginī, the Holy Snake Goddess as is found inscribed in Brāhmī on an image from Sutan, M.P.). A much later image from Birbhum (Bengal) represents her as seven-hooded, two-armed with a double-petalled lotus placed over a jar from which two snakes are seen issuing forth; her bodice also is provided by snakes. Manasā and her many local variants are still worshipped in many villages in India.

Śiva and Pārvatī cults drew close to each other until their merger is symbolically represented by the Ardhanārīśvara image where the gods form two halves of one body. On the philosophical plane this is a creative union of the active and passive principles. We have a description of the Ardhanārīśvara aspect of Śiva in the sectarian Anuśāsanaparvan of the *Mbh.* (XIII: 14: 298–313). In Yama and Yamī we had a primeval bisexual pair, and there are many another pair with bisexual character, and in most cases they are creator divinities.[1] It is one step in advance of the most primitive stage of mythical imagination when the mother-goddess was conceived as the procreatrix without male assistance. Moreover, most of these names are cognates derived from the same root, indicating that the pair is just one single undivided entity, self-cloven into two halves, like the protoplasm, for the sake of creation. For Śiva and Gaurī this was a step to rise to the rank of the primordial pair and also to that of prime creators. It added to their mythological stature and raised them to cosmokrator status. This was essential for two reasons: first, as supreme deities of the Śaiva and Pāśupata cults they had to satisfy the worshipper's innate craving of seeing in their personal god the manifestation of all the cosmic functions; second; as Śiva was assigned the specific task of destruction, his stature would be merely negative if he was not shown to be the creator as well. Here Pārvatī, Jagajjananī (the mother of the universe) became his indispensable helpmate, and with her firmly implanted within his being the task became easier. Śiva in his Ardhanārīśvara personality was a very late mythological embodiment of the primordial bisexual creative principle.

[1] The Egyptian Isis Osiris, Japanese Izanami-Izanagi, Arab Orotalt and Alitat, Mexican Mictlantceutli-Mictlantecuatl, Tonacatecutli-Tonacaciuatl, Ometecutli-Omecuatl, even the Hebrew Adam and Eve in the ancient Rabbinic lore were bisexual. Agdistis is a hermaphrodite monster.

CHAPTER 9

ŚIVA'S RISE TO POWER

In present-day India Śiva is more frequently worshipped in his phallic form than in the iconic. Pebbles smoothed by the Narmadā are called Bāṇaliṅga, phallic emblems of Śiva. The cult is traced to the *ṚV* where the Vedic Aryan seers swear at the 'barbarians' describing them as Śiśnadevas (people to whom the phallus is a god). According to *Nirukta* IV: 19 the word means lustful. Thus the exact import of the word is far from certain. Nor is it certain whether there were actual phallus-worshippers among the non-Vedic population; but this seems a probable assumption, for in Mohenjo Daro and Harappa plenty of clay and stone representations of the male organ are found. Vedic literature is silent about phallic worship and seems to abjure and curse it in a few passages. It is in the epics that we hear of it for the first time. The *Rām.* mentions Rāvaṇa's worship of Rudra in the phallic (liṅga) form (VII: 31: 42–3, also *KP* XXI: 48). By the time the *Mbh.* assumed its present form, phallic worship was an established mode of Śiva worship. Thus we hear that sages and gods have always worshipped the erect phallus (*Mbh.* VII: 200: 92–6, VII: 201: 124–5), and that liṅga worship is an alternative form of image worship (*Mbh.* VII: 201: 140). The Uśanas episode (*Mbh.* XII: 278) emphasizes the significance of the phallus. Upamanyu declining the boon offered by Indra said Śiva was his god because creation was not marked by a lotus (Lakṣmī's symbol) or a disc (Viṣṇu's) or a thunderbolt (Indra's), but by the male and female organs which proves that Śiva and Pārvatī are the supreme deities, and that creation belonged to them (*Mbh.* XIII: 14: 33). Once Pitāmaha Brahman commissioned Śiva for creation. Śiva dived under water to meditate. Brahman, impatient at the delay, appointed another who accomplished creation. When Śiva emerged from under water and saw that another had performed his task he grew furious in indignation, plucked his own procreative organ as superfluous now and planted it on the earth. He told Brahman that through meditation he had procured food for the future creation first, hence the delay. With this he left the place in anger and went away to Mt Muñjavat (*Mbh.* X: 17: 10–26).

The episode definitely and unambiguously connects the phallus with creation. The organ which he planted is the symbol of creative energy charged with the animus produced by meditation—a fit object for veneration. This is the nucleus of a new cult, the worship of the detached phallus iconically reproduced.

Śiva is also worshipped ithyphallically, for he is called Mahaśepha, or Mahaliṅga (ithyphallic).

The cult of the phallus once established tended to obliterate alternate forms of worship. The gods worshipped the phallus of Śiva and none other, Brahman and Viṣṇu both know and worship the phallus of Śiva; all female creatures are stamped with Pārvatī's mark, the mark of the female organ, all males with Śiva's. He who disagrees with this view is foolish for creatures are either male or female, so they are all divided between Śiva and Pārvatī (*Mbh.* XIII: 14: 30–6).

This passage seems to be the rationalization of an already existing cult in order to make it acceptable to the Vedic Indian's mind which had so far abhorred the practice. The phallus as a symbol of male virility must have formed the conceptual basis of even the aboriginal's worship; but in the Aryan pantheon Indra symbolized this virility, frequently indicated by his appellative Vṛṣan, yet Indra was nowhere connected with the phallus worship. Śiva who was gradually assimilating aboriginal gods together with fertility cults naturally supplied the suitable basis upon which the phallus cult could be established. On the other hand the female generative principle was worshipped among the primitives symbolically and was easily absorbed in the totality of the phallic cult, as a complementary cult. The *Śvet. U* calls Śiva Bhageśa (lord of the female organ) thus connecting him with the 'yoni' (the female organ) (VI: 6).[1]

Dionysus also had phallic connections, although he was not directly

[1] Phallic worship is not peculiar to India. Chem, Amun and Munt were worshipped phallically in Egypt. E. A. Wallis Budge (*The gods of the Egyptians*) mentions a passage in the Pyramid Texts where the original form of the worship of Tem seems to be phallic in character. Thus Tem offers a parallel to Śiva who also gradually rose to the lofty altitude of a supreme divinity, and as kosmokrators both were worshipped in the phallic rather than the iconic form. 'Among the most ancient of the Egyptian gods was Min of Koptos who was both a sky and fertility deity' (E. O. James, *The ancient gods*, p. 71). 'The ithyphallic statue of Min was carried in procession on poles by priests beneath a canopy preceded by a white bull' (E. O. James, *Prehistoric religion*, p. 186), and Min too was worshipped ithyphallically. Thus Śiva as a fertility divinity, as accompanied by a bull, and as worshipped ithyphallically, offers a close parallel to this very ancient god of Egypt. Dr Suniti Kumar Chatterji in his Kamala Lectures (entitled *Indianism and the Indian synthesis*), as well as in his *Kirātajanakṛti*, says that the earliest racial substream in the composition of 'the Indian man' was the Negrito or the Negroid stratum. These seem to have travelled from Africa, via Arabia and Iran, to West and South India and then on to the Andamans, Malaya and Indonesia. If that was the case they may have carried the phallic worship of Tem, a god who corresponded to Śiva in other respects too. Later when Śiva began to assimilate similar deities Tem might have contributed this mode of worship.

worshipped phallically. 'The phallus which was carried in the Dionysiac processions belongs to him as a god of fertility; he is never represented as phallic himself, but the Sileni and Satyrs who surround him are' (*Oxford Classical Dictionary*).

The mythical son of Dionysus was Priapus, who was symbolically represented by the phallus. The original phallic divinity in Greece was called Tutunus or Muntunus; only later he was called Priapus (*Encycl. rel. and ethics*, vol. IX, p. 822). According to Pausanius Hermae was worshipped as a phallic god in Cyllene (*ibid.* p. 818). In England and France, too, *ex voto* stones have been discovered which bear phallic figures inscribed on them (*ibid.*). Large stones shaped like the phallus were also discovered in Norway and these belong to the Viking age. Strabo (XIII: 1: 12) and Pausanius (IX: 31: 2) mention the popularity of this cult. In the *Fasti*, Ovid tells us of Ocresia, mother of Servius, who sat on the hearth-ashes marked with the male organ; this perhaps obliquely signifies the cult of the phallus in Rome. Thus after Alexander's conquest of north-western India the cult may have travelled to India with Alexander's followers or successors. Ovid in his *Fasti* and *Metamorphoses* mentions the Priapus cult.

In the *Vedas* Rudra has for his sons only the Rudras and Maruts. In the epics and *Purāṇas* he has other children. The *Rām.* mentions Skanda as a son to Rudra, though not directly begotten by him or in Pārvatī. Agni's seed fell in the Gaṅgā who, unable to bear the heat, deposited it among the bulrushes where Skanda grew up nursed by the six Kṛttikās (I: 39). Hence Agni ever shines among the bulrushes (*Rām.* IV: 44: 72). Now Agni is identified with Rudra, so that the later myth of Kārttikeya being Śiva's son is based on this story. The *Mbh.* gives more elaborate accounts of his birth. The gods needed a heroic general to win their battles against Tāraka the demon. Kārttikeya was born as an answer to their prayer. He is called Kumāra, Skanda, Mahāsena and Kārttikeya. In one anecdote we are told the Aṅgiras's wife Śivā approached Agni. She deposited the seed in a golden pot among reeds (on Śvetaparvata). She assumed the shape of all the seven sages' (Saptarṣi) wives, except that of Arundhatī, and deposited the seed six times. Out of this, Agni's wife Svāhā brought forth a six-headed son. The name Śivā connects the son with Śiva, though indirectly.

Devasenā (an abstraction of the divine army) was looking for a suitable husband, and in Kārttikeya she found her spouse. Kārttikeya killed the nāgas Citra and Airāvata, played with a cock and took Śiva's bow that had destroyed the three cities. The gods gave him gifts (*Mbh.* III: 223).

In a subsequent stanza Rudra is said to have entered Agni and created Skanda (*Mbh.* III: 228: 30–1). This penetration of Agni by Śiva is given its natural corollary in a later passage, where it says that Umā entered Svāhā for the birth of Kārttikeya who would bring relief to all creation (*Mbh.* III: 230: 9: 11). Out of a remainder of the seed different kinds of gaṇas (hosts) were created (*Mbh.* III: 231). Another account says that Śiva's seed fell in Agni. He, unable to bear it, deposited it in the Gaṅgā, who also laid it down by the bulrushes. The Kṛttikā sisters saw it and reared the foetus (vulgate *Mbh.* IX: 44). A still later account has it that at the gods' request Agni deposited his seed in the Gaṅgā who fainted because of its unbearable power and heat. The demons who lived in the water roared, the river was convulsed and refused to bear the seed. Agni asked what it was like, she replied: like Agni, like gold. The seed 'fell' and the child born of it was Skanda (spilled); it was hidden among the bulrushes, hence he is called Guha (hidden) and was reared by the Kṛttikā sisters, so he was called Kārttikeya (vulgate *Mbh.* XIII: 85: 55–82). These different accounts all tend to blur the true origin of Kārttikeya.

One passage gives us the dispute: Some say he is Maheśvara's son, some Vibhāvasu's (i.e Agni's), some say he was born of Umā, others of the Kṛttikās, and still others of Gaṅgā (*Mbh.* IX: 46: 97). The reason why Kārttikeya had to be created is given: Brahman tells the gods, harried by demon Taraka, that the latter cannot be slain except by the son born of Rudra's seed falling in fire and then conceived by Gaṅgā (*Mbh.* XIII: 83: 11–13). Analysing the different accounts we get certain common points: (1) direct begetting of Kārttikeya by Śiva or conception by Umā is avoided; (2) yet in each account Śiva and Umā's indirect parentage is indicated; (3) direct connection is sought to be established between him and Agni, Gaṅgā and the Kṛttikās; (4) he is the destined divine general and the deliverer of the gods from demon Tāraka's menace; (5) in some accounts he is connected with crows (cf. the Krauñcabheda episode), or cocks or peacocks.

It would appear that Kārttikeya enjoyed an independent cult in which he was the supreme god; his relationship with Śiva, therefore, would not be tolerated by this sect until for various reasons the cults coalesced, when he became Śiva's son. He is directly related to Agni, but then Śiva is called Agni in later Vedic literature. In the *Mbh.*, too, Dahana (fire) is one of the eleven Rudras (I: 103: 9). Śiva held the Gaṅgā on his head, later mythology makes her Śiva's wife, whether because Kārttikeya had by then become Śiva's son or vice versa is not known. But Gaṅgā is inseparably connected with Skanda's birth as the receptacle of Agni's seed. This marks the growth of the river in importance through connection with the Śiva cult. Agni is always either the first receptacle or the begetter, and primarily connected with Skanda. This may have been due to emphasizing the power and heat that was mythologically necessary for the creation of a divine general destined to kill Tāraka. Lastly the Kṛttikās are inalienably connected with Skands's birth; they are six in number, so he is six-headed. Alternately Agni mates with Svāhā in the guise of the wives of six of the seven great sages, and so Skanda is six-headed. The Kṛttikās are clearly connected with the rainfall so essential for crops; the month of Kārttika precedes the harvest month (Agrahāyaṇa, lit. 'the first month of the year'; old calendar), and Kārttika is also the month when 'ancestor-worship' is performed. Thus through the Kṛttikās Kārttikeya is essentially bound up with crops and harvest. The reeds are also mentioned in almost every account where Kārttikeya spent the prenatal period.[1]

In most epic accounts Skanda is given the peacock by the gods. It is striking that the *Mbh.* mentions Rohitaka as the habitat of Kārttikeya, and states that that place is inhabited by the Mattamayūraka tribe. We have historical record of a Śaiva clan called the Mattamayūras whose seat was in central India. They appear in history from the seventh century onwards. V. V. Mirashi in his article 'The Śaiva Ācāryas of the Māttamayūra Clan' gives an account of this Śaiva sect (*IHQ*, XXVI, no. 1, 1950). This is a tribe of warrior-folk, the Yaudheyas (lit. fighters, cf. Kārttikeya the general), says the Monier-Williams Lexicon. Thus the relationship between the warrior-god and the peacock—which must have been the totem or mark of the tribe—is established; the epic makes the peacock Skanda's insignia. It seems plausible to conclude that Kārttikeya was the tutelary god of a warlike tribe whose tribal badge was the peacock. Originally, therefore, he enjoyed independent cultic ritual; later, 'worship of Skanda came to be completely merged in that of Śiva in northern India of the post-Gupta period, and separate shrines were seldom dedicated to this deity' (J. N. Banerji, *The development of Hindu iconography*, p. 364).

Skanda's assimilation in the Śiva cult appears to have been principally through Gaṅgā, Agni and the Kṛttikās (who are connected with the vegetation-gods of this group). The Mattamayūraka tribe may have held orgiastic rituals as the word 'matta' (lit. drunk or wild) seems to suggest and, if so, this also must have tended to bring the two gods nearer. The

[1] Strangely enough the Mexican god who answers most closely to the Indian Agni, Huitzilopochtli, has a shield of reeds.

resistance to this fusion (of Śiva and Kārttikeya cults), which is seen reflected in mythology (note that Kārttikeya is hardly ever mentioned as Śiva's direct issue), must have broken down with time. Reluctance to identify him as Śiva's son is finally overcome in the *HV* III: 88, where the Kumārasambhava legend (as Kālidāsa knew it) is given in a nutshell, so that Skanda finally becomes the son of Śiva and Pārvatī. Casual references still state that he is Agni's son, reared by the Kṛttikās among reeds (*HV* III: 41–3). One *Mbh.* passage mentions that at Śiva's marriage, the gods requested him not to deposit his seed in Pārvatī, and he agreed. Umā in mortification cursed them with sonlessness. Agni, who was not present, contained Śiva's seed, etc.[1] This episode seems to rationalize the cultic reluctance to make Kārttikeya Śiva's son.

The *Vedas* do not know a separate Gaṇeśa (lord of the Gaṇas); one or two passages identify Rudra with Gaṇapati.[2] Later Purāṇic mythology knows a pot-bellied, elephant-faced god worshipped as Gaṇeśa. This may be an external projection of that Śiva who rules the hosts (gaṇa). In Yājñavalkya's sūtra we have a Vināyaka (leader, II: 14), which name was later given to Gaṇeśa. The appellatives 'leader', 'leader of the hosts' should properly be Kārttikeya's who led the divine host in battle. But the Vināyaka of the sūtras is a son of Ambikā, and is thus connected with Śiva's family, although only indirectly, for Pārvatī's relationship with Śiva became a *fait accompli* much later. Manuals of iconography lay down that Gaṇapati should be single-tusked, and should hold a wood-apple, a sweetmeat, an elephant driver's goad and a net in his four hands. He should be associated with snakes, should be clad in a tiger-skin and have a snake for a sacred thread. Iconographically Gaṇeśa combines the traits of a Yakṣa and a nāga and it is obvious that the syncretism includes these cults. His pot-belly comes from the Yakṣa side (for in iconography Yakṣas are invariably pot-bellied). His image also has *clear* traces of un-Aryan gods. *Yājñavalkyasmṛti* a late text says that Vināyaka (a synonym of Gaṇeśa; literally 'a general', but actually it means Kārttikeya, the divine general) is a son of Ambikā (i.e. Durgā) (I: 27 ff.). This connects Vināyaka with the Śiva family. In the sixth-century temple at Bhumara we have many sculptures of bird- or animal-faced Gaṇas (= hosts). The Bhitargaon plaque hardly confirms Gaṇeśs's divinity. In the early Gupta relief at Udayagiri the god has no mouse. All this indicates that the syncretistic figure is a much later creation.

[1] Both the gods' request to Śiva and Umā's curse on them indicate that the Śiva cult had fertility associations.

[2] Gaṇānām tvā gaṇapatim havāmahe (*TS* IV: 5: 4), 'I invoke you, Gaṇapati, lord of the gaṇas!' Or, 'let the benefits from Rudra's leadership come (to us)' (*MS* III: 1: 3).

Among his various names are: Herambagaṇapati (gaṇapati of the Heramba), leader of a mad host, leader of a dancing host, gaṇapati of the left-over food. The term 'unmattavināyaka' recalls Kārttikeya's association with the mattamayūras. Thus Nṛtyagaṇapati connects him with Śiva and his dancing host. Ucchiṣṭagaṇapati apparently indicates a cultic practice of eating left-over food as part of a religious discipline. Dr J. N. Banerji's Bengali book *Pañcopāsanā* mentions Śaiva cults with similar practices. The term Heramba is of uncertain origin. 'Hera' means demoniac illusion: 'Heraka' is the name of a demon attending on Śiva; 'Heruka' means both Gaṇeśa and a demon attending on Mahākāla Śiva. Heramba is a name of Gaṇesa, probably, as the leader of the 'demon-host', gaṇa.[1]

Gaṇeśa's elephant trunk is variously explained by the *Purāṇas*; but this obviously connects him with the elephant—for not only is Gaṇeśa himself elephant-faced, he also carries an elephant-rider's hook in his hand, as if to control or punish an elephant. One remembers Śiva killing the elephant-demon, Gajāsura. This exploit may be a mythological record of the victory of the Śiva cult over a section of the Indra cult, for the elephant as Indra's mount symbolized its rider. Indra was the leader of the host of the Maruts, 'marutām gaṇa'. This gaṇa later changed its character and became associated with Śiva, whose son Kārttikeya came to rule them, while the other son Gaṇeśa became their nominal overlord. Kārttikeya performed Indra's function, in leading the divine host against demons, so mythologically he supplanted Indra and inherited the generalship of the heavenly host.

Gaṇeśa is iconographically represented as pot-bellied. This has a suggestive quality, for it evokes the 'lower gods'. Iconography has very precise instructions for the execution of its 'high gods' who are to be siṃhakaṭi (lion-waisted); an exception suggests that the god is primarily a popular god, associated with disreputable followers.

Vaiśravaṇa, i.e. Kuvera, is described iconographically in the *Caturvargacintāmaṇi* as pot-bellied, two-armed, holding a mace and precious gems, and with a drunken appearance (II: I: 138). Kuvera's identity is defined in the Monier-Williams Dictionary as: 'Name of a chief of evil beings or spirits of darkness having the name Vaiśravaṇa.' The *Rām.* makes him Rāvaṇa's brother, a monster by birth. The word *Kuvera* is of uncertain derivation. 'Vera' (or 'bera') means 'body' (cf. 'dhruvavera', permanent images), 'veraṭa' means 'a low man' or 'one of mixed caste'. Thus Kuvera

[1] Heramba also means a buffalo, and this indirectly connects Gaṇeśa both with Yama who rode a buffalo in the epics and *Purāṇas* and with Pārvatī who (in the *Purāṇas*) killed a buffalo demon. Thus through his association with the buffalo Gaṇeśa belongs to the Śiva complex.

would literally mean 'an ugly body'—he is actually sometimes made terrific in appearance and is always made short and pot-bellied. He should have 'apīcyaveśa', i.e. the northerner's dress, and this indicates the original site where the cult must have flourished.

Kuvera is primarily associated with treasure and wealth. His Nidhis (treasures) are nine in number and the Guhyakas (Kuvera's attendants) keep watch over this hidden treasure. One is reminded of the dwarf keeping watch over the hidden Nibelung treasure, Andvari's gold watched over by Fafnir. If there is any connection between these legends preserved in folk memory, then they both must go back to Indo-European times. The Guhyakas are so-called because they 'hide' (from root *guh*) the treasure, and significantly enough Kārttikeya is called Guha, although a different legend is made to attach to his name.

Kuvera is Śiva's particular friend. The *Rām.* knows him as the (divine) Treasurer (dhanādhyakṣa, III: 44: 28), and also the guardian of the north (IV: 44: 4). He was subjugated by his mighty brother Rāvaṇa, who defeated his hosts (V: 78: 4–6, VI: 40: 40); and seized his chariot Vimāna (VI: 106: 9). Kuvera is reported to have dwelt in Laṇkā at first, but when Rāvaṇa's emissary Prahasta came and demanded Laṅkā, he vacated the city and went and made his abode in Kailāsa (VII: 11: 25–50). Now Kailāsa was the place of his friend Śiva. There he offended Umā by looking at her while she was with Śiva; she cursed him and he lost his left eye. This makes Kuvera one-eyed, tradition sometimes makes him three-legged and with eight teeth only. This appearance justifies the exposition of the term Kuvera as 'ugly-bodied'. When Rāvaṇa invaded Kailāsa, Kuvera fought against him, was wounded, but was eventually protected by his 'nidhis' (VII: 15). In the *Mbh.* Śiva took revenge on Uśanas because the latter stole Kuvera's wealth (XII: 278). Marutta's wealth, which actually is the pivot around which a long series of episodes turn, was finally unearthed by Kuvera, Maṇibhadra and Rudra's hosts (*Mbh.* XIV: 64–5). Kuvera's friendship with Śiva is frequently referred to in the epics, Śiva lives in the north, Kailāsa; Kuvera, too, lives there and is moreover the guardian of the north.

Another trait connects Śiva with Kuvera. The *Śilparatnāgama*, a text-book of iconography, lays down that Kuvera may sometimes be represented as with two fangs; he should be shown as riding a chariot drawn by men; hence his name Naravāhana. This cruel feature has something in common with the dread god Śiva to whom human sacrifices were offered, and to Nirṛti (another component of this complex), who also has a man for a mount. Essentially Kuvera, too, like Śiva is a chthonic god, not primarily connected with vegetation, as with the hidden treasure the earth encloses, viz. the minerals. But since wealth was principally agricultural, Kuvera represented vegetation as well. Kuvera and his followers are principally associated with the earth, the mountains and the treasures of the precious stones and metals underground. They are tutelary gods, deriving from the pre-Aryan aboriginal tradition and playing a considerable role in Hindu and early Buddhist folklore. Kuvera's wife is Ṛddhi, prosperity, an extension of the concept behind Kuvera.

Pūṣan is the only solar god, apart from the rather shadowy figure of Vivasvat who is connected with the Śiva group of gods. In the *ṚV* Pūṣan is invoked as the god who helps the worshipper across (the path) and delivers him from sin (*ṚV* VIII: 42: 2; *AV* VI: 112: 3). The path is Pūṣan's special domain—he is to lead us (i.e. our cattle) on to good pastures (*ṚV* VII: 42: 8) he is 'pathaspati', lord of the path (*ṚV* VI: 53: 1). He is born on the path that leads forward (*ṚV* X: 26: 8), he looks after the traveller's welfare, protects him from robbers (*ṚV* VIII: 42: 3) and drives away the evil wolf (*ṚV* I: 42: 2).

He is described as riding on a she-goat (*ṚV* I: 20: 139), and is invoked for food, light, health, intellect and wealth (*ṚV* I: 89: 6, I: 138: 4, VI: 53: 2–8, VI: 55: 1, 3, VI: 58: 2, VIII: 31: 11, VIII: 29: 6, IX: 67: 10, IX: 88: 3). Pūṣan is Prajāpati's son and Indra's brother and helped Indra against Vṛtra (*ṚV* VI: 57: 1–3). He knows the sources of treasure (*ṚV* VIII: 29: 6). In all this Pūṣan is like any other solar divinity, having very little in common with the Śiva group. But Pūṣan's guardianship over the paths does not end with the traveller's welfare; he conducts Sūryā to her bridegroom's house (*ṚV* X: 85: 26). To the departed soul are addressed the words: 'Let Pūṣan carry you hence and hand you over to the fathers' (*ṚV* X: 17: 3), 'as Agni and Savitṛ conduct them to the place of the righteous'.

In rituals, Pūṣan leads the sacrificial horse to the place of sacrifice. The man who has lost his way invokes Pūṣan for leading him back to his path. He is the finder of paths with the swift-footed goat (*ĀGS* III: 7: 9).

Another solar god in Greece was the guardian of paths. In his *Cretan cults and festivals*, R. F. Willets says of Agyieus Apollo, 'There is some evidence to suggest that the cult of the sacred stone side by side with the cult of the guardian of gates and ways which formed the essence of the conception of Agyieus in ancient Greece was paralleled at an earlier date in Anatolia in a way which confirms the oriental origin of Apollo' (p. 259). 'He found cattle who lost their way and strayed from the fold.' He is connected with cattle. 'Die Sage, dass Pūṣan "den König auf bunter

Streu" fand und wie ein verloren gegangenes Tier wieder zutrieb' (Hillebrandt, *Vedische Mythologie*, p. 351). In the *Bṛhaddavatā* Pūṣan is connected with the growth of vegetation (II: 63). His connection with the goat is, according to Keith, his main characteristic: 'The only explanation which is possible...is to regard Pūṣan as in origin an animal god, embodied in the goat, or a vegetation spirit which might be conceived in goat shape' (*Religion and philosophy of the Vedas and Upanisads*, p. 108). But Pūṣan belongs to the Śiva group through his function as the Psychopompos.

In Greek mythology Hermes has this function.[1] In guiding the soul to the fathers, Pūṣan guides them to transmigration because the fathers belong to the chain of existence (Pitṛyāṇa) and this chain is definitely connected with the Śiva group. 'Agni makes over to the gods those who have died' (*ṚV* x: 17: 3), Pūṣan makes over the dead to the fathers (*ṚV* x: 2: 7).

Agni is the god with whom Śiva is frequently identified. But Agni is given dual character in the *Vedas*; he is both benevolent and malevolent, and it is in the latter aspect that he belongs to the Śiva group. Agni is 'purohita', god, priest, giver of wealth, revered by the ancient sages, lord of the house, remover of evils and ever young (*ṚV* I: 1). But it is chiefly as a messenger of the gods that he is invoked, for the gods appointed him as their messenger (*ṚV* v: 8: 6). The sacrificial beast went to heaven along with Agni (*AB* VI: 5). He is called Pravāhaṇa (the Bearer, *TMB* I: 4: 1). 'Having become a horse he does indeed carry the sacrifice to the gods' (*ŚB* I: 4: 1: 30). He carries the libation to the fathers (Agni Kavyavāhana, *GBU* I: 25). The epics also know him as the bearer of the sacrifice.

His habitat is actually threefold: as Mātariśvan he dwells in the highest heaven, as Tanūnapāt he is in the fuel (hence a resident on earth) and lastly as Vāḍava and Apām Napāt he dwells in the water (*ṚV* x: 45: 1).

[1] Sophocles in his *Electra* (121) says, 'Hermes of the Underworld'; Aeschylus in *The Libation Bearers* (1–2) writes, 'Hermes, lord of the dead, who watch over the power of my fathers', again 'Hermes, lord of the dead' (124); Euripides in his *Alcestis* (743), 'Hermes of the world below'; Sophocles, *Oedipus at Colonus*, 'Hither, this way, for this way Hermes leads, the spirit guide' (ll. 1547–8); Sophocles, *Ajax*, 'Hermes I invoke, Born guide of spirits to the nether world' (ll. 832–3); *Electra*, 'Guide of the shades, O Hermes' (l. 111). 'This divine escort of the souls frequently retains the name of Hermes in conformity with the old mythology, for Hermes is the psychopompos who leads the shades to their subterranean abode and moreover summons them and brings them back in another migration to the earth' (Franz Cumont, *After-life in Roman paganism*, p. 163). Thus Hermes forms a link between this life and transmigration via death. There are other similarities between Hermes and Pūṣan. Hermes of Ammon had ram's horns and ears and also pastoral associations. His son by Cyllene was covered with hair and had the horns and feet of a goat. Pan was Hermes' son by Penelope (to whom he came as a he-goat). All this almost certainly indicates the Indo-European infra-structure for the common ancestor of Pūṣan and Hermes.

The Avestan Apām Napāt also lives in the depths of the waters, with demons around him. He is said to have recovered light in the battle between Atar (Avestan Fire) and the dragon and cast the dragon into the ocean. The fire latent in fuel is made to appear through human effort, thus Agni is Dvijanman (twice-born, *ṚV* I: 60: 1) while yet in the firmament the heavenly Agni settled the sun, he watches over nectar, and keeps the heavens fixed (*ṚV* VI: 7: 7). As Vaiśvānara he is the first priest of the sacrifice, the Hotṛ comes after him (*ṚV* VI: 9: 4); while Vaiśvānara is yet wrapped in darkness the gods praise him (*ṚV* VI: 10: 7). He secured Subandhu's mind from Yama (*ṚV* X: 60: 10). When Śayu praised Mitra, Varuṇa and Aryaman, the cow who had left off bearing became rejuvenated at Agni's command (*ṚV* X: 61: 17). Agni helped Atri, Bharadvāja, Gaviṣṭhira Kaṇva and Trasadasyu in battle (*ṚV* X: 151: 5). The *ṚV* hymn X: 191, the last hymn of the collection, is addressed to Samjñāna Agni for harmony of thought and action. When Kutsa had killed the monstress Dīrghajihvī (*TMB* XIII: 6: 9) he purified himself with Śuciguṇa Agni (*ṚV* I: 97). Agni is an earth-dweller because the gods left him behind when they ascended to heaven (*ṚV* II: 4: 3). This connects him with Mārtaṇḍa (derived from the root *mṛ*, another god with a similar mythical history. Like Varuṇa he is connected with spies, for he is invoked for sending the fleetest spy (turṇitamah spaśah, *ṚV* IV: 4: 3).

Agni as the god of nocturnal light is naturally conceived of as the remover of darkness. Thus he is credited with the restoration of sight to Dīrghatamas Māmateya (*ṚV* IV: 4: 13). Sāyaṇa commenting on *ṚV* V: 2: 1 says that Agni had grown dim in the house of the Ikṣvāku because of his partiality, but became blazing again when they conciliated him. Varuṇa, Mitra, Aryaman, the Nāsatyas and Bhaga shine with Agni's light (*ṚV* VIII: 19: 16). Agni is clear-sighted, cf. 'O Agni, the undeceivable, to thee that deceivest the foe' (*TS* I: 1: 10). 'The night is Agni's, cattle are Agni's...he, praised by them, delivered their cattle from night to day...The sun went down from this world to the yonder world; he having gone to yonder world, bethought him again of this world; having returned to this world he had fear of death, for this world, as it were, was yoked with death. He reflected, Let me praise Agni here; he, praised, will make me go to the world of heaven' (*TS* I: 5: 9). The *TS* mentions three Agnis, the bearer of the oblation to the gods, the bearer of the offering to the Pitṛs, and the guardian of the Asuras (II: 5: 9). He is invoked as the slayer of demon Makha (*TS* III: 2: 4).

Agni is one of the five gods whose likeness the kings bear (*Rām.* IV:

17: 26). When Indrajit sacrificed, Agni came and received his oblation (*Rām.* VI: 19: 45). Agni rose with Sītā and confirmed her chastity before Rāma in his assembly (*Rām.* VI: 103: 2–11). The element Agni is thought of when it says that Agni has eternal friendship with Vāyu the wind god for it blazes when fanned (*Rām.* VII: 36: 39). Agni became all-eater because Bhṛgu had cursed him (*Mbh.* I: 7, XII: 329: 43). Satiated with clarified butter and suffering from dyspepsia Agni had consumed the Khāṇḍava forest to restore his appetite and digestion (*Mbh.* I: 214–15). The birds Mandapāla and Jaritāri praised him during the burning of the Khāṇḍava forest (*Mbh.* I: 220, 223). King Nīla of Māhiṣmatī city propitiated Agni, who promised to guard his city from enemies and would not allow Sahadeva to take it (*Mbh.* II: 28). Agni assumed the form of a dove in the Ūśīnara legend (*Mbh.* III: 131), and the dove is a bird associated with the Śiva group of gods.

The story of Agni's love for the wives of the seven sages and subsequently of the birth of Kārttikeya from his seed is told in *Mbh.* III: 214. Agni is said to be born of seven mothers, Kākī, Halimā, Rudrā, Vṛhalī, Āryā, Palālā and Mitrā (*Mbh.* III: 217: 9). Agni gave a cock to Skanda (*Mbh.* III: 218: 31). He found out Indra when the latter lay concealed under a lotus stalk after his defeat at Nahuṣa's hands (*Mbh.* V: 16). Agni is the leader of the Vasus resembling Śiva, leader of other hosts, viz. the Rudras and the Maruts (*Mbh.* VII: 5: 25). Once Agni got lost and the gods found him hiding inside a Śamī tree (*Mbh.* IX: 46). Uttaṅka met Agni (in the shape of a horse) in the realm of the serpents (*Mbh.* XIV: 57). At Agni's request Arjuna cast the discus (which Kṛṣṇa had possessed) and the Gāṇḍīva bow into the water (*Mbh.* XVII: 1). Dhṛṣṭadyumna (the brightly shining one at birth) entered Agni in heaven after his death (*Mbh.* XVIII: 5: 18). Agni desired the daughter of Duryodhana of Māhiṣmatī but the king rejected his suit; the sacrificial fire went out. Priests appealed to Agni who revealed the true cause so that finally the king gave Sudarśanā to Agni. Bhṛgu was born of Brahman's seed (spilled at the sight of the goddesses and their daughters); Varuṇa and Agni claimed him and at the gods' intercession received him in spite of Brahman's claim (*Mbh.* XIII: 85).

Agni is invoked under different names in the Āprī hymns: Susamiddha Pāvaka (purifier), Tanūnapat, Narāśamsa, Ila, Varhis, Dvāro devyāh, Uṣāsānaktā and daivyau hotārau (*RV* I: 13, I: 142, V: 5: 5). Agni is supplicated for wealth, wives, cattle and food (I: 14: 15, 17, 21). He is called Vājasṛt, Annavat and Vasumat (giver of food and wealth) in *MS* II: 1: 10, 11, II: 2: 6.

This aspect of Agni as the giver of wealth connects him with another of Śiva's attendant gods—Kuvera. The gods, when fighting the demons, had deposited their wealth with Agni for fear of losing it if they lost the battle. Agni divided it among cattle, water and the sun (*TB* I: I: 6: I). He moves on the earth providing it with (many kinds of) protection (*TB* I: 2: I: 2). The *GB* knows Agni as the provider of heat (II: 22). He helps man in many ways: 'That mortal, O Agni, whom thou hast helped in battles, whom thou hast strengthened in the contest for booty...thou art lord of food; thou farest with ruddy winds, blessing the household, thou as Pūṣan dost protect thy worshippers with thyself' (*TS* I: 3: 14). 'O Agni, the gods have thee for father' (*TS* I: 5: 10); 'Agni is the lord of vows among the gods' (*TS* I: 6: 7); 'Agni is the begetter of offspring' (*TS* II: 2: 10). The *TMB* has a prayer to Agni for deliverance from earthly dangers (I: 3: 2). Agni, says the *CB*, is to deliver men from death. Agni is connected with the Vasus (*ŚB* III: 4: 2: I), thus he is indirectly the giver of wealth (Vasu).

Dhīra Sātaparṇeya came to Mahāśāla Jābāla and said he knew no other god but Agni, who was everything. Such passages indicate exclusive fire cults which worshipped Agni kathenotheistically. Jābāla became his disciple (*ŚB* X: 3: 3). Agni is the youngest of the gods (*ŚB* I: 4: I: 26), the most attractive of the gods: young and good looking with flaming hair, mighty and heroic, riding a red horse or a goat, a lover of maidens, a husband of women (*ṚV* I: 66: 7, 8). He has many exploits to his credit: he helped Saramā to recover the Aṅgiras' cows, he saved many from demons, helped Indra destroy the ninety cities (*ṚV* III: 12: 6), is the patron of Divodāsa (*ṚV* VI: 15: 19). His horse rose from the sea where he resides as Apām Napāt (son of the waters, *ṚV* II: 35: 6). He is Rudra (*ṚV* III: 2: 5), Śitipṛṣṭha, Nīlapṛṣṭha (*ṚV* III: 7: I, 3, cf. Śitikaṇṭha and Nīlakaṇṭha = Śiva). He is either born on the earth generated by ten maidens (i.e. ten fingers) from the fuel, or born in his Vaidyuta, i.e. lightning, form in the sky, when he is called Mātariśvan. We remember Heimdall in the Edda who also was the son of nine mothers and was associated with the sea (cf. Agni called Apāṃ napāt, son of the waters), and is called the white god (cf. Agni styled 'Śuci' = pure, white). Heimdali indicates the goat and the goat is Agni's mount. There is here perhaps a faint echo of a common Indo-European heritage in mythology.

Cosmic actions are ascribed to the heaven-born fire (*ṚV* VI: 8: 2, X: 12: 7). He is the king of the subjects (or tillers), the wonderful guardian of Dharman (*ṚV* VIII: 43: 24), he is also invoked as the ruddy rohita keeper of Ṛta (*ṚV* X: 5: 2–4, 7, X: 6: 2, X: 8: 5; *TB* II: I: II: I).

It is chiefly in the tenth book of the *ṚV* that we are introduced to the other aspect of Agni—the dark aspect. Agni is supplicated to go with the fathers (x: 15: 10), to offer the oblations to the ancestors who are present and also to those who are not; 'whom we know, and whom we know not' (i.e. immediate and remote ancestors, x: 15: 13). The departed ones are addressed as 'Let your eyes go to Sūrya, your breath to Vāyu, go you to the sky, earth, waters or plants according to your works. Let Agni carry you to pleasant regions' (x: 16: 3, 4). 'Let Agni and Soma restore your limbs which have been gnawed into by crows, ants, snakes and other beasts' (x: 16: 6).

Thus Agni is of two kinds: sacrificial and crematory. The latter aspect of Agni is sinister, and worshippers try to avoid it, for it bears evil (i.e. pollution): 'let it go to Yama, and let the other fire bear oblation to the gods' (*ṚV* x: 16: 9). One remembers the Flamen Dialis, Jupiter's priest, who was forbidden to touch anything connected with death. The offering to the gods is called 'havya', that to the fathers is called 'kavya', the call to Agni when he bears oblation to the gods, is 'svāhā'; that to Agni when he bears libation to the fathers is 'svadhā'. This clearly distinguishes the 'holy' Agni from the 'unholy', for the fire which comes in contact with the corpse, which is said to eat the corpse (kravyād), i.e. consume it by burning, is clearly polluted and quite unsuitable for sacred rituals for gods. Some of the ancestors are said to have become gods gradually and Agni is to bring them to the sacrifice (*ṚV* x: 15: 9). Once Agni sought to avoid sacrifices (*ṚV* x: 51: 4), the gods made him immortal and tempted him back to bear oblations.

Agni kills monsters. When the gods fought the demons Agni advised them to offer to him and they thereby won (*TB* 1: 6: 2: 6). Agni, in order to help the gods against demons, divided himself into three parts—Agni, Rudra and Varuṇa (*TB* 1: 7: 1: 2). This clearly links him with the Śiva group. When immortalized he had to be shown like the other gods who kill demons; Agni, too, kills monsters—he is called Rakṣohan. 'Let Rakṣohan Agni be fed and strengthened by the priests (apparently with offering of ghee) then let him go and kill (pierce, eat up) the monsters' (*ṚV* x: 87: 1). This Rakṣohan has iron teeth (verse 2), he is to bite and attack the Mūradevas (barbarians) and break their arms, pierce their skins, break their joints and give over their bodies to wild beasts; wherever they may be, Rakṣohan Agni is to pierce them with an arrow, and cut off the 'three roots' of the monsters. He is to consume ignorance and iniquity; prick the monsters with arrows of anger and 'discord' (*ṚV* x: 87: 1–13;

AV v: 12). The word used for the phrase 'with arrows' is Śarva, thus recalling Śarva Śiva. This fierce enemy of the monsters is an indirect assistant of sacrifices, through his monster-killing feat. Agni is to kill the worshipper's enemy by his brilliance (*MS* I: 5: 2). What people see near Agni, they see with the eye of demons (*MS* IV: 2: 1). Death himself had challenged Agni, but Agni defeated him with the Anuṣṭubh metre (*AB* III: 3: 12). Agni and Soma had entered Vṛtra, that was why Indra could not hurl his bolt at Vṛtra out of regard for them (*KB* III: 6). Agni is the smiter of the monsters (*KB* III: 4; *ŚB* I: 2: 1: 9). It is chiefly through his Ignis Rogalis aspect (of *AV* XVIII: 4: 1–15) that Agni belongs to the gods of the Śiva group, and is a link in the chain of Pitṛyāṇa (*RV* X: 3: 7). Two paths Devayāna and Pitṛyāṇa are mentioned for the first time in the tenth book of the *ṚV* (X: 88: 15). But even before that we have the corpse-devouring fire (kravyād Agni). In the great sacrifice to ancestors Kavyavāhana is invoked to carry the offerings to the fathers (*ṚV* IV: 7: 11). To this fire is uttered the svadhā call (*TB* I: 3: 10: 3; *AV* XVIII: 4: 71). The *ṚV Brāhmaṇas* are mostly silent about this fire, but the rituals connected with it are taken up again by the *YV Brāhmaṇas*. The *TB* directly links it with the Śiva group by saying that fire should be lighted up under the Kṛttikā constellation, because they belong to Agni (*TB* I: 1: 2: 1, I: 5: 1: 1). The *AV* knows Agni in this function, Agni Kavyavāhana is mentioned in the *GBU* (I: 25). We remember Nirṛti and Pṛthivī frequently mentioned as Yama's wife. The *GB* says: the earth is Agni's wife (*GBU* II: 29), thus equating Agni with Yama and also with Śiva, whose consort Umā is indirectly identified with the earth as the Great Mother.

Agni is directly mentioned in connection with Śiva. Among his various names given in the *AV*, one is Sadyojāta (just born, V: 12) which later became one of the five names of Śiva of the Pāśupata cult. The *GB*, an *AV* Brāhmaṇa (i.e., one of the latest) calls Agni Aghora, another of the five names of Śiva of the above sect. The *TS* calls Agni 'the lord of the hosts of the Maruts' (I: 3: 14), an appellative of Śiva. The *MS* calls Agni Aja Ekapad and Ahirbudhnya and also Rudra—all names of Rudra-Śiva (*MS* I: 2: 16, I: 6: 7; *TB* II: 1: 3: 1; *JB* III: 50). The *AB* account of Agni defeating death aligns him with Mṛtyuñjaya (death-defeating) Śiva. Just as Śiva has two eidons—benign and malign, so we hear of Agni's benevolent eidon—Śivā tanu (*TB* I: 1: 8: 6). The Kṛttikā's are said to be Agni's wife: the Kṛttikas are doubtless Agni's asterism (*ŚB* II: 2: 2: 1), for Agni doubtless is their mate and it is with Agni that they have intercourse (*ŚB* II: 1: 2: 5). This, then, is a variant of the *Mbh.* anecdote of

Agni committing adultery with the six sages' wives, and it is the nucleus of the story of Skanda's birth. Śiva's holding the Gaṅgā on his head and Agni depositing his seed in the river brings them closer. All the gods of this group have ape-sons; Varuṇa (Hemakūṭa and Ṛṣabha), Yama (Sumukha and Durmukha), Vāyu (Hanūmat). Śiva has an ape-shaped associate (cf. Nandin, Vānararūpa, ape-shaped). Agni also has ape-sons, Nīla (*Rām.* IV: 41: 3, V: 1: 47) and Saṃnādana (*Rām.* VI: 3: 25).

Agni hid from the gods and entered the earth in the shape of a mole (*TB* I: 1: 3: 3). The mole is offered to Śiva in the *Śatarudrīya* as Śiva's share and in later mythology it became Gaṇeśa's mount. Thus Agni's assuming that particular shape associates him with Śiva and Gaṇeśa. Of the seven mothers of Agni recorded in the *Mbh.* one is Rudrā, a feminine form of Rudra. But the fact that brings Agni and Rudra closest to each other is the ambiguous parenthood of Kārttikeya, who is called the son of Śiva and Agni in different accounts. The intent seems to have been to say that Śiva in his Agni form begot Kārttikeya. 'Agni at one time cast his eyes on the waters...the seed became gold, for this reason the latter shines like fire' (*ŚB* II: 1: 1: 5). Gold sprang from Agni's seed (*ŚB* III: 9: 4: 1). The *AV* reports that the waters hid the gold (*AV* XIX: 27: 9) and this seems to form the real nucleus of the story of Skanda's birth.

Agni is called Sahasramuṣka (with a thousand scrota) this reminds us of the emphasis on the virility of Śiva, of his Urddhvaliṅga or Mahaśepha image and perhaps indirectly associates Agni with the phallic cult.

Agni has a cult of his own. Oblations to him consist of cakes with clarified butter on them (*ṚV* X: 45: 9); a goat is to be sacrificed to him; he who desires rain should offer a dappled cow to Agni (*MS* II: 5: 7, II: 5: 2; *agnaye'jam TMB* I: 8: 6). Agni's oblations should be offered in the evening (*TB* II: 1: 2: 6)—this is another link between him and the gods of the Śiva group all of whom are associated with the night. A she-goat is said to be the sacrifice of Agni and Soma; a Ruru deer for Agni, because Agni is Ruru (*TMB* I: 8: 6, VII: 5: 10; *JB* III: 49). The he-goat (is to be slaughtered) for Agni (*ŚB* VI: 2: 1: 5). The animal-cake belongs to Agni Vaisvānara (*ŚB* VI: 2: 1: 35). Nothing injures Agni's mouth (*GBU* I: 2).

He who desires heaven should offer the Agniṣṭoma sacrifice, for by it one conquers Yama's region (*MU* VI: 36). The *Purāṇas* lay it down that for wealth Agni should be approached. In the Agnicayana ceremony, some hairs should be cut from the goat and mixed with clay, while the offerer says, 'I mix thee, herein, the well-born Jātavedas'. The goat is thus a symbol of Agni; it is also the mount of Pūṣan, another god of this group.

The conceptual basis of the psychopompos may have been the funeral fire which leads the soul to the next world.

'The night is Agni's' (*TS* I: 5: 9). In this and other similar dark associations Agni resembles the Śiva–Yama–Varuṇa group. Thus a prayer to Agni says: 'Thee, O Agni, with the barren cow have I obtained' (*TS* V: 5: 7, cf. the barren cow offered to Varuṇa, another god of this group). Again 'for Agni the black-necked' (offering; *TS* V: 5: 22). Agni is said to have had three elder brothers. They perished when carrying the offering to the gods. Frightened, Agni hid himself. The gods sought him out, he chose a boon from them: that portion of the offering that falls outside the enclosing sticks became the portion of his brothers (*TS* VI: 2: 8). One remembers Śiva being excluded from the sacrificial portion and Yama and Varuṇa being offered the left-over or cast-off portion of the oblation. Agni is directly said to be the lowest of the gods (*AB* I: I: I).

Agni is a major Ṛgvedic god praised by many priestly families, but we can notice his special devotees and favourite priestly clans. The Kaṇvas are said to be his worshippers from of old (*ṚV* I: 14: 2, 5). The Bhṛgus worshipped Agni for 'divya janman' (divine birth, *ṚV* I: 45: 6). Atharvan's son Dadhyañc lighted Agni of old, so did the sage Pāthya; Agni is the patron of Divodāsa (*ṚV* VI: 16: 14: 15). In *ṚV* VIII: 43: 16 Agni is called Bhṛguvat, Manuṣvat and Aṅgirasvat—connected with Bhṛgu, Manu and Aṅgiras. Now Bhṛgu is connected with Varuṇa (as son or sometimes as father). Manu is Yama's brother and Aṅgiras is connected with both Varuṇa and Yama. The word 'Aṅgiras' may have been derived from the same root as Agni. Agni is said to be created by Atharvan (*ṚV* X: 21: 5). If we remember that the Avestan name for fire is 'Athar', Atharvat (or Atharvan) would mean 'he who has fire' or 'is connected with fire', i.e. a fire-priest. Assuming the existence of a special kind of fire-priests, a common heritage for Indo-Iranian or perhaps Indo-European people, the *ṚV* verse is easily explained: the Athar-priests created fire (by friction) for sacrificial purposes. The Aṅgirases are said to be born of Agni (*ṚV* X: 62: 5). The Bhṛgus sought him out (*ṚV* X: 46: I, X: 122: 5). This sense of discovery is perhaps due to the fact that the fire-sacrifice was invented at a point in history, and popular memory associated this invention with the Bhṛgus. 'Of the two types of offerings the fireless variety would seem to be more primitive' (H. D. Griswold, *The religion of the Rigveda*, p. 158). Thus the later ritual was a speciality of the Bhṛgus. The word *Bhṛgu* seems originally to have been a designation of Agni; the cognate Greek word *Phlegyai* means 'shining'. Thus the fire-priests were supposed to be a human manifestation of the fire-god, similar concepts are not uncommon.

The Aṅgiras-priests, whose functions must have centred round the fire cult, whose existence was essentially bound up with Agni, are naturally thought of as born of Agni. The Bhṛgus, who seem to be a priestly family specialized in the ceremonies of Ignis Rogalis, who were specially connected with the funeral ceremonies, the underworld and eschatology, naturally sought Agni (Kravyād and Kavyavāhana) out, for their domain, i.e. priestly jurisdiction, concerned that aspect of Agni (cf. Bhṛgu's descent into the nether world). In the Cāturmāsya, i.e. seasonal sacrifice of Piṇḍapitṛajña, Kavyavāhana Agni is invoked with Yama at an offering to the fathers. The *YV* mentions three forms of Agni: the eater of raw flesh, eater of corpses and the sacrificial fire (*VS* I: 17).[1] Agni's funerary aspect runs beneath all three words. Agni is said to have been created by heaven and earth, the waters, Tvaṣṭṛ, the Bhṛgus and also by Mātariśvan for the benefit of Manu (*ṚV* X: 47: 9), i.e. for the benefit of man, mānava. Yama has special knowledge regarding Agni (*ṚV* X: 51: 3). Agni protected Jaratkarṇa, burnt Jarūtha, saved Atri and gave offspring to Nṛmedha (*ṚV* X: 80: 3). Sāyaṇa in his commentary on *ṚV* X: 87: 12 says that Atharvavat Dadhyan was a great killer of monsters; thus he was traditionally an assistant of Agni. *ṚV* X: 151: 5 says that Agni helped Atri, Bharadvāja, Gaviṣṭhira, Kaṇva and Trasadasyu in battle. Dīrghatamas Māmateya, Kutsa, Apnavat, Sṛñjaya, Kumāra Somaka Śunahśepa, Vaiyaśva and Sthirayūpa seem to be among Agni's protégés (*ṚV* I: 147: 3, IV: 4: 13, IV: 16: 4, V: 2: 8, VIII: 23: 16, VIII: 23: 24). Uśanas' son Kavi pleased Agni and settled him (Agni) in the house of Manu. Now Uśanas became Śiva's son, and was indirectly associated with the phallus cult as we have seen in the *Mbh.* anecdote. Mārkaṇḍeya narrates the story and says: Agni himself became Aṅgiras (*Mbh.* III: 207: 7). King Nīla of Māhiṣmatī city became associated with Agni (and his cult) through the marriage of his daughter with Agni.

The fire which shines by night acts as the deputy of the sun and hence is called the lord of brilliance (*MS* I: 5: 9); that is why the east is Agni's quarter (*ŚB* VI: 3: 3: 1). An oft-repeated Vedic anecdote connects fire with the sun: the Aṅgirases sent Agni to bid the Ādityas perform a sacrifice to win heaven, but the Ādityas forestalled them, so that the

[1] The word *Kravya* is derived from *Kravis* (= 'carrion'). Greek *Kreas*, Latin *cruentus*, *cruror*, *crudus* or *caro*, Russian *Krovj*, Hebrew *cru*, Lithuanian *Krauja* and Old German *hreo* are cognates with the same or similar meanings. Kavya (oblation to the fathers), a probable cognate of Kravya, seems to be associated with the dark aspect of Agni which devours carrion. *Śava* (a corpse) may also be a cognate from the word at a later period.

Aṅgirases had to officiate for them, much to their indignation. For this the Aṅgirases received the fee of a white horse—the sun (*ŚB* III: 5: 1: 13; *AB* VI: 34; *KB* XXV: 6; *PB* XVI: 12: 1; *GB* II: 6: 14). J. Duchesne-Guillemin in his article 'Fire in Iran and Greece' says

> Pahlavi books, according to which the living species were preserved in the heavenly bodies: men in the sun, the animals in the moon, and the plants in the stars... All this is told mythologically in the Bundahsin: at the death of Gayomart the first man a part of his seed fell on the ground, while another part was collected by the god Neryosang 'Messenger of the humans', who took it to the sun to be purified. In the same way the seed of the primordial Bull was borne to the Moon... the vital seed which transmits life, and hence the warmth is... a species of fire. (*East and West*, new series, vol. 13, nos 2–3, 1962, p. 200.)

The word 'Neryosang' is the same as 'Narāśaṃsa', an epithet of fire; like Agni he also is the messenger of men and like Agni again is connected with Yama (Gayomart).

In *Yasna* 32: 7 fire is the instrument of truth and justice (asa = Ṛta). The connection of Neryosang and Athar with asa is constant. Among the Hatra finds there is an image of Fire in Parthian dress with two snakes in his left hand and an axe in the right; his hair is dishevelled and he has a limp beard. One notices the beard which is a constant feature in Indian images of Agni. The axe and the snakes connect him with the Śiva group.[1] Figures of Agni date from the medieval period of Indian iconography. There is, however, one representation of Agni (in the Mathura museum) which is pre-Gupta. He is represented as a pot-bellied two-armed figure, seated on the goat or ram. A water vessel is usually near his figure, and a rosary in one of his hands. The expression is usually an irate glare. Long and wavy flames emanate from his body. He is usually sparingly decked out with ornaments, but always has a sacred thread indicating that he is a Brahmin. It seems that to a minor sect Agni retained the supreme status that every god attained at some period or other through kathenotheism.

[1] Girru the Babylonian fire-god was primarily the god of the sacrificial fire (cf. *E.R.E.*). In Greece fire was considered as a holy element, kept burning in the temple, at the altar; in Rome fire was kept burning in the temple by the royal palace, although it was not actually deified. In ancient Iran fire was regarded as the most sacred element. It seems that Agni 'the messenger of god' was an older Agni than Agni 'the god'. 'Pre-scientific man was keenly alive to the importance of this element for good or evil, to its demoniac and almost indomitable power, a feature which has, for instance, obtained considerable importance in the Japanese fire-god' (J. Gonda, *Some observations on the relation between 'Gods' and 'Powers'*, p. 38). Agni remained the powerful element even after his deification. Thus waters at the royal consecration are full of Agni. Huitzilopochtli the Nahuan fire-god is fierce, ruthless and terrible. He is also the Mexican fire-god, and because food was obtained by the tribes as booty in war Huitzilopochtli, the god of war, was also the giver of food.

Thus in the *MAU* we read that Puruṣa is none other than Agni Vaiśvānara (II: 2: 6). The *TS* litany to Agni also raises him to a god of paramount importance (*TS* I: 5). The *TB* says that Agni is the nocturnal aspect of Sūrya (II: 1: 2: 6) and that Agni is head of the earth; in heaven there is an Agni, Nāka by name, and Brahman too is Agni (*TB* III: 1: 3: 3, III: 2: 3: 5, III: 12: 2: 7; *JB* II: 233). The *JB* calls Agni the sacrifice (I: 170); Mahāśāla Jābāla recognized Agni as the supreme god (*ŚB* X: 3: 3). Agni is a Brahmin (*ŚB* X: 4: 1: 5), the pioneer (*ŚB* XI: 1: 5: 5), the gold-man (*ŚB* X: 4: 1: 6), Saṃvarga, the despoiler (*ŚB* XII: 4: 4: 5). Thus Agni came to mean various things to the followers of the Agni cult.

Śiva is connected with Agni; also as an alternate form of Agni he had much in common not so much with 'Agni the messenger of the gods or men' as with 'the carrion-devouring Agni' who carried oblations to the fathers. This dark side of Agni was naturally connected with the dark gods of whom Śiva became the head, for Śiva's way to supremacy lay through the mingling of various apparently divergent cults.

In northern India Śiva became associated with the Buddha in the Śākta and Tantric magic cults which spread in China and Tibet. The syncretistic figure emerged as Mahākāla, Bhairava and Bhīma. The Buddhist mother-goddesses also were a conglomeration of abstract concepts, regional and tutelary goddesses and Brāhmaṇical mother-goddesses. In the Tantric cult these came to be known as Vajradhātrī, Locanā, Māmakī, Pāṇḍarā and Tārā; of these Tārā was accepted the most widely (cf. Monier-Williams, *Buddhism*).

A rising cult has to fight many enemies in the shape of rival local cults and already existing supreme gods. The *JB* records these conflicts, before Śiva ascended to the Olympian throne. His immediate rival was Indra. 'Hara surpassed Indra. Indra could only defeat Hara after the gods praised him with the Harivat psalm' (*JB* I: 200). The psalm exalting Rudra, ascribing power and supremacy to him, is the *Jarābodhīya sāman*. By it he obtains overlordship of animals (*JB* III: 11). Indra's pride was crushed by Śiva in the *Mbh.* anecdote recorded in I: 189. The Kirātārjunīya episode also records Śiva's superiority to Indra's (*Mbh.* III: 39, 40). But his over-lordship in heaven had to be established over other rivals—Prajāpati, for instance.

But Prajāpati could hardly be visualized as fighting for his position, so it was best to formulate an equation—Rudra is Puruṣa, i.e. Prajāpati. Rudra, however, did challenge Prajāpati, not as a rival, but as a judge punishing a miscreant. Prajāpati had committed incest with his own daughter in the shape of a deer. Rudra, who had been created for the curbing of excesses, shot Prajāpati (*JB* III: 26: 2–3). Out of the seed which was spilled on the Himalayas different creatures were formed. Here Rudra in his fierce aspect assumes a position from where he can judge even Prajāpati.

The Liṅga cult as a mode of Śiva-worship is very widespread in India. This form of worship, of virility and fertility, has parallels in other mythologies too.

Śiva as Kāla or Mahākāla was a direct rival of Prajāpati, whom the *Brāhmaṇas* identify with Time, the Year (Saṃvatsara). This potential conflict is never brought to a head, they both retain their power, until after the *Brāhmaṇas* Prajāpati increasingly becomes a mere manifestation of Agni and, yielding his personality to Śiva, dwindles into a mere figure-head while Śiva absorbs the form and essence of Time.[1]

The epic Brahman who, when a crisis arises deputes a certain god to accomplish the necessary feat is also a more shadowy figure beside the rising Purāṇic (therefore, sectarian) Śiva. When the gods are molested by Vṛtra, Brahman sends them to Śiva, who removes his in-grown armour (gātraja varman) with which Indra kills Vṛtra (*Mbh.* VII: 69). Here Prajāpati acts as an intermediary in stealing the glory from Indra and lending it to Śiva. When the gods were harried by demon Tāraka, Brahman told them that Śiva's son was the destined divine general who would lead the gods to victory against Tāraka (*Mbh.* XIII: 87), and Brahman asked Śiva to create. Although eventually it was neither Brahman nor Śiva who creates, the anecdote records Brahman's preference for Śiva as a creator, and also Śiva's defiance and real independence of Brahman, for he can show his temper with impunity (*Mbh.* X: 17). The Vedic hymn to Puruṣa when Puruṣa offers himself for the sake of creation has a brief parallel where Śiva is said to have offered all creatures together with his own self in the great Sarvamedha sacrifice (*Mbh.* XII: 122: 4).

This brief passage is doubtless intended to set up Śiva as a rival of Brahman. When Saṃkara (mixture of castes) occurred Brahman asked Śiva to set this right. Śiva created Daṇḍa (punishment) and punished Kṣupa a self-conceived son of Brahman (*Mbh.* XII: 122). This again repeats the

[1] We have an echo of this in the Avestan concept of Zurvan (or Zervan). 'Le sacrifice rétablit Prajāpati, c'est-à-dire, entre autres, restaure le temps perturbé...L'opposition des deux aspects du temps linéaire de l'histoire équivalent à l'époque pendant laquelle le mal exerce son pouvoir. Le dualisme lui-même devient plus prononcé' (M. Molé, *Culte, mythe, et cosmologie*, pp. 529–30). In the Kāla aspect of Śiva we have this same inherent dualism which probably led to the formulation of Prajāpati as infinite time. Illimitability of space and time is the conceptual basis of Brahman, while Śiva personifies the changing aspect of time which ages and destroys the universe.

JB story of Śiva punishing Brahman; but this time the reason is different. Śiva's creating 'asi' (the scimitar) also shows him in his punisher aspect. It is significant that in the later books of the *Mbh.* Śiva becomes gradually independent of Brahman; as in the *Purāṇas*, the rising sectarian god's relationship with Brahman is always one of alliance, never of submission or subordination.

The *HV* psalm of Śiva reads like a praise of the supreme spirit—Brahman. Thus Śiva is one, Puruṣa sanātana (eternal), purātana (ancient) Kaṇāda by name, and aja (unbegotten) (III: 85: 11). All this sets up Śiva as a rival and supplanter of Brahman.

The other rival with whom Śiva had to come to terms before he could become a paramount sectarian god was Viṣṇu or Nārāyaṇa. The solar base of Viṣṇu personified as Sūrya were partly assimilated by Śiva as described in the *Mbh.* litanies. He is called Sūrya or Bhāskara in III: 39: 79, VII: 201: 108, XII: 284: 15 and XIV: 8: 16. Kṛṣṇa as an incarnation of Viṣṇu pays due homage to Śiva and advises Arjuna to do so (*Mbh.* VII: 57). Kṛṣṇa himself approaches Śiva for a son (*Mbh.* XIII: 14). The rivalry must have persisted, not between Śiva and Kṛṣṇa but between Śiva and Viṣṇu. Brahman's attitude of ambivalence regarding the superiority of the one to the other added to the ambiguity of their position. To the two rival sects, Śaiva and Vaiṣṇava—each claiming priority, superiority and the final revelation of the ultimate truth—their own cultic god was the supreme being. Each had a growing following, so there could be no true compromise, no subjugation of one creed by the other. Book XII of the *Mbh.*, the *HV* and the early *Purāṇas* are full of this tussle between Śiva and Viṣṇu. Finally a compromise was arrived at in the Harihara image. It was a sort of coalition of two sects, which had so long vied with each other for supremacy. In books XII and XIII of the *Mbh.*, chapter succeeds chapter on the priority and superiority of either of these gods. Eulogy is usually extracted from the rival god who recognizes the real superiority of his rival, bows to him and extols him as the truly supreme divinity. Sometimes Brahman (masc.) is brought in as arbiter, sometimes superior exploits determine the real worth of the god, at other times other gods, sages and saints justify a devotee's choice of his personal god. Thus in seemingly unending disputes Śiva and Viṣṇu are alternately posed as superior. Behind the literary conflict the real tussle must have been really tough and apparently insoluble. The rising sects had everything at stake—priestly classes with large followings had everything to lose or gain, hence the endless dispute. Until during the time of the composition of the later sectarian *Purāṇas* there was a division of diocese, and each sect was contented with its own following. Traces of conflict are still found in the later *Purāṇas* but a working agreement had been achieved. Harihara may be a symbol of such a compromise.

One of the sources of Śiva's strength was his multifarious manifestations and the peculiar capacity by which antinomies cohere in him. He is the only god who is frequently described with his family—Umā, his wife, Kārttikeya and Gaṇeśa his sons, and in later literature and modern ritual his two daughters Lakṣmī and Sarasvatī. Yet he is portrayed all through epic literature as the god who lives in the cremation ground, with no ties with the outside world—a mendicant *par excellence*—the Yogīśvara.

There is one episode in the *Mbh.* which brings this out very clearly. Maṅkaṇaka the sage of old was wounded with the blade of a Kuśa grass, and vegetable juice came out from the wound. He danced with joy, evidently because his merit and meditation were of such a high order that there was no blood in him—and blood symbolized the natural man with his carnality and cruelty. So Maṅaṇaka, in the apparent success of his meditation, danced with joy. The gods could not tolerate this complacence; they came to Śiva and begged him to stop this unseemly and boastful behaviour. Śiva touched one finger with another, cinder fell out from it. Maṅkaṇaka, thoroughly discomfited, acknowledged his deficiency and sang a hymn to Śiva (*Mbh.* III: 81, repeated in the vulgate edn. in IX: 38: 39, 40). In the second version of the vulgate all earth shook from the boastful laughter of Maṅkaṇaka. Śiva, at the gods' request, came and asked him the reason of his bragging. He displayed his feat, Śiva surpassed with his, and the boasting gave place to praise.

Assuming that Indian religious practices were encouraging vegetarianism at the time (as is quite clear from several other episodes), Maṅkaṇaka's, achievement was of a high order: he had converted his blood into vegetable juice. Such successes belong to Yoga as a discipline. Śiva's own feat was similarly indicative of attaining success of a higher order for ashes symbolize the complete mortification of the flesh, the triumph of the spirit over the world and the flesh, and supreme detachment from all carnal desires. Thus Śiva is shown as the supreme saint—Yogīśvara.

There is another such episode about Rudrakoṭi, a pilgrimage. Once millions of sages demanded a vision of Rudra. Rudra meditated and created millions of Rudras to gratify their desire (vulgate *Mbh.* III. 82: 119–23). Before the burning of the three cities, when the gods approached Śiva, they found him wrapped in meditation (vulgate *Mbh.* VIII: 33: 46). This was one of his normal images. To Dakṣa he discloses the secret of his success: he had performed rigorous austerities. After Brahman betrays him through impatience and gets creation accomplished through another, Śiva went away to Muñjapṛṣṭha for meditation; when Brahman approached him he was delayed under water because of prolonged meditation. There are numerous episodes which describe him as lost in meditation or practising rigid austerities. The *Śvet. U* which praises Śiva kathenotheistically calls him Rudra Maharṣi (the great ascetic, III: 4, IV: 12).

This brings to our minds the Mohenjo Daro seal depicting the proto-Paśupati Śiva. The attitude of sitting with legs flattened under the body is typically Indian and is rarely found in old West Asian art. This may have been the Yogīśvara god of the indigenous population in the region where later the Paśupata Śaiva sect flourished so well, probably because the Yoga tradition was not alien to the region. Śiva thus was Yogīśvara, the supreme monk or Yogādhyakṣa, the supervisor of Yoga, perhaps the central figure of the Pāśupatas. In his Yogīśvara aspect Śiva reflects the Sāṃkhya principle of the non-active Paruṣa of the *Sāṃkhya Kārika* or the 'avyakta' of the *Śvetāśvatara* or *Maitrāyaṇīya Upaniṣads*. Inactivity is stressed because action belongs to Prakṛti (Nature) and is a product of the Guṇas. In the later *HV* and Purāṇic myth of Pārvatī undergoing rigorous penances in order to obtain the meditating and inactive Śiva as her husband, we have a beautiful mythopeic imagination at work—an imagination which transfers the abstract Sāṃkhya principle of the union of Puruṣa and Prakṛti for creation to the field of mythology. No wonder Śiva and Pārvatī are styled 'parents of the universe'. Thus abstract philosophical concepts are absorbed and projected in vivid mythological personalities—a process which adds greater charm and appeal to the Śiva-Pārvatī cult.

Some scholars have suggested that the Muni mentioned in the *ṚV* Keśin-hymn, who drank poison with Rudra, indicates a monastic order which practised rigour for attaining liberation, and that this attitude to life is essentially non-Vedic. There seems to be some truth in the assumption; hermit orders are nowhere mentioned in the *ṚV*, except in the late tenth book, where many elements of non-Vedic practice and ritual have crept in and appear for the first time. The wild attire of the clan or the followers of the cult and their self-torture is something foreign to the Vedic religion which was organised congregational worship, with communal or family sacrifices indicating a homogeneity in religion. But several episodes in the *Mbh.* give us a hint that self-mortification as part of religious discipline was associated with the cult of Śiva. The vulgate *Mbh.* records the story of Atri's wife leaving her husband and worshipping Śiva: she slept on wooden nails and fasted for a hundred years before Śiva blessed her with sons (XIII: 14). The *HV* has the anecdote of Gārgya the preceptor of the Vṛṣṇis and Andhakas who propitiated Śiva by eating iron-dust for long years before Śiva granted him a mighty son. All this reminds us of the present-day practices of self-torture at the time of a Śiva festival (called Caḍaka in Bengal) in many Indian villages. This certainly is a new trait, for the Vedic Aryans' religion knew nothing of mortification of the flesh on this scale.

Probably with the spread of the Upaniṣadic thought, when people questioned the efficacy of the sacrifices, one section of the people took interest in the existing indigenous cults and experimented with practices of self-torture as a means of liberation. Liberation itself is an un-Ṛgvedic goal, for the sacrifices promise mundane bliss or heaven. It is with the *Āraṇyakopaniṣads*, the forest treatises of philosophical enquiries, that we first have a glimpse into the new aspirations, desires and goals—liberation through knowledge, and self-realization through detachment.

On the other hand we have another cult associated with Śiva symbolized by his associates—a macabre host outlandishly dressed with ugly, sub-human and uncouth figures, of unnatural and repulsive behaviour and revolting practices. They sing, dance and make merry. As the leader of this host, Śiva is described as fond of songs, music, dance and dramas, which should be offered to him by way of worship. His followers are wild, fond of meat and wine and thus resemble the Selini Satyrs or Bacchants of Dionysus or the Corybantes of Rhea. They revel in blood and enjoy the pleasures of the flesh.

As Śiva's final theophany is a composite figure which had assimilated many gods, i.e. many cults from very olden times, it is perhaps true that with Pūṣan came a shepherd tribe with their pastoral god. R. N. Dandekar, in his article 'Pūṣan the pastoral god of the Veda' (*NIA*, June 1942), quotes Charpentier's derivation of Pūṣan and says it may be derived from *pśu-san* = *paśusan* = 'acquirer of cattle'. This compares with the Avestic *fsusan*. 'The Bhāradvājas', says Dr Dandekar, 'must have been one of the ancient Vedic tribes whose main occupation was cattle-breeding. And Pūṣan was the god of these nomadic shepherds and cow-herds' (p. 61). Of Karambha, Pūṣan's mess, he says, 'This is obviously intended to assert the dignity of the original Pūṣan religion' (p. 65). Thus one strand of the rich Śiva-skein can be disentangled: pastoral people with their god, his food and cultic practices had joined the Śiva throng. Similarly other component gods must have joined in with their orgiastic practices, dances and intoxicating drinks until the rich Śiva-symphony was composed.

It is Śiva's potentiality as the meeting ground of contradictory attributes that raises him above his rivals. He stands for supreme detachment as also for ritual abandon and indulgence. He is indifferent to worldly ties, yet he himself is the only god with a really convincing family. He lives both in cremation ground and also on a lofty mountain peak and is a friend of Kuvera the god of wealth. He is dressed as a mendicant and is yet the giver of many gifts. Himself the object of meditation, he is ever lost in meditation.

As the husband of Jagajjananī he is the father of the world—and thus enjoys a unique position. Brahman is called Pitāmaha (grandfather), and it is tacitly accepted that Śiva is the father, thus reducing the other gods to a somewhat subsidiary position. He becomes the intermediary between the supreme being personalized in Brahman and the other Ṛgvedic gods who were fast becoming dim and rather unconvincing hierophanies. His children (Kārttikeya, Gaṇapati, and later Lakṣmi and Sarasvatī) are more real and significant than Indra's son Jayanta or Viṣṇu's son Madana.

Śiva's figure in the *ṚV* was sufficiently amorphous and sufficiently suggestive for his subsequent development through syncretism. The potentiality of the too concrete Ṛgvedic gods is soon exhausted; their feats are too well-known, too fully, concretely and frequently described for any different explanation or substantial alteration. They become static after a period because they cannot imbibe new attributes, or incorporate new cultic practices. Indra and the Aśvins are good examples of such gods. Besides, as society moves on with the different cultural needs of different races and ethnic groups, its ritual and spiritual needs also undergo a transformation, its gods are metamorphosed and the contour of its entire pantheon is altered. Neighbouring gods with their cultic demands pay allegiance to the 'high gods', a coalition takes place, new cults are grafted in, become part of the organism and the process goes on until the particular 'high god' is changed beyond recognition. In ancient Egypt and Mesopotamia, in Crete, and Greece and Rome only those gods survived which could go on assimilating regional gods. In mythology, as in life, only the fittest survive. And mythological fitness is determined by the capacity to assimilate. For this there should be appropriate haziness and the necessary vacuum together with one or two suggestive hints which would render the particular god eminently suitable for syncretism. In the *ṚV* Śiva all these elements were present—he was strong and powerful, the benign healer, the bountiful giver, and yet the fierce and wrathful archer whose shafts are sought to be avoided. In both the *VS* and the *TS* of the *YV* where the non-*ṚV* Śiva makes his first appearance this dual potentiality is treated at a great length. He becomes sinister with infinite possibilities for assimilating all the dark chthonic gods into his personality. He is first mentioned as a mountain-god in the *YV*, so that when the *Kenopaniṣad* introduces Umā Haimavatī who later becomes Śiva's consort his potentiality becomes virtually illimitable, for, as the consort of the mother-goddess a hierogamy is formed which serves as the taking-off ground for loftier altitudes. Philosophy and mystery contribute their share and the divine pair becomes the symbol of the infinite, the supreme being.

It is significant that the monistic *Śvet. U* which draws heavily upon Sāṃkhya terminology raises Śiva to the position of the supreme being by attributing solar traits to him (cf. III: 8 which, quoting a *ṚV* stanza, describes him as effulgent) and also elevates him to a status superior to Brahman's. Thus he creates Brahman (III: 4, VI: 18), is the lord of all gods (VI: 11), the multiform all-god (III: 11, IV: 3, VI: 16), the supreme creator (IV: 14) even of the gods (IV: 12, VI: 13), the god of destruction (III: 2, IV: 11, V: 3) and finally the god who grants ultimate release (I: 10, III: 1, 7, IV: 11, 16, V: 14, VI: 6, 13, 16, 18).

With the expansion of population, as village after village was influenced by the Aryanized culture-tract, god after regional god is assimilated to Rudra—some because they are mountain-gods, or associated with snakes or bulls, doves or lions, others because they have primitive mother-goddesses or huntresses, virgins or corn-goddesses as consorts; some because they symbolize yoga, yet others because they are wild, fond of meat, wine and dancing; some death-and-ghost gods come in, fire-and-air gods join company until there emerges a composite godhead with multifarious functions, a symbol of a vast subterranean region of life and a projection of the unplumbed depths of consciousness. Analysing the constituent elements of Rudra-Śiva we have a glimpse into some primitive cultic gods. Alexander's generals in India defeated a tribe which Greek historians have recorded as the Siboi. The people of this tribe wore animal skins and shaved their heads. The Muṇḍas also shaved their heads as their name indicates. Muṇḍa was an epic appellate of Śiva himself (he was visualized with a shaven head), obviously derived from the god of the Muṇḍa sect and their practice of shaving the head—a practice the Śaivas incorporated into their complex and ever-expanding catholic system. Some other aspects of this complex cult are found in the inscriptions on the Kuninda and Audumbara coins. The Kushans, too, seem to have patronized the Śaiva cult, Kadphises called himself a Māheśvara, i.e. a follower of Śiva.

Śiva's Naṭarāja image which shows him as a dancing god, performing the cosmic dance preliminary to final cosmic annihilation, seems also to be the sublimation into philosophy of what originally was a sectarian practice—viz. ritual dance.[1] The fantastic derivation given in the *Brāhmaṇas* connects Rudra with weeping. Before a conflict with the Asuras, the gods deposited their wealth with Agni who went away with it. They sought to take it forcibly. He wept (arodīt) and therefore was called Rudra (*TS* I: 5: I). It is significant that the story identifies Agni with Rudra even though the word Rudra is derived from the root *rud*. Also this Agni-Rudra is shown to be treacherous and thievish by nature. This is in the *TS* (i.e. *YV*)—the time of the coalescence of many allied gods and the first emergence of Rudra-Śiva of the epics and *Purāṇas*. The *Śatarudrīya* Rudra too is false and fickle.

As the names multiply, the god also assumes more facets. In the *YV* and the *Brāhmaṇas* we have Īśāna (*TB* III: 10: 9: 9; *JB* II: 254; *ŚB* VI: I: 3: 17), Hara (*TB* II: 2: 10: I; *JB* I: 200), Śarva, Bhava (*ŚB* I: 7: 3: 8), Mṛḍa (*MS* I: 10: 20), Tryambaka (*VS* XVI; *ŚB* II: 6: 2: 2), Aśani, Mahān Deva, Kumāra (*ŚB* VI: I: 3: 14, 16, 18), Īśānadevatā (*GB* I: 25). Later we have five distinct names by which the Pāśupatas know their Pañcānana, the five-faced god, viz. Sadyojāta, Vāmadeva, Aghora, Tatpuruṣa and Īśāna. In the *Viṣṇudharmottara Purāṇa* we have a different list: there the five faces are made into five elements. Mahādeva is the eastern face, Bhairava, the southern, Naṇḍivaktra, the western, Umāvaktra, the northern and Sadāśiva the top face (bk III, ch. 47, w I–18).

Śiva is also depicted in the Śarabheśa (or Śarabha) mūrti (image). This is a man-bird-beast composition. When Viṣṇu attacked Hiraṇyakaśipu in the Nṛsiṃha (man-lion) form in order to vindicate his devotee Prahlāda's case, Śiva attacked the man-lion in the Śarabheśa form in order to rescue his devotee Hiraṇyakaśipu. This image is seen in many Orissa temples. We clearly see a conflict of two sects. Prahlāda was a devotee of Viṣṇu who attacked his father Hiraṇyakaśipu on Prahlāda's behalf; similarly Hiraṇyakaśipu was a devotee of Śiva's and Śiva felt obliged to come to

[1] Dr Chatterji mentions the Old Tamil word *civan* which means 'red' and *cempu*, 'copper red'. The Tamil words correspond to Sanskrit 'Śiva' and 'Śambhu'. Rudra, according to Dr Chatterji, may have been derived from Rudhra, the name of an old Dravidian divinity, and the word may have meant, the red god. One also remembers the German word *rot* (from which we have English *red*). Red is the colour of fire and wrath, so the original concept may have been one of fierceness.

the former's rescue. Now Viṣṇu had assumed the man-lion form and the lion is the king of animals. The Śarabha is a mythical eight-footed winged animal which is supposed to be mightier than the lion. So Śiva assumed this shape to vanquish Viṣṇu. In this particular myth Śiva comes out victorious and the myth reflects the ascendancy of Śaivism. (In Śarabha we perhaps have a reminiscence of an old Indo-European myth: Odin's horse Sleipnir also was mighty and eight-footed). In the so-called Līlāmūrtis (dalliance images) of Śiva are pointers to the syncretism of several indigenous cults: cf. bhikṣāṭanamūrti (mendicant-form), candraśekhara (moon-crested), nṛtya-mūrti (dancing), gaja-saṃhāra (elephant-slaying), ardhanārīśvara (androgynous, itself the result of the amalgamation of two cults), paśupati (lord of beasts) and saṃhāra (destroyer).

The Ekapāda mūrti or sthāṇumūrti (one-footed or stationary image) may also have been supplied by older sects whose gods corresponded to Śiva in some respects and whose gods were absorbed by the rising Śiva. Thus Śiva was growing in dimension by assimilating neighbouring gods of a similar description.

Śiva is also said to be manifest in eight forms: water, fire, air, sky, earth, the sun and moon and the sacrificer. This may be a list of the eight symbols of Śiva to his different cultic followings, the eight primary forms in which he was worshipped. Pebbles naturally rounded by water-current are worshipped as symbols of Śiva; the bull also is his symbol. Thus the cultic symbols of many sects or clans converged into one composite god who stood for all these various objects.

Mortification of the flesh as well as indulgence in carnal pleasures, the worship of the bull or the phallus, as well as the meditation of a cosmic principle—all converged into the shaping of the epic-Purāṇic Śiva. In the realm of ideas and concepts too Śiva commands lofty altitudes. He is the direct projection of the dual principle of Puruṣa and Prakṛti, of Sāṃkhya in his Hara-Pārvatī or Ardhanārīśvara image as well as the personification of the supremely isolated and supremely abstract Vedantic principle of Brahman in his Yogīśvara aspect. These projections of metaphysical concepts into cultic (i.e. sectarian) gods worshipped in varied rituals was the only tangible way in which the masses of the people could respond to the growing attenuation of the corresponding ideas in the realm of philosophy.

In the Purāṇic triad (Brahman-Viṣṇu-Maheśvara) Śiva stands for final annihilation (saṃhāra). The cosmic Tāṇḍava dance precedes it and Śiva's Tāṇḍava dance indicates the close of an aeon (kalpa). It is quite fitting that the god who created daṇḍa (punishment), asi (sword) and mṛtyu (death), whose component factors are Yama, Agni, Nirṛti and the Maruts should undertake final destruction. This is an inevitable phase in the scheme of things, for destruction makes fresh creation possible, thus Śiva's function is absolutely indispensable. He becomes Brahman's associate in his capacity as the supreme destroyer. Mahākāla (Time the Great) with his consort Mahākālī is in charge of an indispensable third part of the cosmic scheme, namely destruction. Thus a minor *ṚV* god who became an agglomerate of sinister and benign traits in the *YV*, an alien god denied sacrificial share in the *Brāhmaṇas*, is gradually transmuted into an organic god of the Purāṇic triad. And the Purāṇic pantheon has come to stay, for it has since remained essentially unaltered for about a millennium and a half.

PART II

GODS OF THE VIṢṆU GROUP

CHAPTER 10

THE SOLAR GODS

SOLAR GODS are the most numerous in the *ṚV*. We have Sūrya, Savitṛ, the Aśvins, Mitra (sometimes Varuṇa), Vivasvat, Viṣṇu, Bhaga, Aṃśa, Dakṣa, Aryaman, Dhātṛ Mārtaṇḍa, Pūṣan and the goddesses Uṣas and Sūryā.

Not all of these are given distinct individuality, but enough is said to give us a glimpse into the natural phenomenon or idea behind the apotheosis.

SŪRYA

Sūrya, literally the sun, is primarily the orb of the physical sun itself. He is the aid to vision. He is pleaded to remove diseases. 'Cure my heart disease, place my jaundice in the yellow birds' (*ṚV* I: 50: 11: 12). He is the soul of the moving world (*ṚV* I: 115: 1); and the source of Madhuvidyā —the knowledge of honey-therapy as antidote to poison (*ṚV* I: 191). His light lightens the world, his brightness makes men happy. He is golden in appearance, and comes riding a golden chariot drawn by horses called Etaśa (*ṚV* I: 121: 13). Sūrya sees everything that goes on in the world; he is the spy of the world (*ṚV* IV: 13: 3). He supports the sky and is called the pillar of the sky (*ṚV* IV: 13: 5). His knowledge of men's movements gives him the position of a judge of human actions: let him proclaim the innocent before Mitra, Varuṇa, Aryaman and Agni. A familiar idea is that the solar gods enter the fire by night, hence it is that the fire is seen from a distance at night; this fire enters the rising sun at dawn (*ṚV* X: 88: 6). Hence fire is seen only as smoke by day. 'Agni is light, light is the sun, svāhā': this should be the vesper. 'The sun is light and light is Agni: svāhā': this should be the matin (*TB* II: 1: 2: 10). Sūrya is supplicated for progeny, protection, health, light and joy.

Healing is his special province, later tradition also ascribes this function to him. Herodotus records that in Persia 'the citizen who has leprosy or the white sickness may not come into a town or consort with other Persians. They say that he is so afflicted because he has sinned in some wise against the sun' (*The Histories*, I: 138). Sāmba in the *Purāṇas* was cured of leprosy by the grace of the sun. Helios caused blindness and also cured it. The rising sun is addressed and implored for release from the nooses of death (*AV* XVII: 1: 30). Sūrya is to deliver the worshipper from the dangers of the day (*TMB* I: 3: 3: 2). His eye (the orb of the sun) is powerful and nothing injures it (*GBU* I: 2). Sūrya as a sun-god is thought of primarily as the visible orb of light in the firmament; the personification is weak, arrested and unconvincing. He is golden, because that is how he appears; he is a healer because of the obvious healing virtue of sunbeams. His chariot is drawn by seven horses probably because of the seven prismatic colours; the chariot is alternatively drawn by Etaśa, the dappled horse, again, because of the colour of the sunbeams as seen through a prism. Thus the sun as seen in the sky is the image behind Sūrya.

The epic Sūrya is an extension of this image. The *Rām.* knows Sūrya as the observer of everything on the earth (I: 7: 17). His wife is Suvarcalā (V: 25: 26) and his sons are Sugrīva, Śveta and Jyotirmukha (III: 75: 68, VI: 6: 26, VI: 46: 46), evidently because it creates a pedigree for Sugrīva. To Vālin Sūrya gave a divine garland (IV: 12: 18), and blessed Mt Meru with a sun-like brilliance (IV: 43: 43–4). Sūrya is the Āditya *par excellence* to whom the other Ādityas together with other gods bow (IV: 43: 46–7).

In the *Mbh.* Dhaumya enumerates the 108 names of Sūrya (III: 3). We hear that the sun-worshipper can remember his previous birth, and gains memory and a sharp intellect, as well as wealth. The sun is connected with intelligence all over the world; from this may have come the association of the sun and the supernatural knowledge of the oracles in Greece. To this concept again we may finally trace the idea of liberation through knowledge connected with Devayāna, i.e. the path to liberation that lies through knowledge in this life, and through the sun in the other.

The sun is also a giver of food; he granted food to Yudhiṣṭhira with which to feed his Brahmin companions (*Mbh.* III: 4). Karṇa the brave self-confident epic hero is Sūrya's son and Sūrya warned him of Indra's intention of robbing him of the armour and ear-rings (*Mbh.* III: 284). Karṇa's solar bearings are again made clear when in the battle between Karṇa and Arjuna the star-bespangled sky and the Ādityas took his side (*Mbh.* VIII: 50: 39–42). At Karṇa's death the glory escaped from his body to the heavens (*Mbh.* VIII: 67: 27). Karṇa, as the son of Sūrya, is necessarily associated with snakes; his ensign had a serpent girth (*Mbh.* IV: 50: 15). In one passage the king of the nāgas (serpents) is said to draw the sun's chariot (*Mbh.* XII: 345). In the episode of Sūrya and Jamadagni, the sun came down with the gift of a white umbrella in order to placate the irate sage Jamadagni (*Mbh.* XIII: 95). The *HV* has an episode on the brilliance of the sun: King Satrājit was a friend of Sūrya but he could only see the brilliant disc and not the figure of the sun. One day, at his request, Sūrya took off the Syamantaka jewel so that Satrājit could see him as he really was; Satrājit coveted the jewel and Sūrya gave it to him. Later it led to infinite trouble and strife in the Yadu family (*HV* xxxviii: 14–23). The idea that the secret of the sun's brilliance is a jewel is met with for the first time in the later sections of the *Mbh.* where Viṣṇu has the Kaustubha gem, and the *HV* and *Purāṇas* confirm this with the tale of the churning of the ocean whence rose the Kaustubha. This Syamantaka tale seems to be in its origin a variant of the Kaustubha legend—both show a solar god bearing a gem. The later part of the story dealing with the family feud arising from the desire to possess it resembles the story of the Nibelung hoard of wealth which led to similar feuds.

SAVITṚ

Savitṛ as contrasted with Sūrya is more of an idea than a natural phenomenon. Like Sūrya, Savitṛ is golden-armed (*ṚV* i: 22: 5), golden-eyed (*ṚV* i: 35: 8), everything about Savitṛ is golden and beautiful; whole hymns dwell on his beauty and brilliance. He is well-decked in ornaments. Of the three steps of Savitṛ, two are with him, while the third takes the deceased to Yama (*ṚV* i: 35: 6, 9, 10, vi: 71: 1–5, vii: 45: 2). Savitṛ's is the highest heaven which he bestows on the worshippers (*ṚV* i: 35: 6, x: 135: 7; *VS* xii: 63). He is broad-handed (*ṚV* ii: 38: 2), his hands are well-shaped (*ṚV* i: 33: 6), his garments are tawny (*ṚV* iv: 35: 2), his chariot is golden (*ṚV* i: 35: 2, 3, 5), drawn by two red steeds (*ṚV* i: 35: 2, 5), he raises his hands to bless all (*ṚV* ii: 38: 2); he is the son of the waters, like many other gods (apām napāt, *ṚV* i: 22: 6). With his hands Savitṛ leads rivers onwards in their courses (*ṚV* iii: 33: 6), he rules natural elements like the wind and the water (*ṚV* ii: 38: 2). Like the other solar gods he revives drooping life (*ṚV* v: 81: 2, 5). Indigence (amati) is removed through Savitṛ's bounty (*ṚV* iii: 38: 8, vii: 38: 2, vii: 45: 3).

In Egypt we have a god who is conceptually a parallel of Savitṛ. Khepera the sun-god 'is the god of matter which is on the point of passing from inertness into life and also of the dead body from which a spiritual and glorified body is about to burst forth' (E. A. Wallis-Budge, *The book of the dead*, on the hymn to Rā). This tallies with the concept of Savitṛ the progenitor, who turns the inert pseudo-dead matter into consciousness in the morning.

None of the other sun-gods, not even his enemies can measure Savitṛ's dominion (*ṚV* II: 38: 9). He is invoked for wealth and also for the removal of diseases (*ṚV* X: 108: 8). Sūryā is Savitṛ's daughter (*ṚV* X: 85). But the greatest position allocated to Savitṛ is found in the hymn that has symbolized the Indian man's sun-worship through the ages, viz. the Gāyatrī hymn addressed to Savitṛ: we contemplate on the excellent effulgence of the god Savitṛ, may he inspire our intellect (*ṚV* III: 62: 10). Like all the Aryan gods Savitṛ also gives increase to the worshipper's cattle (*AV* XIX: 31). Man crosses indigence by the six spaces while plying the boat of Savitṛ (*AV* XII: 2: 48). Savitṛ is said to have desired the confidence of the gods (*TB* III: 1: 4).

The *TB* knows Sītā as Savitṛ's daughter. Sīta desired Soma who was attached to Śraddhā. Soma had the three *Vedas* in his fist. Sītā in her grief approached Savitṛ who gave her a beauty-ointment. Then Soma desired her and she asked Soma what he had in his fist (*TB* II: 3: 10: 1–3). This story resembles the *Rām.* genealogy only in name; both Savitṛ and Janaka mean progenitor, and both have a daughter named Sītā; beyond this there is no similarity. Sītā means a ploughshare and the *TB* tale perhaps connects the sun with agriculture.

Apart from the common solar characteristics Savitṛ is not portrayed anthropomorphically. He is primarily a golden god, and has two golden steeds. Like all the solar gods he, too, is associated with immortality. Later Vedic literature like the tenth book of the *ṚV* and the *AV* connect Savitṛ with funeral rites (*ṚV* X: 17: 4; *AV* XII: 48). The word 'Savitṛ', like 'Sūrya', is derived from the root 'sū' 'to beget'. The Gāyatrī connects the root with begetting or impelling consciousness. Savitṛ is thought of mainly as the motive power, the awakener; the god who, because he symbolizes light, awakens life, and impels men and creatures to action. As a solar god Savitṛ is connected with truth and norm, Ṛta (*ṚV* X: 34: 8, X: 139: 3). Like Varuṇa he, too, binds the miscreant with fetters (*TS* I: 1: 9) and this leads Dr R. N. Dandekar to conclude that 'Savitṛ is only an aspect of Varuṇa, a hypostasis of Varuṇa' (R. N. Dandekar, 'New Lights on the Vedic God Savitr', *ABORI* XX, 1938–9). But his raising of the arms to rouse and inspire men is his most frequently mentioned trait.

The *Mbh.* and the *Purāṇas* make Savitṛ one-handed. Śiva's wrath provoked at Dakṣa's sacrifice led to the breaking of Savitṛ's arms. The *KB* has the earliest version of the tale: When the gods performed the (sviṣṭakṛt) sacrifice, they kept Brahman's portion for Savitṛ, it cleft his two hands, to him they gave instead two golden ones; therefore he is celebrated as golden-handed (*KB* VI: 13). In classical Sanskrit 'kara' means both arm and beam; the sunbeams are golden, and figuratively they are the arms with which the sun touches the world below; hence the sun is golden-armed. His natural arms must be removed in order to provide room for the golden ones. Later, an outsider, an enemy of the traditional gods, viz. Śiva, was brought in to break off the natural arms.[1]

BHAGA

Bhaga is a minor solar god not invoked alone, but in company with other minor solar gods (of *MS* I: 6: 12). He is a brother to Uṣas (*ṚV* I: 123: 5) whom he and Aryaman chaperons to her bridegroom's house. Bhaga is not described physically, nothing about him is distinctly solar except a few traits which he shares in common with other solar gods. Thus his boat is mentioned (*ṚV* II: 36: 5), like the boats of Savitṛ's, Sūrya's and Āditya's. Bhaga is blind: 'When the gods performed the (sviṣṭakṛt) sacrifice, they kept the Brahman's portion for Savitṛ, it cleft his two hands... They kept it for Bhaga, it destroyed his eyes; therefore they say Bhaga is blind' (*KB* VI: 13). The word 'Bhaga' seems to be very old; we have cognate words in almost all Indo-European languages.[2] By the time the Vedic mythology was being reshuffled on the Indian soil, the god had become a mere shadow of his former Indo-European self, and the substance had altogether vanished, so that not much of his Indo-European personality remained. But at one time he must have been a concrete personality, for the *TB* remembers him as the best of the gods (*TB* III: 1: 1: 8). The *TMB* also records that Bhaga desired supremacy among the gods (III: 1: 4). But of his actual power and prestige we have no record in Indian literature. In the *Rām.*, *Mbh.*, *HV* and the *Purāṇas* Bhaga is included in lists of the twelve Ādityas (*Rām.* II: 25: 21–2; *Mbh.* I: 59; *HV* III: 60–2), but nowhere does he figure independently and mythology altogether ignores his individual existence.

Yet Bhaga has lived on conceptually; Bhāgya (good fortune) is derived from Bhaga. Tracing the associations of bhāgya we have two concepts: sexual bliss and wealth or prosperity. Bhaga means the female organ and

[1] We remember the Eddic parallel of Tyr. 'He is the boldest and most courageous... When the gods tried to persuade the wolf Fenrir to allow the fetter Gleipnir to be placed on him, he did not believe that they would free him until they put Tyr's hand in his mouth as a pledge. Then, when the Aesir would not loose him, he bit off the hand... So Tyr is one-handed' (*Prose Edda*, p. 53). The myths are different but in both we have the one-handed sun-gods who were originally two-handed, a hostile god or enemy led to the loss of the other hand.

[2] In Greek we have Zeus Bagaious, in Zend Bagha, in Old Persian Baga, in Old Church Slavonic Bogu and Bogatu, and in Lithuanian Bogotas and nabagas.

that links the god with sexual happiness and perhaps with progeny too. On the other hand, the classical word *bhagavat* (god, divine being, honourable, i.e. successful man) is also derived from bhaga. Bhagavat actually means one who possesses bhaga. In later literature bhaga is defined as vast wealth, heroism, fame, beauty (or prosperity), knowledge and detachment (*Viṣṇu P* v: 74). In other words, all that raises a man above his fellow creatures is called bhaga. Perhaps, originally, in the Indo-European period, Bhaga dispensed wealth and prosperity to women, or was chiefly worshipped by maidens. Hillebrandt says: 'Auch sein Name geht über die vedische Zeit hinaus und verliert sich in weite Fernen; denn wir finden das Wort in Iran, in dem Phrygischen Zeus Bagaios und bis zu den Slaven hin verbreitet...Wenn beim Traiyambakaopfer die Mädchen die Kuchen in die Luft werfen, in die Hände des Opferers legen und wiedernehmen, sagen sie "Bhaga stha bhagasya vo lapsīya"' (*Vedische Mythologie*, seite 81, 84). Thus Bhaga was the solar god whose function was to grant fertility to women (as also virility to men—a corollary of the former), and his worship as the god who grants fortune may have come from this notion. Bhaga is a bountiful god and tracing the contexts where he is mentioned we come to the conclusion that he brought luck to women, especially in marriage. To men he brought success in assemblies, in dicing and hunting. This power of dispensing luck and success, fertility and virility were considered as attributes of the supreme being in Avesta too where Bagha meant 'god' and the term came to be used as an appellative of Ahura Mazda. In India the concept reached the same semantic stage in *bhagavat* = 'god'.

AṂŚA AND DAKṢA

Aṃśa (mentioned only thrice) and Dakṣa (mentioned only six times) are still less clearly defined figures. They are never mentioned alone but are only found in lists of the Ādityas. They may have been distinct figures in Indo-European times but the *Vedas* hardly recognize them as individual gods. In the *ŚB* Dakṣa became a Prajāpati, father of Umā and also of the twenty-seven stars, the moon's wives. Dakṣa in *ṚV* x: 72: 4, 5 and v: 7 is mentioned as the father of Aditi and also as her son. The word means clever, skilful and is according to Keith 'a product of priestly ingenuity'. The word has Indo-European cognates and seems to go back to that period. The Greek *dexios* and Latin *dexter* meaning 'the right hand' seem to have a common origin with Dakṣa from which later Sanskrit *dakṣiṇa* (right, efficient) is derived. Dakṣa is the efficient and bountiful sun-god, symbolizing the creator-aspect of the sun. It is significant that in post-Vedic mythology we have a progenitor *par excellence*, a Prajāpati by the name of Dakṣa, bearing perhaps faint traces of Dakṣa, the creator sun-god. Aṃśa may be a cognate of aṃśu—scale or beam—indicating the sunbeams. As solar gods these are very dim and indistinct and later mythology drops them altogether.

DHĀTṚ

Dhātṛ figures in the epic lists of the Ādityas. The word means creator, and Dhātṛ may have symbolized the sun in its creative, life-giving aspect. Later Dhātṛ ceases to be a solar god and the word is used as a synonym of Prajāpati, in his creative aspect. Still later Dhātṛ came to be providence or dispenser of destiny, and so shed his direct solar bearings.

VIVASVAT

Vivasvat figures in the later *Saṃhitās* and *Brāhmaṇas*, and is later included in the catalogue of the Ādityas. He is mentioned in the *MS* as the father of Manu and Yama, one of whom rules in this world, and the other in the next (I: 6: 12). In the Purāṇic mythology Vivasvat is a son of Kaśyapa and Dākṣāyaṇī, his wife was Saṃjñā, the daughter of Tvaṣṭṛ (*HV* IX: 1). Their first offspring was Manu, a Prajāpati, lord of the Śrāddha ceremony. Then were born Yama and Yamunā, twins. Chāyā, Saṃjñā's double, was left by Saṃjñā because Vivasvat's brilliance was too much for her. Of Chāyā and Vivasvat were born Sāvarṇi Manu and Śani. Yama was angry at Chāyā's partiality to her own children and reported it to Vivasvat, who, when he knew that Saṃjñā had left him, went to Tvaṣṭṛ. There he was told that Saṃjñā had been unable to bear his brilliance and had left for the Uttarakuru region. Tvaṣṭṛ made him shed some of his brilliance with his lathe (out of the fragments were created the twelve Ādityas: Dhātr, Aryaman, Varuṇa, Aṃśa, Bhaga, Dakṣa, Indra, Vivasvat, Pūsan, Parjanya, Tvaṣṭṛ and Viṣṇu). Then Vivasvat met Saṃjñā as a mare, and himself became a horse. They were united and of this union were born the Aśvins, Nāsatya and Dasra.

This anecdote is repeated with minor variations in the *Purāṇas*, Saṃjñā being alternatively named Saraṇyū.[1] Some traits stand out clearly from

[1] The story of the reluctant mother-goddess fleeing from a pursuing male-god is found in the Greek variants of Kore-Hades, Erinyes-Poseidon and Nemesis-Zeus. The pursuing gods are brothers, i.e. different manifestations of the same theophany. In other words they narrate the cardinal story of Erinyes-Poseidon (or Vivasvat-Saraṇyū) in three different versions. The original myth appears to have been of Indo-European antiquity.

an analysis of this oft-repeated tale. By Saṃjñā (or Saraṇyū) and Chāyā, Vivasvat had many children—Yama, Manu, Sāvarṇi Manu, Śani, Yamunā and the Aśvins. Of these Yama is the ruler of the next world and Manu the first progenitor of the human race. Śani is a satellite, Yamunā a river and the Aśvins are connected with horses. Vivasvat, in other words, is the creator of human, superhuman, subhuman species and also of natural phenomena. This raises him to the rank of a creator-god, and this is Vivasvat's special manifestation—he is the creator aspect of the sun-god. The Vivasvat-Saraṇyū tale is clearly an interpolation by many different and careless hands—Saraṇyū is the daughter of Tvaṣṭṛ and yet out of the splinters of sunbeams (filed off by Tvaṣṭṛ's lathe) were created the twelve Ādityas of whom Tvaṣṭṛ was one and Vivasvat himself another. The sun appears as a horse in many mythologies and the Aśvins, too, have many parallels. Vivasvat as the father of Yama and Manu is the creator of the rulers of both this life and the next, i.e. of both the living and the dead. Yamunā is clearly a Purāṇic metamorphosis of Yamī, and the fact that she is presented as a river is an attempt to gloss over the unsavoury memory of the incest motif; it is also an indication of the Purāṇic sanctity of the river. Śani, too, was figuring rather prominently as a malign astrological phenomenon, hence he, too, figures as Vivasvat's son—an astral double of the Brāhmaṇical Yama. Chāyā's inability to bear the sun's brilliance, and consequently the sun shedding some of his early glory may be traced to the notion that the sun had been brighter in the past. Saṃjñā (consciousness) is Vivasvat's wife, i.e. a concomitant, in Purāṇic language. Her opposite number is Chāyā (shadow), a dim replica of Saṃjñā or Saraṇyū. Vivasvat, literally 'the shining one', is the solar creator-god who awakens men's consciousness and produces life in all levels of existence. Only the later portions of the *ṚV* mention Mārtaṇḍa. The tenth book says that while the gods were dancing in the water, one of them, a piercingly bright beam, escaped. This presumably was the sun who escaped to the sky (*ṚV* x: 72: 6). Aditi had of old gone with seven of her sons, and left Mārtaṇḍa for progeny and death (*ṚV* x: 72: 8, 9).

MĀRTAṆḌA

The *MS* also mentions Mārtaṇḍa among the Ādityas (I: 6: 12). The *ŚB* says: 'There were eight sons of Aditi who were born from her body; with seven she went to the gods, but Mārtaṇḍa she cast off' (III: I: I: 2). The *Mbh.* says Aditi's foetus was killed (mārita), this (dead foetus) became

Mārtaṇḍa Vivasvat, the god of the Śrāddha ceremony (XII: 329: 44). In *Mbh.*, *HV* and Purāṇic lists of twelve Ādityas, Mārtaṇḍa is not usually included. The *Purāṇas* sometimes make an exception. The *Matsya P* apparently following up the *ṚV* and *ŚB* tradition and explaining it, says that Mārtaṇḍa was so named because he was born of a dead egg (II: 36). It is significant that when Mārtaṇḍa is mentioned for the first time (*ṚV* X: 72) he is connected with death or killing, and also that he is mentioned in the latest book of the *ṚV*, which records the first impacts of the cultural amalgamation. Mārtaṇḍa is apparently a euphonic conjunction of Mārta + aṇḍa, and mārta suggests mārita (killed) or mṛta (dead). When Aditi took her divine sons to heaven, she left Mārtaṇḍa behind, for death belongs to this world; the other Ādityas are immortal and dispensers of immortality. As a physical phenomenon Mārtaṇḍa seems to stand for the setting sun with death inherent in him; he sets in the west, and this appears like dropping on to the earth which in mythical language would be 'left behind' on the earth.

ARYAMAN

The early catalogues of the Ādityas mostly include only eight of them, the names of particular gods included sometimes vary, but Bhaga, Savitṛ, Mitra, Varuṇa, Aryaman, Aṃśa, Dakṣa, Viṣṇu and Pūṣan are mostly present. Aryaman as a solar phenomenon is difficult to trace for he does not correspond to any aspect of the sun as such. He, along with Mitra, Varuṇa and Aṃśa, is identified with Agni (*ṚV* II: 1: 4), is included in the Āditya lists (*ṚV* II: 27: 1) and figures chiefly with Mitra and Varuṇa. Aryaman is not physically described. The *TS* says, 'He who desires heaven should offer an oblation to Aryaman, Aryaman is the yonder sun' (II: 3: 4). Thus beyond establishing the solar character of Aryaman the *Vedas* say nothing about him. Consequently we can never know if he ever corresponded to any physical aspect of the sun. In the late tenth book we hear more of him. He is mentioned in the Sūryā hymn (*ṚV* X: 85) where Bhaga and Aryaman escort the couple in safety. He, along with Bhaga, Savitṛ and Pūṣan, is mentioned as a god granting prosperity (*ṚV* X: 85: 36). One hymn says: he who does not feed Aryaman and his friends has wealth in vain (*ṚV* X: 117: 6). This idea is elaborated in the *MS* where Aryaman is identified with charity (II: 3: 6). In the *TB* Aryaman seems to be correlated with Bhaga in a curious way: Aryaman's constellation is Pūrvaphālgunī, Bhaga's Uttaraphālgunī (I: 1: 2: 4). Aryaman's stature increases in that *Brāhmaṇa*; he is called the strong and immortal king and Bhaga the chief of the gods (III: 1: 18). Aryaman is mentioned in the *YV saṃhitās* and *Brāhmaṇas* frequently (cf. *TS* 1: 8: 12; *TB* 1: 7: 6: 6) and also in *TMB* XXV: 12: 3 and like Bhaga he grants a consort to man and woman. Aryaman is prayed to for domestic harmony (*ṚV* X: 85: 43). Later, the epic and Purāṇic literature drops Aryaman except as one of the Ādityas.

The *Avesta* has a parallel to Aryaman in Airyaman, the vow-fulfilling god who gives the righteous man the 'desirable reward that Religion deserves' (Fargard XXI: 20). Of Aryaman (in company with Varuṇa and Mitra) H. Lüders quotes Ed. Meyer's opinion (as set forth in *Geschichte des Altertums*, 1909) and says: 'Varuṇa ist nach ihm eine abstrakte Gottheit ebenso wie Mitra und Aryaman' (*Varuṇa*, Göttingen, 1951, p. 7).[1]

Aryaman is most frequently grouped with Mitra and Varuṇa. Together they stand for Ṛta, oath, order and truth. Mitra and Varuṇa are complementary to each other, and Aryaman is more an abstract idea which acts both as a cohesive element and also as the interpreter of the essence of this group. The word Aryaman seems to be derived from an Indo-European root from which Ṛta and Ārya, Eire, Airem and Airan (Iran) are derived. Conceptually Aryaman corresponds to truth and rectitude, and both Mitra and Varuṇa personify these, but Aryaman is the complete personification of these concepts (cf. derivation Ṛta under Varuṇa, pp. 29–30).

But on the physical plane Aryaman corresponds to the sun whose unvarying and dependable course symbolizes truth, stability and steadfastness. These virtues, according to the Aryans, were characteristics of the Aryans which distinguished them from the barbarians. Truth, law and order expressed by Ṛta were the underlying character of Mitra, Varuṇa and Aryaman which unites them in a group so frequently in the *Vedas*, and they symbolized the ideal of Aryanism and became abstract hero-gods of the Aryans made visible in the sun, whose path also ran straight on, free from obstruction, and this may explain why the *AV* prayer for an easy (i.e. free from obstruction) delivery is addressed to Aryaman and also to Pūṣan, another god of the paths (*AV* 1: 11).

[1] Paul Thieme in his *Mitra and Aryaman* derives the name from *ari* (= 'stranger' = 'guest'); according to him *Aryaman* means 'hospitableness'. In New Persian *erman* means 'a guest'. I find it difficult to agree with an etymology which yields an abstract idea as the only valid meaning. I have discussed my objection in the introduction. I am however prepared to accept 'hospitableness' as one of many component derivations of *Aryaman*.

MITRA

In the *ṚV* there is only one whole hymn (*ṚV* III: 59) given to Mitra, where he is said to bring men together and watch the tillers with unwinking eyes; he also upholds the sky and the earth (III: 59: 1). In other hymns he is usually mentioned together with other solar gods, especially with Varuṇa and Aryaman. He is the great protector, for those under his shelter are never harmed (*ṚV* III: 59: 2). He is addressed as the great Āditya (*ṚV* III: 59: 3, 5). 'Homage to the eye of Mitra and Varuṇa, let the worshipper offer to the great god with truth' (*ṚV* X: 3: 37). Mitra is a god of pure achievements, who, with Varuṇa, thrives in Ṛta and is also a keeper of Ṛta (*ṚV* I: 2: 7, 8, V: 64: 1). These two are also called saṃrāj (emperor) and wield māyā (magic power) with which they hold the sun fixed (*ṚV* V: 64: 4). They are guardians of dharman (the moral order) and are masters of 'asurasya māyā' (the magic power of the mighty) with which they control the universe (*ṚV* V: 64: 7). Mitra and Varuṇa are 'bhūripāśau' with many nooses (*ṚV* VII: 66: 3), they see paths better than human eyes can (*ṚV* VIII: 25: 9); with Aryaman they are invoked in the whole of *ṚV* hymn X: 126.

Mitra creates the firmament, he and Varuṇa are kings of all creation (*ṚV* X: 132: 4). In the *TS* we hear that 'the plants are connected with Mitra and the waters with Varuṇa' (II: 1: 9). 'Mitra is the auspicious one of the gods' (*TS* V: 1: 7). Mitra is 'satyasya pati', lord of truth (*MS* II: 6: 6). Varuṇa is to be offered a hot oblation, but Mitra, as an opposite, is to be given what is cold or cool; he it is who receives what is well-offered as opposed to Varuṇa who receives what is ill-offered (*MS* IV: 5: 8; *JB* II: 230; *ŚB* IV: 5: 1: 6). The day is Mitra (the night, Varuṇa), the waxing fortnight belongs to Mitra, the waning to Varuṇa (*TMB* XXV: 10: 20). Mitra gives rise to the verities; he arrives along the paths of devayāna (*TB* III: 1: 2: 1). In the *ŚB* Mitra is paired with Varuṇa, sometimes as a contrast to Varuṇa, sometimes as a companion. Thus 'Mitra and Varuṇa are his intelligence and will' (IV: 1: 4: 1); 'Mitra is the priesthood, Varuṇa is the nobility. The truth is Mitra since Mitra is the Brahman and the truth is Brahman' (IV: 1: 4: 10). The vessel of the grāha (sacrificial ladle) for Mitra and Varuṇa is goat-like in shape (IV: 1: 5: 19). The worshipper kills a barren 'anubandhyā' cow for Mitra and Varuṇa (IV: 5: 1: 5). That which is self-produced belongs to Mitra (V: 3: 2: 6); what is cooked by hot steam belongs to Mitra (V: 3: 2: 8)—this contrasts with the *MS* rule of offering cold oblations to Mitra, for the hot oblations are usually meant for Varuṇa, but the *ŚB* frequently obliterates the line of demarcation between the domains of Mitra and Varuṇa who are then not conceived as contrary but complementary gods. The word Mitra came to mean a friend in post-Vedic literature. As a physical phenomenon 'Mitra' may have signified the friendly aspect of the sun, perhaps the newly risen sun or the sun in winter when its warmth is most welcome. As the god, or the guardian of contracts Mitra constitutes the basis of good faith on which true friendship is founded. Mitra's career as a solar god terminates with the Vedic literature; he is forgotten in the epics and *Purāṇas*.

The essential characteristic of Mitra is truth: one can find Mitra's approval through keeping Āditya's law (*ṚV* III: 59: I). This concept of Mitra is Indo-Iranian or older still. The invocation of Mithra in the Boghazkeui treaty indicates his connection with truth or faith involved in a treaty. In ancient Iran the Mithra cult flourished till Mithra became the chief divinity of the Messagetae. Mithra as a sun-god is invoked and praised in the tenth Yast in the *Avesta*, known as the *Mihr-Yast*. He was the protector of the faithful, 'the guarantee of orderly international relations' (Paul Thieme, 'The Aryan gods of the Mitanni treaties', *JAOS* 80, no. 4, 1960). The Avestan Mithra is sometimes identified with the sun and is invoked to make the soil fertile. He is strong, sleepless and ever awake. Mitra is closely related to the sun, but not invariably identified with him. The later form of Mithra is Mihir, who is a god of contracts and has a thousand ears and ten thousand eyes, presumably to see and hear all contracts and watch if there is any breach, and to listen to complaints.

In the *Avesta* Mithra is not one of the Amesha Spentas, but a Yazata created by Ahura Mazda. He was a protector of warriors and this latter played an important part in the later Mithraism. In the *Avesta* Mithra had Verethraghna for a companion. 'Oromazes dwells in the domain of eternal light...Ahriman reigns in the realm of darkness and Mithra occupies an intermediary place between them' (Franz Cumont, *The mysteries of Mithra*, p. 7). Babylonian sun-gods who were guardians of truth and faith came to be absorbed into Mithra when the countries became politically related to each other, and the legends were mingled. It was then that 'Mithra became the Sun, Shamash. As Mithra in Persia so Shamash in Babylon is the god of justice...According to Ptolemacus, this solar deity was worshipped in all the countries that stretched from India to Assyria' (*ibid.* p. 10). Zoroaster transformed Mithra into *Mihr Yasht*, a fighter, a god of battles. Mithra came back in the later *Avesta* as a Yazata, or angel, still later as the Sol Invictus of Mithraism.

The Mithra cult which originated in 'the Near East and spread and flourished in Rome as Mithraism consisted in a mystic worship of Mithra. Iconographic representations of Mithra are found all over this region... mystery worships spread enormously throughout the Mediterranean world during the first three centuries A.D. and in the West as much as in the East from where they came' (Michael Grant: *The world of Rome*, pp. 182–3). Here is the secret of Mithra's power and preponderance—at a time of cultural, political and religious turmoil and disintegration his cult offered a focus for the mythological convergence of many concepts, and a unity was achieved in the theological realm which was fast crumbling in other fields. Among the Hatra finds we have a statue of Mithra which Dr Shinji Fukai (in his article 'The artifacts of Hatra and Bactrian art') describes as 'one of the most representative of the artifacts of Hatra'. He is clothed in the attire of a Roman legionary. Behind him is a circle representing the sun in its radiation. He has a pair of necklaces and in the centre of the breast there is a big vermilion medallion; his upper garments also are tucked at shoulders with medallions. On all these medallions there is a spread-eagle. It is noticeable that this Mithra shares some features in common with the sun-gods of India: the necklace and the medallion (Kaustubha), as also the eagle (Garuḍa) are features which are found in Viṣṇu-Kṛṣṇa myth and iconography.

Mediation is another important and significant aspect. The sixteenth or middle day of the month was consecrated to Mithra. He was regarded as a mediator between life and death. His image was accompanied by those of two torchbearers: '...one of them was regarded as symbolizing heat and life, and the other as the emblem of cold and death' (*ibid.* 128–9). The symbols of Mithraism offer significant traits which are associated with those sun-cults which have a kathenotheistic approach to the god. The name Mitra in India also has faint echoes of his role as the mediator, for among the solar gods he alone is Mitra 'friend' (of man).

UṢAS

Uṣas (dawn) is one of the few Vedic goddesses and the only important goddess in the *ṚV*. She is invoked in twenty hymns, sometimes alone, sometimes together with the Aśvins (cf. I: 43). She is the daughter of the sky, a pretty maiden who brightens the world, wakes men up, and gives them food, wealth and prosperity. She is old and ever young (*ṚV* III: 61: 1), is dressed in a red robe and rides golden horses. She is the wife, daughter or sister of Svasara, the sun. When Indra broke Sūrya's chariot wheel, Uṣas fled in fear (*ṚV* IV: 30: 11). She is pretty and fresh, she bares her breast to the worshipper's sight. In a hymn to Uṣas, *ṚV* VIII: 47, verses 15–18 are a charm against evil, for Uṣas as the dawn frustrates the evils attempted by the dark forces of the night. Although mentioned as the sun's wife in one or two passages. Uṣas is mostly portrayed as a maiden and is the prototype of the maiden goddesses. Uṣas is too tangibly the physical phenomenon of the dawn to grow in dimension or to become a richer or more complex personality. Hence her personification is arrested early and post-Ṛgvedic literature forgets her altogether.

SŪRYĀ

Sūryā is a minor goddess and is celebrated in one single hymn—the Sūryā hymn (*ṚV* X: 85), although she is mentioned a few times in other hymns. Bk IX knows her as the sun's daughter who purifies Soma with (her?) hair (*ṚV* IX: 1: 16). She fetched Soma from the sky (*ṚV* IX: 113: 3). In the Sūryā hymn we hear that Savitṛ had intended his daughter for Soma but the Aśvins won the tournament and received Uṣas as the prize. But she is also mentioned as the wife of Soma in which case the Aśvins are her chaperons who convey her to her husband's home. Savitṛ gave her first to Soma, then to Viśvāvasu the Gandharva, who gave her to Agni and finally Agni handed her over to the bridegroom. In some other myths Pūṣan is said to be the bridegroom. The *KB* dwells upon Sūryā's wedding at some length, 'Now when Savitṛ gave Sūryā to Soma the king, he made over to his daughter (whether she was Prajāpati's or his own) on her marriage these thousand verses which were in the possession of these deities; they said "Let us run a race for this thousand"; they ran the race, then the Aśvins were victorious by means of the ass' (*KB* XVIII: 1). The nucleus of this story is found in the *AB*: 'The Aśvins won in the tournament and married Sūryā' (V: 2: 17). The sun's marriage to the moon is a common myth and this would tend to make Sūryā the sun-maiden, for she was intended for Soma, and according to certain myths was actually married to him.

Scholars differ regarding the identity of Sūryā as a distinct personality. E. H. Meyer interprets the Sūryā myths so as to make her a cloud-goddess (*Indogermanishce Mythologie*, vol. II, p. 673). Many scholars regard her as the dawn, identifying her with Uṣas, and interpret her marriage to the Aśvins as the proximity of the morning and evening stars to dawn and dusk. Hillebrandt in his *Vedische Mythologie* identifies Sūryā with Uṣas, and Mannhardt supports this view. Oldenberg, however, is of opinion that Sūryā is the sun-maiden. This view is supported by very old concepts of the feminine sun (cf. *Die Sonne* in German) as she is celebrated in many old Teutonic myths and also in the fairy-tales told by the brothers Grimm. 'The motif of the sun as a goddess instead of as a god is a rare and precious survival from an archaic, apparently once widely diffused, mythological context. The great maternal divinity of South Arabia is the feminine sun Ilat. Throughout Siberia as well as in North America scattered stories survive of a female sun' (Joseph Campbell, *The hero with a thousand faces*, p. 213). The Japanese sun-goddess Amataresu is another example. The sun is mild and pleasant in Siberia, North America and northern Europe and hence the tendency of the mythopoeic mind to imagine it as a maiden who bestows mild warmth is quite understandable, and this may have led to the creation of Sūryā. The sun-goddess of Arinna was sometimes addressed as a god. The transformation of a god into goddess and vice versa is not uncommon in mythology; one remembers the Japanese Kwannon, goddess of mercy, who is just a feminine form of the Avalokiteśvara Buddha transplanted in Japan. Thus Sūrya and Sūryā would appear as the mutually convertible forms of the sun, the conversion only emphasized certain traits: power and brilliance in the masculine form, warmth, charm and mildness in the feminine form.

ĀDITYA

Āditya is sometimes used in the singular number indicating the sun. Thus Āditya is addressed as having got into his hundred-oared boat (*AV* XVIII: 1: 25; *CB* II: 5: 14), or as having beaten off monsters (*MS* IV: 1: 13). In the heart of Āditya dwells this golden man (*MS* VI: 1; *Mait.U.* VI: 34). Ātman is in Āditya (*JB* I: 17). Once Āditya was pierced with darkness by the demon Svarbhānu: the gods delivered him with the Vedic accents—clearly a play on *svar*, 'heaven', and *svara*, 'accent' (*JB* II: 386; *TMB* IV: 5: 2). Āditya enters Agni in the evening, etc. (*TB* II: 1: 2: 10). Āditya is truth (*TB* II: 1: 11: 1). Gold is Āditya's, Āditya is gold (*TB* III: 9: 20: 2). The gods took Āditya to heaven (*TMB* IV: 5: 3). Āditya is the Udgātṛ in the Dīkṣaṇīyeṣṭi (*GB* IV: 3). This Āditya undoubtedly is a generic name for the sun. In the *ṚV* there is not one single Āditya, only the specific names are used. Later in the epics and *Purāṇas* Āditya became a synonym for the sun just as many *ṚV* names of the sun-god lost their specific characteristics and were used indiscriminately as synonyms for Sūrya.

Āditya is used for Sūrya in *Rām.* IV: 43: 46–7. In the *Mbh.* Āditya is said to be the gate to Devayāna (*Mbh.* XIII: 16: 44). In later literature the term lost its early connotation and became another synonym for Sūrya and if it retained any specific meaning it just indicated that Sūrya was Aditi's son.

Analysing the specific characteristics of the solar gods we notice certain features which stand out as significant for an exposition of their essence. The individual gods present different aspects of the sun-god, and most of these solar gods become extinct with time, but they left their traits as a legacy for those of the solar gods who survived. These minor sun-gods are generally neglected by iconography as individuals.

At Sirkap in Taxila there is a sun-icon (published by Marshall). The Bodh-Gaya chariot relief, too, has been identified as Sūrya's by scholars. Also, at Bharhut there is the image of an Indo-Greek prince identified as the sun by Dr J. N. Banerji. In the Bhāja cave there is a first-century B.C. image of the sun on a chariot with one wheel, followed by Ūṣā and Pratyūṣā. The Lala Bhagat image of the sun which belongs to the second century A.D. shows the god riding a four-horse chariot with one wheel. The horses are shown as coming out of a demon's head. The god has an umbrella with a long staff. In the Gandhara black slate figurine Sūrya is shown wearing topboots. In the Mathura museum collection we have a winged Sūrya in a heavy tunic and topboots riding a single-wheeled chariot drawn by four horses. The god holds a lotus bud in his right hand and a scimitar in his left thus anticipating Viṣṇu with lotus and weapons; and the Niyamatpur, Kamarpur and Bhumara sun images closely resemble this one. The earlier images of Sūrya are dressed in non-Indian costume, and Dr J. N. Banerji accounts for this: 'In the extant images of Sūrya of an earlier date, the costume worn by the god is exactly similar to the dress worn by the Kushan kings like Wema Kadphises and Kanishka (cf. the sculptural and numismatic representations of these kings with the Sūrya relief at Bhumara)' (J. N. Banerji, *The development of Hindu iconography*, p. 294).

The Bṛhatsaṃhitā (which contains sections on iconology; a late text) lays down rules for images of Sūrya; in ch. 57, verses 46–8 it says, Sūrya is to have Udīcyaveśa (northern dress) with a close fitting garment, ear-rings, and a crown, two lotuses, a long necklace, a lion-standard and a vyaṅga. This dress is clearly derived from the Iranian. Vyanga, Aiwiyaonghen in Iranian, is a girdle, worn as a mark of initiation by the Iranians. The north Indian dress is obviously of foreign origin, for in the south Indian Sūrya images, there is no vyaṅga or avyaṅga and the god has bare feet; his charioteer Aruṇa and the horses are usually absent. Among the Hatra finds is an image of Ashur Bel, in the heart of the statue is a relief image of the sun-god Shamash with rays emanating from his head. At his feet is the image of Tyche with eagles on both sides. The whole composition is a 'combination of Roman and Oriental' modes. The god is of Assyrian origin. The date of the Hatra finds is placed in the first two centuries A.D.

Considering the foreign dress of the Indian sun-god, its avyaṅga, top-boots and heavy tunic, its Iranian-Mesopotamian look in general, this find may perhaps be regarded as a link in the iconographic tradition.

The sun is everywhere pre-eminently connected with vegetation and this accounts for the supremacy of the solar cult. In rituals, too, there is a predominance of symbolically representing the sun in its full blaze which will ensure good crops. Keith, writing of the conflict of the Śudra and Ārya for the round white skin in the Mahāvrata ritual says: 'The old tradition, already known to the Kāṭhaka equates the skin and the sun... this equation suits admirably the conception of the rite as an attempt to stimulate the sun at the winter solstice both by worship and by magic.' Of the song of the maidens and the musical instruments he says: 'These noises may have been designed, like the gong at Dodona, to drive away evil demons and to protect at once the sun and the performers from their onslaught.' The Mahāvrata 'is a ritual of the Winter Solstice and...it combines within itself the characteristics of a spell to procure the heat of the sun and the fall of rain so as to bring about fertility for the land, while more directly still it is designated to stimulate human and animal productiveness' (*Introduction to the Śāṅkhāyana Āraṇyaka*, pp. 76, 78, 80). Many other ceremonies and rites of the *Vedas* are directed to the same end, viz. to promote the fertility of the land. Indra, a solar god, later became a god of rain, thus combining the two natural phenomena (the sun and rain) necessary for vegetation; and Indra in the epic-Purāṇic period became an agricultural god. The sun is the prime force which makes cultivation possible, for indirectly by generating vapour and cloud, and directly by emitting heat, it makes vegetation possible.

The north Indian Saura (i.e. solar) cult, one of the five cardinal cults of India (viz. Śaiva, Vaiṣṇava, Saura, Śākta and Gāṇapatya) had a foreign origin and is possibly derived from the worship of Iranian Mithra, which again was influenced by the images of the Greek solar gods like Apollo or Helios. At the Nimrud Dagh tumulus one of the five sculptures has the inscription, 'Apollo-Mithras-Helios-Hermes'.

The *Varāha*, *Bhaviṣya* and *Sāmba Purāṇas* tell the story of Sāmba's leprosy and his recovery through the grace of the sun worshipped in the

Śākadvīpin (i.e. east Iranian) manner. Between eastern Iran and north-western India we come across many evidences of a sun-cult. Later it spread to central and western India. Sun-temples at Multan and Mathura represent the god in an alien dress and the manner of worship also was different. The *Bṛhatsaṃhitā* says that the installation of the Sūrya images in the temple was the exclusive privilege of the Magas (an Indianized form of Iranian Magus), priests of the sun-god in Iran. This seems to be a memory of the actual source of the cult. Kings of the Vardhana dynasty in Thaneswar may have adopted this faith as Kings Prabhākaravardhana, Ādityavardhana and Rājyavardhana call themselves Paramādityabhakta (staunch devotees of the sun). Mayūrabhaṭṭa the poet (who was a contemporary of King Harṣavardhana) wrote his famous Sūryaśataka praising the sun as the supreme god. Later the cult spread further east and west.

A *Bhaviṣya Purāṇa* account tells us that 'once the sun chanced to see the maiden Haralīlā and was attracted by her youthful beauty. Finding no other means of enjoying her he entered fire and Haralīlā also transgressed the kindled fire and met the sun' (R. C. Hazra, *Studies in the Upapurāṇas*, pp. 79–80). Fire, urged by the sun, cursed her; her son was called Jaraśabda, or Jaraśastra; his descendants were called the Magas. Thus the origin of the sun-cult with Zarathustra and the Magian priests is recorded here. 'Besides the sun-worshipping Magas and Bhojakas...there came to India in later times other Magas who were the fire-worshipping followers of Zoroaster and must have left Iran as a result of the spread of Islam after the sixth century A.D.' (*ibid.* p. 98). This sun-cult was borrowed from Iran, so when Sūrya (or Mithra) came over to India, the dress, ritual and priests all came with him. 'Something of Mithraism entered India also, for in the first century A.D. and later there was continuous Iranian influence in north India and Hindu sun-worship was carried on almost entirely in accordance with Iranian rules. Magian priests entered India in large numbers and not only became priests in temples of the sun but were also recognized as Brāhmaṇas' (H. D. Griswold, *The religion of the Ṛgveda*, p. 118 n.). Thus the iconographic peculiarity of topboots, heavy tunic and avyaṅga can be accounted for.

The sun-god is symbolically represented by various articles, and the wheel is one of these. In the Vājapeya sacrifice the wheel-shaped cake of grain was placed on top of the post to which the animal victim was tied. The sacrificer mounting the steps said to his wife: 'Come let us both mount to the sun', and some steps up the post he said, 'We have attained the sun, O Gods'. It is clear that the wheel-shaped cake stood for the sun.

A gold plate also symbolized the sun (*ŚB* VII: 4: 1: 10). In the Mahāvrata ceremony the white round skin for which the Śudra and the Ārya fought a mock fight symbolized the sun (*ŚB* XIII: 4: 4: 6; *TMB* V: 5: 15–17). The *TMB* unambiguously states that the round skin is made to resemble the sun. Professor Güntert mentions a rock-painting from Backa near Brastad which shows a manly form with an axe in the raised hand. An exactly similar figure is found in Kinnekule. By the god's side is 'the wheel of the sun' and his footprint. A similar figure is found in southern Caucasus. These sun-figures with the wheels prove the sun-god's association with the wheel-shape which symbolized the sun. This wheel became a fixed mark of the sun and a symbol of kingship. The *HV* describes Sūrya's chariot as having one wheel only and as drawn by a nāga. 'The wheel which later on became the mark of the Chakravartin, the discus of Viṣṇu and the Buddhist Wheel of the Law, originally represented the sun' (A. Coomaraswamy, *History of Indian and Indonesian art*, p. 41).

A gold disc or plate was laid at the time of the piling of the fire-altar to represent the sun (*ŚB* VII: 41: 1: 10). Gold symbolized the sun as we read the description of the gold-coloured bird which resides in the heart of the sun (*MAU* VI: 34), or the 'hiraṇmaya puruṣa', the golden man (*MAU* VI: 1). A torch or gold was symbolic of the sun's brilliance (*ŚB* XII: 4: 4: 6); Savitṛ is described as all golden, presumably because gold reminded one of the sun's brilliance. The Pravargya ceremony is a sun-spell, in it the Mahavīra pot was covered with a golden plate; the pot was filled with milk. The object of the sacrificer in performing the sacrifice was to imbibe the sun's strength. The gold plate covering the white content of the pot may have given rise to a later image: the face of Truth is covered with a gold plate (*ĪU* 15). The sun has been identified with Satya, truth, in *BĀU* V: 5: 1–4. Gold or a firebrand was employed as a symbol of the sun when water had to be drawn after sunset; the absence of the sun in the sky was compensated for by his symbol (i.e. gold or the torch) on earth. 'The disc of gold placed behind the fire-altar to represent the sun may well be the origin of the later prabhāmaṇḍala or śīrṣacakra (nimbus)' (A. Coomaraswamy, *op. cit.* p. 41).

The lotus is found in the hands of sun-images, and it was later taken over by Viṣṇu and the Buddha, both solar gods. Viṣṇu's wife Lakṣmī holds a lotus and is seated on a lotus seat. In the Indian poetic convention the lotus is inseparably connected with the sun, because it blooms only while the sun shines. Iconography associated the lotus with the sun perhaps because the multi-petalled flower resembled the radiant sun.

The bird mount of the sun is absent in the Vedic literature; instead we have Tṛkṣi Trāsadasyava (*ṚV* VI: 46: 8), a real horse later deified. From it was derived Tārkṣya with the epithet (*ṚV* I: 89: 6, X: 178: 1; *KŚS* 73; *Naighanṭuka* I: 14). Later, in a passage which appears to be interpolated (*ṚV* V: 51) and also in *ĀŚS*, Tārkṣya also called Garuḍa or Garutmat became a bird, which it remains through epic and classical literature. The origin of this identification seems to be a *ṚV* passage, where garutman apparently stands for the sun. The course of the sun in the sky resembles the flight of a bird, hence the mythopoeic mind first imagined the sun itself to be a bird flying on golden wings and later imagined the sun to be borne on the back of a golden-winged bird. This was Garuḍa the mount of Viṣṇu in epic and Purāṇic mythology.[1]

A fairly common myth is the sun plying the sky-sea in a golden boat. This myth is found quite frequently in the *AV* (cf. XVII: 1: 26, XVII: 1: 25). The *CB* describes this boat as 'full, blameless and whole which rescues the voyager to safety and wellbeing'. One notices the idea of the sun-god as the saviour through the Devayāna.[2]

Thus Rā the sun-god too stood for final liberation. The *Vedas* also say that the abode of the fathers is the highest point of the sun (*ṚV* I: 115: 1, VII: 76: 2, X: 51: 2: 5, X: 113: 9; *CU* V: 4–10; *BĀU* VI: 2: 9–15) and Pitṛyāna, the path of reincarnation, is through the moon. These ideas are not peculiar to India, for among the Celts there was a soterial creed with the sun as its central object of worship and as an emblem of divine power and constancy, the immortality of the soul was its central doctrine. The end of life's journey is to live in the abode of endless light, the effulgence of the sun; therefore final liberation is through the sun. This is what constitutes the secret of the prominence of the solar cult throughout the world: the sun is the deliverer.

The primitive view regarding the sun is that it is itself a horse brought (i.e. ushered) by Uṣas. In the Ṣoḍaśin sacrifice a horse was placed in the hands of the priest and it symbolized the sun. The horse Dadhikrā of the

[1] Significantly enough, a minor Mexican sun-god called Ipalnemohuani (he by whom men live) has the eagle for his symbol. In the Mithra cult the raven took the place of the eagle; 'mythology made the raven the servitor of the sun' (Franz Cumont, *The mysteries of Mithra*, p. 155); and the raven (*corax*) was the first stage of initiation—symbolically the god's mount—he comes at the lowest rung of the ladder which leads the initiate higher and higher up until he reaches the final stage of the father (*pater*).

[2] One remembers Rā's boat in which the departed soul accompanied Rā. 'He (the deceased) longed to be able to embark in the boat of Rā and to sit in its bows and to sail about with the god for ever' (*The Book of the Dead*, ed. E. A. Wallis Budge). One also remembers the Babylonian god Sin who was called the Ship of Light and whose image was a ship.

Aśvamedha sacrifice was considered an embodiment of the sun. Thus in the horse-sacrifice we probably have a reminiscence of the horse-fetish, as Keith suggests. This myth is actually found in Dadhikrāvan, which is the sun in the shape of the horse. Tṛkṣi Trāsadasyava, from whom is derived Tārkṣya the Garuḍa mount of the solar god Viṣṇu-Nārāyana, was originally a horse. Etaśa the sun's horse may originally have been another solar symbol in horse-form. All solar gods are inalienably connected with the horse. When the Aṅgirases performed a sacrifice on behalf of the Ādityas, they received a white horse as fee (*AB* VI: 34; *KB* XXX: 6; *PB* XVI: 12: 1; *ŚB* III: 5: 1: 13; *GB* II: 6: 14). This white horse is undoubtedly a symbol of the sun.

The horse was the fastest animal and the Aryans ascribed its speed and virility to its solar origin. One remembers the Aśvamedha sacrifice in which the Mahiṣī obtained a valiant son by lying beside the slaughtered horse. We shall see that the horse is everywhere associated with the solar god.[1] Viṣṇu had his Uccaihśravas, the Buddha had his Kaṇṭhaka. Odin had his Sleipnir, the Armenian solar hero Sanasar had his Kurkik Jalali and the Celtic solar god Lugh had his Manaan. Christ at his second coming will come as the Sun of Righteousness; the Revelation describes his advent: 'And I saw heaven opened, and behold a white horse: and he that sat upon him was called Faithful and True and in righteousness he doth judge and make war' (Rev. xix. 11). One remembers that Kalki, the last incarnation of Viṣṇu who is expected to come, will, at the end of the four aeons come riding a white horse, with a drawn sword to destroy the wicked. There are other sun-gods and solar heroes who are inseparably connected with their horses, and these horses are white to symbolize the bright sun. The iconographical representations of Sūrya almost invariably connect him with a horse, or a chariot drawn by one or more (up to seven) horses. The Aśvins, twin solar gods, are born of horse-parents and are themselves connected with riding. Comparable twin solar gods, all over the world, are connected with horses; either are themselves horse-shaped, or born of horses or are fond of riding. Paidva the horse was given to the Aśvins by Pedu.

The horse was the king's mount in the Aryan conception, it was the mark of the victorious king. Hence quite naturally it became associated with the solar gods, who, as we shall see, were prototypes of victorious kings. Horse and kingship are inseparably connected. Of the Messagetae

[1] The high peak of Mount Taygeton was known as Mount Taleton (from Talos, the sun-god). It was sacred to the sun, and horses were among the sacrifices offered there' (R. F. Willets, *Cretan cults and festivals*, p. 52).

Herodotus states that the only god they worship is the sun, to which the horse is offered in sacrifice. The horse thus is an almost invariable concomitant of the sun-god, perhaps because this swift animal was the earthly replica of the sun running across the vast expanse of the sky every day.

Another association of the solar gods is the serpent. Ovid in his *Metamorphoses* says of Aesculapius, the son of Helios, that his symbol was the gold serpent (ch. xv). In ancient Greece the serpent was the symbol of healing—an attribute of the sun-god. Nārāyaṇa reclines on the serpent Ananta, Apollo was connected with the serpent.[1] The Pinturas depict him as stepping down from the sun. In Mithraism, too, we have Aion as a parallel of the sun-god. 'The apotheosis of Time as First Cause and that of the sun, its physical manifestation which maintained on earth heat and light, were highly philosophical conceptions' (Franz Cumont, *The mysteries of Mithra*, p. 148). This Aion (Time), whose manifestation is the sun, was in iconography 'represented in ordinary human guise, was endowed with wings, and entwined with a serpent—because of his endless circling—serpentine course' (Michael Grant, *The world of Rome*, p. 160).[2]

The most characteristic relationship between the sun-god and the serpent, however, is one of fighting. All sun-gods fight and conquer serpents. We remember Indra's fight and triumph over Ahi, Viṣṇu in his Kṛṣṇa incarnation fought and subjugated Kālīya, the water-snake. The Avestan Thraetaona, son of Athwya, conquered Azi (the snake) and bound him to Mount Damavand. Verethraghna also slew Azi Dahaka (later Zohak), the fiendish snake.[3] The Babylonian sun-god Marduk vanquished Tiamat, Apollo vanquished Typhon.

[1] The Mexican Quetzalcoatl was a pre-Nahua sun-god; his symbol was the flying serpent (so admirably described by D. H. Lawrence in *The plumed serpent*). This Quetzalcoatl vanquished the earlier sun-god Tezcatlipoca. Significantly enough Quetzalcoatl was borne on winged serpents from the sea. He was the Nahua and Maya culture-hero and their dawn-god. White in complexion, he was depicted as a traveller with a staff in his hand.

[2] In Egypt, too, there was this association of the sun-god with its serpent. 'The five-headed serpent Asht Hran and on his back lies the dead sun-god' (E. A. Wallis Budge, *Egyptian heaven and hell*, p. 149).

[3] In an Egyptian hymn to Rā we read: 'O come and acclaim ye Rā, the lord of heaven, the prince (life, health, strength)...Thine enemy the serpent hath been given over to the fire, the serpent-headed Seban hath fallen down headlong; his arms have been bound in chains, and his legs hath Rā hacked off from him.' Seban is in reality the name of a legion of devils. 'Rā liveth and the serpent-fiend Nâk is dead.' Nâk is the name of an opponent of the sun-god. Satan is presented as a snake in the garden of Eden (Gen. iii. 1) who outwits the first man Adam and causes his fall but is himself outwitted by Christ in the wilderness (Matt. iv. 11, Mark i. 13, Luke iv. 13) and vanquished by him on the cross and through his resurrection.

This fight and victory is important, for the serpent symbolizes evil, and the sun goodness; and unless man's faith in the final victory of the forces of the good is reinforced, the myth fails to convince and convert. The myth of the sun's victory over the serpent is the reassertion of the victory of light over darkness. In fighting the serpent, the sun-god fights all the enemies of man's happiness, and in conquering him he becomes man's supreme champion. The sun is constant, he does not wax or wane, he never fails man, and when this never-failing god is shown to be victorious over all the forces of darkness—decay, disease and death—the victory has a greater significance, for it becomes eternal. Through it man receives the answer to his deepest doubt regarding the final outcome of human existence. Through the sun-god's triumph man experiences the triumph of his own projected self. More so, because this triumph is not actually experienced in life, but like the katharsis is vicariously experienced, symbolically gone through.

All this partially explains why the sun-gods were the supreme gods in most mythologies. When the *ṚV* says that the sun is the soul of this world the statement is true both physically and spiritually. An agricultural people depends primarily on the sun and the rain (which is caused by the sun indirectly); hence it is quite in place that a people with settled agriculture, like the Vedic Indians, would gradually depend more and more on the sun. This would be expressed by the mythopoeic mind by ascribing mythological paramountcy to the solar gods. The sun is virtually the soul of this material solar universe; it is moreover the centre of man's conceptual world. An Indian school of Vedic commentary holds that all the Vedic gods are fundamentally solar in character. The reason is not far to seek. In Viṣṇuism, the most popular cult of India, most of the important Vedic gods have converged to give rise to the epic-Purāṇic Viṣṇu-Kṛṣṇa. The Ādityas were twelve in number and this number was possibly influenced by the Egyptian mythology. Herodotus says: 'The Egyptians first used the appellations of the twelve gods which the Greeks afterwards borrowed from them' (Herodotus, Loeb edn. p. 279). In the Babylonian pantheon with its triadic and enneadic pattern, the number twelve was early established. In India the number corresponded to that of the months. In Greece, too, the Olympian gods were twelve in number.

Whether one or twelve, the solar god soon captured the throne in the better-known mythologies. Even in Egypt, where death and eschatology played such an important role, Rā was the supreme god. The sun is not a local phenomenon; regarding its central importance and indispensable function there can be no diversity of opinion. Hence he alone can claim universality.[1]

In Celtic mythology we have Lugh, the supreme sun-god. In Greece we have Helios, Apollo and Aesculapius—all enjoying supreme rank. Marduk 'a younger figure in the Pantheon yet finally absorbs all the other gods' (*E.R.E.*). Marduk symbolized the spring sun, his festival fell on the vernal equinox. He was the arbiter of human destiny, an attribute he took over from Nabu. Marduk was the god of healing, too, hence his name was used in exorcism. Gradually he took over the more important traits of many gods and became the god of paramount importance. 'A famous hymn dedicated to Rameses IV to the honour of Osiris recognized the sun as the supreme lord, whose throne Osiris is permitted to share' (H. G. Q. Wales, *The mountain of God*, p. 16). Hammurabi in Babylon compared himself to the sun, thus indicating that the sun is a symbol of kingship and supremacy.

Sectarian gods are always everywhere worshipped kathenotheistically, the sun is the only god who ever gained real universality. 'There was no single god worshipped as alone, supreme, anywhere in Egypt except during the Ikhnaton interlude when Aton, the monotheistic Power manifested in the disk of the sun, was temporarily exalted as the one and only god' (E. O. James, *The ancient gods*, p. 206). In India, too, the only god whose cultic revival swept all over the country was Viṣṇu, the solar god. The cultic revival, however, did not bring back the Vedic Āditya Viṣṇu but the Vāsudeva Kṛṣṇa of the Nārāyaṇīya sect. And what is significant is that they worked into him all the solar traits of all the Vedic Ādityas. Although Śaivsm, too, has a large following, it never attained such supremacy, never evoked such emotional ecstasies as did Vaiṣṇavism. This is perhaps because Viṣṇu is the deliverer *par excellence* in a sense in which Śiva has never been.

While the moon waxes and wanes, the sun is constant and regular, so naturally the moon became the symbol of reincarnation while the sun symbolized liberation, the final release into light and eternal life; 'being with the sun' as the Egyptians imagined, or 'into the constant and ever-lasting Brahman' as the Indians thought. This release from darkness and death is the one dream which has haunted man through the ages. Because

[1] The Hittite sun-god Shamash attained a supreme position. In the Akkadian prayers Shamash is addressed as the merciful lord of judgement, king and merciful, who allots portions, passes through the gates of heaven and illuminates...the below and above. Istanu is another Hittite sun-god who enjoyed similar reverence and had satellites on both sides.

the sun-god symbolized its fulfilment he became man's 'personal god' which no other god could be. Hence it is that solar cults are cults of personal salvation. Rā, Viṣṇu-Kṛṣṇa, Mithra-Mihr, Christ and the Buddha all claim to be personal saviours. Kṛṣṇa says: Abandon thou all other religions and take shelter in me, grieve not, I shall save thee from all sins (*Bh. G* XVIII: 66). Christ says: 'I am the way and the truth, and the life, no man cometh unto the father but by me' (John xiv. 6). Thus the sun-god is the saviour-god, a personal god to whom the devotee approaches with 'bhakti'—devotion and faith.

CHAPTER 11

THE AŚVINS

THE Aśvins hold a unique position in the *ṚV*, for they are the most concrete solar gods. Their solar character is affirmed by their connection with the dawn. They are the early ones in the morning (*ṚV* I: 22: 1). Uṣas comes in their wake (*ṚV* I: 46: 14), and is called their sister (*ṚV* I: 158: 3). She is the daughter of Dyaus and belongs to the same time of the day as the Aśvins. The Aśvins' connection with Sūryā and Savitṛ also confirms their solar bearings. They are always included in the solar group of gods. The *ṚV* describes them as beautiful, golden in appearance and dress, even their chariot is golden—this association with gold also brings out their solar connection. The epics lay particular stress on their physical charm and beauty. Nakula and Sahadeva, the Aśvins' twin sons, were noted for their beauty. Their chariot, all golden (*ṚV* VII: 71: 28, 29, 35) with golden wheels (I: 158: 1), is decked out and fashioned by the Ṛbhus (VI: III: 1); it has a honey-whip, madhukaśā (I: 3: 3) and is ever full of honey (I: 120: 6). The chariot itself is called madhuvāhana, a vehicle of honey (I: 34: 2). With this chariot they created the dawn, days and nights; it goes further than the mind does. The number three is constantly mentioned in connection with the Aśvins; their chariot has all parts triple (I: 34: 2–5, 9); the Aśvins have three steps, a trait they share with Viṣṇu (VIII: 5: 23).

The Aśvins are particularly fond of honey and Soma, although it appears that they were allowed honey but not Soma. They put up a tough fight for the right to a share of the sacrificial Soma. The *ŚB* gives an account of the Aśvins' fight for Soma. 'The gods said, we will not invite you: ye have wandered and mixed much among men, performing cures' (*ŚB* IV: 1: 5: 14). This *Brāhmaṇa* does not tell us how the gods' resistance was overcome, but the *Mbh.* does, although in a different anecdote. The Aśvins rejuvenated Sukanyā's husband Cyavana (when she had refused to accept one of them instead of her senile husband); in return, Cyavana made them participants in the sacrificial oblation of Soma, for they were not soma-drinkers before. But when at Śaryāti's sacrifice Cyavana, officiating as priest, actually offered Soma to the Aśvins, Indra took exception to it, and protested, saying, they could not have a share in the sacrificial Soma, since they were mere physicians and roamed about on the earth curing men (*Mbh.* III: 124: 12). Indra threatened Cyavana with the thunderbolt. Cyavana paralysed his hand and a great demon Mada was created from Cyavana's wrath, so Indra finally yielded and allowed the Aśvins a share in the sacrificial Soma (*Mbh.* II: 123–4).

The story of the Aśvins rejuvenating Cyavana is not an isolated instance; the chief characteristic of the Aśvins is their kind patronage extended to mortals. They gave wealth to Sudās (*ṚV* I: 47: 6); Dīrghaśravas, son of Uśij, received help from the Aśvins in his trade ventures (*ṚV* I: 112: 11). Māndhātṛ, Bharadvāja, Divodāsa and Trasadasyu were also helped by the Aśvins (*ṚV* I: 112: 13, 14). They gave food to the sage Bharadvāja (*ṚV* I: 117: 11) and helped Vamra (son of Vikhānas), the newly-wed Kali, and King Pṛthu who had lost his horse (*ṚV* I: 112: 15). Paṭharvan, Bhujyu, Adhrigu, Kṛśānu, Tuviṣṭi, Dabhīti, Dhvasanti and Purusanti all received help and protection from the Aśvins (*ṚV* I: 112: 17, 20, 21, 23). Pedu pleased the Aśvins and received a strong white horse from them (*ṚV* I: 116: 6), or ninety-nine horses (*ṚV* X: 39: 10)—obvious symbols of the sun-god. Even the horses of young Purukutsa were helped by the Aśvins (*ṚV* I: 112: 26). The refrain of hymn I: 112 is: 'Come, O Aśvins, with those protections of yours'. The *ṚV* only mentions Cyavana's rejuvenation by the Aśvins (I: 116: 10, VII: 68: 6, VII: 69: 7) and also Vandana's (I: 118: 119) and King Kali's (X: 39: 8). The Aśvins helped Sūrya to grow in form and beauty (*ṚV* VI: 62: 6); protected Medhātithi, Vaśa and Gośarya (*ṚV* VIII: 8: 20), as also Mahiṣvat (*ṚV* VII: 68: 5). They gave wealth to the impoverished Vṛka (*ṚV* VII: 68: 8), found the lost cows of Triśoka (*ṚV* I: 112: 11), and ploughed a barley field with a vṛka (= ploughshare, Sāyaṇa) for King Manu (*ṚV* VIII: 22: 6). To Tṛkṣi, son of Trasadasyu, they gave great wealth (*ṚV* VIII: 22: 7), and to sage Vimada a desirable wife (*ṚV* X: 65: 12). An *AV* prayer to the Aśvins asks them to incline the unresponsive woman's mind toward her suitor (II: 30: 2); and they bestowed a husband on Ghoṣā, an old maid in her father's house (*ṚV* X: 39: 3). They took King Purumitra's daughter Śundhyuva on their chariot and conveyed her to Vimada (*ṚV* X: 39: 7). The worshipper praising the Aśvins says: 'There is no fear for him whom you favour with wife, chariots and honour' (*ṚV* X: 39: 11); 'Let them win King Puraya's mares, the hundred cows of King Sumīlha, the food which belongs to King Peruka, and the gold and chariots of King Śāṇḍa. Let them give a hundred horses to King Purupanthan who praises them' (*ṚV* VI: 62: 9, 10). This last prayer clearly brings out the worshipper's faith in the Aśvins' generosity, their belief that the Aśvins rob the unbelieving and non-sacrificing people of their wealth and cattle and bestow these on their devotees. The Aśvins reinstated King Jāhuṣa in his kingdom (*ṚV* VII: 71: 5). They filled a well with water for the thirsty Kṛvi (*ṚV* VIII: 22: 12).

The *JB* praises the Aśvins as 'those who remove the bondage of the gods' (III: 72). This trait of helping men in distress is not peculiar to the Aśvins; the twin gods all over the world display it. 'We see...the origin of the term Dioskouroi, it is no peculiar Greek idea, but one which arose at a very early period of human civilisation...the Dioskouroi came to be regarded as patrons of agriculture and the bestowers of rain' (J. R. Harris, *Cult of the Heavenly Twins*, p. 28).

Like all solar gods the Aśvins are healers too, but healing with them is not a general benevolent gesture like that of the other gods; it is their profession for they are the divine physicians. They healed the decrepit Parāvṛj and the blind Ṛjrāśva (*ṚV* I: 112: 8), as well as the blind seer Kavi (*ṚV* I: 116: 14). They restored the dead Viṣṇāpva to life (*ṚV* I: 117: 7, X: 65: 12). To a leprous sage they gave a pretty wife, restored eyesight to Kaṇva and hearing to the deaf boy Nṛṣad and intelligence and health to Kakṣīvat (*ṚV* I: 117: 8). They also cured King Paktha, Adhrigu and Vabhru (*ṚV* VIII: 22: 10); Ghoṣā they cured of leprosy so that she could marry (*ṚV* I: 117: 7). To the barren Vadhrīmatī they gave a son, Śyāva Hiraṇyahasta (*ṚV* X: 65: 12). Viśpalā had lost her leg in battle, the Aśvins gave her an iron leg (*ṚV* I: 117: 11). The sage Syāva was killed by the demons and his body cut into three; the Aśvins revived him (*ṚV* I: 117: 24). Cyavana was rejuvenated with the Viṅka saman (*TMB* XIV: 6: 10). King Śayu's cow was rejuvenated by them (*ṚV* X: 39: 13). The Aśvins put out the fire which the demons had lighted around Kakṣīvat (*ṚV* I: 116: 8). They are supplicated for protection and (the cure of) the waters, plants and trees (*ṚV* VIII: 9: 2).

They are expressly called the divine physicians (*GBU* II: 6). The *Mbh.* (III: 81: 14) knows them as gods who can give good favour and charm to devotees even if they only bathe in the Aśvina-tīrtha (the pilgrimage of the Aśvins). Upamanyu, blind in the well, regained his vision by praising the Aśvins (*Mbh.* I: 3). To Upamanyu they offered a cake which he refused to eat before offering it to his preceptor. Pleased at this they gave his preceptor golden teeth in place of the black iron ones that he had; they also restored Upamanyu's vision (*Mbh.* I: 3). The Aśvins, together with Sarasvatī, restored power and function to Indra's arm (which Cyavana had paralysed) with the help of an amulet (*VS* XIX: 80–95).

The connection of the Aśvins with healing is not peculiar to the Indian pantheon. As solar gods they symbolize the sun's healing power. In Pindar's *Pythian Ode* we read:

Apollo gave it (his child by Koromis) to the Magnesian Centaur to teach it how to heal mortal men of painful maladies...and those whosoever came suffering from the sores of nature or with their limbs wounded either by grey bronze of by far-hurled stones or with bodies wasting away with summer's heat or winter's cold, he loosed and delivered divers of them from diverse pains, tending some of them with kindly incantations, giving to others a soothing potion, or haply swathing their limbs with simples or restoring others by the knife.

The *JB* knows a different version of the Cyavana story: the Aśvins rejuvenated Cyavana for a share in the gods' sacrifice which had become truncated because Āditya had cut its head off (*JB* III: 120–7).

The *Mbh.* account of the rejuvenation of Cyavana is significant. The Aśvins restored Cyavana's youth and, although the sage had in gratitude agreed to make them partakers of Soma, Indra raised an objection and relented only when his hand was paralysed. Indra's objection was very clear: you two roam about the earth, curing people and assuming different shapes, how can you claim a share of the sacrificial Soma? In other words, the Aśvins behaved in a fashion unworthy of the gods: they had direct contact with men and their beneficent gestures were not words of blessing uttered from the Olympian altitude, but they 'actively' (cf. karmakarau) cured the sick. The pollution of the sick, the active touch or surgery (cf. Viśpalā or Śyāva) degraded them from the rank of true gods. The *ŚB* account also tallies with this: the gods said, 'We will not invite you, you have wandered and mixed among men, performing cures' (IV: 1: 15: 4). The social taboo against the Aśvins is understood better if we remember the position of doctors in ancient Indian society. In *TS* VI: 4: 9 and *MS* IV: 6: 2 a Brahmin is forbidden to heal. A *Mbh.* passage says that offerings to a Brahmin who practises medicine become pus and blood (vulgate XIII: 90: 14). Manu also lays down that a physician should be avoided in a sacrifice (*Manusaṃhitā* III: 152). The *Vaśiṣtha Dharmaśāstra* says that a doctor may not be invited to sacred ceremonies (LXXXII: 9). The *ĀpDS* prohibits the partaking of a physician's food (I: 4: 18, XIX: 15). Even the Buddhists and Jains were forbidden the medical profession (*Tevijja Sutta* II: 7). Behind this objection one notices that Soma was not the Aśvins' portion originally; they forced the gods (by inflicting paralysis on Indra) into alloting them a share of Soma. Decoding the language of mythology we may say that the cult of the Aśvins fought and won against the opposition of the prevalent Indra cult.

One remembers the case of Rudra-Śiva, who was denied the sacrificial oblation by Dakṣa; he could only get it by taking revenge on Dakṣa and his sacrifice. The reason, as we have seen, is the non-Aryan element in the composition of the god. This is a case in point, for the Aśvins, too, may have some such antecedents. Yāska, writing his *Nirukta* in the last centuries B.C., says: 'Then, who are these Aśvins? Heaven and earth, say some; the day and the night, say others; the sun and the moon, say (yet) others; but historians say that they are pious kings' (*Daivatakāṇḍa* 5–8). These historians apparently belonged to the euhemeristic school of thought and the Aśvins in their opinion were originally human kings (or leaders) who went about doing good to people and who, because of their piety, were deified. But obviously there was protest at the apotheosis: the worshippers of the orthodox pantheon could hardly be expected to render these intruders a share of the sacrificial Soma; and like Rudra they were kept out for a time. But because the Aśvins had a large following these objections were brushed aside and they were given due share of Soma.

Before they received Soma they had been fond of madhu, honey (or mead, a cognate of madhu), which they carried in their chariot. They are frequently called to come and drink honey (*ṚV* 1: 34: 10), their fondness for honey is recorded in *ṚV* 1: 47. In a curious tale we are told that Dadhyañc had taught them the secret of the honey-lore, madhuvidyā; they cut off Dadhyañc's head and joined a horse's head to the truncated body to trick Indra out of killing him. Indra, angry at Dadhyañc for divulging the secret of the honey-lore, struck off the horse's head which he took for Dadhyañc's own and then the Aśvins restored the real head to its position (*ṚV* 1: 116: 121). In a slightly different version the tale is retold in *ṚV* 1: 117: 22, where Dadhyañc becomes Dadhīca. All this indicates that (i) the Aśvins were good surgeons, (ii) they were excessively fond of mead (madhu), perhaps an intoxicating drink to which they had been addicted before they were entitled to a share of Soma, and (iii) Indra, who did not wish mere mortals to become endowed with the knowledge of (brewing?) mead, took vengeance on the traitor, Dadhyañc. Here, too, Indra's objection to the Aśvins being treated as gods is clear.

The objection was to their profession of healing as well as to their intimacy with mere mortals. They were naturally kind to men and whenever somebody in distress cried out to them they flew to the rescue. Atri, we are told was tormented by the demons in a hundred-door contraption where he was being burned to death; he called out for help; the Aśvins immediately quenched the fire with a jet of water (*ṚV* 1: 112: 16, 1: 158: 4,

VIII: 73: 3). When Vimada, the gods' protégé, won a pretty wife, the disappointed suitors assaulted her. The Aśvins came to her rescue (*ṚV* I: 116: 1). Tugra's son Bhujyu was drowning in a shipwreck and the Aśvins rescued him; they also saved him from enemy assault (*ṚV* I: 116: 5, I: 158: 3, VI: 62: 6, VII: 68: 7). Kakṣīvat was being burned to death by the demons, but thanks to the timely help from the Aśvins he was brought to safety (*ṚV* I: 116: 8). The demons had cast Rebha in a well where he languished for nine long days, but on the tenth the Aśvins came and rescued him (*ṚV* I: 117: 12, X: 39: 9). They saved the hen bird Vartikā from a wolf (*ṚV* I: 112: 8, I: 117: 16). The sage Kaṇva fell into the hands of the demons, the Aśvins saved him (*ṚV* VIII: 5: 23); they also saved Aṃśu and Agastya (*ṚV* VII: 71: 26). Saptavadhri was shut up in a chest (apparently by the demons) but the Aśvins came to his rescue (*ṚV* VIII: 73: 9, X: 39: 9). Vandana's wife died. Mad with grief Vandana threw himself into a well, but the Aśvins came and saved the poor distraught man (*ṚV* X: 39: 8). On behalf of their protégé Atri, the Aśvins rescued Ṛvisa from fire.

The Aśvins supreme feat of power and prowess is their winning of Sūryā who was originally intended for Soma by Savitṛ her father (*ṚV* I: 116: 17). In *ṚV* I: 182 we hear that they won Sūryā in a tournament with a thousand *Ṛc* stanzas; begged by the runners-up they surrendered a part of these hymns to each of them, but they set Sūryā on their chariot and left. The *AB* tells the same story: they had won Sūryā in a tournament and had married her, but because they had ignored the claims of the other rivals, they yielded a share of the Āśvinaśastra (their special litanies) to Agni, Uṣas and Indra (*AB* IV: 2 (17)). They are actually addressed as husbands (or protectors) of Sūryā (*ṚV* IV: 43: 6). Sūryā, says another hymn, when she was given in marriage to Soma rode in the Aśvins' chariot (*ṚV* VI: 62: 5). But the longest account is found in the Sūryā hymn (*ṚV* X: 85: 6 ff.). Here we are told that Soma desired a wife and that Savitṛ, Sūryā's father, contemplated giving her in marriage to Soma. But the Aśvins came as suitors; Bṛhaspati went to Savitṛ with their proposal (6–9) and the Aśvins became her husband (14). Their chariot was red, decked out with spring flowers, and Sūryā was requested to get up into it and reach her husbands' home (20). Viśvāvasu the Gandharva, a suitor who had been waiting patiently, is requested to rise and seek another wife since Sūryā is married already (21–2). 'Let Bhaga and Aryaman escort her (23), let Indra send her fortune (25). Let the Aśvins take the bride home and let Pūṣan grant her safe conduct (26).' We are told that Sūryā was first given to Soma, who handed her over to the Gandharva (i.e Viśvāvasu), who again gave her to Agni and finally from Agni she came to 'him born of men' (manuṣyajah). This is rather peculiar, for, in some accounts Sūryā is either intended for Soma (*ṚV* I: 116: 17) or is actually called Soma's wife (*ṚV* VI: 62: 5); in the rest either she is said to be intended for the Aśvins, or they are called her husbands. Gandharva Viśvāvasu and Agni appear only in *ṚV* X: 86. And the tenth book is the latest, composed after the Indian culture was already a mixed product of Aryan and non-Aryan factors. It would perhaps not seem too far-fetched to suggest that the Soma-Sūryā, or Aśvinau-Sūryā pair was Indo-European in origin, but the claims of the Gandharva or Agni appeared later. In support of this view one remembers that the hierogamy of the sun and the moon is a very common myth found almost all over the world; and, gods corresponding to the Aśvins are married to goddesses of the Sūryā type in other Indo-European mythologies.

Altogether fifty-four hymns are addressed to the Aśvins in the *ṚV* and over half of these are found in books I and VIII, and they are mentioned more than 400 times. The *ṚV* has a generic name, Aśvinau, for both of them; sometimes they are called Nāsatyau; in later Vedic literature the two are frequently referred to by two individual names—Nāsatya and Dasra. Dasra in *ṚV* language means bright or shining. In the Boghaz-keui treaty (*c.* fifteenth century B.C.) we have Nāsatya (Nāoṅhaithya in the *Avesta* who together with Indra and Saurva is a counterpart of Asha Vahiṣṭha and opposes the Spenta Aramaiti because he is a demon of discontent). In the *Vedas*, however, the singular number for Aśvins is unknown; they are always referred to in the dual.

The Pravargya ceremony, a solar rite, has oblations which the sacrificer offers exclusively to the Aśvins for strength; they are mentioned as harbingers of the morning. Sometimes the mid-day and evening oblations were offered to them, rarely, the dawn-oblation too; but they were particularly recipients of the morning litany. They were generally deprived of Soma, so the special offering made to secure their favour consisted of surā and madhu (wine and honey) (*ŚB* IV: 1: 5). Red-white animals were slaughtered for the Aśvins. The Aśvins also had fertility associations—blessed by the Aśvins the barren cow calved, the eunuch had a child and the barren woman conceived. They gave an old maid a husband, and this, too, implies their power of bestowing fertility. 'The Aśvins are closely connected with love, courtship, marriage, virility and offspring' (H. D. Griswold, *The religion of the Rigveda*, p. 256). As fertility-gods the Aśvins were also related to ploughing and milking.

In the *ṚV* there is no trace of the Aśvins as horsemen; they ride a chariot. But their name signifies that 'they possessed horses'. From the *Vedas* down to the *Purāṇas* we have an anecdote whose *ṚV* skeleton filled out with time till it reached full dimensions in the *Purāṇas*. It tells us of Vivasvat and Saraṇyū whose first children were Yama, Yamī and Manu and when Saraṇyū, unable to bear the sun's glory, fled, leaving Chāyā (her double) behind, Sāvarṇi, Śani and others were born. Vivasvat came to know of Saraṇyū's flight, went to the Uttarakurus, found her in the shape of a mare, himself assumed horse-shape and was united with her—the Aśvins were born (see Vivasvat). The epics, *HV* and the *Purāṇas* call them Aśvinīkumāras, sons of a mare, but do not say that they were horse-shaped gods. It is clear that the Indians remembered that these gods had some connection with horses, but the Vedic Indian mythology either forgot or chose to forget their actual connection with horses. Poseidon, the Greek sea-god, was associated with horses. He once pursued Demeter in horse-shape; they had two children—a horse and a girl. Again, Apollo the sun-god (corresponding to Vivasvat) pursued Leto to the land of the Hyperboreans (corresponding to Uttarakuru); she left that country in the shape of a she-wolf (cf. Saraṇyū fleeing from Vivasvat as a mare). One can almost notice an Indo-European myth split into several bits and retained in folk-memory, altered and modified by time and place.

The horse is, as we have seen, a solar symbol, and the Vivasvat-Saraṇyū episode is one of the few instances of a major god assuming a sub-human shape and begetting children. In the Greek mythology Zeus was united with Leda who assumed the form of a swan. In Vedic mythology, too, swans as well as eagles and buffaloes are said to draw the Aśvins' chariot (lambs are their favourite animals). One remembers the twin lambs which Urvaśī kept tied to her bed (*ŚB*) and she herself was a swan-nymph. These may not have been accidental connections. As Castor and Pollux (or Polydeuces) these twin gods are intimately connected with horses, and racing. They won Sūryā in a chariot-race, and this may well have been a horse race in the Indo-European proto-Aśvina mythology. One remembers that at the gate of the ancient hippodromes statues of Castor and Pollux were situated. Castor was famous for his skill in taming horses and Pollux for his skill in boxing. They are usually represented in iconography, poetry and painting as young horsemen and were regarded as patrons by equites.

From parallels in Greece, Rome and north European mythology it is clear that the Aśvins were not isolated Indian gods; their origin is at least as old as the Indo-European period. The Tyndaridae of the Greeks or the

Castores of the Romans have a beginning which perhaps goes back to an even more ancient period. Like the Dioscouri (Diokcouroi, cf. Lettish *dewa deli*, Lithuanian *diewo sunelei*) the Aśvins are the sons of the supreme sky-god. We have the Lettish myth of two sons of a god, helpers in time of need. Both the Aśvins and the Dioscouri are helpers of men. There must have been similar gods in pre-Zoroastrian Iran; and in Semitic mythology, too, we have parallel gods.[1]

In the Spartan myth Castor was murdered (because he was the son of a mortal, Tyndareus), and when Polydeuces called on Zeus, Zeus gave Polydeuces the choice of living on Olympus or passing one day on earth and the next in heaven. He chose the second one and Castor and he became stars who twinkle, the Gemini, who are bright and dim alternately. The Aśvins are twins but they are both immortal, and according to Yāska both had been mortal, benevolent kings.[2] Thus the mortal–immortal composition is constant and the one myth is a variant of the other. C. G. Jung in his *Psychology of the unconscious* writes: 'the sun is a pair of brothers, one being mortal, the other immortal' (p. 125). This is the fundamental concept of the Aśvins and their parallels all over the world.

'Castor', we read in Pindar, 'was slain in war, Polydeuces preferred this life to being wholly a god dwelling in heaven' (*Nemean Ode*, Loeb edn.). The solar god Nārāyaṇa with the mortal 'nara' (= 'man') may have been a reflection or sublimation of this solar mortal–immortal pair.

In all mythologies these brothers are helpers of men: 'Swift riders who intervene whenever men in distress invoke them as helpers and deliverers in the emergencies of the battlefield but still more often in the perils of the sea...If they bring aid to a ship in danger of the winter gales, they do not appear as horsemen but as gods of earlier days often revealed themselves in the shape of winged celestial beings' (C. Kerényi, *The heroes of the Greeks*, p. 112). Hesiod, too, in his *Theogony* gives an account of the Dioscouri which is similar to that of the *ṚV* Aśvins; 'They are children

[1] In most mythologies they are twin brothers, sometimes they are simply brothers. Ismenos and Kaaithos (or Kaanthos) were brothers of Melia the nymph, Ismenos was her favourite and Kaanthos killed him. In the myth of Samothrace Antiope had twins Amphion and Zethon; in the Spartan mythology Leda had twins, Kastor and Polydeuces, who rode on white stallions and were regarded as divine riders.

[2] The Aśvins' association with the horse, gold and kingship, and the same associations with analogous gods in other mythologies go back to the period of Homer and Hesiod in Greece and that of the earlier *Brāhmaṇas* in India. Significantly enough gold, the horse and kingship are connected in time: the Bronze Age introduced them all. If we remember that the conquering hero riding the horse-drawn chariot (still later, riding the horse) became the king of the settled agricultural population and thus the earthly replica of the sun in the firmament, things become somewhat clearer.

who are deliverers of men on earth and of swift-going ships when stormy gales rage over the ruthless sea.' This is one special manifestation of the solar gods, the helpers in need—they still the waves and calm the tempest. They themselves say: 'We...the Twins born with your mother, named sons of Zeus...We come to Argos having turned the rolling storm of a sea-tossed ship to quiet.' Of Phoebus (says Castor)

> '...yet he is my lord.
> we two must rush to Sicilian seas;
> rescue the salt-smashed prows of the fleet...'
>
> (Euripides, *Electra*, 1349 ff.)

The natural substratum of the Aśvins is hard to determine. Scholars are not in agreement regarding their identity. Weber says they are the twin stars Gemini and this view is supported by many others. Goldstücker regards them as the morning and evening twilight. V. H. Vader supports this theory, he considers the Aśvins to be the Zodiacal Light and Gegenschein. 'The path of the Aśvins is the Devayāna or the portion of the Zodiacal belt visible in the Polar regions' ('The twin gods Aśvinau', *IHQ*, 1932, p. 276). The *ṚV* also bears this out as it invokes the Aśvins to come via the Devayāna (I: 183: 6, III: 58: 5). Mannhardt and Oldenberg regard them as the morning and evening stars. These views may have originated from the Greek and Roman myths of the brothers becoming mortal and immortal alternately. The theories of the morning and evening star who are never visible together, or the Zodiacal Light and the Gegenschein may have arisen from these myths, or the identification of the brothers with the astral bodies or celestial lights may have been explained by these myths. In any case the twin stars or twilights were early identified with the twin brothers. Because of their beneficent mission among men they were given the highest honour by the mythopoeic imagination of the ancient poets, viz. the identification with stars or heavenly lights which still shine brightly as if blessing and shedding grace and favour to the world of men below. Whatever be the original natural substratum of the Aśvins, all these phenomena may have come to be associated with them in different places and at different times.

The Dioscouri were a very common feature on the coins of the Greek rulers, and also on the coins of the Bactrian kings, a particular dynasty of the Bactrians looked upon them as their tutelary gods.

'Eucratides I and Diomedos represented them on horseback, the pilos on their heads surmounted by a star, each with a palm, the long lance poised, on galloping horses.' There is another type of Dioscouri figures in which these are shown standing by one another, swords at their sides, in the position of leaning on their spear. Both types, standing and on horseback, were adopted by the Saka Pahlava. In the Gandhara art of the Swat valley we have...two standing male figures on the panel...similar in both attitude and body position...These two personages are thus represented once and always together; they may be nude, with only a cloak over their shoulders, or semi-nude, with a short skirt...at least one of them holds a spear and sometimes carries a shield as well. Their classical aspect is clear and comes above all from the dressing of the hair, for the sandals and for the cloak. Their identification is too obvious: we are dealing with an image of Dioscuri. The iconography of this panel, and the analogous pieces found in the same excavation, takes us quite suddenly into the full Hellenistic environment. (Gherardo Gnoli, 'The Tyche and the Dioscuri in ancient sculptures from the Valley of Swat, *East and West* 14, nos. 1 and 2, March–June 1963.)

It is interesting to note that the Aśvins do not figure in the iconography of the Indian pantheon. Post-Vedic literature dropped them almost unceremoniously and if the names persist in the epics and *Purāṇas* they are remembered as the handsome gods of healing whom the sick and the distressed invoked. Gradually they faded out in the epic-Purāṇic pantheon.

The identification of the Aśvins, as we have seen, is a complicated business. Authorities are divided in their opinions, each emphasizing one aspect of their personality as fundamental. But Yāska gives us another angle: the Aśvins, he says, were originally beneficent kings. They may actually have gone about healing the sick, rescuing men in distress or salvaging those in shipwreck. They may have been kings who were fast riders and fond of their horses so that they came to be inseparably connected with them. Later, after their death, people wishing to cherish their memories and remembering their innumerable kind acts deified them. Naturally there was opposition and violent resistance by the worshippers of the orthodox pantheon, devotees of respectable gods like Indra, on the ground that these were mere men with no sanction of tradition or antiquity to their credit, whose human history was recent and still fresh in men's minds and whose achievements (viz. healing the sick and helping those in distress) were unworthy of bona fide divinities. For, as the *JB*, *ŚB* and *Mbh.* say, they moved too much among men and did not maintain an Olympian distance from mere mortals. Even in the Homeric–Hesiodic period these gods were regarded as not very distant. Herodotus says that Euphorion received Castor and Pollux under his own roof. This resistance was overcome gradually; a section of the people started worshipping them, others followed and the Aśvins received their due share of the Soma-libation. All this may have taken place in the dim Indo-European antiquity, for when the Vedic Aryans arrived in India they brought the Aśvins with their pantheon.

The Aśvins and the parallel gods were associated with a goddess—their mother, sister or wife according to the different versions—who rode the same chariot with them or who accompanied them on horseback. They are 'always represented at the side of a feminine divinity, either Ūṣā, goddess of Dawn or Sūryā; the Dioscuri also accompanied a female figure, their mother or sister, Castor and Pollux accompanied Helen, Amphion and Zethos their mother, Antiope, Herakles and Iphikles their mother Alcmene, Diardanos, and Iason, Harmonica' (M. Eliade, *Patterns in comparative religion*, p. 97). 'Die Verbindung der Aśvins mit Sūryā, die der Dioskuren mit Helena und die Beziehung sowohl der Aśvins als der Dioskuren zum Meer weist auf einen gemeinsamen Hintergrund' (A. Hillebrandt, *Vedische Mythologie*, seite 15). Sūryā in the Sūryā-hymn was intended by Savitṛ her father for Soma; later, however, the Aśvins got her. The anecdote has a parallel in Graeco-Roman mythology. 'Castor and Pollux, sons of Tyndareus carried off Phoebe and Hilaria, daughters of Leucippus, betrothed to Idas and Lynceus' (J. G. Frazer's footnote on p. 312, Loeb edn. of Ovid's *Fasti*).

In their twin character of brothers-in-arms, acting as brave champions of men, they may have had prototypes in Gilgamesh and Enkidu. This friendship has a very deep David-and-Absalom kind of appeal, and Castor and Polydeuces and the Aśvins who go about helping men thus belong to an archetypal pattern which accounts for the response to the image. In the *Mbh.*, too, we are frequently told of Nara and Nārāyaṇa (of whom the former was human and the latter divine) who were absorbed in meditation in Badarikāśrama 'for the good of men' from times immemorial. This reference to an ageless pair of a god and a man who are engaged in some activity for the good of men has an eternal appeal. The *Mbh.* pair of Kṛṣṇa and Arjuna, we are told, are nothing but a reincarnation of that pair and this is the source of their power, the invincibility. Behind this image is the potent concept of God working in unison with man for the benefit of the world, a real friendship between man and god. The memory of one of the Aśvins being mortal may have grown dim by the time of the composition or compilation of the Vedic anthology, but their human antecedents, though not recorded in the hymns is indirectly hinted at by Yāska whose euhemeristic theory makes both of them mortals originally, as also by the resistance to their inclusion in the existing pantheon on the ground of their close association with men. It may easily have been the case that Dasra ('the shining') was originally thought to be divine and Nāsatya (perhaps from *na+asatya*, 'not false', i.e. 'true to his promise' of help) was a mortal.

The twin brothers with Sūryā on their chariot is also a familiar image. Kastor and Polydeukes had Helen on their chariot. The *Padmapurāṇa* mentions a similar trio—Kṛṣṇa, Balarāma and Subhadrā (*Utkalakhaṇḍa* XIX: 11–17, 45–6), the images in the famous Jagannatha temple at Puri. We read in Hesiod's *Theogony*, 'horse-taming Castor and prize-winning Polydeuces, desiring to be the husband of rich haired Helen'. The image of the Aśvins with Sūryā between them in their chariot has a parallel here.

As the *Mbh.* introduced the Kṛṣṇa–Arjuna pair and the *HV* the Kṛṣṇa–Balarāma pair they mythologically supplanted the earlier pair of the Aśvins who vanished from the pantheon. The cult underwent great transmutation, but the Aśvins–Sūryā trio is still worshipped in a different guise, because in mythology hardly ever do we find any significant god completely disappearing. Gods reappear again and again in changed garbs to suit the altered needs of the times.

CHAPTER 12

INDRA (1)

INDRA is the chief god of the *Ṛ V*; over a quarter of the hymns in the collection are addressed to him. The reason is, as we have seen, that he is a warrior, a leader of the Aryans.

He has been described as a mighty man with well-formed jaws (suśipra, *ṚV* I: 9: 3), son of valour (sahasah sunū), riding a chariot drawn by mighty and splendid horses (*ṚV* I: 10: 3) called Hari (I: 6: 2). His might and valour are emphasized and frequently dwelt upon. He is an undaunted soldier who has numerous victories and conquests to his credit. His worshippers express confidence in his strength, his enemies are in constant fear of it.

Prayers are addressed to Indra imploring his help in vanquishing the enemy, capturing their cattle and acquiring the enemies' wealth. He is the giver of cows—godā (I: 2: 2). He is besought to win the enemy's cows and to bestow them on his worshipper, for 'kine are of no use to the non-sacrificing Kīkaṭas, give them over to us' (III: 53: 14). He filled the earth with food for the sake of Turvīti and Vayya (IV: 19: 6). There was apparently a clamour over Indra's favour, 'he has already been purchased by his followers and cannot be purchased by others', says a devotee seeking to monopolize his favour (IV: 25: 9, 10). Kutsa was Indra's friend and at Indra's advice Kutsa went to heaven, where Indra's wife was confused at his resemblance to her husband (IV: 16: 10). Agru's blind son Parāvṛkta was being devoured by white ants, Indra rescued him from the anthill, restored his vision and made whole the limbs which the ants had made limp (IV: 19: 9). To Parāvṛkta Indra gave a share in the sacrifice and rendered Yadu and Turvaśa worthy of sacrificial oblation (IV: 30: 16, 17). Indra showed favours to Evara who had offered him Soma (VIII: 45: 38).

Indra was fond of the Vaikhānasas; the demon Rahasyu killed them at a place called Munimaraṇa. The gods told Indra where they were; Indra found and revived them with a sāman (hymn, *TMB* XIV: 4: 7).

Vaśiṣṭha's sons forced Indra to leave the sacrifice of Paśadyumna and to come to Sūdas's where they were performing a sacrifice. Indra protected King Sudās against the ten kings because Vaśiṣṭha's sons had interceded on Sudās's behalf. Indra heard the praise of Vaśiṣṭha's priests and helped by Varuṇa rescued the besieged Sudās from the ten kings. Varuṇa also helped Indra (*ṚV* VII: 33: 3–6, VII: 82 the whole hymn, and VII: 83: 1–8). This episode, mentioned so frequently, seems to have had a historical basis. To a blind man Indra restored his sight, and strength to a lame man (IV: 30: 19). Indra conquered 100 cities with stone walls from Śambara and gave them to Divodāsa (IV: 30: 20). Namuci the demon attacked the sleeping Nami, Indra protected him by crushing the demon's head (VI: 20: 6). He killed Śipru of the magic power and distributed his wealth among his own followers (VI: 20: 7). Indra tamed Vetasu, Daśoni, Tugra Ibha and Tutuji on King Dyotana's behalf (VI: 20: 8). Seven cities of the demon Śarat were conquered by Indra who made a gift of these to King Purukutsa (VI: 20: 10). He killed Uśanas's enemy Navavāstva and gave his wealth to Uśanas (VI: 20: 11). Waters held up by Dhuni were released by Indra. Turvaśa and Yadu were helped to cross the sea (VI: 20: 12). Indra killed Vetasu's enemy Tugra on Vetasu's behalf, King Tuji was made to prosper because he praised Indra (VI: 26: 4). Dabhīti was favoured by Indra, who killed Cumuri for him as well as 6,000 of his enemies (VI: 27: 6). King Kṣattraśrī, son of Pratardana, prospered through Indra's grace (VI: 27: 8). At the time of Indra's fight with demon Varaśikha, the terrible noise of his thunderbolt killed a valiant son of the demon who died on the other side of Hariyūpīya (identified by some with Harappa) when Indra was killing Vṛcīvat for Sṛñjaya on this side in order to give his wealth to King Abhyavartin (VI: 28: 4, 5, 7). The hundred cities of Śambara which Indra destroyed were rich; this wealth he gave to Divodāsa and Bharadvāja (VI: 30: 4). When Etaśa fought against his enemy Saurāśva Indra helped him to win a victory (I: 61: 15)—Indra saved his follower, King Tuvaryāṇa, against Kutsa Atithigva and Āyu (I: 53: 10). A prayer to Indra begs him to give Druhyu's and Puru's strength to his devotees (VI: 46: 8). At Udavraja Indra slew Varcin and Śambara and received ten horses, ten jars, ten garments and ten ingots of gold—these he gave to Divodāsa (VI: 47: 23). To Prastoka of the Atharvans he gave ten chariots and hundreds of cows (VI: 47: 24). Indra helped Sudās to cross the Paruṣṇī, the Maruts were then sent to his aid by their mother Pṛśni (VII: 18: 10: 11). He drowned Śruta, Kavaṣa, Vṛddha and Druhyu in water, forcibly entered their cities and gave Anu's wealth to Tṛtsu (VII: 18: 12). To Kutsa, son of Arjuni, Indra gave wealth and subjugated Kuyava and Śuṣṇa (VII: 19: 2–3). Kings Puru, Ruśama, Śyāvaka and Kṛpa are counted among Indra's protégés (VIII: 3: 12). The worshipper prays to Indra for gifts similar to those given to Nahuṣa's descendants, and to protect him and his as he did the Daśagvas and Adhrigu (VIII: 20: 20, 24). In the Vālakhilya hymns we hear prayers for protecting the votary. He fetched the enemy king Pravat's wealth for his follower Śarabha (VIII: 98: 6). A prayer says 'Let Indra win hundreds and thousands of horses and milch cows and give them to his devotees' (X: 48: 4). He never gives Aryan wealth to the Dasyus but protects the Vetasus like a father (*ṚV* X: 49: 3, 4). 'He who desires a village', says the *TS*, 'should offer on eleven potsherds to Indra' (*TS* II: 2: 11), but one should not sacrifice to Mahendra if one is not prosperous (*TS* V: 5: 1). Indra's bounty is frequently mentioned: he is the giver of the best (*MS* II: 2: 13) and the deliverer from sin (*MS* II: 2: 10).

In the epics Indra is the benign bestower of blessings and weapons. To Daśaratha he gave a jewel which the king later gave to Sītā (*Rām.* V: 67: 5). Indra's discus was given to Rāma by Viśvāmitra (*Rām.* I: 30: 6). He dissuaded King Vasu of the Cedis from his endeavour to become Indra, made him sky-rover (uparicara) and gave him a lotus-garland that would never wither, also a bamboo-pole, the royal insignia; he even shared his seat with Vasu. This last he dug into the earth and this event is celebrated every year (*Mbh.* I: 57, XII: 322: 21). When all Yudhiṣṭhira's brothers and Draupadī had dropped dead Indra appeared before Yudhiṣṭhira and asked him to get into his chariot and reach heaven. Yudhiṣṭhira declined the offer, argued, said he could not leave the faithful dog behind. Then Dharma confessed that he had been testing Yudhiṣṭhira's loyalty in the shape of a dog and Indra took Yudhiṣṭhira to heaven (*Mbh.* XVIII: 2, 3). Once Indra found a parrot clinging to a withering tree because it would not leave the tree which had sheltered him for so long; touched by the parrot's loyalty Indra revived the tree (*Mbh.* XIII: 5). Mataṅga was practising stiff penance in order to achieve Brahminhood, Indra tried hard to dissuade him and at last succeeded by offering him power and fame (*Mbh.* XIII: 29). The kine of Indra's devotees had been stolen by the Paṇis: Indra sent Saramā (the dog of the gods) as an emissary to retrieve them (*ṚV* X: 67: 6, X: 108). Some scholars see in Saramā a replica of the Greek Hermes, but the anecdotes in the two mythologies seem to have quite different slants. Indra as the champion of the Aryans helps them to recover their lost property.

The most important trait of the Vedic Indra was his demon-killing and the *ṚV* is full of these accounts. Among the minor demons slain by Indra we hear of Ilīviṣa, Śuṣṇa (I: 33: 12, I: 101: 2), Pipru (I: 51: 5)—whom he killed with his Māyā, magic power—and Śambara (I: 51: 6, I: 53: 4). When fighting the enemies of his devotee Purukutsa, Indra destroyed seven cities and won demon Aṃh's wealth for Sudās (I: 63: 7). He killed Rauhiṇa

(I: 103: 2) while the latter was ascending the sky (II: 12: 12), also the demon Kṛṣṇa who dwelt by the river Aṃśumatī (I: 130: 8), Śuṣṇa and some other demons he killed with the sun's chariot-wheel (I: 130: 9, I: 175: 4). Demon Kuyavāc was another of Indra's victims, so was Dhuni (I: 174: 7, 9). Śambara eluded Indra, who hunted him for forty years till he found him hiding in a cave and killed him (II: 12: 11). He killed demons Nārmara, Sahavasu and Jātuṣṭhira (II: 13: 8, 11), Dṛbhīka, Uraṇa, Arbuda, Aśna and Rudhrīka, Pipru and Mṛgaya (II: 13: 8: 11, II: 14: 3–5, IV: 16: 15). He destroyed the cities of enemies and slaughtered thousands of demons. He rescued Dabhīti by throwing the arms of the latter's enemies into the fire (II: 15: 3). He slew Dhuni and Cumuri to protect Dabhīti and to the latter's doorkeeper he gave the demons' wealth (II: 16: 9). He chased Krivi with his thunderbolt and made him sleep on the ground (II: 17: 6). Assisted by Agni, Indra destroyed ninety enemy cities in one attempt (III: 30: 9); this probably is a reference to the incendiary to which he took recourse in order to crush demon prosperity. He is called Pūrbhid (III: 34: 1) and Purandara, because he forced entry into the enemy fortresses. He subjugated Vidatha's son Ṛjīśvan, destroyed fifty black enemies and captured Śambara's cities (IV: 16: 13). Thor, the Eddic parallel of Indra, killed giants (like Hrungrir, Thrym, Hymir, Geirrod and Midgard) who were huge, powerful and evil beings, especially jealous of the Aesirs' (i.e. the gods') possessions. Thor was actually struggling for mankind and, like Indra, was a culture-hero who helped civilization in a precarious moment, the civilization which the invaders (both Indian and Norwegian) had created after their victory over the indigenous population.

When Indra was born, Kuṣavā, a monstress, came to devour the new-born child, but Indra killed her (IV: 18: 8). This episode reminds us of Kṛṣṇa another solar hero of a later age who, as an infant, slew Pūtanā the monstress. We shall see later that Kṛṣṇa waxed in stature and power by borrowing much of Indra's exploits, i.e. by imitating them on another plane of mythology. Vyaṃśa, the monster, devoured Indra's jaws but Indra slew him with his thunderbolt (IV: 18: 9). Indra destroyed ninety-nine cities of Śambara, made a hundred cities over to Divodāsa (IV: 26: 3), and slew Śambara (son of Kulītara), by stretching him on a mountain (IV: 30: 14). Five hundred of the followers of the demon Varcin were slain by Indra (IV: 30: 15). Indra forced his way into demon Kuvitsa's cowshed (VI: 45: 24). Thousands of enemy soldiers fell in battle. Ajāsa, Śipru and Yakṣu brought the heads of horses dead in battle to offer to the victor Indra (VII: 18: 14, 19). Devaka the son of Manyamāna was an enemy (of the

Aryans), Indra killed him (VII: 14: 20), as Ahnavayya too was enemy to Yadu and Turvasu and the latter were Indra's protégés, Indra killed Ahnavayya (VIII: 45: 27). The new-born Indra asked his mother: 'Who are the strong, who are the famous?' She replied: 'There yet remain the demons Aurṇavābha and Mahīśuva, destroy these and others too.' Indra broke them as one breaks chariot-wheels with rope (VIII: 77: 1–3). When he killed the demons Parṇaya and Karañja in battle, he made the Guṅgus yield to Atithigva Divodasa (X: 48: 8). Atka he killed for Kavi Uśanas (X: 49: 3), Mṛgaya he defeated for Śrutarvaṇi, Vesa for Āyu and Paṅgabhi for Savya; he also destroyed Navavāstva and Bṛhadratha (X: 49: 5, 6). Once he is simply mentioned as the killer of seven great demons (X: 120: 6).

It is true that Sāyaṇa's commentary does not enlighten us regarding the identity of those whom Indra killed, he designates some as 'asuras' others as enemy kings. Historically it may be safe to assume that Indra's enemies (the asuras) were the non-Aryan (i.e. pre-Aryan on Indian soil) chiefs who offered resistance to the hordes of the Aryans; some may even have been rival tribal leaders among the Aryans. The numerous demons seem to have been indigenous tribal heads, rulers of petty principalities whom Indra had to defeat one by one in order that the Aryan army could have access to their wealth and land.

The *TS* gives an interesting account of the Asura power: 'The Asuras indeed at first owned the earth, the gods had so much as one seated can espy.' The gods asked for a share; the Asuras agreed to give them as much as a Sālāvṛkī can thrice run around. Indra (in the shape of a Sālāvṛkī, i.e. wolf-hound) did so on all sides of the earth (*TS* VI: 2: 4). One is reminded of the Edda account of the Deluding of Gylfi.

> It is told of him (King Gylfi) that he gave a ploughland in his kingdom, the size four oxen could plough in a day and a night, to a beggar-woman... This woman, was of the family of the Aesir... From the north of Giantland she took four oxen and yoked them to a plough, but those were her sons by a giant. The plough went in so hard and deep that it loosened the land and the oxen dragged it westwards into the sea... The Gefjon set the land for good and gave it a name, calling it Zealand (*Prose Edda*, p. 29).

Here as in the *TS* we perhaps have the same account of the Indo-Europeans deluding the indigenous population and occupying their land where sheer might would be of no avail and fraud alone could secure the end, the Vedic poets would call it māyā which Indra frequently employed in deluding his enemies.

The *Brāhmaṇas* mention other demons whom Indra killed—the Arurmaghas (*AB* VII: 2)—but there Indra usually kills demons with sacrifices, and with Sāmans (in the *Sāmaveda Brāhmaṇas*). Thus he at first could not kill Dīrghajihvī the monstress, asked Kutsa and Sumitra for help and aided by them killed her with the Saumitra sāman (which Sumatra used) (*TMB* XIII: 6: 9). The Dīrghajihvī episode is retold in the *Rām.* (I: 28: 18–19), but there she is called Dīrghajihvā. The epics give Indra other victims; thus Indra kills the demon Vipracitti (*Mbh.* VI: 90) and even Tāraka (*Mbh.* VI: 91).

Tvaṣṭṛ in the *ṚV* helps Vṛtra by fashioning his thunderbolt for him. But in the *YV*, i.e. in the *MS*, Indra requites this in a curious fashion: he kills Tvaṣṭṛ's son Viśvarūpa (*MS* II: 4: 1). In the *Brāhmaṇas* the episode is mentioned. The *ŚB* mentions it among the five sins of Indra (VII: 2), and says that Indra killed Tvaṣṭṛ's three-headed son Viśvarūpa (I: 6: 3: 1 ff.). As a result Indra was cut off from his share of Soma. He partook of it stealthily; Tvaṣṭṛ said to that desecrated Soma, 'let Indra's enemy grow'; it rolled on and became Vṛtra, Indra's greatest enemy (*ŚB* I: 6: 3). Another passage says, 'Indra killed Tvaṣṭṛ's son Viśvarūpa and Tvaṣṭṛ exorcized him' (*ŚB* XII: 7: 1: 1). The *JB* says: 'Tvaṣṭṛ's son (Viśvarūpa) was three-headed, Indra struck the heads off; they turned into birds: Kapiñjala (heathcock), Kalaviṅka (cuckoo) and a Tittiri (partridge). The bereaved Tvaṣṭṛ performed a sacrifice and uttered his desire: "Grow thou the enemy of Indra, out of the sacrifice Vṛtra was created"' (II: 153–5).

The *Mbh.* gives the longest account of this event. Tvaṣṭṛ created Viśvarūpa Triśiras an an adversary of Indra. One of his three heads was for the study of the *Vedas*, another for drinking wine and the third was for watching the world. Viśvarūpa practised penance and Indra sent nymphs to distract him for fear of losing his overlordship to him. But the nymphs failed. Then Indra slew him with his thunderbolt. But the corpse shone so bright that Indra ordered a takṣan (smith) to strike the heads off. At first he would not agree, but was tempted into obeying Indra when he promised to make the smith's tools like his own thunderbolt and also to give him a share in the animal sacrifice. The smith struck off the heads out of which flew the three birds. Tvaṣṭṛ, enraged at this, created Vṛtra (*Mbh.* V: 9).

Indra's feat of killing Viśvarūpa has parallels in other mythologies. In the *Avesta* Thrita Athwya (Trita Aptya) and Thraetaona (commonly called Traitona) are names of the fire-god. Thraetaona killed a three-headed, six-eyed fiend and let loose confined cows. Thraetaona Athwya killed Azi Dahâka, the most beautiful fiend created by Angra Mainyu, and released the cows. Keith says that in the earlier legends Trita Aptya was the slayer of Viśvarūpa. Indra assumed the authorship of this feat when he became the supreme god in India. This explains the Thraetaona myth. In Greece Heracles killed a three-headed or three-bodied monster called Geryones, and in the Roman mythology Hercules killed Cacus, the son of Vulcan. Now Tvaṣṭṛ is the Indian parallel of Vulcan; thus from the Greek and Roman myths emerges the figure of a solar hero (a culture hero) who slays a monster-son of the divine smith. The myth seems to be of Indo-European origin; the *Brāhmaṇas* filled it out with details to suit the needs of a hieratic religion and connected it with the Vṛtra myth.

The *ṚV* frequently mentions Indra as killing Ahi and releasing the waters (I: 32: 1), or releasing the seven rivers (II: 12: 3), or cutting a path for the rivers by slaying Ahi (II: 15: 1–3). Sometimes Indra wins cows after killing Ahi with a thunderbolt (IV: 17: 10). Even after his hands and feet were struck off Ahi lay hiding in a cave where Indra slew him (I: 32: 7). The killing of Ahi was a fearful event, the sky bowed down when Ahi was slain (VI: 17: 10).

The word Ahi has cognate Greek forms *Ophis* or *Echis*—'serpent'. This meaning persists in later Vedic texts, where Ahi is constantly referred to as a serpent. The Midgard Serpent was the most powerful adversary of Thor, Indra's Eddic parallel. In these early Vedic texts another meaning of the word Ahi may also have been intended—'one who does not release'—for Ahi does not release the waters until Indra kills him.

If the above derivation formed a hidden substratum in the concept of Ahi then Ahi becomes a synonym of Namuci, 'one who does not release'. Namuci is mentioned in the lists of Indra's victims (*ṚV* II: 14: 3–5), another variant of the Geryones/Cacus myth. Indra protected the sleeping sage Nami by crushing Namuci's head (*ṚV* VI: 20: 6). Again, Indra is said to have killed Namuci with foam (*ṚV* VIII: 14: 13).

Cows were recovered when Ahi or Namuci was killed. The Namuci episode, however, was elaborated in the *Brāhmaṇas*. Indra and Namuci discussed the manner in which the latter could be killed, and Indra killed Namuci with foam, during twilight (first mentioned in *ṚV* VIII: 14: 13, also in *TMB* XII: 6: 8). Indra killed Vṛtra and Namuci with 'foam of the waters' on a 'neither-dry-nor-wet' thing at the juncture of day and night (*TB* I: 7: 1: 6, 7), for Indra swore to Namuci that he would kill him 'neither by day nor by night...neither with the dry nor with the moist'. So Indra asked the Aśvins for help, they agreed in return for a share (of oblations). They poured out foam at early dawn and Indra struck off

Namuci's head (*ŚB* XII: 7: 3: 1–2). The *Rām.* mentions a great duel between Indra and Namuci (IV: 9: 54). In the *Mbh.* Namuci is one of the demon overlords whom Indra found fallen from glory and asked whether he mourned his lot. Namuci said that Fate was ineluctible, one should submit to it with inner equanimity (XII: 219).

Indra had apparently failed to kill or defeat the powerful Namuci by sheer valour, arms or might, for the latter had magic power (*ṚV* I: 53: 7). With the help of the Aśvins, and with guile and trick he killed Namuci and retrieved wealth, waters and cows. Needless to say these are won as booty.

Enemy chiefs, because they belong to the soil, can withhold the water supply to an invading enemy and thus virtually create the conditions of a siege (for the invader) and maintain these conditions indefinitely. In later mythology cosmic interpretations were given to what was perhaps originally a military situation. Thus in Sāyaṇa all the demons are demons of drought, and Indra's demon-killing feats are simply acts by which he releases rain-water. This became his cosmic function, when his military prowess had ceased to retain the former glory because the invaders were already settled in the land. Once they had become a peacefully settled agricultural people, the memory of early warfare became transmuted to suit the needs of the day. Indra was still great, not because he was an invincible general but because he was a luminary, a solar god, a culture-hero who poured down rain-water, the natural phenomenon vitally important to an agrarian population.

Another demon slain by Indra is Vala (*ṚV* I: 53: 5, II: 14: 3). Vala, the leader of the Paṇis (*ṚV* VIII: 4: 8) who lay hidden in a cave, and Kuyava, another demon hidden in water, were both hunted down and slain by Indra (*ṚV* X: 148: 2). Vala is also said to have hidden in a hole hiding cows (*ṚV* I: 11: 5). 'The cave itself, Vala, becomes in time personified as a cave-demon' (H. D. Griswold, *The religion of the Rigveda*, p. 88). Indra tore Vala up with his hands, destroyed the Paṇis and retrieved the cows (*ṚV* X: 67: 6). The solar hero killing a demon hiding in a cave is a common myth in many countries, and the solar hero hunting out an adversary hiding in water is perhaps repeated in the Pāṇḍavas' hunting Duryodhana out of Lake Dvaipāyana. The image of the solar hero retrieving lost cows had gained such popularity that the *Mbh.* also offers a parallel episode in Arjuna retrieving the cows of his temporary patron King Virāṭa from the Kauravas (*Mbh.* IV).

Śuṣṇa was a demon, i.e. an enemy of the Aryans, whom Indra killed even though he hid in water (*ṚV* V: 31: 9) for his magic availed not before

Indra (*ṚV* VI: 20: 4). Sāyaṇa explains his identity as a demon of drought withholding waters and cows from the Aryan invaders. Indra stole one of the two chariot-wheels of Sūrya and killed Śuṣṇa with it (*ṚV* I: 175: 4), and in this feat Indra becomes the prototype of Viṣṇu with his discus.

The arch-enemy of Indra, however, was Vṛtra, for he it is who fought Indra longest, so that after his slaughter Indra assumed the designation Vṛtrahan.

Indra killed Vṛtra by striking off his arms (*ṚV* I: 32: 5). Vṛtra's mother lay covering him but Indra slew him even there and released the waters whose current had been arrested by Vṛtra (*ṚV* I: 32: 11). Moreover, Vṛtra owned ninety-nine cities which Indra eventually destroyed with a thunderbolt fashioned from Dadhīca's bones (*ṚV* I: 84: 13). Vṛtra had to be killed to oblige Purukutsa (*ṚV* I: 174: 2), and he, too, was slain while hiding in water (*ṚV* II: 11: 9). All these enemies slain while hiding in water had left such an abiding impression on the popular mind that the epic battle in the *Mbh.* had to end in a similar fashion: Duryodhana, the last enemy, had to be taunted into emerging from his hiding place in water before he is killed.

Vṛtra fled from Indra in the shape of a deer (*ṚV* V: 29: 4, VIII: 93: 14). When Indra had slain Vṛtra his seed fell on herbs; cows ate it and produced milk (*ṚV* VIII: 6: 20). This indicates the virility of the solar hero Indra, who in one of his epiphanies is a vegetation-god. It is significant that this virility is manifested after he performs the most wonderful feat of killing Vṛtra. 'Indra slew Vṛtra; the gods said of him; Great hath he become who hath slain Vṛtra, that is how Mahendra (the great Indra) has his name' (*TS* VI: 5: 5). The Maruts were Indra's faithful comrades, for 'when Indra killed Vṛtra, all the deities left him...only the Maruts, his true comrades, did not leave him' (*AB* III: 16).

Gradually with the rise of the priestly hierarchy Indra's feat of Vṛtra-killing is differently explained—he did not do it alone, other gods helped him and he did it through sacrifices. Thus he is said to have done it with the help of Agni and Soma (*AB* II: 3: 5). The *TB* says Indra slew Vṛtra with the foam of water as he did Namuci (I: 7: 1: 6, 7). But Vṛtra had not been an easy enemy to kill. Once Indra hid in a hole out of fear of Vṛtra. Then the daughters of Tvaṣṭṛ succoured him with the Tvāṣṭrī sāman (*TMB* XII: 5: 21).

The cosmic interpretation of the identity of Vṛtra perhaps originated with the *ŚB* account: 'Vṛtra in truth lay covering all this (space) which here extends between heaven and earth. And because he lay covering all this, (root *vṛ* = to cover), therefore his name is Vṛtra. Him Indra slew' (*ŚB* I: I: 3: 4, 5). 'For Indra, when he was battling with Vṛtra, did choose them (the waters) and with their help he killed him' (*ŚB* I: I: 4: 8). Indra enticed Agni and Soma to follow him. He killed Vṛtra who said, 'thou art now what I (was before). Only cut me in twain' (*ŚB* I: 6: 3 ff.). Of the Śākamedha offering it is said 'therewith indeed the gods slew Vṛtra' (*ŚB* II: 5: 3: I). Again, 'Verily by means of the Great Oblation the gods slew Vṛtra...For before the slaying of Vṛtra he was indeed Indra but after slaying Vṛtra he became Mahendra even as (a king becomes) a mahārāja after obtaining the victory' (*ŚB* II: 5: 4: I, 9). It is significant that the *Brāhmaṇas* tend to substitute Indra's valour and prowess with sacrifices; even demons were killed through sacrifices; Indra's victories are still remembered but his individual achievements are steadily being minimized. The Vedic Indra was primarily a warrior-god, and consequently champion of the Kṣattriyas. At a time when the clergy were a rising class Indra's achievements would naturally be explained as fruits of sacrifices, the Śākamedha for example.

His Kṣattriya characteristics are stated in the *TB* (III: 9: 16: 3). Again 'the sacrificer is Indra...because he is a Kṣattriya and because he is a sacrificer' (*ŚB* V: 4: 3: 8). As a Kṣattriya he is inferior to the priests whose supremacy had to be established not only in the spiritual realm but also in the mundane; hence Indra slew demons aided by the power arising out of sacrifices. Thus the *JB* says Indra hurled his thunderbolt 'through the (merit of) the Uṣṇij and Kakubh sāmans' (*JB* I: 58). This point is most clearly expressed in another *JB* passage: Indra attempted to slay Vṛtra with his vajra (thunderbolt), but could not until he 'saw' the hymn 'pra itya', etc. (I: 182). Again, Indra killed Vṛtra with the Śakkarī hymns (*JB* I: 194). He did not accomplish the task unaided, for he asked the Maruts to play with axes (paraśu) in their hands so that he could kill Vṛtra fearlessly (*JB* II: 232). He became Mahendra after killing Vṛtra (*JB* II: 234). But the *TMB* says that he became the great victor through the Mahāvrata sacrifice (*TMB* XXIII: 10: 2). When Indra was about to kill Vṛtra, the latter offered his strength to Indra, which Viṣṇu thrice received on Indra's behalf. This strength was the thousand cows which they divided into three parts; Indra took two parts and Viṣṇu one (*TMB* XX: 15: 6, 7).

The epics refer to the killing of Vṛtra as a well-known historical event and even use it in imagery. Vṛtra was burnt by the thunderbolt (*Rām.* III: 56: 25, VI: 32: 35). The *Mbh.* reduces the importance and significance of this episode. Tvaṣṭṛ, enraged at his son's death, created Vṛtra who had once swallowed Indra; the gods created the yawn, so that Indra escaped through Vṛtra's gaping mouth (*Mbh.* v: 9). Afterwards Viṣṇu entered Indra's thunderbolt, but Vṛtra said he would be killed on neither-dry-nor-moist ground, neither in the day nor at night. Then Indra sought and found a loophole in the conditions and killed him (*Mbh.* v: 10). That Indra became Mahendra by killing Vṛtra is still remembered (*Mbh.* XII: 15: 15).

In the sixth book of the *Mbh.*, Bhīṣma described the manner of Indra's slaughter of Vṛtra. At first Indra felt weak due to Vṛtra's māyā, magic power, and was overwhelmed by Vṛtra's prowess till Vaśiṣṭha provoked him into action. Later Śiva's power created a fever in Vṛtra and Viṣṇu's power entered Indra's thunderbolt. Then, while Vṛtra was in fever, Indra hurled his bolt. It entered Vṛtra's gaping mouth and slew him (*Mbh.* XII: 272–3). In this account Indra's credit is visibly diminishing, for his achievement is being usurped by the two rising sectarian gods of the epic-Purāṇic pantheon, viz. Viṣṇu and Śiva, who between them share the glory which belonged to the *ṚV* Indra.

In another account, when Indra sought to kill Vṛtra the latter took shelter in element after element till at last he entered Indra's body and Indra slew him with a sword (*Mbh.* XIV: 11). Significant is the weapon: the sword, instead of the thunderbolt, for Vṛtra is a far less formidable foe than he was in the Vedic times and the use of the thunderbolt is hardly called for.

Indra's solar bearings are expressed in his demon-slaying feats. Together these monsters recall Typhon whom Apollo slew. Ahi, too, was identified with the serpent in later literature.[1]

In other mythologies, too, the solar hero has to conquer a snake or snake-fiend. Apollo kills the Python, St George kills the dragon, Thor killed the Midgard serpent, Indra and all his successors do the same. Indra as a solar god fights darkness, as a rain-god fights drought, and as a culture-hero fights indigence and wins cows.[2]

[1] The Avestan Indra was a demon, but Verethraghna (Bahram) was an assistant of Ahura Mazda, who killed Azi Dahâka (Zohâk), literally 'the fiendish snake'; 'he was the snake of the storm-cloud and a counterpart of Ahi or Vṛtra' (Introduction to the *Zend Avesta*, part II, Yasts and Sirozahs).

[2] According to Hillebrandt this feat had a primary reference to natural phenomena, 'dass in seiner ursprunglichen Form der Mythus doch ein Gewittermythus war, dass Wolkenquellen waren, bei welchen die Schlange lagerte, dass seinem ursprunglichen Wesen nach der Vajra die Blitzwaffe war, lassen die Tatsachen der vergleichenden nicht zweifelhaft' (*Vedische Mythologie*, seite 145). On the import of Indra's fight against Vṛtra Hillebrandt seems to be sure that the waters which Vṛtra had arrested and which Indra released were earthly not heavenly: 'Es sind aber fast überall die irdischen, nicht die himmlischen Wasser, die Vṛtra umlagert, die irdische Ströme und die irdische Berge' (*op. cit.* seite 159).

In the *TS* we are told that 'Indra gave the Yatis to the Sālāvṛkas, them they ate on the right side of the high altar' (VI: 2: 7). The *AB* repeating the five sins of Indra mentions this act (VII: 2). The *TMB* gives a full account: Indra gave the Yatis to the Sālāvṛkas; three survived, Rāyovāja Bṛhadgiri and Pṛthuraśmi; they said, 'who will feed our sons?' 'I shall', said Indra to them, and did so with the Trikakubh sāman (VIII: 1: 4). The *KUB*, too, mentions this among his sins which failed to harm him in any way (III: 1). When Indra offered boons to the Yatis, Pṛthuraśmi got Kṣatra (the warrior's valour), Bṛhadgiri, Brahmavarcasa (the Brahmin's power), and Rāyovāja, paśu, animals (*TMB* VIII: 1: 4, XIII: 4: 17). The *Mbh.*, too, records this act of delivering the Yatis to the Sālāvṛkas as one of Indra's sins (*Mbh.* XII: 15: 15).

The myth may perhaps be interpreted as an acceptance of the surviving Yatis into the Aryan community. The names are significant and may have been those of clans rather than individuals. Thus the name 'Bṛhadgiri', who (or which clan) was accepted among the Brahmins, has *Bṛhat* (from the same root from which 'Brāhmaṇa' is derived). 'Pṛthuraśmi' means 'great glory' and he got Kṣattra was naturally included among the Kṣattryas, whereas 'Rāyovāja' which means 'wealth and strength' was assimilated with the herdsmen (i.e. Vaiśya, cf. he got 'paśu', 'cattle'). This myth throws light on the composition of the Yati groups who were considered as equivalent of the Aryans and were not treated as Dāsas or Dasyns.

The Yatis perhaps formed a pre-Aryan hermit brotherhood who had opposed or refused to accept the Aryan culture or religion and paid with their lives. Significantly enough they do not appear in the earlier sections of the Vedic literature but only in that part in which the cultural and racial commingling of the Aryans and non-Aryans is an accepted fact. Even in the *Mbh.* we have records of the conflict between the merits of sacrifice and the merits of meditation, between 'karman', in other words, and 'jñāna' or 'bhakti' (i.e. between action and knowledge or devotion). The Yatis and what they stood for constituted a challenge to the sacrificing Aryans, hence the inevitable conflict and the defeat of the weak at the hands of the mighty. Their faith and practice, however, did not die out (there were survivors as the narrative states); the *Upaniṣads* secure a compromise by recognizing the intellectual approach to release. The Varṇāśramadharma (the four stages of life) effected another compromise by recognizing the last two stages of life (of which the last is called Yati) as periods to be devoted to a search for the fundamental truth through retirement and comparative non-action. Thus the Yatis won a late victory.

The Sālāvṛkas are usually translated as hyenas, but Monier-Williams' dictionary has 'house-wolves' (?)—they might have been wolf-hounds—or fierce domestic dogs who tore the Yatis up into pieces. In the *TS* the account of how the gods received the lion's share of the Asura territories, by Indra's assuming the shape of a Sālāvṛkī and thrice running round the desired territory, would perhaps point more to a wolf-hound (a domestic dog) rather than to a wild hyena (*TS* VI: 2: 4).

Vedic and post-Vedic literature records the unique self-sacrifice of a sage called Dadhīca and perhaps another, Dadhyañc. *ṚV* I: 80: 16 mentions Dadhyañc as a sage, and I: 139: 9 mentions him as a sacrificer. In *ṚV* I: 84: 13 and *TMB* XII: 8, we hear that Indra destroyed ninety-nine cities of Vṛtra with the thunderbolt made from Dadhīca's bones. The next verse says Indra found the horse's (or Dadhīca's?) head which lay hidden in a cave. In another passage we are told that Indra struck off Dadhyañc's head because Dadhyañc had divulged the honey-lore (madhuvidyā) to the Aśvins in spite of Indra's warning (see the Aśvins). Indra retrieved the cows from Ahi, usurped demon wealth and gave it to Dadhīca, son of Mātariśvan (*ṚV* X: 48: 2, 3). *ṚV* VI: 16: 14 calls Dadhyañc the son of Atharvan. The account of the horse's head and Dadhyañc is repeated in *ṚV* I: 116 and 119, and *ṚV* IX: 108: 4. Indra favoured Dadhyañc (*ṚV* X: 48: 2). Dadhyañc as the propounder of the honey-lore is mentioned in *ŚB* IV, and XIV, 'When Visnu's head was cut off the sacrifice became truncated and only Dadhyañc Ātharvaṇa knew how to restore it; but Indra had promised to cut off Dadhyañc's head if he divulged the secret (i.e. honey-lore) to anybody. The Aśvins learned it by putting away Dadhyañc's head and joining a horse's head to the torso which Indra duly cut off, after which they restored his own head' (*ŚB* XIV: 1: 1: 18–24). The *Mbh.* mentions the anecdote of Dadhīca, where he offered his bones to Indra. The thunderbolt was fashioned from them, and with it Indra slew the Kālakeya demons, the chief of whom was Vṛtra (*Mbh.* III: 98). Probably the intention of the author of this anecdote was to point out the merits of meditation; for Dadhīca's meditations or their merits clung to his bones and made the bolt fashioned from it such an irresistible weapon.

The episode of the Aśvins, honey-lore and Dadhyañc seems to be distinct from Dadhīca, from whose bones Tvaṣṭṛ fashioned the thunderbolt with which Indra killed Vṛtra. This story is repeated in the epics and *Purāṇas*. The other episode is hardly mentioned in later literature (except in the *Bhaviṣyapurāṇa*). In the Dadhīca episode Indra is shown as indebted to a man, a sage, for his supreme feat of killing Vṛtra. In the Dadhyañc episode his jealousy regarding the honey-lore and his enmity towards the Aśvins is recorded. Of this anecdote we perhaps have a parallel in the Eddic mythology:

Mimir is...the Kentaur Mimas; and the wisdom of the Kentaur, it may be noted, became a proverb. In one story Mimir is sent by the Asas to the Vanir, who cut off his head and sent it back to them. Wuotan utters a charm over it and the head, which never wastes away becomes his counsellor—a legend which can scarcely fail to remind us of the myth of Memnon's head with its prophetic powers localized in Egypt. (Sir G. W. Cox, *The mythology of the Aryan nations*, vol. II, pp. 18–19n.)

The Eddic Mimir had to pledge one of his eyes before he got a draught from the water which imparts wisdom. These anecdotes are close parallels of the Indian honey-lore legends, and perhaps belong to a world-wide stock of such legends.

In the *ṚV* Indra is indisputably the greatest of the gods—because of his courage, might and demon-killing feats, also because he secured wealth (booty) for the Aryans. In the *Brāhmaṇas* his reputation declines. We are told that Indra attained his position only after Prajāpati performed the Vājapeya sacrifice on his behalf (*TB* I: 3: 2: 2). The gods requested Prajāpati to lend them his eldest son Indra to be their general, so that they could defeat the demons (*TB* I: 9: 1). Indra is still regarded as the eldest, the general (*TB* I: 7: 4: 1, II: 5: 7: 4). By killing Vṛtra he became the greatest, the leader of the gods (*TB* II: 8: 3: 8). He desired to be firm, not shaky (*TB* III: 1: 5: 9), and offered a sacrifice to Varuṇa the doctor who cured him (*TB* II: 6: 4: 1, III: 1: 5: 9). Indra was the king of the gods, he was the emperor (while) Varuṇa was the king (*TB* III: 7: 9: 6, 7); oblations are offered to the gods whose chief is Indra, whose king is Varuna. Indra is Kṣattra, the warrior, the lord of might (*TB* III: 9: 16: 3), he is the victor (*TB* III: 9: 16: 3; III: 11: 4: 2; *TMB* VII: 5: 14). He was praised by all creatures; he asked sage Śiśumāra to praise him as many times as there were drops of water. There was great commotion in the water, so in order to cope with it the sage praised Indra with the Śārkara sāman (*TMB* XIV: 5: 15).

His overlordship, however, was not universally accepted, for Sauśravasa Upagu was Kutsa's priest and Kutsa promised to kill anyone who sacrificed to Indra. At this Indra took some cakes to Kutsa and said that Sauśravasa had offered them to him. Kutsa killed Sauśravasa's son, who was officiating in his father's stead in the sacrifice. Sauśravasa complained to Indra, who joined the head to the trunk with the Sauśravasa sāman (*TMB* XIV: 6: 8). The *JB* has a different tale: Kutsa was born from Indra's thigh and desired to become like Indra (III: 199). Due to Kutsa's fault he was punished with baldness by Indra. Upagu was drowned by Kutsa; Indra, assuming the shape of a Rohita (a chestnut horse or deer), drank Soma from his mouth. He revived and praised Indra (*JB* III: 199–202). Indra desired 'hara' (the power to subjugate others) and practised penance, and obtained his object through the Hārāyaṇa sāman (*TMB* XIV: 9: 34). The sages could not see Indra face to face until they sang the Nihaya sāman (*TMB* XV: 5: 24). Of Trita Āptya and others it says that 'they roamed about with Indra even as nowadays a Brāhmin follows in the train of a king' (*ŚB* I: 2: 3: 2). He came to dominate both warfare and sacrifice; the thunderbolt hurled by Indra became the 'sphya', 'yūpa', 'ratha' and 'śara' (a sacrificial implement, the sacrificial post, a chariot and an arrow). 'In consequence of this priests make use of two (of these pieces) at the sacrifice and men of the military caste also make use of two of them in battle' (*ŚB* I: 2: 4: 2).

In the age of the *Brāhmaṇas* Indra's supremacy is sought to be maintained by connecting him with the sacrifice in various ways. Thus 'the sacrificer is Indra' (*ŚB* III: 4: 2: 16); 'the sadas (seat) belongs to Indra' (*ŚB* III: 6: 1: 22). 'Indra means power and vigour' (*ŚB* III: 9: 1: 15). His warrior antecedents are still remembered and he is primarily connected with the Kṣattriyas: 'Indra is nobility' (*ŚB* III: 9: 1: 18); a ram is to be sacrificed to Indra in the Ṣoḍaśin sacrifice. 'Indra seized upon the strength and fury (hara) of his enemies, the aśuras' (*ŚB* IV: 5: 3: 4). 'Indra is "vimṛdh", the averter of scorn' (*ŚB* IV: 6: 4: 4). 'He (obtained for his share) two-thirds;...the Ṛces and saman are Indra's' (*ŚB* IV: 6: 7: 3). 'He is Kṣattra (warrior) and jyeṣṭha, the eldest, and people should offer to him for his lordship' (*ŚB* V: 1: 1: 11, V: 3: 3: 6, V: 3: 3: 11). 'The sacrificer is Indra... because he is a Kṣattriya and because he is a sacrificer' (*ŚB* V: 4: 3: 8). 'Indra surely is equal to all the gods' (*ŚB* VIII: 7: 3: 8); 'to him should the bull be slaughtered' (*ŚB* VI: 2: 1: 5). It is clear that Indra's prestige of the Samhitā period diminishes to suit the needs of the age of the *Brāhmaṇas* and he is equated with various elements of the sacrifice to elevate the sacrificial ritual to one of supreme importance.

Indra's thunderbolt is called āyasa (of iron?, *ṚV* I: 51: 8, X: 96: 4, X: 113: 5); with it he slew the demons and enemies. Tvaṣṭṛ fashioned it for him (*ṚV* I: 32: 2, X: 48: 3) In *ṚV* I: 84: 13 and *TMB* XII: 8 we are told that this thunderbolt was fashioned from Dadhīca's bones. The Ṛbhus are also said to have fashioned it. Whatever be the material it was made of, it was undoubtedly a powerful weapon and with it Indra struck terror in the hearts of his enemies. It would appear that much of the Aryan victory and prestige was due to this thunderbolt.[1]

The physical aspect of Indra as a mighty general is forgotten or less remembered in the epics. Thus the *Rām.* refers to his achievements as accomplished facts without describing them, they also ascribe some new feats to him. Indra had killed demons on ascending the throne (I: 46: 34). His thunderbolt is not mentioned by name but as the Aindrāstra (I: 57: 5). His prowess is minimized to a certain extent, for unable to kill Śambara single-handed he begs Daśaratha to help him (II: 9: 25). He killed demons not on his own initiative but at his mother's behest (II: 18: 24–5). The gods blessed him when he set out to kill Vṛtra (II: 25: 24). His valour and invincibility are still mentioned, especially in imagery, 'like Indra in heroism' (II: 1: 21; II: 1: 219; II: 27: 14). His thunderbolt, too, appears in imagery (II: 111: 9). The epic heroes are frequently described as like Indra and Varuṇa. He becomes a liberal donor of arms; to Agastya he gave his arrows and arrow-case as also clothes and weapons which Rāma received from Agastya (III: 18: 42). Pāka and Maya are demons whom Indra kills in his epic career. The rainbow is called his bow (III: 32: 19, III: 34: 25, 29).

But in the epics Indra alone is the guardian of the east, a position which was not exclusively his before. The east is variously called 'Indra's direction'. It is there that his capital is situated, for he is also the king of heaven and the king of the gods now.

This new position at once elevates and diminishes his rank, for while the *ṚV* Indra was more a general than a king, more engaged in campaigns than in reigning, the epic Indra is a king *par excellence*; stationary, with a fixed capital where he reigns amidst glory and splendour. He is devarāja reigning in Amarāvati (*Rām.* V: 8: 23), surrounded by the Maruts (*Rām.* V: 1: 13). The heavenly court of Indra is described in *Mbh.* II: 7; it is won by deeds. But his role as king is comparatively tame and quiet; he does not fight formidable enemies in tough battles, nor does he destroy demons, or win cattle and wealth or light and water; but sitting on his throne he rules like an emperor who enjoys courtly luxuries after his expeditions are successfully carried through. The epic Indra, even as a king, is more a

[1] It is just possible that the thunderbolt was made of iron. Indra as the leader of the invading Vedic Aryans introduced this new metal, and this perhaps accounts for his victory over a bronze-using people. Recent radiocarbon tests prove the earliest traces of iron in India *c.* 1000 B.C. which practically tallies with the advent of the major group of Vedic Aryans. Indo-European invaders of Greece of the same time (Middle Helladic) brought iron to Greece. Zeus with the thunderbolt (perhaps another missile of iron) is their victorious leader.

titular head than an actual administrator. We are told that warriors killed in battle go to Indra's heaven (*Mbh.* VI: 17: 8, VII: 18: 36).

Between the Vedic and epic ages Buddhism had intervened with its own mythology.

> Above the lowest heaven and on the highest summit of the world's axis, Meru, is enthroned the god Śakra (Indra)...He is lord of a heaven of his own and no god is more popular among the Buddhists or oftener named in their legends; yet he is inferior to Mahābrahma and to Māra. Buddha himself was Indra in some of his births...Hence we may infer that in the early days of Buddhism Indra...was still the formidable god of the people. His heaven forms the second tier, reckoning from the lowest upwards, and is called Trāyastriṃśa, that of the thirty-three divinities. (Monier-Williams, *Buddhism*, p. 207.)

This degradation of Indra in Buddhism appears to be a direct reflection of his status in Brāhmaṇical mythology, where he had sunk considerably. The east was his quarter in the epics, but under Buddhism its guardian is Dhṛtarāṣṭra, king of the Gandharvas. Thus Indra's position was usurped and he became a god of secondary importance.

This is borne out by his chequered epic career. The Brāhmaṇical Indra wins through sacrifices and priestly intervention where the Vedic Indra won by sheer valour and heroism. But in the epics Indra is harassed, defeated by mere mortals, and suffers many discomfitures. His defeat is mentioned in *Rām.* VI: 20: 25; Rāvaṇa is frequently described as having actually defeated Indra (*Rām.* V: 52: 17). When Rāvaṇa came to King Marutta's sacrifice, Indra, frightened, turned himself into a peacock (*Rām.* VII: 18: 5). When he heard that Rāvaṇa was advancing against him he ordered the heavenly host to muster strength for an encounter, but felt so unnerved himself that he went to Viṣṇu in fear and trembling and admitted his inferiority (*Rām.* VII: 27: 3–13). He was actually defeated in the battle that followed. Brahman explained his defeat to him as inevitable on account of a previous sin (*Rām.* VII: 30). The whole episode is extremely unlike everything that the Vedic Indra represented: he is a coward, admits his inferiority and suffers defeat.

In the *Mbh.* we hear of Indra hiding himself in a pond from fear of Nahuṣa, who had usurped his heavenly throne and demanded his wife. At Indra's advice his wife Śacī asked Nahuṣa for a chariot drawn by sages; Nahuṣa complied, but in his impatience touched Agastya with his toe. Agastya cursed him into a serpent. The gods, then, at Viṣṇu's advice performed a horse-sacrifice for the remission and atonement of Indra's sins, and reinstated Indra on the throne (*Mbh.* XII: 329). In the *HV* King Raji's sons persecuted and deposed Indra. Deprived of sacrificial oblations Indra was famished; he begged Bṛhaspati for a cake (puroḍāśa) as big as a plum. Brahman reinstated Indra in power by creating atheism to allure and deceive the demons (*HV* I: 28). Indra's discomfiture at the hands of Kṛṣṇa is described in the Pārijāta-haraṇa (stealing of the heavenly flower Pārijāta) episode (*HV* II: 27). In the battle between the gods and demons Indra was dissuaded from fighting against Vali by a voice in the sky (*HV* III: 64). The whole epic-Purāṇic portrait of Indra is utterly unlike all we have known him to be, it is the picture of a retired soldier.

CHAPTER 13

INDRA (2)

THE transmutation of Indra in the epic-Purāṇic age is along specific lines which were already noticeable in the Vedic period but which became clearer and more significant during the later stage of his career.

Indra's solar character is clear in the *ṚV* and in passages like: 'He (the sun) indeed is Indra' (*ŚB* IV: 5: 9: 4; IV: 6: 7: 11). He is called Arkavat (having the sun) in *MS* II: 2: 9.

In the whole of *ṚV* hymn VII: 82, Indra, together with Varuṇa is called the author of cosmic deeds. In *ṚV* V: 29: 4 Indra is said to have torn asunder a demon who held heaven and earth together, and separated them. He is called Viśvakarman (fashioner of everything, *ŚB* IV: 6: 4: 6). He settled the earth in the firmament (*ṚV* X: 119: 9). One of his wings is in the sky and the other on the earth (*ṚV* X: 119: 11). He calmed the river Paruṣṇī (*ṚV* II: 15: 5), turned the course of another river (*ṚV* II: 15: 6) and fixed the mountains in their places. Indra, together with Bṛhaspati, fetched Soma from the river Aṃśumatī where Soma lay hiding (*ṚV* VIII: 96: 13–15). His feat of fixing the mountains in their places is frequently retold as the cutting off of the mountains' wings (*MS* I: 10: 13). Indra also controls the moon in the sky and regulates days, nights and seasons (*ṚV* VI: 39: 3).

We hear of Indra breaking one of the sun's chariot-wheels; sometimes he kills demons with it (*ṚV* I: 130: 9), Śuṣṇa was killed with it (*ṚV* I: 175: 4). Indra's relationship with the other solar gods is interesting. Once he is even said to have begotten Sūrya (*ṚV* I: 32: 4) and Uṣas (*ṚV* II: 12: 7). He made a path for Sūrya in the sky (*ṚV* X: 111: 3). He placed Uṣas in her region (*ṚV* VI: 17: 5), and the sun in the sky (*ṚV* I: 7: 3). He is invoked to reveal the sun (*ṚV* VI: 17: 13). He made the sun and other luminaries shine brightly (*ṚV* VIII: 98: 2, X: 54: 6). He also fixed the firmaments (*ṚV* II: 15: 1, 2).

The most important cosmic act ascribed to Indra is the releasing of the waters or light and both feats have been interpreted as winning cows.

Indra charged Sūrya's wheel with power (*ṚV* IV: 17: 14), he stole Sūrya's chariot-wheel (*ṚV* IV: 28: 2) and also fought Sūrya on Kutsa's behalf (*ṚV* IV: 30: 4), protected Etaśa against Sūrya, killed Uṣas (*ṚV* IV:

28: 4, 6, 8), broke off a wheel from the sun's chariot and fought demons with it (*ṚV* v: 31: 11).

This enmity of Indra towards Sūrya is rather striking as they both are solar in character and are two of the most important Vedic gods. The mystery clears a little if we refer to Ovid's *Metamorphoses* (ch. 1), where Jove, the Roman parallel of Indra, is said to have broken the sun's chariot with his three-pronged thunderbolt. As the Roman Jove is a parallel of Indra it is significant that these particular myths should correspond. What is Indra that there should be this enmity between him and Sūrya and Uṣas? For we notice that although he is called the begetter of Sūrya and Uṣas he is opposed to both. The answer seems to lie in the exact solar identity of Sūrya. In his cosmic and culture-hero aspect Indra resembles Zeus, whose 'name in the language of the ancient Cretans, who had not yet learnt Greek, meant the Sun, and in Crete Zeus also had the same name, as Zeus Tallaois. In the story of Europea "Zeus" obviously meant the Cretan sun-god' (C. Kerényi, *The gods of the Greeks*, p. 110). The various names of the sun-god are not an isolated Vedic phenomenon. In Graeco-Roman mythologies, too, the sun is conceived of as many gods. The Greeks had, besides Zeus (who later became the storm-god): Hyperion and his son Helios, Phaeton, son of Helios, Apollo and his son Aesculapius. In the later Vedic pantheon we have twelve Ādityas, all different phases or aspects of the sun. And these similarities are not accidental; the Indo-Europeans, primarily a sun-worshipping people, deified and anthropomorphized the different epiphanies of their central godhead. Of these manifestations Zeus, Jove or Indra were the most important and they symbolize the blazing midday sun. Because of Indra's power and might he was early identified with this phase of the sun's course; the mighty warrior easily resembled the sun at its peak-point of splendour and heat. As the midday sun seems to remain stationary for some time in the sky, the mythopoeic mind imagines him as breaking the sun's chariot-wheel, so that the chariot cannot move, and the sun's course through the sky is temporarily arrested. Again as midday follows morning, Indra is imagined to kill Uṣas, the dawn, and to fight Sūrya the early phase of the sun in the sky. As the blazing midday sun, he takes the longest time to be born; thus Indra is said to have remained a long time in his mother Aditi's womb. Aditi was delivered of the child through much pain and suffering; she regarded her child Indra as shameful, but when he was born he filled heaven and earth with his dazzling brilliance (*ṚV* iv: 18: 4, 5). Hence he broke the sun's chariot wheel, hence also is the midday pressing of Soma exclusively for Indra for Indra is the midday sun (*ṚV* x: 96: 13). Like Zeus he caught his own father by the feet and killed him (*ṚV* iii: 48: 4, iv: 18: 12), and this father must have been the early morning sun.

As a god of heat and light Indra is the brother of Agni. To the Vedic poets' imagination all light-and-heat manifestations are complementary to each other. What the sun is by day, Agni is by night. Thus Indra and Agni are twins born of Aditi (*ṚV* vi: 59: 2), together they are said to be the mightiest among the gods (*TMB* xxiv: 17: 3). The *ŚŚS* speaks of images of Indra and Agni with a prominent navel, possibly to indicate their solar character.

Like all solar gods Indra came to be a vegetation-god. The first clear mention of Indra's connection with agriculture is found in the *TB* where he is said to be worshipped with the offering of an ox and with songs by the husbandmen (*TB* ii: 4: 7: 2), for Indra is the god of the tillers (*TB* ii: 4: 3: 11). The *TS* knows Indra as Śunāsīra (*MS* iv: 3: 3), a compound of Śunā (share) and sīra (plough), and the name goes down to the later literature. It is as an agricultural deity that Indra fights his epic-Purāṇic rival Kṛṣṇa in the *HV* and in the *Purāṇas*. Indra resented it when Kṛṣṇa prohibited Indramaha and instituted Giriyajña (*HV* ii: 18). In the *Purāṇas* we have the fight between Indra and Kṛṣṇa. The herdsmen say, 'Of what use is Mahendra to us, our gods are the cows and the hills'. The Brahmins worship with chants and sacrifices, the ploughmen perform the sacrifice with ploughshares and on the hills (*Viṣṇu P* v: 10: 36–7). Here Kṛṣṇa is a rival who not merely disputes his predecessor's claim but first absorbs all those characteristics which were still felt to be mythologically potent. Thus like Indra Kṛṣṇa is a god associated with cattle, he tends them where Indra won them, for cows still constitute one of the essential factors of an agrarian community's wealth. (See Kṛṣṇa, pp. 309–10.)

It is as an agricultural deity that Indra became the god of rain and storm. Even in the *ṚV* he was credited with defeating the demon of drought and releasing the waters. This trait was developed in later literature, so that when Indra ceases to be a solar god he retains his dominion over agriculture as a rain-god. It is in this aspect that his epiphany is presented in the epic-Purāṇic age. The *Rām.* mentions the festival of Indra in the rainy season (ii: 84: 23) and describes him as actually pouring rain for four months in the rainy season (ii: 122: 18), and also as the god of rain in iv: 13: 39, iv: 29: 7 and iv: 39: 2. It is said that Indra appears on the top of Mount Mahendra in fixed seasons (*Rām.* iv: 41: 33). Kadrū praises Indra as the god of rain (*Mbh.* i: 22). The *HV* records his connection with cloud and thunder (I: 44: 6) and calls him the god of thunder, cloud and rain. This cosmic phenomenon is his feat, his sacrifice (*HV* II: 15: 4–6). Furious at Kṛṣṇa's forbidding the Giriyajña, Indra had taken revenge by sending a continuous downpour for seven days to drown the entire cowherd community (*HV* II: 18). The *Viṣṇu P*, too, remembers Indra solely as the god of clouds and rain, and only nominally as a king of the gods (V: 10: 19).

The advent of the rainy season in India is usually accompanied with great tumult and noise, and resembles the advance of a royal army. Even to Kālidāsa the whole scene evoked the advance of a victorious king (*Ṛtusaṃhāra* II: 1).

In his function as the rain-god, his associates are the Maruts who are called his gaṇa, troops (*ṚV* I: 6: 8); also his brothers, born of the same mother Aditi (*ṚV* I: 170: 2). He is invoked with the Maruts (*ṚV* I: 23: 7–12). The sacrificer invites him together with the Maruts. They were sent to his aid by their mother Pṛśni. Indra is also said to have created the Maruts (*ṚV* VII: 18: 10, 11), they had praised Indra in the past (*ṚV* VIII: 3: 7). They are called Indra's ministers (*AB* III: 9: 12). In later literature the Vasus are Indra's assistants, who surround him in his heavenly court. In the epics and *Purāṇas*, the Maruts and Vasus are used indiscriminately and appear to be interchangeable.

Indra is said to have been born through his mother's side. She is called Niṣṭigrī (*ṚV* X: 101: 12) or Śavasī ('the strong'). The *AV* calls her Ekāṣṭakā, daughter of Prajāpati. In the *Brāhmaṇas*, epics and *Purāṇas* she is Aditi, and he, the mightiest of the Ādityas. His father is Tvaṣṭṛ or Dyaus whom he killed in order to obtain Soma (*ṚV* IV: 18: 12).

Indra's wife in the Vedic period was Indrāṇī who stayed at home (*ṚV* III: 53: 6). 'Indrāṇī, beyond other women, I have heard to be favoured with a spouse, for never at any time shall her husband die of old age' (*TS* I: 7: 13)—this may have been a reference to Indra's solar, and hence immortal, character or it may refer to Indra's inexhaustible youthfulness and vigour.

The *AB* calls Indra's wife Prāsahā (the enduring one) (III: 22); she was his beloved and the chief (vāvātā) queen, also called Senā (army), her father-in-law (i.e. Indra's father) was Ka (Prajāpati) (*AB* III: 11). The *TB* calls her Śrī (III: 11: 4: 20).

It is significant that in later literature Śrī (or Lakṣmī, as she came to be known) became Viṣṇu's wife. This is quite natural because Viṣṇu was Indra's mythological heir. The *GBU* also calls Senā the wife of Indra (II: 9). In the *ṚV* Indra's wife wants her husband to go to sacrifices and desires to go herself (v: 37: 3). In the Vṛṣākapi hymn (*ṚV* x: 86) she is a vigorous personality reminding us somewhat of Hera, the querulous wife of Zeus. In *ṚV* viii: 21: 3 we are told that Sītā is Indra's wife. This is probably because she corresponds to his character as the fertility-god, for he is called Urvarāpati (lord of the field) in that passage. His epic heir Rāma's wife was called Sītā.

One is reminded of Kārttikeya, commonly called Devasenāpati (lord of the divine army), who actually inherits Indra's role as the divine general and is also provided with an apparently invincible demon-foe, Tāraka. But in spite of the epic-Purāṇic attempts the story never becomes as convincing as Indra's killing of Vṛtra. Kārttikeya's early biography has faint echoes of Zeus, who was abandoned in infancy and brought up by Amalthea, a nymph according to some traditions and thus corresponding to the Kṛttikās. But Kārttikeya's demon-slaying myth is thin compared with Indra's, perhaps because the social background of the myth was different. Indra not only slew demons but was at the same time the author of titanic cosmic feats.

The secret of Indra's cosmic acts and demon-killing is ascribed to his māyā, magic power. He killed demons through māyā (*ṚV* i: 51: 5), even Vṛtra was thus killed (*ṚV* i: 80: 7) also Pipru (*ṚV* vi: 20: 7). Others also were killed through magic power. Indra's almost supernatural heroism and might may have created this notion of his magic power. But we remember that Varuṇa, the supreme divinity before Indra, was also conceived of as reigning with the help of magic. The dominant gods of ancient mythologies all had this mysterious power.

Vedic texts refer to two kinds of magic—the magic of the gods, and of the Asuras. 'Yātu', another word for magic, is also twofold. In the *Kāṭhaka-Saṃhitā* (xxxvii: 14) we are given the difference between Brahmayātu or Devayātu (Brāhmaṇic or divine magic) and Asurayātu (demonic magic). *MS* iii: 1: 9 says: 'it was the māyā of the Asuras which the gods dispelled by a yajus formula'. *TMB* xix: 1: 1 says: 'the ungodly māyās captured Indra, but Indra, in order to suppress demonic magic wields a magic all his own'. It was with the help of this māyā that he quells the might of the more difficult of his demon adversaries.

With the help of māyā Indra assumed different shapes (*ṚV* vi: 47: 18). He is invoked as Kapiñjala in *ṚV* ii: 43: 44. He assumed the shape of a sheep and came to drink Medhātithi's Soma (*ṚV* i: 51: 1, viii: 97: 12). He also assumed the shape of a quail (*ṚV* x: 119), of a Sālāvṛkī (hyena or wolf hound) (*TS* vi: 2: 7). The *JB* and *ŚB* give a list of the shapes Indra assumed to achieve his ends. He assumed the shape of a ram (*ṚV* VIII: 97: 12), also the shape of Menā, the daughter of Vṛṣaṇāśva (*ŚB* III: 3: 4: 8; *JB* II: 79), the shape of a deer, as well as of Ahalyā's husband Gautama (*ŚB* III: 2: 2).

A curious anecdote says: 'In the battle between Pratardana and the ten kings Indra came with a balance with cakes and posset on its two sides and danced before the Kṣattriya Pratardana's wife Upamā Sāvedasī, while she was churning curd. When she told her husband of this he immediately knew that it was Indra in disguise and felt assured of victory in the ensuing battle' (*ṚV* IX: 101: 1; *JB* III: 244–6). He came to Ahalyā assuming her husband's shape and enjoyed her (*Rām.* I: 49: 15–50). At Marutta's sacrifice Indra assumed the shape of a peacock (*Rām.* VII: 18: 5). In the Ūśīnara episode he became an eagle (*Mbh.* III: 164). After he was polluted with the sin of killing a Brahmin he reduced himself to a microscopic size and hid under a lotus (*Mbh.* V: 13). Once Indra appeared as a bird before a group of hermits and explained to them the comparative inferiority of renunciation in relation to the normal life of a householder (*Mbh.* XII: 11).

His power of assuming various shapes was well recognized in the epic period; the *Mbh.* states it clearly (XIII: 40: 24). When Indra fell in love with King Janamejaya's wife Kāśyā, he enjoyed her by entering the slaughtered horse of the Aśvamedha sacrifice (*HV* III: 5). He assumed various shapes including those of a leech, a parrot and a cat. His ability to adopt different shapes is mentioned in *ṚV* VI: 47: 15–17, and *PB* IX: 2: 22.[1]

In this characteristic Indra resembles Zeus, who also assumed many different shapes. But Zeus mostly did so in order to enjoy mortal women and to escape the vigilance of the jealous Hera. One remembers his affair with Europa whom he visited as a bull, with Leda whom he enjoyed as a swan, and with Danae to whom he came as a shower of gold. Indra, too, went as a ram to Medhātithi, as Vṛṣaṇāśva's daughter in the former's house, as Gautama to enjoy Ahalyā. One remembers that Zeus seduced Alcmene in her husband, Amphitryon's, shape. The *Mbh.* tells us that he has a lascivious nature and desires others' wives (*Mbh.* XIII: 40: 19). He even fell in love with the demoness Viliṣṭeṅgā and went to live among the demons as a male among men and a female among women (*AV* VII: 32: 8). He fell in love with the female monster Dīrghajihvī who licked Soma

[1] The myths of Indra assuming different shapes are mostly found in post-Ṛgvedic literature and are probably accounts of different cults—totemistic or otherwise—which converged in the Indra cult in the period of the early *Brāhmaṇas*.

(with her long tongue) and had unlimited organs of sex (*JB* 1: 162; *PB* xiii: 6: 9 ff.). Thus he behaved with different women, but when later his own son Kutsa (called Aurva, because he was born from Indra's thigh) appeared before Śacī in Indra's shape (*ṚV* iv: 16: 10), Indra punished Kutsa for his sins (*JB* iii: 199 ff.).

This adulterous career is nothing unusual for a solar god and a culture-hero; it only proves his extraordinary virility—a necessary characteristic for an agricultural god, and a god who, for a period at least, dominates the pantheon. Hence Zeus and Indra, and later Kṛṣṇa, are shown as philanderers and sometimes even as lascivious characters.

Such a character cannot and should not be morally judged, since to his followers he represents the life force at work. He flouts the common ethical code and thereby attains his own ends, and for this he is shown quite frequently to be cheating others.

Thus when he was deprived of Soma on account of his sins he snatched Tvaṣṭṛ's share of Soma (*AB* vii: 2, 35). The *TMB* tells us that a non-divine māyā or magic (i.e. an unholy supernatural power called adevyā māyā) clung to Indra and he could not shake it off until he performed the Vighana sacrifice (*TMB* xix: 19: 1). The Kālakañja demons were once attempting to reach heaven by piling bricks on an altar. Indra, alarmed at the prospect, came and placed a brick in the pile, and then when the altar was nearly complete he took it away and the structure collapsed (*TB* 1: 1: 2: 4–6). Here the end must have justified the means. With Namuci Indra sought to violate his contract. The slaughter of Viśvarūpa Tvaṣṭṛ's son was utterly unprovoked. Indra became polluted with the killing of demons, many of whom he killed through guile, and asked sages to purify him by singing hymns. They did so (*JB* iii: 228). By the time of the *Upaniṣads* his sins had become so numerous and well-known that in the *KU* we have a sort of defence of Indra who, in spite of his sins, is stated to be supreme (iii: 1).

Diti desired an avenger of the death of her demon-sons slain by Indra. Indra deceitfully entered her womb and cut up the foetus of the future avenger into forty-nine parts; these became the Maruts (*Rām.* 1: 47: 1, 1: 48: 12). He sent Rambhā to disturb Ṛṣyaśṛṅga's meditation (*Rām.* 1: 65: 16) and commissioned Menakā to distract Agastya (*Rām.* 1: 65: 33). This becomes his habit in epic-Purāṇic and classical literature. Whenever a sage seems to store merits or a king performs nearly a hundred sacrifices Indra in his anxiety for his own status hurries to the spot to dissuade the aspirant or sends a pretty nymph to distract him. King Raji had fought on the gods' behalf on condition that if he conquered the demons he would become the king of the gods. After victory was won, however, Indra went back on his promise and deceived him. Raji's son persecuted Indra and deposed him. Brahman restored Indra to his throne by deluding the demons with atheism which he then created (*HV* I: 28). Thus Indra was not very scrupulous regarding the means he employed to gain his ends. It was because of his sins that Indra was regarded as a far from ideal character. For the Buddhists in the post-Vedic period he was not a god of a very high order. 'Sakka, the ruler of the devas, was the person whose rāga, doṣa and moha...had not left him and therefore he was much inferior to the Bhikkhu who had reached Arhatship and was free from the defects of ordinary beings' (B. C. Law, *Heaven and hell in Buddhist perspective*, p. 11).

Morality, in the human sense, is not his strong point; he has bigger stakes to play for. Demons have to be slain, his people have to be provided with cattle, land, food and wealth, his country and kingdom have to be established, so he can hardly afford to concern himself with the niceties of conduct. He needs superhuman strength and this he derives from Soma, and the *Vedas* are full of accounts of his addiction to it. He has a strong neck, a big belly and fine arms; he kills enemies when drunk with Soma (*ṚV* VIII: 17: 8). 'Indra's share of Soma was fixed by the gods in the past'—this is the refrain of the first part of the hymn *ṚV* VIII: 36. Kadrū, Yadu and Turvaśa offered Soma to Indra; drunk with it, Indra killed their enemies (*ṚV* VIII: 45: 26: 27). He slew his father for Soma (*ṚV* III: 48: 4, IV: 18: 12).

Indra together with Bṛhaspati actually fetched Soma from near the Aṃśumatī river. There Soma lay hidden and mistook Indra for Vṛtra until Bṛhaspati assured him (*ṚV* VIII: 96: 13–15). Soma became Indra's very own after he had withstood the demons' magic (*ṚV* V: 98: 5). According to another account Soma was stolen from heaven by an eagle (*ṚV* VIII: 89: 8). In the *Avesta* Verethraghna drinks Haoma (Avestan for Soma) and brings it down from heaven in the shape of a bird. Hence the myth seems to be old, at least of Indo-Iranian antiquity.

Indra is presented as jealous of his right to Soma. He denies it to the Aśvins. When he is himself forbidden the drink he partakes of it by stealth, and he assumes the form of a deer to drink it from Kutsa's mouth.

Meat and barley cakes are among other oblations mentioned in connection with Indra, and incidentally these together with an intoxicating drink appear to have constituted the staple diet of the early Vedic Indian. Indra's followers invite him to a repast of cooked beef and Soma. 'If Indra came to our sacrifice he would eat roasted barley and drink pressed Soma' (*ṚV* x: 28: 1). In the Vṛṣākapi hymn buffalo meat is offered to Indra. Male animals are to be offered to Indra (*TS* v: 5: 1), wheaten-cakes are also his (*MS* iii: 10: 6); a ram is to be offered to Indra in the Ṣoḍaśin sacrifice. The bull is to be slaughtered for Indra (*ŚB* vi: 2: 1: 5) as also the ox (*TB* ii: 4: 7: 2).

As the central god of the Vedic Indian pantheon Indra enjoyed undisputed supremacy for a time, but even when his importance lessened he remained a cult-god for a long time.

Significantly enough one *ṚV* passage seems to indicate the use of a fetish in connection with Indra. In *ṚV* iv: 24: 10 we read: 'Who will buy this my Indra with ten cows; when he has slain your enemies then return him to me.' The passage may be construed to mean various things, but the obvious meaning, as long as it contradicts no vital basic concept, should not be rejected. True there were no temples in those distant days, but a fighting people who had great faith in their leader can easily be conceived to have faith in a fetish or effigy of Indra which they regarded to be charged with magic power. The previous verse, too (verse 9), mentions buying and selling; of what? Probably of this fetish or effigy which would ensure victory. The ambitious or prosperous man should worship him (*TS* ii: 2: 11, ii: 5: 5); if a warrior performs a sacrifice it is to Indra that he offers (*MS* iii: 4: 3). When Indra had become an agricultural deity, the tiller worshipped him 'with songs and bullocks which they offered to him' (*TB* ii: 5: 7: 4). The *ŚSS* mentions images of Indra; this is anticipated by the *ṚV* passage where a fetish of Indra is mentioned.

By the time of the epics a definite cultic practice with Indra as the central fertility-god seems to have been established and we have Indramaha or Indramahotsava (worship of Indra, or Indra-festival), where a pole was raised in his honour (presumably to celebrate his victory over the demons of drought) in the rainy season and oblations were placed near it on the ground (*Rām.* ii: 76: 32, ii: 84: 8, ii: 84: 33). His temple is described where pennants are hung in his honour (*Rām.* ii: 87: 25). The ensign of Indra is frequently mentioned (*Rām.* iii: 32: 19, iii: 34: 25). The bamboo-stick is mentioned as his royal insignia (*Mbh.* i: 57). The *Silappadigaram*, a work of the eighth century A.D., refers to an Indra festival which began on the full-moon day of the Vaiśākha and continued for twenty-eight days. Apart from the fact that the Vaiśākha full-moon day was the birthday of the Buddha, the latest solar hero in the line, this period coincides with the first advent of the nor'westers and showers and establishes the fact that Indra had been firmly entrenched in his position as the rain-god and was worshipped for the showers, presumably by the tillers.

In the *HV* Kṛṣṇa prohibited Indra-worship and instituted Giriyajña instead. Indra, the champion of a losing cause, fought Kṛṣṇa and ultimately achieved a compromise (*HV* II: 18, 19). The *Purāṇas* have relegated Indra to the status of a deity of ploughmen from whom he goes on enjoying worship as a minor divinity.

The Vṛṣākapi hymn (*ṚV* x: 86) gives us a dialogue between Indra, Indrāṇī and Vṛṣākapi. On the identity of the last-named creature scholars are divided in opinion. Sāyaṇa explains him as Indra because he pours showers of desired objects, and can go wherever he wishes. Elsewhere Sāyaṇa says Vṛṣākapi is Indra's son (introduction to the hymn).

Commenting on the first verse of the hymn Sāyaṇa gives us a hint as to the real purport of the hymn. Indra says, 'Worshippers sent (or commanded) by me did not worship me but praised my son Vṛṣākapi' (*ṚV* x: 86: 1, Sāyaṇa's commentary). Sāyaṇa quotes Mādhavabhaṭṭa who holds that Vṛṣākapi had somehow polluted the oblation intended for Indrāṇī (*ṚV* x: 86: 1, Sāyaṇa's commentary). The first few verses are spoken by Indrāṇī who blames Indra for pampering Vṛṣākapi when Indra himself is supreme. 'Indra is above everything' is the refrain of the entire hymn. She calls Vṛṣākapi the beloved (son) of Indra (verse 4), and describes her as a 'yellow ape' or animal (verse 3). The hymn is in general an adverse portrait and accusation of Vṛṣākapi by Indrāṇī, who resents the fact that through Indra's indulgence Vṛṣākapi is coming into prominence, when Indra is yet the indisputably supreme god with exceptional male vigour and virility (verses 16–17). Indra tries to placate her, says he cannot be happy without his friend Vṛṣākapi (*ṚV* x: 86: 12). Then Vṛṣākapi himself endeavours to appease the angry Indrāṇī by calling Indrāṇī 'mother' (verse 13) and a compromise seems to be obtained; they share oblations in Indra's house. It is true that much in the hymn is obscure, but those portions which are obviously clear and yield a coherent meaning need not be complicated by tortuous expositions. Taking Indrāṇī's description of Vṛṣākapi—yellow beast, i.e. the ape—literally we can easily understand her resentment at his growing importance.

The *JB* recounts an episode where Indra stole Aiṣakṛta Śitivāhu's Soma in the shape of a monkey (I: 363). The Vṛṣākapi hymn occurs in the tenth and latest book, where the non-Aryan element of the population were already making their impact felt in religion, social institutions and other spheres of culture, and the Aryans, too, were moving towards the south-eastern part of the country from the Punjab, and were probably settled in the present U.P.—an old seat of monkey-worship—so that the sudden intrusion of the monkey cult and the resulting opposition is better understood. The monkey cult was a powerful pre-Aryan influence over a vast tract which the Vedic Indians had to combat, and eventually come to terms with. This cult mingled with the solar cult of Indra, Viṣṇu and their incarnations. Thus Arjuna, the solar hero of the *Mbh.*, was Kapidhvaja, with the monkey-ensign; and Rāma the solar hero of the *Rāmāyaṇa* won the victory over his enemies with the help of the monkeys. The monkey cult, whether of totemic origin or not, had come to stay and Hanūmat is worshipped by a vast population even in present-day India. We perhaps see its first advent and inclusion in the Indian religion in the Vṛṣākapi hymn, where, because the pantheon then was indisputably predominantly Vedic, the refrain emphasizes the supremacy of Indra. Dr S. K. Chatterji in his book *Indianism and the Indian synthesis* says that the word 'hanūmat' ('hanūmant') is probably derived from Tamil *An-manti* meaning 'male monkey'. This would be a literal synonym of Vṛṣākapi (*vṛṣa* = 'male', *kapi* = 'monkey'). As noted earlier Indrāṇī describes him as 'harito mṛgah'—the yellow ape—and institutes an oblique and insidious comparison between Vṛṣākapi and Indra in points of male virility, naturally in Indra's favour. Thus the monkey was being interpreted as an epiphany of the solar god and was being introduced in the Vedic Aryan pantheon, and the Vedic Aryan's revulsion is recorded in the hymn through Indrāṇī's protests against his admission.

Both Indra and Viṣṇu are Ṛgvedic solar gods, Indra the god in power and Viṣṇu the incipient divinity. In the *Brāhmaṇas* Viṣṇu is seen as the rising power and Indra as almost a spent force, although he remains the nominal sovereign of heaven. When Vṛtra offered his strength to Indra, Viṣṇu received it on Indra's behalf (*TMB* XX: 15: 6). The epics see this process of emphasizing Viṣṇu's role at Indra's cost. Thus when Indra feels polluted he has to perform a Vaiṣṇava sacrifice before he can re-enter heaven (*Rām.* VII: 49–50). When Indra hears of Rāvaṇa's advance he becomes flustered at the news and anxiously seeks Viṣṇu's advice and confesses his inferiority (*Rām.* VII: 27: 3–13). Prior to killing Vṛtra Indra acknowledged Viṣṇu's superiority and asked for his help. What is still more astounding is that armed with only one-third of Viṣṇu's strength he slays Vṛtra, but immediately after is consumed with the anguish of guilt-consciousness and has to offer a horse-sacrifice for atonement and purgation (*Rām.* VII: 84, 85).

It is significant that all these passages indicating Viṣṇu's rise at Indra's expense are found in the seventh, interpolated, book of the *Rām.* This book, as also the first half of the first book, is late and has a Purāṇic flavour of the time when the sectarian gods are on the rise, especially the Viṣṇu Nārāyaṇa of the Vaiṣṇavas and Bhāgavatas.

The *Rām.* actually says that Rāma is Indra Padmanābha (VI: 102: 16). Garuḍa, who later became Viṣṇu's mount, was 'the Indra of the birds' (*Mbh.* I: 27), and he is Viṣṇu's bird-epiphany. Indra fetched Soma through an eagle (*ṚV* VIII: 98: 7), Viṣṇu fetched Amṛta (nectar) in his bird-personality. Indra's demon-killing was inherited by all Viṣṇu's incarnations. They all slew their arch-enemies, demons in different shapes and with different names. In the *Bhagavadgītā*, Kṛṣṇa says that his purpose in incarnation is the destruction of the miscreant—and this was Indra's prime achievement. Indra had friends among men like Kutsa or Divodāsa; Viṣṇu in his incarnations is quite frequently assisted by men in his task of demon-killing. Indra is inalienably connected with Soma, Viṣṇu with Amṛta. Indra wins cattle, destroys enemy cities and brings demon-wealth over to his Aryan followers; Viṣṇu, too, destroys demons or the property of monsters and enriches his devotees. Indra's vajra or thunderbolt changes shape and name and becomes the 'sudarśana-cakra' in Viṣṇu's hands, but it is always there as his invincible weapon. Indra's Śacī becomes Viṣṇu's Śrī in a different guise. Indra's philandering, too, is imitated by Viṣṇu in his Kṛṣṇa incarnation. Indra's assuming the forms of all things in the universe (*ṚV* VI: 47: 18) is the prototype of the Viśvarūpadarśana (transfiguration) of Kṛṣṇa as seen by Arjuna (*Gītā* XI). This *Mbh.* (*Gītā*) episode perhaps has another prototype in the *JB.* Indra reveals to the ṛṣis (sages) the Akūpāra tortoise which is of immeasurable dimension (*JB* III: 203, 272). This tortoise finds the earth in the ocean and is thus a precursor of Viṣṇu in his Kūrma incarnation; and also of Kṛṣṇa in his transfiguration in the *Gītā* (bk. XI). Sītā mentioned as Indra's wife (*ṚV* VIII: 21: 3) also foreshadows Sītā, the wife of Rāma, one of Viṣṇu's incarnations. Again, Indra is called Pāñcajanya in *ṚV* V: 32: 11. Sāyaṇa explains this as pañcajanebhyo hita—beneficent to the five races of men. This term later came to be associated with Kṛṣṇa's conch-shell which he won from the demon Pañcajana, an obvious later gloss. Thus Viṣṇu and his successor-incarnates borrowed attributes and associations from Indra. The *ṚV* hymn X: 47 is addressed to Vaikuṇṭha Indra and in the epic-Purāṇic age Vaikuṇṭha became Viṣṇu's habitat; it also connects Indra with Viṣṇu.

In the epic battle in the *Mbh.* Kṛṣṇa remained a passive onlooker, the charioteer of Arjuna. Therefore the task of slaying enemies devolved on Arjuna—and Arjuna was Indra's son and Kṛṣṇa's friend. Thus Indra discharged his duty of demon-killing or slaying the wicked through his own son. The *VS* tells us that Indra's secret name was Arjuna. This seems to be the nucleus of the epic relationship of Indra and Arjuna. When we remember the saying that a man himself is born (again as) his son, then this incarnation of Indra as Arjuna seems quite natural. In Arjuna Indra himself was born as the national hero. The *ŚB* tells us: 'The Phālgunīs are Indra's asterism and even correspond to his name; for indeed Indra is called Arjuna, this being his mystic name, and they (the Phālgunīs) are also called Ārjunīs' (*ŚB* II: 1: 2: 11). Phālgunī was one of Arjuna's names in the *Mbh.* Thus Indra is a prototype of Arjuna. In the *Mbh.* we are told that Brahman said to Indra that he (Indra) in another body would rout the Nivātakavaca demons, and this prophecy was fulfilled through Arjuna (*Mbh.* III: 169). All through the epic Indra assisted his mortal son Arjuna, took him to heaven, blessed him and even begged Karṇa's armour and ear-rings in order to ensure Arjuna's victory. Only once, during the burning of the Khāṇḍava forest (*Mbh.* I: 218), he fought Arjuna on his friend Takṣaka's behalf. In the *HV*, too, Indra fought Arjuna, trying in vain to secure his position against the rising cult of Viṣṇu (*HV* II: 18, 19). When a compromise had been agreed upon, Indra commissioned Kṛṣṇa to kill the demon Naraka and be friendly to his son Arjuna (*HV* II: 193). Indra put up this one last fight against Kṛṣṇa, his spiritual descendant, before he relinquished his claim to sovereignty.

As the prototype of the Viṣṇu or solar group of gods Indra was the natural enemy of Śiva, the central deity of the lunar group. The *JB* tells us that Indra overcame Hara only when the gods praised him with Harivat hymns (I: 200). Hara later became an epithet of Śiva. According to the *TMB* Indra desired 'hara' (power, glory) and received it through penance and through the Hārāyana hymns (XIV: 9: 34). Another anecdote tells us that the sage Viśvamanasa was possessed by a monster. Indra coming to know of it asked him who had possessed him. He replied 'Sthāṇu' (a name of Śiva). Indra gave him a straw charged with virtue with which he split the monster's skull. Then Sthāṇu possessed Indra and was finally vanquished by the Vaiśvamanasa hymn (*TMB* XV: 5: 24). Thus the first inkling of the rivalry between the cults of Śiva and Viṣṇu can be traced already in the *Brāhmaṇas* where Indra is yet the prototype of his Viṣṇu group of successors and where Śiva of the epic-Purāṇic age makes his personality felt for the first time.

Indra appears as Zeus on the coins of Eucratides with an elephant[1] and seated on a throne. Images of Indra are comparatively rare, perhaps because the Indra-cult was a minor cult and quite in the background and by the time images and temples had come into vogue Indra's importance had dwindled almost to insignificance. In present-day Bengal we have the worship of Viśvakarman, and this god like the epic-Purāṇic Indra is seated on an elephant, and his festival like the Indramaha falls in the rainy season. The *ṚV* ascribes cosmic activities, including the creation of the universe, to Indra. Gods corresponding to Indra in other mythologies are the sons of craftsmen (cf. C. G. Jung, *Psychology of the unconscious*, p. 202), as was Viśvakarman as Tvaṣṭṛ in the Vedic period. In the Bhaja cave Vedic Indra and Sūrya appear respectively as symbols of the Buddha's temporal and spiritual powers.

Indra the great solar-god, the culture-hero of the Vedic Indians, had a parallel in almost every mythology. In *ṚV* x: 38: 5 Indra is invoked to free himself from the hundred knots of leathern straps with which Kutsa and Luśa had bound him in the former's sacrifice. The episode is mentioned also in *PB* ix: 2: 22. The image of the hero bound with strong knots tearing himself free recalls those of Prometheus and Samson, culture-heroes of the Greeks and the Jews respectively. The elephant-headed rain-god who combined the traits of both Indra and Ahi was called Chac among the Mayas and Tlaloc among the Aztecs. George Eliot Smith in *The evolution of the dragon*, pp. 84–5, says: 'I reproduce here a remarkable drawing from the *Codex Troana*, in which this god, whom the Maya people called Chac, is shown pouring the rain out of a water-jar...and putting his foot down upon the head of a serpent who is preventing the rain from reaching the earth...The Māyā Chac is, in fact Indra transferred to the other side of the Pacific and there only thinly disguised by a veneer of American stylistic design.' Marduk, Thor and Zeus are better known parallels of Indra, Egyptian Rā was also a serpent-killer.[2] The Iranian Verethraghna was also a demon corresponding to the Indian Vṛtraghna, i.e. Indra. Thor's hair was lovelier than gold. One remembers Indra's description as Harikeśa, golden-haired. Thor is the strongest of all gods

[1] Indra as a rain-god is symbolized by the elephant which fills its trunk with water and sprays it. Later mythology places elephants in the sky which pour rain-water on the earth.

[2] Even in China we have a remote parallel. 'When the artist diviner of the Shang Era desired not a character but a concrete image of the Dragon for display in the service of prayers for rain or to ascertain when rain would fall or hold off, he had recourse for his model to the contemporary alligator' (L. C. Hopkins: 'The dragon terrestrial and the dragon celestial', *IHQ*, ix, 1933). The alligator answers to the Indian elephant who is seen as a mass of rain cloud and which pours water through its snout.

and men...He also owns three precious things. One is the hammer Mjöllnir (= Crusher). The frost-ogres and cliff-giants know since he has cracked the skulls of many of their kith and kin. Thor is also a great drinker; he entered in a drinking competition with Utgard Loki and won. But his greatest achievement was against the Midgard Serpent. (*Prose Edda*. pp. 50–1, 80.)

Thus in possessing unique weapons, in his fondness for drinks and in the feat of serpent-killing, Thor resembles Indra.

Indra's power lies in his being the culture-hero of the Vedic Aryans. They needed a god in whom they could project their aspirations and experiences, a god who symbolized their national dreams. They created Indra in their own image, and he grew with them in stature and power. Thus Indra appears as the national hero-god of the Vedic Aryans. He shares their experiences and is a pioneer of the advancing hordes of the Aryans. But simultaneously with his mundane career he symbolizes the cosmic creator. The resultant figure is 'a most complex personality composed of sometimes even contradictory traits...Traits of a human hero but also the world-creator to whom mankind owes the fundamental necessities of life—light, fire, water and milk' (Paul Thieme, 'The Aryan gods of the Mitanni treaties', *JAOS*, no. 4, 1960).

Vṛtra appears to have been the most formidable enemy of the advancing Aryans, who surmounted this obstacle through the prowess of their general, Indra. Naturally whole hymns extol this most famous act of Indra. Pūrbhid or Purandara is Indra's title because he broke into the fortified cities of the indigenous principalities. The demons who exercised māyā (magic power) seem to be the gods of the vanquished races and the Dāsas or Dasyus, the conquered people themselves. Equipped with unusually powerful weapons and armour he achieved victory after resounding victory, leading his army into the heart of the country, taking fortresses, releasing the dammed up water supply, winning cattle and wealth, bringing slaves and booty—and thus being regarded as divine.

Divinity was ascribed to the leader of the Aryan hordes long before they entered India, for the Hittite treaty knows an Indra and the *Avesta* knows a Verethraghna. Hence it would appear that the Indo-Europeans had such a warrior leader, the prototype of Thor, Zeus and Indra. In India the name must have been regarded as hereditary, applied to the general of the invading army.

In support of this theory we notice in the epics a notion that Indra is not an individual name, but a title, a post. When Indra is downcast at his discomfiture at the hands of Rāvaṇa, Brahman consoles him saying; 'No one remains an Indra permanently' (*Rām.* VII: 30: 35). Śiva once crushed Indra's pride by showing him previous Indras (*Mbh.* I: 189). When Indra found Vali in the shape of an ass, he laughed and asked Vali if he (Vali) felt shame and remorse at the loss of kingship. Vali replied that he had known glory and fame just like Indra's and he could take his present ignominy in his stride. (*Mbh.* XII: 217: 54.) In the vulgate *Mbh.* the dialogue between Vali and Indra is longer and many of Vali's statements there confirm the notion that Vali, Nahuṣa and Indra are but three sovereigns and that the title Indra was a post given to the best leader for a specific period; when he failed, the glory departed and some fitter person succeeded him. Vali tells Indra that Indra was powerless before and had somehow become strong, that Vali himself had once been like Indra, that Indra had become Indra because it was his turn then, and not because he had earned it (*Mbh.* XII: 227: 22–36). 'You and I and all others who come after us will go the way of the former Indras, all these had performed a hundred sacrifices, all had been mighty warriors; Vali had been deposed from being Indra and Indra had succeeded him' (*Mbh.* XIII: 227: 39–41). In the *Brahmavaivarta Purāṇa* we have an anecdote where the boy Kṛṣṇa laughs at a long array of ants. Indra who was present asked him the reason; Kṛṣṇa replied: these were all Indras at some time or other, through their actions they are now ants. (Kṛṣṇajanmakhaṇḍa, XLVII: 50–161.) The transitory nature of divine sovereignty is brought home through anecdotes like this.

This concept is somewhat unusual for a Vedic god, who is commonly thought of as eternal. Some gods grew dim and unimportant but the divinity or authority of none was usurped by another so openly. Yet for a long time Indra dominated the pantheon. When he sees Śrī retiring from Vali's body and kingdom he questions her and is told that heavenly sovereigns did not rule by 'divine right', they waxed and waned, and others ousted them from their positions (*Mbh.* XII: 221). Significantly enough Śrī later becomes the wife of Viṣṇu, Indra's mythological heir.

One is tempted to think that the thousands of Indras referred to by Vali were the kings who ruled the India before Indra, the Aryan conqueror, Kings whose material prosperity and administration were superior to those of the Aryans. These the Aryans subjugated, seizing their land and wealth from them; but public memory, operative through the mythopoeic mind, wished to retain the chastening memory of these rulers who succumbed to Ineluctable Fate just as Indra some day would do.

Sir Mortimer Wheeler throws out a plausible conjecture regarding the end of the Mohenjo Daro civilization. In his book *Prehistory from the earth* he says that from some of the ruins at Mohenjo Daro and Harappa it would appear that Indra stood condemned for the destruction and ruin of this civilization.

After dominating the Aryan pantheon for a long time Indra's mythological potentialities were exhausted. The myth lost the power to grow and change with time so that the image was gradually reduced to a mere shell. But mythology, like nature, abhors a vacuum, and other gods filled the role of the culture-hero till their places were occupied by others. Thus Indra's powers and functions, features and attributes were distributed among the Viṣṇu-group of solar gods and the culture-hero continued as the central figure of the pantheon, although under a different name.

CHAPTER 14

VIṢṆU

VIṢṆU is a minor god in the *ṚV* with only five whole hymns addressed to him. He is not physically described but is said to be strong as a ferocious animal and to live in mountains (*ṚV* I: 154: 2). His solar identity is clear from the hymns; he is always grouped with the solar gods. The *ŚB* says: 'Now he who is Viṣṇu is the sacrifice and he who is this sacrifice is yonder Āditya' (XIV: I: I: 6–7). The *Mait. U* says of him: '(He is) the sacrificer, the enjoyer of oblations, the (sacrificial) formula, the sacrifice, Viṣṇu and Prajāpati. (He is) all, the lord, the witness—he who shines in the yonder orb' (VI: 16). The *AV* invokes Viṣṇu to give heat (V: 26: 7), thus proving his solar character. The *ŚB* says that Viṣṇu's head was cut off and it became the sun (XIV: I: I: I). Bhīṣma praises Kṛṣṇa, an incarnation of Viṣṇu, as the sun (*Mbh.* XII: 47: 27). In the *HV* he is called the lord of the Ādityas (I: 4: 5). Chāyā, Sūrya's wife in earlier literature is said to be Viṣṇu's wife in the *HV* (I: 41: 35). The catalogue of the Ādityas varies but Viṣṇu is included in every list. Ghaṇṭākarṇa praises Viṣṇu in the *HV* as 'the brilliance of the sun'. His orb is the sun by day and the moon by night says the *HV* (III: 28: 45–8).

Viṣṇu's three strides are mentioned frequently in the *Vedas* as his most important feat (*ṚV* I: 23: 17, 18, 20, I: 154: 1–3, VII: 99: 7, VIII: 12: 27, VIII: 29: 7). We are told that his two steps are visible but the third is inscrutable. This third step seems to be his highest achievement, in it lies the fountain of honey (*ṚV* I: 154: 5). This stride is called the highest, parama (*ṚV* I: 23: 10, 21). Because of these strides Viṣṇu is styled urugāya or urukrama (having a movement of magnitude, *ṚV* I: 155: 5). By these strides Viṣṇu reached the gods' region (*ṚV* VIII: 29: 7). 'We know the two regions, Viṣṇu, you know the uppermost (parama) region' (*ṚV* VII: 99: 1). For this feat he is to be offered sacrificial cakes on three potsherds in the Agniṣṭoma sacrifice. 'Viṣṇu takes his strides, being Viṣṇu he conquers these (three) regions' (*TB* I: 7: 4: 4). Scholars are divided in their opinion regarding the identity of Viṣṇu's three steps. No interpretation is given in the *Vedas*. The *MS* and *TS* alone among the *Saṃhitās* seem to suggest that the three strides covered the three regions (*TB* III: I: 2: 6), thus establishing his overlordship of the three regions.

By the time of the epics the three strides had already been an accepted myth and are frequently mentioned in connection with Viṣṇu (*Rām.* IV: 40: 62, V: 5: 3, V: 13: 23, VI: 38: 2, VI: 51: 7, VI: 52: 7). The *Mbh.* has an anecdote: when Viṣṇu was taking the three strides he came upon the sage Bharadvāja in the celestial Gaṅgā. Bharadvāja smote Viṣṇu on the chest with the water in his hand, it left a mark there. (*Mbh.* XII: 329: 42.) Vali's yielding the three steps to Viṣṇu is mentioned in the *HV* III: 71.

The *AB* version of the story mentions Indra with whose help Viṣṇu deludes the Asura, for in three strides Viṣṇu wins the worlds, the Vedas and Vāc (speech) (*AB* VI: 15). The Purāṇic story of the three strides of the dwarf by which Viṣṇu conquered the three worlds is anticipated in *TS* II: 1: 3: 1. It is also referred to, though rather vaguely, in *ŚB* I: 2: 5: 1. V. Machek in his article 'Origin of the god Viṣṇu' says,

> His three strides and his dwarfish likeness suggest that Viṣṇu's original character emerges from the realm of witchcraft, from the world of fairy-beings and charms. The *Mait.U* describes the Supreme Being as 'as high as a third of the thumb'. Here we cannot help thinking of that type of fairy tale in which some magician helps the hero of the fairy tale not with his physical strength but with his witchcraft (*Archiv Orientalni*, 1960, vol. 28, pp. 107–8).

One remembers the Eddic story of the Deluding of the Gylfi where the Aesir won land by the two giants disguised as oxen. In Celtic mythology the dwarf was the man of the sun who emerges from the cosmic egg.[1]

The Eddic parallel appears to be the *ṚV* version of the three strides where it says that Viṣṇu's strides gained land for the sacrificer (*ṚV* VII: 100: 4). This feat is ascribed to Indra in the *Brāhmaṇas* and the idea seems to be an old one. After the dissemination of the Indo-European peoples they gained land from the indigenous population wherever they settled, and guile may have helped them in their struggle for land. Demons and Asuras were without doubt the aboriginal population and there are many tales in which they were deluded into yielding what was originally theirs.

We have a Finnish parallel of the story of the three strides in the third rune of the *Kalevala*. The hero Wainämöinen doubts the ability of the dwarf who comes from the sea to fell the oak tree which obstructs sunlight and moonlight from reaching the earth. The dwarf turns into an enormous giant and fells the tree. (*Kalevala*, Everyman edn. vol. I, lines 111–224.) Here the actual strides are absent but the dwarf turning into a giant to accomplish a superhuman task links this account with the dwarf story.

[1] 'In Yucatan dwarfs were sacred to the sun-god and were occasionally sacrificed to him, for reasons which appear obscure' (Lewis Spence, *The myths of Mexico and Peru*, p. 194).

The Celtic god Cuchulain's leap across the bridge is also comparable to these feats.[1]

The *ṚV* does not connect Viṣṇu with the dwarf in any way. The *TS* does, and in the *TS* we first notice non-Vedic influences insidiously making their way into the Vedic pantheon. Thus we read, 'He to whom the sacrifice does not come should offer a dwarf to Viṣṇu' (*TS* II: 1: 8). In the *MS*, too, this connection is repeated, 'the dwarf belongs to Viṣṇu', 'the gods saw this dwarf animal, it should be slaughtered for Viṣṇu' (*MS* II: 1: 7). The *ŚB* also says, 'Now Viṣṇu was a dwarf' (*ŚB* I: 2: 5: 5).

This anecdote was filled out into the elaborate story of the dwarf incarnation of the epics and *Purāṇas*. In the *Rām.* we are told the story at some length; Viṣṇu assumed the shape of a dwarf and asked for only as much land as he could cover in three strides. The unsuspecting Vali granted his request. Viṣṇu magnified his dimensions, covered heaven, atmosphere and the earth and pushed Vali into hell. Thus the episode is but demon-vanquishing in another form, for he is said to have brought the three worlds under the gods (*Rām.* VII: 11: 8). The *Mbh.* mentions his dwarf incarnation in III: 100. Aditi gave birth to the Ādityas of whom Viṣṇu was a dwarf. 'From his strides the gods' prosperity increased and the demons were defeated' (*Mbh.* XII: 200: 26–7). The *HV* includes the dwarf in its lists of incarnations (cf. I: 41: 104, II: 48: 16–22). The story of the dwarf incarnation and the destruction of Vali is given in *HV* III: 31. The dwarf shape is explained in the *JB*: 'Once the gods slept, demons stole their strength, Viṣṇu saw it and consoled the gods. They offered the Vyāhṛtis to Viṣṇu, hence he is short' (III: 354). Viṣṇu's shortness is thus due to spiritual greatness.

The Teutonic parallel of Viṣṇu is Frey who 'can appear in the shape of a dwarf, he is the ruler of the dwarfs and elves. Frey kills practically unharmed the giant Beli'[2] (V. Machek, Origin of the god Viṣṇu', *Archiv Orientalni*, vol. 28, 1960).

This tripādavikrama, as this feat of Viṣṇu is commonly known, is immortalized in the cult by the worship of his footprints in many forms. One

[1] The Eskimo myths of the dwarf Kâgssagssuk who performed miraculous deeds is another illustration (*Eskimo folk tales*). St Moling (in Celtic mythology) asked a boon of his fosterer: Let me have my three steps...The first step...he looked no bigger than a crow...The second leap...they saw him not at all and they knew not whether he had gone into heaven or into earth. The third step...he alighted on the earth (mentioned by A. and B. Rees in *Celtic heritage*). Here, too, we notice the same motif of the three steps. In Chinese mythology P'an Ku was originally a dwarf. He grew for 18,000 years, increasing his height by six feet every day, changing himself into a giant. After his death, the universe was created from his body. Here we have the dwarf as a Kosmokrator.

[2] The name Beli in the Teutonic myth is akin to its Indian counterpart, Vali.

remembers the Viṣṇupāda at Gaya where his supposed footprints are daily worshipped by pilgrims. Also the footprints of the Buddha, of St Patrick or St Columba in Ireland are relevant parallels; so are Tezcatlipoca's footprints (on flour) in Aztec ceremony and he is the sun-god of Mexico.

The dwarf-motif is common all over the world and is accompanied by the notion of superhuman cleverness. One remembers the clever dwarf Andvari, keeper of the Nibelung treasure, who changed shapes to elude enemies. The Homunculi are spread all over the world. In mythology they are either the custodians of treasure or solar gods in dwarf disguise who win this treasure, or both, as in the *Nibelungenlied*. 'In folk-lore the child-motif appears in the guise of the dwarf or the elf as personifications of the hidden forces of nature' (C. G. Jung and C. Kerényi, *Introduction to a science of mythology*, p. 106). The Asuras, demons or dwarfs are usually wealthier than the Aryan people to whom the solar hero belongs, but he usurps their land, wealth or power by might and by guile. In India the Asuras may have been primitive iron-smelters or miners, as some scholars suggest. These dwarfs who hide their hoarded treasure in caves or under the ground may actually have been smelters or miners who were wealthy and who knew the art of making ornaments.

Among other incarnate forms, the boar is mentioned in the *TS* in connection with Viṣṇu. 'The sacrifice went away from the gods in the form of Viṣṇu and entered the earth. Indra told him that a boar kept the demons' wealth. Viṣṇu smote him with a bunch of Darbha (Kuśa grass) which smote the seven hills' (VI: 2: 4). Here we notice that what became one of Viṣṇu's incarnation-forms was originally the shape of his adversary. It is also striking that the boar was a custodian of the demon treasure. The first direct idea of the boar as an incarnation of Viṣṇu performing the specific task of rescuing the earth is mentioned in the *ŚB*: 'A boar called Emūṣa raised her (the earth) up and he was her lord Prajāpati' (XIV: 1: 2: 12). Thus the nucleus of the story of the god rescuing the earth in the boar-shape is found here. The *ṚV* reference is rather confusing. It says Viṣṇu carried off a hundred buffaloes and drank a milk-draught which belonged to the boar, and Vṛtra shot the boar (I: 61: 7, VIII: 77: 10).[1]

The *HV* raises the epiphany of Viṣṇu to cosmic proportions (I: 41: 35),

[1] It is significant that in all these myths Viṣṇu's role is the same: he deludes the original owners of wealth (as of buffaloes and milk-draught as in the *ṚV* myth) and appropriates it either for himself or for his people, the Aryans. Whether as a dwarf or as a boar Viṣṇu's function is to usurp demon property. Comparing this with the later myth of Viṣṇu stealing nectar from the demons we have a uniform character of Viṣṇu, the usurper of demon (i.e. Pre-Aryan, indigenous) wealth by fraud, guile, disguise or magic power.

and in II: 48: 16–22 lists it as one of the six past incarnations. The story is narrated fully in *HV* III: 34. The *Purāṇas* describe this incarnation (as in *Matsya P*, ch. 247; *Viṣṇu P* V: 29: 23). The *Mbh.*, *HV* and *Purāṇas* mention Viṣṇu's slaughter of demon Hiraṇyākṣa in his boar incarnation. We have an iconographic representation of this incarnation in Udaygiri of *c.* A.D. 400, where the boar is shown as 'overcoming the great serpent-king, who with folded hands implores his mercy'.

Parallels of the boar incarnation are found in other mythologies too. 'The divine magician (such as Viṣṇu) is to be found also among the Teutons of the North. There he is called Frey. His war-animal (Kampf-tier) is the boar, just as in the case of Viṣṇu' (V. Machek, 'Origin of the god Visnu', *Archiv Orientalni*, Praha, vol. 28, 1960, p. 123).

In iconography the boar incarnation is represented in Udaygiri (*c.* A.D. 400) and in the fifth-century Bhitargaon plaque. The stone-boar of Eran belongs to fifth-to-sixth century A.D. The Damodarpur inscription (fifth century) refers to it as 'the white boar lord'. Seal no. 54 at Basarh has an image of the boar-incarnation.

It is interesting that M. Kuiper, in his article 'An Austro-Asiatic myth in the Rigveda' (*Mededeelingen d. Kroninkl. Nederl. Akd. van Wetenschappen*, 1950, no. 7), mentions the slaughter of a boar Emūṣa by an archer-god who uses his 'drumbhūlī'. This would explain the name Emūṣa. In *MS* III: 8: 3 we have the term 'Drumbhūlī', it means a kind of reed or stalk: probably a reed with which the arrow was made which killed Emūṣa. One remembers the *TS* reference to the Kuśa grass used for killing the boar. This Saṃhitā is late and incorporates non-Aryan material as is evident from the *Śatarudrīya*. Thus the incarnation stories may have been partially contributed by the pre-Aryan myths of India.

The fish incarnation has its first mention in the *ŚB* where Manu is saved by a fish during the deluge (*ŚB* I: 8: 1: 1). The identity of the fish is not given in the *Brāhmaṇas*, and the epics do not connect this episode with Viṣṇu. The *Mbh.* makes Prajāpati the fish. The epic or *HV* lists of the incarnations do not mention the fish. The *Purāṇas* identify Manu's fish as Viṣṇu. Thus the fish incarnation was clearly borrowed by the Vaiṣṇava sect and then appropriated in order to extol their god. As an incarnation story it is of late origin.

The Greek parallel of the fish-incarnation is found in the image of Apollo Delphinios. In Hesiod we read of Phoebus Apollo: 'in the open sea he sprang upon the swift ship, like a dolphin in shape and lay there' (Homeric hymn to Pythian Apollo, ll. 399–402).

The *Brāhmaṇas* mention the cosmic tortoise. In *JB* III: 272 and *ŚB* VII: 5: 1: 1 Prajāpati is the Akūpāra tortoise who assumes cosmic proportions. It is not mentioned in connection with Viṣṇu either in the *Brāhmaṇas* or in the epics. Only in the *Purāṇas* do we hear of Viṣṇu's descent in the shape of a tortoise to support Mount Mandara at the time of the churning of the ocean (*Nṛsimhapurāṇa*). The word 'Akūpāra' means 'unbounded' (as in *ṚV* V: 39: 2, X: 109: 1). In the *Bh.P* 'Akūpāra' becomes the tortoise which upholds the earth. The tortoise becomes one of Viṣṇu's incarnations in the age of the *Purāṇas*.

The Nṛshṃha (man-lion) incarnation has no Vedic antecedent. The *Mbh.*, *HV* and *Purāṇas* introduce it. The *HV* gives a full account. With his disc Viṣṇu slew Hiraṇyākṣa (in the shape of Dīrghavaktra) whom Brahman had blessed with virtual immortality (*HV* III: 74). The gods requested Viṣṇu to destroy Hiraṇyakaśipu. Viṣṇu agreed and descended in the man-lion form. Prahlāda the prince warned the king, his father, but the latter paid no heed. The demon fought Nṛsiṃha with famous weapons, which were of no avail. Finally Viṣṇu vanquished and slew him (*HV* III: 43–6). The man-lion incarnation is represented in seal no. 191 in the Basarh Besnagar inscriptions of the sixth century (in the Gwalior museum). It appears to indicate that the worshippers of Nṛsiṃha were a small sect.

The first few incarnations—Matsya (fish), Kūrma (tortoise), Varāha (boar), Nṛsiṃha (man-lion) and Vāmana (dwarf)—seem to indicate an evolution: the small fish (as it first appeared to Manu) and the tortoise, both of these aquatic; the quadruped boar, Nṛsiṃha the cross between man and animal, and the dwarf—these seem to develop through an evolution. Of the next incarnations, Paraśurāma, Rāma and Balārama are supposed to belong to mythical epochs—the first two to Tretā and the last one to Dvāpara. The Buddha is clearly a later addition, an attempt to include the historical hero-figure who in the Mahāyāna system had been solarized and hence represents to the Buddhists what Viṣṇu does to the Vaiṣṇava. The Eddic solar god has many traits in common with these incarnations: thus he has a chariot fashioned by the dwarfs, he is associated with the horse, has the boat Gullinbursti and the ship Skidbladnir.

As Paraśurāma, Viṣṇu came down to destroy Kārtavīryārjuna as also to annihilate the Kṣattriyas as a class. And he did extirpate the Kṣattriyas twenty-one times; and this symbolizes the conflict between the *Brāhmaṇas* and the warriors. He is solidly on the side of the Brahmins and seems to be a product of priestly imagination. The accepted Kṣattriya values of courage, heroism and the militant temperament combine with the wrath and zeal of a mortified Brahmin. The result is an impressive hero. The Kṣattriyas were shown as a threat to the Brāhmaṇical values, and Paraśurāma by extirpating the Kṣattriyas saved these values. In this he performs the task of a solar-hero god.

Rāmacandra descended to destroy Rāvaṇa, the wicked and powerful monster-king of Laṅkā. The impact of the story has much in common with the Vedic tales of demon-killing. Sītā is Lakṣmī's incarnation in the spurious portions of the *Rām.*, and this associated Rāma with Viṣṇu. Like Nārāyaṇa of old, Rāma, too, is assisted by his brother Lakṣmaṇa, who appears as less divine (at least in the later parts of the epic) than Rāma. They remind us of Nara and Nārāyaṇa. The mighty adversary Rāvaṇa, rendered almost invincible through divine boons, is a parallel of Vṛtra and Namuci. Thus Rāma is in the direct line of the progressive unfolding of the solar hero of the Indra-Viṣṇu epiphany. The agricultural associations of these gods are preserved in Sītā, who rose in the cornfield ploughed up by the ploughshares. The epic pattern presupposes a different treatment of the myths and introduces new emotional and ideological impacts; but underneath it all remains the substratum of the ancient mythologem which assumes fresh vitality and force through the richer and more complex, hence aesthetically more satisfying, treatment.

Balarāma, or Haladhara as we know him, is a comparatively obscure hero in the *Mbh.* We are told that the gods, before their incarnation as the five Pāṇḍavas went to Nārāyaṇa, who pulled out two hairs, one white the other black; these hairs entered Rohiṇī and Devakī respectively and were born as Balarāma and Kṛṣṇa (*Mbh.* 1: 189). Their almost twin nature is brought out in this passage. Inherent in the concept of these two brothers is the idea of the one remaining semi-neutral and the other more active.

Balārama is called Saṃkarṣaṇa. He carries a ploughshare and is associated with agriculture. As a personification of the Śeṣanāga he was probably a god of the nāga-worshippers and in the Saṃkarṣaṇa-Vāsudeva we perhaps have an amalgamation of the Nāga and Kṛṣṇa cults. The Mauṣalaparvan of the *Mbh.* gives an account of Balarāma's death: he sat meditating, and Kṛṣṇa saw a huge white serpent escaping from his body and entering the sea (ch. IV). This identifies Balārama with the Śeṣanāga and perhaps establishes the connection between nāga-worshippers and the Balarāma sect (the 'white' serpent indicates his 'sattvaguṇa', detachment). Significantly enough Viṣṇu is said to recline his head on the Śeṣa or Ananta in the bottom of the ocean. The image of the two brothers, metamorphosed, continues in the myth. In the epic war Balarāma remains a conscientious objector and does not participate in it. He is sometimes represented by the Ananta or Śeṣa serpent on whose hood Nārāyaṇa reclines while he sleeps between creations. In his human shape he is Kṛṣṇa's brother and Revatī's husband. With his wife he indulges in drinks. 'In one form, he is a sort of bucolic deity connected with agriculture and harvests' (J. N. Banerji, *The development of Hindu iconography*, p. 420). Unlike the other incarnations he kills no demons and fights no battle singly; together with Kṛṣṇa, however, he is engaged in many encounters.

Kṛṣṇa is not included in the earlier list of the incarnations because he is a Purṇāvatāra, the total incarnation of Viṣṇu unlike the others who represent him only partially (aṃśāvatāra). Kṛṣṇa is the divine hero of one epic as Rāma is of the other. Balarāma seems to have been the central figure of an agricultural people with their separate cult and ritual who was later solarized and brought into line with the other incarnations. We have an inscription at Ghurundi of *c.* 150 B.C. which mentions the construction of a temple dedicated to Saṃkarṣaṇa and Vāsudeva. This seems to point to the existence of a cult of the two brothers.

The theory of incarnation is a reflection of human reincarnation on the sublime and divine plane. The *Purāṇas* belong to the period when all the divergent rituals, cults, sects with their theorics and practices were brought together and harmonized into one religion. The different epiphanies of the sun-god and the regional hero-cults were thus relegated to their proper places in the Purāṇic religion. The totem-worshippers, the animists, the hero-worshippers, all had to find their respective places in this Neo-Brāhmaṇical religion. This could only be done by acknowledging them as manifestations of one fundamental theophany. With the idea of metempsychosis accepted on the human level, it needed but one step of sublimation to transfer it on to the divine, and thus unite the different cults and people into one fold by harmonizing their faiths. None was denied a place, all felt that they worshipped the supreme being in onc or other of its manifestations.

The Ṛgvedic Viṣṇu lacked facets which could be developed into the attributes of a major god. Not only was he a minor god with few hymns but his achievements and characteristics too were so limited that they had very little mythological potentiality. It is only in the *Brāhmaṇas*—the product of the first encounters with the non-Vedic and non-Aryan culture—that Viṣṇu's stature is magnified and he comes into the limelight. One of the methods of emphasizing his role and importance was to identify him with the sacrifice. The *Brāhmaṇas* never tire of repeating the formula:

'Viṣṇu is the sacrifice' or 'the sacrifice is Viṣṇu'. 'He to whom the sacrifice does not come should offer to Viṣṇu' (*TS* II: 1: 8). The *TB* states the formula the sacrifice is Viṣṇu (1: 2: 5: 1). 'The sacrifice is the undefeated (i.e. unsurrendered) realm...Viṣṇu protects the oblation' (*TB* III: 3: 7: 7, III: 7: 4: 18). The Yajña-Viṣṇu equation is also repeated in the *JB* (II: 68). 'Viṣṇu', says the *ŚB*, 'is the upper half of the sacrifice' (III: 1: 3: 1). 'The Soma-cart belongs to Viṣṇu' (*ŚB* III: 5: 3: 15). 'Viṣṇu (obtained for his share) one-third...the yajña is Viṣṇu's' (*ŚB* IV: 6: 7: 3). 'Viṣṇu is the sacrifice' (*ŚB* V: 4: 5: 1). 'They (the gods) spake, "Whoever of us through austerity, fervour, faith, sacrifice and oblations shall first compass the end of the sacrifice, he shall be the most excellent of us and shall then be in common to us all". "So be it", they said. Viṣṇu first attained it. Now he who is Viṣṇu is the sacrifice and he who is this sacrifice is yonder Āditya' (*ŚB* XIV: 1: 1: 4–7).

This equation of Yajña and Viṣṇu was important in order to bring Viṣṇu into power and prominence, for the age of the *Brāhmaṇas* was pre-eminently an age of sacrifices, and the god who symbolized the sacrifice in his person assumed supreme importance. His meagre *Saṃhitā* antecedents were forgotten. After the Brāhamaṇical age Viṣṇu needed no propaganda, for he was already supreme. So the epics do not repeat the Yajña-Viṣṇu equation. It is forgotten except for rare exceptions. In his incarnate form Kṛṣṇa is praised kathenotheistically and his identity as the sacrifice adds to his spiritual stature as in *MU* VI: 16, where he is called the sacrificial priest, the oblation, the hymn and the sacrifice. The Vaiṣṇava Yajña which Karṇa describes to Duryodhana (and none has performed it except Viṣṇu himself, III: 241), is, however, a pastoral ritual. The *Mbh.*, especially the *Gītā*, also identifies Viṣṇu with the sacrifice in order to enhance his spiritual grandeur. The *HV* too repeats this formula in a semi-mechanical manner (1: 41: 3–9).

Although the Ṛgvedic Viṣṇu is not credited with warlike activities, he assists Indra in his encounters with demons (*ṚV* VII: 99: 4), particularly with Vṛtra. The *Brāhmaṇas* are not keen to bring out this aspect of Viṣṇu, they would rather see him as the sacrifice personified. This warrior-trait of Viṣṇu recurs in the epics where he is the killer of the demon Madhu (*Rām.* 1: 77: 49), or Hayagrīva (*Rām.* IV: 43: 34). He destroyed the glory of the Asuras in his three strides (*Rām.* V: 13: 22); he is the mighty warrior (*Rām.* V: 31: 48) who killed Tāraka (*Rām.* IV: 48: 7). In the *Purāṇas* Tāraka was killed by Kārttikeya. He also killed Hiraṇyakaśipu, Namuci, Kālanemi, Rādheya, Hārdikya, Śumbha and Niśumbha (*Rām.* VII: 6: 34–5).

In the *Mbh.* Viṣṇu killed Madhu and Kaiṭabha (III: 194), Hiraṇyākṣa (VII: 13: 44) and Hiraṇyakaśipu. In the *HV* Viṣṇu is called the central figure and the indisputable leader of the divine army (I: 44: 35–42). Nārada tells Viṣṇu that all the demons and enemies he had killed in his previous incarnation are born as fierce demons in the Dvāpara age; hence Viṣṇu had to descend in order to destroy them (*HV* I: 52: 54). Rāma had received his bow from Agastya with which he won Śrī (*Rām.* III: 18: 40) and killed monsters in the forest and won the battle in Laṅkā. Kṛṣṇa had his Śārṅga bow in the *Mbh.* and *HV*. But the Vedic and epic-Purāṇic Viṣṇu's distinctive weapon was the disc or wheel, the cakra. The *ṚV* mentions it (I: 155: 6) and there it undoubtedly stands for the solar disc. The *Brāhmaṇas*, describing the sacrificial ritual, say that a gold plate symbolizes the sun and the dazzling Puruṣa who is later identified with Viṣṇu (*ŚB* X: 5: 4: 15, X: 6: 3: 2). His cakra is mentioned in the *Rām.*, where Viṣṇu is said to carry it (*Rām.* I: 57: 9) and Rāma received it from Viśvāmitra (*Rām.* I: 30: 6). It is mentioned elsewhere too; with it Viṣṇu cut off Hiraṇyākṣa's head and it seems to have become inseparably associated with Viṣṇu. In the *Mbh.* Viṣṇu killed demons Madhu and Kaiṭabha with it. Significantly enough the wheel is associated with the Buddha, too, and the Buddha is Viṣṇu's ninth incarnation and also a solar hero. The Buddha set the Dharmacakra (the wheel of Law) in motion which automatically annihilates the powers of evil and darkness—a task the solar disc of the Vedic Viṣṇu performed in his person as the sun's orb; and in the epic-Purāṇic incarnations the killing of demons, the forces of evil, is performed with this symbolic weapon.

Brahman told the gods that Kṛṣṇa and Arjuna are none other than Nara and Nārāyaṇa of old (*Mbh.* V: 48). They had undertaken hard penance in the hermitage at Badarikā, where they lived in a pretty eight-wheeled golden cart. Emaciated, with knotted veins standing out, they meditated there, and only those whom they favoured could see them for they were invisible. (*Mbh.* XII: 321: 10–12.) The mention of the 'golden' cart brings out the solar character of Nara and Nārāyaṇa. King Vasu Uparicara was Nārāyaṇa's friend. Nārāyaṇa accepted an oblation in his horse-sacrifice (*Mbh.* XII: 322). Of Nara and Nārāyaṇa we hear that Rudra chased them with his śūla (spike); Nara hurled an arrow sanctified with a charm, it became an axe, but when it hit Rudra it broke (*Mbh.* XII: 330). This last part of the myth is clearly a late Śaiva gloss aimed at glorifying Rudra. Nārada had a glimpse of Nara and Nārāyaṇa at Badarikāśrama and there Nārāyaṇa congratulated him (*Mbh.* XII: 332).

Strangely enough all through later literature, especially in the *Purāṇas*, the word Nārāyaṇa is derived from water. The *Mbh.* account does not mention Nārāyaṇa in connection with water; at least not when he is mentioned with Nara, for then they are invariably described as undergoing penance in the hermitage of Badarikā. Nārāyaṇa derived from the water may be an afterthought suggested by the description of the god lying under water.

Nara-Nārāyaṇa linked as a divine and a human being is an important phenomenon, because it holds the germ of the incarnation theory. From the Gilgamesh-Enkidu pair or the Dioscouri, with one immortal and one mortal brother, the idea is there. Of this pair the divine personality does nothing, kills no demons, performs no feats without the help of the mortal; together they are credited with superhuman achievements. In the *HV* Kṛṣṇa and Balarāma or *Mbh.* Kṛṣṇa and Arjuna we have a replica of this group, in Rāma and Lakṣmaṇa of the *Rām.* perhaps another, but the best, poetically most impressive and mythologically most gripping is the Kṛṣṇa and Arjuna pair. Of them we are told that they are none but Nara and Nārāyaṇa of old. Hence Nara-Nārāyaṇa is the archetypal pattern behind these concepts. The principle of an active and a passive agent had been introduced in the Sāṃkya system—Kṛṣṇa does not fight but leads the warrior, supplies the motive, the urge and the impelling force. In other words, he discharges the functions of the sun, the awakener. This image of Kṛṣṇa and Arjuna was so effective aesthetically, and so satisfying philosophically that the hazy concept of the god-man pair was transmuted into a concrete archetype in Nara-Nārāyaṇa which explains the power of the Kṛṣṇa-Arjuna image.

The ancient sage Nārāyaṇa is also identified with the sage Kapila of old. Indra tells Lomaśa 'this Madhusūdana on earth is none other than the Supreme Hari, the god Kapila' (*Mbh.* III: 45: 25). In the Sāgara episode this Kapila is identical with Vāsudeva (*Mbh.* III: 106: 2). This identification of Nārāyaṇa with Kapila, found only in the third book of the *Mbh.*, is perhaps due to the influence of the Bhāgavata school to whom Kapila was the fifth incarnation of Viṣṇu.

In the Dvāpara age Kṛṣṇa, a full incarnation of Viṣṇu, joined hands with Indra's son Arjuna. We are reminded of the *ṚV* description of Viṣṇu as friend and ally of Indra (*ṚV* I: 23: 19). Indra, even in the *ṚV* and the *Brāhmaṇas*, had more human attributes than divine—the brave fighter, the wily and crafty general, the Soma-drinker and the philanderer, the gay and mighty hero, with unmistakable human traits even when he was praised as a god. But Viṣṇu had no human counterpart, he was a god from the beginning, symbolizing the sun's disc in its power, brilliance and celestial course. We remember the creation of Gilgamesh the solar hero: 'Two-thirds they made him god and one-third man' (*The epic of Gilgamesh*, Penguin edn. p. 59). In the incarnation in the *Mbh.* Viṣṇu as Kṛṣṇa is more divine than human. Arjuna, son of the man-like god Indra, is a man with superhuman zeal and courage as well as with divine weapons. One remembers the creation of Enkidu. Aruru, the goddess of creation 'dipped her hands in water, pinched off clay, she let it fall in the wilderness, and noble Enkidu was created' (*ibid.* pp. 60–1). The prototype image holds good even in the case of Arjuna, who has more of the mortal in him but is allied to a divine hero and is the direct descendant of Indra.

At Arjuna's request Kṛṣṇa reveals his divine identity as he does to nobody else (*Mbh.* VI: 54, XII: 328). As a solar hero's chief task is to rout enemies, Kṛṣṇa of the *Mbh.* is engaged in the task of defeating the wicked sons of Dhṛtarāṣṭra, although he does not fight them himself. As the hero of the *HV*, however, he fights the demons which he had destroyed in his previous incarnations, but which are now born as mighty demons in various shapes (*HV* I: 54). But in both these works Kṛṣṇa has a human ally, a mighty hero-friend in the *Mbh.* and a hero brother in the *HV*. Kṛṣṇa and Arjuna fighting together are like Indra and Viṣṇu fighting demons and discharging cosmic responsibilities as they are invoked as Indrāviṣṇū in *ṚV* I: 155.

The *ṚV* Viṣṇu is not the overlord in any physical sense; supremacy in the *ṚV* belongs to Indra. Viṣṇu in the *Brāhmaṇas* enjoys prominence on account of his identity with the sacrifice. Thus 'Viṣṇu (is) the highest of the gods' (*AB* I: 1). 'As Viṣṇu he conquers these regions' (*TB* I: 7: 4: 4). He becomes superior to Indra, for Indra is the king of heaven, whereas Viṣṇu is the lord of the three worlds. The *Brāhmaṇas* by interpreting Viṣṇu's three strides pave the way to his sovereignty over the three worlds. In the epics this sovereignty is an established fact. He is mentioned as Trailokyanātha, lord of the three realms (*Rām.* II: 14: 22). He is said to have brought the three worlds under the gods' dominion (*Rām.* VII: 11: 8). One passage tells us of his suzerainty in heaven and his partial incarnation on the earth (*Rām.* VII: 85: 4–7). His superiority to the Vedic overlord Indra is gradually built up. Thus it says that when Indra failed to defeat Vṛtra the gods went to Viṣṇu who promised to enter Indra's bolt; he also entered the foam with which Vṛtra was finally killed (*Mbh.* V: 48). Indra's overlordship is remembered as when Kṛṣṇa says to Arjuna: 'Give the earth to the king as Hari (did) to Śakra' (*Mbh.* VIII: 51: 53). Śiva created Daṇḍa (punishment, or the rod) and after he had destroyed evil with it Brahman gave it to Viṣṇu (*Mbh.* XII: 160), the god in charge of the preservation of the universe.

As a solar hero Viṣṇu had to be king. He was so as Rāma and Kṛṣṇa, the heroes of the *Rām.* and the *HV* which are the *Purāṇas* (i.e. sectarian scriptures) of these gods. In the *Mbh.* the hero's role is divided into three: Yudhiṣṭhira, who stood for eternal humanistic values, dharma; Arjuna, who stood for the Kṣattriya warrior's values; and Kṛṣṇa, who stood for the transcendental spiritual values. In the *Rām.*, however, Rāma embodies the Kṣattriya and humanistic values in his own person.

This kingship of Viṣṇu becomes apparent through his relation with the earth. The earth in Indian mythology is not the mere expanse of land, but its vegetation, wealth and prosperity. Hence she is Śrī (cf. the cognate Latin word 'Ceres' corresponding to the Greek 'Demeter') in a material shape. This Śrī belonged to Indra in the later Vedic literature; the *Purāṇas* also record this. In the epics and *Purāṇas* we hear of an infinite number of Indras, and Śrī passes from each to the next ruler. In the *Purāṇas* Śrī and Pṛthivī are mentioned as Viṣṇu's wife. They both symbolize kingship and prosperity in the abstract, conceived as a woman. The *Mbh.* episode of Indrāṇī suffering at the hands of Nahuṣa, the usurper king of heaven, because Indra had been deposed (*Mbh.* V: 11 ff.) is the precursor or perhaps the reflex of this concept: this Indrāṇī anticipates Lakṣmī. In the *Rām.* we are clearly told that Lakṣmī holding the lotus is the wife of Madhusūdana (*Rām.* II: 13: 8). Lakṣmī, like Venus, rose from the sea, thus establishing Nārāyaṇa's connection with the sea. In Phoenician mythology, too, 'El...appears...as a sun-god. He had a wife Asherat-of-the-sea, conceived of...as the mother-goddess' (Donald Harden, *The Phoenicians*, p. 82). The concepts of Lakṣmī as a goddess of wealth and of Śrī as a goddess of prosperity (of the soil and harvest) are blended in one epiphany presented as the sun-god's wife. Śrī is said to follow her husband (*Rām.* II: 60: 17). The transition of Śrī from Indra to Viṣṇu, too, seems to be indicated in one passage (*Rām.* II: 60: 13). Sinīvālī is said to be Viṣṇu's wife in *AV* VIII: 46: 3. Thus we know that the earth changed hands. Once Pṛthivī approached the assembly of gods soliciting redress for the heavy burden she was forced to bear. Viṣṇu replied, that Duryodhana would cause the weight to diminish (through slaughter and carnage) at Kurukṣetra (*Mbh.* XI: 8). The *HV* has a variant of this episode. The earth feels the pressure of too many men and too much evil on her and appeals to the gods for relief. She narrates the story of Madhu and Kaiṭabha. We hear that Jāmadagnya had offered the earth to Kaśyapa to whom she had complained and asked for a worthy husband. Then she was offered to Manu and later to the Ikṣvāku line. Worthy rulers became rare, so she came to Viṣṇu for relief. Nārada tells Viṣṇu that all the demons he (Viṣṇu) had killed in the Dvāpara age have been born again on the earth so a full incarnation is called for. Thus it is assumed that Viṣṇu as the prototype of kings is the husband of the earth. Kingship, as we know, is an attribute of the solar god, and so Viṣṇu is the true lord and husband of the earth. After Indra's decline he inherits the earth as the solar successor and rescues and enjoys her in different incarnations.

In the *ṚV* Viṣṇu is an ally of Indra, but a minor ally, for Indra was the more powerful hero. Indra and Viṣṇu together constitute the earliest Indian prototype of Nara-Nārāyaṇa, for the *ṚV* Indra is conceived as almost a human hero, whereas the *ṚV* Viṣṇu has nothing human about him; he is a divine ally of Indra (*ṚV* I: 23: 19). In the *Brāhmaṇas*, with Indra's gradual decline and Viṣṇu's rise, the tables are turned and Viṣṇu steadily advances to the forefront. In the epics, Indra is assigned a very limited task and position and Viṣṇu in his different incarnations is the major figure. The Vedic friendship of Viṣṇu and Indra is still remembered; Rāma with Lakṣmaṇa is like Viṣṇu and Vāsava, i.e. Indra (*Rām.* VI: 79: 40). When Viṣṇu is approached by Indra for the killing of Vṛtra, Viṣṇu says that he and Vṛtra are sworn friends, so he cannot kill Vṛtra himself but lends one-third of his power to Indra for the task (*Rām.* VII: 85: 4–7).

As Viṣṇu-Kṛṣṇa's stature grew in mythology it became necessary to assert his supremacy over Indra. Thus in the *HV* we read Māyāvatī says to Pradyumna, 'your father (i.e. Kṛṣṇa) is superior even to Indra' (*HV* II: 104: 28). But Indra had commanded the allegiance and respect of an entire people too long to be summarily dismissed. Thus a sort of compromise was forged by calling Viṣṇu Upendra (i.e. minor Indra). Indra was called Mahendra (Indra the great). This name occurs in the epics (*Rām.* I: 1: 6). As the youngest of the Ādityas he is called the younger brother of Indra, perhaps because he ascends the throne after the mythological death of his elder Āditya (= solar) brother Indra. The *HV* calls Viṣṇu the younger brother of Indra (*HV* I: 42: 5).

Whether Viṣṇu enjoyed a separate cult as Viṣṇu is not very clear from the scriptures, but that the various incarnations, especially the later ones, became centres of cultic rituals is clear. In the *ŚB* we read, 'Viṣṇu (obtained for his share) one-third...the Yajus are Viṣṇu' (*ŚB* IV: 6: 7: 3); also the

Soma cult belongs to Viṣṇu (*ŚB* III: 5: 3: 15). Later, as Rāma, Kṛṣṇa and Buddha, Viṣṇu became the central figure of many cults. Pebbles smoothed and rounded by the river Gaṇḍakī are called Śālagrāma, stone symbols of Nārāyana and are worshipped as substitutes for images.

As a sectarian god the most powerful rival of Viṣṇu was Rudra. This rivalry was absent in the Vedic literature, where both were minor gods. From the time of the later *Brāhmaṇas* they came to have cults of their own. But in the epics where both rise to prominence the rivalry becomes sharp and irreconcilable. As both sects drew more and more followers, each found it profitable to invent myths in which the god of the rival sect paid homage to its own. Thus of the Suvarṇākṣatīrtha we hear that there Viṣṇu had worshipped Śiva for the latter's favour (*Mbh.* III: 82: 16). The entire thirteenth book of the *Mbh.* is fraught with the sectarian rivalry expressed through anecdotes in which Śiva and Viṣṇu vie with each other for power and prominence. Sectarian proselytizing activity must have been carried on with fierce rivalry at this period.

Later some kind of harmony emerged. Thus in the *HV* we read that these two gods are essentially one (*HV* III: 73: 5).

Viṣṇu is called Śipiviṣṭa in *ṚV* VII: 99: 6. Sāyaṇa interprets the term as 'residing in (the solar) rays'. The term occurs in *TS* II: 4: 5, IV: 4: 9, VII: 3: 15; *MS* II: 2: 13 and is used as an appellative of Viṣṇu. The *ŚB* too calls Viṣṇu Śipiviṣṭa in XI: 1: 4, 3. The meaning of the term is not clear, but as the sun symbolizes procreative energy, *śipi* may perhaps be explained as 'in the male organ' (*śip* in the locative singular, *śepa* and *śepha*, the male organ, may be derivatives from it). This would be a spiritual equivalent of the liṅga cult of the rival sect.

Viṣṇu's solar antecedents are clear from his many associations—Garuḍa, serpents, the lotus and gold. The *Vedas* do not know Garuḍa although we hear of the 'divya suparṇa' (the divine bird). This bird steals or carries Soma. The sun is easily conceived of as a bird which flies across the sky. The Soma-stealing bird becomes, in later mythology, the nectar-stealing Garuḍa. The *Mbh.* gives us the story of Garuḍa; his father was Kaśyapa, and his mother Vinatā, sold in slavery to Kadrū, the co-wife. Garuḍa was sent by his mother to fetch nectar, the price of her freedom. He meets Viṣṇu in the sky and is offered a boon. Garuḍa chooses to stay on top of Viṣṇu and in return offers Viṣṇu a boon. Viṣṇu asks Garuḍa to be his mount. A compromise is arrived at, Garuḍa does become Viṣṇu's mount but Garuḍa's image is placed on Viṣṇu's ensign; hence he is called Garuḍadhvaja (*Mbh.* I: 29).

When Sumukha the Nāga's span of life was increased by Indra, Garuḍa resented the gesture for he felt cheated of his food. While he boasted before Viṣṇu, the latter leaned slightly on him and he fainted immediately. This convinced him of Viṣṇu's infinite superiority (*Mbh.* v: 103).

Garuḍa lived on snakes, and in this he performs the same task as Viṣṇu does, for Viṣṇu in his incarnations is also a killer of demons, especially of serpent-demons. The struggle between the eagle and the snake is a symbolic representation of the struggle between the solar hero and his adversary. Thus Garuḍa the mount of Viṣṇu becomes an ornithomorphic form of Viṣṇu himself, just as the bull is a theriomorphic epiphany of Śiva.

These two aspects of Viṣṇu, his Garuḍa manifestation and his relationship with the serpent are found together in the Mexican god Quetzalcoatl, a pre-Nahua god of the sun, who is borne on serpents over the sea (cf. Viṣṇu in the sea reclining on the serpent Ananta) with the eagle and the serpent as his emblem. In the Pinturas he is shown as stepping down from the sun. In Mithraism, too, 'mythology made the raven the servitor of the sun' (Franz Cumont, *The mysteries of Mithra*, p. 155). The theme is very old and in almost all mythologies we have accounts of this struggle. 'The heavenly bird ravaging the serpent symbolized...the victory of the patriarchal masculine heavenly order...over the female principle', says Zimmer (in *Myths and symbols in Indian art and civilisation*, p. 74). More than that, in the sun-bird's victory over the serpent we have the victory of the solar god over the lunar hierophany, for the serpent is an inseparable association of the chthonic and lunar group of gods: Śiva, Durgā, Yama, Nirṛti and Varuṇa.

Viṣṇu kills the serpent, and that is his prime achievement. This feat is not ascribed to the Vedic Viṣṇu, it is a special trait of the epic god. But Viṣṇu's relationship with the serpent is apparently ambiguous, for the *Mbh.* and the *Purāṇas* describe him as sleeping on Vāsuki's head under the ocean. Thus we read in the *Rām.* of 'Viṣṇu rising from his serpent-bed' used in a simile. The *PGS* says that the celestial serpents belong to Sūrya (II: 19: 9). Thus Viṣṇu, a solar god, is naturally connected with celestial serpents. In Indian mythology he is connected with aquatic, especially marine serpents. The association of the solar god with serpents is a common theme in all mythologies. 'The sun and the serpent appear to have been everywhere connected with sea, rivers, lakes and in fact with the waters generally' (C. F. Oldham, *The sun and serpent*, p. 52).

Once Viṣṇu's association with the ocean became an established fact, the serpent image became a natural corollary, especially as the rolling waves rushing towards the shore actually look like a myriad-hooded serpent. To say that the supreme spirit dwells in the bottom of the ocean, passively reclining on the many-hooded Endless (Ananta) serpent, is in mythological language to associate him with the ultimate potential energy and the unfathomable mystery of the universe. The picture evokes the latent and potential energy which lies dormant between two creations (Kalpa). 'This multi-headed snake is an animal counterpart of the anthropomorphic sleeper himself. It is named Endless (Ananta) also the Remainder (Śeṣa)' (H. Zimmer, *Myths and symbols in Indian art and civilisation*, p. 62). In Buddhist mythology, too, we have a parallel in the Mucalinda serpent, the prodigious cobra 'with the expanse of his giant snake-hood he sheltered as an umbrella the blessed head' of the Buddha.

Viṣṇu is connected with the lotus both conceptually in mythology and iconographically in sculpture. He holds a lotus in one of his four hands; from his navel rises a lotus-stalk on which Brahman was seated. Mārkaṇḍeya saw Viṣṇu as a child on a lotus-leaf. His wife Lakṣmī is seated on a lotus. The dhyānamantra (the image for meditation) says: 'Viṣṇu should be conceived as (residing) in the solar disc seated on a lotus'. The lotus as well as the conch-shell have aquatic and solar associations. One remembers Horus as a child seated on a lotus-flower, and Horus, too, has solar bearings.

Gold also directly symbolizes the sun. Viṣṇu is invariably well decked out in ornaments in iconography. This is indicative of kingship. The dhyānamantra, too, says 'Nārāyaṇa should be imagined as golden-bodied wearing gold ornaments, bangles, ear-rings, a diadem, and a gold chain around his neck'. The sun-god's association with gold is borne out by the Greek myth of Phoebus Apollo of whom we read: 'The braided band around the swaddling clothes was of gold...Delos shone golden and the island blossomed...the foundations of Delos turned to gold and all day the round pool on the island shone golden. The leaves of olive turned to gold...The river Inopus overflowed with gold' (C. Kerényi, *The gods of the Greeks*, p. 134). The only difference between the Indian myth and the Greek is that while Viṣṇu has gold on his person, Apollo turns everything to gold. Both the myths seem to be based on the golden sun-beams at whose touch all creation turns into gold.

CHAPTER 15

KṚṢṆA

THE Viṣṇu-concept reaches it culmination in Kṛṣṇa because, as Kṛṣṇa, his anthropomorphism is most complete, full-blooded and hence most convincing and emotionally satisfying. The *HV*, which aims at creating a Kṛṣṇa-Purāṇa (just as the *Rām.* is a Rāma-Purāṇa, and the *Mbh.* is the blue-print of the Kṛṣṇa-Purāṇa of the *HV*), largely succeeds because it creates a fully human and yet fully divine hero—a hero who is born, grows up, fights, marries, loves and finally dies. Each phase satisfies the soul's craving for one particular hierophany, to satisfy particular inclinations of individual needs. Moreover the Kṛṣṇa cult is a point where various cults converge.

The *CU* mentions Kṛṣṇa, son of Devakī, a Brahmin student. This is perhaps the earliest reference to Kṛṣṇa. Kṛṣṇa's birth is supernatural. The *Mbh.*, the *HV* and the *Bhāgavata Purāṇa* give a complete biography of Kṛṣṇa. His supernatural birth is nothing unusual—all solar heroes have miraculous birth. Christ is immaculately born, the Buddha, Kṛṣṇa, Rāma, Apollo and other Western solar gods are all miraculously born. In the Armenian epic of David of Sasun, Sanasar the hero was born miraculously of a virgin mother, Lusik. Most of these heroes' lives are threatened in infancy. Kaṃsa threatened Kṛṣṇa's life, Herod Christ's, Pharaoh's law Moses', and Balor threatened Lugh the Celtic solar-hero's life. Perhaps the sun rising suddenly out of the dark night appears as an unaccountable and mysterious creation which in these myths has been translated into miraculous births.

After their births most solar heroes are abandoned. Kṛṣṇa was taken to the cowherd quarters, Karṇa to the charioteer Adhiratha, Bhīṣma was left on the banks of the Gaṅgā, Moses among the bulrushes. This abandonment is necessary because the hero in order to evoke pity, awe and wonder must be shown in his heroic isolation; it adds more glamour to his heroic feats. 'More than once we find a god actually represented as a baby abandoned by his mother and reared either by a supernatural being, such as a nymph, or by some beast which suckles him' (A. J. B. Wace and F. H. Stubbings, *A companion to Homer*, p. 473). We remember Zeus suckled by the goat Amalthea, and Kārttikeya (the demon-killer and hence faintly resembling the solar gods) reared by nymphs.

The solar hero has two supreme tasks: on the physical plane he is the dragon-killer, and on the spiritual plane he is a deliverer. Usually the solar hero is an infant prodigy with wondrous feats to his credit, for he is frequently a boy-god. Thus Hermes is a boy-god. Christ defeats his seniors in a theological discussion as a boy. Moses kills an Egyptian as a boy. Sanasar and Pal'tasar, the Armenian solar culture-heroes have feats to their credit while yet mere boys, David kills Goliath while yet a boy, Samson performs feats while quite young. Arjuna, Karṇa and Rāma are infant prodigies who kill monsters or perform wonderful tasks before they attain manhood. Kṛṣṇa in one of his important hierophanies is a boy-god. Louis Renou in his *Religions of India* says: 'Most of the Indian themes, apart from that of asceticism, are found in this complex legend (of Kṛṣṇa) which alone provides a consistent narrative of the hero's "enfances", like the mediaeval "chansons de geste"' (p. 64). The *HV* which gives a full biography, tells us of his various infant feats: he kills the ass Dhenuka, the bull-demon Ariṣṭa (II: 20), the horse-demon Keśin (II: 24), he destroys the twin Arjuna trees (yamalārjuna), slays demon Pralamba, kills the monstress Pūtanā (or Śakunī, II: 23) the elephant-demon Kuvalāyapīḍa (II: 29), the demon Cāṇūra (while Balarāma kills Muṣṭika, II: 30). He tears the rope with which he was bound and hence was called Dāmodara (II: 27). He also fought and subjugated the serpent Kālīya; but his greatest deed was his slaughter of Kaṃsa.

In these episodes perhaps we 'have the accounts of the subjugation of some of the lower cults by the higher one which was soon to be accepted as authoritative by the orthodox Vedic section of the people' (J. N. Banerji, *op. cit.* p. 102). Various cults with theriomorphic gods prevalent among pastoral people, perhaps with totemic worship of the ass, the bull, the snake and the elephant, the indigenous people's dendrolatry (symbolized perhaps by the Yamalārjuna episode, as Mackay suggests), ophiolatry (as symbolized by Kālīya), ornitholatry (as perhaps symbolized by Śakunī) are all crushed by the rising cult of Kṛṣṇa. The people's faith in various kinds of demons had to be canalized, Kṛṣṇa the solar god had to be shown as vanquishing the forces of darkness. Through these feats the new god was presented as supreme in power and rank. Vegetation-worship, and beast-worship, the dark and fearful cults of ghost-and-demon worship, all bowed to this new manifestation of the solar god.

In the *Mbh.* we read that when Bhagadatta hurled the Vaiṣṇava weapon at Arjuna, Kṛṣṇa bore it and it became a garland on his chest (VII: 28). The *Purāṇas* tells us that Kṛṣṇa rescued his teacher Sandīpana's dead son from Yama after defeating the latter. The *HV* says that Kṛṣṇa fought and defeated Jvara in Bāṇa's capital Śoṇitapura and finally granted him a boon: divided into four Jvara enters all creation (*HV* II: 123). Kṛṣṇa was about to kill Bāṇa but dissuaded by Umā he let the demon live on after cutting off his thousand arms. Kṛṣṇa also defeated King Pauṇḍra who attempted to usurp his position at Dvarakā (*HV* III: 94). He also killed the boastful Kaṃsa (*HV* III: 128).

Of Kṛṣṇa's feats two deserve greater attention—Kālīya and Pūtanā—because these have greater significance. Kṛṣṇa fought the fierce snake Kālīya who lived in the Yamunā, defeated him and permitted him to escape to the sea. The account is found in the *HV*, the *Viṣṇu* and *Vāyu Purāṇa* and mentioned in the *Mbh.* and other *Purāṇas*. Description and iconography have made the image of Kṛṣṇa vanquishing and trampling over the serpent vivid and lasting. This image of the sun-god defeating personified evil in its most widely acknowledged form corresponds to an archetypal pattern and is, therefore, the richest in evocative power. Thus Apollo's destruction of the Typhaon, Thretaona's victory over Azi Dahâka, Keresâspa's conquest of the sea-monster Gandarewa and the Christ-child's conquest of the serpent-dragon (Rev. xiii).[1] In actuality the Kṛṣṇa cult's victory over an old snake cult may have inspired the Kālīya tale.

This tale has a variant in the infant Kṛṣṇa's slaughter of Pūtanā. Kṛṣṇa was threatened with death in infancy when the female monster Pūtanā offered him her poisoned breast, but he sucked the life out of her. We find a prototype for this in the female monster Kuṣavā seeking to kill the new-born Indra. One remembers Typhaon or Python, the serpent-monster destroyed by Apollo at Delphi.

> The Python which guarded the shrine and which was slain by Apollo was symbolic of this primitive goddess. Thus a pre-deistic snake-cult, indigenous also in Minoan Crete, was drawn into the cult of the Delphic Apollo; and according to the legend, Pytho was so called from the rotting serpent. (R. F. Willets, *Cretan cults and festivals*, p. 268.)

This element of putrefaction connected with Typhaon (i.e. Python) is first given by Hesiod:

> Now rot here upon the soil that feeds man!...here shall the Earth and shining Hyperion make you rot...And the holy strength of Helios made her rot away there; wherefore the place is now called Pytho and men call the lord Apollo by another name, Pythian, because on that spot the power of piercing Helios made the monster rot away. (Hesiod: Homeric hymn to Pythian Apollo, ll. 363–9.)

[1] Rā defeating the serpent-headed Seban and the snake-fiend Nâk, as Marduk vanquishing Tiamat, and Heracles the water-snake Hydra, all belong to feats of this category.

This element of rot or poison is symbolized by the poisoned breast of Pūtanā.

One notices the similarity in the names of Pytho and Pūtanā. They both mean rotting and putrefaction which is destroyed by the sun and both Apollo and Kṛṣṇa are solar heroes.[1]

Apollo's or Kṛṣṇa's feat of slaying Pūtanā or Python even while he was an infant is thus a symbolic account of the sun's victory over what is evil or putrid.

The sun-god in his youth usually goes out and wins a bride and sometimes he goes on winning many brides. The *HV* describes Kṛṣṇa's marriage with Rukmiṇī after he had stolen her (II: 59–60). Besides Rukmiṇī Kṛṣṇa married many other wives (II: 60: 36, II: 41–3); and besides the wives we hear of innumerable cowherdesses with whom he was in love (*HV* II: 20).

We are told Lakṣmī coveted Kṛṣṇa's frame and was his wife (*HV* II: 33). In the *Purāṇas* we are introduced to Rādhā as his favourite cowherdess (*Vāyu P* CIV: 52). In the *Bhāgavata Purāṇa* this side of Kṛṣṇa's character receives fuller attention, but the *Bhāgavata Purāṇa* is rather late. In the Pahaḍpur sculptures of the Gupta age we have Kṛṣṇa's Gopikāvilāsa depicted, so that the myths were already established by the fifth or sixth century A.D. Bhāsa in his Bālacarita gives an account of the erotic sports of Kṛṣṇa, and Bhasa belongs to the early centuries A.D. The *Viṣṇu P* depicts Kṛṣṇa's amorous dalliances. We are reminded of Apollo dancing with the Muses.

One remembers the Greek sun-god Apollo in a similar role. Hesiod in the *Hymn to Delian Apollo* says: 'there the long-robed Ionians gather in your honour with their...shy wives', 'the girls of Delos, handmaidens of the Far-shooter', 'Shall I sing of you as wooer in the fields of love, how you went wooing the daughters of Azan'. (*Theogony*, Loeb edn. pp. 333–6.) Ovid in his *Metamorphoses* mentions the Sun's love for Leucothoe, who corresponds to the beautiful Rukmiṇī. In chapter IV of the *Metamorphoses* we hear of the many wives of Apollo—Daphne, Kyrene, Biobeis and Koronis—and are reminded of the many wives of Kṛṣṇa.

The solar god is a vegetation-god and is mostly polygamous and this indicates the fertility aspect of the sun, hence both Indra and Kṛṣṇa are shown as husbands of many wives and lovers of many women. Kṛṣṇa is the father of many children, too.

[1] Both *Pytho* and *Pūtanā* are derived from a root from which is derived *Pūti* which means 'rotting'; it has cognates in other languages, too. Thus the Zend has the root *pu, puiti*; Greek *púon, putho*; Latin, *pus, puteo*; Lithuanian, *púti*; Gothic, *fúls*; Germanic, *Faul*; English, *foul*.

Kṛṣṇa, unlike his solar predecessors, dies, but in Viṣṇu there is the anticipation of the manner of Kṛṣṇa's death. The *ŚB* gives a full account of Viṣṇu's death. 'Taking his bow, together with three arrows, he stepped forth. He stood, resting his head on the end of the bow. (The gods sat thinking. The ants were suborned by the gods to gnaw the bowstring.) When it was cut, the ends of the bow, springing asunder, cut off Viṣṇu's head...on falling it became the yonder sun' (XIV: 1: 1: 4–10). This account is found in *TA* V: 1 ff. and *PB* VII: 5: 6–16. In the *PB* version Makha, instead of Viṣṇu, is the god's victim. But 'makha' means sacrifice and Viṣṇu is the sacrifice. Indra, Agni and Rudra kill him because of his inordinate pride. Makha means 'sacrifice' and Viṣṇu is equated with the sacrifice, so the *PB* tale is but a variant of the *ŚB* account.

The *Mbh.* and *HV* describe Kṛṣṇa's death in a different manner. The Yadu line had been cursed with extinction by three sages. At Balarāma's death Kṛṣṇa sat meditating; a hunter, Jarā, pierced Kṛṣṇa's feet by mistake, but afterwards, recognizing the hero, repented. Kṛṣṇa left his body and entered heaven where he was greeted by the gods. Jarā, a cognate of the Greek *Geras*, means old age. Now, the natural explanation would be Kṛṣṇa died of old age, but in the Vedic tales Viṣṇu's death anticipates this end of Kṛṣṇa: in both he is attacked unawares and is prematurely killed.

In the *ŚB* account Viṣṇu's solar character is specifically brought out because it says the severed head became the sun. One remembers the burning pyre where Heracles perished which symbolized the setting sun. The *Mauṣalaparvan*, a late book, makes Kṛṣṇa become Viṣṇu at death, thus establishing his solar character.

One remembers similar deaths of Achilles, Sigurd and Samson and it becomes clear that solar heroes do not die natural deaths, but are always 'killed by others'.

E. M. Butler in *The myth of the magus* says that the ritual hero has ten stock features of which many are applicable to Kṛṣṇa. Thus he has supernatural origin, with portents at birth, perils menacing him in infancy (Pūtanā), initiation, wanderings, a magical contest (cf. Kaṃsavadha and the Kuvalayāpīḍā episode), trial or persecution (by Kaṃsa and his followers), a violent or mysterious death and resurrection or ascension (cf. the *HV* account of his ascent to heaven).

One remembers one brief, almost passing, reference to a Kṛṣṇa, a demon in the *ṚV* (VIII: 85: 13–15) who lay hidden in the river Aṃśumatī and whom Indra slew. Thus we have the nucleus, cultic and mythological, of a hostility between Indra and Kṛṣṇa. There may have been demon, i.e. aboriginal, sects who worshipped Kṛṣṇa, an enemy tribe subjugated by the Vedic Aryans.

> [They] held sacred the Naga or hooded serpent, sometimes represented with many heads...their religious dances, their sacrificial rites...their communication with the deities through the medium of inspired prophets...their use of tribal emblems or totems...seem to connect them with the very early civilisation Turanian or otherwise—which we find amongst so many of the peoples of extreme antiquity. They had, in fact, much in common with the early inhabitants of Babylonia and perhaps even more with those of Elam and the neighbouring countries. (C. F. Oldham, *The sun and the serpent*, pp. 54–5.)

Thus the *ṚV* account may have preserved the memory of an actual contest between the Aryan invaders with Indra as their general and an ancient tribe with Kṛṣṇa as their leader-god.

Kṛṣṇa describes himself as the younger brother of Indra (*HV* II: 68: 33). Nārada says he has come to see the younger brother of Mahendra, the most illustrious among the sons of Kaśyapa (*HV* II: 69: 24). This fact of Kṛṣṇa's being the younger brother of Indra has a twofold importance: mythologically he is presented as the final Messiah, the ultimate fulfilment of the Indra-theophany, and cultically a new god usurps the worship of Indra and the solar gods. Thus the *HV* account of Kṛṣṇa fighting the Indra-cult, instructing the cowherds to abandon the old ritual and to worship the mountain and cattle, is only a record of the superimposition of the new Vāsudeva-Kṛṣṇa cult on the old, worn-out Indra-cult. Kṛṣṇa inherits most of Viṣṇu's Vedic epithets; thus he is Gopā (cf. Viṣṇu so-called in *ṚV* I: 22: 18), Śipiviṣṭa (Visnu in *ṚV* VII: 99: 5, 6) and Dāmodara (Viṣṇu in *Baudhāyana Dharma Sūtra* II: 5: 24).

Vaiṣṇavism, which carries on this new tradition in practice, has certain distinctive features of its own. It is quiet, the ritual consists of fruits, leaves, flowers and water given 'with devotion' (*Mbh.* VI: 31: 22, XII: 257: 10). The god accepts it because of the devotion. This form of worship is entirely non-Vedic, it avoids sacrifices and its strong predilection for non-violence precludes offerings of living creatures. This new mode of worship is essentially epic-Purāṇic; i.e. it is seen in a nebulous form in the epics and is clearly defined and established in the *Purāṇas* when Neo-Brāhmaṇism assumed its final shape in Hinduism.

This Kṛṣṇa is a sectarian god, and the only other god who commanded the worship of another sect was Śiva, hence Kṛṣṇa fights Śiva as a rival. In this struggle there were short-lived truces and temporary alliances, even capitulation of one god before the other. Thus the thirteenth book of the

Mbh. is full of accounts of the struggle where victory changes sides frequently. The *HV* says that Viṣṇu and Śiva are ultimately one (II: 125), again Kṛṣṇa is praised by Śiva as the supreme principle almost in the vein of the Viśvarūpadarśana (*Gītā*, ch. XI) and bows before him (*HV* III: 88). But the issue is never finally clinched and the struggle remains undecided. In spite of attempts at coalition the gods remain separate and distinct, perhaps because they symbolized different sectors of life and commanded homage from different types of devotees.

Incarnation is a special feature of the Viṣṇu-Kṛṣṇa hierophany. In Greece the sun-gods are many—Helios, Apollo Aesculapius, Phaeton and Hyperion are all different aspects of the sun and some are the sons of the others. But in the solar gods of the Indian pantheon we have real incarnation of Viṣṇu in a gradual upward incline: fish, tortoise, boar, man-lion, dwarf and then three legendary and one historical figures with another yet to come.

There seems to have been at least two influences on the growth of this concept of incarnation, and the first of these is Buddhism. The *Jātakas* were mostly ancient folk-tales that were appropriated by Buddhism through an influence of the Vaiṣṇava concept of divine incarnation. In early Buddhism there was the idea of the Buddhas of the past, who in earlier cosmic cycles came to earth to lead men to salvation. Thus Vaiṣṇavism and Buddhism influenced each other in framing the Jātaka stories and moulding the avatāra-myths. Archaeology gives us data for the earliest representations of Viṣṇu's incarnations only from the Gupta age. The *Jātakas* go back somewhat earlier in time, so that during the early centuries A.D. there was brisk interchange of ideas which became operative both in Hindu and Buddhist mythology. The theory of avatāras, incarnation, is a product and characteristic of the Pāñcarātra sect. Vāsudevism had two kinds of votaries: the orthodox Brāhmaṇical followers and the Ābhīras from central India, together with the Magas and Śakas. The orthodox sections's attempt at harmonizing the various approaches to the supreme god—the different philosophical positions, emotional responses and intellectual ratiocinations—is found in the *Bh.G*, and herein lies the secret of its tremendous appeal and impact. The non-orthodox un-Brāhmaṇical section gave rise to the five Vṛṣṇivīras, Vāsudeva, Balarāma, Pradyumna, Aniruddha and Śāmba, and wove a sectarian doctrine around these semi-legendary figures.

The other formative influence on the development of the incarnation theory is the wide acceptance of the theory of rebirth. Viṣṇu became an objective demonstration of the same spiritual essence being manifested in different bodies—the lower forms of life (fish, tortoise, boar) assumed by him became an affirmation of metempsychosis on the human level. Incarnation and metempsychosis seem to have interacted, each confirming the other. Whereas a man is reborn because of his own spiritual shortcomings, Viṣṇu was reincarnated to redeem man and creation. This again brings out his sun-god-deliverer role, as he himself states in the *Gītā* that he descends to rescue the good and to destroy evil. We hear that he has had many incarnations and will yet have many more (*HV* I: 41: 10–11).

The chief difference between Śiva and Viṣṇu is that Śiva, except in some exclusively sectarian and late texts, does not promise final release. We have seen how men and women received boons from him which bear fruit in the next life (on earth) thus connecting him with chains of existence; while Viṣṇu's devotees approach him for and receive from him release from saṃsāra—i.e. rebirth. One significant episode makes this very clear: Ghaṇṭākarṇa, a demon, had appeased Śiva and begged for release from Saṃsāra. Śiva refused and said only Viṣṇu could grant it. He praised Viṣṇu, attained samādhi (the final stage of yoga), saw Viṣṇu transfigured, and praised him henotheistically giving a summary of his different incarnations, emphasizing the significance of the Kṛṣṇa incarnation (*HV* III: 80–82). All solar gods are redeemers, or we could reverse the statement and say all redeemer-gods are shown as having solar traits. Viṣṇu-Kṛṣṇa, Mithra, Marduk, Rā, Christ, Buddha, Zarathustra and some heroes with solar characteristics like Heracles, Sanasar, Pal'tasar Mher, David of Sasun, Phokr Mher, Karṇa, Arjuna, Moses, Noah—they are all both solar heroes and redeemer figures.

These figures are all culture-heroes, around whom a people weave their spiritual and material experiences and aspirations. They both symbolize and inspire a people's progress by mobilizing and channelling their vital energy. They are thus solar gods, signifying vegetation, growth, cultivation, stock-breeding and prosperity on the material plane, man's fight against darkness and the forces of evil, his struggle and victory over disease, decay, death, indigence and decrepitude, and his craving and attainment of the Ultimate Light and Truth; his release from bondage—on the spiritual plane. Their message is: 'I am the Truth, the way, the life, no man cometh unto the Father, but by me', as Christ stated it; or 'Leave all religions and follow me, I shall redeem thee' (*Gītā* XVIII: 66) as Kṛṣṇa formulated it. We also remember the *Matsya Purāṇa* instruction: 'desire release from Janārdana' (LXVIII: 41) or the statement in *Viṣṇu P* which says, 'who ever obtains release without worshipping Vāsudeva?' (XI: 4: 18). An entire people project their hopes and aspirations on to such a hero, concretize him through myths and legends until the apotheosis is complete and then he becomes their 'ideal ego', their dream-self and can mould their communal life through his rich and complex hierophany.

Jainism teaches the cyclical movement of time, i.e. history. Civilization deteriorates till at certain points of history the Saviour appears, who significantly enough is also the first king. He teaches mankind the necessary arts of writing, arithmetic, cooking or pottery-making and preaches the Law. After him comes another age of progressive deterioration followed by the rise of another Saviour. This theory contains some reflection of real history which agrees with the concept of 'avatāras' or culture-heroes who appear at critical junctures of history to raise civilization to the next higher stage.

Kṛṣṇa's hero-figure was given the Saṃvartakahala, ploughshare, the Saunanda muṣala, the Śārṅga bow, the Kaumodakī club, the Syamantaka and the Kaustubha gems, the Pāñcajanya conch-shell, the Sudarśana disc—all these are divine weapons, so that he is divinely equipped, but his prowess, courage, enterprise and feats are described in a human fashion and he becomes the meeting point of the divine and the human. And this again is an essential feature of culture-heroes and solar redeemers. Of all of them it can be said 'the Word was made flesh and dwelt among us and we beheld his glory, the glory as of the only begotten of the Father, full of grace and truth' (John i. 14).

Viṣṇu and Kṛṣṇa taken together have much in common with the Greek solar hero Heracles. In vague outlines Viṣṇu-Kṛṣṇa is associated with lion (nṛsiṃha), boar (varāha), serpent (Kālīya, Vāsuki), horse (Keśin), the cattle (of the cowherd king) and elephant (Kuvalayāpīḍa). The elephant is substituted by the bull of Minos in the case of Heracles, he also is connected with the Nemean lion, the Erymanthian boar, the Hydra serpent, the horses of Thracian Diomedes and the cattle of Geryoneus, and although the actual feats differ in details, the symbol of vanquishing rival cults may have formed the substratum beneath both the Greek and Indian myths.

The Vāsudeva-Kṛṣṇa cults seems to have originated among pastoral folk, and his amorous career has a typical flavour of pastoral love-poetry. He is pre-eminently a cowherd, and no myth of the *HV* and the *Bhāgavata Purāṇa* loses sight of his earthly origin. Thus he belongs to a community of stock-breeders, is dressed like one of them, behaves like one of them, their interests are dear to his heart, and he fights demons and enemies primarily on their behalf. And yet all this is sublimated into a superb allegory, for he is called Govinda (lit. the obtainer of cattle), and we are told that above manuṣyaloka (the world of men) is devaloka (the world of the gods), above that is Brahmaloka (the world of Brahmins) and even above that is the highest region, Goloka (the world of cattle), beyond which there is no region. This world is ruled by Kṛṣṇa because he gave shelter to the cows (*HV* II: 19: 30).

Thus Kṛṣṇa is clearly conceived on two levels of significance—on the human, regional and historical level he is the cowherd-hero, and on the spiritual level he is the supreme being. And these two layers of meaning tend mutually to enhance each other's significance. His feat of holding Mount Govardhana (lit. the increase of cattle), is another case in point.

The *Saṃhitās* present the indistinct sketch of a potentially great god, the *Brāhmaṇas* magnify his stature by equating him with the sacrifice, the most important and potent social action, but it is only in the epics and *Purāṇas* that his figure is purposefully built up as that of the supreme being. The purpose was supplied by sectarian motives and interests. He is described as the author of numerous feats, the demon-killer, the king, hero leader and the god of paramount importance. The supreme being must be shown as the author of cosmic deeds, and the epic-Purāṇic Viṣṇu is the preserver of the universe. Thus after the deluge of annihilation, Mārkaṇḍeya saw Nārāyaṇa as a boy sitting on the leaf of a banyan-tree; inside his body was the world. Nārāyaṇa revealed his true identity; the supreme one in whom is contained the other worlds (*Mbh.* III: 187, XII: 161). Viṣṇu created the four castes (*Mbh.* XII: 200: 31, 32), thus he is shown as the foundation of the social system as well. He alone knows Brahman (*Mbh.* XII: 203: 21). Sanatkumāra at Uśanas' request describes Viṣṇu to Vṛtra: he is the all-powerful creator and Preserver. Immanent, all the gods inhere in him, all the guṇas too (*Mbh.* XII: 271). He is the twenty-fifth principle of Sāṃkhya, according to the hierarchy of the Sāṃkyha principles (*Mbh.* XII: 291: 37), this again establishes his supremacy. At Arjuna's request Nārāyana reveals himself as the god who has been described and praised as supreme from *ṚV* downwards (*Mbh.* XII: 328). All the other gods are but partial manifestations of him; he is both immanent and transcendental. As Vāḍavamukha Viṣṇu is the creator of the sea, the largest expanse on the earth (*Mbh.* XII: 329: 48). He *is* the Ātman (*Mbh.* XII: 334: 7). Viṣṇu offered three piṇḍas (food to the Manes) in the hope that Pitā (father), Pitāmaha (grandfather) and Prapitāmaha (great grandfather) should be created for enjoying the piṇḍas (*Mbh.* XII: 334); this indicates that there was no Being beyond Viṣṇu, ancestors had to be created because he was the First Cause. He came out of Brahman's ears as the latter was contemplating creation, taught Brahman laws, especially the Sātvata law. He is self-created (*Mbh.* XIV: 40: 9). We hear of a fire that escaped from Kṛṣṇa's body, burnt a mountain, touched Viṣṇu's feet in heaven and returned to Kṛṣṇa (*Mbh.* XIII: 139). Later Kṛṣṇa's gracious glance restored the mountain to its former shape. In *Mbh.* XIII: 147–9 Śiva sings a hymn praising Viṣṇu as the supreme lord.

The Syamantaka gem, like the Kaustubha, is a symbol of the sun and in the *HV* Kṛṣṇa considered himself as its rightful owner (*HV* I: 39). His transfiguration before the demons (*HV* I: 42: 21–8) led to their defeat. Indra paid a compliment to Kṛṣṇa when the Govardhana hill was raised by the latter, saying he (Kṛṣṇa) was suppressing his full brilliance (*HV* II: 19: 18). He had been white in the Kṛta age, red in Treta, yellow in Dvāpara and dark in Kali (*HV* II: 71: 31). This makes Kṛṣṇa co-eternal with the Eternal Essence, for he was there through all aeons. Śiva praises him as the supreme lord (*HV* III: 88). He offered the *Vedas* to Brahman (*HV* III: 72: 77). He is the prime dispenser of release (*HV* III: 79). Brahman appoints him as the remover of the earth's distress (*HV* I: 51). He is Hari (the redeemer) in all ages, Vaikuṇṭha among the gods and Kṛṣṇa among men (*HV* I: 42: 1). He has been all the gods (*HV* I: 42: 3–5). His capacity is infinite and his functions and achievements are many and varied. He is the author of cosmic acts and yet among the cowherds he tends cattle and fights for their well-being. Thus a figure is presented whose supremacy becomes unchallenged, because he has been so many things through the ages. Achievements which cannot be packed into one lifetime have been distributed among the different incarnations. Indra the ruler of heaven, the leader of armies, divine and human, has almost disappeared in the period when Viṣṇu-Kṛṣṇa's figure is being played up. Indra, together with the other gods, is said to have attained heaven through Kṛṣṇa's favour (*Mbh.* VI: 21: 16). He is even described as the supreme creator out of chaos (*Mbh.* VI: 31); Nārāyaṇa-Kṛṣṇa, the god in the *Mbh.*, is described as the primeval creator (*Mbh.* VI: 63), even Prajāpati worshipped him.

Slowly a figure emerges who is unrivalled in the epic pantheon. Before his supreme grandeur Śiva pales, for Śiva had no incarnations and hence his feats are less numerous, his manifestations are limited, less varied and amazing. Viṣṇu's feat of destroying the six Asura towns or Ṣaṭpura (six cities; described in *HV* II: 82–5) is clearly introduced to raise him above Śiva who destroyed only three (tripura).

Viṣṇu's brilliance is described in the sectarian sections of the *Mbh.* Thus we hear that Kṛṣṇa's brilliance would equal that of a thousand suns rising simultaneously in the sky (*Mbh.* VI: 33: 12). Kṛṣṇa says of himself that he is quadruple-formed, existing for the well-being of creation; one form meditates on the earth, another watches the world performing good and evil deeds, yet another performs actions in the world of men, the fourth sleeps for a thousand years (*Mbh.* VII: 28: 23–5).

Viṣṇu, like Indra, is the master of magic power, māyā, We are told that māyā is born of Viṣṇu's body (*HV* I: 50: 32). Sleep which envelopes the world becomes Viṣṇu's māyā when he wakes to destroy evil. Māyā is equated with sleep in *HV* I: 50: 33. Thus his association with magic power is actually an association with sleep but this sleep is personified in *HV* as supernatural energy or power in a feminine shape who escaped from Kṛṣṇa's body (*HV* I: 50: 27). The early solar prototype of Viṣṇu in his early Āditya phase was also connected with Māyā, the magic creative power. Māyā has always remained the monopoly of the central solar god. The solar gods are all associated with magic power and it may not be quite accidental that the Buddha's mother was called Māyādevī. V. R. Ram. Ch. Diksitar, in his article 'Kṛṣṇa in early Tamil literature', says that there was an old god of the herdsmen called Mayon or Mayavan (= the black god) who like Kṛṣṇa was associated with the flute and cattle and whose birth star was Rohiṇī (*IC*, 1937–8). The name 'Viṣuṇa' (a dialect form of Viṣṇu) means 'changing' and thus connects him with māyā.

Viṣṇu's relationship with Brahman is extremely ambiguous. Once Nārāyaṇa says, 'Half of my body is the Universal Grandfather; I am Nārāyaṇa by name who holds the conch-shell, the disc and the mace' (*Mbh.* III: 187: 38). Mythology has it that Brahman was created from the navel-lotus of Viṣṇu, which attaches greater importance to Viṣṇu. This, as we shall later see, is the product of the Vaiṣṇava sects' rise to power; but whatever the cause may be, it led to Viṣṇu's aggrandisement, for Brahman, otherwise conceived as supreme, is made subservient—at least etiologically dependent—on Viṣṇu.

> Thus Viṣṇu having risen to the position of the Highest Being and being revered as the creator, protector and destroyer of the gods and the universe is, apart from his avatāras and heroic exploits in destroying the enemies of gods and men, in the epic and puranic mythology, constantly praised on account of the yeoman's service he always renders to the world: he restores peace by destroying all evil. (J. Gonda, *Aspects of early Viṣṇuism*, p. 121.)

Thus through his power of being incarnated (and hence frequently visiting the earth to remove its distress) Kṛṣṇa enjoys superiority over Brahman and Śiva.

But part of his power is derived from his equivocal relationship with Brahman: he is Brahman, a creature of Brahman, and when necessary, the creator of Brahman.

Bhakti (devotion), images, temples, personal attachment to one incarnate form or another, communal democracy (cf. castelessness), ecstatic experience, music and the predominance of aesthetic ritual, dance—all these characterize the Viṣṇu-Kṛṣṇa cult. Some are shared by the Śaiva cult, too, but together they are symptoms of the epic-Purāṇic religion—worship of a visible image, and approach through devotion. On the other hand, when Vedānta leaned towards a compromise formula with a less abstruse approach to reality, when from the rarified atmosphere of Absolute Monism Advaita philosophy stooped to Dvaitādvaita or Dvaita level, it joined hands with Vaiṣṇavism. For the *HV* Bhāgavata-Kṛṣṇa, Rādhā symbolized the second principle necessary for duality; interpreters came forward, Jīvātman and Paramātman were formulated and found symbolized in the couple, and the image became an archetype. Māyā, the wife or feminine principle of Viṣṇu, took the place of Māyā of Vedanta and once again we approach the suppressed equation of Brahman and Viṣṇu.

PART III

GODS OF THE BRAHMAN GROUP

CHAPTER 16

COMPONENT VEDIC GODS

FUNCTIONALLY Brahman is the first god of the Indian trinity, for he is the creator. The concept of Brahman as one god can only be inferentially gathered from the *ṚV*, it is not categorically stated, defined or named. The *ṚV* actually has many gods which contributed to the growth of Brahman, the other *Saṃhitās* presented some others, the *Brāhmaṇas* put forward still others and finally the epics and *Purāṇas* saw some gods declining, others growing, changing and developing till the mythological Brahman emerged. In the present work we are concerned with the masculine Brahman (i.e. Brahmā), the creator-god of the epic-Purāṇic triad.

BRAHMAṆASPATI

The earliest sections of the *ṚV* know a Brahmaṇaspati, the lord of prayer. To him are addressed prayers like: 'Present the sacrificer to the gods as you did Kakṣīvat, son of Uśij' (*ṚV* I: 18: 1). He is invoked with Dakṣiṇā (sacrificial fees). He utters mantras in which the gods dwell; he also helps the devotees in all his endeavours (*ṚV* I: 40: 5–8). Prayers for protection are addressed to him (*ṚV* II: 23: 5). In *ṚV* II: 23 he is invoked (together with Bṛhaspati in alternate verses) for victory. Tvaṣṭṛ created him as the supreme overlord (*ṚV* II: 23: 17); he shook the firm mountains and weakened trees (*ṚV* II: 24: 3). He is identified with Brahman (*MS* II: 2: 3). The Aṅgirases, created by Brahmaṇaspati, recovered cows stolen by the Paṇis, they also destroyed the latter's dwelling place (*ṚV* II: 24: 6). In the later books of the *ṚV* Brahmaṇaspati becomes increasingly rare. This power of prayer personified by Brahmaṇaspati seems to be the precursor of the power of sacrifices as embodied in the Apūrva of the *Pūrva-mīmaṃsa*. Brahmaṇaspati, as the lord of prayer, is half an abstraction, a power which ensures the result or effect of the sacrifice, we are reminded of Bhīmācārya's definition of Apūrva—the virtue (or power) born of sacrifices which creates (i.e. leads one to) heaven.

Bṛhaspati or Brahmaṇaspati has eleven hymns addressed to him and is mentioned 170 times. His rise is concomitant with Varuṇa's decline. Brahmaṇaspati's appearance is like that of Agni's—he is pure and beautiful in form with a ruddy appearance, has a clear voice, seven mouths, a beautiful tongue, sharp horns, a hundred wings, and holds an iron axe (*ṚV* VIII: 29: 3) in his hands. He is said to be born of a great light and thunder in the highest heaven, and is himself the progenitor of the gods. His bowstring is Ṛta.

The *AB* makes Brahmaṇaspati the god of the hymn 'I invoke the lord of the Gaṇa's'. This description of Brahmaṇaspati as Gaṇapati naturally reminds us of the epic-Purāṇic Gaṇeśa who became the dispenser of success in men's endeavours, thus reflecting the original function of Brahmaṇaspati who ensured the success of sacrifices. Gaṇapati and Kārttikeya are but two facets of the same hierophany, they are both lords of 'gaṇas' and in South India Kārttikeya is called Subrahmaṇya. The name recalls Brahmaṇaspati's and may really be an echo of the Vedic god's name.

The personification in Brahmaṇaspati is weak. The physical description is hardly vivid and is primarily directed to emphasizing his brilliance and sanctity. He fades out even in the *ṚV* literature, and his place is taken by other gods. Another minor god is Sadasaspati (*ṚV* I: 18: 6), the lord of the assembly (at a sacrifice); he is perhaps just another name of Brahmaṇaspati. Without Sadasaspati a sacrifice cannot be offered. Agni and Indra are usually meant by this appellative.

BṚHASPATI

Bṛhaspati is one of the two major Vedic precursors of the epic-Purāṇic Brahman. He is the chief offerer of prayers and sacrifices and is, therefore, of the priestly order. He is the Purohita (priest) of the gods with whom he intercedes for men. Bṛhaspati or Vācaspati as he is called in some later texts is an abstraction of priesthood as Brahmaṇaspati is of prayer. In the *ṚV* he sometimes figures as an almost concrete person. He heard Trita calling out to him from a well (*ṚV* I: 105: 17). This is a corroboration of the concept of being 'the power of prayer' and the priest is the official channel of communal prayer. In some hymns Brahmaṇaspati is just another name for Bṛhaspati. Bṛhaspati rides a cow called Viśvarūpā (*ṚV* I: 161: 6). *ṚV* V: 43 describes him as Nīlapṛṣṭha, Hiraṇyavarṇa and Vedhas (blue-backed, golden-complexioned and the creator). In this description we have a clearer glimpse of him. He is the blue-tipped golden flame of the sacrificial fire. Gold belongs to Bṛhaspati (*MS* I: 8: 6). This connects him with the solar gods, especially with Viṣṇu.

Bṛhaspati destroyed enemy cities and won wealth (*ṚV* VI: 76: 2, 3). He is called Anarvaṇa, the irresistible (*ṚV* VII: 97: 5); he recovered two-thirds of the cows stolen and hidden by the Paṇis, for the remaining third hidden in darkness he created the sun (*ṚV* X: 67: 4, 5). Prayers are offered to him for crossing evil and danger, also for peace and prosperity. He dispenses peace to the sacrificer (*ṚV* X: 182: 1). *ṚV* hymn X: 71, a late hymn, extols him as the supreme principle. All plants, fruitful and fruitless, flowering and flowerless, are created by Bṛahaspati (*ṚV* X: 97: 16); he also created medicinal herbs (*ṚV* X: 97: 19). In the *AV* the upper direction is made Bṛhaspati's (*AV* XII: 4: 57). He is an Aṅgirasa (*AV* XI: 10: 10) and is also called Atharvan, father, friend of the gods, the creator of all, to him oblations should be offered (*AV* IV: 1: 7). 'Bṛhaspati is the holy power (Brahman) of the gods' (*TS* I: 5: 4). 'To Bṛhaspati he (the sacrificer offers an oblation in the house of the Brahman priest; the sacrificial fee is a white-backed animal' (*TS* I: 8: 9). We hear of 'Bṛhaspati of speech' (*TS* I: 8: 10). A prayer says 'O Bṛhaspati, instigator, awake him...when, O Bṛhaspati, thou didst free from life yonder, from Yama's enmity, the Aśvins removed death from him' (*TS* IV: 1: 7). 'Bṛhaspati was the purohita of the gods' (*MS* I: 11: 5). Many passages equate Bṛhaspati with Brahman (*AB* I: 4: 3, II: 3, IV: 5: 17). The gods did not acknowledge Indra's supremacy until Bṛhaspati performed the Dvādaśāha sacrifice on the latter's behalf (*AB* IV: 3: 19). Bṛhaspati is the god's Brahman (priest) (*TB* I: 3: 8: 4; *TS* III: 7: 6: 3). In this aspect he resembles the creative word, *logos*. This 'word' is, in Indian mythology, the sacrificial formula which calls forth the cosmos out of chaos. It is this word which is Vāc, the Mānasakanyā of Brahman, who came out of the latter's head (i.e. thought). With her he committed incest and created. In other words this was the creative word. Bṛhaspati as the potent power behind the sacrificial formula is the lord of this word; he is vācaspati (*TB* I: 7: 4: 7, II: 6: 19: 2), the hotṛ of ten hotṛ priests (*TMB* III: 12: 5: 1). He has an alternate name, Brahmaṇaspati (*TB* III: 11: 4: 2). Clothes should be offered to him (*TMB* I: 8: 10). One prayer says 'Let Bṛhaspati bestow upon you the heat of Agni and the brilliance of the sun' (*TMB* I: 3: 7: 5). Bṛhaspati desired to become the divine priest and became one through the Bṛhaspatisava (*TMB* XVII: 11: 4).

The clue to Bṛhaspati's identification with Brahman is supplied by the *ŚB*, which says 'Bṛhaspati is the Brahman' (*ŚB* X: 2: 3: 3) and 'the Brahman is the sacrifice' (V: 3: 2: 4). The ascendency of Bṛhaspati is most clearly noticeable in the *ŚB*. 'Bṛhaspati for speech' (V: 3: 5: 31), 'to Bṛhaspati belongs the upper regions' (V: 5: 1: 12). The *GB* says, 'Bṛhaspati is Aṅgirasa, the Brahman (priest) of the gods' (*GBU* I: 1, I: 4). The *JB* says

Bṛhaspati 'was' the priest of the gods (I: 125). Brahman is identified with Agni and Bṛhaspati (*ŚB* IX: 2: 3: 3), by him is creation accomplished (*MS* III: 4: 3). The *JB* in a rather striking anecdote somewhat modifies the story of Sūryā's wedding, for, we are told, Prajāpati intended his daughter Uṣas for Bṛhaspati, then the gods competed in a tournament for her; the Aśvins won her (*JB* I: 257). Here Uṣas takes the place of Sūryā, and Bṛhaspati that of Soma.

In the epics and *Purāṇas* the picture changes considerably, for there we have two distinct personalities: Bṛhaspati, the priest of the gods, and Brahman, the grandfather. This Bṛhaspati, priest of the gods, is the most intelligent (*Rām.* II: I: 24, IV: 54: 4). He is not only the gods' priest, but their counsellor, too, especially Indra's (*Rām.* II: 4: 22, IV: 54: 4). He treated the gods whom the demons wounded in battle, and restored the dead to life with magic spells (*Rām.* VI: 26: 3). His son was Kuśadhvaja and daughter Vedavatī, who became incarnated as Sītā in order to ruin Rāvaṇa because the latter had caught her hair (*Rām.* VII: 17). In the *Mbh.*, too, Bṛhaspati figures as the divine priest and counsellor. His son Kaca went to Uśanas (Śukra), Bṛhaspati's opposite number among the demons, to learn the art of reviving the dead. The episode indicates a slight fall in Bṛhaspati's prestige, for formerly he himself knew the art, but now has to send his son to the enemy's camp to learn the magic art. Droṇa, who was the priest and adviser of the Kauravas, entered Bṛhaspati after his death.

Keith, in his article 'Brahman' (*Jha Comm.* vol. 1937), says that it is improbable that he (Bṛhaspati) is the 'lord of the high heaven', because the word seems to be a late formation and probably denotes rather 'the lord of prayer' like Brahmaṇaspati. From *ṚV* I: 18 and X: 182 Bṛhaspati seems to be the same as the Narāśaṃsa fire. Bṛhaspati's deification is a product of the *Brāhmaṇas* and it was arrested after that period, for in the epic-Purāṇic literature he is merely the gods' priest and adviser. His status was higher when identified with the sacrifice, i.e. the sacrificial fire and the power of prayer; then he was more an abstract spiritual force and less an actual priest.

TVAṢṬṚ AND VIŚVAKARMAN

Tvaṣṭṛ or Viśvakarman definitely belongs to the creator-group of gods. Tvaṣṭṛ is derived from the root *tvakṣ* which has a parallel in *Avesta* and which later became the root *taks*, meaning to form or fashion. He fashions forms (rūpa) of creatures and this sense is expressed in Viśvakarman (the all-fashioner) too. He, Tvaṣṭṛ, created Brahmaṇaspati (*ṚV* II: 23: 17), his hands are skilful or dexterous (*ṚV* III: 54: 12). He carries an axe in his hand, probably because in those days timber was more in vogue as building material. His prime function is to express or reveal the forms of all creatures (*ṚV* I: 189: 9; *TB* I: 8: 1: 2). Vāyu is Tvaṣṭṛ's son-in-law (*ṚV* VIII: 27: 22). Tvaṣṭṛ is almost invariably connected with the wives of the gods (*ṚV* X: 64: 10, X: 66: 3). One is reminded of his Greek and Roman parallel Hephaestos' affair with Ares' wife Aphrodite. In the Āprī hymns Tvaṣṭṛ is prayed to for children (*ṚV* X: 81, 82). He is invoked for helping the pregnant woman, presumably to fashion and deliver the child (*AV* VI: 81: 3). He created the bride and the bridegroom (*AV* VI: 78: 3; *TB* III: 7: 4: 3). This is as is expected, for the creator-god who creates 'forms' also creates the couple who will ensure the continuity of the species. He is also the father of Vivasvat's wife Saraṇyū, the mother of various species of creatures. Viśvarūpa was Tvaṣṭṛ's three-headed son. He promised sacrificial shares openly to the gods, and secretly to the demons (to whom he was a cousin). Frightened at this, Indra struck his heads off, but bore the guilt for a year (*TS* II: 5: 1). The name Viśvarūpa, as also Viśvarūpā the cow, his *ṚV* mount, associates him with Viśvakarman, Tvaṣṭṛ's *alter ego*. Viśvakarman is identified with the all-embracing Prajāpati (*MS* I: 3: 34). Prajāpati became Viśvakarman after he created the universe (*AB* IV: 8: 18; *ŚB* VII: 4: 2: 5, VIII: 2: 3: 13). Viśvakarman was the first creator (*TB* I: 1: 1: 5); he is sometimes described as the ubiquitous, illimitable, immanent principle. He is lord of the sense-organs and of creation (*ṚV* X: 82: 1), is called Dhātṛ and Vidhātṛ and is identified with the supreme spirit (verses 2, 3). He created and named the other gods, therefore his true identity is unknown. He is above heaven and earth, gods and demons. Thus Viśvakarman is raised to the supreme god's rank. The above passage reads like the transfiguration passage in the *Gītā* (ch. XI) and may well be the prototype for the later passage. The creative principle is extolled in the most glowing language in these hymns, and it is the climax in Viśvakarman's mythological career, for afterwards he dwindles into comparative insignificance.

Viśvakarman Prajāpati is 'not merely the material cause but also the efficient cause of the world' (H. G. Narahari, *Atman in the pre-Upanisadic Vedic literature*, p. 114).

Tvaṣṭṛ gradually becomes the lord of all creation, animate and inanimate. Thus he is the lord even of fuel (*TB* III: 11: 4: 1). To him should be offered the multiform (dappled?) animal, for he is the author of the change in form of creatures (*TMB* IX: 10: 3). Viśvakarman was given a potsherd in sacrifice for completing the sacred work of slaying Vṛtra (*ŚB* II: 5: 4: 10). Human offerings are also to be made to Viśvakarman (*ŚB* VI: 2: 1: 5). Mares are offered to Tvaṣṭṛ by anyone desiring progeny, for in that shape Prajāpati, desiring to create, saw the second pair (of creatures) (*GBU* II: 1).

This creator-god of the *Vedas* dwindles in importance in the epic-Purāṇic literature where creation becomes the specific task of Brahman, and Tvaṣṭṛ disappears leaving Viśvakarman in a clearly minor and subordinate position. The epic-Purāṇic Viśvakarman fashions this man's bow (cf. Agastya's, *Rām.* III: 8: 37) and that man's chariot. He planned and laid out Laṅkā, Rāvaṇa's capital, as well as the palace of the monkey-kingdom of Vālin and Sugrīva. Maya, the Viśvakarman of the demons, was his opposite number just as Uśanas (or Śukra) was Bṛhaspati's. Yudhiṣṭhira's palace at Indraprastha was constructed by him. The epic Viśvakarman is an artificer, like the Vedic Ṛbhus, and is perceptibly shrunk in stature. He has nothing in common with the creator-gods.

PRAJĀPATI

The most important epiphany of Brahman is found in his Prajāpati aspect. As early as the *ṚV* he is styled Prajāpati, the lord or preserver of creatures. In the *ṚV* the epithet is applied to Savitṛ, Soma, Agni and Indra. Later it came to indicate a god with control over procreation, a supreme god. In the epic-Purāṇic period it indicated both the sectarian gods Śiva and Viṣṇu. Still later the term meant also the ten primeval progenitors created by Brahman—Marīci, Atri, Aṅgiras, Pulastya, Pulaha, Kratu, Vaśiṣṭha, Pracetas or Dakṣa, Bhṛgu and Nārada. In Purāṇic and classical literature Prajāpati is a name of Brahman.

In the *ṚV* Prajāpati appears in the late tenth Maṇḍala. He too is supplicated for children (*ṚV* X: 85: 43). Dakṣiṇā is Prajāpati's daughter. Hiraṇyagarbha, the son of Prajāpati, is the seer of hymn *ṚV* X: 121. The hymn begins with the praise of Hiraṇyagarbha, but ends with a prayer to Prajāpati, 'O Prajāpati, creatures are not outside thee, give us the things we desire, may we become lords of wealth' (*ṚV* X: 121: 10). Hymn X: 130 is ascribed to Yajña, son of Prajāpati, and the god invoked is said to be Prajāpati himself. But the hymn itself does not mention Prajāpati, it expresses doubt and wonder regarding the act of creation and seeks in it a symbolic interpretation of the sacrifice and the incantatory spells. It also seeks to imagine a primordial sacrifice from which creation stems. Similarly hymn x: 121 usually known as Prajāpatisūkta, because Sāyaṇa explained it thus, mentions Hiraṇyagarbha. Sāyaṇa's interpretation is based on an equation of 'Ka' with Prajāpati. But that is clearly untenable if only on grammatical grounds, for, the refrain reads, to which god should we offer oblations? And if 'Ka' meant Prajāpati there would be the noun-inflexion (kāya) instead of the pronoun-inflexion which is actually used. The hymn thus expresses doubt and has no direct bearing on Prajāpati. One reason is that Prajāpati as a distinct god had not yet emerged; the tenth maṇḍala sees his shadowy beginnings; it was in the *Brāhmaṇas* that he really assumes full dimensions.

The *TS* sees the gradual rise of Prajāpati. 'Prajāpati is unlimited' (I: 7: 3), 'Prajāpati's world is called Vibhān' (I: 7: 5). 'Cattle belong to Prajāpati; their overlord is Rudra' (III: I: 5). 'The eye of Prajāpati swelled, that fell away, that became a horse' (*TS* V: 3: 12; *ŚB* XIII: 4: 2: 3). 'His is the horse' (*TB* I: I: 5: 5). 'Indra was, as it were, loose and unfixed. He ran up to Prajāpati; he gave him this (rite) of fifteen nights as a bolt' (*TS* VII: 3: 7). 'His forms in animals are (called) Śipiviṣṭa' (*MS* I: 11: 19). 'The other gods are exhausted, Prajāpati alone is unexhausted' (*MS* IV: 8: 9). 'He should be worshipped before the other gods' (*TB* II: 8: I: 4). It is in the *YV* that we are told of Prajāpati's incest with his own daughter Uṣas (*MS* IV: 2: 12). 'Prajāpati conceived a passion for his own daughter—either the Sky or the Dawn' (*ŚB* I: 7: 4 ff.). 'Prajāpati felt love towards his own daughter, some call her the sky, others, Uṣas. Having become a stag he approached her in the form of a deer. The gods saw him. They condemned it and put their most dreaded forms together. The name contains Bhūta; he chose the overlordship of cattle. He pierced Prajāpati who flew upwards. The female deer was Rohiṇī. His seed fell; the gods said "mā duṣa" (pollute not), it became mānuṣa (man). They surrounded it with Agni, the Maruts blew upon it; Agni Vaiśvānara caused it to move. The first part of the seed became Āditya, the second part Bhṛgu, him Varuṇa took; the third part became Aṅgiras in that the ember after being quenched blazed forth again, Bṛhaspati came into being' (*AB* III: 33: 34). Prajāpati became 'Kavi' through the Nivid chants (*AB* II: I: 10).

Sāyaṇa's interpretation of Prajāpati as 'Ka' is based on an *AB* passage 'After the slaughter of Vṛtra, Indra told Prajāpati that he, Prajāpati, would be what Indra was. Prajāpati said "Ko'ham" (who am I?) Indra replied, "you shall be what you said" (i.e. 'Ka', who; *AB* III: 10; *ŚB* IV: 5: 6: 4). The passage may also be interpreted as 'Prajāpati's identity will remain an enigma'.

Prajāpati arranged a tournament for the suitors for Savitṛ's daughter Sūryā's hand (*AB* IV: 6). After creation Prajāpati became Viśvakarman. The gods' subservience to Prajāpati is brought out when he is said to have anointed Indra, King Soma, Varuṇa, Yama and Manu (*AB* VIII: 3). He created gods and demons, but not Indra. The gods asked him to create Indra. He said 'you create him with meditation'. They meditated and saw Indra within them and asked him to be born. He asked them 'what shall be my portion?' They offered time, men and animals. He asked them to offer these in a sacrifice to him. He was born of that sacrifice (*TB* II: 2: 3: 3–5). Prajāpati created the demons and was not pleased, hence the dull gold. Gods pleased him, hence the bright gold (*AB* II: 2: 4: 4–5). Besides human offering he is to be given elephant, boar and grains (*TMB* I: 8: 15). The elephant connects him with the Purāṇic Viśvakarman and the boar with Viṣṇu. Human offerings are to be given to Prajāpati (*TB* II: 2: 5: 3). He is the father of the gods, the progenitor of men, the lord of all the world (*TB* II: 8: 1: 3; *JB* III: 135). Rohiṇī is said to be Prajāpati's wife. He desired her and instituted an offering to Prajāpati and Rohiṇī of old (*TB* III: 1: 4: 2). Prajāpati is called 'a friend', 'the protector of the world, may he deliver us from sin' (*TB* III: 7: 7: 2). The gods offered Prajāpati in a sacrifice (*TB* III: 9: 22: 1). He is for all the gods and is ineffable and sovereign (*TMB* XIX: 12: 3; *JB* II: 86).

His creative act is raised to loftier altitudes in the later *Brāhmaṇas*. 'I shall be many and reproduce; he saw the atirātra sacrifice, offered it, and created day and night' (*TMB* IV: 1: 4). A constant refrain in the *Brāhmaṇas* and in the *Upaniṣads* is that Prajāpati was All in the beginning; he desired to become many for creation; (there is or was) only one god, the self-created Prajāpati (*JB* III: 341, I: 68–9). 'Prajāpati became pregnant with all beings. Whilst they were in his womb, evil, death seized him.' With the help of the gods he freed these beings from evil (*ŚB* VIII: 4: 2: 1–2). He created men and animals at Brahman's behest who told him to create and preserve. He offered himself in a sacrifice, but the gods clamoured for their shares and finally agreed to a competition thus creating the ājya (*TMB* VII: 2: 1). He who offers the Vājapaya sacrifice attains Prajāpati (*TMB* XVIII: 6: 4).

Agni went away from the gods and entered the water. The gods said to Prajāpati:

Go thou in search of him! to thee his own father, he will reveal himself. He became a white horse and went in search of him. He found him on a lotus-leaf, having crept forth from the water. He eyed him and he (Agni) scorched him, hence the white horse has as it were a scorched mouth, and indeed is apt to become weak-eyed... He is Prajāpati, he is Agni, he is the sacrificer...He is made of gold, for gold is light and fire is light; gold is immortality. It is a man, for Prajāpati is the man. (*ŚB* VII: 3: 2: 15; VII: 4: 1: 18.)

One notices that Prajāpati's identification with Viṣṇu is suggested by finding Agni on a 'lotus-leaf' and assuming the shape of a white horse (the horse is the sungod Viṣṇu's symbol). The *TB* identifies him with fire; Prajāpati is Agni. Viśvakarman is Agni (*ŚB* IX: 2: 3: 3). The *JB* identifies him with Indra, the sun and time (*JB* III: 372: 386, I: 167, II: 56), and with Puruṣa and the year. Gradually he is identified with the eternal entities. Thus, we hear, he is the sky, he is death (*JB* III: 351). He is ancient, hence the heavenly region is old (*JB* III: 286).

The gods discovered the Vājapeya sacrifice and entered a competition as to who should offer the sacrifice. Prajāpati won and performed it and became the lord of his region. At Indra's request he performed it on Indra's behalf and Indra became the oldest of the gods (*TB* I: 3: 2: 1–2). Thus Prajāpati is shown as the bestower of antiquity on Indra. In the beginning there was water in which Prajāpati wished to have a firm foothold (pratiṣṭhā). He created and consolidated this earth. Hence, it was called Pṛthivī (root *prath* = establish). He became the all-enveloping (*JB* III: 318).

'Prajāpati, tired out, saw a lotus-leaf on water and guessed that it must have some support under the water. He assumed the shape of a boar, dived under and found soil, he brought it up and placed it on the lotus-leaf. Then was creation accomplished' (*TB* I: 1: 3: 6). One remembers Viṣṇu's assuming the boar-shape and rescuing the earth from under the cosmic waters in his third incarnation. A further passage suggests Viṣṇu's identification with Prajāpati. 'That man in yonder orb is no other than this gold man (on the altar)...His feet are that gold plate and the lotus-leaf, (that is) the water, and the sun's orb' (*ŚB* X: 5: 2: 6, X: 5: 4: 15). Yet another passage says, 'by the Viṣṇu strides Prajāpati created this world' (*ŚB* VI: 7: 4: 7). A further passage indicates the assumption of this identification of Prajāpati with Viṣṇu, 'as to its being called Kūrma, Prajāpati having assumed that form created living beings and Kūrma (being the same as Kaśyapa), therefore all creatures are said to be descended from Kaśyapa. Now this tortoise is the same as the yonder sun' (*ŚB* VII: 5: 1: 5–6). Thus we notice that the dwarf (cf. the Viṣṇu strides), the boar and the tortoise incarnations are being shared by Prajāpati and Viṣṇu. 'This gold man, below the centre of the first layer, on a gold plate, representing the sun, lying itself on the lotus-leaf...the womb whence Agni springs. And this gold man in the altar is thus no other than Agni-Prajāpati and the sacrificer' (Eggeling's introdn. to the translation of the *ŚB*, *SBE*, pt. IV, vol. XLIII, p. xxiv).

We are told that 'mysterious is Prajāpati' (*ŚB* V: 3: 5: 31). His creative act is variously described. He touched the cosmic egg and said, 'Let it exist, let it exist and multiply'. From it the Brahman (neuter) was first created and the triple science. Hence they say 'The Brahman (n.) is the first born of the All' (*ŚB* V: 1: 1: 10). He is the whole, Brahman (*ŚB* VII: 3: 1: 42). He is both the gods and men (*ŚB* VI: 8: 1: 4); the all-shaper (*ŚB* VIII: 1: 1: 43), he produced creatures (*ŚB* VII: 1: 2: 1). He created men without food and supplied food through some hymns (*JB* III: 148). He is food (*ŚB* VII: 1: 2: 4). Gods and demons were both his children; the demons were the elder and stronger; the gods gained ascendancy over the demons through the Upahavya sacrifice which he provided for them (*TMB* XVIII: 1: 8). Prajāpati found himself alone in the beginning, looked around, saw another who said he was Brahman (n.). Prajāpati proposed they should be together. Brahman refused and said that Prajāpati was sinful, so at Prajāpati's request Brahman cut him in three places which became the cow, dream and shadow. Afterwards he cut him in eight places and Prajāpati became sinless, the sun (*JB* II: 369–70).

Prajāpati ministers to the spiritual needs of men. Men approach the region of Prajāpati sailing by the golden boat of Svadhā. He leads or draws men (unto himself) (*JB* I: 139). He created creatures by the Agniṣṭoma sacrifice (*JB* I: 67), Prajāpati fought with death (presumably on behalf of men); when men perform sacrifices, chant spells and offer oblations they strengthen Prajāpati, when they sing and dance they strengthen death (*JB* II: 69). They fought long till at last Prajāpati performed a sacrifice and won. 'Prajāpati evaded Death (who lay in wait for him) by laying the stoma bricks' (*ŚB* VIII: 4: 4: 2). 'Now one half of that Prajāpati was mortal and the other half immortal: with that part of him which was mortal he was afraid of death and being afraid he became twofold, clay and water, and entered this earth' (*ŚB* X: 1: 3: 2). 'Death scorched him, a brick of clay and water, and the gods made him immortal. Now at the beginning Prajāpati was both these, the mortal and the immortal' (*ŚB* X: 1: 4: 1). 'When Prajāpati was creating living beings, Death, that evil, overpowered him. He practised austerities and conquered evil' (*ŚB* X: 4: 4: 1).

In such passages we have a new concept of godhead, for here is a god who like the Buddha or the Christ came to grips with death, and had to conquer death before assuming power. In his creator-aspect he encounters the opposite force, viz. death, which is called evil and which, like the Avestan Angra Mainyu, challenges the positive creation by a set of corresponding negatives. Prajāpati is the only god who is actually described in his creative activity and has therefore to be shown as grappling with death or destruction, i.e. the negative principle threatening creation. 'He wished to cross death, he did so and ascended via Kāma, Suvar, Suvata and Nāka. These regions can be seen as one sees a higher place by climbing on something high' (*JB* III: 346). 'From the upper vital airs he created the gods and from the lower vital airs the mortal creatures' (*ŚB* VI: 1: 2: 11). 'He was alone in the beginning' (*ŚB* VI: 6: 3: 1). 'The gods and Asuras, both of them sprung from Parjāpati' (*ŚB* I: 2: 4: 8, I: 2: 5: 1). 'After Prajāpati had created the living beings his joints were relaxed. Now Prajāpati, doubtless, is the year and his joints are the junctures of day and night, the full moon and the new moon and the beginning of the seasons' (*ŚB* I: 6: 3: 35).[1] 'The lord of speech is doubtless Prajāpati' (*ŚB* III: 1: 3: 22). 'By speech Prajāpati then again strengthened himself (*ŚB* III: 9: 1: 7), also 'by cattle' (10), 'by priesthood' (11). 'The she-goat is Prajāpati's kind' (*ŚB* III: 3: 3: 8). 'The goat sprang from Prajāpati's head' (*ŚB* VI: 5: 4: 6); 'Truly the he-goat is no other than Prajāpati' (*ŚB* V: 2: 2: 3); 'the goats and sheep are most conspicuously of Prajāpati' (*ŚB* IV: 5: 5: 6). This is perhaps so because Prajāpati is thought of as the creator-god, and these species are noted for their prolificity. One also remembers the *Śvet. U* passage where the creative couple is compared to the goat and the she-goat. Thus 'Prajāpati means productiveness' (*ŚB* V: 1: 3: 13).

'There are thirty-three gods, and Prajāpati is the thirty-fourth' (*ŚB* IV: 5: 7: 2). We are told of the twelve bodies of Prajāpati: the eater of food and the mistress of food, the happy and glorious, the abodeless and dauntless, the unattained and unattainable; the invincible and irresistible; the unpreceded and unmatched (Eggeling's footnote on *ŚB* IV: 6: 9: 21). 'Sevenfold is Prajāpati' (*ŚB* V: 2: 2: 3). Quite frequently we are told that Prajāpati is the seventeenth (principle). All this adds an element of mystery to the concept of Prajāpati. Prajāpati, we are told, is unlimited (*AB* II: 17). 'Kauṣītaki used to say: "the morning litany is Prajāpati, Prajāpati is incommensurable"' (*KB* XI: 7). Thus slowly but surely emerges a figure who is ubiquitous, omniscient, omnipotent and immanent. He is the

[1] In *La Doctrine du sacrifice dans les Brāhmaṇas* (Paris, 1899) Sylvain Levi wrote: 'Prajāpati est le temps; il est aussi le père des deva et des asura' (p. 16). 'La lutte entre eux a comme enjeu l'année. L'essentiel des idées cosmogoniques Mazdéennes est là' (M. Molé, *Culte, mythe et cosmologie*, p. 226).

Dvādaśāha, the Udgātṛ, the Yajamāna, the man in the sun, the man in the soul: 'for him who knows him thus all the *Vedas* and the regions yield the desired objects' (*JB* III: 379). He is Savitṛ, the all-god. When one offers oblations to the all-god they are offered to Prajāpati (*JB* I: 126).

The *GB*, perhaps the latest of the *Brāhmaṇas* (and therefore contemporaneous with the *Āraṇyakopaniṣads*) records the meditation of Prajāpati, 'he created the Brahmaudana (the sacrificial food for the Brahmin) through meditation' (*GB* II: 16).

The *Rām.* gives a list of ancient Prajāpatis: Kardama, Vikrīta, Śeṣa, Suvrata, Vahuputra, Sthāṇu, Marīci, Atri, Kratu, Pulastya, Pulaha, Pracetas, Dakṣa, Vivasvat, Ariṣṭanemi and Kaśyapa (III: 20: 6–9). From these descended the gods, men and all creatures. The genealogies or lists of primeval progenitors are by no means final. Thus Dakṣa, one of these sixteen, had fifty daughters, out of whom he gave eight (or thirteen, according to other accounts) to Kaśyapa another of the Prajāpatis. Of these wives Aditi gave birth to the thirty-three gods—twelve Ādityas, eight Vasus, eleven Rudras and the Aśvins. Prajāpati created the creatures out of water; they asked him what they should do. 'Protect mankind', said Prajāpati; they agreed, said 'rakṣāma, yakṣāma' (we shall protect, we shall sacrifice) and so were created the Rakṣas and Yakṣas (*Rām.* VII: 4: 9–13). When people suffered because Vāyu, angry at Hanūmat's humiliation at Indra's hands, had hidden himself, Prajāpati besought Vāyu on men's behalf and he came out. Prajāpati touched and revived Hanūmat (*Ram.* VII: 35: 53–65, VII: 36: 3–5). Here we notice that Prajāpati's cosmic activities have become less significant. He acts more as an arbiter for gods and men. When something goes wrong he settles the dispute or sees the distressed through their predicament. His stature and functions are limited and consequently the mythological concept becomes indistinct.

In the *Mbh.* Prajāpati is a minor assistant of Brahman and we mostly hear of a number of Prajāpatis who carried out Brahman's command and created the different species. The specific figure of a Prajāpati is no longer remembered, sometimes the name is used as a synonym of Brahman as in Nārada's hymn to Brahman (*Mbh.* XII: 322–4). If there is any real connotation it is bound up with the concept of creation and reproduction. We are told that one can please Prajāpati by raising a family (*Mbh.* XII: 184: 13). There is also a subtle distinction made between Brahman (n.) and Prajāpati. 'Religion characterized by detachment is the eternal Brahman and that characterized by attachment (propagated by) Prajāpati' (*Mbh.* XII: 210: 3, 4). Thus Brahman is abstract while Prajāpati is conceptually more tangible. In the *HV* Āpava Prajapati is mentioned. He is a Manu and his wife is Śatarūpā (*HV* II: 1–3), a conceptual counterpart of Viśvarūpā. Ten Prajāpatis are mentioned in *HV* III: 16. Prajāpati is also mentioned as the archetypal creator (*HV* III: 36: 5).

In order to emphasize Prajāpati's transcendence he is called the seventeenth element beside the sixteen or the thirty-fourth above the thirty-three gods. He is the lord of the three worlds and is yet above them. In *TA* I: 23 we are given an account of the creative process. 'The waters existed as the primeval element, Prajāpati was on the waters, he desired to create, and through fervour created the universe. His first creation was the tortoise, the Puruṣa, who was actually prior to Prajāpati himself. From Prajāpati's cast-off flesh was created Aruṇaketu who took over the task of creation. Because of his desire, meditation and creative fervour Prajāpati is equated with Manas, the mind' (*JB* I: 269; *BĀU* III: 2: 7). In the first stage of the evolution of the concept of Brahman, Prajāpati, Brahman's precursor in the *Brāhmaṇas* discharged the duties of creator and preserver. And this perhaps explains his similarity with Viṣṇu who later became the preserver, for in Prajāpati we have the functions of Brahman (m.) and Viṣṇu combined. 'The Pravargya makes the Mahāvīra pot a symbol of the sun...As the sun is the head of the universe—or in figurative language the head of Prajāpati, the world-man—so its earthly and earthen counterpart, the Mahāvīra pot is the head of Viṣṇu, the sacrificial man and the sacrificer' (Eggeling, *Introduction to the ŚB*). Thus in rituals, too, Prajāpati combines the functions, i.e. the symbols, of Viṣṇu and the prime creator. He belongs to the first phase of the development of Brahman (n.) and is thus less abstract and nebulous and has more mythological potentialities than his successor. As the name indicates, the creation of the different species, of the elements and of the prime progenitors themselves (Prajāpatis)—these are his specific connotation. He meditates and performs sacrifices thus symbolizing both 'yoga' and 'karman'. Later there is a bifurcation into these two as separate approaches. From the first evolved the philosophical Brahman (n.) and from the second, the mythological Brahman (m.).

VIRĀJ

In an *ṚV* passage we read that Virāj was born from Puruṣa and Puruṣa from Virāj (*ṚV* X: 90: 5). One is reminded of a similar creation of Dakṣa and Aditi from each other. In *AV* VIII: 10: 24 and XI: 8: 30 Virāj is a female and is regarded as a cow. Virāj dies mythologically after the Saṃhitā period but is revived in the Vedānta philosophy as an imaginary aggregate of gross bodies. As a base for the production of Puruṣa, Virāj perhaps symbolizes the cosmic waters. Like Brahman Virāj connotes vastness or all-pervasiveness.

Creation is a graded art in early Indian mythologies. Brahman split himself into two principles male and female, and they were united. Out of this union Virāj was born. This Virāj practised austerity (lit. fervour) and created Manu, the prime progenitor of mankind (*MS* I: 32: 33). From Manu came the Prajāpatis. In all the myths Virāj is an intermediary stage in the long creative process. The personification of Virāj was never seriously attempted and thus he remains utterly unconvincing.

HIRAṆYAGARBHA

Hiraṇyagarbha is one of the two or three concrete components of Brahman. The name implies the golden germ (or foetus) and here, too, there is a vague connection with Viṣṇu through the gold-association. Bṛhaspati is described as Hiraṇyapṛṣṭha, golden-backed in *ṚV* V: 43: 12. The only hymn which really launches a separate epiphany of Brahman calling him Hiraṇyagarbha is the late *ṚV* hymn X: 121. Here we are told that in the beginning there was Hiraṇyagarbha, the sole lord of all beings; 'he upheld the earth and heaven—to which god shall we offer oblation?' (*ṚV* X: 121: 1). It goes on to ascribe different stages of creation to him, so that the total 'mythological image' becomes sufficiently amorphous to justify the refrain. His supremacy and sovereignty are emphasized frequently. We are told that he is the supreme god above the gods. The seer of the hymn is Hiraṇyagarbha, son of Prajāpati, and this makes his position a little clearer, for he is second in rank to Prajāpati at least. Hiraṇyagarbha evokes the image of the primordial cosmic egg, which is golden, and out of which was born Brahman the Creator.[1]

[1] The concept of the universe being created from a cosmic egg is found in Egyptian mythology too. 'Ptah...was originally represented in the Memphite theology as anterior to the sun-god Atum...By thinking as the "heart" and commanding as the "tongue" Ptah fashioned an egg on his potter's wheel from which the earth was hatched' (E. O. James, *The ancient gods*, p. 201). Strangely enough the creation of the universe from a cosmic egg is the special function of the supreme god in all mythologies. In Egypt as in India gods did not retain their power eternally and there was a time when Thoth was considered the supreme being. At that time Thoth 'laid an egg on the waters of Nun out of which the sun-god appeared' (*ibid.* p. 205). In China P'an Ku is 'the ancestor of Heaven and Earth and all that live, move and have their being'. '"P'an" means the shell of an egg and "ku" 'to secure', "solid" referring to P'an Ku being hatched from out of Chaos' (E. T. Chalmers-Werner, *Myths and legends of China*, p. 76). The cosmic egg is found in

The egg perhaps connects Brahman-Prajāpati with the swan he rides on in later mythology or his description 'haṃsa' in the *Upaniṣads*. This bird is associated with the sky, the earth and the water, and thus symbolizes creation at all three levels.

'The gander is the animal mask of the creative principle which is anthropomorphically embodied in Brahman...the homeless, free wanderer between the upper celestial and lower earthly spheres at ease in both, but not bound te either. Hence it symbolizes the divine essence' (H. Zimmer, *Myths and symbols in Indian art and civilisation*, p. 48).[1]

The gold recalls Viṣṇu with whom the creator-god is conjointly conceived. The *Brāhmaṇas* do not mention Hiraṇyagarbha as a separate epiphany except as a phase in the complex and graded creative process. The *Upaniṣads* present the various creative-phases of the supreme principle as different manifestations through different divinities (*MU* VI: 8). The *HV* tells us that Hiraṇyagarbha was born from Brahman's mouth as the latter contemplated creation (*HV* II: 36: 2–5).

SKAMBHA

In the *AV* we get another manifestation of Brahman-Skambha. In hymn X: 7 he is called 'the universal support'. We are told that in him inheres all creation, all virtues, properties of things, time, seasons, Ṛta and truth, death and immortality. He is called Puruṣa, Brahman, Parameṣṭhin, Prajāpati, Hiraṇyagarbha and Skambha. Vedic hymns, the gods themselves, past, present and future, all are contained in him.

It is clear that here the transcendental essence of Brahman is presented, but at the same time Skambha the fulcrum is shown to be the stable, eternal, timeless support of all creation. Creation exists because it has an uncreated support. Here Brahman's creator-aspect is not so much

the mythologies of Polynesia, Indonesia, Iran, Latvia, Esthonia and Phoenicia; in the language of mythology the cosmic egg is the equivalent of the metaphysical First Cause. The Samoans relate that the high-god Tangaloa-Langi lived in an egg which he eventually broke into pieces and shed the shell bit by bit. In Tahiti, too, a similar tale of the creator-god is told; he broke the enclosing shell and created the universe out of it. S. Reinach in his *Orpheus* gives an account of a Phoenician myth: 'Chaos, fertilized by divine breath produced two principles, male and female, from which came an egg; this broke and so constituted earth and heaven' (p. 45).

[1] The golden egg recalls the golden orb of the sun. Speaking of the golden egg shaped Ptah, E. A. W. Budge says: 'The god referred to as being in the Egg is of course a form of the Sun-god' (*The Egyptian heaven and hell*, p. 119). Gelo in Egyptian mythology produced a cosmic egg painted as a man with a goose head, with a crown. One notices the points of similarity: the goose association, the solar essence (symbolized by the disc) and supremacy (cf. the crown).

emphasized, but as the universe is conceived as a huge edifice Brahman or Skambha is imagined to be its stable support. The *JB* reflects this notion. It identifies Brahman with the sun, an eternal support of all creation, and calls this manifestation of Brahman time with a thousand pillars; the word Skambha means a pillar. The image as we have noticed is one of an illimitably vast structure which is supported by the eternal entities, like pillars—the sun, time and light which hold creation together and prevent it from collapsing. Skambha is the abstraction of these supports, they are but manifestations of Skambha.

PARAMEṢṬHIN

Parameṣṭhin is an epithet of the supreme principle indicating its rank or region. The name, which literally means 'dwelling in the highest (station)', associates him with Viṣṇu whose 'parama', final or highest station, is frequently mentioned in the *Vedas*. In Viṣṇu's ultimate station is the fountain of honey (*ṚV* I: 154: 5). This aspect of Brahman is therefore merely indicative of his transcendence. Parameṣṭhin is included in the list of the creator-gods who followed Brahman in changing places (*AV* XV: 7: 25). The *AV* mentions Parameṣṭhin more than the other *Saṃhitās* do. All regions belong to Parameṣṭhin. In a prayer for peace and tranquillity we read, 'This goddess of speech Parameṣṭhinī, inhered in Brahman, by whom terror was created, may peace descend through it to us' (*AV* XIX: 9: 3, 4). 'In time is held fervour, in time the primeval, in time Brahman. Kāla, time became Brahman and holds (or supports) Parameṣṭhin' (*AV* XIX: 53: 9). The *ŚB* says, 'Parameṣṭhin Prajāpati was created out of Prajāpati (along with Agni, Indra and Soma)' (XI: I: 6: 14). Also 'Parameṣṭhin was the son of Prajāpati' (*ŚB* XI: I: 6: 16). The reason of this subservience and posteriority of Parameṣṭhin to Prajāpati is perhaps not far to seek. Mythologically Parameṣṭhin did not amount to much, while Prajāpati's stature was increasing in dimension in the *Brāhmaṇas*. Hence the one grew at the cost of the other. Parameṣṭhin, by becoming a son of Prajāpati, was converted—mythologically at least—into an epithet of Prajāpati and raised to the highest rank. In the age of the predominance of sacrifices when Prajāpati was frequently identified with sacrifice his stature would inevitably grow. His rank became exalted and Parameṣṭhin became a descriptive appellation of this exalted station of Prajāpati.

SVAYAMBHŪ

Svayambhū as an epiphany of Brahman is rather late in making his appearance. In the *ŚB* we hear of Brahman Svayambhū who was performing penances. 'He said this much, "Verily there is not perpetuity in austerities; well, then, I will offer up mine own self in creatures and the creatures in mine own self"' (XIII: 7: 1: 1). The result was the Sarvamedha sacrifice in which he offered himself for the creatures and the creatures in his own self. As Brahman is usually described as rising out of a lotus from Viṣṇu's navel, strictly speaking he is not Svayambhū. Hence the *Mbh.* says that Svayambhū created a luminous lotus in which appeared Brahman called Ahaṃkāra, composed of the five elements (*Mbh.* XII: 175: 14–16). This Svayambhū, we are told, is Viṣṇu (verse 20). It is clear that whether the luminous lotus is in his navel or not Viṣṇu is the creator of Brahman, and since he is self-created the epic knows him as Svayambhū. Thus the *ŚB* Svayambhū who was an aspect of Brahman is now equated with Viṣṇu who eclipses several other aspects of Brahman, too.

CHAPTER 17

VEDIC AND EPIC BRAHMAN

PURUṢA, as a manifestation of Brahman, appears in the late *ṚV* x: 90. The hymn is called *Puruṣa* hymn and has cosmological import. We hear of 'a thousand-headed, thousand-eyed Puruṣa who envelops the whole earth and is yet taller by a span' (verse 1). This is a symbolic expression of the god being both immanent and transcendental. 'He is the lord of immortality, he is all that is and all that will be' (2). 'All creation is but a quarter of that Being, three-quarters of him is immortal in heaven—this is his magnitude, his superiority' (3). We remember Viṣṇu whose two strides are visible, but the third belonging to the highest heaven is not, and in that highest region is the fountain of honey. Both these scriptures emphasize the transcendence and illimitability of the god. In the *Gītā* Kṛṣṇa, too, says 'I transcend the entire universe with only a fragment of myself' (x: 42). 'From this Being was born Virāj, from and on Virāj Puruṣa appeared transcending everything and creating the earth' (5). In the *Nṛsiṃha Tāpanīyopaniṣad* we read, 'He created the creatures, sense-organs, Virāj, the gods, the cases (or containers), entered (them), and though wise, behaved as if he was otherwise' (II: 1: 9). This combination of immanence and transcendence is a special feature of Puruṣa. He is the universe and yet is above and more than it. 'The gods offered him as oblation in a sacrifice, spring was the ājya for it, summer the fuel, and autumn the libation' (6). This Puruṣa the gods sprinkled on the grass as an oblation and together with the Sādhyas and saints, offered him in sacrifice (7). From this sacrifice were created all the birds and beasts of the air, the forest and the village (8). From this cosmic sacrifice were created the Ṛces, Sāmans, the metres and the Yajus (9)—in other words, the verbal ingredients of a sacrifice were created. From him were created horses, cows, sheep and goats (10). Who knows how Puruṣa was distributed—what is his mouth, arms, thighs and feet? (11). The next verses supply the answer.

His mouth became the Brāhmaṇa, his arms, the Rājanya, his thighs, the Vaiśya and his feet the Śūdra (12). From his mind was created the moon, from the eye the sun, from the mouth Indra and Agni, from his life Vāyu (13); from the navel, the ether, from the head the sky, from the feet the land, from the ears the directions and the regions (14). Seven are the enclosures, seven fuel (sticks) of the sacrifice where the gods offered Puruṣa as the sacrificial animal (15).

'The gods offered a sacrifice with a sacrifice (i.e. with Puruṣa as the sacrificial animal). These were the primordial religious rituals. Thus they (the gods) obtained heaven where the Sādhyas are gods' (16). The self-immolation of the demiurge is conceived in many mythologies to be an essential prerequisite of creation. In Christian mythology the corrupt creation is restored to its pristine glory through Christ's self-sacrifice, which is like a second creation. The result is the 'new heaven and the new earth' of the Book of Revelation. 'Creation cannot take place except from a living being who is immolated' (Mircea Eliade, *Patterns in comparative religion*, p. 183).

The tenth book of the *ṚV* is a precursor of the *Brāhmaṇas* and it is significant that in this hymn Puruṣa is identified with the sacrifice in a very important way—he was offered in the sacrifice as an oblation. The Brāhmaṇical formula 'Prajāpati is the sacrifice' presupposes this hymn, for in it Puruṣa is vitally connected with the sacrifice.

In the age of the elaboration and prevalence of the sacrifice it was felt that the sacrifice, through the supernatural energy that it releases (Apūrva in the *Pūrva Mīmaṃsā*) evokes the non-existent into being. Thus it gives sons to the sonless, brings rain in times of drought, gives wealth to the indigent and so on. In principle, therefore, the sacrifice 'creates'. Hence the primeval creation must have been from a primeval sacrifice. It is this primordial cosmic sacrifice that the Puruṣa hymn sings of. In order to produce the universe, the metaphysical essence of the universe, i.e. the prototype of the universe, had to be offered as the oblation, and Puruṣa was this essence, the final cause.

Puruṣa is absent in the other *Saṃhitās*. The *JB* takes up the subject again. 'Puruṣa is Prajāpati; Prajāpati is the Year; this Puruṣa is the same as in the ether, in the sky' (*JB* II: 56). The emphasis in this image is on the invisible categories of entities; time, ether, sky. The *GB* also identifies Puruṣa with time (*GB* V: 23). 'He is the Puruṣa in the sun, in the moon. In this luminous halo he is the brilliant, the rhythmic one. He is life, Prajāpati and the initiate' (*JB* II: 62). In the *ŚB* we are told of Puruṣa that

> even as a grain of rice, or a grain of barley or a grain of millet, so is this golden Puruṣa in the heart; even as a smokeless light; it is greater than the sky, greater than the ether, greater than the earth, greater than all existing things; that self of the spirit (breath) is my self: on passing away from hence I shall obtain that self. Verily, whosoever has this trust (buddhi) for him there is no uncertainty. (*ŚB* X: 6: 3: 1.)

This passage is very important, for it transforms the theological Brahman (Puruṣa) into the metaphysical Brahman (n.) and posits the fundamental equation of Brahman and Ātman, the basis of Vedānta. Life, we are told, is established in Puruṣa (*JB* III: 372). In *TA* I: 23 Puruṣa is identified with the boundless tortoise, thus emphasizing his identity as Brahman and suggesting the substratum of Viṣṇu in the concept.

In Puruṣa, especially of the Puruṣa hymn, we touch the nadir of the concept of Brahman—he is the macrocosm and yet is beyond the categories of thought and in this he foreshadows the metaphysical Brahman. Of this Puruṣa the *Kaṭhopaniṣad* says, 'Beyond Puruṣa there is nothing' (III: 11). The *ŚB* passage emphasizes his microcosmic essence, we are reminded of the 'Puruṣa as big as a thumb' who resides in the human heart. In Puruṣa, because he is sufficiently vague mythologically, we are face to face with a semi-abstract prime spirit who stands at a cross-roads; on one side is infinite possibility for him to develop metaphysically, on the other side is a blind alley in mythology. He cannot evoke an image, visual or audial, for by his very nature he is beyond the categories of thought. Hence mythologically he is already a spent force. In Brahman we meet a last chance of making this image a concrete reality which is successful up to a point.

In this work we are concerned with the masculine Brahman. He has a neuter predecessor in the *Vedas* which stands for 'a sacred word, prayer, mantra, oṃkāra or a chant used as a spell' (cf. Brahman is the holy power, *AB* I: 30). Brahmaṇaspati was lord of this Logos-Brahman. Beyond this the *ṚV* does not mention a masculine Brahman.

Brahman is a growth from Prajāpati on the one hand and from Bṛhaspati or Brahmaṇaspati on the other. 'Prajāpati was gradually displaced by Brahman, and finally the most definite expression for the object of man's search was found in the concept of the "ātman"' (P. Denssen, *Philosophy of the Upaniṣads*, p. 81). Ātman is the microcosmic obverse of the coin of which Brahman is the macrocosm-reverse. And Brahman is a slow and steady growth from the abstract associations of the semi-concrete demiurges of the *ṚV*. The *TS* says that Brahman is the holy power (I: 5: 4) and by it is meant the neuter Brahman. The *MS* says Brahman (n.) is Brahmaṇaspati (II: 2: 3); here we see the neuter and abstract Brahman equated with its more concrete hierophany. 'Twofold are the forms of Brahman (n.); Kāla and Akāla, one should worship Kāla as Brahman' (*MS* VI: 14). The neuter Brahman is also identified with Bṛhaspati (*AB* IV: 5; *ŚB* V: 3: 2: 4) and we notice the effort to make it into something concrete. In the *TB* we have a masculine Brahman who is said to be Bṛhaspati (II: 6: 19: 2). But this is clearly an imposition of the masculine gender on the neuter word because functionally he becomes a male force. Thus Brahman (n.)

'begot the gods, is this whole world, from it is created Kṣatra, its self is the Brāhmaṇa, in it inheres these regions, in it the universe, it is the eldest of creatures, who can challenge it? Brahman (n.) is the thirty-three gods, Brahman (n.) is Indra and Prajāpati, Brahman (n.) is all the creatures' (*TB* II: 8: 8: 8, 9). Thus, although the form is neuter, the concept is actually masculine. The same happens in the *JB* too. We are told that 'Brahman is Agni, Bṛhaspati, everything was created by Brahman' (II: 230). 'Prajāpati wished to create in collaboration with Brahman, the latter declined, for Prajāpati had sinned. At Prajāpati's request Brahman cut off his limbs' (II: 369–70). Here again the form (of the word Brahman) is neuter but the concept is clearly that of a male agent.

In the *Upaniṣads* we have a male Brahman. Thus in the 'Kautsāyanī stuti' we hear, 'Thou are Brahman (n.) thou Viṣṇu, Rudra, Prajāpati, Agni, Varuṇa, Vāyu, Indra and the moon' (*MU* V: 1). Again in the *Kauṣītaki Bṛāhmaṇa Upaniṣad* where we are introduced to the different regions of the different gods, Brahman (n.) is mentioned.

A man, coming on the path of Devayāna goes to the region of Agni, Vāyu, Varuṇa, Indra, Prajāpati, Brahman (n.). In that region Ara is the lake...Vijarā is the river, Ilya the tree...undefeated the region, Indra and Prajāpati, the gate-keepers... Vicakṣaṇa the chair, Amitauja the bedstead and Mānasī Pratirūpā the bride...Five hundred nymphs attend on him, a hundred carrying fruits, a hundred with unguents, a hundred with garlands, a hundred with attires and a hundred with powder, these adorn that Brahman (n.). (*KB* I: 3, 4.)

By the time of the epics mythology has shaken off its hesitation and uncertainty and meets Brahman (m.) squarely. He is a synonym for all the hierophanies dealt with so far and is, together with Prajāpati, the most concrete god of this group. He is a demiurge with actions and speeches attributed to him. In the *Rām.* Brahman commands Vālmīki to compose the epic (I: 2: 25–41). He actually appears to receive oblations at Daśaratha's horse-sacrifice (I: 14: 4). The gods approach him for the creation of Rāma; he agrees (I: 14: 12–20, 21–2). Then Svayambhū Brahman convenes an assembly of gods, where he proposes that they should help Viṣṇu when he is incarnated (I: 20: 1–6). He creates Lake Mānasa (I: 27: 7). The gods approach him for a general, he plans the creation of Kārttikeya (I: 39: 2–9). Harassed by Sagara's grandsons the gods appeal to Brahman (I: 41: 25, I: 42: 1–3), who appears to Bhagīratha and blesses him with the descent of the Gaṅgā (I: 45: 16–53). Brahman appears to Viśvāmitra when the latter practises penances to become a Brahmin and refuses to make him one (I: 65: 1–27). He is the lord of all the worlds (II: 25: 36), the prime creator (II: 119: 3). He had blessed Virādha with invulnerability (III: 7: 21).

Brahmaloka is above the region of the gods (III: 9: 39). Śarabhaṅga saw Brahman there surrounded by attendants (III: 9: 37). Brahman supplied the arrows for the bow which Agastya gave to Rāma. He commanded Indra to succour Sītā with nectar (III: 63: 1–17), and blessed Kabandha with a long life (III: 75: 25). Rāvana became a terror through Brahman's boon (IV: 10: 4). The ape Jambavat is Brahman's son (IV: 41: 2, VI: 6: 20). 'In a spot in the farthest north he (Brahman) dwells—the highest, ubiquitous god' (*Rām.* IV: 44: 120). He had allowed the apes Mainda and Dvivida to drink nectar (VI: 4: 7). Kumbhakarṇa had been cursed by Brahman (VI: 37: 14) but the curse was modified at Rāvaṇa's request (VI: 38: 28–31). Brahman blessed Rāvaṇa with immortality but made him vulnerable to a man's weapon (VII: 10: 12–26). He is styled Svayambhū in VI: 52: 47, VI: 53: 4, VI: 64: 12). He came and blessed Rāma after Rāvaṇa was killed (VI: 102: 3). The Vimāna chariot was fashioned by Brahman with a mere wish (VI: 111: 25, 32). He is called 'the old grandfather' in VII: 23: 11. He came to dissuade Rāma from self-immolation (VII: 98: 11–23). Śruti, i.e. the *Vedas*, follow him (VII: 96: 11). When Rāma left his body in the Sarayū, Brahman welcomed him to heaven (VII: 110: 8).

The *Mbh.* says that Brahman, the creator was born of an egg (I: 1: 29–30). He blessed Śeṣanāga, who had practised hard penances, and commissioned him to hold the earth (I: 32). He ordained that Āstīka would save the serpents from total annihilation in the Sarpayajña (I: 34). In *Mbh.* III: 38: 39, 40 Brahman is distinguished from Prajāpati. Brahman existed before and is superior to Prajāpati. He is a negation of opposites and the essence and source of all that exists. Sanatsujāta says 'only saints see the eternal god' (V: 45: 12). He is Prajāpati Brahman, the grandfather who was in the beginning; he created all men, gods, demons, monsters and serpents (XII: 121: 55). He appeared out of the primeval waters (XII: 175: 34). The Uncreate (Aja) Brahman creates the gods, saints, fathers and men (XII: 224: 45). He assumed the shape of a golden swan and he encloses the three worlds (XII: 288: 3). In that swan-shape he had a dialogue with the Sādhyas a species of sondergötter.

Nārada's hymn to Brahman (missing in many manuscripts) is a cryptic hymn of single epithets. Many of these epithets deserve special attention. Thus he is called the lord of valour and speech, the giver of wealth and pūrvanivāsa—a former abode. He is the Brahman priest, he is Yāmya (relating to Yama) and is tuṣita, Mahātuṣita and parinirmita—three classes of celestial beings in Buddhist theology. He is Vaikuṇṭha and Hayaśiras (appellatives of Viṣṇu), Sāṃkhyayoga (systems of philosophy), Sāmikavratadhara (observing the vow of the sāmānists). He is called Phenapācārya (the preceptor of the foam-drinking sect of mendicants), Vālakhilya (another class of mythical thumbsized saints), Vaikhānasa (anchorite)—and these connect him with different anchorite brotherhoods and indirectly connect him with Śiva, who unlike Viṣṇu is associated with such hermit brotherhoods. Thus Brahman is said to practise extremely stiff self-control and penance. He is called Citraśikhaṇḍin, an appellative of the Seven Sages and perhaps a description of another anchorite-sect. His association with sacrifices is clear from epithets like recipient-of-the-sacrificial-cake, born-of-the-sacrifice or observing-the-five-sacrifices. His association with detachment as a means to liberation is made clear in epithets like he-who-has-finished-his-course, he-whose-desire-is-broken, he-whose-doubts-are-removed, he-who-has-withdrawn-from-everything (*Mbh.* XII: 322, 325–7).

In the hymn we notice the attempt at unifying all the various sects and creeds under an abstraction which, through its manifold manifestations, is raised to the rank of the supreme being. After Nārada finishes the hymn Brahman reveals himself to Nārada as a synthesis of opposites (*Mbh.* XII: 326) and is called Vāsudeva the Eternal Spirit. A little later in that chapter we have Brahman (n.) and Brahman (m.) belonging to the same chain; Brahman (n.)–Saṃkarṣaṇa–Pradyumna–Aniruddha–Brahman (m.), born of the primordial lotus—the material creation (XII: 326: 68–70). This series connects Brahman with Vāsudeva-Kṛṣṇa and through him with Viṣṇu.

In the *HV*, too, Brahman is born of a golden egg. The universe is created out of the broken bits of the shell (I: 29–32). He created the prime progenitors, and gods, the *Vedas*, man and woman out of his two parts (I: 34–44). He praises Viṣṇu after Kālanemi is slain. He orders the gods to descend to the earth (in partial incarnation) in the Bhārata line (I: 53: 12–13). He cursed Kaśyapa, saying the latter would be born on the earth as a cowherd and his two cows Aditi and Surabhi would be his two wives. This was King Vasudeva with his wives Rohiṇī and Devakī (I: 55: 40–5). Balarāma praises Brahman as the father of the gods and demons (*HV* II: 109: 6). This hymn is known as the *Maṅgalāṣṭaśata*, it makes Brahman the creator of the cosmos. Brahman intervened when Kṛṣṇa and Śiva fought over the Bāṇāsura issue. With his mind and thought properly expressed (in words) he created (*HV* III: 20: 7). At Puṣkara Brahman offered a sacrifice. Bṛhaspati, who was none other than Brahman, acted as Hotṛ and they worshipped Viṣṇu there (III: 23: 32–3). The *GB* also tells us that Brahman (n.) created Brahman (m.) at Puṣkara. The created Brahman pondered, 'how can I, with one letter, experience all the desires, regions,

Vedas, sacrifices, sounds, awakenings, creatures, everything that is static and everything that moves' (*GB* I: 16). When Dakṣa's sacrifice escaped in the shape of a deer, Brahman made it the deer in the moon (III: 32: 26–30). 'As Brahman sat contemplating creation, Hiraṇyagarbha was born of his mouth' (III: 36: 2–5).

Kaśyapa praised Brahman in a long hymn (*HV* III: 68). He calls Brahman by some names which are Śiva's and by others which are Viṣṇu's. Thus he calls him Dharma, Dharmarāja, Kakudmin, Muñjakeśa, Sthavira, Śambhu (Śiva's names) as well as Vṛṣṇija, Hṛṣīkeśa, Viriñci, Puruṣottama, Hiraṇyanārāyaṇa (Viṣṇu's names). Strangely enough this praise was accepted by Nārāyaṇa. Here, too, there are some specific epithets of Brahman which connect him with the detached hermit.

The *Matsya P* describes creation by Brahman (I: 3): 'When he sat meditating there were created from his body Sāvitrī, Śatarūpā, Sarasvatī or Brahmāṇī with whom he committed incest' (I: 4). It was not a sin because she was but part of his body (I: 5). The *Vāyu P* associates Brahman with Rajas (the active principle) (V: 15). In the beginning of the Kalpa he is moved by Rajas and creates (*Vāyu P* VII: 68). He was born of the lotus rising out of Viṣṇu's navel (*Vāyu P* CVI: 2). The *Viṣṇu P* clearly states that Brahman's essence is Nārāyaṇa (I: 3: 24).

The *Saṃhitās* or *Brāhmaṇas* do not know Pitāmaha, even as an appellate of Brahman. It is in the epics that he appears for the first time. Thus the *Rām.* quite frequently uses the word Pitāmaha as a synonym for Brahman. In the *Mbh.* Vedī (altar) is called the wife of Pitāmaha (V: 115: 10). Brahman, Pitāmaha and Prajāpati are synonyms all through the epics. This may indicate a very old concept (that of a creator-grandfather), perhaps obtaining from pre-Aryan times, which, when the Aryans adopted it was still remembered as old by the term Pitāmaha. The *Purāṇas* use Brahman, Svayambhū, Prajāpati and Pitāmaha indiscriminately to denote the same personality. The sectarian gods like Śiva or Viṣṇu are mentioned quite frequently and they are created by Brahman who thus becomes their father. Hence, from the human point of view, the creator of father-gods quite naturally becomes the Pitāmaha. But a better exposition would be to take him as 'the father of the fathers (i.e. ancestors, Pitarah)' which also would push his origin to an extreme and inconceivable past. Ancestor-worship as a ritual may have created this 'grandfather-god', the creator even of those who have passed on.

In tracing the evolution of the Brahman concept, reference should be made to the *ŚB* passage which states that from not-being (asat) Prajāpati was created, from him Puruṣa and from Puruṣa, Brahman (VI: 1: 1). Prajāpati is primarily the creator of life (i.e. living beings) out of non-life, while Tvaṣṭṛ, Dakṣa or Viśvakarman is conceived of as the fashioner of the inanimate world, and also that aspect of the creator-god who calls forth 'form' out of non-form (cf. tvaṣṭā rūpāṇi vikaroti, *TB* 1: 8: 1: 2), i.e. he gives distinctive shapes to things and creatures. Tvaṣṭṛ creates a cosmos out of chaos but Prajāpati creates life out of dead matter. How does he do it? The answer begins to be given from the tenth Maṇḍala of the *ṚV* and is variously given in the *Brāhmaṇas*. But this age (from *ṚV* x to the end of the *Brahmaṇas*) was one of the predominance of sacrifice, and sacrifice, as we have seen, was the creative ritual. Hence Prajāpati, who had been identified with Bṛhaspati or Brahmaṇaspati, the power of prayer and the incantations, was made to appear as the sacrifice itself. This aspect of the Prajāpati is Puruṣa. If one is permitted to differentiate between Prajāpati and Puruṣa one may say that while Prajāpati 'performs' sacrifices for creation, Puruṣa 'is' the sacrifice. He offers himself as an oblation and thus becomes not only the impelling energy behind the creative act, but the material ingredient of the universe too.[1]

Bṛhaspati or Brahmaṇaspati have a common origin with Brahman and Bṛhat and the concept behind the word seems to be one of vastness as also of strength. The sacrifice performed in time and place produced an effect much vaster than the causal act itself, the supernatural power which produced this disproportionate effect was 'Bṛh'. The theophany which wielded 'Bṛh' was Bṛhaspati, he who possessed it was Bṛh + man (from suffix *ṃat*) (= Brahman). Since the abstract Brahman (n.) meant 'pious

[1] One notices the derivation of *Bṛhaspati* and *Brahmaṇaspati* from a similar root *bṛh*. Without going into the controversy of the origin of the word—whether from *Baresman* or *Bricht* or *Bhraj* (cf. S. K. Belvelkar, 'Brahman–Baresman–Bricht–Bhraj', Fourth Oriental Conference, Allahabad, 1928)—one may safely state that the root means to expand, include, envelop, or pervade. *Virāj* also suggests the same sense. In identifying Brahman with life breath in 'Brahman Knowledge', L. D. Barnett perhaps intended to derive it from the same root as 'breath'. If we were to look for a cosmic infra-structure for the concept of Brahman, we would find it in the boundless sky (cf. the root *bṛh* = vast). Dyaus was dim because he was neither fully anthropomorphozed nor fully conceptualized. Besides, he failed to answer to the mythological needs of a warring, invading people, for whom even Varuṇa (the sky-god in the earliest Vedic hymns) was unsuitable and Indra alone was satisfactory. After the *Upaniṣads* and Buddhism there was a renewed mythological interest in the sky, which was seen as boundless and shapeless, uncreate and endless, the best mythological parallel and counterpart of the supreme being of absolute monism. The concepts associated with the sky were also valid for Brahman—cf. uncreate (aja), everlasting (nitya), beyond attributes (nirañjana), supreme (para), formless (nirākāra), all-pervasive (sarvagata) and free from all qualities (nirguṇa). Anthropomorphism was easier on the conceptual level, but very difficult in mythology, because the sky hardly lends itself to personification; hence Brahman remained vague, undistinguished and mythologically unconvincing.

uttering of the sacrificial formula' and the power it contained, or the strength it bestowed, he who was its lord was Brahmaṇaspati. 'According to the poets of the *ṚV* Brahman may be in the possession of the gods or, at least be connected with them (VII: 33: 11). They are strengthened by it (II: 12: 14, I: 31: 18). Priests are able to make a brahman for the gods (III: 53: 13). Indra stimulated his impetuousity by the brahman of the singer (II: 17: 3)' (J. Gonda, *Notes on Brahman*, p. 13).

At a definite stage of the evolution of Brahman, the demiurge Brahman arose out gf the abstract concept. 'When, by a well-known gradual process this neuter Brahman (nom. Brahma) is changed into masculine (nom. Brahmā), it comes to mean a man conversant with Brahman, i.e. a member of the priestly class'; 'a priest charged with the special duty of superintending the sacrifice, but likewise the personal creator, the universal force conceived as a personal god, the same as Prajāpati and in later times one of the Trimūrti, Brahman, Viṣṇu and Śiva' (Max Müller, *Introduction to the Aitareya Āraṇyaka*). This creative force embodied in Brahman which brings the non-existent into being led to the growth of the metaphysical entity, Brahman the supreme being. Brahman is beyond all limiting conditions of phenomenal being, it is metaphysically existent though empirically non-existent. This potential energy is something like Parmenides' concept of a single universal being which is thought (*Nous*). Conceptually it is the point where thought and matter are one; the sacrificer by disturbing the balance at this point generates 'apūrva' which converts thought into matter.

Brahman (n.) is actually used to mean the vital breath in *BĀU* I: 5: 4; *CU* I: 9: 5, V: 1: 6, VI: 7, VII: 15; *Praśna Up.* VI: 3. In the sense of 'creator' it is used in *BĀU* II: 1: 20; *Śvet. U* VI: 10; *MU* I: 1: 7, II: 1: 1. It is also used to mean the Eternal Being as in *BĀU* I: 6: 3, II: 4: 12; *CU* III: 15: 1, IV: 4–9, VI: 13. As Asat or non-being it is used in *BĀU* II: 3: 1; *CU* III: 19: 1; *TU* II: 4–7.

Bṛhaspati as we have seen is the priestly power, the lord of Bṛh, the power behind the sacrifice. Brahman, as he arises out of this priestly power, Bṛhaspati, may have given rise to the Brahman priest. Dumézil in his '*Flamen-Brahman*' has investigated the conceptual basis of the Brahman-priest. Keith in his article 'New theories as to Brahman' (*Jhā Comm. Vol.*) quotes Dumézil, who asks if the word Brahman denotes that unlike the other priests he is consubstantial with the sacrifice which he himself once was. Bṛhaspati actually is the sacrifice and the Brahman priest arising out of Bṛhaspati was a personification of the sacrifice. This epiphany of the sacrifice is Puruṣa.

The abstract concept is converted into a concrete personality by adding a 'pati' as in Bṛhaspati, Vācaspati, Brahmaṇaspati or Prajāpati. In Prajāpati we reach a definite stage in the evolution of the concept of Brahman, for he replaced his predecessors, i.e. the creator demiurges, and foreshadowed his semi-abstract successor Brahman. When sacrifice replaced Varuṇa and the nature-gods under Brahmanic influence between 800 and 600 B.C., (i.e. in the age of the predominance of sacrifices) replaced Prajāpati became the personification of the creative principle, at once creator and creation. Svayambhū, Parameṣṭhin or Skambha become mere descriptive appellatives. The transformation of the abstract neuter Brahman into a personality was necessary for the sacrificer for in this power he (the sacrificer) visualized the cosmic creator. 'The manifestation of brahman among men was called brahman. Hence the statement that he who knows the Imperishable is a brahman, for to know something on this level of civilisation means to have control over it, to be unified with it' (J. Gonda, *Notes on Brahman*, p. 54).

Kaśyapa is one of the ten Prajāpatis. By his thirteen wives he was the father of gods, men, birds, beasts, reptiles and all the intermediary species between gods and men. By Aditi he was the father of the Ādityas, the solar gods, and by Diti, of the Daityas or demons. Bearing in mind the chronic strife between these two species we see in Kaśyapa the embryo of the dualism inherent in creation. He is the father of the good and the bad. Kaśyapa further means a tortoise, 'Kacchapa', and this would seem to suggest that he was the Akūpāra, the cosmic tortoise. The tortoise in its association with water would recall Viṣṇu (who was actually incarnated in that form) and who like the tortoise lies under water. Thus Kaśyapa is a conceptual prototype of Brahman.

The relationship between Brahman and Viṣṇu is ambiguous. One is shown to be just another manifestation of the other. We hear that Prajāpati worshipped Nārāyaṇa at Gandhamādana before the gods and sages (*Mbh.* VI: 61: 6). Nārāyaṇa as Kṛṣṇa is the supreme being (*Mbh.* XII: 121: 50); Brahman is Viṣṇu (*Mbh.* XII: 175: 20). Like Viṣṇu, Brahman too rose out of the waters (*Mbh.* XII: 175: 34). Nārāyaṇa described and praised Brahman (*Mbh.* XII: 321: 28–40). Brahman in the shape of a fish saved Manu (*Mbh.* III: 185). In all this it becomes clear that Viṣṇu and Brhaman were almost interchangeable in mythology. Nārada's praise of Brahman or Kaśyapa's includes epithets which usually signified Viṣṇu. The *Viṣṇu P* says, Brahman is the supreme lord. '...in his last aspect, nay in his own and true aspect in which the sacrificer himself will come to share—that of pure intellectuality, pure spirituality—he is Mind, such is the ultimate source of being, the one self, the Puruṣa, the Brahman' (Eggeling's *Introduction to the ŚB*, p. xxiv).

This very ambiguity of the relationship between Brahman and Viṣṇu is, however, significant. In an age when Viṣṇu played a predominant role, Brahman's only path to prominence lay through his identification with Viṣṇu. Besides, Viṣṇu's own image was gradually assuming such dimensions that it overlapped with Brahman's. Consequently they became increasingly indistinguishable. Moreover, through Devayāna Viṣṇu was connected with Brahman, for the aim of Devayāna was a merger with Brahman, and Puruṣa was the last stage before this merger. 'Those who give up cruelty, and perform wise deeds move towards rays, from rays to the day, the waxing fortnight, the upward path, the sphere of the gods, of the sun, lightning and the mind; then becoming Puruṣa they move to the region of Brahman and return nevermore' (*Niruktapariśiṣṭa* II, pp. 38–9). When we remember that Brahman was called Puruṣa, and Viṣṇu Puruṣottama, the relationship becomes closer still.[1]

In the age when the Brahman mythologem was fast crumbling at the 'cold touch of philosophy' with its parallel figure of Brahman (n.), and when Viṣṇu with his varied manifestations was speedily gaining ground, this ambiguity may have been the only way to keep the Brahman myth alive a little longer. Functionally they are the reverse and obverse of the same demiurge, for in the *Purāṇas* Viṣṇu is quite frequently the creator-god. Later, when the division of cosmic labour had been finally recognized, Viṣṇu was pensioned off from an active role and was described as superintending the preservation of the universe through his latent consciousness in Yoganidrā (the sleep of meditation). 'One might venture the hypothesis that Viṣṇu was, in a sense, also Prajāpati's successor in being the sacrifice. Yet a variety of facts might, on the other hand, induce us to suppose him to have been at the same time the creator god's competitor' (J. Gonda, *Aspects of early Visnuism*, p. 79). Thus the inner conflict and essential identity of the gods make their relationship more complex. In the Ṛgvedic period they were more or less distinct hierophanies, for Viṣṇu was a minor god then. With the *Brāhmaṇas* inserting equivocal myth after myth the two figures drew closer to each other till the lines of demarcation became blurred and they became the alternate epiphanies of the same essence.

The *Mārkaṇḍeya Purāṇa* says, 'when in the water lies the thousand-eyed thousand-footed, thousand-headed Puruṣa the golden-complexioned Being beyond perception, then it is Brahman called Nārāyaṇa' (VI: 2, 3).

[1] The close relation of Viṣṇu and Brahman is reflected in the development of the Vedānta philosophy. This philosophy started by reducing all existence to Brahman (n.) which it calls 'padārtha' (entity), but with its further development at the hands of Rāmānuja, Madhva and Nimbārka it leaned more and more towards Vaiṣṇavism.

In the *Purāṇas* and Vaiṣṇava theology Māyā is one of the nine śaktis (functional energies) of Viṣṇu. The association of Māyā with the solar god is found in other mythologies, too. In Apollodorus' *Bibliotheca* we read that Circe was a daughter of the sun...and she was skilled in enchantment. Brahman's māyā may have been a by-product of his latent solar nature. In Vedānta, Māyā is illusion, the source of the visible and phenomenal universe. Fundamentally the Māyā or Yogamāyā of Viṣṇu is similar to the Vedāntists' concept of Māyā. The cosmic illusion is the manifestation of Māyā in both. Viṣṇu, sleeping the apparent sleep of inaction and watching over the universe through the magical power of abstract meditation (cf. *Bhaviṣya Purāṇa*), is just a concretized replica of the apparently inactive Puruṣa of Sāṃkhya with Prakṛti to discharge the function of creation and preservation, or of the Brahman (n.) of Vedānta, with Māyā to maintain the cosmic illusion.

We have noticed that Brahman in mythology is the product of the merger of various creator-gods into one. This led to the creative act being ascribed to him in the epic-Purāṇic age. These component figures by their primordial character, cosmic and eternal essence and creative function are easily transmutable into a teleological essence, an abstract entity who is mythologically indistinct and obscure. As cosmic beings these component gods cannot be described with any degree of vividness or given truly visible traits or dimensions. They can only be visualized as forms of the sun-god. As eternal beings they are ageless and, mythologically speaking, without any potentiality for growth and development. This very indistinctness was the most vitally necessary trait for the growth of the abstract principle, the metaphysical Brahman who is beyond speech and thought. Such a cosmic principle cannot be created out of distinct outlines.

Hence towards the close of the Brahmanical period we have a clear bifurcation—the metaphysical Brahman of the *Upaniṣads* and the mythological Brahman of the epics and *Purāṇas*. Of these the first has infinite potentiality for development in Vedānta and has a long span while the other dwindles visibly and remains a thin, attenuated figure, the vague and obscure creator god of the epic-Purāṇic triad. These two products were ambiguously conceived in the first phase of their separation and were easily confused, not only by the layman but also by the seers. This uncertainty became creative in the case of the metaphysical Brahman and led to its being divested of all attributes. It became a timeless impersonal principle, invisible because insubstantial, incomprehensible because it is beyond the mind, omnipresent, omniscient, immanent yet transcendental. But this vagueness became fatal to the mythological Brahman.

That the god Brahman had a popular base is attested by its mention in the Buddhist scriptures. Tarapada Bhattacharyya in *The cult of Brahman* has a theory about the history and evolution of the Brahman cult and says that it was essentially a very old institution. Vedism and, later, Brāhmaṇism sought to suppress it. It achieved a compromise with the Vaiṣṇava Pañcarātra cult and insidiously and tortuously returned to power via the identification of Viṣṇu with Brahman. In Buddhism it struck a decisive note of victory, for the strong predilection for ancestor-worship (cf. the Buddha's enlightenment came after he had worshipped the ancestors) is part of the cult of Pitāmaha, who is so-called because he is the father even of the fathers, the Pitarah, i.e. the Manes. But when Mahāyānism pushed Hīnayāna beyond the territories of India the old Rātra cult with its emphasis on Pitṛkārya (ancestor ritual) lost ground. 'The name Brahman', he says, 'appears to have been the popular name of the creator-god in the Brahmāvarta region, other parts called him by other names. Regarding Puruṣa it may be said that he is the production of the philosophical tendency of the *ṚV* Indians'. Whether this was the actual history of the Brahman cult or not is quite uncertain, but the cult may have imbibed certain traits of ancestor-worship and have thus revived some characteristics of a pre-Vedic religion.

In the *Majjhima Nikāya*, the *Āssalayana Sutta* (no. 93) claims that the Brahmins are the real sons of Brahmā, they came from his mouth and were his real heirs. In the *Milinda Pañha* (IV: 5: 20) we hear that Brahman is the highest and most worshipped of the gods. The same work states that all men of those days—monks, itinerant teachers and Brahmins—were worshippers of Brahman (IV: 5: 37). Of the three tiers in the first dhyāna in the Buddhist cosmic scheme, the lowest grade is the world of the Brahman. In it the first group is the retinue of the Mahābrahmā, the second is the ministers of Mahābrahmā and the third is the Mahābrahmās, of whom the Mahābrahmā is the chief. Together these are called Brahmakāyika gods of whom the chief Mahābrahmā is called Brahmā, lord of the sufferers. It is true that Brahman is inferior to the Buddha, but he is superior to Sakka (Indra) and if this is any reflection of the cultic hierarchy of that time, then Indra was making an exit from the Brāhmaṇical pantheon while Brahman still retained a hold on the people and their rituals. One reason why the Buddhist Brahman was superior to Indra (Sakka) is perhaps because while Indra had violent deeds to his credit, Brahman had none, and a religion of non-violence could accept him more easily. Another reason may have been the insidious and imperceptible influence of philosophies of monism and asceticism.

A sure proof of the existence of the cult of a god is found in iconography where he is produced in plastic art, for the urge to reproduce a god iconically springs from a desire to worship him. In the *Mbh.* we are told that Brahman and Viṣṇu were competing with each other in plumbing the depth and scaling the height of the Sthāṇumūrti of Śiva. Brahman falsely claimed to have reached the top of the column; Śiva cursed him saying that he would never have a cult of his own. This is clearly a later mythological gloss attempting to explain the actual absence or comparative rarity of the Brahman cult. He has no success as a cultic god.

Brahman figures are found in the coins of the Kushan period. Guy E. Swanson in *The birth of the gods* says of the nature of the high gods, 'Men may commemorate them, but worship and sacrifice are not directed towards these distant, disinterested beings' (p. 56). Thus Brahman's altitude, magnitude and detachment—attributes which render him a particularly suitable object of contemplation—are just the attributes which stand in the way of a convincing mythology being built up around him. The neutrality and inactivity of the Atharva–Vedic Brahman-priest in the sacrifice also foreshadow the neutral and inactive Brahman–Pitāmaha in mythology and Brahman (n.) in Vedānta. Inaction is detrimental to the growth of a myth, it leads to vagueness, and cosmogonic actions performed through the mind or thought alone are not conducive to the creation of ritual or mythology.

The concept of Brahman as the supreme overlord may have been a reflex of the growth of monarchies of considerable size and power. In Egypt we perhaps have a parallel situation. Breasted suggests that monotheistic beliefs may have grown out of the experience of powerful rulers of great, consolidated and complex, kingdoms and empires with a centralized administration (*The dawn of conscience*, pp. 60–1). The Egyptians did evolve the notion of a high god (in the period of the powerful Pharaoh Ikhnaton) who superintended human morality and was the lord of the universe.

In the Dula Deo temple of Brahman at Khajuraho the god is represented with a sacrificial ladle (symbolizing his essence as Puruṣa or Prajāpati, the sacrifice), a book (he is to be approached through wisdom), the rosary (he is to be contemplated and meditated upon), Kamaṇḍalu, the small waterjug (symbolic of the mendicant's life), and the bull-mount (connecting him with Śiva; elsewhere he has the Garuḍa or horse-mount connecting him with Viṣṇu). Sometimes he has a swan for a mount as in the temple at Puṣkara near Ajmer, or is seated in a chariot drawn by seven swans. This reflects his description as Haṃsa in the *Upaniṣads*, and also connects him with Sarasvatī, his daughter who also has a swan for a mount. Brahman is always white-bodied, has white garments and jewelled ear-rings. He is shown as Śiva's charioteer in the latter's Tripurāntakamūrti, or as his wedding-priest in his Kalyāṇasundaramūrti. In Śiva and Viṣṇu's Ekapādamūrti Brahman is shown as bowing to them. Brahman has four heads presumably to signify his solar character, for the sun is all-seeing; and this in iconography and mythology is sometimes symbolized by a multiplicity of heads. Thus Janus is two-headed and the Gaulish sun-god is three-headed. But the number four also indicates that Brahman is an anthropomorphism of the sky (with its four directions); more precisely of space and also of time which his solar essence inevitably epitomizes. Brahman becomes an abstraction too difficult for iconography to personalize. because of his vague and vast cosmic substratum.

This last gesture indicates his subservience to the two gods whose cults are raising them to exalted positions while his own lack renders him insignificant beside them. In him the rival cults seem to find a meeting ground. The Tantric worshippers regard Śakti as the Māyā of Brahman. The Śaivas worship Rudra-Śiva as the spiritual son of Brahman. Thus Brahman became the name for the final realization of all sects.

The supreme principle has to be shown as the meeting point of all contradictory principles. 'The oriental mind cannot conceive perfection unless all opposites are present in their fulness...a unity which signifies not the chaos that existed before any forms were created but the undifferentiated being in which all forms are merged' (M. Eliade, *Patterns in comparative religion*, p. 420).

The concept of the mythological Brahman seeks to present him as an ideal god dwelling in a loftier altitude than the other gods and maintaining an Olympian distance from them. This is achieved by making him Pitāmaha, removed from the mortals by a whole generation of gods, and thus at two removes from men. He does not participate in any strife and is free from their petty jealousies and struggles. But this distance left him mythologically denuded and unconvincing.

Xenophanes (*c.* 570–548 B.C.), the founder of the Eleatic school of philosophy, dismissed the gods of Homer and Hesiod as thieves, cheats and adulterers and substituted for them a timeless, eternal Being, intelligent and ruling the universe by the power of thought alone. This supreme being resembles Brahman. But such a being by its very ideal detachment discourages mythology and the result is 'an idea' divested of myths. Brahman suffers this fate and remains a dim, shadowy personality.

PART IV
THE EPIC-PURĀṆIC TRIAD

CHAPTER 18

THE NEO-BRĀHMANIC TRIAD

THE original religion of the Indo-European-speaking tribes (if such a thing ever existed) is entirely conjectural. We only have its residues in the mythologies of Indian, Iranian, Greek, Roman, Celtic and certain North European countries. When the proto-Aryans were on their way to India they lived in Iran for a while and their mythology underwent some change there. Later, when the *Avesta* was composed we have a new element in religion; a complete opposition in the character of certain Vedic and Avestan demiurges. Those who are gods in India became demons (daevas) in the *Avesta* and vice versa. M. Molé investigating these differences says,

> Où est alors la différence entre les Gāthās at le Véda? Elle est dans le caractère exclusif du choix opéré—certaines divinités sont non seulement préférées, mais seules reconnues, certaines autres non seulement passées sous silence, mais recusées (sans que leur existence soit niée). Elle est dans la subordination de tous les dieux à un seul dont les autres ne peuvent qu'être messagers. Elle est dans la croyance en une crise finale vers laquelle tout converge, qui doit être préparée et qui rénovera l'existence. Leur concomitance constitue le fond de la doctrine gathique; mais celle-ci s'exprime dans un langage ritualiste qui est le même des deux côtés de l'Hindukouch. (*Culte, mythe, et cosmologie*, p. 172.)

This duality inherent yet concealed in the Indo-European religion became explicit in the Avestic pantheon. In the Vedic pantheon there was an early bifurcation between gods and demons. The former had 'ṛta' (law and order) while the latter wielded 'māyā' (magic power). Vedic religion did not admit evil as such within its pantheon. Varuṇa had dark traits, so had Nirṛti, it is true, but Varuṇa was the moral judge and punisher and that both explained and exhausted his evil associations. Nirṛti symbolized the sinister side of chthonic and expiatory rites and she steadily grew in power, stature and malignity until the hierophany became so static and gruesome that it lost mythological potentiality and had to be dropped.

Later, the village deities embodied sinister traits but the orthodox pantheon had nothing to do with them, except in Śiva and gods in the lunar complex. But it was necessary to defend evil on the metaphysical plane, for a god could not be evil. Philosophical systems which codified and classified concepts came to supply a *raison d'être* for a malevolent or dark divinity, for undeniably Śiva had much that conflicted with the Vedic notion of a god.

Cosmic principles admitted all systems of metaphysics and were fundamentally expressions of three spiritual conditions, sattva, rajas and tamas. Brahman the cosmokrator personifies 'rajas', the active and good principle; Viṣṇu the preserver embodies 'sattva', the passive and good principle, while Śiva the destroyer is a personalization of 'tamas', the active, evil principle (*Mārkaṇḍeya Purāṇa* LXVI: 105: 8). Brahman here is deistic, he becomes passive after creation and remains so throughout a Kalpa (aeon). So is Viṣṇu, apparently slumbering in the depths of the ocean; and we have seen that in the later post-Vedic scriptures (epics and *Purāṇas*) Viṣṇu and Brahman tended to come closer till they merged into one personality, their individual traits hardly distinguishable any longer. So then we are brought back to the original dichotomy of two fundamental principles—now personalized in the two sectarian gods Śiva and Viṣṇu.

In the late sections of the *Rām.* (i.e. the first part of book I, and the whole of book VII), the late Brāhmaṇical sections of the *Mbh.* and the *Purāṇas* we find a new pantheon, the product of a new theological consciousness. Old Vedic gods like Varuṇa, the Aśvins and Uṣas become extinct. Indra or Agni lose their rank and significance, Rudra and Yama change almost beyond recognition, and Viṣṇu assumes unpredictably greater dimensions. Gods of comparatively late origin like Durgā, Kālī, Gaṇeśa, Kārttikeya, Lakṣmī, Kāma, were new arrivals and gradually became firmly entrenched in power. Rich and complex rituals and myths grew around them.

Worship had also changed its character by then, for instead of sacrifices we have pūjā of idols in and out of temples. The mode of the ritual is different, the oblations and priests are different. Animal sacrifice is still there, but the animals are not strangled to death as in Vedic times but slaughtered with a scimitar. Instead of twelve or sixteen priests officiating we usually have one, sometimes with an assistant or two. Oblations are different, formulas are different too.

Pilgrimages and vows play an important role. Spread all over India are numerous pilgrimages, some grew around ancient legends and hero cults, but most were sanctified by particular epiphanies of gods and goddesses. These are usually by rivers or on mountains or hills, on the confluence of rivers or by the seaside. We are frequently told that if one fasts, bathes and offers oblations to the particular god of the pilgrimage and gives gifts to Brahmins one acquires the merit of many sacrifices (like the Aśvamedha, Vājapeya, etc.). It indicates that the old sacrifices were becoming obsolescent and were gradually being displaced by these new modes of religious practices. Dakṣiṇā, bounty to Brahmins, is also praised as producing the merits of many sacrifices. Vows (vrata) were also coming into vogue, they bring the desired object as sacrifices did in olden times. The Pañcayajña of the Purāṇic times clearly show the trend of the age: study in Brahmayajña (Vedic recitation), Tarpaṇa (offering libation to the ancestors) is Pitṛyajña (elaborate rituals for ancestors in Vedic times), Homa (offering clarified butter into the fire) is sacrifice to the gods, Vali (or gifts to living beings) is Bhūtayajña (sacrifice to creatures) and hospitality is nṛyajña (sacrifice to men). Thus a householder becomes the offerer of the five great and compulsory sacrifices without tears, so to speak, for none of these is a real sacrifice in the old sense of the term. The trouble, expense and complexity are eliminated and yet the sense of having performed the necessary rituals is created. The entire outlook of the age is changed, for, although man still seems to believe in the efficacy of sacrifices and does not feel satisfied unless he feels he has offered them, the sacrifices themselves are entirely different. Hence the scriptures are full of formulas of substitution. If one visits a pilgrimage and performs the necessary penances for two or three days, one collects the merit of this or that sacrifice. If one takes and fulfils a vow one also gains the merit of a sacrifice. If one gives proper dakṣiṇās to worthy Brahmins one acquires the merits of other sacrifices. Thus the merits of sacrifices (the only kind yet valid to the religious consciousness) are obtained through easier modes of religious practices.

Many social factors contribute to this change of outlook. Even before Buddhism arose, the violence and bloodshed involved in animal sacrifices had been questioned (cf. the *Mbh.* episode of King Vasu Uparicara's conversation with the sages). Even in the *Brāhmaṇas* cereals, not meat, had been shown to be the proper sacrificial offerings. Numerous tales in the twelfth and thirteenth books of the *Mbh.* had this import, viz. to point out the sin involved in violence even in religious sacrifices. Buddhism had dealt the death-blow to animal sacrifices and for a long time human consciousness was left troubled and tormented on this issue. Non-violence as a spiritual value had unquestionably greater appeal to the public imagination, and a revaluation of old religious values went on. Bloody sacrifices were not actually substituted but the old mode of worship lost favour.

With the advent of Mahāyānism Buddhism sought a rapprochement with the orthodox religion and much of the doctrinal dogma was sacrificed for a more acceptable form of doctrine. Meanwhile, the orthodox religion, too, was not in a static condition, but fast changing its configuration.

Values were being weighed, some were rejected. The inner metabolism of religion was releasing forces which acted as formative influences during this period of vital and far-reaching changes.

Metempsychosis and the theory of Karman (work) were changing the contour of the official religion. These presuppose a different end, for now—unlike in the Vedic period—the end of life is not 'to live a hundred autumns' and 'to see the sun longer', but to be released from the cycle of reincarnation and not to see any autumn at all. Man is in bondage with the prospect of an unending chain of rebirth, and the aim of one's religious practices is to be released from this chain. New legends were created in order to impress upon the people this new theory of reincarnation. The last sections of the *Mbh.*, the *HV* and the *Purāṇas* abound in such legends. The best known is perhaps the seven hunter brothers in Daśārṇa who were reborn as deer at Mount Kālañjara, as cakrāvakas in Śaradvīpa, swans in Lake Mānasa. In the last incarnation they were born at Kurukṣetra as Brahmins conversant with the *Vedas* and were liberated because of their detachment and piety.

An element of fatalism seems to have crept in the general attitude to life. It is all right to claim to be the architect of one's own fate, but in real practice gods embodying Fate in their person grow in stature. Śiva is Kāla with Yama called Kṛtānta (a synonym for fate) as his assistant. With the enunciation of Tantra-metaphysics, Śiva was raised to the position of the supreme being in whom inhere all cosmic entities. Kṛṣṇa the supreme god of the Vaiṣṇavas calls himself Kāla, the destroyer of men or worlds (lokakṣayakṛt). People now saw themselves as victims of an unknown and ineluctable power, which may actually be works performed in a previous birth, but which appear as Fate, a dark and mysterious force in this life, if only because knowledge is withheld and the causal relation is not discernible. Thus rebirth and Karman left a deep, indelible impression of fatalism on people's minds which is palpable even to-day.

The path to release from recurring life lay through knowledge, devotion or works. These were advocated by one or the other rising school of religious thought and practice. Knowledge belonged primarily to the domain of metaphysics and meditation. Works were pious deeds and observance of religious ceremonies. Bhakti or devotion was a somewhat new approach because it was a substitute for ritual performances.

Devotion means reliance on a personal god for attaining the ultimate goal. These personal gods were foreign to the Vedic religion where all gods were objects of communal worship, and where the end was worldly bliss.

With Janmāntaravāda (theory of reincarnation) this bliss was regarded as illusory and attachment began to be condemned as the root-cause of reincarnation. Gods therefore were primarily sought as liberators although wealth, prosperity and longevity still constituted the subjects of prayers. Men seeking liberation approached personal gods with utter abandon.

Of these new gods only two deserve special attention, for they alone fully satisfied the new demands of this age. These are Śiva and Viṣṇu—old gods whose origins are found in the *ṚV* but who have grown and undergone transformation in order to become personal gods able to fulfil these new desires. The rise of sectarian gods is a complex phenomenon for each of the rising gods has to fight hard for a greater number of converts.

There is something conceptually irreconcilable between these two gods, probably because fundamentally they symbolize two contrary principles—the lunar and solar. In ritual details, too, one notices this incompatibility. Let us take a few significant instances. 'Bilva' leaves are sacred to the Śiva-worshipper and taboo to certain sections of Vaiṣṇavas. Tulasī leaves are similarly sacred to the Vaiṣṇavas (they are Rādhikā, Kṛṣṇa's lover in leaf-form, known also as Viṣṇupriyā, Viṣṇu's favourite) and are taboo to the Śāktas. Dūrvā grass is offered *without* the inner shoot to Śiva and the Manes; *with* the inner shoot to Viṣṇu and the solar deities. The Śālagrāma (stone-emblem of Viṣṇu) and Śiva-liṅga (stone-emblem of Śiva) are mutually exclusive taboos to the two sects. 'Yantras' are metal plaques with intricate diagrams and formulas, but *without figures* worshipped by the Śaktas; 'Paṭṭas' are such plaques *with figures* of Viṣṇu and his ten incarnations worshipped by the Vaiṣṇavas.

The Śaivas, particularly the Pāśupatas—were great adversaries of the Vaiṣṇavas. Even the cultic practices were opposed to each other. The *Nārada Pañcarātra Saṃhitā* says, 'by the Tantrikas who practise magic Śiva should be worshipped with fierce vows, with corpses, fuel, cow-dung and ashes' (IV: 45). Hari on the other hand is fond of worship offered with purity (V: 20). The official pūjā of Viṣṇu has more aesthetically pleasing votive offerings than that of Śiva. Śiva-rites are comparatively simple. The Śālagrāma stone, symbol of Viṣṇu, may not be touched by women and the Śūdras (*Padmapurāṇa*: Kṛṣṇajanmakhaṇḍa, ch. XX), while the Śivaliṅga may be touched by all. The Āgamic and popular base of the Śiva cult and the Vedic-Brahmanical and hence comparatively aristocratic and hieratic following of the Viṣṇu cult is clear from the distinction regarding the stone-symbols of the two gods. It is of course true that in both cults there was much which can be regarded as exceptions to this, but these do not remove the basic difference. All this is ritual language for expressing the inner antinomy between the two sects.

Time softened much of the sharp edge of this rivalry and each sect in its attempt to elevate its god to the supreme altitude felt obliged to incorporate some traits of the rival sect's god. Yet enough remained and still remains to bear out our basic contention that there was a conceptual antinomy which goes deeper than the history of the rivalry of the sects and that this rivalry was merely an expression of this antinomy. The lunar (and chthonic) character of Śiva and solar character of Viṣṇu is the difference between rebirth and liberation, between Pitṛyāṇa and Devayāna. Viṣṇu is associated with cults whose keynote is devotion while the Śaiva and Śākta cults generally lay greater stress on knowledge and works.

With the advent of metempsychosis, clearly formulated for the first time in the *Upaniṣads*, the spiritual aim took a new turn. Yājñavalkya appears to be the first propounder of this theory although the germs might have lain dormant from a much earlier time. With this, the need for release from rebirth was felt more keenly, as the immutable laws of 'karman' would drag a man down even from heaven. It is here that the sectarian gods Viṣṇu and Śiva came in. Each in his all-god aspect promised salvation to the devotee. The *Bhāgavata Purāṇa* says that Bhakti arose among the Dravidians (in the south). But it must have been in an incipient stage even in the north, for ever since the early centuries A.D. we have traces of the Vāsudeva and Bhāgavata sects whose approach is through bhakti. For three or four centuries sectarian worship spread and the Gupta empire saw the emergence of a new phase of religion which later history called Hinduism.

With the spread of sectarian worship the solar and lunar principles solidified separately. Vedic gods were for a long time being gradually absorbed by Śiva or Viṣṇu, now they disappeared as individual theophanies. Brahman as the shadow-figure was brought in to co-ordinate these three cosmic principles of creation, preservation and destruction. Thus was born the triad, recognized as the fixed and final form of the 'high' tradition of the Indian pantheon by the later Gupta and post-Gupta scriptures, viz. the *Purāṇas*.

But mythology can hardly ever remain linear and formular in character. Whereas Brahman, Viṣṇu and Śiva were the mythological correlatives of metaphysical and cosmic concepts, religion was much less easily formulated on the popular or 'folk' level, for the religious need of the common man is much less articulate, cerebral and clear and craves much more varied mundane satisfaction. Just as the *AV* records the religious mores and needs of the common man of the Vedic period and has a greater variety of the modes and objects of worship, so do the *Purāṇas* at a later time uphold the three supreme gods. Thus Viṣṇu and Śiva had to symbolize as many aspects of the human experiences as possible and at the same time remain distinct theophanies. Their success as sectarian gods is due to their ability to fulfil these two conditions. They grew immensely in the epic-Purāṇic age and in the end they came to command the respect and devotion of an entire people, and are the central godheads (though with slight variations and sometimes through different epiphanies and with different names) of many major and innumerable minor cults.

It was, however, necessary in order to raise any sectarian god to a supreme position and make him independent of other theophanies with spiritual sufficiency at all levels of cosmic activity and for all levels of the human consciousness, to show that Viṣṇu, Śiva and Brahman could each discharge all three functions of creation, preservation and destruction.

The *Mbh.* has anecdotes to show these three gods acting in unison to perform deeds of cosmic significance or acting in a crisis. Sometimes Śiva is shown as born of Brahman or vice versa. At other times Viṣṇu is created by Brahman or vice versa. Each of the two sectarian gods is shown as paying homage to the other, both to Brahman, Brahman to each and to both. Thus no clear line of demarcation can be drawn to separate their stations or functions. But the mention of these three gods at critical junctures proves that they have a status more exalted than the other gods.

In the *Purāṇas* the triad is a more clearly recognized thing and there are numerous passages which show them as in charge of these three functions. Thus in the *Matsya P* we read 'Brahman creates all living beings and inanimate matter, Viṣṇu preserves them and bestows growth on them, at the end of an aeon Rudra destroys creation' (CXI: 3–4). The three gods are distinguished by the spiritual attributes which are peculiar to them: Rajas, the creative, active principle inheres in Brahman. Sattva, the unattached, passive attribute belongs to Visnu; and Tamas, the dark and fierce attribute, is Śiva's (*Vāyu P* V: 15). In the *Mārkaṇḍeya Purāṇa* Śiva says to Viṣṇu: 'Know thyself as Prakṛti and me as Śiva the Puruṣa: Thou art half my body, so am I thine' (XXV: 24). In one passage we hear that of Brahman's rajas-self was made Marīci Kaśyapa; of his tamas-self, Bhava (i.e. Śiva) the annihilator; of his sattva the Puruṣa-self, Viṣṇu (*Mārkaṇḍeya P* LXVI: 105–6). Thus Marīci Kasyapa substitutes Brahman the creator, and we have noticed before Kaśyapa is the Brahman of mythology, for he is the progenitor of all species of creatures and thus performs the task of a creator-god. Besides, this Kaśyapa is a rather vague personality, wrapped in meditation and not participating in any task actively. His shadowy figure is a replica of Brahman's.

In some passages the triad appears as three distinct personalities as in the *Viṣṇu P* passage where it says 'The creator creates his own self (in creation), Viṣṇu preserves and in the end the Ender annihilates' (II: 67). In the *Mbh.*, too, we meet three distinct personalities. Mythology needs them, for separate tasks are allotted to them and they play different parts in mythological anecdotes. They themselves differentiate their roles. Thus Viṣṇu says: 'Brahman creates, I preserve, and Śiva destroys' (*KP* II: 90). Mythology maintains the difference; they stand for different guṇas (attributes), perform different cosmic functions and always act differently in different situations.

It is in the cosmogonic myths and the metaphysical sections that we are told that the three characters are but three manifestations of the same essence. 'As Brahman he creates the creatures, as Kāla destroys them, as Puruṣa he remains indifferent—these are the three stages of Prajāpati' (*Vāyu P* V: 30, 31). Or, 'the one Self-create Kāla performs three tasks in three (forms): creates, kindly preserves creatures and destroys them (too)' (*Mārkaṇḍeya P* CXVI: 108).

Vedānta had launched a Brahman who was, by himself, free of the guṇas; the illusory functions of creation, preservation and destruction attributed to him are actually performed when he becomes Īśvara through the illusory superimposition of the attributes. This supreme being is made to say 'One pervading power manifests itself as many. Thus it assumes the shape of Brahman (which inheres in Me, and is essentially Me) and creates the universe of varied shapes. The other Great Power becomes the Endless Nārāyaṇa, the lord of the world and immanent in the world. The third Great Power destroys all creation, it is my Tamas-form called Kāla and has Rudra's form' (*KP* IV: 29–31). Or, 'three are (His) forms, the cause of creation, preservation and destruction, the Sattva-self is the Lord Viṣṇu who ever stabilizes creation; Brahman, the Rajas-self creates and Hara the Tāmasa destroys' (*KP* XXII: 26, 27). With the rise of Viṣṇuism Viṣṇu is said to be the essence behind these three manifestations. Hence in the *Viṣṇu Purāṇa* we are told that Janārdana is the power that creates, preserves and destroys and is manifest as Brahman, Viṣṇu and Śiva (*Viṣṇu P* II: 66); in the Śaiva Purāṇas and Tantras all this is attributed to Śiva or Śakti, i.e. Kālī. The reason why the one essence is split into three is also given—the division is functional. Thus metaphysics and religion join hands in the exposition of this group of three gods as both triadic and triunal (*KP* II: 97).

The epic-Purāṇic pantheon is the pantheon of the present-day India. Around the second or third century of this era we have signs of radical changes which convert the ancient Brāhmaṇical religion into Hinduism. The introduction of sectarian religion in place of the Vedic-Brāhmaṇical community-worship is the main sign of this change. The objects and modes or worship, priestly hierarchy, purpose of worship had all changed, but the most evident change is found in the gods and their natures. Viṣṇu and Śiva had emerged as the leading godheads. When Buddhism was on the wane on the Indian soil the neo-Brāhmaṇical religion found a new impetus, as also new patronage under the Guptas who commanded vaster territories than their predecessors. Inscriptions, coins and literature all bear out this new revivalism. Theoretically it was a revival of the old religion, but in actual practice what we have under the Guptas is new wine in old bottles.

Pūjā as opposed to yajña presupposes plastic images of the godhead and a personal (as opposed to communal) relationship with the god. In Viṣṇu and Śiva people found their personal gods. The South Indian devotional lyrics of the Naynars (or Nayanmars) and Alwars are examples of this attitude, and the *Purāṇas* are its scriptures. The *Purāṇas*, besides consolidating the images of these sectarian gods, Viṣṇu and Śiva, also introduce many minor gods as distinct epiphanies of these two. Thus we have Kārttikeya, Gaṇapati, Kuvera, Durgā, Kāma and Kāla in the Śiva group and Lakṣmī and the several incarnations of Viṣṇu in the Viṣṇu group.

Some of these minor gods had predecessors in the Vedic and Brāhmaṇical literatures, others are developed from casual references. Behind these we can trace the millennium-old Āgamic gods, gods of the indigenous population in India even before the Aryans' advent. With the arrival of the more powerful invaders with a predominantly solar and patriarchal pantheon, these gods had gone underground. Thus the first nine Maṇḍalas of the *ṚV* record in almost pure and unmixed form the religion of the invading Aryans, while from the tenth Maṇḍala, the *YV* and *AV Saṃhitās* we have the mention of these minor gods. In the *Khila Sūktas* (late supplementary verses) we have Lakṣmī, the *YV* presents a new Rudra and the *AV* Kāla and minor epiphanies of gods of the Śiva group. In the *Brāhmaṇas* the germs of the incarnations of Viṣṇu are presented; the

Śvet. U presents a Śiva who is a paramount lord. The *Mbh.* develops these new aspects till in it and the *Purāṇas* the canonical scripture of the sectarian gods is finally composed.

Brahman, as we have seen, is an intermediary between the conflicting divinities Śiva and Viṣṇu and is at the same time above them both. They symbolize birth, life (growth) and death. But each tends to symbolize all three phases in himself because 'every high god is, in some sense, the determiner of all events which occur' (G. E. Swanson, *The birth of the gods*, p. 57). In their potential ability to fulfil these demands lies the way to their success as sectarian gods. To Viṣṇu's and Śiva's devotees their gods are all-mighty and all-comprehensive, they control birth, life and death. Brahman fails here; hence Viṣṇu and Śiva have flourishing sects and cultic rituals while Brahman lacks them.

In these three gods we have a pantheon of the truly 'high gods' of India, the gods of the orthodox religion. All the other gods are shown as reducible to these three. A religion attempting to harmonize all the various religious theories and practices of India (northern and southern) was formulated. The lunar gods were reduced to Śiva, the solar gods to Viṣṇu, the creator-gods to Brahman and the mother-goddesses to Durgā, with Lakṣmī as a minor epiphany. The multiple gods continued to be worshipped among the people but the Purāṇa theologists explained them as epiphanies of one or other of these gods.

The Hindu pantheon, as it came to be called, was largely matriarchal and in the mother-goddess we see a revival of the mother-goddess at Lauriya Nandangarh (where the female figurine is interpreted as a mother-goddess by Sir John Marshall) at Mohenjo Daro, Harappa and Lothal. After long centuries of obscurity these gods dominated the pantheon. In the resurgence of the mother-goddesses as the Matṛkās we have the various aspects of the fundamental feminine divinity assuming new dimensions. Thus Brahmāṇī, Maheśvarī, Kaumārī, Vaiṣṇavī, Vārāhī, Indrāṇī and Cāmuṇḍā are expressions of the changed needs of the times when goddesses largely replaced their consorts in rituals.

Where the Brāhmaṇical religion stopped short Hinduism or this neo-Brāhamaṇism came forward after the intervention of Buddhism. In the pantheon of this new religion we have the triad conceived as an essential triunal manifestation of the supreme being. Innumerable minor, local gods are also raised to the ranks of demiurges—village deities, tutelary gods and goddesses of specific regions (like cremation grounds, temples, mounds), disease-goddesses, fierce spirits, tree or animal spirits, ancestor-spirits, sanctuary spirits, local-spirits, all came into their own. In Buddhism we have the funerary-mounds converted into sanctuaries (caityas or maṭhas) and tree-worship was revived (cf. the Bodhi tree at Gaya). These attitudes must always have been there, for they are timeless and world-wide. They were pushed into the background in the Vedic religion for some centuries. But the ethnic miscegenation and cultural commingling of the invaders with the indigenous population led to a compromise with the existing practices. In Buddhism some of these beliefs received official recognition, and when Neo-Brāhmaṇism was consolidated it incorporated these.

History never repeats itself; if it seems to do so the resemblance is always superficial. Delving deeper we find that what appeared resemblance is always a reappearance on a different plane which alters the contour of the event and its true import. And this new plane is always much more significant than the apparent repetition, because it is much more complex. Thus in Indian religion the reappearance of the old gods on a new level of significance had the greater bearing and impact because the level is so very different and the context of the significance so much more complex. Hence we find that when the old gods reappear they are vastly different in what they signify, how their worshippers approach them and what they bestow on the devotees. Communal gods re-emerge as personal gods, abstract divinity-concepts are replaced by visible images, sacrifices give way to pūjās. Society has moved on since the days of the sacrifices. But even though the Vedic antecedents of these gods can be traced in their Purāṇic successors, the new gods, whose name is legion, are more significant because they now command obligatory rituals from the vast majority of the common people. One suspects they had always been there, demanding worship from certain sections of the people. Under neo-Brāhmaṇism they are recognized on the popular level and are granted not a grudging morsel but seasonal or occasional rites.[1] Thus while on the one hand we have a high trinity with obvious metaphysical associations, with cosmic functions of the first magnitude, and the truly 'high' appeal to the imagination and intellect, on the other hand we have these innumerable 'low gods' which dominate the popular imagination and fill the hiatus between an erudite minority, and the vast majority of the people to whom gods are chiefly functional and worshipped for the sake of expediency. Although the various regional and functional deities, the 'low gods', are sought to be explained

[1] The Vedic word 'Ṛtvij' (priest) perhaps indicates seasonal sacrifices. Thus it is formed from *Ṛtu* (season) + *ij* (from the root *yaj*). Under neo-Brāhmaṇism the seasonal sacrifices became different in character but the ritual is as old as Vedic religion.

as manifestations of the 'high gods', the actual worshippers are very little bothered with this exposition.

The triad, therefore, remained a rationalized pattern of religious thought at a time when all the various philosophies were endeavouring to enumerate exhaustively and classify completely their various 'tattvas' or 'padārthas' (essence and entity). The three gods are reduced to one because of the great philosophical predilection for the One. The inherent duality of Brahman and Māyā (on the empirical plane, at least), or of Puruṣa and Prakṛti (on the philosophical), is reflected in Tantra and popular religion in each male god having a projection in a female principle, his Śakti.

One is amazed when one analyses these, for here in India we have all the known elements of all stages of religion—from the primitive to the most advanced. Thus we have ancestor-worship (in Śrāddha, piṇḍapitṛyajña and Yama-worship connected with these), worship of spirits (Dākinī, Śākinī, piśāca, yakṣa, rakṣa, Sādhya, Gandharva, and Kinnara), worship of cosmic elements (in Agni Sūrya, Soma, Uṣas, Vāyu, Dyaus and Pṛthivī), the mother-goddess (Pṛthivī, Aditi, Durgā, Kālī and Ambikā), euhemeristic worship of culture-heroes (Indra, the Aśvins, Vāsudeva-Kṛṣṇa, Pradyumna, Aniruddha Śāmba and the Buddha), worship of the dwarf (Vāmana), the child (the boy Kṛṣṇa), theriolatry (the monkey in the Vedic Vṛṣākapi and epic Hanūmat, Saramā, matsya (fish), the akūpara tortoise, Śiva's bull and Pārvatī's lion, other minor cultic birds or beasts surviving as mounts, like the swan of Brahman and Sarasvatī, the peacock of Kārttikeya, the elephant of Indra, Garuḍa the eagle of Viṣṇu, the mouse of the *TS* Rudra and the Purāṇic Gaṇeśa, the buffalo connected with Yama and Durgā, etc.), ophiolatry (Vedic Ahi or Ahirbudhnya, epic nāgas, epic-Purāṇic Vāsuki and Ananta), tree-worship (in the sanctity of the banyan, Bodhidruma, Bilva, Pipul trees and the Tulasī plant),[1] stone-worship (in the Śālagrāma stone of Viṣṇu, the Śivaliṅga or Bāṇaliṅga of Śiva and the Śoṇa-smoothed pebbles sacred to Gaṇeśa). Between Vedism and the epic-Purāṇic triad there were the 'high gods' (like Dyaus, Varuṇa or Brahman) and in the final stage, absolute monism of Vedānta (with Brahman as the sole entity) and the utter negation of Buddhism. The fundamental catholicity of Indian religion (arising perhaps from the absence of a widely accepted and clearly enunciated doctrine) denies nothing and is intolerant of no level or phase of religious consciousness.

Mythology has preserved records of this infinitely rich and varied

[1] The Aśvattha is Viṣṇu, Vaṭa is Rudra, and Palāśa is Brahman (*Padmapurāṇa Utkalakhaṇḍa*, ch. CIX).

development of religious awareness at various levels spread over three and a half millennia and over a vast subcontinent. There is no clear-cut system, no theology as such but a rich storehouse of mythological material such as no other religion can boast of.

Thus the cults and creeds of the various religious tracts are brought under a homogeneous religion which recognized the 'high gods' at the top level as well as the 'low gods' at the bottom. This catholicity of attitude, this elasticity and resilience succeeded in unifying India as a country as she had never before been unified. And neo-Brāhmaṇism is largely responsible for the conceptual unification of the country that the Gupta era saw emerging.

SELECT BIBLIOGRAPHY

A. SOURCE MATERIAL

Aeschylus. *Agamemnon* (Loeb edn.).
Eumenides (Loeb edn.).
Prometheus Bound (Loeb edn.).
The Libation Bearers (Loeb edn.).
Agnipurāṇa (Anandasrama Sanskrit series no. 41).
Aiteraya Brāhmaṇa (ed. A. K. Shastri, Travancore, 1942).
Āpastamba Dharmaśastra (Bombay Sanskrit series, 1932).
Āpastamba Gṛhysūtra (ed. C. Shastri, Chowkhamba Sanskrit series, 1928; also Vienna, 1887).
Āpastamba Śrautasūtra (Baroda Oriental Institute, 1955).
Apollodorus: *Bibliotheca* (Loeb edn.).
Apuleius: *The Golden Ass* (Loeb edn.).
Āśvalayana Gṛhyasūtra (ed. P. Shastri, Poona, 1936).
Āśvalayana Śrautasūtra (Anandasrama series, 1913).
Atharvaveda Saṃhitā (Svadhyayamandala series, Bombay).
Atharvaveda Saṃhitā (Harvard Oriental series, vols. VII and VIII).
Avesta (ed. J. Darmesteter, Sacred Books of the East Series, vols. IV and XXIII).
Baudhāyana Dharmasūtra (Chowkhamba Sanskrit series, 1934).
Baudhāyana Śrautasūtra (ed. Caland, Bibliotheca Indica, 1907).
Bhaviṣya Purāṇa (Gita Press, Gorokhpur).
Chāndogya Brāhmaṇa (Sanskrit College Research Series, 1957).
Egyptian Book of the Dead, The (Kegan Paul, 1901).
Euripides: Bacchae (Loeb edn.).
Hippolytus (Loeb edn.).
Iphigenia in Tauris (Loeb edn.).
The Libation Bearers (Loeb edn.).
Garuḍa Purāṇa (ed. M. N. Datta, Calcutta, 1908).
Gautama Dharmasūtra (ed. G. Buhler, Bombay, 1892).
Gilgamesh, The Epic of (Eng. tr. by W. K. Sanders, Penguin, 1960).
Gobhila Gṛhya Sūtra (Calcutta, 1936).
Gopatha Brāhmaṇa (E. J. Brill, Leyden, 1919).
Harivaṃśa (Calcutta, 1839).
Herodotus: *The Histories* (Loeb edn.).
Hesiod: *Theogony* (Loeb edn.).
Holy Bible, The (Authorized Version).
Homer: *The Iliad* (Loeb edn.).
The Odyssey (Loeb edn.). Also Oxford University Press, New York, 1946.
Īśādi Upaniṣads (The 28 Upaniṣads, Nirnayasagar Press 1946; also 11 Upaniṣads, Bibl. Ind. 1935).
Jaiminīya Brāhmaṇa (Nagpur International Academy of Indian Culture, 1954).
Kauṣītaki Brāhmaṇa (Bibliotheca Indica, 1861).
Kūrma Purāṇa (Calcutta, 1926).

Liṅga Purāṇa (Venkateswara Press, Bombay, 1924).
Mahābhārata (Critical Text, Poona).
Maitrāyaṇī Saṃhitā (Svadhyayamandala series, Bombay).
Mārkaṇḍeya Purāṇa (Varanasi, 1961).
Matsya Purāṇa (Venkatesvara Press Bombay, 1923).
Nārada Purāṇa (Gita Press, Gorakhpur).
Nibelungenlied (Penguin, 1965).
Ovid: *Fasti* (Loeb edn.).
Metamorphoses (Loeb edn.).
Padma Purāṇa (Gurumandala Press, Calcutta, 1957).
Pāraskara Gṛhyasūtra (Benares, 1938).
Rāmāyaṇa (Vālmīki's ed. G. Bhatt, Baroda Oriental Institute, 1960); also G. Gorresio's Critical Text, Parigi Stamberia Imperiale, Roma, 1843–1867).
Ṛgveda Saṃhitā (Vaidik Samsodhana Mandala, Poona).
Śatapatha Brāhmaṇa (Bibliotheca Indica, 1903).
Śāṅkhāyana Gṛhya Sūtra (Delhi, 1960).
Śāṅkhāyana Śrauta Sūtra (Bibliotheca Indica, 1888–99).
Sophocles: *Oedipus the King* (Loeb edn.).
Oedipus at Colonus (Loeb edn.).
Antigone (Loeb edn.).
Ajax (Loeb edn.).
Electra (Loeb edn.).
Taittirīya Brāhmaṇa (Bibliotheca Indica, 1890).
Taittirīya Saṃhitā (Svadhyayamandala, Bombay).
Talmud (tr. and ed. P. Blackman, London, 1951).
Tāṇḍya Mahābrāhmaṇa (Bibliotheca Indica, 1874).
Vaikhānasa Śrautasūtra (Biblotheca Indica, 1924).
Vājasaneyī Saṃhitā (Svadhyayamandala, Bombay).
Varāha Purāna (Benares, 1936).
Vaśiṣṭha Dharma Sūtra (ed. G. Buhler, Bombay, 1892).
Vāyu Purāṇa (Poona, 1905).
Viṣṇu Purāṇa (Venkatesvara Press Bombay, 1904).

B. REFERENCE BOOKS

Abbott, J.: *Keys of power* (Methuen, London, 1932).
Aiyyar, C. V. N.: *Origin and early history of Śaivism* (Madras University Press, 1936).
Albright, W. F.: *From Stone Age to Christianity* (Johns Hopkins, Balitmore, 1946).
Apte, V. M.: *Social and religious life in the Gṛhyasūtras* (Ahmedabad, 1939).
Arbman, E.: *Rudra* (Uppsala, 1922).
Atkins, G. G.: *Procession of the gods* (Constable and Co. 1931).
Atkins, S. D.; *Pūṣan in the Ṛgveda* (Princeton, 1941).
Bagchi, P. C.: *Studies in the Tantras* (Calcutta, 1939).
Banerji, A. C.: *Studies in the Brāhmaṇas* (Delhi, 1963).
Banerji, G. N.: *Hellenism in ancient India* (Butterworth, London, 1920).
Banerji, J. N.: *Development of Hindu iconography* (Calcutta University Press, 1956).
Banerji, S. C.: *A Glossary to Smṛti literature* (Calcutta, 1963).
Banton, M.: *Anthropological approaches to the study of religion* (London, 1966).

BIBLIOGRAPHY

Barnett, L. D.: *Brahman knowledge* (London, 1907).
Hindu gods and heroes (London, 1922).
Hinduism (London, 1906).
Barry, W. T. (ed.): *Sources of Indian tradition* (Columbia University Press, 1958).
Barth, A.: *The religions of India* (London, 1882).
Barua, B.: *A history of pre-Buddhistic Indian philosophy* (Calcutta University Press, 1921).
Bellamy, H. S.: *Moons, myths and man* (London, 1948).
Belvalkar, S. K. and Ranade, R. D.: *History of Indian philosophy* (Poona, 1927).
Bergaigne, A : *La Religion védique d'après les hymnes de Ṛgveda* (Paris, 1878–97).
Bhandarkar, R. G.: *Vaiṣṇavism, Śaivism and minor religious systems* (Strasbourg, 1913).
Bhattacharyya, T.: *The cult of Brahma* (Patna, 1957).
Bhattacharyya, B.: *Buddhist iconography* (Oxford, 1924).
Bloomfield, M.: *The Atharvaveda and the Gopatha Brāhmaṇa* (Strasbourg, 1899).
The religion of the Vedas (New York, 1908).
Cerberus the dog of Hades (Chicago, 1905).
Brandon, S. G. F.: (ed.) *The saviour god* (Manchester University Press, 1963).
Legends of the ancient Near East (Hodder and Stoughton, 1963).
Man and his destiny in the great religions (Manchester, 1963).
Bray, O.: *The Elder Edda* (Viking Club, 1908).
Breasted, J. H.: *The dawn of conscience* (New York, 1933).
Brunnhofer, G. H.: *Arische Urzeit* (Berne, 1910).
Budge, E. A. W.: *The gods of the Egyptians*, 2 vols. (Methuen, 1904).
The Egyptian heaven and hell (Kegan Paul, 1906).
Egyptian religion (London, 1908).
Egyptian ideas of future life (London, 1899).
From fetish to god in ancient Egypt (Oxford, 1934).
Burgh, W. G. D.: *The legacy of the ancient world*, 2 vols. (London, 1923).
Burrow, T.: *The Sanskrit language* (Faber, 1955).
Butler, E. M.: *The myth of the magus* (Cambridge University Press, 1948).
Cameron, G. G.: *History of early Iran* (Chicago University Press, 1935).
Campbell, J.: *The masks of God*, 2 vols. (Secker and Warburg, 1962).
The hero with a thousand faces (Meridian Press, New York, 1956).
Cassirir, B.: *Buddhism, its essence and development* (Oxford, 1951).
Chadwick, N.: *Russian heroic poetry* (Cambridge University Press, 1932).
Stories and ballads of the Far East (Cambridge University Press, 1921).
The Druids (Cardiff, 1966).
Chakladar, H.: *Social life in ancient India* (Calcutta, 1929).
Chakravarty, C.: *Tantras, studies in their religion & literature* (Calcutta, 1963).
Chalmers-Warner, E. T.: *Myths & legends of China* (Harrap, 1922).
Chanda, R.: *The Indo-Aryan races* (Varendra Research Society, Dacca, 1916).
Chatterji, S. K.: *Indianism and the Indian synthesis* (Calcutta, 1953).
Chatterji, S.: *The evolution of the theistic sects in ancient India* (Calcutta, 1962).
Early history of north India (200 B.C. to A.D. 650) (Calcutta, 1958).
Clemen, C.: *Religions of the world* (Harrap, 1931).
Conze, E.: *Buddhist thought in India* (Allen and Unwin, 1962).

Cook, A. B.: *Zeus, the Indo-European sky-god* (Cambridge University Press, 1914–40).
Coomaraswamy, A. K.: *The aims of Indian art* (Broad Campden, 1908).
Elements of Buddhist iconography (Cambridge, Mass. 1935).
Hinduism and Buddhism (New York, 1943).
History of Indian and Indonesian art (London, 1927).
Myths of the Hindus and Buddhists (London, 1913).
Coulanges, F. de: *La Cité antique* (Paris, 1905).
Cox, Sir G.: *The mythology of the Aryan nations* (Kegan Paul, 1878).
Coyajee, J.: *Cults and legends of ancient Iran and China* (Bombay, 1936).
Crooke, W.: *Religion and folklore in northern India* (Oxford University Press, 1926).
Cumont, F.: *After-life in Roman paganism* (reprint, Dover, New York, 1959).
The oriental religions in Roman paganism (New York, 1957).
The mysteries of Mithra (New York, 1956).
Davis, F. H.: *Myths and legends of Japan* (London, 1917).
De Groot, V: *The religious system of China* (Leyden, 1892).
Deshmukh, P. R.: *Indus civilization in the Ṛgveda* (Yeotmal, 1954).
Deshmukh, P. S.: *The origin and development of religion in Vedic literature* (Oxford University Press, 1933).
Deussen, P.: *Philosophy of the Upaniṣads* (Edinburgh, 1905).
Dietrich, B. C.: *Death, fate and the gods* (London, 1965).
Duchesne-Guillemin, J.: *Symbols and values in Zoroastrianism* (New York, 1966).
Dumézil, G.: *Flamen-Brahman* (Paris, 1935).
Ouranos-Varuṇa (Paris, 1934).
Mitra-Varuṇa (Leiden, 1943).
Durkheim, E.: *Primitive classification* (London, 1963).
The elementary forms of religious life (reprint, London, 1915).
The rules of sociological method (Chicago, 1938).
Eggeling, J.: *Introduction to the Śatapatha Brāhmaṇa* (part IV, vol. XLIII, Sacred Books of the East).
Eliade, M.: *The history of religions* (Chicago, 1959).
Myth and reality (London, 1964).
Patterns in comparative religion (Sheed and Ward, 1958).
Images and symbols (London, 1961).
The two and the one (London, 1965).
Birth and rebirth (New York, 1960).
Shamanism (London, 1964).
From primitives to Zen (London, 1967).
Eliot, Sir C.: *Hinduism and Buddhism*, vol. I (London, 1954).
Elmore, W. T.: *Dravidian gods in modern Hinduism* (Madras, 1925).
Elwin, V.: *Myths of middle India* (Oxford University Press, 1941).
Myths of the north east frontier of India (Shillong, 1958).
Farquhar, J. N.: *An outline of the religious literature of India* (Oxford University Press, 1920).
Filip, J.: *Celtic civilization and its heritage* (Prague, 1960, Eng. tr. 1962).
Frankfort, H.: *The birth of civilization in the Near East* (New York, 1950).
Kingship and the gods (Chicago, 1948).

Franklin, H. B.: *Wake of the gods* (Stanford, California, 1963).
Frazer, Sir J. G.: *Fear of the dead in primitive religion* (London, 1936).
Myths of the origin of fire (Macmillan, 1930).
The golden bough (London, 1911–15).
Lecture on the early history of immortality (London, 1927).
Freud, S.: *Moses and monotheism* (London, 1939).
Totem and taboo (London, 1919).
Freund, P.: *Myths of creation* (London, 1964).
Fuchs, S.: *The origin of man and his culture* (New York, 1963).
Gaster, T. H.: *Thespis* (Schuman, New York, 1959).
Getty, A.: *The gods of northern Buddhism* (London, 1914).
Ginzberg, L.: *The legends of the Jews* (Philadelphia, 1909–13).
Gladstone, M. S.: *Viṣṇu in the Ṛgveda* (Cambridge University Press, 1928).
Glasenapp, H. von: *Die Philosophie der Indien* (Stuttgart, 1949).
Die Religions Indiens (Stuttgart, 1943).
Die Literaturen Indiens von ihren Anfängen bis zur Gegenwart (Stuttgart, 1961).
Goetz, H.: *Epochen der Indische Kultur* (Leipzig, 1929).
Gonda, J.: *Notes on Brahman* (Utrecht, 1950).
Ancient Indian kingship from the religious point of view (Leiden, 1966).
Some observations on the relations between gods and power in the Vedas (Mouton, 1957).
The vision of the Vedic poets (The Hague, 1963).
Aspects of early Viṣṇuism (Utrecht, 1954).
Change and continuity in Indian religion (The Hague, 1965).
Goodrich, N. L.: *Ancient myths* (Mentor, 1960).
Gopal. R.: *India of the Kalpasūtras* (Delhi, 1959).
Gowen, H. H.: *History of Indian literature* (New York and London, 1931).
Grant, M.: *The world of Rome* (reprint, Mentor, 1961).
Gray, L. H.: *Baltic mythology* (Boston, 1918).
Greene, W. C.: *Moira, fate, good and evil in Greek thought* (Harvard, 1948).
Griswold, H. D.: *The religion of Ṛgveda* (Oxford University Press, 1923).
Guthrie, W. K. C.: *The Greeks and their gods* (London, 1957).
Hackin, J.: *Asiatic mythology* (Harrap, 1932).
Hall, H. R.: *The ancient history of the Near East* (Methuen, 1932).
Halliday, W. R.: *Indo-European folk tales and Greek legends* (Cambridge, 1933).
Harden, D.: *The Phoenicians* (Thames and Hudson, London, 1962).
Hariyappa, H. L.: *Ṛgvedic legends through the ages* (Poona, 1953).
Harris, J. R.: *Cult of the Heavenly Twins* (Cambridge University Press, 1906).
Origins of the cult of Aphrodite (Manchester University Press, 1960).
Harrison, J. B.: *Themis* (1st edn., Cambridge University Press, 1912).
Prolegomena to the study of Greek religion (Cambridge University Press, 1922)
Hawkes, J.: *Man and the sun* (London, 1962).
Hazra, R. C.: *Studies in the Upapurāṇas* (Sanskrit College, Calcutta, 1958).
Heidel: *The Babylonian Genesis* (Cambridge University Press, 1951).
Henning, W. B.: *Brahman* (Trans. Phil. Soc. London, 1945).
Heras, Fr.: *Studies in the proto-Indo-Mediterranean culture* (Bombay, 1953).
Hillebrandt, A.: *Vedische mythologie*, vol. II (Breslau, 1929).
Hiriyanna, M.: *Indian philosophical studies* (Mysore, 1957).

Hooke, S. H.: *Myth, ritual and kingship* (Oxford, 1958).
(ed.) *Myth and ritual* (Oxford University Press, 1933).
Hopkins, E. W.: *Gods and saints of the great Brāhmaṇa* (Trans. Connecticut Academy of Arts and Sciences, vol. 15, 1909).
The great epic of India (Yale University Press, 1920).
The religions of India (Boston, 1895).
Epic mythology (Strasbourg, 1905).
Hughes, E. R.: *Religion in China* (Hutchinson, 1950).
Hume, R. E.: *The thirteen principal Upanisads* (Oxford University Press, 1921).
Iversen, E.: *The myth of Egypt and its hieroglyphs* (Copenhagen, 1961).
Jairazbhoy, R. A.: *Foreign influence in ancient India* (Asia Publishing House, 1963).
James, E. O.: *The ancient gods* (Weidenfeld, 1960).
Prehistoric religion (Thames, 1957).
Beginnings of religion (Hutchinson, 1948).
The worship of the sky-god (Athlone Press, University of London, 1963).
Jaspers, K.: *The origin and role of history* (Routledge, 1963).
Jastrow, R.: *The civilization of Babylonia and Assyria* (Philadelphia, 1915).
Jayne, W. A.: *The healing gods of ancient civilization* (University Books, New York, 1962).
Johnson, F. E.: *Religious symbolism* (Harper, New York, 1953).
Jung, C. G.: *Psychology and the unconscious* (Kegan Paul, 1933).
The archetypes and the collective unconscious (London, 1959).
Psychology and religion (New Haven, 1938).
Man and his symbols (London, 1964).
Freud and psychoanalysis (London, 1961).
Jung, C. G. and Kerényi, C.: *Introduction to a science of mythology* (Routledge, 1951).
Kanbawala, S. C.: *Cultural history of the Matsyapurāṇa* (M.S. University Press, Baroda, 1964).
Kane, P. V.: *History of the Dharmaśāstra* (Poona, 1930–62).
Karsten, R.: *The origins of religion* (Routledge, 1935).
Katre, S. L.: *Avātaras of the gods* (Allahabad University Studies, 1940).
Keith, A. B.: *Introduction to the Ṛgvedic Brāhmaṇas*, Sacred Books of the East, vol. II.
Indian mythology (*Myths of all races*, vol. IV, part I, Boston, 1917).
Religion and philosophy in the Vedas and Upaniṣads. 2 vols. (Cambridge, Mass. 1925).
Kellett, E. E.: *The northern saga* (London, 1929).
A short history of religions (Gollancz, 1933).
Ker, W. P.: *Epic and romance* (reprint, Dover, New York, 1957).
Kérenyi, C.: *The heroes of the Greeks* (Grove, New York, 1960).
The gods of the Greeks (London, 1951).
Religions of the Greeks and Romans (Thames, 1960).
Kern, W.: *Manual of Indian Buddhism* (Strasbourg, 1896).
Konow, S. and Tuxen, P.: *Religions of India* (Copenhagen, 1949).
Kramer, S. N.: *Mythologies of the ancient world* (New York, 1961).
Sumerian mythology (Philadelphia, 1944).
Lamotte, E.: *Spirit of ancient Buddhism* (Ist. per la Collaborazione Culturale, Paris, 1961).

— Law, B. C.: *Heaven and hell in Buddhist perspective* (Thacker and Spink, Calcutta, 1935).
Leeuw, G. van der: *Religion, its essence and manifestation* (London, 1938).
Leger, L.: *Etudes de mythologie slave* (no. II, Brill, Leiden, 1896).
Lévi-Strauss, C.: *Le Totéisme aujourd'hui* (Paris, 1962).
Le Cru et le Cuit (Paris, 1964).
La Pensée Sauvage (Paris, 1966).
A World on the Wane (London, 1961).
Structural Anthropology (New York, 1964).
Liddell, R.: *Byzantium and Istanbul* (Cape, London, 1956).
Lowie, G.: *Primitive religion* (London, 1936).
Luders, H. L.: *Varuṇa* (Göttingen, 1951).
Macdonell, A.: (ed.) *Bṛhaddevatā of Śaunaka* (Harvard Oriental Series, vols. V and VI).
Vedic mythology (Strasbourg, 1897).
Lectures on Comparative Religion (London, 1925).
Malinowski, B.: *Myth in primitive psychology* (London, 1926).
(ed. R. Redfield) *Magic, science and religion* (New York, 1955).
Marshall, J. H.: *Mohenjo Daro and the Indus civilization* (London, 1931).
Mehta, P. D.: *Early Indian religious thought* (Luzac, London, 1956).
Mendelssohn, I:. *Religions of the ancient Near East* (New York, 1955).
Meyer, J. J.: *Gesetzbuch und Purāna* (Breslau, 1929).
Mode, H.: *Indische Frühkulturen* (Basel, 1944).
Das Frühe Indien (Weimar, 1960).
Molé, M.: *Culte, mythe et cosmologie dans l'Iran ancien* (Paris, 1963).
Morgan, K. W.: *The religion of the Hindus* (New York, 1953).
Munch, P. A.: *Norse mythology* (New York, 1926).
Murphy, J.: *Origins and history of religions* (Manchester University Press, 1949).
Murray, M. A.: *Five stages of Greek religion* (London, 1935).
The genesis of religion (Routledge and Kegan Paul, 1963).
Narahari, H. G.: *Ātman in the pre-Upaniṣadic Vedic literature* (Adyar Library, Madras, 1944).
Nariman, G. K.: *Literary history of Buddhist Sanskrit* (Taraporewala, 1920).
Nilsson, M. P.: *Greek popular religion* (New York, 1940).
The Mycenaean origins of Greek mythology (Berkeley, 1933).
Oberman, J.: *Ugaritic mythology* (Yale University Press, 1948).
Oldham, C. G.: *The sun and the serpent* (Constable, 1905).
O'Malley, L. S. S.: *Popular Hinduism* (Cambridge University Press, 1935).
Palmer, R. B.: *Dionysus, myth and cult* (Indiana University Press, 1965).
Pargiter, F. E.: *The Purāṇa Texts of the dynasties of the Kali Age* (Oxford University Press, 1913).
Ancient Indian historical traditions (Oxford University Press, 1922).
— Pathak, V. S.: *History of Śaiva cults in northern India* (Benares, 1960).
Perry, B. E.: *The ancient Romans* (University of California, 1967).
Perry, W. J.: *The children of the sun* (London, 1923).
Pettazzoni, R.: *Essays on the history of religion* (Leyden, 1954).
The all-knowing God (tr. H. J. Rose, London, 1956).
The labyrinth (New York, 1935).

Piggott, S.: *Prehistoric India* (Pelican, 1950).
Pillai, G. S.: *Tree Worship and Ophiolatry* (Trichinopoly, 1948).
—Potdar, K. R.: *Sacrifice in the ṚgVeda* (Bombay, 1953).
Powell, T. G. E.: *The Celts* (Thames, 1959).
Pritchard, J. B.: *Ancient Near Eastern texts* (Princeton University, 1959).
Pusalkar, A. D.: *Studies in the epics and Purāṇas* (Delhi, 1955).
Radin, P.: *Primitive religion* (Dover, New York, 1957).
Monotheism among primitive peoples (Allen and Unwin, 1955).
Raglan, Lord: *The hero* (London, 1949).
The origins of religion (London, 1949).
Rao, G.: *Elements of Hindu iconography* (Madras, 1916).
Rassmussen: *Eskimo folk tales* (Copenhagen, 1921).
— Ray Chaudhuri, H. C.: *Materials for the early history of the Vaiṣṇava sect* (Calcutta University Press, 1936).
Redfield, R.: *Present society and culture* (Chicago University Press, 1955).
The little tradition (Chicago University Press, 1960).
The primitive world and its transformations (New York, 1953).
Rees, A. B.: *Celtic heritage* (Thames, 1961).
Reinach, S.: *Orpheus* (Routledge, 1931).
Renou, L.: *Religions of ancient India* (Athlone Press, 1953).
Vṛtra et Verethragna (Paris, 1935).
Vedic India (Calcutta, 1957).
La Poésie religieuse de l'Inde antique (Paris, 1942).
Rice, T. T.: *The Scythians* (Thames, 1958).
Rohde, E.: *Psyche* (London, 1925).
Ruben, W.: *Beginn der Philosophie in Indien* (Berlin, 1956).
Eisenschmiede und Dämonen in Indien (Leiden, 1939).
Rugg-Gunn, A.: *Osiris and Odin* (London, 1940).
Saxl, F.: *Mithras* (Berlin, 1932).
Schmidt, W.: *Der Ursprung der Gottesidee* (Münster, 1912).
Schrader, F. C.: *Introduction to the Ahirbudhnya Saṃhitā* (Madras, 1916).
Schwab, G.: *Gods and heroes* (Routledge, 1950).
Seznec, J.: *The survival of pagan gods* (Harper, 1961).
— Shastri, S. R.: *Origin and development of the rituals of ancestor-worship in India* (Calcutta, 1963).
— Shende, N. J.: *Religion and philosophy of the Atharvaveda* (Poona, 1952).
Shorter, A. W.: *The Egyptian gods* (London, 1937).
An introduction to Egyptian religion (London, 1931).
Slater, G.: *The Dravidian element in Indian culture* (London, 1924).
Smith, G. E.: *The birth of the gods* (Longmans, 1919).
Starr, C. G.: *Origins of Greek civilization (1100–650 B.C.)* (Cape, London, 1962).
Swanson, G. E.: *The birth of the gods* (Ann Arbor, University of Michigan Press, 1960).
Thieme, P.: *Mitra and Aryaman* (Yale University Press, 1957).
Thomas, E. J.: *Early Buddhist scriptures* (Kegan Paul, 1935).
Turnville Petre, E. O. G.: *Myth and religion of the north* (Weidenfeld and Nicolson, 1964).
Vetter, G.: *Magic and religion* (Phil. Lib. New York, 1958).

Vogel, J. P.: *The goose in Indian religion and art* (E. J. Brill, 1962).
Indian serpent lore (London, 1926).
Wace, C. S.: *Serpent-worship and other essays* (Redway, London, 1888).
Waisbard, S. and R.: *Masks, mummies and magicians* (London, 1965).
Wales, H. G. Q.: *The mountain of God* (London, 1953).
Prehistory and religion in South-East Asia (London, 1957).
Warren, T.: *Buddhism in translation* (Cambridge, Mass. 1896).
Weber, M.: *Religions in China* (Allen and Unwin, 1952).
Wheeler, Sir M.: *Early India and Pakistan* (Taraporewala, Bombay, 1959).
The Indus civilization (Supp. to Cambridge History of India, 1953).
Wheeler, P. W.: *The sacred scriptures of the Japanese* (Allen and Unwin, 1953).
Whitehead, H.: *Village deities of South India* (Calcutta, 1921).
Willets, R. F.: *Cretan cults and festivals* (Routledge, 1962).
Winternitz, M.: *History of Indian literature*, 3 vols. (Calcutta University Press, 1927).
Index volume to The sacred books of the east (Oxford, 1910).
Winternitz, M. and Nariman, G. K.: *Literary history of Sanskrit Buddhism* (Bombay, 1920).
Woodroff, Sir J.: *Shakti and Shakta* (Luzac, London, 1920).
Wright, A. F.: *Buddhism in Chinese history* (Stanford University Press, 1959).
Zaehner, R. C.: *A Zoroastrian dilemma* (Oxford, 1955).
Zehrin, E.: *The crescent and the bull* (Sidgwick and Jackson, 1962).
Zimmer, H.: *The art of Indian Asia* (New York, 1955).
Philosophies of India (London, 1952).
Maya der Indische Mythos (Stuttgart, 1936).
Myths and symbols in Indian art and civilization (New York, 1962).
Zurcher, E.: *The Buddhist conquest of China*, 2 vols. (Brill, Leiden, 1959).

C. ARTICLES IN JOURNALS

Banerji-Sastri, A.: Iconism in India (*Ind. Hist. Quart.* vol. XII, June 1932).
Belvalkar, S. K.: Brahman-Berêsman-Bricht-Bhraj (*Proceedings of the Fourth Oriental Conference.* Allahabad, 1928).
Bhattacharya, V.: The phallus worship in India (*Ind. Hist. Quart.* 1933).
Bose, J.: The prototype of Śiva in the prehistoric age (*Calcutta Rev.* 1940).
Boyce, M.: Some reflections on Zurvanism (*Bull. School of Oriental and African Studies, London*, vol. XIX, 1957).
Briggs, G. W.: Brief outline of Indo-Iranian contracts (*Perry Comm. Vol.* London, 1933).
Brough, J.: The tripartite ideology of the Indo-Europeans (*Bull. School of Oriental and African Studies, London*, vol. XXII, 1959).
Brown, W. N.: The ṚgVedic equivalent for hell (*JAOS*, vol. 61, 1941).
Bühler, W.: Indian palaeography (*Ind. Antiq.* vol. XXXIII).
Chakladar, H. C.: Problem of the racial composition of the Indian people (*Man in India*, Apr.–Sept. 1936).
Chandavarkar, G. L.: Aśvins as historical figures (*J. Bombay Univ.* 1935).
Chandhuri, N. M.: Rudra-Śiva as an agricultural deity (*Ind. Hist. Quart.* 1939).
— The Indian cowherd god (*J. Bhand. Oriental Res. Soc.* 1942).
The sun as a folk god (*Man in India*, Jan.–Mar. 1941).

Chatterji, S.: Buddhist survivals in Bengal (*B. C. Law Comm.* vol. I, 1965).
Chatterji, S. K.: Armenian hero legends and the epic of David of Sassun (*J. Asiatic Soc.* vol. I, no. 3, 1963).
Chaudhury, S. K.: The mythology and folklore of central Asia (*Calcutta Review*, 1944).
Collitz, V.: König Yima und Saturn (*Parry Comm. Vol.* London, 1933).
Dandekar, R. N.: Asura Varuṇa (*Ann. Bhaend. Or. Res. Inst.* vol. XXI, 1939–40).
Pūṣan the pastoral god of the Veda (*New Ind. Ant.* June 1942).
New light on the Vedic god Savitṛ (*Ann. Bhand. Or. Res. Inst.* XX, 1938–9).
Viṣṇu in the Veda (*Festschrift for Prof. P. V. Kane*. Poona, 1941).
Rudra (*AIOC*, vol. XII, Benares, 1943–4).
De, S. K.: Vedic and epic Kṛṣṇa (*Ind. Hist. Quart.* vol. XIX, 1942).
Dikshitar, V. R. R. C.: Kriṣṇa in early Tamil Literature (*Ind. Culture*, 1937–8).
Duchesne-Guillemin: Fire in Iran and Greece (*East and West*, new series, vol. 13, nos. 2 and 3).
Dumézil, G.: Review of *Déesses Latines et myths védiques*, Bruxelles (*JAOS*, vol. 80, no. 1, 1960).
Dumont, P. E.: The Indic god Aja Ekapad (*JAOS*, 1933).
Fuchs, S.: Tracing monotheism in India (*New Review*, Aug. 1940).
Fukai, S.: The artifacts of Hatra and Bactrian art (*East and West*, vol. II, June–Sept. 1960).
Gadri, A.: A note on a unique image of Yama (*New Ind. ant.* vol. II, 1939–40).
Ghose, E. N.: The twin gods of the ṚgVeda (*Ind. Hist. Quart.* 1933).
Ghosh, B. K.: Varuṇa (*JGIS*, 1941).
Birth of the gods (*Ind. Culture*, 1940).
Gnoli, G.: The Tyche and the Dioscuri in ancient sculptures from the valley of Swat (*East and West*, vol. 14, nos. 1 and 2, 1963).
Grierson: The Nārāyaṇīya and the Bhāgavata (*Ind. Antiq.* Sept. 1908).
Guterbrock, A.: The composition of Hittite prayers to the sun (*JAOS*, vol. 78, no. 4, 1958).
Hillebrandt, A.: Brahman (*Festgabe Jacobi, Beitrage zur Litt.* Bonn, 1925).
Hopkins, E. W.: Epic view of the earth (*J. Ind. School Vedic Res.* no. 1).
Horton, R.: A definition of religion and its uses (*J. Royal Anthr. Inst.* no. 90, 1961).
Karmarker, A. P.: Some nude gods in the Indian pantheon (*Ann. Bhand. Or. Res. Inst.* XXXIII, 1942).
Katre, S. L.: Kṛṣṇa and Jarāsandha (*Ind. Hist. Quart.* 1939).
Keith, A. B.: The god Varuṇa (*Ind. Hist. Quart.* 1933).
Indra and Vṛtra (*Ind. Cult.* 1935).
The origin of Aryan gods (*JRAS*, 1933, 1937).
Varuṇa and Ouranos (*Ind. Cult.* 1937–8).
New theories as to Brahman (*Jha Comm. Vol.* 1937).
Kramrisch, S.: Pūṣan (*JAOS*, vol. 81, no. 2, 1961).
Machek, V.: Origin of the god Viṣṇu (*Archiv. Orientalni*, vol. 8, 1960).
Meyer, J. J.: The monotheistic religion of ancient India (*Asiatic Quart. review*, no. 28, 1909).
Ojha, R.: The Indra-Vṛtra war (*J. Bhand. Or. Res. Soc.* 1942).
Perry, E. D.: Indra in the ṚgVeda (*JAOS*, Oct. 1880).
Peterson, M.: Varuṇa (*Tagner Comm. Vol.* 1918).

Przyluski, J.: Varuṇa god of sea and sky (*JRAS*, 1931).
The great Goddess in India and Iran (*Ind. Hist. Quart.* 1934).
Renou, L.: Sur la notion de Brahman (*J. Asiatique*, 1949).
Ronnow, K.: Viśvarūpa (*Rapson Comm. Vol.* 1930–2).
Sur, A. K.: Pre-Aryan elements in Indian culture (*Ind. Hist. Quart.* 1934).
Thieme, P.: The Aryan gods of the Mitanni treaties (*JAOS*, vol. 80, no. 4, 1960).
Thomas, F. W.: The expansion of Indianism (*Oriental Congress*, 1937).
Vader, V. H.: Twin gods Aśvinau (*Ind. Hist. Quart.* 1932).
Wesendonk, O. G. von: The Kālavāda and the Zervanite system (*JRAS*, 1931).
Winternitz, M.: Race and religion (*Prabuddha Bhārata*, Aug. 1937).
Zimmerman, H.: God in the Gathas and in the *ṚV* (*JCOI*, 1932).

D. DICTIONARIES AND ENCYCLOPAEDIAS

Real-encyclopaedia der klassischen Altertumswissenschaft (A. Pauly and G. Wissowa).
The new Schaff-Herzog encyclopaedia of religious knowledge (Michigan, 1958).
Hastings' encyclopaedia of religion and ethics (1958).
International bibliography of the history of religions (ed. C. J. Blecker, Leiden).
Larousse encyclopaedia of mythology (London, 1954).
Standard dictionary of folk-lore, mythology and legend (Leach and Fried, 1949–50).
Motiv-index in folk-lore literature (ed. S. Thompson, Indiana).
Concise encyclopaedia of living faiths (R. C. Zaehner, Hutchinson, 1959).
Oxford classical dictionary (Clarendon Press, Oxford).
Sanskrit–English dictionary (M. Monier-Williams, Clarendon Press, Oxford).
The encyclopaedia of myths and legends of all nations (H. S. Robinson and K. Wilson, London, 1962).
Civilizations past and present (ed. T. W. Walbank and A. M. Taylor, Chicago, 1949).

INDEX

The reader should refer to the analytical list of contents for the treatment of the major themes. The references to the Mahābhārata, the Rāmāyaṇa, the Ṛgveda, and other sources, are so frequent that it would serve no purpose to include them in this index.

INDEX

Fafnir, 185
Fenrir, 215 n.
Fiji, 32, 95
Finnish mythology, 285
flagellation, ritual, 166–7
Flamen Dialis, 191
France, 180
Fravashi, 76
Frazer, Sir James G., 1, 2, 97 n., 129, 247
Frey, 96, 286, 288
Fukai, Shinji, 115, 165

Gadhi, 37
Gaia, 23, 38, 47, 82–3, 94 n.
Gajāsura, 184
Gālava, 127
Gallis, 267
Gaṇapati, 3, 145, 183, 203, 317, 359
Gāṇapayta sect, 14, 227
Gaṇḍakī, 298
Gandara art, 246
Gandhamādana, 343
Gāndhāri, 67, 146, 153, 226
Gandarvas, 65, 139, 224, 241–2, 265
Gāṇḍīva, 189
Gaṇeśa, 14, 39, 141, 159, 183–4, 193, 200, 318, 352, 362
Gaṅgā, 39, 40, 125, 180–2, 193, 285, 301, 337
Gaṅgāmmā, 92, 167
Garga, 127
Gārgya, 140, 202
Gārhapatya fire, 56, 73, 84, 105
Gārhasthya, 18
Garuḍa, 15, 39, 223, 230–1, 298–9, 347, 362
Garuḍadhvaja, 298
Gau, 131
Gaurī, 39, 133, 159, 162, 177
Gautama, 52, 63–4, 272
Gautami, 53
Gavedhuka, 116
Gaviṣṭhira, 188, 195
Gaya, 287, 361
Gāyatrī hymn, 27, 214
Gayomart, 196
Geb, 23
Gefjon, 253
Gegenschein, 245
Geirrod, 252
Gemini, 244–5
Geras, 82
Geryones, 255, 309
Ghaṇṭākarṇa, 184, 308
Ghorā, 176
Ghoṣā, 237–8
Ghosh, M. M., 29
Ghoṣiṇīs, 11 n.
Ghṛta, 96
Ghurundi, 291
Gilgamesh epic, 88, 115, 247, 294–5
Giricara, 152
Giriśa, 152
Giritra, 152
Giriyajña, 269–70
Girru, 196 n.
Gleipnir, 215
Glover, T. R., 175
Gnoli, G., 246
Goliath, 302
Goloka, 310
Gonda, J., 1, 2, 342–4
Gopā, 306
Gopalī, 140
Gopendrasyānujā, 164
Gopikāvilāsa, 304
Gośarya, 237
Govardhana, Mount, 310–11
Govinda, 309
Govṛṣeśvara, 116
Graeae, the, 70
Grāhi, 101
Great Mother cult, 176, 192
Greek mythology: *see* separate gods and goddesses
Gṛhyasūtras, 18, 69, 147, 150
Grim, 34
Grimm, the brothers, 225
Griswold, H. D., 228, 242
Gṛtsamada, 127
Guha, 181, 185
Guhyakas, 185
Gullinbursti, 289
Guṇas, 201
Guṇaviṣṇu, 55
Gundestrap, 115
Guṅgus, 253
Gupta age, 5, 13, 19, 69, 85, 99, 111, 128, 162, 182, 196, 304, 307, 356, 359, 362
Gwalior, 289
Gylfi, 253, 285

Hades, 163, 217 n.
Hagia Triada, 92, 168 n.
Haimavatī, 165
Haladhara, 290
Halimā, 189
Hammurabi, 47, 234
Haṃsa, 119, 303, 347
Hanūmat, 118, 131, 193, 277, 308, 362
Haoma, 156, 274
Hara, 134, 197, 205–6, 279, 358
Haralīlā, 228

Kālīya, 232, 302–3, 309
Kalki, 15, 145, 231
Kalpa, 300, 340, 352
Kalyāṇasundaramūrti, 348
Kāma, 3, 106–7, 163, 171–2, 327, 352, 359
Kamalāksa, 120
Kāmanāśaka, 172
Kamaṇḍalu, 347
Kamarpur, 226
Kami gods, 93 n.
Kampf-tier, 288
Kaṃsa, 173, 301–2, 305
Kaṃsavadha, 305
Kaṇāda, 199
Kanishka, King, 226
Kaniska, 112, 131
Kannon, 102
Kāntarvāsinī, 167
Kaṇṭhaka, 231
Kaṇva, 194–5, 238, 241
Kanyākumāri, 158, 164
Kapālin, 133–4
Kapardin, 109, 134
Kapidhvaja, 277
Kapila, 89, 109, 294
Kapilapatnī, 89, 162
Kapiñjala, 254, 271
Kapota, 72, 170
Kapotalubdhakakathā, 58
Kapoteśvara, 170
Karālī, 85, 158, 171
Karambha, 202
Karaṇa putra, 102
Karañja, 253
Karbara, 71
Kardama, 161, 328
Karīṣiṇī, 161
Karkemish, 115
Karman, 6, 53, 57, 61, 65, 73, 107, 354, 356
Karmavāda, 61
Karṇa, 119–20, 212, 279, 292, 301–2, 308
Karṇikāra garden, 110, 141, 159
Kārtavīryārjuna, 289
Kārttika, 97–8, 182
Kārttikeya, 3, 139, 159, 180–1, 183–5, 189, 193, 200, 203, 271, 292, 301, 318, 337, 352, 359, 362
Kāśīnātha, 125
Kāśyā, 272
Kaśyapa, 4, 58, 134, 160, 217, 298, 306, 325, 328, 339–40, 343, 358
Katachthonioi Theoi, 86
Kaṭha, 18
Kāṭhaka, 227
Kaṭhiawar, 148
Kaṭhopaniṣad, 59, 336
Kātyāyanī, 158
Kaumāri, 360
Kaumodakī, 309
Kauravas, 64, 85, 149, 256, 320
Kauśika, 57, 173
Kauṣītakī, 18, 145, 327
Kaustubha, 213, 223, 309, 311
Kautsāyanistuti, 337
Kavaṣa, 250
Kavi, 26, 195, 323
Kavi Uśanas, 253
Kavya, 70, 191
Kavyavāhana, 7, 77, 106, 192, 195
Keith, A. B., 30, 32, 75, 227, 255, 320, 342
Kena, 18
Kenopaniṣad, 158, 204
Kentaur Mimes, 262
Ker, 82, 86
Kerberos, 71, 104
Kerényi, C., 82–3, 147, 244, 268, 287, 300
Keresâspa, 151, 303
Késin, 139–40, 152, 201, 302, 309
Khaḍga, 119
Khajuraho, 347
Khāṇḍava, 189, 279
Khepera, 213
Khila Sūktas, 161
Kīkaṭas, 249
Kinnekule, 229
Kirātārjunīya, 197
Knossos, 169
Kojiki, 93 n.
Kokamukhā, 170
Kolita, 68
Kore, 217 n.
Koronis, 239, 304
Kośas, 135
Kratu, 322, 328
Krauṅcabheda, 181
Kravyād, 7, 105, 195
Krivi, 109, 252
Kronos, 64, 94 n., 100, 165
Kṛpa, 250
Kṛśānu, 237
Kṛṣṇa, 6, 164, 168, 189, 247–8, 252, 273, 290–1, 301–16, 334, 339, 343, 362; and Varuṇa, 37–9, 41; and Yama, 58, 101; and Śiva, 119, 126, 144, 149, 173; and Viṣṇu, 199, 223, 232, 235, 284, 292, 294–8; and Indra, 266, 269–70, 276–9, 282
Kṛṣṇachavisamakṛṣṇā, 173
Kṛṣṇajanmakhaṇḍa, 282, 355
Kṛṣṇa-Purāṇa, 19, 301

Mahaśepha, 193
Mahātuṣita, 338
Mahāvastu, 68
Mahāvīra, 229, 329
Mahāvrata ceremony, 227, 229, 258
Mahāvyutpatti, 39
Mahāyāna, 11, 15, 162, 173, 174, 289, 346, 353
Mahendra, 74, 251, 257–9, 269, 306
Māheśvara, 124, 172, 182, 205–6, 360
Mahiṣamardinī Durgā, 165
Mahiṣī, 231
Māhiṣmatī, 189, 195
Mahīśuva, 253
Mahiṣvat, 237
Mahundra, 297
Mainda, 338
Maitrāyaṇīya, 18, 201
Majjhima Nilāya, 346
Makha, 305
Mallikā, 162
Māmaki, 197
Mamallapuram, 166
Māmateya, 195
Manaan, 231
Managarm, 71
Manalūra, 126
Manas, 329
Manasā, 85, 128, 151–2, 177, 337, 354
Mānasakanyā, 319
Manasāmaṅgala, 152
Mānasī Pratirūpā, 337
Maṇḍala, 5, 36, 108, 322, 341, 359
Mandapāla, 57, 189
Mandara, 119, 289
Māndhātṛ, 237
Māṇḍūkya, 18
Manes, 16, 67, 310, 346, 355
Maṅgalakāvyas, 177
Maṅgalāṣṭaśata, 339
Maniar Math, 151
Maṇibhadra, 185
Manichaism, 157
Maṇi Nāga, 151
Mañjiṣṭhā, 162
Maṅkaṇaka, 200
Manu, 102–3, 113, 176, 195, 217–18, 237, 239, 243, 288–9, 324, 329, 330, 343
Manuṣvat, 194
Manyamāna, 252
Manyu, 135, 137, 141
Māra, 106–7, 265
Marduk, 47, 232, 234, 280, 303 n., 308
Mariāmman, 92, 167
Marīci, 322, 328
Marīci Kaśyapa, 357
Mariyāttal, 92, 167
Mārkaṇḍeya, 161, 166, 172, 195, 300, 310, 344, 357–8
Mars, 91, 168
Marshall, Sir John, 113, 360
Mārtaṇḍa, 3, 8, 85, 100, 132, 188, 218–19
Marutah, 130
Maruts, the, 14, 48, 112, 130–2, 135, 180, 184, 189, 192, 207, 257–8, 264, 270, 273, 323
Marutta, 38, 142, 185, 265, 272
Maski, 12
Mātali, 70
Mataṅga, 251
Mātariśvan, 13, 187, 190, 261
Mathura, 196, 226, 228
Matsya, 28, 289, 357
Mattamayūras, 182
Maurya age, 82, 162, 169
Mauṣalapatvan, 290
Maya people, 280
Māyā, 35–6, 232, 251, 264, 312–13, 322, 345, 348, 362
Māyādevi, 312
Mayavan, 312
Māyāvatī, 297
Māyin, 35
Mayon, 312
Mayūrabhaṭṭa, 228
Mazda, 61, 69
Medhātithi, 237, 271–2
Medusa, 165
Megasthenes, 144
Meghayantī, 97
Melia, 244 n.
Memphis, 148
Men, 106
Menā, 158, 272
Menakā, 273
Meru, Mount, 141, 153, 159, 265
Mesopotamian mythology, 24, 34, 47, 82, 157, 203, 227
Messagetae, 222, 231–2
Mexican mythology, 94 n., 141 n., 177 n., 182 n., 196 n., 230 n., 232 n., 280, 285 n., 287, 299
Mictecaciutli, 94 n., 177 n.
Midgard, 151, 252, 255, 259
Mīḍhuṣī, 10, 142, 147, 159, 169
Mihir, 222
Mihiragula, 149
Milinda Pañha, 346
Milton, John, 66, 105
Mimir, 262
Min, 128, 148, 179 n.
Minerva, 91, 164

Śarva, 54, 104, 117–18, 130, 133, 135–7, 140, 142, 192, 205
Śaryāṇavat, 132, 154
Śaryāti's sacrifice, 236
Sasun, 301, 308
Śatamakha, 119
Śatapatha Brāhmaṇa, 20
Śatarudrīya, 109, 117, 135–7, 149, 205
Śatarūpā, 329, 340
Satayavatī, 37, 52
Saṭpura, 311
Satra sacrifice, 113
Satrājit, King, 213
Sattva, 357
Saturn, 62, 91
Sātvata, 311
Satyavat, 58, 66, 73
Satyrs, 180, 202
Śaunaka, 6, 19
Saunanda, 309
Saura cult, 6, 14, 227
Saurāśva, 250
Sauru, 130, 242
Sauśravasa Upagu, 262
Sāvaṇa, 323
Sāvarni, 126, 218, 243
Sāvarṇi Manu, 103, 217
Śavasī, 270
Savitṛ, 3, 8, 13, 14, 134, 219, 224; as solar god, 25, 211, 213–15, 229; and Varuṇa, 40; and Yama, 52, 57–8, 65–6, 74; and Prajāpati, 122–3, 322, 324; and the Asvins, 236, 241, 247; and Brahman, 340
Sāyaṇa, 17, 55, 102, 132, 188, 195, 253, 256–7, 276, 278, 323
Śayu, 188, 238
Scruta, 250
Ścrutāyudha, 27
Scythians, 148–9
Seban, 232 n., 303 n.
Selene, 170
Semitic mythology, 244, 280, 301
Senā, 270
Servius, 180
Śeṣa, 290–1, 300, 328
Śeṣanāga, 39, 290, 338
Shakespeare, William, 32
Shamash, 222, 227, 234
Shame, 47
Siberia, 225
Siboi, 204
Sidhumanṃsapaśupriyā, 167
Sigurd, 305
Śikaṇḍi, 95
Śikhaṇḍa, 95
Silappadigaram, 275
Sileni, 180
Śilparatnāgama, 185
Siṃhavāhinī, 168
Sin, 157
Sindhu, the, 37
Singin, 135
Sinīvalī, 296
Śipiviṣṭa, 118, 298, 306, 323
Śipru, 250, 252
Śira, 143
Śirima Devatā, 161
Sirkap, 226
Sīsara, 70–1
Śiśnadevas, 178
Śiśumāra, 262
Sītā, 189, 214, 251, 271, 290, 320, 338
Sītalā, 85, 90
Śitikaṇṭha, 109, 190
Śiva, 3, 6, 7, 10, 12, 14, 19, 76, 89, 214–15, 322, 342, 351, 356, 358–60, 362; and Viṣṇu, 15, 16, 199, 234, 259, 298–9; and Varuṇa, 38–40, 194; names, 53, 95, 109, 177, 187, 205–6, 340; and Yama, 67, 70, 73, 104, 107–8, 194, 354; and Nirṛti, 85, 129; iconography, 111–12, 127–8, 139, 157, 178–9, 201, 205–6, 355; and Durga, 158, 174–5; and Brahman, 198–9, 207, 347; and Indra, 279, 282; and Kṛṣṇa, 306–8, 311, 339
Śivadūti, 89
Śivaliṅga, 128, 355, 362
Śiva-Pasúpati, 117
Skambha, 4, 331–2, 343
Skanda, 180–3, 193
Skidbhadnir, 289
Sleipnir, 112, 206, 231
Smṛtis, 6
snake (serpent), 15, 34, 39, 80, 82, 149–52, 165, 176–7, 196, 212, 232–3, 298–9, 306
Ṣoḍaśin, 230, 263, 275
Sol Invictus, 222
Soma, 13, 25, 49, 65, 75, 80–1, 120, 214, 224, 241–2, 320, 322, 324, 332, 362; and Varuna, 27, 31, 35–7, 40; and Yama, 73, 105–6; food or drink, 96, 156, 236–7, 239–40, 246, 263; and Rudra, 109, 111, 117–18, 129, 132, 152–4; and Indra, 253, 257–8, 267, 270, 272–8; and Visnu, 292, 294, 298
Somaka, King, 57, 195
Soma Kavyavāhana, 77
Somakrayaṇī, 80
Soma Pitṛmat, 106
Somātman, 104
Somavantah, 105